Interpreting Southern History

SANFORD W. HIGGINBOTHAM

Interpreting Southern History

*Historiographical Essays in Honor of
Sanford W. Higginbotham*

Edited by
JOHN B. BOLES
and
EVELYN THOMAS NOLEN

Louisiana State University Press
Baton Rouge and London

Copyright © 1987 by Louisiana State University Press
All rights reserved
Manufactured in the United States of America

Designer: Christopher Wilcox
Typeface: Sabon
Typesetter: G & S Typesetters
Printer: Thomson-Shore, Inc.
Binder: John Dekker & Sons, Inc.

Library of Congress Cataloging-in-Publication Data

Interpreting southern history.
  Includes index.
  1. Southern States—Historiography.   2. Southern States—History.
3. Higginbotham, Sanford W.   I. Boles, John B.   II. Nolen, Evelyn Thomas.
III. Higginbotham, Sanford W.
F208.2.I57   1986   975'.0072   86-10370
ISBN 0-8071-1318-2
ISBN 0-8071-1361-1 (pbk.)

Portions of John B. Boles's essay "The Discovery of Southern Religious History"
originally appeared as "Religion in the South: A Tradition Recovered," in *Maryland
Historical Magazine,* LXIX (April, 1984), 64–85.

Publication of this book has been assisted by a grant from the Burkitt Foundation.

Frontispiece courtesy of Rice University.

Louisiana Paperback Edition, 1987
96 95 94 93 92 91 90   5 4 3 2

Contents

CONTENTS

Preface and Acknowledgments

Probably no field of American history has been more transformed by recent scholarship than the study of the South. Methodologically innovative work has pushed the beginning of southern history back almost two centuries before Eli Whitney's invention of the cotton gin in 1793, and the chronological boundary ending the antebellum period blurs as the evolving roles of planters and freedmen have been followed through the Civil War and into the era of Reconstruction. The beginning of Reconstruction itself has slipped back to 1862, when Union forces first began conquering parts of the South. Moreover, the new research on blacks in particular has created a "new" Old South that bears little resemblance to the historical portrayals offered only a generation ago.

The changes in historical interpretation of the period after the Civil War have been just as marked. Politics has been far less a concern, and issues of race and economics predominate. Hardly a trace remains of the old passions associated with images of a "Tragic Era." When politics has been the central topic, the subject has usually been agrarian or middle-class reform—the Populists and the Progressives. The old debate over whether southern history during the era of the Civil War and Reconstruction represented more continuity or discontinuity goes on, but its terms have been changed and refined as scholars untangle the origins of sharecropping, for example, or probe the persistence of planter control.

In the mid-1980s, as the "recent" South since the Second World War reaches four decades of existence, historians are discovering that *that* war might have been as great a watershed for the South as was the Civil War. Slowly the characteristics of an older South, which was poor, rural, and racist, recede as publicists celebrate the Sun Belt and southerners once more are elected to the White House. These momentous changes have attracted the attention of historians as well as social scientists, with the result that southern history begins earlier and is far more inclusive—free blacks, women, skilled slaves, sharecroppers, factory workers, and urban dwellers—than would have been imaginable only twenty-five years ago. Simply by comparing the table of contents and index of this volume with those in a similar historiographical tribute, Arthur S. Link and Rembert W. Patrick's *Writing Southern History* (1965), one will see dramatically the changes in the field of southern history. These dramatic differences in how southern history is conceived, taught, and written are the concerns of this book, *Interpreting Southern History*.

The changes have not been merely chronological and topical, although two new separate topics, women and religion, do set this volume apart from its predecessor. The history that is now being written has been more nearly social and intellectual—and intellectual history that emphasizes not the ideas of an elite but the *mentalité* of the people—and far less military and political in a traditional sense. There has been a sophisticated effort to understand the culture of the various Souths: the culture of eighteenth-century evangelicals, of antebellum planters and slaves, of late-nineteenth-century Populists. As with much of American history, there has been a shift away from narrative history and a rise in quantitative scholarship, with a significant increase in local studies. Sensitivity to issues of race, class, and gender has increased, as has attention to regional variation. There is much less talk of a Solid South in any sense of the term, yet correspondingly the search continues for those overarching themes that somehow have created a popular conception of "the South" out of many different Souths.

Despite this outpouring of written history that has transformed our understanding of the South, there seems to be no diminution of interest in the subject. And there are still topics that lie fallow. The lines of inquiry taken up forty years ago by Frank L. Owsley remain insufficiently followed, and as a result we know far less about yeomen whites than about planters or slaves. Yeoman culture in general is starved for scholarship. The histories of women and religion are new but now very active subfields, and those of science and medicine are growing. We need to know more about southern education, urbanization, and popular culture. Too much southern historical scholarship has centered on the Atlantic seaboard states, so we can look forward to the testing of theses and interpretations with data drawn from the more western sections of the South. Southern history is such a dynamic field that we can expect future transformations of our conceptions as far-reaching as those that have occurred in the past generation. Of one thing we can be sure—this will not be the last summing up of the historiography of the South.

Sanford W. Higginbotham served as managing editor of the *Journal of Southern History* from 1965 to 1983, when he retired on June 30. In commemoration of his tenure, Rice University sponsored a symposium entitled "Interpreting Southern History," held on February 18–19, 1983. Historians who had served on the editorial board of the *Journal* under Higginbotham were invited to prepare papers on the significant recent scholarship on southern history and present the results of their research first in brief form in panel discussions at the symposium and then in extended historiographical essays for this book. Moderators Harold M. Hyman and Allen J. Matusow of Rice University and Edwin A. Miles of the University of Houston kept the panel discussions lively and invited questions from the floor. The quality of the panelists' remarks and the participation of the audience made the symposium an intellectual feast.

Now, three years after that event, the papers are completed and edited. That last word requires elaboration. The co-editors of this volume worked with Higginbotham for a total of fifteen years, Boles as associate editor and Nolen as assistant editor of the *Journal of Southern History*. We have followed his editorial procedures, which means checking every quotation, verifying every footnote, double-checking every title. As each author in this volume knows—and every author published in the *Journal* has learned—such care often brings momentary frustration, a fleeting sense of embarrassment, even anger, and some delay, but we trust the resulting accuracy redeems the procedure in everyone's mind. It is that kind of precision Higginbotham practiced and taught. This volume is as much a celebration of his professionalism as it is a celebration of the remarkably rich scholarship on southern history published since 1965, the year "Hig" became *Journal* editor and *Writing Southern History* was published. That landmark volume, a festschrift for Fletcher M. Green, a master teacher, included literature up to about 1963; this volume, honoring a master editor, generally begins with titles published after that date. *Interpreting Southern History* is conceived as a companion piece to *Writing Southern History*.

A number of individuals helped make the symposium and this volume possible. The co-editors want especially to thank Gale Stokes, Ira D. Gruber, and Allen J. Matusow of the Department of History at

Rice; Lynda Crist and Mary Dix of the *Papers of Jefferson Davis* project at Rice; Bennett H. Wall of the Southern Historical Association; Kathy Tomasic-Carrazedo, Darlene Butler, and Tami Chappel, who helped with typing and details; Cathy S. Monholland, who helped proofread; Dean James and Elizabeth H. Turner, who assisted with the editing; and Dee Pipes, who compiled the index. Barbara O'Neil Phillips, our editor at LSU Press, has been unfailingly accurate, meticulous, and cooperative. To her, and to Beverly Jarrett, who has been so supportive, thanks. Rice University underwrote the cost of the symposium and of preparing the manuscript, with additional funds from the Burkitt Foundation and the Texas Committee for the Humanities. The co-editors also acknowledge with gratitude the cooperation, patience, and active assistance of their respective spouses, Nancy G. Boles and Roy L. Nolen.

Interpreting Southern History

Introduction
Reflections on Sanford W. Higginbotham and the
Journal of Southern History

BENNETT H. WALL

Natives of Fordyce, Arkansas, seem to have a penchant for sustained achievement. The retirement of Sanford Wilson Higginbotham as managing editor of the *Journal of Southern History* on June 30, 1983, a position he held longer than any other editor, marked the end of an era just as certainly as did the retirement two years before of a second distinguished native of that town, Paul "Bear" Bryant, who had at the time won more collegiate football games than any other coach.

I was secretary-treasurer of the Southern Historical Association for more than thirty years and have known the editor even longer. Initially, when "Hig," as he is universally known, served as professor and university editor at the University of Mississippi, we met often at professional meetings but telephoned or wrote each other rarely; however, when he became director of the bureau of research, publication, and records of the Pennsylvania Historical and Museum Commission, our exchanges increased. At that time engrossed in research on a biography of William Goebel of Kentucky, I sought Hig's assistance in looking for Goebel's Pennsylvania birth record. (After many exchanges and much effort on his part, he finally announced that no such record existed.) When Hig moved to Rice University in 1961, our contacts continued.

He and I usually managed to breakfast together at professional meetings. During these *ad hoc* sessions we discussed principally the profession and southern history—not necessarily in that order—and when Rice University nominated Hig for the editorship of the *Journal of Southern History,* I was delighted. Prior to that time I had worked with four editors in eleven years, and, while all of them had been friends, the lack of a continuous relationship between the two key SHA offices had been apparent. In 1965, Hig became editor, and we began to work together. When he became emeritus editor in 1983, that valuable relationship slowed down but did not end.

We two SHA officers believed earnestly in and worked hard to

1

achieve harmony between our respective positions. Problems of the association (and of the changing historical profession) received constant, thorough discussion through telephone calls and letters. Both of us at times took adamant positions, but after discussing a matter, we usually tempered our views. Neither of us ever meddled in the operations of the other's office—but we spoke about what went on and thus informed each other.

Hig chose the editorial board of the *Journal,* as was his prerogative; however, on occasion he asked me, "What kind of historian do you think _____ is?" These conversations usually elicited some response, but I listened more and talked less, for these decisions were the editor's responsibility. Likewise, when, as secretary, I had financial or membership decisions to make, I consulted the editor, realizing, however, that the responsibility was mine. We worked together that way, and both of us believe it to have been effective.

In my opinion, a close relationship and an understanding between both officers of what takes place in the office of editor and in the office of secretary-treasurer is basic to the smooth functioning of any historical association. For eighteen years, the SHA had that, and no change in that relationship occurred when Hig retired.

The SHA in 1965 had 2,969 members and library subscribers. Today it has 4,537 members and subscribers. In 1965 it had just entered its third decade as a scholarly organization. Hig was the first editor in some years to drive his editorial board hard and the first editor (since 1948) who served long enough to tie these scholars into his editorial scheme. Further, his annual editorial board breakfasts became arenas for debate and exchange. To these he often invited editors of other professional journals, who freely gave their opinions.

Gradually the word went out: Hig would give an honest and, at times, blunt appraisal of an article submitted. Nor did the writers wonder for months whether he had received and considered their work; he acknowledged receipt of their articles and accepted or rejected manuscripts in a reasonable length of time. All of this proved to be a factor in increasing the number of SHA members—and, more important, in keeping them. The prestige of the *Journal of Southern History* is testimony to his handling of the editorship and his office.

Hig's excellence as an editor quickly became obvious to me. In conversations at meetings of other historical groups and in discussion with many editors and officers of those bodies, I heard nothing but praise for his work. Martin Ridge, distinguished editor of the *Journal of American History* for more than a decade, often remarked to me how fortunate the SHA was to have Hig as editor. When asked to recall some of those conversations, Ridge wrote, "So far as my comment about Hig is concerned, I guess I have always said that he was and is the best editor in the profession; the JSH has been a model magazine, and that Hig is an editor's editor. You may quote any or all of the above. I will stick by it."

Across eighteen years of working in partnership, not one letter from a responsible person complaining about Hig's editing ever reached me. The two crank letters received went into the special file. On the contrary, scores of persons wrote praising the *Journal,* and numerous authors of articles told me how Hig had helped them say what they attempted to say in the first place.

So what did the two SHA officers discuss in their telephone calls and letters? The usual question had to do with association finances—should it build up a surplus to invest? Without much debate we agreed that a nonprofit, tax-exempt, educational organization, heavily underwritten by universities (at first, Tulane and Rice; later, the University of Georgia and Rice), should not attempt to develop portfolios of stocks. We agreed upon, and supported in the Executive Council meetings, minimal dues increases with all changes based on demonstrable need: charges for printing, postal increases, and the wages of the secretary's staff.

Shortly after Hig became editor, the Executive Council elected the two of us the finance committee of the association. Together, we moved cautiously on association finances. Hig read every *Journal* printing bill as though Internal Revenue Service agents waited outside the door. And he found errors. Despite his congenial attitude and far from overpowering stature, he often proved a straight talker when printing errors or billing errors occurred.

Both of us usually made inspection trips to prospective *Journal* printers. For me, these proved to be educational as I listened to Hig and the printers discuss every advance in printing from Johann Gutenberg to the use of the laser beam in reading copy. Despite my presence, the editor alone chose the printers and decided when to change. Only after Hig had made his decision on *Journal* printing did I discuss the printing of the annual meeting program.

Time after time, Hig and I reviewed the work of members active in the association. Our collective judgment enabled either of us, when asked by the vice-president, to recommend reliable and conscientious persons for committee assignments.

Across eighteen years, we observed and discussed the Southern

Historical Association's annual meeting. Both of us sought to make it interesting and accessible as to program, location, and, of course, sleeping-room charges. In an age when universities continually reduce travel benefits, and in a region where many of the smaller institutions have practically no benefits—and a disproportionate number of blacks and women teach in such institutions—we have made every effort to keep the total cost of attending the annual meeting as low as possible. We have long believed that the annual meeting should be a forum for the free exchange of ideas among equals. We have both pressed to the extent of our influence to have the best possible programs and participants. To this end, we opposed restricting participation to members of the association, believing that non-members had much of value to offer. We also sought to keep the informality and friendliness that had become outstanding characteristics of the annual meetings of the association from the early years—there should be no strangers at Southern Historical Association meetings.

Hig has been a stabilizing force on me, for at times complaints and demands have caused eruptions of—anger, is a good term. In eighteen years, we have had no quarrel and only one misunderstanding, the reason for which neither of us can recall.

Just how many articles Hig read in his eighteen years of editing the *Journal* will ever remain unknown. In those years, he edited more than 288 (including the presidential addresses and reports of the secretary-treasurer). So devoted is he to the *Journal* that during his tenure as editor he vacationed very little and then usually when issue number three, the August issue, had been prepared for printing. His careful editing and helpful comments aided scores of beginning scholars as well as those with reputations to preserve. He is a good friend to many of these persons because of the care and consideration he gave their work. Justifiably, several of the editorial board members who labored with him to keep the quality of the *Journal* high here contribute essays for a volume in his honor. Nothing could be more fitting, though I wonder just how the editors, John B. Boles and Evelyn T. Nolen, managed to keep Hig from penciling his comments on the manuscripts.

After reflecting on more than three decades of friendship and almost two decades of working together, I realize the experience is one to be cherished and not yet consigned to memory, because the relationship will continue.

Sanford Wilson Higginbotham was born April 19, 1913, in Fordyce, Arkansas. He received his B.A. from the then Rice Institute in 1934, his M.A. from Louisiana State University (where he was a graduate assistant for the *Journal of Southern History*) in 1941, and his Ph.D. from the University of Pennsylvania in 1949, studying under Roy F. Nichols. From 1947 to 1956 he taught at the University of Mississippi, rising to professor and serving as university editor. Then he moved to Harrisburg, Pennsylvania, to become director of the bureau of research, publication, and records of the Pennsylvania Historical and Museum Commission. In 1961 he returned to Rice University as professor of history and became managing editor of the *Journal of Southern History* in 1965. He retired on June 30, 1983, and now is a voluntary staff member of the *Papers of Jefferson Davis* project at Rice. Among his published works is *Keystone in the Democratic Arch: Pennsylvania Politics, 1800–1816* (Harrisburg: Pennsylvania Historical and Museum Commission, 1952).

The South Before 1800

GEORGE C. ROGERS, JR.

A History of the South, published by the Louisiana State University Press, was planned four decades ago as a ten-volume series. The only volume that has not appeared is "The Southern Colonies in the Eighteenth Century, 1689–1763." Why? Perhaps because the historical profession has produced too much fractured work, and the two authors directly concerned have been of the most conscientious type. Clarence Ver Steeg clearly understands the need to put the mosaic pieces together but has done so only for four aspects of the South Carolina and Georgia story. Peter Wood has probably fallen under the influence of the ethnographers and consequently is trying to understand every gesture—every twitch and wink.[1] Rhys Isaac, the author of the most distinguished recent book on this period of southern history, says that the reader must be satisfied with the "nodal events," that he can never have the whole. "Yet it is not to be supposed that the writer mistakes the world for a stage. Limited aspects of life may be illuminated, but the whole (no matter what the pushers of systems may affirm) can never be summed up in any interpretive scheme."[2] The answer is that each historian must set before his or her reader the whole as he or she sees it.

During the past twenty years, since the work published in 1962 and 1963, there has been a joyous breaking down of the wholes into the discrete facts—each family, each demographic instant—but now it is time to reassemble the past. Historians have recently been concerned with lines, boundaries, frontiers and have been looking at the points where two or more cultures meet—savagery and civilization;

1. Wendell Holmes Stephenson and E. Merton Coulter (eds.), *A History of the South* (10 vols.; Baton Rouge: Louisiana State University Press, 1947–); Clarence L. Ver Steeg, *Origins of a Southern Mosaic: Studies of Early Carolina and Georgia* (Athens: University of Georgia Press, 1975). Peter Wood is now writing this volume in the series.

2. Rhys Isaac, *The Transformation of Virginia, 1740–1790* (Chapel Hill: University of North Carolina Press, 1982), 332, 326.

English and Spanish; French and English; English, Spanish, and French; or red, white, and black—the configurations are indeed kaleidoscopic. Earlier historians had not failed to look at frontiers; but the new studies observe and understand frontiers and the people on both sides of these lines. The urge is to embrace both sides, yet historians still have an either/or mind-set. In studying the period before 1800, one is concerned with beginnings. Therefore topics are fairly recognizable. But surely one must also probe for a spirit or an ethos that at some point before 1800 begins to give a sense of order to disparate facts and developments. Bertram Wyatt-Brown, author of a recent, innovative book on the South, has presented the concept of "southern honor" in order to pull all the discrete facts together.[3] Like the poet, one must perhaps feel rather than see things clearly.

There does seem to be a sea change taking place in our studies. We might mark the beginning at January, 1981, when the *William and Mary Quarterly: A Magazine of Early American History* added the two words *and Culture* to its subtitle. On that occasion the editors noted that the magazine had been publishing material on literary history and ethnohistory, which essays it would now increase but at the same time add articles on material culture and the arts.[4] One would have thought that the word *history* could have embraced quite easily these newer emphases, but one suspects the desire is for more fundamental change. The historical enterprise has been greatly broadened to include new topics and methodologies, and these developments, for all their promise, complicate the problem of conceptualizing and narrating the whole.

But first historians need facts, and the key to the study of the colonial period in the South since 1962 has been the organization of the state archives. Ernst Posner, in his book *American State Archives* (1964), which Lester Cappon called "this notable book," said that "records have become an important source to which the social scientist must turn in his attempt to diagnose and interpret the past for the benefit of the present and the future."[5] In 1961, Philip Hamer as president of the Society of American Archivists was instrumental in choos-

3. Bertram Wyatt-Brown, *Southern Honor: Ethics and Behavior in the Old South* (New York: Oxford University Press, 1982).

4. "Editorial," *William and Mary Quarterly*, 3rd Ser., XXXVIII (January, 1981), 147. The January, 1982, issue was devoted to the family in early America. See particularly the lead article by Daniel Blake Smith, "The Study of the Family in Early America: Trends, Problems, and Prospects," *William and Mary Quarterly*, 3rd Ser., XXXIX (January, 1982), 3–28.

5. Ernst Posner, *American State Archives* (Chicago: University of Chicago Press,

ing Posner to survey state archives. A central purpose of this survey was "to contribute to the standardization of archival work and procedure throughout the Nation and to the maturation of the archival profession."[6] Vast contributions to the study of the colonial South have been made by archivists—Morris L. Radoff and Edward C. Papenfuse of Maryland, Christopher Crittenden and H. G. Jones of North Carolina, J. Harold Easterby and Charles Lee of South Carolina, Mary Givens Bryan and Carroll Hart of Georgia.

The flourishing Chesapeake school of local history seems to have been predestined. The records of colonial Maryland were the first to be retained, organized, and housed. Lord Baltimore in 1637 appointed John Lewger secretary and keeper of the acts for the first general assembly of Maryland, which met in January, 1638, in St. Mary's City. In 1666, Maryland authorized a building for housing the records of the province and an office for the secretary. The Historical Records Survey of the 1930s accomplished much and in the process trained many who would lead the archival movement of the next generation. In 1934–1935, Maryland built the Hall of Records and in 1935 created the Hall of Records Commission. Enthusiasm for these changes was sparked by the tercentenary of Maryland's founding.[7] Morris Radoff, who was appointed archivist in 1939, pushed the Hall of Records' outstanding publication program.

Court Records of Prince Georges County, Maryland, 1696–1699, edited by Joseph H. Smith and Philip A. Crowl and published in 1964, called attention to the rich harvests that the new social historians could glean. The social relationships of twelve hundred persons mentioned in these court records provided an introduction to the nature of society in early America.[8]

The records of colonial Virginia had suffered far greater losses than had those of Maryland. Virginia wisely undertook, as part of the 350th anniversary celebration of the founding of Jamestown, the Virginia Colonial Records Project, an attempt to reconstitute those records by microfilming all documents pertaining to the early history

---

1964), 1; Lester J. Cappon, Review of Posner's *American State Archives*, in *William and Mary Quarterly*, 3rd Ser., XXII (October, 1965), 678–80 (quotation on p. 678).

6. Posner, *American State Archives*, 3.

7. *Ibid.*, 8, 29–30.

8. Joseph H. Smith and Philip A. Crowl (eds.), *Court Records of Prince Georges County, Maryland, 1696–1699* (Washington, D.C.: American Historical Association, 1964).

of Virginia that could be found in the British Public Record Office and other British depositories.[9]

The North Carolina Historical Commission, established in 1903, made great progress, and in 1934, R. D. W. Connor left the commission to become the first archivist of the United States. In 1934 the Department of Archives and History was established, and with the impetus of North Carolina's tercentenary celebration a new building was authorized and completed in 1965.[10] Mattie Erma Parker's edition of the North Carolina charters initiated a new era in the publication of North Carolina colonial records and was quickly followed by letterpress editions of a series of North Carolina court records.[11] H. G. Jones's *For History's Sake: The Preservation and Publication of North Carolina History, 1663–1903* (1966) told the exciting story of the attempts to bring the records of North Carolina together.[12] With the 400th anniversary of the Roanoke voyages, early North Carolina studies are undergoing a new revival.

In South Carolina the story has been one not of assembling, but of housing and inventorying. J. Harold Easterby laid the plans for a new building, and Charles Lee, since 1961 when the building opened, has carried forward the inventorying and the preparation of finding aids. The publication of the colonial records that was well under way was interrupted until one could be sure that all was under expert control, and the last works planned by Easterby were not published until well into the period under consideration here—William Edwin Hemphill and Wylma Anne Wates's records of provincial congresses and Wil-

9. Posner, *American State Archives*, 284.

10. *Ibid.*, 204–205.

11. Mattie Erma Edwards Parker (ed.), *North Carolina Charters and Constitutions, 1578–1698* (Raleigh: Carolina Charter Tercentenary Commission, 1963), Parker (ed.), *North Carolina Higher-Court Records, 1670–1696* (Raleigh: State Department of Archives and History, 1968), and Parker (ed.), *North Carolina Higher-Court Records, 1697–1701* (Raleigh: State Department of Archives and History, 1971); William S. Price, Jr. (ed.), *North Carolina Higher-Court Records, 1702–1708* (Raleigh: State Department of Archives and History, 1974), and Price (ed.), *North Carolina Higher-Court Minutes, 1709–1723* (Raleigh: Department of Cultural Resources, Division of Archives and History, 1974); Robert J. Cain (ed.), *North Carolina Higher-Court Minutes, 1724–1730* (Raleigh: Department of Cultural Resources, Division of Archives and History, 1981).

12. For a mixed review of Jones's account of North Carolina historical records, see Morris L. Radoff, Review of H. G. Jones's *For History's Sake*, in *William and Mary Quarterly*, 3rd Ser., XXIV (April, 1967), 330–31.

liam L. McDowell's books on Indian affairs.[13] R. Nicholas Olsberg and Terry W. Lipscomb's editions of Commons House of Assembly journals and Adele Stanton Edwards' *Journals of the Privy Council*,[14] most recently buttressed by the impressive work of Theodora J. Thompson, Lark Emerson Adams, and Michael Stevens on the house of representatives of the 1780s, show that the Colonial and the State Records series are now fully under way again.[15]

In Georgia a new building and the continuation of an old series have prepared early Georgia studies for a resurgence,[16] exemplified in the conference staged in February, 1983, in Savannah on the occasion of that city's 250th anniversary.

But the South is not limited to the southeastern states. Most broadly defined, it is the region between Annapolis and Santa Fe, and this study includes all persons who lived within this region prior to 1800. One must begin with the Indians, the true native Americans.

The original occupants migrated to the Americas over the land bridge that once joined Siberia with Alaska. J. Leitch Wright, Jr., in *The Only Land They Knew* (1981), wrote that underwater archaeologists have found evidence that natives were at Tampa Bay thirteen thousand years ago. The number of natives in America prior to the

13. William Edwin Hemphill and Wylma Anne Wates (eds.), *Extracts from the Journals of the Provincial Congresses of South Carolina, 1775–1776* (Columbia: South Carolina Archives Department, 1960). See also William Edwin Hemphill, Wylma Anne Wates, and R. Nicholas Olsberg (eds.), *Journals of the General Assembly and House of Representatives, 1776–1780* (Columbia: University of South Carolina Press, 1970). W. L. McDowell (ed.), *Journals of the Commissioners of the Indian Trade, September 20, 1710–August 28, 1718* (Columbia: South Carolina Archives Department, 1955), McDowell (ed.), *Documents Relating to Indian Affairs, May 21, 1750–August 7, 1754* (Columbia: South Carolina Archives Department, 1958), and McDowell (ed.), *Documents Relating to Indian Affairs, 1754–1765* (Columbia: University of South Carolina Press, 1970).

14. R. Nicholas Olsberg (ed.), *The Journal of the Commons House of Assembly, 23 April 1750–31 August 1751* (Columbia: University of South Carolina Press, 1974); Terry W. Lipscomb and Olsberg (eds.), *The Journal of the Commons House of Assembly, November 14, 1751–October 7, 1752* (Columbia: University of South Carolina Press, 1977); Adele Stanton Edwards (ed.), *Journals of the Privy Council, 1783–1789* (Columbia: University of South Carolina Press, 1971).

15. Theodora J. Thompson (ed.), *Journals of the House of Representatives, 1783–1784* (Columbia: University of South Carolina Press, 1977); Lark Emerson Adams (ed.), *Journals of the House of Representatives, 1785–1786* (Columbia: University of South Carolina Press, 1979); Michael E. Stevens (ed.), *Journals of the House of Representatives, 1787–1788* (Columbia: University of South Carolina Press, 1981).

16. Kenneth Coleman and Milton Ready (eds.), *Original Papers of Governors Reynolds, Ellis, Wright, and Others, 1757–1763* (Athens: University of Georgia Press,

European discovery of the continent was far greater than was once imagined. Wilbur R. Jacobs, in "The Tip of an Iceberg," pointed out in 1974 that the Indians' contact with white Europeans caused rapid decline in their numbers. William McNeill in *Plagues and People* (1976) provided the worldwide setting by identifying the disease pools. Charles M. Hudson, in a 1983 paper, addressed the question of how many Indians there were at the time of their initial contact with Europeans.[17]

Conclusions reached in these studies explain the anger with which many have written the history of the Indians. A whole school arose out of the cases brought in the late 1940s and early 1950s by Indians trying to recover damages for lands they considered stolen. Wilcomb Washburn's *Red Man's Land/White Man's Law* (1971) highlights the legal aspect of this story. The traditional or Puritan view of the Indian has been undermined by many of these studies, including Francis Jennings' angry book, *The Invasion of America* (1975).[18] Bernard W. Sheehan, from the time of his review essay "Indian-White Relations in Early America" (April, 1969), has focused on the dichotomy of savagism versus civility. In "Paradise and the Noble Savage in Jeffersonian Thought" (July, 1969) and in *Seeds of Extinction* (1973) and *Savagism and Civility* (1980), Sheehan analyzed perceptions, particularly those of Englishmen "trapped by the disjunction between savagism and civility."[19] Gary B. Nash also pursued the conflicting

1976), and Coleman and Ready (eds.), *Original Papers of Governor John Reynolds, 1754–1756* (Athens: University of Georgia Press, 1977).

17. J. Leitch Wright, Jr., *The Only Land They Knew: The Tragic Story of the American Indians in the Old South* (New York: Free Press, 1981), 3; Wilbur R. Jacobs, "The Tip of an Iceberg: Pre-Columbian Indian Demography and Some Implications for Revisionism," *William and Mary Quarterly*, 3rd Ser., XXXI (January, 1974), 123–32; William Hardy McNeill, *Plagues and People* (Garden City, N.Y.: Anchor Press, 1976). Charles M. Hudson, who had written extensively on the Indians of the southeastern United States, delivered his paper at the February, 1983, Savannah, Ga., conference. See also Hudson (ed.), *Four Centuries of Southern Indians* (Athens: University of Georgia Press, 1975), and Hudson, *The Southeastern Indians* (Knoxville: University of Tennessee Press, 1976). Peter Wood put into context the relative populations of whites and Indians in his "The Eighteenth-Century South: An Overview" (Paper presented at the annual meeting of the Southern Historical Association, Memphis, Tenn., November 5, 1982).

18. Wilcomb E. Washburn, *Red Man's Land/White Man's Law: A Study of the Past and Present Status of the American Indian* (New York: Charles Scribner's Sons, 1971); Francis Jennings, *The Invasion of America: Indians, Colonialism, and the Cant of Conquest* (Chapel Hill: University of North Carolina Press, 1975).

19. Bernard W. Sheehan, "Indian-White Relations in Early America: A Review Es-

images in the English mind in his article "The Image of the Indian in the Southern Colonial Mind" (April, 1972). What Indians thought of Englishmen is a more difficult riddle to unravel, although Nancy O. Lurie just prior to our period made a helpful start on this problem, and James Merrell discussed Indians' attitudes toward blacks in "The Racial Education of the Catawba Indians" (1984).[20]

No action could have fixed more permanently in the colonial mind the sharp division between Englishmen and Indians than the Proclamation of 1763, which attempted to establish a precise line between the two cultures. Louis De Vorsey described the painful steps that the authorities took in order to make that line a reality. Stitt Robinson, in the tradition of Thomas Perkins Abernethy's *Three Virginia Frontiers* (1940), wrote of the moving southern Indian frontier.[21]

More work should be done on the great Indian confederacies that occupied an ever-shrinking area surrounded by the English, the Spanish, and the French. David Corkran studied the Cherokee and Creek frontiers and pointed out that the Cherokee power was broken as early as 1760 and 1761. James H. O'Donnell made the history of these southern Indian tribes during the American Revolution his special subject. Jerry Cashion assessed the effect of greed for land on the relations between North Carolina and the Cherokees.[22]

---

say," *William and Mary Quarterly*, 3rd Ser., XXVI (April, 1969), 267–86, "Paradise and the Noble Savage in Jeffersonian Thought," *William and Mary Quarterly*, 3rd Ser., XXVI (July, 1969), 327–59, *Seeds of Extinction: Jeffersonian Philanthropy and the American Indian* (Chapel Hill: University of North Carolina Press, 1973), and *Savagism and Civility: Indians and Englishmen in Colonial Virginia* (Cambridge, England: Cambridge University Press, 1980), ix.

20. Gary B. Nash, "The Image of the Indian in the Southern Colonial Mind," *William and Mary Quarterly*, 3rd Ser., XXIX (April, 1972), 197–230; Nancy Oestreich Lurie, "Indian Cultural Adjustment to European Civilization," in James Morton Smith (ed.), *Seventeenth-Century America: Essays in Colonial History* (Chapel Hill: University of North Carolina Press, 1959), 33–60; James H. Merrell, "The Racial Education of the Catawba Indians," *Journal of Southern History*, L (August, 1984), 363–84.

21. Louis De Vorsey, Jr., *The Indian Boundary in the Southern Colonies, 1763– 1775* (Chapel Hill: University of North Carolina Press, 1961); W. Stitt Robinson, *The Southern Colonial Frontier, 1607–1763* (Albuquerque: University of New Mexico Press, 1979).

22. David H. Corkran, *The Cherokee Frontier: Conflict and Survival, 1740–62* (Norman: University of Oklahoma Press, 1962), and *The Creek Frontier, 1540–1783* (Norman: University of Oklahoma Press, 1967); James H. O'Donnell III, *Southern Indians in the American Revolution* (Knoxville: University of Tennessee Press, 1973); Jerry Clyde Cashion, "North Carolina and the Cherokee: The Quest for Land on the Eve of the American Revolution, 1754–1776" (Ph.D. dissertation, University of North Carolina, 1979).

In a sense we need more local Indian history, that is, studies of the smaller tribes. Alan Calmes wrote perceptively of the Cusabo Indians who lived along the coasts of South Carolina and Georgia, and Gene Waddell identified at least seventeen Cusabo tribes.[23] Others might study the Yamassee, Guale, and Timucua Indians.

Major works that assess the perceptions of the three races are Wesley Craven's *White, Red, and Black* (1971) and Gary Nash's *Red, White, and Black* (1974).[24] The first European thrust into the region was by Spanish explorers and settlers who entered through Florida. The Florida story is part of a larger picture that was painted by J. H. Parry in *The Spanish Seaborne Empire* (1966) and by Charles Gibson in *Spain in America* (1966).[25] John J. TePaske, in a pamphlet he edited in 1967, taught us to think in terms of three American empires. He had already opened up administrative history by the publication in 1964 of *The Governorship of Spanish Florida, 1700–1763*.[26] Eugene Lyon, by using the family of Pedro Menendez de Avilés, analyzed the kinship network that "became the basis for the later socioeconomic structure of Spanish Florida." Thus by looking at the private side, we are at last entering the area of local history. How far the student can go in this direction is illustrated by Charles W. Arnade's 1961 article, "Cattle Raising in Spanish Florida, 1513–1763," and by Joyce Harman's 1969 study of Spanish Florida's illicit trade in local products with Virginia, Georgia, South Carolina, and New York.[27]

23. Alan Royse Calmes, "Indian Cultural Traditions and European Conquest of the Georgia–South Carolina Coastal Plain, 3000 B.C.–1733 A.D.: A Combined Archaeological and Historical Investigation" (Ph.D. dissertation, University of South Carolina, 1968); Gene Waddell, *Indians of the South Carolina Lowcountry, 1562–1751* (Spartanburg, S.C.: Reprint Co., 1980).

24. Wesley Frank Craven, *White, Red, and Black: The Seventeenth-Century Virginian* (Charlottesville: University Press of Virginia, 1971); Gary B. Nash, *Red, White, and Black: The Peoples of Early America* (Englewood Cliffs, N.J.: Prentice-Hall, 1974).

25. J. H. Parry, *The Spanish Seaborne Empire* (New York: Knopf, 1966); Charles Gibson, *Spain in America* (New York: Harper & Row, 1966).

26. John J. TePaske (ed.), *Three American Empires* (New York: Harper & Row, 1967), and TePaske, *The Governorship of Spanish Florida, 1700–1763* (Durham: Duke University Press, 1964).

27. Eugene Lyon, *The Enterprise of Florida: Pedro Menendez de Avilés and the Spanish Conquest of 1565–1568* (Gainesville: University Presses of Florida, 1976), vi; Charles W. Arnade, "Cattle Raising in Spanish Florida, 1513–1763," *Agricultural History*, XXXV (July, 1961), 116–24; Joyce Elizabeth Harman, *Trade and Privateering in Spanish Florida, 1732–1763* (St. Augustine: St. Augustine Historical Society, 1969). For a good study of fiscal matters, see Amy Bushnell, *The King's Coffer: Pro-*

As counterpoint to the Spanish story in Florida, Charles Bennett wrote of René Goulaine de Laudonnière and Fort Caroline (1964) and translated Laudonnière's journals of his three voyages (1975). Paul Hulton's new work (1977) on Jacques Le Moyne reintroduces the student to that artist who provided us with the best visual presentations of the St. Augustine Spanish and Indians. Literary evidence and the artifacts provided by archaeologists can be tied together only by the pictures from an artist like Le Moyne.[28] Paul Hoffman provided the freshest reinvestigation of the Spanish in the Southeast in the sixteenth century in *The Spanish Crown and the Defense of the Caribbean, 1535–1585* (1980), which displays broad vision and the most particular research. Michael V. Gannon went much further than earlier historians in revealing the full story of the Spanish missions in Guale and Apalache in the seventeenth century, but his title indicates the uncertain foundations of this research—*The Cross in the Sand* (1965).[29]

Gannon, in an article in the *William and Mary Quarterly* in October, 1981, surveyed the accessibility of documents for the study of the borderlands. Four separate collections at the University of Florida have been calendared. Small collections as yet uncalendared are at Loyola University of the South in New Orleans; at the University of Alabama at Birmingham; at the University of Southwestern Louisiana; at the Louisiana State Museum in New Orleans; and at the University of West Florida. The Bancroft Library at the University of California at Berkeley is still the best place to study the western Spanish borderlands, and the University of Texas at Austin is the best for the vast Texas borderlands. A guide to published studies on the Spanish borderlands can be found in the publication to which Samuel

---

prietors of the Spanish Florida Treasury, 1565–1702 (Gainesville: University Presses of Florida, 1981).

28. Charles E. Bennett, *Laudonnière and Fort Caroline: History and Documents* (Gainesville: University of Florida Press, 1964); René Laudonnière, *Three Voyages*, trans. Charles E. Bennett (Gainesville: University Presses of Florida, 1975); Paul Hulton, *The Work of Jacques Le Moyne de Morgues* (2 vols.; London: British Museum Publications for the Trustees of the British Museum, 1977). See also Kathleen A. Deagan, *Spanish St. Augustine: The Archaeology of a Colonial Creole Community* (New York: Academic Press, 1983).

29. Paul E. Hoffman, *The Spanish Crown and the Defense of the Caribbean, 1535–1585: Precedent, Patrimonialism, and Royal Parsimony* (Baton Rouge: Louisiana State University Press, 1980); Michael V. Gannon, *The Cross in the Sand: The Early Catholic Church in Florida, 1513–1870* (Gainesville: University Presses of Florida, 1965).

Proctor (University of Florida), J. Leitch Wright, Jr. (Florida State), William S. Coker (University of West Florida), and Jack D. L. Holmes (University of Alabama at Birmingham) contributed.[30] During the American Revolution bicentennial, Proctor coordinated annual conferences at which papers were read, and these have been published.[31]

William Coker, with his edition of the papers of Panton, Leslie & Company, showed how a Scottish firm trading with the Florida Indians maintained its footing in ever-changing situations. Robert L. Gold, in *Borderland Empires in Transition* (1969), discussed the multinational complexities of Florida's colonial history.[32]

The work of J. Leitch Wright, Jr., on the eastern borderlands in the period of the American Revolution and after is notable. His *William Augustus Bowles* (1967) was the first of his books on this large subject. *Anglo-Spanish Rivalry in North America* (1971) provides the larger context, and *Florida in the American Revolution* (1975) identifies the countless lesser subjects that need investigation. And his most recent *The Only Land They Knew* (1981) puts the native Americans into the picture.[33] Wright's work illuminates the eastern borderlands story in the late eighteenth century as the historical and archaeological work at St. Augustine sheds new light on the sixteenth and seventeenth centuries.

France entered the American West from Canada by way of the Great Lakes and the Mississippi River. Jacques Marquette and Louis Jolliet first and René Robert Cavelier, Sieur de La Salle, a few years

---

30. Michael V. Gannon, "Documents of the Spanish Florida Borderlands: A Calendaring Project at the University of Florida," *William and Mary Quarterly*, 3rd Ser., XXXVIII (October, 1981), 718–22; "Topical Review: Research in the Spanish Borderlands," *Latin American Research Review*, VII (Summer, 1972), 3–94.

31. Samuel Proctor (ed.), *Eighteenth-Century Florida and Its Borderlands* (Gainesville: University Presses of Florida, 1975), Proctor (ed.), *Eighteenth-Century Florida: Life on the Frontier* (Gainesville: University Presses of Florida, 1976), Proctor (ed.), *Eighteenth-Century Florida and the Revolutionary South* (Gainesville: University Presses of Florida, 1978), and Proctor (ed.), *Eighteenth-Century Florida: The Impact of the American Revolution* (Gainesville: University Presses of Florida, 1978).

32. William S. Coker and Thomas D. Watson (eds.), *Indian Traders of the Southeastern Spanish Borderlands: Panton, Leslie & Company and John Forbes & Company, 1783–1847* (Gainesville: University of West Florida Press, 1985); Robert L. Gold, *Borderland Empires in Transition: The Triple-Nation Transfer of Florida* (Carbondale: Southern Illinois University Press, 1969).

33. J. Leitch Wright, Jr., *William Augustus Bowles: Director General of the Creek Nation* (Athens: University of Georgia Press, 1967), *Anglo-Spanish Rivalry in North America* (Athens: University of Georgia Press, 1971), *Florida in the American Revolution* (Gainesville: University Presses of Florida, 1975), and *The Only Land They Knew.*

later led the French advance, but the arrival of Pierre Le Moyne, Sieur d'Iberville, and Jean Baptiste Le Moyne, Sieur de Bienville, around 1700 on the Gulf Coast was the beginning of permanent settlements at Mobile and Biloxi. Not much has been written recently about the explorations downriver, but the reprinting of Iberville's 1699 journal and his journals of the three voyages between 1699 and 1702 represent renewed interest in early Louisiana history.[34]

The translation (1974) of Marcel Giraud's splendid volume on the early eighteenth century from *A History of French Louisiana* gives us a view from the French sources to place against Verner W. Crane's 1928 classic. Charles E. O'Neill's *Church and State in French Colonial Louisiana* (1966) provides a mine of historical information on this early period, and John G. Clark's *New Orleans, 1718–1812* (1970) constructs the economic framework of the French and later Spanish efforts. Patricia Dillon Woods's *French-Indian Relations on the Southern Frontier, 1699–1762* (1980) concentrates on the pro-French Choctaws and pro-English Chickasaws but also describes the destruction of the Natchez.[35] When one reads these books, one can understand why South Carolinians like Thomas Nairne and John Barnwell took the French threat at New Orleans seriously.

Spanish Louisiana has been discussed in the works of John Preston Moore and Jack D. L. Holmes. Moore studied (1976) the revolt in Louisiana in the late 1760s as a convenient comparison to the English colonial revolt of the 1770s, and Holmes produced in 1965 a biography of Manuel Gayoso de Lemos that proceeds beyond the study of one key figure to a study of the region itself.[36]

34. Carl A. Brasseaux (ed. and trans.), *A Comparative View of French Louisiana, 1699 and 1762: The Journals of Pierre Le Moyne d'Iberville and Jean-Jacques-Blaise d'Abbadie* (Lafayette: Center for Louisiana Studies, University of Southwestern Louisiana, 1979); Richebourg Gaillard McWilliams (ed. and trans.), *Iberville's Gulf Journals* (University: University of Alabama Press, 1981). Patricia K. Galloway recently edited *La Salle and His Legacy: Frenchmen and Indians in the Lower Mississippi Valley* (Jackson: University Press of Mississippi, 1982).

35. Marcel Giraud, *The Reign of Louis XIV, 1698–1715*, trans. Joseph C. Lambert (Baton Rouge: Louisiana State University Press, 1974), vol. I of Giraud, *A History of French Louisiana*, 5 vols. projected; Verner W. Crane, *The Southern Frontier, 1670–1732* (Durham: Duke University Press, 1928); Charles Edwards O'Neill, *Church and State in French Colonial Louisiana: Policy and Politics to 1732* (New Haven: Yale University Press, 1966); John G. Clark, *New Orleans, 1718–1812: An Economic History* (Baton Rouge: Louisiana State University Press, 1970); Patricia Dillon Woods, *French-Indian Relations on the Southern Frontier, 1699–1762* (Ann Arbor: UMI Research Press, 1980).

36. John Preston Moore, *Revolt in Louisiana: The Spanish Occupation, 1766–*

Abraham Nasatir, who has made the study of Spanish Louisiana and Spanish Illinois his life's work, summed up his thoughts in *Borderland in Retreat* (1976). Oakah L. Jones, Jr., in *Los Paisanos* (1979), wrote of the farmer, the day laborer, the soldier on the northernmost frontier of Spanish America, little people who planted a culture that now burgeons.[37]

Joseph T. Hatfield described the Americanization of the Louisiana frontier in his biography of William Claiborne (1976). An excellent book that reveals the full extent of the English settlers' rapaciousness for land is Peter Magrath's volume on the Yazoo case (1966). Although this is most valuable for the study of American constitutional history, it also implies that between 1795 and 1810 a flood of settlers swept across the Creek and Choctaw lands.[38]

What Verner Crane accomplished for the borderlands, Lawrence Henry Gipson tried for the British Empire as a whole—as Richard Morris has called it, Gipson's "spacious empire."[39] The last five volumes of Gipson's history of the great war for the empire appeared after 1962.[40] Thus his opus represents the culmination of the old school. He had a desire to embrace all—in terms of geography, institutions, national interest—and the research was meticulous. Jackson T. Main summed up: "He still discovers and effectively utilizes seldom used and even previously unknown primary sources, while

1770 (Baton Rouge: Louisiana State University Press, 1976); Jack D. L. Holmes, *Gayoso: The Life of a Spanish Governor in the Mississippi Valley, 1789–1799* (Baton Rouge: Louisiana State University Press, 1965).

37. Abraham P. Nasatir, *Borderland in Retreat: From Spanish Louisiana to the Far Southwest* (Albuquerque: University of New Mexico Press, 1976); Oakah L. Jones, Jr., *Los Paisanos: Spanish Settlers on the Northern Frontier of New Spain* (Norman: University of Oklahoma Press, 1979).

38. Joseph T. Hatfield, *William Claiborne: Jeffersonian Centurion in the American Southwest* (Lafayette: University of Southwestern Louisiana, 1976); C. Peter Magrath, *Yazoo: Law and Politics in the New Republic, The Case of Fletcher v. Peck* (Providence, R.I.: Brown University Press, 1966).

39. Richard B. Morris, "The Spacious Empire of Lawrence Henry Gipson," *William and Mary Quarterly*, 3rd Ser., XXIV (April, 1967), 169–89.

40. Lawrence Henry Gipson, *The British Empire before the American Revolution*, Vol. XI, *The Triumphant Empire: The Rumbling of the Coming Storm, 1766–1770*, Vol. XII, *The Triumphant Empire: Britain Sails into the Storm, 1770–1779*, Vol. XIII, *The Triumphant Empire*, Part I: *The Empire Beyond the Storm, 1770–1776*, Part II: *A Summary of the Series*, Part III: *Historiography*, Vol. XIV, *A Bibliographical Guide to the History of the British Empire, 1748–1776*, Vol. XV, *A Guide to Manuscripts Relating to the History of the British Empire, 1748–1776* (New York: Knopf, 1965, 1967, 1968, 1969, 1970).

absorbing fully the very latest secondary books and articles. Throughout, the reader feels the comfortable assurance that he is in the hands of a master craftsman."[41] Gipson's modern stance, if we can call it that, was an attempt to see both sides. He was understanding of the English government, believing that the rebels had not only rights but also obligations, and he recognized maturing American nationalism as a catalyst for revolution. These grand themes may grate upon the nerves of the new social historians, but they were based on searches in 235 repositories and 5,400 bibliographical entries. Although the work is now out of date, it was a noble try. We love to dig deeply, but we do not have the dedication or the stamina to write history in this grand manner.

Twenty-five years ago this article would have begun, as indeed Hugh Rankin began his in *Writing Southern History,* with the arrival of the English in Virginia. But David Quinn, the modern Hakluyt, pushed our knowledge of English explorations along the south Atlantic coast back almost one hundred years. Quinn recently wrote a book on the Lost Colony for the 400th anniversary of the Roanoke voyages, and his five-volume documentary history (1979) has become the indispensable starting point for the investigation of explorations in the southeastern United States. His article "Thomas Hariot and the Virginia Voyages of 1602" (1970) is a case in point. The renewed interest in Thomas Hariot as in Jacques Le Moyne reflects the emphasis on the study of material culture. One product is *Thomas Harriot: Renaissance Scientist,* edited by John W. Shirley (1974).[42] Hariot was the first scientist of note to set foot in the New World.

The hackneyed figure of Captain John Smith apparently must be reinvestigated. In 1972, Wesley Frank Craven told us that we should be pleased that a new edition of Captain Smith's works had been planned, with Philip L. Barbour as editor. Smith had come to life in the pages of Barbour's bulky *The Three Worlds of Captain John Smith*

41. Jackson Turner Main, Review of Gipson's *The Triumphant Empire,* XI, XII, in *William and Mary Quarterly,* 3rd Ser., XXIII (July, 1966), 489–91.

42. Hugh F. Rankin, "The Colonial South," in Arthur S. Link and Rembert W. Patrick (eds.), *Writing Southern History: Essays in Historiography in Honor of Fletcher M. Green* (Baton Rouge: Louisiana State University Press, 1965), 3–37; David B. Quinn, *Set Fair for Roanoke: Voyages and Colonies, 1584–1606* (Chapel Hill: University of North Carolina Press, 1985), Quinn (ed.), *New American World: A Documentary History of North America to 1612* (5 vols.; New York: Arno Press, 1979), and Quinn, "Thomas Hariot and the Virginia Voyages of 1602," *William and Mary Quarterly,* 3rd Ser., XXVII (April, 1970), 268–81; John W. Shirley (ed.), *Thomas Harriot: Renaissance Scientist* (Oxford: Clarendon Press, 1974).

(1964), the best study of that enigmatic man. Alden T. Vaughan provided a synthesis of the man and his times in *American Genesis* (1975). More understandable is the interest in the Massacre of 1622. More and more work implies that Indians did not massacre whites as often as whites massacred Indians. For Vaughan, 1622 was important because by then all prospects for an integrated society had come to an end.[43]

The early 1960s saw a number of publications that carried forward the interests of Charles S. Sydnor, whose *Gentlemen Freeholders* (1952) remains a classic. Perhaps Hugh Rankin unknowingly introduced the new historiography by commenting on Sydnor's work as "a study deceptive in its depth because of its readability."[44] Robert E. Brown and B. Katherine Brown's rather peevish work, *Virginia, 1705– 1786: Democracy or Aristocracy?* (1964), is a good introduction to the historiography of the 1960s, but it has not stood the test of time very well. Lucille Griffith, in *Virginia House of Burgesses* (1963), was less ambitious than the Browns but still saw the power structure rooted in the Tidewater aristocracy.[45] Oliver Chitwood on Richard Henry Lee (1967), Robert D. Meade on Patrick Henry (1969), John Alden on Governor Dinwiddie (1973), and Emory Evans on Thomas Nelson (1975) represent a continuing interest in biography, although none is a memorable portrait.[46]

The reinvigoration of Virginia studies was launched by an older,

---

43. Wesley Frank Craven, "A New Edition of the Works of Captain John Smith," *William and Mary Quarterly*, 3rd Ser., XXIX (July, 1972), 479–86; Philip L. Barbour (ed.), *The Complete Works of Captain John Smith* (3 vols.; Chapel Hill: University of North Carolina Press for the Institute of Early American History and Culture, 1986), and Barbour, *The Three Worlds of Captain John Smith* (Boston: Houghton Mifflin, 1964); Alden T. Vaughan, *American Genesis: Captain John Smith and the Founding of Virginia* (Boston: Little, Brown, 1975), and "'Expulsion of the Salvages': English Policy and the Virginia Massacre of 1622," *William and Mary Quarterly*, 3rd Ser., XXXV (January, 1978), 57–84.

44. Charles S. Sydnor, *American Revolutionaries in the Making: Political Practices in Washington's Virginia* (New York: Collier Books, 1962), originally published as *Gentlemen Freeholders: Political Practices in Washington's Virginia* (Chapel Hill: University of North Carolina Press, 1952); Rankin, "The Colonial South," in Link and Patrick (eds.), *Writing Southern History*, 14.

45. Robert E. Brown and B. Katherine Brown, *Virginia, 1705–1786: Democracy or Aristocracy?* (East Lansing: Michigan State University Press, 1964); Lucille Griffith, *Virginia House of Burgesses, 1750–1774* (Northport, Ala.: Colonial Press, 1963).

46. Oliver Perry Chitwood, *Richard Henry Lee: Statesman of the Revolution* (Morgantown: West Virginia University Library, 1967); Robert Douthat Meade, *Patrick Henry: Practical Revolutionary* (Philadelphia: Lippincott, 1969); John Richard

more traditional historian, Edmund S. Morgan. His article in April, 1971, on the first American boom (1618–1630) highlighted the labor problem. One could get rich off tobacco, but one had to have a labor force. Thus the interest in white and black indentured servants and ultimately in black slaves. The question was when and why did the Virginians turn to black slavery? This line of inquiry led ultimately to one of the great books written during this period, Morgan's *American Slavery—American Freedom* (1975), which perceptively connects slavery and the increase in racial consciousness to the development of democratic tendencies among the whites—hence American *slavery*, American (white) *freedom*.[47] The importance of this book for slavery studies is discussed in Charles B. Dew's essay later in this volume.

Younger scholars poured into the field. Warren M. Billings, in "The Cases of Fernando and Elizabeth Key" (1973) and "The Growth of Political Institutions in Virginia, 1634 to 1676" (1974), essayed the history of seventeenth-century institutions. John Rainbolt (1974) and Mark Egnal (1980) investigated the economy, and Emory Evans became the authority on indebtedness. Richard Beeman provided us with a more analytical study of Patrick Henry (1974) than Meade's 1969 biography. Drew McCoy examined the political economy of Jefferson's Virginia (1976).[48] T. H. Breen pondered the cultural signifi-

---

Alden, *Robert Dinwiddie: Servant of the Crown* (Williamsburg: Colonial Williamsburg Foundation, 1973); Emory G. Evans, *Thomas Nelson of Yorktown: Revolutionary Virginian* (Williamsburg: Colonial Williamsburg Foundation, 1975).

47. Edmund S. Morgan, "The First American Boom: Virginia 1618 to 1630," *William and Mary Quarterly*, 3rd Ser., XXVIII (April, 1971), 169–98, and *American Slavery—American Freedom: The Ordeal of Colonial Virginia* (New York: Norton, 1975).

48. Warren M. Billings, "The Cases of Fernando and Elizabeth Key: A Note on the Status of Blacks in Seventeenth-Century Virginia," *William and Mary Quarterly*, 3rd Ser., XXX (July, 1973), 467–74, and "The Growth of Political Institutions in Virginia, 1634 to 1676," *William and Mary Quarterly*, 3rd Ser., XXXI (April, 1974), 225–42; John C. Rainbolt, *From Prescription to Persuasion: Manipulation of Eighteenth Century Virginia Economy* (Port Washington, N.Y.: Kennikat Press, 1974); Mark Egnal, "The Origins of the Revolution in Virginia: A Reinterpretation," *William and Mary Quarterly*, 3rd Ser., XXXVII (July, 1980), 401–28; Emory G. Evans, "Private Indebtedness and the Revolution in Virginia, 1776 to 1796," *William and Mary Quarterly*, 3rd Ser., XXVIII (July, 1971), 349–74; Richard R. Beeman, *Patrick Henry: A Biography* (New York: McGraw-Hill, 1974); Drew Randall McCoy, "The Republican Revolution: Political Economy in Jeffersonian America, 1776 to 1817" (Ph.D. dissertation, University of Virginia, 1976), published as *The Elusive Republic: Political Economy in Jeffersonian America* (Chapel Hill: University of North Carolina Press, 1980).

cance of gambling among the gentry (1977), and with such a study we entered the age of the ethnographer and the search for meaning in gestures. A. G. Roeber's "Authority, Law, and Custom: The Ritual of Court Day in Tidewater Virginia, 1720 to 1750" (1980) is another example of this trend.[49]

The history of colonial North Carolina has always been difficult to pull together into clearly recognizable major themes. Robert Ramsey, in *Carolina Cradle* (1964), described the Piedmont as a spawning ground for further movement to the west. Lawrence Lee portrayed the lower Cape Fear (1965) as an extension of the South Carolina world of rice and naval stores. James Morrill tried to make sense of fiat finance (1969); Robert Ganyard of the election of 1776 (1967). Don Higginbotham, in editing the papers of James Iredell (1976), and William Masterson, in editing those of John Gray Blount (1965), were both laying the basis for a better understanding of the Federalist period in North Carolina.[50] The Regulation draws the most interest and causes the most heated debates. Marvin L. Michael Kay's "The North Carolina Regulation, 1766–1776: A Class Conflict" (1976) builds upon the older view of Elisha Douglass in *Rebels and Democrats* (1955) that the Regulation pitted the yeomen farmers of the interior against the gentlemen of the coast. Yet Kay perceived the class struggle as inherent in the backcountry society itself. James P. Whittenburg carried the analysis of social change further in his 1977 article "Planters, Merchants, and Lawyers: Social Change and the Origins of the North Carolina Regulation." Some culmination of this debate may be found in A. Roger Ekirch's "*Poor Carolina*"

49. T. H. Breen, "Horses and Gentlemen: The Cultural Significance of Gambling among the Gentry of Virginia," *William and Mary Quarterly*, 3rd Ser., XXXIV (April, 1977), 239–57; A. G. Roeber, "Authority, Law, and Custom: The Ritual of Court Day in Tidewater Virginia, 1720 to 1750," *William and Mary Quarterly*, 3rd Ser., XXXVII (January, 1980), 29–52.

50. Robert W. Ramsey, *Carolina Cradle: Settlement of the Northwest Carolina Frontier, 1747–1762* (Chapel Hill: University of North Carolina Press, 1964); Lawrence Lee, *The Lower Cape Fear in Colonial Days* (Chapel Hill: University of North Carolina Press, 1965); James R. Morrill, *The Practice and Politics of Fiat Finance: North Carolina in the Confederation, 1783–1789* (Chapel Hill: University of North Carolina Press, 1969); Robert L. Ganyard, "Radicals and Conservatives in Revolutionary North Carolina: A Point at Issue, the October Election, 1776," *William and Mary Quarterly*, 3rd Ser., XXIV (October, 1967), 568–87; Don Higginbotham (ed.), *The Papers of James Iredell* (2 vols.; Raleigh: Department of Cultural Resources, Division of Archives and History, 1976); William H. Masterson (ed.), *The John Gray Blount Papers*, Vol. III, *1796–1802* (Raleigh: State Department of Archives and History, 1965).

(1981), where the concentration is on the question of corruption in the eighteenth-century English and American society. The itch to get rich permeated all groups. Focusing on royal patronage and courthouse cliques produces a complex picture in which social distinctions may not be so great as the simple dichotomy of a class struggle implies. Hugh T. Lefler and William S. Powell, who have been for the last two generations the preeminent authorities on North Carolina history, published in 1973 *Colonial North Carolina: A History*. This is a largely successful attempt to embrace all subjects, although slavery, women, and demography are shortchanged in light of the new interests of historians.[51]

Colonial South Carolina (1966), Eugene Sirmans' excellent book, grew out of his study of the Bull family, which he had written as a doctoral dissertation under Wesley Frank Craven. The Bull family was central to the political history of South Carolina and continues to fascinate authors, as the forthcoming works by Geraldine Meroney and Kinloch Bull prove. Sirmans' book opened the new era. Contemporaneous publications such as William Dabney and Marion Dargan's *William Henry Drayton* (1962), Richard Sherman's *Robert Johnson* (1966), and George Frakes's *Laboratory for Liberty* (1970) are less successful than Sirmans' work.[52] Unfortunately Sirmans died at an early age. Dr. Joseph Waring made a distinct contribution to the history of medicine in South Carolina (1964), and Converse

51. Marvin L. Michael Kay, "The North Carolina Regulation, 1766–1776: A Class Conflict," in Alfred F. Young (ed.), *The American Revolution: Explorations in the History of American Radicalism* (DeKalb: Northern Illinois University Press, 1976), 71–123; Elisha P. Douglass, *Rebels and Democrats: The Struggle for Equal Political Rights and Majority Rule During the American Revolution* (Chapel Hill: University of North Carolina Press, 1955); James P. Whittenburg, "Planters, Merchants, and Lawyers: Social Change and the Origins of the North Carolina Regulation," *William and Mary Quarterly*, 3rd Ser., XXXIV (April, 1977), 215–38; A. Roger Ekirch, *"Poor Carolina": Politics and Society in Colonial North Carolina, 1729–1776* (Chapel Hill: University of North Carolina Press, 1981); Hugh T. Lefler and William S. Powell, *Colonial North Carolina: A History* (New York: Charles Scribner's Sons, 1973).

52. M. Eugene Sirmans, *Colonial South Carolina: A Political History, 1663–1763* (Chapel Hill: University of North Carolina Press, 1966), and "Masters of Ashley Hall: A Study of the Bull Family in Colonial South Carolina, 1670–1737" (Ph.D. dissertation, Princeton University, 1959); William M. Dabney and Marion Dargan, *William Henry Drayton & the American Revolution* (Albuquerque: University of New Mexico Press, 1962); Richard P. Sherman, *Robert Johnson: Proprietary & Royal Governor of South Carolina* (Columbia: University of South Carolina Press, 1966); George Edward Frakes, *Laboratory for Liberty: The South Carolina Legislative Committee System, 1719–1776* (Lexington: University Press of Kentucky, 1970).

Clowse closely examined the history of the port activity of Charleston (1981).[53]

Jack P. Greene and two of his students, Robert Weir and Robert Calhoon, have presented penetrating analyses of the Carolina political world. Greene's articles on the Gadsden and Wilkes crises are model dissections of the political scene. Weir's dissertation on the Stamp Act crisis in South Carolina (1966) led to his article with Calhoon, "'The Scandalous History of Sir Egerton Leigh,'" and to his own "'The Harmony We Were Famous For'" (both published in 1969).[54] *The Papers of Henry Laurens* has provided grist for these mills, but in the area of analysis, there has been nothing more exciting than the contributions by Weir. His essay on southern newspapers (1980) and his consideration of rebelliousness as a motivating factor in the Revolution are models of this genre. His recent *Colonial South Carolina* (1983) is a major reconsideration of the important questions that historians have been asking about South Carolina. Only Peter Wood's *Black Majority* (1974) is in this class, but this pathbreaking book in black history is appropriately discussed by Charles Dew in his essay in this volume.[55]

53. Joseph Ioor Waring, *A History of Medicine in South Carolina, 1670–1825* (Columbia, S.C.: R. L. Bryan Co., 1964); Converse D. Clowse, *Economic Beginnings in Colonial South Carolina 1670–1730* (Columbia: University of South Carolina Press, 1971), and *Measuring Charleston's Overseas Commerce, 1717–1767: Statistics from the Port's Naval Lists* (Washington, D.C.: University Press of America, 1981).

54. Jack P. Greene, "The Gadsden Election Controversy and the Revolutionary Movement in South Carolina," *Mississippi Valley Historical Review*, XLVI (December, 1959), 469–92, and "Bridge to Revolution: The Wilkes Fund Controversy in South Carolina, 1769–1775," *Journal of Southern History*, XXIX (February, 1963), 19–52. See also Greene (ed.), *The Nature of Colony Constitutions: Two Pamphlets on the Wilkes Fund Controversy in South Carolina By Sir Egerton Leigh and Arthur Lee* (Columbia: University of South Carolina Press, 1970); Robert McColloch Weir, "'Liberty and Property, and No Stamps': South Carolina and the Stamp Act Crisis" (Ph.D. dissertation, [Case] Western Reserve University, 1966); Robert M. Calhoon and Weir, "'The Scandalous History of Sir Egerton Leigh,'" *William and Mary Quarterly*, 3rd Ser., XXVI (January, 1969), 47–74; Weir, "'The Harmony We Were Famous For': An Interpretation of Pre-Revolutionary South Carolina Politics," *William and Mary Quarterly*, 3rd Ser., XXVI (October, 1969), 473–501.

55. Philip M. Hamer, George C. Rogers, Jr., and David R. Chesnutt (eds.), *The Papers of Henry Laurens* (10 vols. to date; Columbia: University of South Carolina Press, 1968–); Robert M. Weir, "The Role of the Newspaper Press in the Southern Colonies on the Eve of the Revolution: An Interpretation," in Bernard Bailyn and John B. Hench (eds.), *The Press & the American Revolution* (Worcester: American Antiquarian Society, 1980), 99–150, "Rebelliousness: Personality Development and the American Revolution in the Southern Colonies," in Jeffrey J. Crow and Larry E. Tise (eds.), *The Southern Experience in the American Revolution* (Chapel Hill: Uni-

Richard Maxwell Brown's *The South Carolina Regulators* (1963) is the seminal work on that backcountry phenomenon, but two recent studies not yet published have successfully built upon Brown's foundation. Rachel Klein beautifully dissected the chaos of the backcountry. Her Yale dissertation contains a memorable portrait of the banditti, and the result is a clear explanation of how the backcountry farmers were transformed into cotton planters. The motivation was a desire not only for law and order but also for status equal to that of lowcountry magnates. Ronald Bridwell used Wade Hampton I to tell an individual story that stands as a model against which to measure the careers of other aspiring yeomen and shopkeepers.[56]

There is a vast amount of new social history recently published. Philip Morgan's essay on the task system (1982), Peter Coclanis' placement of South Carolina (1982) in the market economy of that day, and George Terry's demographic study of the parish of St. Johns Berkeley (1982) are a few examples. The sources are not as rich as are those for New England, nor is there the constant conferencing of the Chesapeake school, but the group is on its way and has been using the rich resources of the South Carolina Department of Archives and History. A different kind of local history, an attempt at the total picture, is *The History of Georgetown County, South Carolina* (1970) by George C. Rogers, Jr., and a projected *History of Beaufort County, South Carolina* by Rogers and Lawrence S. Rowland.[57]

The connections of the South Carolina Federalists with the na-

---

versity of North Carolina Press, 1978), 25–54, and *Colonial South Carolina: A History* (Millwood, N.Y.: KTO Press, 1983); Peter H. Wood, *Black Majority: Negroes in Colonial South Carolina from 1670 through the Stono Rebellion* (New York: Knopf, 1974).

56. Richard Maxwell Brown, *The South Carolina Regulators* (Cambridge: Belknap Press, 1963); Rachel Klein, "The Rise of the Planters in the South Carolina Backcountry, 1767–1808" (Ph.D. dissertation, Yale University, 1979); Ronald Edward Bridwell, "The South's Wealthiest Planter: Wade Hampton I of South Carolina, 1754–1835" (Ph.D. dissertation, University of South Carolina, 1980).

57. Philip D. Morgan, "Work and Culture: The Task System and the World of Lowcountry Blacks, 1700 to 1880," *William and Mary Quarterly*, 3rd Ser., XXXIX (October, 1982), 563–99; Peter A. Coclanis, "Rice Prices in the 1720s and the Evolution of the South Carolina Economy," *Journal of Southern History*, XLVIII (November, 1982), 531–44; George D. Terry, "'Champaign Country': A Social History of an Eighteenth Century Lowcountry Parish in South Carolina, St. Johns Berkeley County" (Ph.D. dissertation, University of South Carolina, 1981); George C. Rogers, Jr., *The History of Georgetown County, South Carolina* (Columbia: University of South Carolina Press, 1970).

tional party figures were traced by Rogers in his biography of William Loughton Smith (1962), by Marvin Zahniser in *Charles Cotesworth Pinckney* (1967), and by Joseph W. Cox in his biography of Robert Goodloe Harper (1972). More comprehensive treatments of southern Federalists have been presented by Lisle A. Rose (1968) and James H. Broussard (1978).[58]

The great vigor presently manifest in Georgia studies was apparent on February 8–10, 1983, at a symposium on colonial Georgia entitled "Forty Years of Diversity" held in Savannah on the occasion of the 250th anniversary of the founding of that city. The first topic was the Georgia Plan, which Milton Ready examined in its economic aspects, Larry Ivers in its military aspects, and Betty Wood from the stance of the earl of Egmont in London.[59]

The second session was on Oglethorpe and the Indians. Phinizy Spalding, in "James Edward Oglethorpe's Quest for an American Zion," used a novel approach by comparing early Georgia with early Massachusetts. Charles Hudson drew upon his recent, thorough analysis of the marches of Hernando de Soto and Juan Pardo through the southeastern region in his paper "The Genesis of Georgia's Indians."[60] On the eve of de Soto's arrival the Indians were numerous;

58. George C. Rogers, Jr., *Evolution of a Federalist: William Loughton Smith of Charleston (1758–1812)* (Columbia: University of South Carolina Press, 1962); Marvin R. Zahniser, *Charles Cotesworth Pinckney, Founding Father* (Chapel Hill: University of North Carolina Press, 1967); Joseph W. Cox, *Champion of Southern Federalism: Robert Goodloe Harper of South Carolina* (Port Washington, N.Y.: Kennikat Press, 1972); Lisle A. Rose, *Prologue to Democracy: The Federalists in the South, 1789–1800* (Lexington: University of Kentucky Press, 1968); James H. Broussard, *The Southern Federalists, 1800–1816* (Baton Rouge: Louisiana State University Press, 1978).

59. Milton L. Ready, "Philanthropy and the Origins of Georgia," Larry E. Ivers, "Rangers, Scouts, and Tythingmen," and Betty Wood, "The Earl of Egmont and the Georgia Colony," all in Harvey H. Jackson and Phinizy Spalding (eds.), *Forty Years of Diversity: Essays on Colonial Georgia* (Athens: University of Georgia Press, 1984), 46–59, 152–62, 80–100. Other works by these historians include Coleman and Ready (eds.), *Original Papers of Governors Reynolds, Ellis, Wright, and Others* and *Original Papers of Governor John Reynolds;* Larry E. Ivers, *British Drums on the Southern Frontier: The Military Colonization of Georgia, 1733–1749* (Chapel Hill: University of North Carolina Press, 1974); and Betty Wood, *Slavery in Colonial Georgia, 1730–1775* (Athens: University of Georgia Press, 1984).

60. Phinizy Spalding, "James Edward Oglethorpe's Quest for an American Zion," and Charles M. Hudson, "The Genesis of Georgia's Indians," both in Jackson and Spalding (eds.), *Forty Years of Diversity,* 60–79, 25–45. Spalding has also written *Oglethorpe in America* (Chicago: University of Chicago Press, 1977). Chester B. De-

by the time of Oglethorpe's arrival few remained. Disease, vicious slave-trading, and the rivalries of the great powers had decimated the native population. Noteworthy was Hudson's description of Indian migrations. No wonder Tomochichi clung to Oglethorpe during this ongoing holocaust.

In the third session, John Reps reconsidered the origins of the town plan of Savannah. He suggested that Benjamin Martyn might have been the principal author. The frontispiece for the program was a view of Savannah taken from a Benjamin Martyn pamphlet. Reps also speculated that Londonderry and Coleraine in Northern Ireland were precedents as were the newly fashionable squares of London's West End, particularly Hanover Square. George Fenwick Jones, who has made a major contribution to Georgia history by his translations and editing of the Salzburger manuscripts, presented the career of John Adam Treutlen, the first governor of Georgia of German descent, and demonstrated what can be accomplished by meticulous research.[61]

In a session devoted to the social and political life of the colony, Calvin Smith drew material from his dissertation on the Habersham family, the most important merchant family of Georgia's colonial period. Lee Ann Caldwell searched colonial wills in order to find whether or not women could inherit real property. She punctured the idea that they could not.[62]

The backcountry-lowcountry contrasts were perceptively presented by Edward Cashin and Harvey Jackson. Cashin focused on the Augusta traders and argued that rivalry between traders and settlers

Pratter, Charles M. Hudson, and Marvin T. Smith, "The Route of Juan Pardo's Explorations in the Interior Southeast, 1566–1568," *Florida Historical Quarterly*, LXII (October, 1983), 125–58.

61. John W. Reps, "$C^2 + L^2 = S^2$? Another Look at the Origins of Savannah's Town Plan," and George Fenwick Jones, "John Adams Treutlen's Origin and Rise to Prominence," both in Jackson and Spalding (eds.), *Forty Years of Diversity*, 101–51, 217–28. Reps is also the author of Jones (ed.), *Detailed Reports on the Salzburger Emigrants Who Settled in America . . . Edited by Samuel Urlsperger* (8 vols. to date; Athens: University of Georgia Press, 1968–), and Jones, *The Salzburger Saga: Religious Exiles and Other Germans Along the Savannah* (Athens: University of Georgia Press, 1984).

62. W. Calvin Smith, "The Habershams: The Merchant Experience in Georgia," and Lee Ann Caldwell, "Women Landholders of Colonial Georgia," both in Jackson and Spalding (eds.), *Forty Years of Diversity*, 198–216, 183–97. See also Smith, "Georgia Gentlemen: The Habershams of Eighteenth-Century Savannah" (Ph.D. dissertation, University of North Carolina, 1971).

after the land cession of 1773 had raised the passions of these interior folk before British troops arrived. Jackson examined the beginnings of Georgia Whiggery on the coast.[63]

Kenneth Coleman, whose *Colonial Georgia* (1976) is the most recent summary view of the colony, was the opening-night speaker and expertly set the scene for all the papers that followed. Jack Greene, final speaker, tried to fit Georgia into his scheme that pertains to the self-perceptions of the Virginia, South Carolina, and Jamaica planters. All were anxious for profit and status, and thus they established, even more than New Englanders did, the model for future Americans.[64]

The historian of the pre-1800 South must consider the southern colonies and states in their relationship to the British West Indies. The most direct connection was South Carolina as an offshoot of Barbadian culture. The work of Richard Dunn in his analysis (1969) of the Barbados census of 1680 and his *Sugar and Slaves* (1972), with his conclusion that South Carolina was settled by the younger sons of Barbadian planters, suggests the transfer of plantation models. In the same way, Richard Sheridan's *Sugar and Slavery* (1973) provides points of comparison for the rice and indigo cultures of the southern colonies.[65]

More should be written on the world of the pirates, who ranged over the West Indies and the American coast. Marcus Rediker's ar-

63. Edward J. Cashin, "Sowing the Wind: Governor Wright and the Georgia Backcountry on the Eve of the Revolution," and Harvey H. Jackson, "Georgia Whiggery: The Origins and Effects of a Many-faceted Movement," both in Jackson and Spalding (eds.), *Forty Years of Diversity*, 233–50, 251–73. See also Cashin and Heard Robertson, *Augusta and the American Revolution: Events in the Georgia Back Country, 1773–1783* (Darien, Ga.: Ashantilly Press, 1975); and Jackson, *Lachlan McIntosh and the Politics of Revolutionary Georgia* (Athens: University of Georgia Press, 1979).

64. Kenneth Coleman, "The Founding of Georgia," and Jack P. Greene, "Travails of an Infant Colony: The Search for Viability, Coherence, and Identity in Colonial Georgia," both in Jackson and Spalding (eds.), *Forty Years of Diversity*, 4–20, 278–309. Coleman has also written *Colonial Georgia: A History* (New York: Charles Scribner's Sons, 1976).

65. Richard S. Dunn, "The Barbados Census of 1680: Profile of the Richest Colony in English America," *William and Mary Quarterly*, 3rd Ser., XXVI (January, 1969), 3–30, and *Sugar and Slaves: The Rise of the Planter Class in the English West Indies, 1624–1713* (Chapel Hill: University of North Carolina Press, 1972). Peter Wood in his *Black Majority* also emphasizes that South Carolina was a colony of another colony, Barbados. Richard B. Sheridan, *Sugar and Slavery: An Economic History of the British West Indies, 1623–1775* (Baltimore: Johns Hopkins University Press, 1973).

ticle (1981) is an interesting attempt at social analysis of the pirates' hierarchical world. Hugh Rankin provided an overview in *The Golden Age of Piracy* (1969). Further work on the maroon societies of the West Indies and the southern colonies would be a great challenge to a young scholar.[66]

Following the Revolution the Loyalists left South Carolina and Georgia, taking their slaves with them. After they successfully produced Sea Island cotton in the Bahamas in the 1780s, their seeds and know-how were soon transferred back to the mainland and sparked the great cotton boom. The religious map of the West Indies was changed with the arrival of black Baptists among the slaves who left Savannah for Kingston and New Providence. James Walker's *The Black Loyalists* (1976) is a seminal contribution in this area. Richard Sheridan's article (1976) on provision crops and the problems of subsistence after the British West Indies were closed to American sailing vessels in 1783 shows the integral connection that existed between the two areas.[67]

And much work is under way comparing Virginia, South Carolina, Jamaica, Bermuda, and Barbados plantations. Richard Dunn, Michael Craton and James Walvin, Michael Mullin, Virginia Bernhard, and Jack Greene have all spent time and effort in this fertile field of comparative history.[68] Such studies will certainly change the way we look at the southern colonies.

66. Marcus Rediker, "'Under the Banner of King Death': The Social World of Anglo-American Pirates, 1716 to 1726," *William and Mary Quarterly*, 3rd Ser., XXXVIII (April, 1981), 203–27; Hugh F. Rankin, *The Golden Age of Piracy* (Williamsburg: Colonial Williamsburg, 1969); Barbara Klamon Kopytoff, "The Early Political Development of Jamaican Maroon Societies," *William and Mary Quarterly*, 3rd Ser., XXXV (April, 1978), 287–307; Richard Price (ed.), *Maroon Societies: Rebel Slave Communities in the Americas* (Garden City, N.Y.: Anchor Press, 1973).

67. James W. St. G. Walker, *The Black Loyalists: The Search for a Promised Land in Nova Scotia and Sierra Leone, 1783–1870* (New York: Africana Publishing Co., 1976); Richard B. Sheridan, "The Crisis of Slave Subsistence in the British West Indies during and after the American Revolution," *William and Mary Quarterly*, 3rd Ser., XXXIII (October, 1976), 615–41.

68. Richard S. Dunn, "A Tale of Two Plantations: Slave Life at Mesopotamia in Jamaica and Mount Airy in Virginia, 1799 to 1828," *William and Mary Quarterly*, 3rd Ser., XXXIV (January, 1977), 32–65; Michael Craton and James Walvin, *A Jamaican Plantation: The History of Worthy Park, 1670–1970* (Toronto: University of Toronto Press, 1970); Michael Mullin, "British Caribbean and North American Slaves in an Era of War and Revolution, 1775–1807," in Crow and Tise (eds.), *The Southern Experience in the American Revolution*, 235–67; Virginia Bernhard, "Bermuda and Virginia in the Seventeenth Century: A Comparative View," *Journal of Social History*,

Thomas O. Ott, in *The Haitian Revolution* (1973), and George Terry, in his thesis (1979) on South Carolina and the insurrections in Saint-Domingue, have begun an assessment of the impact of the French Revolution and its West Indian repercussions upon the southern mind.[69]

There are a number of valuable studies on the military and naval history of the American Revolution, but they generally deal with the whole continental struggle. Of course, they cannot ignore the southern scene as so many studies of the Revolution once did. Stephen Saunders Webb's *The Governors-General* (1979) is a good introduction, as it emphasizes military considerations in the shaping of the empire. More immediate background for the Revolution is found in John Shy's *Toward Lexington* (1965), which charts the stationing and withdrawal of British troops in the southern colonies. A reviewer has called Shy's *A People Numerous and Armed* (1976) "one of the most thoughtful and worthwhile books on the military struggle for American independence."[70]

The growing interest among historians in analyzing deeply held perceptions is reflected in Charles Royster's *A Revolutionary People at War* (1979), a book that picks up some hints from Shy's *A People Numerous and Armed*. Royster selected Light-Horse Harry Lee as the subject of an individual study (1981) in order to explore the connection between the Revolution and character. Sylvia R. Frey produced a more matter-of-fact account in *The British Soldier in America* (1981). A southern emphasis and a traditional approach are traits of Hugh Rankin's study *The North Carolina Continentals* (1971), and Rankin's biography of Francis Marion (1973) is the standard ac-

---

XIX (Fall, 1985), 57–70; and Jack P. Greene's forthcoming study of Virginia, South Carolina, and Jamaica.

69. Thomas O. Ott, *The Haitian Revolution, 1789–1804* (Knoxville: University of Tennessee Press, 1973); George D. Terry, "A Study of the Impact of the French Revolution and the Insurrections in Saint-Domingue upon South Carolina: 1790–1805" (M.A. thesis, University of South Carolina, 1973).

70. Stephen Saunders Webb, *The Governors-General: The English Army and the Definition of the Empire, 1569–1681* (Chapel Hill: University of North Carolina Press, 1979); John Shy, *Toward Lexington: The Role of the British Army in the Coming of the American Revolution* (Princeton: Princeton University Press, 1965), and *A People Numerous and Armed: Reflections on the Military Struggle for American Independence* (New York: Oxford University Press, 1976); Franklin B. Wickwire, Review of Shy's *A People Numerous and Armed*, in *William and Mary Quarterly*, 3rd Ser., XXXIV (April, 1977), 326.

count of that always intriguing military figure. Clyde Ferguson's fine dissertation (1960) on Andrew Pickens should be published.[71]

One would naturally expect to find much of importance on southern military campaigns in the festschrift for John Alden (1979). John Cavanagh on Benjamin Lincoln and Paul Nelson on Horatio Gates are successful assessments of these two military leaders, but Richard Hargrove's attempt at a portrait of that romantic Carolinian John Laurens is a great missed opportunity. Ira D. Gruber's "Britain's Southern Strategy" is an excellent brief account with penetrating comments: "Differences of opinion—aggravated by distance, personal pique, and pressure from London—kept Clinton and Cornwallis from acting together until the French intervened finally and decisively at Yorktown."[72] After that statement, one may not need to follow William B. Willcox through his psychological investigations of Clinton's character (1962). Franklin Wickwire and Mary Wickwire's biography of Cornwallis (1971) is more popular but less probing of the human psyche. The freshest item in the Alden festschrift is Clyde Ferguson's interpretation of the role of the state militia. Ferguson was critical of Russell Weigley's grand theme in *The Partisan War* (1970), a book which, if it is wrong, is gloriously wrong. Weigley's comparison of the American Revolution in the South with the Vietnam War is brilliant. And M. F. Treacy's *Prelude to Yorktown* (1963) is the best showing of Nathanael Greene's talents as a delaying-surviving general.[73]

71. Charles Royster, *A Revolutionary People at War: The Continental Army and American Character, 1775–1783* (Chapel Hill: University of North Carolina Press, 1979), and *Light-Horse Harry Lee: The Legacy of the American Revolution* (New York: Knopf, 1981); Sylvia R. Frey, *The British Soldier in America: A Social History of Military Life in the Revolutionary Period* (Austin: University of Texas Press, 1981); Hugh F. Rankin, *The North Carolina Continentals* (Chapel Hill: University of North Carolina Press, 1971), and *Francis Marion: The Swamp Fox* (New York: Thomas Y. Crowell, 1973); Clyde R. Ferguson, "General Andrew Pickens" (Ph.D. dissertation, Duke University, 1960).

72. John C. Cavanagh, "American Military Leadership in the Southern Campaign: Benjamin Lincoln," Paul David Nelson, "Major General Horatio Gates as a Military Leader: The Southern Experience," Richard J. Hargrove, "Portrait of a Southern Patriot: The Life and Death of John Laurens," and Ira D. Gruber, "Britain's Southern Strategy," all in W. Robert Higgins (ed.), *The Revolutionary War in the South: Power, Conflict, and Leadership. Essays in Honor of John Richard Alden* (Durham: Duke University Press, 1979), 101–31, 132–58, 182–202, 205–38 (quotation on p. 237). Gruber has much to say on the reasons for the failure of British strategy in the American Revolution in his *The Howe Brothers & the American Revolution* (Chapel Hill: University of North Carolina Press, 1972).

73. William B. Willcox, *Portrait of a General: Sir Henry Clinton in the War of*

Neil R. Stout on the Royal Navy in America (1973), Jonathan R. Dull on the French navy and the American Revolution (1975), and Ernest McNeill Eller, as editor, on American naval activities in the Chesapeake (1981) go a long way in introducing the student to the naval side of these southern campaigns. The eight volumes of the *Naval Documents of the American Revolution* (begun in 1964), which carry the war up to 1777, contain important information on the southern phase of American naval history.[74]

The study of the American Loyalists is a national question, but the southern aspect of this story is its most important segment. Paul Smith's fine study, *Loyalists and Redcoats* (1964), shows to what extent British strategy rested on the presence of numerous Loyalists in the southern colonies. This subject does not lend itself easily to quantification, as Wallace Brown's two books, *The King's Friends* (1965) and *The Good Americans* (1969), prove. A prosopographical approach would yield more enduring results. A Loyalist generally changed sides several times, and thus the career line of each individual must be studied. It was not necessarily true that wives and children followed the head of the family. There is a vast corpus of materials to be mastered, and the Loyalists of each state should be studied in turn. Only after such work is completed will the definitive book be possible. Mary Beth Norton's general account of the British-Americans in England (1972) will not be helpful to the prosopographer because individual stories are avoided in favor of generalization. Robert Calhoon selected a well-known few to begin the attempt and did valuable service in providing examples of varying paths through the Revolution (1973). Anne Zimmer, in her biography of Jonathan

---

Independence (New York: Knopf, 1962); Franklin Wickwire and Mary Wickwire, *Cornwallis and the War of Independence* (London: Faber & Faber, 1971); Clyde R. Ferguson, "Functions of the Partisan-Militia in the South During the American Revolution: An Interpretation," in Higgins (ed.), *The Revolutionary War in the South*, 239–58; Russell F. Weigley, *The Partisan War: The South Carolina Campaign of 1780–1782* (Columbia: University of South Carolina Press, 1970); M. F. Treacy, *Prelude to Yorktown: The Southern Campaign of Nathanael Greene, 1780–1781* (Chapel Hill: University of North Carolina Press, 1963).

74. Neil R. Stout, *The Royal Navy in America, 1760–1775: A Study of Enforcement of British Colonial Policy in the Era of the American Revolution* (Annapolis: Naval Institute Press, 1973); Jonathan R. Dull, *The French Navy and American Independence: A Study of Arms and Diplomacy, 1774–1787* (Princeton: Princeton University Press, 1975); Ernest McNeill Eller (ed.), *Chesapeake Bay in the American Revolution* (Centreville, Md.: Tidewater Publishers, 1981); William Bell Clark and William James Morgan (eds.), *Naval Documents of the American Revolution* (8 vols. to date; Washington, D.C.: U.S. Government Printing Office, 1964–).

Boucher (1978), did the best job, but do we have the time to provide studies of such magnitude for every Loyalist?[75]

H. James Henderson's *Party Politics in the Continental Congress* (1974) must be considered here because Henderson saw a fundamental division in the Congress between sections, and in his third period, from 1783 to 1789, the southern bloc was in the ascendancy. Was this the true First South? Henderson's roll-call analysis works in this situation, which involves a small group of people, and each of them is individually known. By using traditional sources, that is, correspondence, as well as the roll-call analysis, the author achieved a nice blend. And yet the irritation of the South at the Jay-Gardoqui negotiations may be overemphasized.[76]

Republicanism is certainly the most important subject for the student of eighteenth-century American history. What was the proper structure for the Republic and upon what principles of human nature was it based? No amount of the new social history will be revealing unless it is rooted in this context. And this is a southern topic, as a study of eighteenth-century southerners would prove.

The preeminent figure in contemporary historiography is Bernard Bailyn. Many of his students, such as Gordon Wood and Pauline Maier, carry on his work. Wood's "Rhetoric and Reality in the American Revolution," published in January, 1966, emphasized the primacy of intellectual history, but of ideas continuously undergoing transformation. His *The Creation of the American Republic* (1969) concentrates upon the dialogue that was background to the work of 1787. Maier, in "The Charleston Mob and the Evolution of Popular Politics in Revolutionary South Carolina, 1765–1784" (1970),

75. Paul H. Smith, *Loyalists and Redcoats: A Study in British Revolutionary Policy* (Chapel Hill: University of North Carolina Press, 1964); Wallace Brown, *The King's Friends: The Composition and Motives of the American Loyalist Claimants* (Providence, R.I.: Brown University Press, 1965), and *The Good Americans: The Loyalists in the American Revolution* (New York: Morrow, 1969); Mary Beth Norton, *The British-Americans: The Loyalist Exiles in England, 1774–1789* (Boston: Little, Brown, 1972); Robert McCluer Calhoon, *The Loyalists in Revolutionary America, 1760–1781* (New York: Harcourt Brace Jovanovich, 1973); Anne Y. Zimmer, *Jonathan Boucher: Loyalist in Exile* (Detroit: Wayne State University Press, 1978).

76. H. James Henderson, *Party Politics in the Continental Congress* (New York: McGraw-Hill, 1974). Jack N. Rakove, *The Beginnings of National Politics: An Interpretive History of the Continental Congress* (New York: Knopf, 1979), challenges Henderson's thesis and supports the "nationalist" interpretation of the origins of the American Union. Every student of the Congress should begin with Paul H. Smith *et al.* (eds.), *Letters of Delegates to Congress, 1774–1789* (10 vols. to date; Washington, D.C.: U.S. Government Printing Office, 1976–).

showed how out-of-doors actions supplemented and deepened the movement toward new republican forms. Her *From Resistance to Revolution* (1972) gives us the larger picture.[77] But the school of Bailyn could not have made such an impact without the work in English history of Caroline Robbins, Trevor Colbourn, Isaac Kramnick, and especially J. G. A. Pocock. Robbins first traced the connections between the English Civil War and the American Revolution (1959); Colbourn worked on the genealogy of commonwealth ideas (1965); Kramnick introduced us to Bolingbroke and his circle, who fathered the country party (1968); and Pocock (1975) saw how all culminated in the Machiavellian moment of 1787.[78]

No one has helped the student of republicanism more than Robert E. Shalhope in his series of historiographical essays. In January, 1972, he published "Toward a Republican Synthesis: The Emergence of an Understanding of Republicanism in American Historiography." In 1974, Colbourn, Robbins, and Shalhope combined their efforts to make the work of Douglass Adair more accessible to scholars. *Fame and the Founding Fathers: Essays by Douglass Adair* made the eclectic efforts of an older scholar the natural prelude to these reconsiderations of republicanism. In April, 1982, Shalhope returned to his subject in "Republicanism and Early American Historiography," and in his recent biography of John Taylor of Caroline (1980), he made the major point that the ideals of the country party lived on in the South. Pauline Maier, in "The Road Not Taken: Nullification, John C. Calhoun, and the Revolutionary Tradition in South Carolina" (1981), reassessed

---

77. Bernard Bailyn, *The Ideological Origins of the American Revolution* (Cambridge: Belknap Press of Harvard University Press, 1967); Gordon S. Wood, "Rhetoric and Reality in the American Revolution," *William and Mary Quarterly*, 3rd Ser., XXIII (January, 1966), 3–32, and *The Creation of the American Republic, 1776–1787* (Chapel Hill: University of North Carolina Press, 1969); Pauline Maier, "The Charleston Mob and the Evolution of Popular Politics in Revolutionary South Carolina, 1765–1784," *Perspectives in American History*, IV (1970), 173–96, and *From Resistance to Revolution: Colonial Radicals and the Development of American Opposition to Britain, 1765–1776* (New York: Knopf, 1972).

78. Caroline Robbins, *The Eighteenth-Century Commonwealthman: Studies in the Transmission, Development and Circumstance of English Liberal Thought from the Restoration of Charles II until the War with the Thirteen Colonies* (Cambridge: Harvard University Press, 1959); H. Trevor Colbourn, *The Lamp of Experience: Whig History and the Intellectual Origins of the American Revolution* (Chapel Hill: University of North Carolina Press, 1965); Isaac Kramnick, *Bolingbroke and His Circle: The Politics of Nostalgia in the Age of Walpole* (Cambridge: Harvard University Press, 1968); J. G. A. Pocock, *The Machiavellian Moment: Florentine Political Thought and the Atlantic Republican Tradition* (Princeton: Princeton University Press, 1975).

Calhoun in light of this tradition. And George C. Rogers, Jr., recently tried to stretch this tradition to the present in "A Southern Political Tradition" (1981).[79] This subject alone deserves study in the manner of a Robbins or a Pocock.

Richard Beale Davis merits separate treatment for his magisterial three-volume *Intellectual Life in the Colonial South* (1978), which was the culmination of a life's work. It blankets the field of southern literary history. Davis was determined to prove that there was "a far greater literary activity in the colonial South than has been recognized in the past." According to one reviewer, Davis "has done for the southern mind, although in a different way, what scholars such as Samuel Eliot Morison and Perry Miller did for the New England mind." Davis' study is more factual, less interpretative, of course, than Perry Miller's intricately wrought intellectual history. As Edwin Wolf II wrote, Davis was the South's "most masterful cultural interpreter."[80] Davis' principal point will always be debatable, but in the future the debate must begin with his work.

In spite of George Tindall's calling our attention in *The Ethnic Southerners* (1976) to the various ethnic groups that went into the southern melting pot, there have not been many studies of the ethnic groups present in the southern colonies in the eighteenth century. R. J. Dickson wrote of the ethnic background of many southerners in

79. Robert E. Shalhope, "Toward a Republican Synthesis: The Emergence of an Understanding of Republicanism in American Historiography," *William and Mary Quarterly*, 3rd Ser., XXIX (January, 1972), 49–80; Trevor Colbourn (ed.), *Fame and the Founding Fathers: Essays by Douglass Adair* (New York: Norton, 1974). Caroline Robbins contributed a personal memoir and Robert E. Shalhope a bibliographical essay. Shalhope, "Republicanism and Early American Historiography," *William and Mary Quarterly*, 3rd Ser., XXXIX (April, 1982), 334–56, and *John Taylor of Caroline: Pastoral Republican* (Columbia: University of South Carolina Press, 1980); Pauline Maier, "The Road Not Taken: Nullification, John C. Calhoun, and the Revolutionary Tradition in South Carolina," *South Carolina Historical Magazine*, LXXXII (January, 1981), 1–19; George C. Rogers, Jr., "A Southern Political Tradition," in *Why the South Will Survive by Fifteen Southerners* (Athens: University of Georgia Press, 1981), 81–90.

80. Richard Beale Davis, *Intellectual Life in the Colonial South, 1585–1763* (3 vols.; Knoxville: University of Tennessee Press, 1978). The publication in 1964 of his *Intellectual Life in Jefferson's Virginia, 1790–1830* (Chapel Hill: University of North Carolina Press) was the important prelude to this larger effort. Pierre Marambaud, Review of Davis' *Intellectual Life in the Colonial South*, in *William and Mary Quarterly*, 3rd Ser., XXXVI (July, 1979), 469–72; Edwin Wolf II, Review of Richard Beale Davis' *A Colonial Bookshelf*, in *William and Mary Quarterly*, 3rd Ser., XXXVII (April, 1980), 350–53.

Ulster Emigration to Colonial America (1966). Klaus Wust, in *The Virginia Germans* (1969), took the story of that group to the twentieth century. There have been dissertations on the French Huguenots and the Purrysburgh Swiss, two South Carolina ethnic groups. And Daniel Littlefield, in *Rice and Slaves* (1981), considered black ethnic groups. Only Forrest McDonald and Ellen Shapiro McDonald, in their article "The Ethnic Origins of the American People, 1790" (1980), have tried to raise their subject to the level of a formative influence upon the entire history of the South, but seeing the South as simply a Celtic offshoot is a view through a distorted lens.[81]

There is still no work on women in the colonial period to take the place of Julia Cherry Spruill's old (1938) but still valuable study. The three-volume *Notable American Women, 1607–1950,* edited by Edward T. James, Janet W. James, and Paul S. Boyer, contains admirable short accounts of a few southern women: Virginia Dare, Martha Logan, Eliza Lucas Pinckney, Pocahontas, and Martha Laurens Ramsay. Joan Hoff Wilson suggested a number of approaches to the study of women in the American revolutionary period in "The Illusion of Change: Women and the American Revolution" (1976). Mary Beth Norton's *Liberty's Daughters* (1980) and Linda Kerber's *Women of the Republic* (1980), which use southern examples, assess the changing place of women, particularly with reference to the goals of the Revolution and the training of the young for their own roles in the new republican society. Catherine Clinton's *The Plantation Mistress* (1982) attempts to get beneath the myths about the white mistresses of southern plantations but draws far more upon antebellum examples than upon colonial ones.[82]

81. George Brown Tindall, *The Ethnic Southerners* (Baton Rouge: Louisiana State University Press, 1976); R. J. Dickson, *Ulster Emigration to Colonial America, 1718– 1775* (London: Routledge & Kegan Paul, 1966); Klaus Wust, *The Virginia Germans* (Charlottesville: University Press of Virginia, 1969); Amy Ellen Friedlander, "Carolina Huguenots: A Study in Cultural Pluralism in the Low Country, 1679–1768" (Ph.D. dissertation, Emory University, 1979); Arlin Charles Migliazzo, "Ethnic Diversity on the Southern Frontier: A Social History of Purrysburgh, South Carolina, 1732–1792" (Ph.D. dissertation, Washington State University, 1982); Daniel C. Littlefield, *Rice and Slaves: Ethnicity and the Slave Trade in Colonial South Carolina* (Baton Rouge: Louisiana State University Press, 1981); Forrest McDonald and Ellen Shapiro McDonald, "The Ethnic Origins of the American People, 1790," *William and Mary Quarterly*, 3rd Ser., XXXVII (April, 1980), 179–99.

82. Julia Cherry Spruill, *Women's Life and Work in the Southern Colonies* (Chapel Hill: University of North Carolina Press, 1938). For a detailed analysis of the historiography of women in the South, see the essay in this volume by Jacquelyn Dowd Hall and Anne Firor Scott. Edward T. James, Janet Wilson James, and Paul S. Boyer (eds.),

In the study of colonial education, one effort towers above all others. Lawrence A. Cremin, in his two volumes entitled *American Education* (1970, 1980), provided a magnificent overview in the grand tradition. There is, however, little attention paid to the southern side of the story. Yet anyone wishing to write on the eighteenth-century practice of sending the young to the dissenting academies in England or on the postrevolutionary practice of hiring northern tutors or establishing rural academies (three subjects crying out for authors) would have an excellent interpretative framework within which to place his or her own investigation.[83]

The history of science in the colonies has thus far been a study of the Anglo-American natural history circle. In 1970, Raymond Phineas Stearns published his life's work, *Science in the British Colonies of America* (with chapters entitled "The Royal Society's Early Promotions: Virginia" and "The Southern Mainland Colonies"), which Whitfield J. Bell, Jr., described as "a triumphant climax of one period in the historiography of American science, and an indispensable reference for all future historians of science in the British colonies of America." Stearns's emphasis was on individual men of science. He had already published, with George F. Frick, *Mark Catesby: The Colonial Audubon* (1961). The interest, of course, was in botany, the discovery of plants and the attempts to organize the knowledge of a worldwide system of plants. Edmund Berkeley and Dorothy Berkeley have most persistently followed this traditional approach to science. In 1963 they brought out their study *John Clayton: Pioneer of American Botany* and then wrote studies of Dr. Alexander Garden

---

Notable American Women, 1607–1950: A Biographical Dictionary (3 vols.; Cambridge: Belknap Press of Harvard University Press, 1971). A new volume to this series has been added. Barbara Sicherman and Carol Hurd Green (eds.), *Notable American Women: The Modern Period: A Biographical Dictionary* (Cambridge: Belknap Press of Harvard University Press, 1980). Joan Hoff Wilson, "The Illusion of Change: Women and the American Revolution," in Young (ed.), *The American Revolution,* 383–445; Mary Beth Norton, *Liberty's Daughters: The Revolutionary Experience of American Women, 1750–1800* (Boston: Little, Brown, 1980); Linda K. Kerber, *Women of the Republic: Intellect and Ideology in Revolutionary America* (Chapel Hill: University of North Carolina Press, 1980); Catherine Clinton, *The Plantation Mistress: Woman's World in the Old South* (New York: Pantheon, 1982).

83. Lawrence A. Cremin, *American Education: The Colonial Experience, 1607–1783* (New York: Harper & Row, 1970), and *American Education: The National Experience, 1783–1876* (New York: Harper & Row, 1980). For a good introduction to the northern tutor, see Elizabeth Brown Pryor, "An Anomalous Person: The Northern Tutor in Plantation Society, 1773–1860," *Journal of Southern History,* XLVII (August, 1981), 363–92.

(1969), Dr. John Mitchell (1974), and John Bartram (1982).[84] It is time now to have histories of particular scientific problems (experiments in electricity, for example) rather than further biographical studies.

The arts in colonial America need a major study, although Kenneth Silverman's *A Cultural History of the American Revolution* (1976) is a good introduction to the period from 1763 to 1789.[85] When the work of assembling information at the Museum of Early Southern Decorative Arts in Winston-Salem, North Carolina, has been completed, the facts will be available for a full-scale survey of the arts in the southern colonies. The work that has already been done in that institution on the history of southern colonial furniture is a good harbinger.

Anna Wells Rutledge broke the ground in 1949 with her *Artists in the Life of Charleston* (reprinted in 1980). Margaret Middleton gave us studies of Jeremiah Theus (1953) and Henrietta Johnston (1966), both of Charleston. Perhaps no strictly southern artist deserves the treatment that Jules David Prown gave to John Singleton Copley (1966) or that Robert C. Alberts has recently provided for Benjamin West (1978) and Irma B. Jaffe for John Trumbull (1975).[86] Although

---

84. Raymond Phineas Stearns, *Science in the British Colonies of America* (Urbana: University of Illinois Press, 1970); Whitfield J. Bell, Jr., Review of Stearns's *Science in the British Colonies of America,* in *William and Mary Quarterly,* 3rd Ser., XXIX (January, 1972), 163–65; George F. Frick and Stearns, *Mark Catesby, the Colonial Audubon* (Urbana: University of Illinois Press, 1961); Edmund Berkeley and Dorothy Smith Berkeley, *John Clayton: Pioneer of American Botany* (Chapel Hill: University of North Carolina Press, 1963), *Dr. Alexander Garden of Charles Town* (Chapel Hill: University of North Carolina Press, 1969), *Dr. John Mitchell: The Man Who Made the Map of North America* (Chapel Hill: University of North Carolina Press, 1974), and *The Life and Travels of John Bartram: From Lake Ontario to the River St. John* (Tallahassee: University Presses of Florida, 1982).

85. Kenneth Silverman, *A Cultural History of the American Revolution: Painting, Music, Literature, and the Theatre in the Colonies and the United States from the Treaty of Paris to the Inauguration of George Washington, 1763–1789* (New York: Thomas Y. Crowell, 1976). The first three chapters of Jessie Poesch, *Art of the Old South* (New York: Knopf, 1983), which cover the colonial South, indicate how valuable a nationwide history of the arts in the colonial period would be.

86. Anna Wells Rutledge, *Artists in the Life of Charleston, Through Colony and State from Restoration to Reconstruction* (Columbia: University of South Carolina Press, 1980), first published in 1949 by the American Philosophical Society; Margaret Simons Middleton, *Jeremiah Theus: Colonial Artist of Charles Town* (Columbia: University of South Carolina Press, 1953), and *Henrietta Johnston of Charles Town, South Carolina: America's First Pastellist* (Columbia: University of South Carolina Press, 1966); Jules David Prown, *John Singleton Copley* (2 vols.; Cambridge: Harvard

more national than southern in interest, Lillian Miller's work on the Peale family and Edward Carter's edition of the Benjamin Latrobe papers are superior. The Gibbes Art Gallery's spring 1983 exhibition of Charles Fraser marshals the resources of a number of southern institutions in its study of that Charleston artist. George W. Williams' study of sacred music in Charleston (1971) remains a model for the field of musicology. Hugh Rankin wrote *The Theater in Colonial America* (1960), but there is still much to be done concerning the stage in southern towns during the eighteenth century.[87] Someone should do for the arts in the South what Richard Beale Davis has done for literature.

Hugh Rankin stated in *Writing Southern History*: "Studies of colonial culture in the South have always been limited, by the nature of the sources, to the upper classes; and only an extensive use of the extant legal records and reliance upon contemporary observations can restore any kind of balance." As I pointed out earlier, there are more recorded facts than we realized, and they have become more accessible, but the chief shift in the last twenty years has been to new methodologies and new approaches. Lawrence Stone, in a paper delivered at Vanderbilt University in 1975, delineated the new fields and some of the new techniques. The six major fields of historical inquiry that are still in their heroic phase of primary exploration are the history of science, demographic history, history of social change, history of mass culture (*mentalités*), urban history, and history of the family.[88]

University Press, 1966); Robert C. Alberts, *Benjamin West: A Biography* (Boston: Houghton Mifflin, 1978); Irma B. Jaffe, *John Trumbull: Patriot-Artist of the American Revolution* (Boston: New York Graphic Society, 1975).

87. Lillian B. Miller (ed.), *The Collected Papers of Charles Willson Peale and His Family*, Microfiche (Millwood, N.Y.: Kraus Microform, 1980); Edward C. Carter (ed.), *The Papers of Benjamin Henry Latrobe*, Microfiche (Clifton, N.J.: James T. White & Co. for the Maryland Historical Society, 1976); Martha R. Severens and Charles L. Wyrick, Jr. (eds.), *Charles Fraser of Charleston: Essays on the Man, His Art and His Times* (Charleston: Carolina Art Association, 1983); George W. Williams, *Jacob Eckhard's Choirmaster's Book of 1809* (Columbia: University of South Carolina Press, 1971); Hugh F. Rankin, *The Theater in Colonial America* (Chapel Hill: University of North Carolina Press, 1960). See also Kathryn Painter Ward, "The First Professional Theater in Maryland in Its Colonial Setting," *Maryland Historical Magazine*, LXX (Spring, 1975), 29–44; David Ritchey, "The Philadelphia Company Performs in Baltimore," *Maryland Historical Magazine*, LXXI (Spring, 1976), 80–85; and Ward, "The Maryland Theatrical Season of 1760," *Maryland Historical Magazine*, LXXII (Fall, 1977), 335–45.

88. Rankin, "The Colonial South," in Link and Patrick (eds.), *Writing Southern History*, 36; Lawrence Stone, "History and the Social Sciences in the Twentieth Cen-

It takes time to develop these new fields, but interest is stimulated, and the latest findings are circulated by the symposia and colloquiums that have proliferated in the last two decades. The Institute of Early American History and Culture has had a long series of conferences. The meeting at Rice University in 1983 is the latest in another group—the festschriften. The essays that appeared in the book in honor of Fletcher M. Green were prepared only for publication and not oral presentation. In 1964 the students of Thomas Perkins Abernethy produced a volume in his honor.[89] When John Edwin Pomfret, a man who has been called the real founder of the Institute of Early American History and Culture, retired, a group of scholars who had been connected with the institute and with the Huntington Library contributed to a reinterpretation of early American history (1966). In 1973 the students of Bernard Mayo honored their mentor, as did those of Merrill Jensen in 1976.[90] The festschrift for John Alden has been considered earlier.

There is another category of conferences, the reassessment of important topics, that often leads to publication of important essays. *The Southern Experience in the American Revolution*, edited by Jeffrey J. Crow and Larry E. Tise, is an excellent example. Stephen G. Kurtz and James H. Hutson's edition of *Essays on the American Revolution* (1973); Alfred F. Young's edition of *The American Revolution;* Charles F. Delzell's edition of *The Future of History;* and John Higham and Paul K. Conkin's *New Directions in American Intellectual History* (1979) contain insights for both American and southern history.[91]

---

tury," in Charles F. Delzell (ed.), *The Future of History: Essays in the Vanderbilt Centennial Symposium* (Nashville: Vanderbilt University Press, 1977), 22–23.

89. Link and Patrick (eds.), *Writing Southern History;* Darrett B. Rutman (ed.), *The Old Dominion: Essays for Thomas Perkins Abernethy* (Charlottesville: University Press of Virginia, 1964). Eleven essays were contributed by William M. E. Rachal, Darrett B. Rutman, Emory G. Evans, Jane Carson, John C. Matthews, William M. Dabney, W. Stitt Robinson, Francis L. Berkeley, Jr., Newton B. Jones, Elizabeth Cometti, and Alan Schaffer.

90. Ray Allen Billington (ed.), *The Reinterpretation of Early American History: Essays in honor of John Edwin Pomfret* (San Marino, Calif.: Huntington Library, 1966); John B. Boles (ed.), *America: The Middle Period. Essays in Honor of Bernard Mayo* (Charlottesville: University Press of Virginia, 1973); James Kirby Martin (ed.), *The Human Dimensions of Nation Making: Essays on Colonial and Revolutionary America* (Madison: State Historical Society of Wisconsin, 1976).

91. Crow and Tise (eds.), *The Southern Experience in the American Revolution;* Stephen G. Kurtz and James H. Hutson (eds.), *Essays on the American Revolution* (Chapel Hill: University of North Carolina Press, 1973); Young (ed.), *The American Revolution;* Delzell (ed.), *The Future of History;* John Higham and Paul K. Conkin

The history of science in colonial America has not yet felt the winds of change. As was explained above, it is largely the history of botanical studies, but historical archaeology has come of age, principally through the work of Ivor Noël Hume at Williamsburg and of Stanley South in North Carolina and South Carolina. Noël Hume has published continuously and, with access to the vast resources that Colonial Williamsburg can marshal, has been digging steadily. *Martin's Hundred* (1982) is a work that should excite any historian. The fruits have been unexpected, the light thrown on the Massacre of 1622 important, and the joy of treasure hunting raised to the level of a high art.[92] Stanley South at Brunswick, North Carolina, Old Charles Town, South Carolina, and now the fort and town of San Marcos on Parris Island, South Carolina, has unearthed the sites of our earliest Spanish and English settlements. These efforts and those described by Kathleen Deagan that have taken place at St. Augustine, when combined with the work of David Quinn, Eugene Lyon, and Paul Hoffman in the literary records (all mentioned earlier), are adding to our knowledge. There is no area of our work where more sophisticated techniques are being used to probe the past.

According to Lawrence Stone, urban history is a subject in search of a problem. The motives for the development of villages and clustered settlements of the seventeenth and eighteenth centuries have been investigated. Joseph Ernst and Roy Merrens considered the "process of urbanization" when they examined the history of Camden, South Carolina's first interior town (1973). Camden grew because of the fortuitous coincidence of a trade path with the distributive functions represented by "flour milling and the wheat trade" as well as mercantile connections with Philadelphia. Hermann Wellenreuther rebutted (1974), focusing on the personal initiative of landholders who wanted to improve the value of their lands as the most important motive for settlement. Surely the many "lost towns" of the South Carolina and Georgia coast would indicate that land speculation was a primary incentive.[93]

(eds.), *New Directions in American Intellectual History* (Baltimore: Johns Hopkins University Press, 1979).

92. Ivor Noël Hume, *Martin's Hundred* (New York: Knopf, 1982). See also Noël Hume's *Here Lies Virginia: An Archaeologist's View of Colonial Life and History* (New York: Knopf, 1963) and *Historical Archaeology* (New York: Knopf, 1969).

93. Joseph A. Ernst and H. Roy Merrens, "'Camden's turrets pierce the skies!': The Urban Process in the Southern Colonies during the Eighteenth Century," *William and Mary Quarterly,* 3rd Ser., XXX (October, 1973), 549–74 (quotation on p. 562); Her-

We need a complete study of town incorporation in the colonial and early national period—the motives, the kinds of government, and a thorough, systematic search for records, such as the Wilmington Town Book. Town plans have been studied. The work of John Reps towers above all others in this area of interest. In *Tidewater Towns* (1972), Reps goes back to Britain to investigate the origins of colonial town plans. He compliments Francis Nicholson (who needs a full-scale biographical study) on his siting of both Annapolis and Williamsburg. Most town plans followed the grid plan, although Joan Sears shows (1979) how the common plan was variously adapted in Georgia. No one, however, has come up with an overarching work on the colonial cities to take the place of Bridenbaugh's classics, *Cities in the Wilderness* (1938) and *Cities in Revolt* (1955).[94]

Kenneth Lockridge made us aware of the enormously important generalizations that stem from the study of demography and the family. But he also warned us of the dangers. He frightened us with the image of Robert Fogel in his laboratory calling for: "Numbers, numbers, give me more numbers!" and confessed that quantitative approaches do not reveal "the great resonances of human life."[95] But this quantitative historical effort will continue.

Much of the work in American demography and family history has been done in New England, for there the local records are ample.

---

mann Wellenreuther, "Urbanization in the Colonial South: A Critique," *William and Mary Quarterly*, 3rd Ser., XXXI (October, 1974), 653–71; Henry A. M. Smith, "Some Forgotten Towns in Lower South Carolina," *South Carolina Historical Magazine*, XIV (July, 1913), 134–46, (October, 1913), 198–208; Charles C. Jones, Jr., *The Dead Towns of Georgia* (Savannah: Morning News Steam Printing House, 1878). See Carville Earle and Ronald Hoffman, "The Urban South: The First Two Centuries," in Blaine A. Brownell and David R. Goldfield (eds.), *The City in Southern History: The Growth of Urban Civilization in the South* (Port Washington, N.Y.: Kennikat Press, 1977), 27–51.

94. Donald R. Lennon and Ida Brooks Kellam (eds.), *The Wilmington Town Book, 1743–1778* (Raleigh: Department of Cultural Resources, Division of Archives and History, 1973); John W. Reps, *Tidewater Towns: City Planning in Colonial Virginia and Maryland* (Williamsburg: Colonial Williamsburg Foundation, 1972); see also John C. Rainbolt, "The Absence of Towns in Seventeenth-Century Virginia," *Journal of Southern History*, XXXV (August, 1969), 343–60; Joan Niles Sears, *The First One Hundred Years of Town Planning in Georgia* (Atlanta: Cherokee Publishing Co., 1979); Carl Bridenbaugh, *Cities in the Wilderness: The First Century of Urban Life in America, 1625–1742* (New York: Ronald Press Co., 1938), and *Cities in Revolt: Urban Life in America, 1743–1776* (New York: Knopf, 1955).

95. Kenneth A. Lockridge, "Historical Demography," in Delzell (ed.), *The Future of History*, 61.

Philip J. Greven, Jr., while working on Andover (1966), began to formulate the questions: "How many children people had, how long people lived, at what ages did they marry, how much control did fathers have over their children, and to what extent and under what conditions did children remain in their parents' community?" He described the modified extended family that was patriarchal as well. More questions flowed from the pen of David J. Rothman in "A Note on the Study of the Colonial Family" (1966). By July, 1967, Greven could write an essay review—"Historical Demography and Colonial America"—that informed his American readers of the work of those who had established in England the Cambridge Group for the History of Population and Social Structure. By October, 1970, Demos on Plymouth, Greven on Andover, and Lockridge on Dedham could be reviewed at the same time. And by 1976, Herbert G. Gutman had presented a sweeping reassessment of the black family.[96]

The professional success and acclaim that came to these authors was too great for those who were investigating southern social history to ignore. Demographic and family studies were spreading like wildfire, but where could the historian of the South find the necessary facts? Presumably in Maryland, which had well-preserved, voluminous records for the colonial period.

This new school burst upon the scene with the January, 1973, issue of the *William and Mary Quarterly* entirely devoted to the Chesapeake Society and an ensuing conference on the seventeenth-century Chesapeake held on November 1–2, 1974, at the University of Maryland at College Park and St. Mary's City, Maryland. The St. Mary's City Commission would soon rival the Institute of Early American History and Culture at Williamsburg. It was appropriate that Rhys Isaac should write the lead article in the January, 1973, issue because his later work would be greatly influenced by the new scholarship making its publishing debut in the issue. Noteworthy were the new documents coming under scrutiny and the new ways of looking at

96. Philip J. Greven, Jr., "Family Structure in Seventeenth-Century Andover, Massachusetts," *William and Mary Quarterly*, 3rd Ser., XXIII (April, 1966), 234; David J. Rothman, "A Note on the Study of the Colonial Family," *William and Mary Quarterly*, 3rd Ser., XXIII (October, 1966), 627–34; Greven, "Historical Demography and Colonial America," *William and Mary Quarterly*, 3rd Ser., XXIV (July, 1967), 438–54; John J. Waters, Review of Demos' *A Little Commonwealth*, Greven's *Four Generations*, and Lockridge's *A New England Town*, in *William and Mary Quarterly*, 3rd Ser., XXVII (October, 1970), 657–62; Herbert G. Gutman, *The Black Family in Slavery and Freedom, 1750–1925* (New York: Pantheon, 1976).

traditional materials. Russell R. Menard used land and probate records to investigate status mobility, the shift from servant to freeholder. The Muster of 1624/25 and early proslavery petitions were discussed in articles by Irene Hecht and by Frederika Schmidt and Barbara Wilhelm.[97]

The fact that the papers from the 1974 conference on the seventeenth-century Chesapeake did not appear in print until 1979 is an indication of the difficulties involved in launching a new school. Thad W. Tate and David L. Ammerman's edited volume, *The Chesapeake in the Seventeenth Century,* became the starting point for work in this new field. Tate's historiographical essay set the scene; James Horn wrote on servant emigration in the seventeenth century; Carville V. Earle looked at the environment, disease, and mortality in early Virginia; Lorena S. Walsh, the family and marriage; Darrett B. Rutman and Anita H. Rutman, parental death in a Virginia county; Kevin P. Kelly, the settlement patterns in seventeenth-century Virginia; Lois Green Carr and Russell R. Menard, freemen in early Maryland; and David W. Jordan and Carole Shammas, new approaches to the English and Creole elites.[98]

Since 1973 and 1974, there has been a veritable flood of work on Maryland: David Curtis Skaggs, *Roots of Maryland Democracy* (1973); Russell R. Menard, "The Maryland Slave Population" (January, 1975); Ronald Hoffman, *A Spirit of Dissension* (1974); Lois Green Carr and David W. Jordan, *Maryland's Revolution of Government* (1974); Darrett B. Rutman and Anita H. Rutman, "Of Agues and Fevers" (January, 1976); Edward C. Papenfuse, *In Pursuit of Profit* (1975); Carville V. Earle, *The Evolution of a Tidewater Settlement System* (1975); Lois Carr and Lorena Walsh, "The Plant-

---

97. Rhys Isaac, "Religion and Authority: Problems of the Anglican Establishment in Virginia in the Era of the Great Awakening and the Parsons' Cause," Russell R. Menard, "From Servant to Freeholder: Status Mobility and Property Accumulation in Seventeenth-Century Maryland," Irene W. D. Hecht, "The Virginia Muster of 1624/5 As a Source for Demographic History," David Curtis Skaggs, "Thomas Cradock and the Chesapeake Golden Age," Edward C. Papenfuse and Gregory A. Stiverson, "General Smallwood's Recruits: The Peacetime Career of the Revolutionary War Private," and Frederika Teute Schmidt and Barbara Ripel Wilhelm, "Early Proslavery Petitions in Virginia," all in *William and Mary Quarterly,* 3rd Ser., XXX (January, 1973). Also see the articles in the St. Mary's City Commission special issue of the *Maryland Historical Magazine,* LXIX (Summer, 1974), 123–227.

98. Thad W. Tate and David L. Ammerman (eds.), *The Chesapeake in the Seventeenth Century: Essays on Anglo-American Society* (Chapel Hill: University of North Carolina Press, 1979).

er's Wife" (October, 1977); Allan Kulikoff, "The Origins of Afro-American Society" (April, 1978); Norman K. Risjord, *Chesapeake Politics* (1978); and Russell R. Menard, "Five Maryland Censuses" (October, 1980).[99] These works, characterized by the depth of their research and the sophistication of their methodologies, transformed the early history of the South and perhaps made the seventeenth-century Chesapeake the subject of more sustained scholarly work than was Puritan Massachusetts. The most magisterial work of all, however, has been that of Jacob Price on the Chesapeake tobacco trade, although it is somewhat more traditional in methodology. His *France and the Chesapeake* (2 vols.; 1973), along with his continuing articles on the Glasgow tobacco merchants, will remain a monument of scholarship. And finally Aubrey C. Land, the dean of the Maryland historians, in his *Colonial Maryland* (1981) summed up the work of two generations of historians.[100]

The national stories of the First (1740) and the Second (1801)

99. David Curtis Skaggs, *Roots of Maryland Democracy, 1753–1776* (Westport, Conn.: Greenwood Press, 1973); Russell R. Menard, "The Maryland Slave Population, 1658 to 1730: A Demographic Profile of Blacks in Four Counties," *William and Mary Quarterly*, 3rd Ser., XXXII (January, 1975), 29–54; Ronald Hoffman, *A Spirit of Dissension: Economics, Politics, and the Revolution in Maryland* (Baltimore: Johns Hopkins University Press, 1974); Lois Green Carr and David W. Jordan, *Maryland's Revolution of Government, 1689–1692* (Ithaca: Cornell University Press, 1974); Darrett B. Rutman and Anita H. Rutman, "Of Agues and Fevers: Malaria in the Early Chesapeake," *William and Mary Quarterly*, 3rd Ser., XXXIII (January, 1976), 31–60; Edward C. Papenfuse, *In Pursuit of Profit: The Annapolis Merchants in the Era of the American Revolution, 1763–1805* (Baltimore: Johns Hopkins University Press, 1975); Carville V. Earle, *The Evolution of a Tidewater Settlement System: All Hallow's Parish, Maryland, 1650–1783* (Chicago: Department of Geography, University of Chicago, 1975); Lois Green Carr and Lorena S. Walsh, "The Planter's Wife: The Experience of White Women in Seventeenth-Century Maryland," *William and Mary Quarterly*, 3rd Ser., XXXIV (October, 1977), 542–71; Allan Kulikoff, "The Origins of Afro-American Society in Tidewater Maryland and Virginia, 1700–1790," *William and Mary Quarterly*, 3rd Ser., XXXV (April, 1978), 226–59; see also Kulikoff, "The Colonial Chesapeake: Seedbed of Antebellum Southern Culture?" *Journal of Southern History*, XLV (November, 1979), 513–40; Norman K. Risjord, *Chesapeake Politics, 1781–1800* (New York: Columbia University Press, 1978); Russell R. Menard, "Five Maryland Censuses, 1700 to 1712: A Note on the Quality of the Quantities," *William and Mary Quarterly*, 3rd Ser., XXXVII (October, 1980), 616–26.

100. Jacob M. Price, *France and the Chesapeake: A History of the French Tobacco Monopoly, 1674–1791, and of Its Relationship to the British and American Tobacco Trades* (2 vols.; Ann Arbor: University of Michigan Press, 1973), and "Buchanan & Simson, 1759–1763: A Different Kind of Glasgow Firm Trading to the Chesapeake," *William and Mary Quarterly*, 3rd Ser., XL (January, 1983), 3–41; Aubrey C. Land, *Colonial Maryland: A History* (Millwood, N.Y.: KTO Press, 1981).

Great Awakenings are well known if not perfectly understood, but much more work could be done on these revivals as they made themselves manifest in the Southeast. Twenty years ago, Hugh Rankin made the flat statement that there was little religious activity among the slaves, a statement that cannot be made today. Donald G. Mathews, in his excellent book *Religion in the Old South* (1977), provided the historian of the South with a schema that, if not acceptable to all, at least provides a convenient foil.[101] The work of John Wesley and George Whitefield, particularly the latter, in Georgia and South Carolina must be reexamined. Frank Baker's *From Wesley to Asbury* (1976) is a good starting place, as is William Howland Kenney's "Alexander Garden and George Whitefield" (January, 1970). The Salzburger records of Georgia give evidence that religious messages reached the slaves. A study of Whitefield's activities would reveal the very early preaching to the slaves, the forerunners of the black Baptists, and provide a gloss on the kind of Anglicanism that prevailed in the South among the white population. Bridenbaugh's *Mitre and Sceptre* (1962) and Mills's *Bishop by Ballot* (1978) should have already warned us that southern Anglicanism was different from that of New England and of Old England as well.[102]

Donald Mathews suggested the radicalization that took place among the white population at the end of the eighteenth century, but Rhys Isaac documented the transformation that took place in Virginia. George William Pilcher, in his study of Samuel Davies (1971), made a contribution, but Isaac described the shift from Anglican society to Dissenter society in Virginia. How this culminated by the end of the century is set forth by John B. Boles in his key work on the Second Great Awakening (1972).[103] This story is at the center of south-

101. Rankin, "The Colonial South," in Link and Patrick (eds.), *Writing Southern History*, 32; Donald G. Mathews, *Religion in the Old South* (Chicago: University of Chicago Press, 1977). For the historiography of southern religion, see the essay in this volume by John B. Boles.

102. Frank Baker, *From Wesley to Asbury: Studies in Early American Methodism* (Durham: Duke University Press, 1976); William Howland Kenney III, "Alexander Garden and George Whitefield: The Significance of Revivalism in South Carolina, 1738–1741," *South Carolina Historical Magazine*, LXXI (January, 1970), 1–16; G. F. Jones (ed.), *Detailed Reports on the Salzburger Emigrants;* Carl Bridenbaugh, *Mitre and Sceptre: Transatlantic Faiths, Ideas, Personalities, and Politics, 1689–1775* (New York: Oxford University Press, 1962); Frederick V. Mills, Jr., *Bishop by Ballot: An Eighteenth-Century Ecclesiastical Revolution* (New York: Oxford University Press, 1978).

103. Mathews, *Religion in the Old South*, 250; Isaac, *The Transformation of Vir-*

ern culture. For the white population, it was a story of the eighteenth century; for the black population, it would be of the nineteenth.

If there is a future for fractured history, it rests with those historians who have responded to the call of the ethnographers. That call is most clearly stated in the first chapter of Clifford Geertz's *The Interpretation of Cultures* (1973), where he urges his readers to avoid "academic bemusements with formal symmetry." Geertz describes his "concept of culture" as "essentially a semiotic one. Believing, with Max Weber, that man is an animal suspended in webs of significance he himself has spun, I take culture to be those webs, and the analysis of it to be therefore not an experimental science in search of law but an interpretive one in search of meaning. It is explication I am after, construing social expressions on their surface enigmatical." Thus one should concentrate on the study of signs and symbols. The results will be "thick description," and our knowledge will grow "in spurts." [104]

Rhys Isaac, responding to such calls after having been deeply immersed in the new social history, particularly the Chesapeake school, produced a pathbreaking book. His *The Transformation of Virginia, 1740–1790* begins with illustrations, the signs and symbols of early Virginia. As he writes he evokes landscape images, those that would come to the attention of Virginians at various levels of the local hierarchy. The Anglican society is perceived not continuously but on special occasions—court days, race meetings, militia musters, election days. Thus one comes to feel the texture of the community. The written word gives way as source to oral culture. The great written documents are downplayed; the *tableaux vivants* replace them. There is more meaning in a camp meeting than in the Declaration of Independence. "Through extempore preaching in search of 'liberty,' the oral culture of the people was surfacing in a form of rebellion against the dominance of the literary culture of the gentry." [105] The revivals had transformed the Anglican world by 1790.

Both sides of the transformation can be studied by using these new methods. The resonances of community life are continuously under

---

ginia; George William Pilcher, *Samuel Davies: Apostle of Dissent in Colonial Virginia* (Knoxville: University of Tennessee Press, 1971); John B. Boles, *The Great Revival, 1787–1805: The Origins of the Southern Evangelical Mind* (Lexington: University Press of Kentucky, 1972).

104. Clifford Geertz, *The Interpretation of Cultures: Selected Essays* (New York: Basic Books, 1973), 24, 5, 6, 25.

105. Isaac, *The Transformation of Virginia,* 263.

examination. "The patriots attested their participation in revitalized community by signing self-denying 'Associations.' The evangelicals did so by bringing to meeting the humble testimony of hearts regenerated by God's grace." The emphasis is, however, on the side of being able to probe the nonliterate culture more deeply than ever before—and thus place it on the same level with the literate. There is communication that we should not miss going on every moment. Thus the need to study "gesture, demeanor, dress, architecture, and all the codes by which those who share in the culture convey meanings and significance to each other." [106]

The tremendous influences upon Isaac are the theater and films. The planter's mansion, the yeoman's farmhouse, the slaves' quarters are treated as stages upon which the actors play their parts. The episodes are treated as segments of a scenario for a film. This is an extraordinary reconstruction of the past. It is immensely appealing and no doubt will be endlessly imitated. It can be entertaining, amusing, enriching. But the mind still wants "formal symmetry"—the larger picture. A Raphael tapestry has both richness of texture and one story. Historians should be grateful to Isaac for trying to achieve a historical tapestry worthy of a Raphael.

106. *Ibid.*, 267, 325.

Planters and Plain Folks
The Social Structure of the Antebellum South

RANDOLPH B. CAMPBELL

From contemporary observers to late-twentieth-century historians, those who would interpret the antebellum South have generally held strong views concerning the region's social structure. Frederick Law Olmsted, who remains the most widely read antislavery and anti-southern writer of the 1850s, insisted that the South had essentially three classes: a ruling elite of slaveholding planters, an impoverished mass of degraded whites, and the enslaved blacks. On the other hand, Daniel R. Hundley of Alabama claimed that the southern states contained eight social groups: southern gentlemen, the middle classes, southern yankees, cotton snobs, southern yeomen, southern bullies, poor white trash, and Negro slaves. Hundley's characterization of antebellum social structure was as defensive as Olmsted's was critical, but it was significant for the number of classes described and especially for the emphasis on the middle class.[1]

When *Writing Southern History* appeared in 1965, James C. Bonner's essay "Plantation and Farm: The Agricultural South" explained how these different views had entered and shaped historical interpretations of the antebellum period in the years since the Civil War. Somewhat ironically, southern-born historians such as Ulrich B. Phillips and William E. Dodd, joined by Lewis C. Gray, took the lead in arguing that slaveholding planters dominated the Old South. According to the Phillips-Gray-Dodd thesis, members of the planter

---

1. Olmsted's famed travel accounts published during the 1850s are now being supplemented by an edition of his letters and lesser-known publications. The relevant volume here is Charles E. Beveridge and Charles Capen McLaughlin (eds.), *Slavery and the South, 1852–1857* (Baltimore: Johns Hopkins University Press, 1981), vol. II of *The Papers of Frederick Law Olmsted,* 12 vols. projected. Hundley's book, which appeared first in 1860, has been reprinted with a useful introduction by the editor, William J. Cooper, Jr. See Daniel R. Hundley, *Social Relations in Our Southern States,* ed. William J. Cooper, Jr. (Baton Rouge: Louisiana State University Press, 1979). For a recent summary of Hundley's views on social structure, see Tommy W. Rogers, "D. R. Hundley: A Multi-Class Thesis of Social Stratification in the Antebellum South," *Mississippi Quarterly,* XXIII (Spring, 1970), 135–54.

class owned, in addition to their slaves, more and better land than did their small farmer counterparts, exercised political control disproportionate to their numbers, and represented the social ideal for all southerners. Phillips, Gray, and Dodd, of course, recognized the existence of numerous small slaveholders, nonslaveholding farmers, and poor whites, but their works gave little attention to these classes and assigned them a relatively insignificant role in antebellum society.[2]

Much as defenders of the Old South were certain to answer antislavery critics during the 1850s, it was almost inevitable that champions of the plain folk would arise to attack the planter-dominance thesis. The challenge came during the 1940s under the leadership of Frank L. Owsley and his students at Vanderbilt University. Relying heavily on data from the United States census returns, the Owsley group argued that middle-class farmers constituted the backbone of antebellum southern society. These yeomen, who were generally nonslaveholders, owned their fair share of land, comparable in quality to that owned by planters, and as a class they prospered and expanded during the 1850s. Reasonably well educated, middle-class farmers enjoyed and exercised the franchise in a democratic fashion. In the eyes of Owsley and his students, then, the Old South, regardless of slavery and plantations, was essentially a plain-folk democracy.[3]

The yeoman-democracy thesis drew criticism immediately. Writing in the *Journal of Negro History* in 1946, Fabian Linden pointed out that the Owsley group had not shown the exact proportions of the

2. James C. Bonner, "Plantation and Farm: The Agricultural South," in Arthur S. Link and Rembert W. Patrick (eds.), *Writing Southern History: Essays in Historiography in Honor of Fletcher M. Green* (Baton Rouge: Louisiana State University Press, 1965), 147–53, cites and summarizes the most important works stating the Phillips-Gray-Dodd thesis. These include Ulrich B. Phillips, "The Origin and Growth of the Southern Black Belts," *American Historical Review*, XI (July, 1906), 798–816; Lewis C. Gray, *History of Agriculture in the Southern United States to 1860* (2 vols. paged consecutively; Washington, D.C.: Carnegie Institution of Washington, 1933), I, 444–45, 474, 532–37; and William E. Dodd, *The Cotton Kingdom: A Chronicle of the Old South* (New Haven: Yale University Press, 1920), 24–47.

3. The yeoman-democracy thesis is summarized and the major works published by Owsley and his students are cited in Bonner, "Plantation and Farm," in Link and Patrick (eds.), *Writing Southern History*, 153–56. These works include Frank L. Owsley and Harriet C. Owsley, "The Economic Basis of Society in the Late Ante-Bellum South," *Journal of Southern History*, VI (February, 1940), 24–45; Frank L. Owsley, *Plain Folk of the Old South* (Baton Rouge: Louisiana State University Press, 1949); Herbert Weaver, *Mississippi Farmers, 1850–1860* (Nashville: Vanderbilt University Press, 1945); and Blanche Henry Clark, *The Tennessee Yeomen, 1840–1860* (Nashville: Vanderbilt University Press, 1942).

general population constituted by each class and that, in any case, the mere existence of numerous farmers did not prove that they actually had economic strength or political power comparable to that of the planters. It would be more revealing, he said, to determine the proportions of plain folk and planters in society as a whole and then compare the proportions of all forms of wealth, property, and agricultural production belonging to each.[4] In 1949, three years after Linden's article appeared, Owsley's major work, *Plain Folk of the Old South*, was published, but then there was a hiatus in the seemingly promising debate between planter-dominance and yeoman-democracy views of the Old South. Perhaps the decade of the 1950s was not a time for historical interpretations that emphasized the differences between plain folk and the upper class.

Bonner's 1965 essay described the historiography of the planter-dominance and yeoman-democracy theses but offered little by way of a critical summary of the debate to that point. Owsley and his students were given credit for "a minor revolution in historical interpretation" because they directed attention to middle-class farmers and demonstrated the value of manuscript census data for the study of economic and social questions. At the same time, Bonner recognized that Linden's criticisms had not been answered. Thus, by implication at least, his essay suggested that existing historical studies of planters and plain folk were hardly definitive. This judgment was affirmed by David M. Potter in 1967. Writing in *Perspectives on the South*, he pointed out that southern historians are "far from agreeing about so basic a question as the nature of ante-bellum society." Further investigations of the subject constituted a fundamental challenge to historical scholarship, Potter said.[5]

4. Fabian Linden, "Economic Democracy in the Slave South: An Appraisal of Some Recent Views," *Journal of Negro History*, XXXI (April, 1946), 140–89. Linden's article dealt only with Alabama, Louisiana, and Mississippi. And in a sense he talked past Owsley and his students by focusing on *slave* ownership rather than *land* ownership, which was their point. James Oakes, *The Ruling Race: A History of American Slaveholders* (New York: Knopf, 1982), 259, suggests that Linden's article has been uncritically accepted by many. Nevertheless, Linden performed a service in asking for greater methodological rigor and greater care in the interpretation of statistical data.

5. Bonner, "Plantation and Farm," in Link and Patrick (eds.), *Writing Southern History*, 156–57 (quotation on p. 156); David M. Potter, "Depletion and Renewal in Southern History," in Edgar T. Thompson (ed.), *Perspectives on the South: Agenda for Research* (Durham: Duke University Press, 1967), 84–85 (quotation on p. 84). Another historiographical survey, Morton Rothstein, "The Cotton Frontier of the Antebellum United States: A Methodological Battleground," *Agricultural History*, XLIV (January, 1970), 160–61, essentially agreed with Bonner and Potter, concluding that

Bonner and Potter wrote nearly twenty years ago. Since then, historians have developed several general interpretations of the Old South that offer new or revised explanations of antebellum social structure and class relationships. There have also been numerous studies of sectionalism and secession that depend in varying degrees on concepts of class consciousness and social tension to explain rising southern separatism and the decision for disunion. These writings provide a departure point for examining the recent historiography of planters and plain folk in the Old South. First, the general accounts and studies of southern sectionalism will be surveyed, with emphasis on how they have portrayed antebellum social structure and based their interpretations on those portrayals. Then, it will be possible to offer an assessment, with reference to works that have focused more narrowly on particular aspects of the problem, of the progress made during the past twenty years in determining the basic nature of antebellum southern society and the relationships among the various classes composing that society.

During the 1960s, even as Bonner and Potter indicated that research on antebellum economic and social structure was anything but complete, Eugene D. Genovese began to publish his celebrated reinterpretation of the Old South. *The Political Economy of Slavery* (1965) and *The World the Slaveholders Made* (1969), plus a number of major articles, broke new ground in southern historiography, particularly because Genovese worked within the analytical framework of Marxism. This meant, of course, that his studies were grounded on a particular view of the South's economic-social classes and the relationships between those classes. (It has never been easy, but Genovese, as a Marxist, has always had to argue that class somehow outweighed race as a force shaping the antebellum South.)[6]

"there is still uncertainty as to whether they [large slaveholders] dominated the cotton frontier in any sense: political, economic, or social" (p. 160).

6. Eugene D. Genovese, *The Political Economy of Slavery: Studies in the Economy & Society of the Slave South* (New York: Pantheon, 1965), *The World the Slaveholders Made: Two Essays in Interpretation* (New York: Pantheon, 1969), and "Race and Class in Southern History: An Appraisal of the Work of Ulrich Bonnell Phillips," *Agricultural History*, XLI (October, 1967), 345–58. Interestingly, just as Genovese's work began to appear in the early 1960s, C. Vann Woodward, *American Counterpoint: Slavery and Racism in the North-South Dialogue* (Boston: Little, Brown, 1971), 261–83, gently suggested that W. J. Cash, one of the most famous commentators on southern society, may have exaggerated the lack of class consciousness in the region. For criticism of Genovese's views on class and race, see Kenneth M. Stampp, "Reconsidering U. B. Phillips: A Comment," *Agricultural History*, XLI (October, 1967),

The antebellum South, according to Genovese, was a precapitalist, "seigneurial" society. This was not to say that it had no capitalist institutions such as banks or that its upper class was uninterested in accumulating wealth; banks existed, and planters wanted money. But, Genovese argued, the South was fundamentally precapitalist because slavery gave it a "dependent labor force" that held "some claim to the means of production," whereas capitalism has wage labor and separates the labor force from the means of production. The South's labor system, thus understood, was the key to an economic *and* social structure far different from that of the northern United States. To Genovese, antebellum southern society consisted of three major classes—slaveholders, nonslaveholding whites, and black slaves— and a "small commercial bourgeoisie." And it was dominated utterly by the slaveholders, who were in turn led by the large planters among them. "The hegemony of the slaveholders," he wrote in *The Political Economy of Slavery,* "presupposing the social and economic preponderance of the great slave plantations, determined the character of the South."[7]

Genovese left no room for misunderstanding his concept of planter hegemony. He praised the work of Ulrich B. Phillips "for its brilliant descriptions of a proud and tough people who forged themselves into a ruling class and imposed their values as well as their will on society at large." Through paternal neighborliness, planters dominated the nonslaveholders who lived among them, lending aid when needed, inquiring about the family (which often included some of the planters' relatives), and taking care not to act "better" than the plain folk. Backcountry yeomen who lived apart from slaveholding districts were simply left alone by the planters. Thus the nonslaveholding farmer majority either accepted or acquiesced in planter rule.[8] The

---

365–68; and Stanley M. Elkins, "Class and Race: A Comment," *Agricultural History,* XLI (October, 1967), 369–71. Robert E. Shalhope, "Race, Class, Slavery, and the Antebellum Southern Mind," *Journal of Southern History,* XXXVII (November, 1971), 557–74, sought to determine the relative importance of race and class in the thought of those Confederates who exiled themselves to Mexico in 1865. His conclusion gave equal emphasis to both concepts, but obviously this group was hardly typical of southerners in general.

7. Genovese, *The World the Slaveholders Made,* 16–20 (quotations on p. 16), and *The Political Economy of Slavery,* 13–23 (quotations on pp. 20, 13).

8. Genovese, "Race and Class in Southern History," 358, and "Yeomen Farmers in a Slaveholders' Democracy," *Agricultural History,* XLIX (April, 1975), 331–42. Bertram Wyatt-Brown, "W. J. Cash and Southern Culture," in Walter J. Fraser, Jr., and Winfred B. Moore, Jr. (eds.), *From the Old South to the New: Essays on the Transi-*

South's small commercial class was so dependent on the patronage of the slaveholders that its members had no opportunity to follow divergent economic interests, and "the merchants either became planters themselves or assumed a servile attitude toward the planters."[9] The final proof of planter domination came in secession and the Civil War. Slaveholders, believing that their system had to expand or die, refused to accept a Republican administration and opted "to stake everything on an uncompromising fight for regional independence." They took the entire South with them and, in the process, came closer to establishing themselves as a ruling, slaveholding class than did any other group in the New World.[10]

Genovese's interpretation was seconded and placed in a breathtakingly broad context during the 1970s by the Italian military historian Raimondo Luraghi. In *The Rise and Fall of the Plantation South* (1978), Luraghi traced the "premodern," "seigneurial" civilization of the planters to the Italian Renaissance. Southern planters provided not only a ruling aristocracy but a "political class" as well—a class able to transcend narrow interests and rule by consensus. Thus they exercised hegemony over the people of the Old South.[11]

Genovese's and Luraghi's Marxist analyses of antebellum social structure placed virtually complete emphasis on the planter class. But as was the case during the 1940s, the plain folk could not be obscured indefinitely in the background of the historiographical picture. A 1975 article on antebellum southern herdsmen by Forrest

---

tional South (Westport, Conn.: Greenwood Press, 1981), 195–214, has pointed out that Genovese, although a critic of W. J. Cash's *The Mind of the South* for its insistence that southerners generally lacked class consciousness, came by 1975 (in the article on yeomen farmers) to accept a view of "class bondings" in the Old South very similar to that presented by Cash.

9. Genovese, *The Political Economy of Slavery*, 20. George D. Green, *Finance and Economic Development in the Old South: Louisiana Banking, 1804–1861* (Stanford: Stanford University Press, 1972), 177–78, has argued that in Louisiana bankers and merchants combined with the planter class to promote common interests, so they were not dominated by precapitalist slaveholders.

10. Genovese, *The World the Slaveholders Made*, 101–102 (quotation on p. 101). Shearer Davis Bowman, "Antebellum Planters and Vormärz Junkers in Comparative Perspective," *American Historical Review*, LXXXV (October, 1980), 779–808, supports Genovese by citing the Civil War as evidence that antebellum planters may have been more truly conservative than even the Prussian Junker class.

11. Raimondo Luraghi, *The Rise and Fall of the Plantation South* (New York: New Viewpoints, 1978), 15, 64–82, and "The Civil War and the Modernization of American Society: Social Structure and Industrial Revolution in the Old South before and during the War," *Civil War History*, XVIII (September, 1972), 230–50.

McDonald and Grady McWhiney of the University of Alabama was the first step in the development of a provocative new thesis concerning the nonslaveholding majority.

McDonald and McWhiney, though not denying a certain type of planter domination, argued that the plain folk had exactly the sort of economic-social life they wanted and that they were critical in shaping southern character. Their explanation was ethnocultural. The great majority of white southerners, they contended, were of Celtic extraction—Welsh, Scots, Irish, and Scotch-Irish—or had originated on the Celtic frontier of England. And this made southerners very different from the English and German peoples of the northern United States. Specifically, the plain folk preferred a pastoral life as herdsmen, with as little tilling of the soil as possible, and they did not believe in working hard to maximize profits. By northern standards, southern plain folk were lazy; in more charitable words, they favored a "leisure ethic" over the Puritan work ethic. And yet the plain folk, again by their own standards, were not poor. Their houses were run-down, and their farms looked anything but prosperous. Still, they had enough pork, beef, corn, and garden vegetables to be "lavishly self-sufficient." Moreover, surplus livestock could be sold to provide cash, if necessary, for the liquor and tobacco so essential to a leisurely way of life. They did not emulate the planters by investing in slaves and producing cotton and other cash crops because they simply did not choose to do so.[12]

Southern plain folk of Celtic extraction, according to McDonald and McWhiney, were "unhurried" in every way. They were "courteous, modest, and even deferential" but "deadly if provoked." And the quickest way to provoke them was to be disrespectful toward an individual or his kin. Plain folk were not class conscious in a Marxian sense, but they had strong ethnic and racial prejudices and were very suspicious of outsiders and governmental restraints. Celts tended toward extremism in everything, and this affected even their performance in war. They fought great single battles but lacked the willing-

---

12. Forrest McDonald and Grady McWhiney, "The Antebellum Southern Herdsman: A Reinterpretation," *Journal of Southern History,* XLI (May, 1975), 147–66. This ethnocultural thesis was elaborated and broadened to southern farmers in general in McDonald and McWhiney, "The South from Self-Sufficiency to Peonage: An Interpretation," *American Historical Review,* LXXXV (December, 1980), 1095–1118. The beginnings of the Celtic South are explained in Forrest McDonald and Ellen Shapiro McDonald, "The Ethnic Origins of the American People, 1790," *William and Mary Quarterly,* 3rd Ser., XXXVII (April, 1980), 179–99.

ness to persist through a long contest. *Attack and Die* (1982) by Mc-Whiney and Perry D. Jamieson explains the Confederacy's military fortunes to a large extent in terms of this interpretation of Celtic character.[13]

The McDonald-McWhiney view of plain-folk character, though not necessarily its ethnocultural basis, has been seconded in several recent articles. John Solomon Otto studied slaveholding general farmers in Yell County, Arkansas, and found that there was little difference between the small slaveholders and their nonslaveholding neighbors in areas dominated by the latter. The small slaveholders also valued self-sufficiency and leisure over wealth. In fact, their form of subsistence agriculture, based on livestock herding and planting corn among girdled trees, required so little labor from their slaves that they could be considered "easy" masters. Wayne Mixon pointed out in 1977 that at least one important southern writer, Joel Chandler Harris, was not overcome by the myth of the planter class during the 1880s. Harris wrote fondly of the yeomen farmers' down-to-earth, unhurried ways. Questioning progress if it meant industry and cities, Harris' antebellum plain folk valued their independence far more than money.[14]

The interpretation of the plain folk's economic and social lives as a product of culture and tradition was questioned by Gavin Wright, an economist who has written extensively on the nineteenth-century cotton South, even as it was being elaborated during the 1970s. Small farmers in the cotton South, Wright argued, focused on self-sufficiency not from any particular attitude or cultural characteristic but as a matter of deliberate economic choice. "Consider," he wrote, "the two alternative methods of meeting basic food needs: the farm can plant corn for its own consumption or it can plant cotton and purchase the corn and meat required." Plain folk chose the "safety-first" strategy of producing enough bread and meat and then planting cotton if possible. Wright admitted that his argument did not refute interpretations based on culture and tradition, but as an economist, he preferred an explanation of behavior "as a response to differing circumstances, rather than a reflection of variation in

13. McDonald and McWhiney, "The Antebellum Southern Herdsman," 166; Grady McWhiney and Perry D. Jamieson, *Attack and Die: Civil War Military Tactics and the Southern Heritage* (University: University of Alabama Press, 1982).

14. John Solomon Otto, "Slaveholding General Farmers in a 'Cotton County,'" *Agricultural History*, LV (April, 1981), 167–78; Wayne Mixon, "Joel Chandler Harris, the Yeoman Tradition, and the New South Movement," *Georgia Historical Quarterly*, LXI (Winter, 1977), 308–17.

psychologies or social conventions." Moreover, Wright said, non-economic interpretations seemed to posit a bipolar economy of subsistence farmers on one hand and staple-producing plantations on the other while there was, in fact, a corn/cotton crop mix continuum from smaller to larger (*i.e.*, slaveholding) agricultural operations throughout the cotton South. Individuals varied in economic status and behavior, but they shared an "essential unity" in the region. Much of Wright's argument is supported by James D. Foust, another economist, in *The Yeoman Farmer and Westward Expansion of U. S. Cotton Production* (1975). Foust found that smaller farmers played a major role in settling the southwestern cotton frontier and that they did not all remain simply herders or subsistence farmers. "In fact," he wrote, the small farmer "was able to raise food crops in proportions greater than his share of the total population and have land and labor left over to devote to the production of cotton." Thus, while there was an adjustment of economic behavior according to circumstances, small farmers on the cotton frontier were not likely to be pushed out of their new homes by larger planters.[15]

These broad interpretations, though each touched at least by implication on the themes of planter dominance and yeoman democracy, offered little or no evidence of class conflict in the Old South. Genovese and Luraghi asserted the hegemony of the planter class, and McDonald and McWhiney did not really disagree. Their plain folk had little class consciousness and were "deferential" unless of-

15. Gavin Wright, *The Political Economy of the Cotton South: Households, Markets, and Wealth in the Nineteenth Century* (New York: Norton, 1978), 22–24, 62–74 (quotations on pp. 63, 69). For an earlier statement of the "safety-first" idea, see Gavin Wright and Howard Kunreuther, "Cotton, Corn and Risk in the Nineteenth Century," *Journal of Economic History*, XXXV (September, 1975), 526–51. This thesis is criticized in Robert McGuire and Robert Higgs, "Cotton, Corn, and Risk in the Nineteenth Century: Another View," *Explorations in Economic History*, XIV (April, 1977), 167–82. Sam Bowers Hilliard, *Hog Meat and Hoecake: Food Supply in the Old South, 1840–1860* (Carbondale: Southern Illinois University Press, 1972), 151, argued that small farmers in the cotton belt concentrated on cotton almost as much as did the planters. At the other extreme is the idea that the South had a "dual economy," with planters living as market-oriented businessmen and yeomen as tradition-bound, noncommercial farmers. See Morton Rothstein, "The Antebellum South as a Dual Economy: A Tentative Hypothesis," *Agricultural History*, XLI (October, 1967), 373–82. James D. Foust, *The Yeoman Farmer and Westward Expansion of U. S. Cotton Production* (New York: Arno Press, 1975), 201. In contrast to Foust, Julia Floyd Smith, *Slavery and Plantation Growth in Antebellum Florida, 1821–1860* (Gainesville: University Presses of Florida, 1973), found that planters rather than yeomen were the first to arrive in Florida's plantation region.

fended by a lack of respect. Wright found a basic unity of interests among farmers in the cotton South. Several recent accounts of southern sectionalism, secession, and the Civil War, however, have made social tension and class conflict an integral part of their story. We must now consider how the planters and plain folk appear in these interpretations.

William W. Freehling issued one of the first calls for relating antebellum social structure to secession in a 1970 review essay of George Reese's edition of the *Proceedings of the Virginia State Convention of 1861*. Impressed by the "concern about internal opposition to slavery" among Virginia secessionists, he asked for "a fresh look at sectional and class divisions in the Old South." That same year, Steven A. Channing, in *Crisis of Fear*, also mentioned the theme of internal conflict. Planters and their defenders, he wrote, were very disturbed over the matter of nonslaveholder loyalty. And he quoted the fear expressed by Daniel Hamilton of Charleston: "Think you that 360,000 Slaveholders will dictate terms for 3,000,000 of non-slaveholders at the South—I fear not, I mistrust our own people more than I fear all of the efforts of the Abolitionists." Class conflict was not, however, central to Channing's interpretation of disunion, which emphasized the South's "irrational perception" of northern intentions. William L. Barney, in *The Secessionist Impulse* (1974), also touched on fears of class conflict in the antebellum period. He delineated two groups, yeomen and poor whites, who owned no bondsmen, and pointed out that the slave system rendered them "economically superfluous" and therefore a potential threat to that system. Barney quoted Daniel Hamilton, too, and indicated that many slaveholders found southern nationalism attractive "as a means of assuring home rule in both class and racial matters." Nevertheless, the idea of tension between slaveholders and nonslaveholders does not appear really vital to his interpretation either. Instead, he argued that young radical planters with expansionistic ambitions sparked secession in Alabama and Mississippi, and he found the most important internal divisions to have been those within the planter class, whose older, established members were more conservative.[16]

16. William W. Freehling, "The Editorial Revolution, Virginia, and the Coming of the Civil War: A Review Essay," *Civil War History*, XVI (March, 1970), 64–72 (quotations on pp. 68, 71); Steven A. Channing, *Crisis of Fear: Secession in South Carolina* (New York: Simon & Schuster, 1970), 254–56 (quotation on p. 256); William L. Barney, *The Secessionist Impulse: Alabama and Mississippi in 1860* (Princeton: Princeton University Press, 1974), 38–49 (quotation on p. 49), 267–316.

In *Toward a Patriarchal Republic,* published in 1977, Michael P. Johnson carried the thesis of internal class struggle much further than had either Channing or Barney. While agreeing with Genovese that secession was the ultimate test of planter hegemony, he argued that disunion "was necessary precisely because the hegemony of slave-holders was not secure." Secessionists, fearing that nonslaveholders would accept Republican patronage and use their power in numbers to overthrow the plantation regime from within, translated their fear into a "double revolution"—one for home rule against the external threat and one for those who ruled at home to prevent realization of the internal threat. According to Johnson, then, secession was moti-vated as much by class struggle or the threat of class struggle as by Republican and abolitionist opposition to the interests of slave-holders. Steven H. Hahn's work on yeomen farmers in Georgia's Upper Piedmont agreed essentially with that of Johnson. The under-lying class and regional tensions between slaveholders in the planta-tion belt and yeomen in the Piedmont, Hahn argued, did not threaten slavery but erupted with enough force during the Civil War to bring the Confederacy "to the edge of internal collapse." [17]

In 1978, J. Mills Thornton III published a much-acclaimed new approach to the study of secession. *Politics and Power in a Slave So-ciety: Alabama, 1800–1860* put disunion within the context of Jack-sonian ideology and insisted that contemporary perceptions were the key to understanding the crisis of the 1850s. As Thornton presented it, Alabamians, reared on the rhetoric of the Jacksonians, had long feared any loss of liberty and autonomy to the rich and powerful and jealously guarded against such "enslavement." Serious difficulties then developed during the 1850s when the state government began to take actions to support commerce and industry and to enlarge its role in the lives of the people. Planters generally approved of state support for banks and railroads, but farmers felt that their autonomy was threatened. At the same time, however, concern over northern opposition to slavery reached crisis proportions, and Alabama poli-

---

17. Michael P. Johnson, *Toward a Patriarchal Republic: The Secession of Georgia* (Baton Rouge: Louisiana State University Press, 1977), xx (both quotations), 79–87; Steven Howard Hahn, "The Roots of Southern Populism: Yeomen Farmers and the Transformation of Georgia's Upper Piedmont, 1850–1890," (Ph.D. dissertation, Yale University, 1979), and "The Yeomanry of the Nonplantation South: Upper Piedmont Georgia, 1850–1860," in Orville Vernon Burton and Robert C. McMath, Jr. (eds.), *Class, Conflict, and Consensus: Antebellum Southern Community Studies* (Westport, Conn.: Greenwood Press, 1982), 41–47 (quotation on p. 47).

ticians were able to convince the voting majority that the real threat was external. To Thornton, the small farmers of Alabama, more than the planters, felt that they were under assault. Secession was almost a yeomen's crusade to protect against a loss of liberty and autonomy.[18]

Thornton contended that his interpretation went beyond the planter-dominance versus yeoman-democracy debate, which he said was "increasingly barren." In fact, he argued, questions of social structure and wealth distribution are actually beside the point. Whatever the real social structure, voters and politicians responded in terms of their "social ideology." Thus, "the definition of southern reality . . . must begin with an understanding of the southern perception of reality." Regardless, however, of this point of view, Thornton's interpretation does depend to some extent on the existence of class consciousness in Alabama, and his work was taken by reviewers as a challenge to the concept of planter hegemony.[19]

More recently, James Oakes's *The Ruling Race* (1982), though concentrating on describing the entire slaveholding class rather than explaining secession, also touched on the importance of class divisions in the late antebellum period. Oakes argued that generally there was "substantial mobility into and out of the slaveholding class" and that "physical movement, upward mobility, and social fluidity shaped the destinies of the vast majority of American slaveholders." Nonslaveholders could hope to become participants in the slave economy or at least share in its proceeds. After 1830, however, population expansion and rising prices caused a decline in the percentage of families owning slaves and, coupled with potential restriction of the westward expansion of slavery, threatened to close off opportunities for material advance by nonslaveholders. "Whether they were justified or not," Oakes wrote, "slaveholders approached the secession crisis fearful of an uncertain consensus among free Southerners."[20]

While Freehling, Channing, Barney, Johnson, Thornton, and Oakes called attention, with varying degrees of emphasis, to the role of

18. J. Mills Thornton III, *Politics and Power in a Slave Society: Alabama, 1800–1860* (Baton Rouge: Louisiana State University Press, 1978), xvii–xxi, 442–61.

19. *Ibid.*, 479. For a reviewer who saw conflict between Thornton and Genovese, see Robert J. Brugger, Review of Thornton's *Politics and Power in a Slave Society*, in *Journal of American History*, LXVI (June, 1979), 154–55.

20. Oakes, *The Ruling Race*, 67–68, 229–32 (quotations on pp. 67, 68, 229). For a critique of Oakes's contention that there was significant movement into and out of slavery, see Randolph B. Campbell, "Intermittent Slave Ownership: Texas as a Test Case," *Journal of Southern History*, LI (February, 1985), 15–30.

threatening internal class divisions in the decision for secession, several other historians found such tensions evident earlier in the antebellum period. Ronald T. Takaki's study of the crusade to reopen the African slave trade depended heavily on the idea that proponents of this movement, especially those in South Carolina, were motivated by a desire to reduce tensions between slaveholders and nonslaveholders. Without a new supply of slaves, prices would continue to rise, and nonslaveholders would be consigned to the lower class forever. The resulting conflict would endanger the whole social structure. Fred Siegel tested the planter-hegemony thesis by examining the 1831–1832 debate on slavery in the Virginia legislature following Nat Turner's rebellion. He found that spokesmen for the yeomen strongly opposed the planters and concluded that the planter class had its way not by some sort of social hegemony but by plain old politics. Siegel also found class tension rising in late antebellum Georgia when white artisans in towns such as Augusta and Savannah sought to prevent competition from slave labor. This opposition frightened slaveholders about support for slavery in general—a fear that became much greater when Lincoln's election brought to office a party that would try to appeal to southern nonslaveholders.[21]

What, then, of class relationships during the Civil War? If there was internal tension before disunion, surely the pressures of war and defeat would exacerbate the situation. Stephen E. Ambrose concluded, in a 1962 *Civil War History* article, that impressment of farm products, the tax-in-kind, and the twenty-slave exemption from conscription alienated the yeomen by the end of 1863 to the point that they were either unresponsive or hostile to the Confederacy. Paul D. Escott went further in 1978, arguing that the "latent" class conflict between planters and plain folk became a reality during the war.

21. Ronald T. Takaki, *A Pro-Slavery Crusade: The Agitation to Reopen the African Slave Trade* (New York: Free Press, 1971), 43–58; Fred Siegel, "The Paternalist Thesis: Virginia as a Test Case," *Civil War History*, XXV (September, 1979), 246–61, and "Artisans and Immigrants in the Politics of Late Antebellum Georgia," *Civil War History*, XXVII (September, 1981), 221–30. John B. Boles, "Tension in a Slave Society: The Trial of the Reverend Jacob Gruber," *Southern Studies*, XVIII (Summer, 1979), 179–97, found the threat of internal division between slaveholders and nonslaveholders present as early as 1818 in the case of a minister accused of inciting slave rebellion in Maryland. John McCardell, *The Idea of a Southern Nation: Southern Nationalists and Southern Nationalism, 1830–1860* (New York: Norton, 1979), 73–74, 325–26, touched on the fears of some leaders of the movement that increasing concentration of slave property would alienate the lower classes and create discontent the Republicans could exploit.

The common people did not develop a commitment to Confederate nationalism, according to Escott, and their "quiet rebellion" seriously weakened the South's cause. James Smallwood found widespread Unionism in largely nonslaveholding areas of north Texas, and Marc W. Kruman concluded that a good many North Carolinians came to see the Confederacy as a military despotism intent on destroying their liberty. Smallwood's and Kruman's studies were not cast in terms of yeoman disaffection from a planters' war, but the implications are the same.[22]

During the 1970s, then, questions about the Old South's social structure and internal unity became increasingly important to the historiography of sectionalism, secession, and the Civil War. Eric Foner called in 1974 for a new look at antebellum economic-social structure as a basis for deciding the issues of planter hegemony and nonslaveholder loyalty. By 1980, Paul Goodman concluded that the "Slave Power" had indeed faced an enemy within and contended that a new synthesis of the causes of the Civil War would have to recognize the long-neglected yeomen opponents of slavery and their impact on the planters. Not all historians, however, emphasized class conflict over social unity in the Old South. William R. Brock's study of political parties during the 1840s, while recognizing the possibilities "of a movement against slavery in the South itself," concluded that the aspirations of the "rural middle class" to move with slaves to new land led to general support for the "Peculiar Institution" and allowed planter politicians to speak for a "united society." Carl N. Degler's The Other South (1974), in spite of its focus on those who dissented from traditional southern views and values, was presented as a book about "losers." It emphasized "the ways class has been subordinated to race in the life of nineteenth-century Southerners." A 1978 study of class and party during the secession crisis in the Deep South by Peyton McCrary and others concluded, "Our search yielded little clear-cut evidence of class alignments in voting behavior on the brink of Civil War." James L. Roark's study of planters during the Civil War

22. Stephen E. Ambrose, "Yeoman Discontent in the Confederacy," *Civil War History*, VIII (September, 1962), 259–68; Paul D. Escott, *After Secession: Jefferson Davis and the Failure of Confederate Nationalism* (Baton Rouge: Louisiana State University Press, 1978), 94–134, and "Southern Yeomen and the Confederacy," *South Atlantic Quarterly*, LXXVII (Spring, 1978), 146–58; James Smallwood, "Disaffection in Confederate Texas: The Great Hanging at Gainesville," *Civil War History*, XXII (December, 1976), 349–60; Marc W. Kruman, "Dissent in the Confederacy: The North Carolina Experience," *Civil War History*, XXVII (December, 1981), 293–313.

and Reconstruction found that the slaveholders' fears about non-slaveholders' disloyalty were without basis. The plain folk turned against the war because of privation and defeat, not because of heightened class consciousness. Moreover, they simply quit; they did not confront the planters with torches or even ballots. The yeomen wanted peace rather than the planters' hides. Incidentally, even then the planters were upset because of plain folks' willingness to sacrifice slavery to end the war.[23]

The two major syntheses dealing with sectionalism, secession, and the war that appeared during the late 1970s tended to endorse the concepts of planter hegemony and social unity rather than internal struggle and class conflict. David M. Potter's *The Impending Crisis, 1848–1861* (1976) described the South's idealization of the plantation and slavery and explained how "doctrines of race served to minimize the potentially serious economic divisions between slaveholders and nonslaveholders." Emory M. Thomas, in *The Confederate Nation, 1861–1865* (1979), went into some detail on the "broad-based status pyramid" of southern society and mentioned "potential tension between aristocracy and democracy in the social structure of the Old South." But he concluded that the planter class dominated. Planters pursued their interests and "for the most part led the rest of the South into the same course." Plain folk deferred to their "betters" and accepted "planter values and ideology." "United by the series of personal relationships which characterize folk culture, planters and plain folk formed an essentially solid Southern society." Thomas also found that, although the Civil War heightened class consciousness among yeomen, planters maintained control without great difficulty.

23. Eric Foner, "The Causes of the American Civil War: Recent Interpretations and New Directions," *Civil War History*, XX (September, 1974), 209–12; Paul Goodman, "White Over White: Planters, Yeomen, and the Coming of the Civil War: A Review Essay," *Agricultural History*, LIV (July, 1980), 450–52; William R. Brock, *Parties and Political Conscience: American Dilemmas, 1840–1850* (Millwood, N.Y.: KTO Press, 1979), xiii, 270–75 (quotations on pp. 270, 274, 275); Carl N. Degler, *The Other South: Southern Dissenters in the Nineteenth Century* (New York: Harper & Row, 1974), 1–7 (quotation on p. 7); Peyton McCrary, Clark Miller, and Dale Baum, "Class and Party in the Secession Crisis: Voting Behavior in the Deep South, 1856–1861," *Journal of Interdisciplinary History*, VIII (Winter, 1978), 456; James L. Roark, *Masters Without Slaves: Southern Planters in the Civil War and Reconstruction* (New York: Norton, 1977), 55–56. William J. Cooper, Jr., *The South and the Politics of Slavery, 1828–1856* (Baton Rouge: Louisiana State University Press, 1978), also emphasizes unity based on the defense of slavery as the dominant factor in southern political life.

"The Confederate quest for home rule," he wrote, "never became a contest over who should rule at home."[24]

From the foregoing survey, it is obvious that questions of social structure, the distribution of wealth among social classes, and the relationships between those classes have been vital to interpretations of the antebellum South, secession, and the Civil War during the past twenty years. We must ask, therefore, what progress historians have made in dealing with these matters. (1) Is there a consensus concerning antebellum social structure based on reasonably precise definitions of each class? (2) What can we say with a fair degree of certainty about the distribution of wealth in the Old South? (3) Was the section essentially unified socially and politically under planter hegemony, or did the plain folk battle the slaveholding upper class for control? These questions are sufficiently distinct that the recent historiography of each may now be dealt with in turn.

Historians have not developed precise, generally accepted definitions of social classes in the Old South. Joseph G. Tregle, Jr., pointed to this fundamental weakness in our understanding of antebellum social structure in a 1976 critique of Roger W. Shugg's still-acclaimed and oft-cited work, *Origins of Class Struggle in Louisiana* (1939). Shugg obviously based his interpretation on the existence of distinct social classes, but, according to Tregle, he never decided exactly what he meant by *planter, farmer,* and *yeoman.*[25] Genovese's studies demonstrate this difficulty, too. Intent on his sweeping Marxist analysis, he largely presupposed slaveholders as the ruling class. In the process, he came close to placing small farmers owning one or two Negroes in the same class with the great planters and also close to perpetuating the idea that the Old South had only two classes of free whites. Forrest McDonald and Grady McWhiney began writing about the "herdsman" in 1975 and expanded to the "plain folk" by 1980 without any particular delineation of that class in contrast to the planters or poor whites. Surely members of other classes shared the Celtic cultural heritage of the plain folk and should, therefore,

24. David M. Potter, *The Impending Crisis, 1848–1861* (New York: Harper & Row, 1976), 458–59; Emory M. Thomas, *The Confederate Nation, 1861–1865* (New York: Harper & Row, 1979), 6 (first two quotations), 8, 9, 10, 233–34 (last quotation on p. 234).

25. Joseph G. Tregle, Jr., "Another Look at Shugg's Louisiana," *Louisiana History,* XVII (Summer, 1976), 245–81; Roger W. Shugg, *Origins of Class Struggle in Louisiana: A Social History of White Farmers and Laborers During Slavery and After, 1840–1875* (Baton Rouge: Louisiana State University Press, 1939).

have been like the latter unless other factors were involved. The studies of secession by Channing, Barney, Johnson, and Thornton generally portrayed a white South composed of two classes, slaveholders and nonslaveholders, and, except for Barney's division of the latter group into a middle class of yeomen farmers and urban tradesmen and a lower class of landless poor whites, made little further effort to analyze antebellum social structure.

Gavin Wright, in *The Political Economy of the Cotton South* (1978), argued that social classes should be defined explicitly in terms of "wealth-holding categories" and named "planters, small slaveowners, yeoman farmers, tenants, and landless wage earners" as the relevant groups. He did not, however, offer definitions by wealth to determine membership in these classes, choosing instead to analyze the cotton South primarily in terms of slaveholding planters and nonslaveholding farmers. In their preface to *The Southern Common People* (1980), editors Edward Magdol and Jon L. Wakelyn suggested even more specific definitions of antebellum social classes. "Planters who owned more than twenty slaves and who grew staple crops" were part of the elite; the lower class consisted of day laborers and factory workers. The "common people" were farmers and small slaveholders with fewer than twenty bondsmen, herdsmen, storekeepers, urban mechanics, and the "professional middle class" composed of lawyers, doctors, merchants, clerks, and factory managers. Unfortunately, after this promising preface, Magdol and Wakelyn's collection contained mostly older studies rather than new contributions to a more careful delineation of social classes in the Old South.[26]

Can historians actually apply precise wealth-holding categories, as suggested by Wright, to determine the social structure of antebellum southern communities? Do the three classes—planters, common people, and poor whites—as defined by Magdol and Wakelyn, properly describe the people of the Old South? Answering these questions will likely prove difficult and frustrating. First, there will be the problem of agreeing on wealth-holding categories. This has appeared in recent attempts to measure the impact of the Civil War and Reconstruction on the antebellum planter elite. Jonathan Wiener defined this group in the Alabama Black Belt as the 236 planters who reported the greatest wealth in real estate in the United States censuses

26. Wright, *The Political Economy of the Cotton South*, 37; Edward Magdol and Jon L. Wakelyn (eds.), *The Southern Common People: Studies in Nineteenth-Century Social History* (Westport, Conn.: Greenwood Press, 1980), ix–xii (quotation on p. xi).

of 1850 and 1860. Individuals who qualified in 1850 had at least $10,000 in real property value; in 1860, the required total was $32,000. A. Jane Townes's study of the planter elite in Nelson and Goochland counties, Virginia, dealt with all those who paid taxes on five hundred or more acres of land in 1860. In examining this group in Harrison County, Texas, Randolph B. Campbell included those who comprised the wealthiest 5 percent of taxpayers in 1850 and in 1860.[27] Such differences in the definition of classes will probably be magnified when efforts are made to draw precise lines of wealth-holding between groups that were lower on the social ladder. Second, it is not likely that the people of any particular antebellum community will fall neatly enough into the classes suggested by Magdol and Wakelyn. For example, Campbell argued that the free population of Harrison County in 1850 and 1860 consisted of five classes: large planters owning twenty or more slaves, small planters holding ten to nineteen bondsmen, yeomen farmers who were both small slaveholders with fewer than ten Negroes and nonslaveholding farmers, poor whites who were generally landless farmers, and non-farmers who were primarily townspeople. These classes seemed reasonable, given the population of that particular community, but obviously they do not square perfectly with those suggested by Magdol and Wakelyn. Small planters, for example, were as numerous as large slaveholders and seemed to constitute a class having more in common with the latter than with other groups defined as the common people.[28] In short, any categorization by quantitative data is ar-

27. Jonathan M. Wiener, "Planter Persistence and Social Change: Alabama, 1850–1870," *Journal of Interdisciplinary History,* VII (Autumn, 1976), 235–60; A. Jane Townes, "The Effect of Emancipation on Large Landholdings, Nelson and Goochland Counties, Virginia," *Journal of Southern History,* XLV (August, 1979), 403–12; Randolph B. Campbell, "Population Persistence and Social Change in Nineteenth-Century Texas: Harrison County, 1850–1880," *Journal of Southern History,* XLVIII (May, 1982), 185–204. Lee W. Formwalt, "Antebellum Planter Persistence: Southwest Georgia—A Case Study," *Plantation Society in the Americas,* I (October, 1981), 410–29, duplicated the approach taken by Wiener.

28. Randolph B. Campbell, *A Southern Community in Crisis: Harrison County, Texas, 1850–1880* (Austin: Texas State Historical Association, 1983). Frank J. Huffman, Jr., "Town and Country in the South, 1850–1880: A Comparison of Urban and Rural Social Structures," *South Atlantic Quarterly,* LXXVI (Summer, 1977), 366–81, suggested yet another problem in the delineation of antebellum social classes by pointing out that townspeople had a greater variety of occupations than did individuals in rural areas. Perhaps, then, urban social structure based on varying groups of white- and blue-collar workers should be considered apart from rural social structure based on planters, yeomen, and so on.

bitrary and will not fit every antebellum community in the same way.

Thus, while most historians will agree that southern society was a good deal more complex than the three-tiered arrangement of planters, poor whites, and slaves, generally accepted, precise definitions of social classes are not yet available. There are problems and dangers in being too "scientific" and reducing the whole to quantitative measurements. James Oakes, for example, discusses slaveholders in terms of small owners, middle-class masters, and the planter aristocracy but insists that "the slaveholding class was fluid." "Most slaveholders," he wrote, "spent their lives defying the statistical boundaries historians so emphatically establish." Also, to Oakes, "it is futile to locate clearly delineated boundaries between slaveholders and nonslaveholders, just as it is difficult to draw simple numerical distinctions between small slaveholders and planters."[29] His point is well taken. We must not only recognize social fluidity but also, as Daniel R. Hundley would remind us, remember that class distinctions always depend on more than simple property holding. Nevertheless, increased emphasis on understanding social classes at any given time as wealth-holding categories and the testing of those definitions by applying them to particular communities over extended periods of time should provide greater precision than any other approach. At least, attempts to be more precise will stand as warnings against using terms such as *farmer, yeoman,* and *common people* loosely and remind us of work yet to be done.

In contrast to the analysis of antebellum class structure, a great deal of progress has been made during the past twenty years in studying the distribution of wealth in the Old South. Robert E. Gallman's 1969 paper, "Trends in the Size Distribution of Wealth in the Nineteenth Century," provided measures of wealth-holding concentration in Louisiana (representative of the Deep South) and Maryland (representative of the border states) in 1860. Excluding New Orleans and Baltimore, Gallman found a high degree of concentration of wealth in both states. For example, the wealthiest 10 percent of families in Louisiana held nearly 74 percent of the state's gross wealth in 1860. Gallman pointed out that wealth was nearly as concentrated in the United States as a whole (the wealthiest decile in his national sample for 1860 held 71 percent of all wealth). Nevertheless, his findings tended to support the idea that planters, as the wealthiest class in the South,

---

29. Oakes, *The Ruling Race,* 52–67 (first two quotations on p. 52; third quotation on p. 67).

dominated that region. In 1970, Gavin Wright published a study of the concentration of agricultural wealth in the cotton South in 1850 and 1860. Using quantitative data samples from the manuscript censuses of 1850 and 1860, he found distributions of agricultural property and production generally in line with the statistics on wealth-holding presented by Gallman. For example, Wright concluded that improved farm acreage was substantially concentrated in the cotton South, that farm value was even more concentrated than was improved acreage (suggesting that planters owned better, as well as more, land), and that slaves and cotton production were also distributed very unequally. The degree of concentration remained high during the 1850s, though there was no general pattern of increase during the decade. Lee Soltow's *Men and Wealth in the United States, 1850–1870* (1975), in the portions devoted to the South, reinforced the findings of Gallman and Wright. Soltow found concentration in the ownership of land and slave property and concluded: "The extreme inequality in distribution of slaves among slaveholders in the South caused a great deal of general inequality even among whites."[30]

Two studies published in 1977 gave greater depth and clarity to the picture of wealth concentration in the antebellum South. Albert W. Niemi, Jr., pointing out that Wright had concentrated on cotton-producing regions, examined inequality in the distribution of slave wealth in other southern agricultural areas. He found the concentration of slave property to be as great in noncotton as in cotton regions. Randolph B. Campbell and Richard G. Lowe, in *Wealth and Power in Antebellum Texas* (1977), investigated all facets of wealth distribution among the entire population of the Lone Star State. Basing their work on samples of five thousand heads of families from the censuses of 1850 and 1860 each, Campbell and Lowe found that "all important forms of wealth—real and personal property, slaves, and total wealth—were concentrated in the hands of a small group con-

30. Robert E. Gallman, "Trends in the Size Distribution of Wealth in the Nineteenth Century: Some Speculations," in Lee Soltow (ed.), *Six Papers on the Size Distribution of Wealth and Income* (New York: National Bureau of Economic Research, distributed by Columbia University Press, 1969), 1–30; Gavin Wright, "'Economic Democracy' and the Concentration of Agricultural Wealth in the Cotton South, 1850–1860," *Agricultural History*, XLIV (January, 1970), 63–93; Lee Soltow, *Men and Wealth in the United States, 1850–1870* (New Haven: Yale University Press, 1975), 124–46 (quotation on p. 146). In an earlier study, Soltow concluded that the distribution of slave property had demonstrated consistent inequality since 1790 ("Economic Inequality in the United States in the Period from 1790 to 1860," *Journal of Economic History*, XXXI [December, 1971], 822–39).

stituting less than 10 percent of all free Texans." They also engaged in a counterfactual exercise of "freeing" the slaves and considering the freedmen as potential property holders rather than as property themselves. The subtraction of wealth in slaves from the holdings of the upper class did not, however, significantly affect indexes of concentration. Wealth was no more unequally distributed in Texas than in other areas of the antebellum United States; nevertheless, the evidence seemed conclusive that even on the cotton frontier the upper economic class held a greatly disproportionate share of all property.[31]

In at least one important way the studies of Gallman, Wright, Soltow, Niemi, and Campbell and Lowe did not address themselves directly to the planter-dominance versus yeoman-democracy debate. They examined wealth distributions in a variety of ways but made no attempt to divide the populations under investigation into economic-social classes and study the proportions of property held by each. Their support for the planter-dominance thesis was, in a sense then, found in the implication, albeit a very strong one, that if wealth was concentrated, it had to be in the hands of large slaveholding planters. Certainly they all tended to endorse the suggestion made by Fabian Linden in 1946: the Old South may have had a large middle class, but this class did not hold a proportionate share of any form of wealth.

The argument does not end here, however, for several historians have warned against accepting evidence of concentration in wealth-holding as final proof that the Old South had an especially oligarchic economic-social structure. Edward Pessen has reminded us that inequality was nationwide rather than peculiarly southern during the antebellum "Era of the Common Man." His studies, such as *Riches, Class, and Power Before the Civil War* (1973), which deals with wealth distributions in Boston, New York, Brooklyn, and Philadelphia, have concentrated on the North. But by comparing his work with similar studies of the South, he has concluded that in spite of slavery, the two sections were far more similar economically and socially than is generally recognized. Concentrated wealth and power

31. Albert W. Niemi, Jr., "Inequality in the Distribution of Slave Wealth: The Cotton South and Other Southern Agricultural Regions," *Journal of Economic History*, XXXVII (September, 1977), 747–54; Randolph B. Campbell and Richard G. Lowe, *Wealth and Power in Antebellum Texas* (College Station: Texas A&M University Press, 1977), 135 (quotation), 146–53. Michael P. Johnson, "Wealth and Class in Charleston in 1860," in Fraser and Moore (eds.), *From the Old South to the New*, 65–80, found that the distribution of wealth in South Carolina's leading city could be summarized in one word: "unequal."

were American rather than simply southern characteristics. Otto H. Olsen made essentially the same point in 1972 when he pointed out that too much emphasis on how few southerners owned slaves and how few of those had planter-sized holdings could be misleading. He argued that the meaning of narrow or broad ownership of property is relative and indicated that in our modern capitalist system, only a small proportion of families own stock in corporations or live as employers rather than as employees. The Old South, therefore, was no more oligarchic than the antebellum North or the contemporary United States, and slavery created no more of a class rule system there than it did elsewhere.[32] Actually, most of those who studied southern wealth distributions found that property was similarly concentrated outside the South and in this way agreed with Pessen and Olsen. The difference was a matter of emphasis and interpretation.

Conclusions drawn from data on the distribution of wealth should be qualified also by considerations of the economic-social mobility of those involved. Robert E. Gallman made this point in commenting on Pessen's *Riches, Class, and Power Before the Civil War.* He suggested that the great degree of inequality Pessen found in major northeastern cities may have resulted to a large extent from age differences rather than a class system. Older people who had accumulated property over a longer period of time outnumbered younger people in the upper class; many of the latter could expect to rise as the years passed. Gallman's comments, though not directed to conditions in the Old South, probably apply there, too. Campbell and Lowe, for example, found that size of wealth-holding was positively related to advancing age in antebellum Texas. In Donald Schaefer's study, yeomen (defined as nonslaveholding farmers) in Kentucky and Tennessee from 1850 to 1860 "were experiencing difficulty in advancing relative to wealthier farmers and planters." On the other hand, however, they were not being pushed off the land, and their

---

32. Edward Pessen, "The Egalitarian Myth and the American Social Reality: Wealth, Mobility, and Equality in the 'Era of the Common Man,'" *American Historical Review,* LXXVI (October, 1971), 989–1034, *Riches, Class, and Power Before the Civil War* (Lexington, Mass.: Heath, 1973), and "How Different from Each Other Were the Antebellum North and South?" *American Historical Review,* LXXXV (December, 1980), 1119–49; Otto H. Olsen, "Historians and the Extent of Slave Ownership in the Southern United States," *Civil War History,* XVIII (June, 1972), 101–16. An article by D. L. A. Hackett, "The Social Structure of Jacksonian Louisiana," *Louisiana Studies,* XII (Spring, 1973), 351–52, emphasizes how widespread slaveholding was in rural Louisiana during the 1830s and 1840s and thus tends to support Olsen.

wealth grew at a rate comparable to that enjoyed by slaveholders. Carl H. Moneyhon's 1981 analysis of "economic democracy" in Phillips County, Arkansas, concluded that while large planters improved their position relative to other groups during the 1850s, all classes were unstable, and individuals exhibited a great deal of mobility within the larger structure. In short, though wealth distributions based on census data help clarify the economic class structure at a particular time, we must remember that the membership of these classes was not static and that the wealth-holding status of individuals in each changed, too.[33]

Finally, there is the matter of political relationships among the people who composed the various economic-social classes of the Old South. On this subject, as is the case with the distribution of wealth, significant progress has been made but definitive conclusions are not available. Ralph A. Wooster has made a major contribution in this area of investigation with systematic studies of the structure and personnel of state and local governments in all the slaveholding states except Delaware. *The People in Power* (1969) and *Politicians, Planters and Plain Folk* (1975) reveal that a majority of the southern states had essentially democratic political institutions by the last antebellum decade. Adult white males had the right to vote and hold office to such an extent that Wooster classified only North and South Carolina as "Aristocratic" and Louisiana and Maryland as "Moderately Aristocratic." George M. Fredrickson seconded Wooster's conclusions, albeit in a different context, in *The Black Image in the*

33. Robert E. Gallman, "Professor Pessen on the 'Egalitarian Myth,'" *Social Science History,* II (Winter, 1978), 194–207. Pessen replied to Gallman, and the ensuing debate continued into 1982. See Pessen, "On a Recent Cliometric Attempt To Resurrect the Myth of Antebellum Egalitarianism," *Social Science History,* III (Winter, 1979), 208–27; Gallman, "The 'Egalitarian Myth,' Once Again," *Social Science History,* V (Spring, 1981), 223–34; and Pessen, "The Beleaguered Myth of Antebellum Egalitarianism," *Social Science History,* VI (Winter, 1982), 111–28. For other studies dealing with questions of mobility, see Campbell and Lowe, *Wealth and Power,* 57–59; Donald Schaefer, "Yeoman Farmers and Economic Democracy: A Study of Wealth and Economic Mobility in the Western Tobacco Region, 1850 to 1860," *Explorations in Economic History,* XV (October, 1978), 435–37 (quotation on p. 435); and Carl H. Moneyhon, "Economic Democracy in Antebellum Arkansas, Phillips County, 1850–1860," *Arkansas Historical Quarterly,* XL (Summer, 1981), 154–72. Marriages between men and women of different social classes may also have affected mobility, but systematic study of this subject is very difficult. Nancy C. Roberson, "Social Mobility in Ante-Bellum Alabama," *Alabama Review,* XIII (April, 1960), 135–45, found numerous marriages across class lines in five Alabama counties during the years from 1851 to 1855.

White Mind (1971). The plain folk, Fredrickson wrote, were "fiercely democratic in their political and social thinking" and would not accept any philosophy of southern society or defense of slavery based on class differences. And "with the extension of the suffrage in the 1830s, this element acquired a political leverage that required some upper-class accommodation." Therefore, Negro slavery had to be justified in terms of race, and "the planter class, whatever its own inner feelings, endeavored to maintain its *de facto* hegemony by making a 'democratic' appeal, one which took into account the beliefs, desires, and phobias of an enfranchised nonslaveholding majority." White southerners saw their political system as a "*Herrenvolk*" democracy.[34]

Democratic structures and upper-class rhetoric supporting popular rule by whites do not tell the whole story of antebellum politics, however; there is also the matter of office holding and the actual exercise of power. Wooster found that those who held office were much more likely to be property holders and slaveholders than was typical of adult males among the general population. Virtually all the governors were slaveholders, and in 1860, slaveholders constituted a majority in the legislatures of every southern state except Missouri and Arkansas. Even on county courts, slaveholders had majority control in all the lower South states and in Virginia and Kentucky. The number of slaveholders and planters holding office tended to increase during the 1850s. Wooster did not argue that the increasing control of state and local offices by slaveholders was more important than the democratic structure of government in shaping southern politics. But he concluded: "Certainly the influence of the planters was greater than their numbers among the general population or southern officeholders would indicate."[35]

34. Ralph A. Wooster, *The People in Power: Courthouse and Statehouse in the Lower South, 1850–1860* (Knoxville: University of Tennessee Press, 1969), 116–17, and *Politicians, Planters and Plain Folk: Courthouse and Statehouse in the Upper South, 1850–1860* (Knoxville: University of Tennessee Press, 1975), 123–29; George M. Fredrickson, *The Black Image in the White Mind: The Debate on Afro-American Character and Destiny, 1817–1914* (New York: Harper & Row, 1971), 64–69 (first two quotations on p. 67; third on p. 68).

35. Wooster, *The People in Power*, 54, and *Politicians, Planters and Plain Folk*, 39, 63, 116, 127 (quotation). On the personnel of local government in Kentucky, see Robert M. Ireland, *The County Courts in Antebellum Kentucky* (Lexington: University Press of Kentucky, 1972), 12–17. In a recent study, Wooster wrote that "the higher the level of political organization the greater the involvement by men of wealth" ("Wealthy Southerners on the Eve of the Civil War," in Gary W. Gallagher [ed.], *Es-*

Campbell and Lowe, in their study of antebellum Texas, sought to measure the relationship of wealth-holding to political power by comparing the economic status of officeholders and political leaders with that of household heads among the population in general. They identified more than one thousand federal, state, and local office-holders from 1850 to 1860 and found them to be, in general, much wealthier than the average adult male Texan and more likely to be a slaveholder and a larger slaveholder at that. Texas, they concluded, had democratic political institutions, but "those who actually wielded political power at all levels of government were members of the slaveholding economic elite." [36]

It is true, as Gavin Wright argued in *The Political Economy of the Cotton South,* that such evidence is "circumstantial" and tells about the personnel of government rather than the exercise of power by constituent groups. Historians have not shown, Wright argues, "that slaveowners were able to extract resources from small farmers by political means, nor, with the possible exception of secession itself, enact any program to which there was significant small-farmer opposition." John Hebron Moore recently made a similar point in an article on government in antebellum Mississippi. Planters may have held office, he wrote, but they did so only by appealing for farmer votes. On the other hand, those who hold office have immediate control of making and implementing policy. William L. Barney made this point well in *The Secessionist Impulse.* "The vote cannot automatically be equated with political power, particularly when the voter represents a class with next to no influence in the decision-making process. . . . When the yeoman farmer voted, and most did, there was little for him to decide. Both candidates were more likely than not to represent slaveholding interests." Studies of the structure and rhetoric of antebellum southern politics thus favor the yeoman-democracy thesis while examinations of office holding point toward planter domination. A choice between the two depends on the development and application of a broadly acceptable definition of power. Gail W. O'Brien has made some useful suggestions on the subject in a paper entitled

says on Southern History Written in Honor of Barnes F. Lathrop [Austin: General Libraries of the University of Texas, 1980], 150).

36. Campbell and Lowe, *Wealth and Power,* 107–23 (quotation on p. 122). Randolph B. Campbell, "Planters and Plain Folk: Harrison County, Texas, as a Test Case, 1850–1860," *Journal of Southern History,* XL (August, 1974), 369–98, studied political activists as well as officeholders and reached similar conclusions.

"The Systematic Study of Power in the Nineteenth-Century South," but reaching a consensus will be difficult indeed.[37]

On balance, the weight of recent historical scholarship concerning antebellum southern society appears to lean toward the planter-dominance thesis. Eugene D. Genovese's Marxist interpretation, for example, depends on the idea of rule by the planter class. Studies of wealth distributions, though generally not concerned with social classes as such, have found high degrees of concentration in the ownership of both land and slaves. Economic historians have shown that those who utilized slave labor produced a huge percentage of the South's cash crops such as cotton. It has even been suggested that the region had a dual economy with large slaveholders engaging in commercial agriculture while the plain-folk majority existed on a subsistence basis. Finally, investigations of antebellum politics reveal that slaveholders constituted a greatly disproportionate share of those who held state and local offices across the South.

The plain folk have not gone without attention from historians during the past twenty years, but studies of the middle class do not really contradict the concept of planter dominance. Instead, the tendency is to explain the lives of small farmers and nonslaveholders in ways that show how the southern common people were able to "get along" in a society controlled by planters. McDonald and McWhiney, for example, indicate that the plain folk were essentially satisfied as long as they had individual autonomy, enough to eat, and plenty of leisure. Dickson D. Bruce, Jr., in *And They All Sang Hallelujah* (1974), presents plain-folk camp-meeting religion as an escape for an oppressed people who could not understand or combat planter control of their society.[38] Studies of political arrangements

37. Wright, *The Political Economy of the Cotton South,* 40–41 (quotation on p. 41); John Hebron Moore, "Local and State Governments of Antebellum Mississippi," *Journal of Mississippi History,* XLIV (May, 1982), 104–35; Barney, *The Secessionist Impulse,* 91; Gail W. O'Brien, "The Systematic Study of Power in the Nineteenth-Century South," in Burton and McMath (eds.), *Class, Conflict, and Consensus,* 263–89. For an application of O'Brien's ideas, see O'Brien, "Power and Influence in Mecklenburg County, 1850–1880," *North Carolina Historical Review,* LIV (Spring, 1977), 120–44.

38. Dickson D. Bruce, Jr., *And They All Sang Hallelujah: Plain-Folk Camp-Meeting Religion, 1800–1845* (Knoxville: University of Tennessee Press, 1974), 15–35. J. Crawford King, Jr., "The Closing of the Southern Range: An Exploratory Study," *Journal of Southern History,* XLVIII (February, 1982), 53–70, argues that the inability of planters to destroy the open-range tradition calls into question their sup-

and practices indicate that the structure of government was democratic in most states but that the plain folk apparently were to a large extent willing to allow slaveholders to hold the important offices. No doubt they objected to planter policies and pretensions at times, but there was no revolt to make the South more of a yeoman democracy. Class alignments did not determine political leadership or voting behavior in the Old South.

Studies of secession that emphasize class tension in explaining disunion also seem to accept the planter-dominance thesis. This is implicit in the argument that members of the ruling class were motivated in part by a perceived threat to their position from disgruntled nonslaveholders. Reviewers have generally been unconvinced by the class-tension interpretation of secession, but their doubts do not arise from the implications of planter dominance. Instead, the difficulty lies in the possibility that this interpretation may be mistaking secessionist rhetoric about the appeal of Republicanism to nonslaveholders for evidence that enough class tension actually existed to allow the development of significant antiplanter, antislavery views in the South.[39] In some cases, too, there appears to be a problem in interpreting as class conflict sectional tension between plantation areas and nonslaveholding backcountry regions in states such as Virginia and North Carolina. Even in these states, the great majority of plain folk in the backcountry showed no desire to abolish slavery or to become Republicans. This conclusion is supported in several studies, including *Southern Mountain Republicans* (1978), which argues that the chances of building a Republican party in antebellum Virginia, Tennessee, Kentucky, and North Carolina were "remote."[40] More-

posed domination of antebellum society. His study, however, focuses on the postbellum years and does not show conclusively that planters in the antebellum period wished to close the open range.

39. For reviewers who have not been entirely convinced by the internal-tension interpretation of secession, see Joel H. Silbey, Review of Johnson's *Toward a Patriarchal Republic*, in *Journal of American History*, LXVI (June, 1979), 155–56; and William W. Freehling, Review of Thornton's *Politics and Power in a Slave Society*, in *Journal of Southern History*, XLV (February, 1979), 116–18. Harold D. Woodman, "The Old South: Global and Local Perspectives on Power, Politics, and Ideology," *Civil War History*, XXV (December, 1979), 339–51, suggests that if yeomen were unhappy during the 1850s, it was only because they faced greater and greater difficulty in becoming planters themselves.

40. Gordon B. McKinney, *Southern Mountain Republicans, 1865–1900: Politics and the Appalachian Community* (Chapel Hill: University of North Carolina Press, 1978), 12–13.

over, according to Emory M. Thomas and James L. Roark, not even the strains of defeat in the Civil War created enough class conflict to produce an attempt by the plain folk to overthrow the planter class.

Although it seemingly has won general acceptance, the planter-dominance view of the Old South is still based on less than full knowledge of antebellum social structure. The planter class obviously included the wealthiest slaveholders, but there remain significant differences of opinion over the requirements for entry into this group. Some historians appear to include all slaveholders when they speak of "planters." Surely this is too encompassing, but where should the line be drawn? Would it be appropriate to divide this class into large planters who owned twenty or more slaves and small planters who held ten to nineteen bondsmen and then place small slaveholders with the plain folk? These problems of definition affect the size of the dominant minority and thus our view of social structure. At least, since this upper class clearly included those with twenty or more slaves, we know a good deal about these large planters' wealth, culture, control of public office, and success in leading the South into disunion.[41]

We know far less, however, about the plain folk. A number of important questions remain unanswered. In the first place, definitions of this class are anything but precise. Was it composed entirely of nonslaveholders, or were small slaveholding farmers and townspeople included? Second, was there a distinctive plain-folk culture? Third, there is the matter of mobility. Did the plain folk expect to move up the social ladder, and could they? Fourth, what was the attitude of the plain folk toward control of public office by the planters? Answers to these questions will depend on systematic new histories of the Old South's plain folk that look three or four decades back into the antebellum period.

Calling for new studies of the plain folk is easy; the execution of these works will be extremely difficult. Obviously, the task will depend heavily on information from the manuscript census returns, but these data can explain only part of what we need to know. Traditional

41. The broader culture of this class is revealed in accounts such as Robert Manson Myers (ed.), *The Children of Pride: A True Story of Georgia and the Civil War* (New Haven: Yale University Press, 1972), based on the papers of the Charles Colcock Jones family. This book moved Ludwell H. Johnson to comment that the planter world depicted by Thomas Nelson Page and Margaret Mitchell did indeed exist. It was "not the product of weak-minded romanticizing" (Review of Myers [ed.], *The Children of Pride*, in *Civil War History*, XIX [September, 1973], 280–85 [quotation on p. 280]).

nonquantitative sources will be essential, too, in investigating questions of plain-folk culture, social attitudes, and political views. Manuscript materials are available primarily for the planter class, and only the most assiduous and imaginative researcher can hope to find similar sources for the plain folk. Perhaps, as John Solomon Otto and Ben Wayne Banks have recently suggested, information derived from oral traditions can become a key to describing and understanding the historical experience of the South's common people.[42] Again, it is not an easy matter, but every effort must be made to escape overdependence on "elite" sources in describing antebellum southern society.

Research on the plain folk of the sort suggested here will probably have to be carried on at the local and state level. It is difficult to imagine such a project covering the whole South. Local studies, those dealing with one county, for example, have both advantages and limitations. They afford an opportunity to examine a relatively small population in depth and become thoroughly familiar with the plain folk as a class and ideally, in some cases, as individuals. On the other hand, a great many such local studies are necessary to the formulation of any general interpretation, and their contributions may be limited, too, by inconsistencies in methodology. State-level investigations, by covering large geographical areas, will allow consideration of sectional variations in social structure and the relationships among classes. A thorough study of the plain folk of Virginia, Georgia, or Louisiana, for example, should prove worth all the methodological problems, burdens of data collection, and other difficulties to be found along the way.[43]

42. John Solomon Otto and Ben Wayne Banks, "The Banks Family of Yell County, Arkansas: A 'Plain Folk' Family of the Highland South," *Arkansas Historical Quarterly,* XLI (Summer, 1982), 146–67.

43. This is hardly an original suggestion. Bonner concluded his essay in *Writing Southern History* with a call for more and better local histories dealing "with the entire range of social and economic life." In 1977, Ira Berlin wrote of "the decisive need for a social history of the nonslaveholding white majority" and suggested that historians "push back the frontier of historiographical concern beyond the 1850 census" ("White Majority," *Social History,* II [May, 1977], 653–60 [quotations on p. 659]). Woodman's 1979 review essay "The Old South" asked for additional local studies and more in-depth work on the yeomanry. Keith L. Bryant, Jr., "The Role and Status of the Female Yeomanry in the Antebellum South: The Literary View," *Southern Quarterly,* XVIII (Winter, 1980), 73–88, pointed out that middle-class women have been even more neglected than men. The chapter entitled "Shades of Ma and Pa: The Obscured Ancestors," in Virginia Van der Veer Hamilton, *Alabama: A Bicentennial History* (New York: Norton, 1977), 3–54, is an excellent general look at the role of the plain folk in one state. Scholars wishing to investigate this class in greater depth for the ante-

In short, interpretations of the antebellum South have tended to outpace knowledge of the region's social structure. Many historians appear willing to accept the planter-dominance view without pursuing and attempting to "settle" the original debate between the Phillips-Gray-Dodd and the Owsley theses. Some may even consider the older argument irrelevant when in fact a better understanding of antebellum social structure—of who dominated the Old South economically, politically, and socially, and of how that domination was exercised—is critical to interpreting the role of class relationships in developments such as secession. There is a need for agreement on more precise definitions of the various classes and for application of those definitions through a combination of quantitative and traditional historical sources in local and state studies. This need is especially clear in the case of the plain folk. We still need to know a great deal more about who they were, where and how they lived, what share of wealth they held, what their aspirations were, how often they achieved those ambitions, and whether or not they lived in essential unity with the planter class. The agenda for research established by David M. Potter in 1967 challenges us yet.

---

bellum period should consult Hamilton's chapter. There are important suggestions about plain-folk culture and the role of this class in settling the Old South's frontier in Milton Newton, "Cultural Preadaptation and the Upland South," in H. J. Walker and W. G. Haag (eds.), *Geoscience and Man*, V (1974), 143–54.

Studies that attempt to distinguish between the plain folk and the planters will also have to consider making a distinction between the white middle class and the poor whites. The first two chapters of J. Wayne Flynt, *Dixie's Forgotten People: The South's Poor Whites* (Bloomington: Indiana University Press, 1979), provide a good point of departure for this undertaking.

The Peculiar South Revisited
White Society, Culture, and Politics in the Antebellum Period, 1800–1860

DREW GILPIN FAUST

The past twenty years have witnessed the transformation of the South—and of its image in the American mind. Two decades ago, much of the region was still rigidly segregated, a "closed society," in the words of one of its interpreters. The North, by contrast, considered itself liberal and egalitarian; blacks, it insisted, were treated like any other citizens. By 1983, this had changed. Federal legislation had brought blacks into most dimensions of southern life. But in less visible ways the North had been transformed as well. In the course of attacking southern racism, the North exposed its own. No longer was the burden of guilt left to the South alone; no longer could the North claim its innocence in what C. Vann Woodward has called the national morality play. Instead, the North began to recognize how much it shared with the South; it too began to feel the burden of southern history.[1]

These changes have had an important impact upon scholarly interpretations of the antebellum South. The issue of regional distinctiveness, long a staple within southern historiography, has become far more complex. As scholars have illuminated the details of numerous substantive similarities between the sections, the North has been compelled to reevaluate not only its understanding of the South but its own consoling sense of peculiarity.

In a 1967 speculation on the future of research on the South, David M. Potter remarked that the task of the southern historian was "to identify and investigate the distinctive features of Southern society." A fascination with the special character of the region had in

1. James W. Silver, *Mississippi: The Closed Society* (New York: Harcourt, Brace & World, 1964); C. Vann Woodward, *The Burden of Southern History* (Baton Rouge: Louisiana State University Press, 1960), and *American Counterpoint: Slavery and Racism in the North-South Dialogue* (Boston: Little, Brown, 1971); William R. Taylor, *Cavalier and Yankee: The Old South and American National Character* (New York: George Braziller, 1961). I am grateful to Charles Rosenberg, Steven Hahn, John B. Boles, Evelyn T. Nolen, and Jennifer Garlid for comments and assistance.

fact long preoccupied historians and has continued to do so in the years since Potter's essay. Increasingly, however, the historiography of the Old South has been dedicated not just to illuminating distinctiveness but to evaluating how meaningful the peculiarities of southern civilization really were. Even Potter concluded that North-South differences could not be regarded as sufficiently important to warrant designating the regions as separate cultures. And in succeeding years, debate over the nature and significance of these differences has become both more sophisticated and more intense. Advances in theory and method have profoundly altered the terms of the argument.[2]

The most dramatic and influential contribution has been the work of Eugene D. Genovese. His writings have given a special generational cast to this century-old controversy. Emphasizing what he sees as the fundamental differences between North and South, Genovese has explained southern distinctiveness as the product of its prebourgeois society. Within the Marxian framework of his analysis, the relationship between master and slave has become the determining factor within southern civilization, affecting class relationships and social structures and defining the ideology of power that gave meaning to every action within the precapitalist social order. Like Ulrich B. Phillips, Genovese has placed the planter and the plantation community at the center of southern life; like Arthur Cole, Genovese has postulated an irrepressible conflict between North and South that resulted inevitably in the Civil War. But unlike his predecessors, Genovese has placed these notions in a far broader context. In treating the master-slave relationship as southern history's newest "central theme," Genovese has been able to construct an explanation of nearly every aspect of the southern way of life. And while he has sharply differentiated the North from the South, he has not designated the region as unique. Instead, Genovese has placed the South within an implicitly—and often explicitly—comparative framework, for his Marxism has necessarily implied the similarity of the antebellum South to societies of its own and other eras that also possessed unfree labor systems.[3]

2. David M. Potter, "Depletion and Renewal in Southern History," in Edgar T. Thompson (ed.), *Perspectives on the South: Agenda for Research* (Durham: Duke University Press, 1967), 78, *The Impending Crisis, 1848–1861* (New York: Harper & Row, 1976), and *The South and the Sectional Conflict* (Baton Rouge: Louisiana State University Press, 1968).

3. Eugene D. Genovese, *The Political Economy of Slavery: Studies in the Economy & Society of the Slave South* (New York: Pantheon, 1965), *The World the Slaveholders*

Genovese's interpretation has set the agenda for much of the research on antebellum southern history undertaken in the past two
decades. Scholars such as Carl N. Degler and James Oakes have devoted books specifically to refuting Genovese's thesis.[4] And a remarkable number of articles and monographs have related their findings to
his broad-gauged assertions, casting their particular conclusions as
"test cases" of Genovese's individual contentions. Even those who
have dissented most vigorously from his arguments have confirmed
the importance of Genovese's interpretation in their eagerness to
deny its validity. The appeal of his thesis has derived to a considerable
degree from the Gramscian character of his Marxism, from his growing interest over the past two decades in the ideological as well as the
material realities of southern life. His own work moved rapidly from
consideration of slavery's political economy (1965) to an exploration
of the world view of the master class in *The World the Slaveholders
Made* (1969) to an examination of a central component of this belief
system in his discussion of paternalism in *Roll, Jordan, Roll* (1974).
He has been concerned with a master class that possessed not just
"material interests" but "moral sensibility, ideological commitment,
and social psychology" worthy of the historian's attention. With his
notions of "paternalism" and planter "hegemony," Genovese has
offered a new perspective on the continuing enigma of the "mind of
the South." By means of a theoretical framework that specifies often-
elusive links between ideas and behavior, Genovese has provided

---

Made: Two Essays in Interpretation (New York: Pantheon, 1969), and *In Red and
Black: Marxian Explorations in Southern and Afro-American History* (New York:
Pantheon, 1971); Laura Foner and Eugene D. Genovese (eds.), *Slavery in the New
World: A Reader in Comparative History* (Englewood Cliffs, N.J.: Prentice-Hall,
1969); Eugene D. Genovese, *Roll, Jordan, Roll: The World the Slaves Made* (New
York: Pantheon, 1974), and *From Rebellion to Revolution: Afro-American Slave Re-
volts in the Making of the Modern World* (Baton Rouge: Louisiana State University
Press, 1979); Elizabeth Fox-Genovese and Eugene D. Genovese, *Fruits of Merchant
Capital: Slavery and Bourgeois Property in the Rise and Expansion of Capitalism*
(New York: Oxford University Press, 1983). For another Marxist approach to the Old
South, see Raimondo Luraghi, *The Rise and Fall of the Plantation South* (New York:
New Viewpoints, 1978).

4. Carl N. Degler, *Place Over Time: The Continuity of Southern Distinctiveness*
(Baton Rouge: Louisiana State University Press, 1977); James Oakes, *The Ruling
Race: A History of American Slaveholders* (New York: Knopf, 1982). Much of this
criticism has been addressed to the issue of planter hegemony and the nature of relations between planters and plain folk. On this question, see Randolph Campbell's essay in this volume.

a multifaceted and holistic interpretation of antebellum southern culture.

It is this very holism that has made Genovese's interpretation so resistant to the many attacks that have been launched upon it. In response to critics, Genovese has continuously refined his analysis without substantially changing its basic contours. Acknowledging recent empirical findings that emphasize certain objective similarities between North and South in, for example, patterns of urbanization or rates of per capita income growth, Genovese has insisted that the broader context of southern life, with its slave-based economy and society, meant that seemingly objective similarities were in fact perceived and experienced differently in the two sections. Those "interpretations that assume that the slaveholders lived, thought, and acted as ordinary bourgeois assume everything they must prove."[5] Moreover, he has readily accepted the importance of capitalist influences in southern society, devoting increasing attention to the contradictions generated by the participation of the southern economy in the world market for its highly commercial agricultural staples. But the reality of planter power and the pervasive influence of a master class world view, Genovese has continued to argue, defined the antebellum South as distinct.

Although some criticism of Genovese has been offered by scholars who have accepted southern distinctiveness but dissented from his particular description of southern peculiarity, the most elaborate attacks on his interpretation have come from those arguing that the South was not so profoundly different from the North as to be considered a separate culture. Some historians have always stressed the similarities between the sections, but in recent years, there has been an increase in their number and visibility. In a 1980 article entitled "How Different from Each Other Were the Antebellum North and South?," Edward Pessen has summarized much of this literature. Directing particular attention to the economy, politics, and society of the two regions, he found them "far more alike than the conventional scholarly wisdom has led us to believe."[6]

Recent work in economic history has made a major contribution to this conclusion, bringing the formidable legitimating power of

---

5. Eugene D. Genovese and Elizabeth Fox-Genovese, "The Slave Economies in Political Perspective," *Journal of American History,* LXVI (June, 1979), 9, 10.

6. Edward Pessen, "How Different from Each Other Were the Antebellum North and South?" *American Historical Review,* LXXXV (December, 1980), 1119–49.

the new cliometrics to enhance the arguments of those challenging southern distinctiveness. Although most widely discussed because of its iconoclastic assertions about the slave experience, Robert William Fogel and Stanley L. Engerman's *Time on the Cross* (1974) also questioned many traditional assumptions about southern prosperity and economic growth.[7] Piecing more than a decade of econometric studies into a comprehensive portrait of the South, Fogel and Engerman depicted a society neither backward nor stagnant. The South, Fogel

7. Robert William Fogel and Stanley L. Engerman, *Time on the Cross: The Economics of American Negro Slavery* (Boston: Little, Brown, 1974). The entry of econometrics into the study of the antebellum South must be dated from Alfred H. Conrad and John R. Meyer, "The Economics of Slavery in the Ante Bellum South," *Journal of Political Economy*, LXVI (April, 1958), 95–130; and Douglass C. North, *The Economic Growth of the United States, 1790–1860* (Englewood Cliffs, N.J.: Prentice-Hall, 1961), both of which stress dimensions of southern economic health. Richard A. Easterlin, "Regional Income Trends, 1840–1950," in Seymour E. Harris (ed.), *American Economic History* (New York: McGraw-Hill, 1961), 525–47, suggested the basic equivalence of North and South. Robert E. Gallman, "Trends in the Size Distribution of Wealth in the Nineteenth Century: Some Speculations," in Lee Soltow (ed.), *Six Papers on the Size Distribution of Wealth and Income* (New York: National Bureau of Economic Research, distributed by Columbia University Press, 1969), 1–30, and Lee Soltow, "Economic Inequality in the United States in the Period from 1790 to 1860," *Journal of Economic History*, XXXI (December, 1971), 822–39, also stress regional similarities. See also Robert E. Gallman, "Gross National Product in the United States, 1834–1909," in Conference on Research in Income and Wealth, *Output, Employment and Productivity in the United States After 1800* (New York: National Bureau of Economic Research, distributed by Columbia University Press, 1966), 3–76; Stanley L. Engerman, "The Effects of Slavery Upon the Southern Economy: A Review of the Recent Debate," *Explorations in Entrepreneurial History*, IV (Winter, 1967), 71–97, and "The Antebellum South: What Probably Was and What Should Have Been," *Agricultural History*, XLIV (January, 1970), 127–42; Robert W. Fogel and Stanley L. Engerman, "The Economics of Slavery," in Fogel and Engerman (eds.), *The Reinterpretation of American Economic History* (New York: Harper & Row, 1971), 311–41; Stanley L. Engerman, "A Reconsideration of Southern Economic Growth, 1770–1860," *Agricultural History*, XLIX (April, 1975), 343–61; Robert W. Fogel and Stanley L. Engerman, "The Relative Efficiency of Slavery: A Comparison of Northern and Southern Agriculture in 1860," *Explorations in Economic History*, VIII (Spring, 1971), 353–67.

For overviews of the evolving debate, see Alfred H. Conrad, "Econometrics and Southern History," *Explorations in Entrepreneurial History*, 2nd Ser., VI (Fall, 1968), 34–53; Morton Rothstein, "The Cotton Frontier of the Antebellum United States: A Methodological Battleground," *Agricultural History*, XLIV (January, 1970), 149–65; Harold D. Woodman (ed.), *Slavery and the Southern Economy: Sources and Readings* (New York: Harcourt, Brace & World, 1966), and "Economic History and Economic Theory: The New Economic History in America," *Journal of Interdisciplinary History*, III (Autumn, 1972), 323–50.

and Engerman argued, as they had already suggested in their earlier articles, was as prosperous as the North and was growing between 1840 and 1860 at a rate as rapid as that of any other area of the nation.[8] The traditional portrait of the South as stunted by limited urbanization and industrialization, one-crop agriculture, underdeveloped financial institutions, and economic dependence upon the North was replaced by a portrait of thriving regional economy. Other scholars have joined Fogel and Engerman in challenging the image of slavery as a detrimental economic force. Countering views held even by many antebellum southerners themselves as well as by succeeding generations of historians, quantifiers have shown the Old South to have been largely self-sufficient in foodstuffs rather than woefully dependent upon importations from the North and West.[9] Not only was

8. Fogel and Engerman even go so far as to argue greater productive efficiency for the South. See refutation of this claim by Gavin Wright, *The Political Economy of the Cotton South: Households, Markets, and Wealth in the Nineteenth Century* (New York: Norton, 1978), 87–88, and "Prosperity, Progress, and American Slavery," in Paul A. David *et al., Reckoning with Slavery: A Critical Study in the Quantitative History of American Negro Slavery* (New York: Oxford University Press, 1976), 302–36; Paul A. David and Peter Temin, "Slavery: The Progressive Institution?" in David *et al., Reckoning with Slavery,* 165–230; Woodman, "Economic History and Economic Theory"; Gavin Wright, "The Efficiency of Slavery: Another Interpretation," *American Economic Review,* LXIX (March, 1979), 219–26. See also Franklee Gilbert Whartenby, *Land and Labor Productivity in United States Cotton Production, 1800–1840* (New York: Arno Press, 1977).

9. Robert E. Gallman, "Self-Sufficiency in the Cotton Economy of the Antebellum South," *Agricultural History,* XLIV (January, 1970), 5–23; Raymond C. Battalio and John Kagel, "The Structure of Antebellum Southern Agriculture: South Carolina, a Case Study," *Agricultural History,* XLIV (January, 1970), 25–37; Diane Lindstrom, "Southern Dependence upon Interregional Grain Supplies: A Review of the Trade Flows, 1840–1860," *Agricultural History,* XLIV (January, 1970), 101–13; Colleen M. Callahan and William K. Hutchinson, "Antebellum Interregional Trade in Agricultural Goods: Preliminary Results," *Journal of Economic History,* XL (March, 1980), 25–31; William K. Hutchinson and Samuel H. Williamson, "The Self-Sufficiency of the Antebellum South: Estimates of the Food Supply," *Journal of Economic History,* XXXI (September, 1971), 591–612. Sam Bowers Hilliard, *Hog Meat and Hoecake: Food Supply in the Old South, 1840–1860* (Carbondale: Southern Illinois University Press, 1972), also addresses the issue of self-sufficiency, but his analysis is more qualitative.

The issue of financial dependence upon the North has been less fully explored. Harold D. Woodman finds agriculture heavily reliant on outside sources of financing in *King Cotton & His Retainers: Financing & Marketing the Cotton Crop of the South, 1800–1925* (Lexington: University of Kentucky Press, 1968). George D. Green, *Finance and Economic Development in the Old South: Louisiana Banking, 1804–1861* (Stanford: Stanford University Press, 1972), finds otherwise for Louisiana, arguing

slavery itself profitable both in its annual return to individual slave-holders and to the region more generally, it was part of a dynamic and healthy economic order.[10] Even the relative absence of industrial development, seen by historians from Ulrich B. Phillips to Eugene Genovese as a systemic deformity, has appeared in the new econometric literature not as weakness but as evidence of strength. Southerners, Gavin Wright argued in *The Political Economy of the Cotton South* (1978), chose plantation agriculture because of its profitability and its comparative advantage over manufacturing in southern society, where the constraints on the size of the labor force present on the North's free family farms did not exist.[11]

Those contributing to this rosy portrait of the southern economy differ in many significant particulars. Wright, for example, has viewed southern economic prosperity as the product of the peculiarly intense worldwide cotton demand between 1820 and 1860, not as proof of the economic viability that Fogel and Engerman claimed for slavery. In fact, like Genovese, Wright has regarded the South as moving inevitably toward crisis, though he has argued that slavery might have survived its internal contradictions until the 1930s. But most of these econometric scholars have shared a belief in the economic rationality of an essentially bourgeois planter class, which made the proper choices for immediate profit maximization under the circumstances prevailing in the Old South. Wright might have accused the southern elite of shortsightedness but would certainly not attribute to them an economic "irrationality" originating in a noncommercial social order.[12]

---

against both factor and planter domination of investment and banking decisions. His identification of a commercial spirit and his discovery of a well-developed banking system are, however, probably not generalizable to the whole South. J. Mauldin Lesesne's *The Bank of the State of South Carolina: A General and Political History* (Columbia: University of South Carolina Press, 1970) deals chiefly with the political battles banking engendered within the state. However, these battles do reveal considerable anti-commercial spirit.

10. Conrad and Meyer, "The Economics of Slavery." For the recent debate on profitability, see Edward Saraydar, "A Note on the Profitability of Ante Bellum Slavery," *Southern Economic Journal*, XXX (April, 1964), 325–32; Richard Sutch, "The Profitability of Ante Bellum Slavery—Revisited," *Southern Economic Journal*, XXXI (April, 1965), 365–67; Harold D. Woodman, "The Profitability of Slavery: A Historical Perennial," *Journal of Southern History*, XXIX (August, 1963), 303–25; Richard K. Vedder and David C. Stockdale, "The Profitability of Slavery Revisited: A Different Approach," *Agricultural History*, XLIX (April, 1975), 392–404.

11. Wright, *The Political Economy of the Cotton South*, Chap. 3 (pp. 43–88).

12. Wright, "Prosperity, Progress, and American Slavery," in David *et al.*, *Reckoning with Slavery*, 332–33.

Yet, as Harold D. Woodman, Eugene Genovese, and others have shown in response to the findings of the econometricians, the picture of a prosperous and modern South does not necessarily follow from this impressive array of new quantitative evidence. For all their apparent objectivity, numbers too must be interpreted. And the cliometricians, Woodman and Genovese have found, interpreted their statistics within a framework of unproven assumptions, which then have appeared as part of their conclusions. In fact, Gavin Wright has readily acknowledged this, admitting that "most of the existing research in econometric history" has assumed profit maximization to be an explanatory given. Genovese and his followers have dissented from this presupposition, insisting that these behavioral assumptions are appropriate only within a capitalist culture. Such motivations, they have argued, cannot automatically be attributed to planters in the Old South.[13]

Recently, Harold Woodman has recast many of the most important econometric findings within a Genovesean matrix. He has questioned whether income statistics are a valid basis for asserting the South's economic equality with the North, because the South's apparent prosperity was in fact largely a statistical artifact, a result of the comparatively slow increase in population, rather than of the rapid growth of regional income. Southern economic expansion "arose as a result of the failure to attract immigration because of limited opportunities. This is hardly a description of a land of opportunity." Per capita income figures are also misleading, in Woodman's view, because they tell little about market realities and resulting social and economic structures. Because such statistics do not distinguish between the value of crops produced for sale and those grown for home consumption, they offer no insight into the role of the mar-

13. Woodman, "Economic History and Economic Theory," 332; and "New Perspectives on Southern Economic Development: A Comment," *Agricultural History,* XLIX (April, 1975), 374–80; Genovese and Fox-Genovese, "The Slave Economies in Political Perspective"; Wright, *The Political Economy of the Cotton South,* 3. See how Genovese accepts much of the econometricians' evidence yet reinterprets its significance in "Commentary: A Historian's View," *Agricultural History,* XLIV (January, 1970), 143–47. Interest in the "rationality" of the southern planter has led to new examinations of plantation management. See William Kauffman Scarborough, *The Overseer: Plantation Management in the Old South* (Baton Rouge: Louisiana State University Press, 1966); Jacob Metzer, "Rational Management, Modern Business Practices, and Economies of Scale in the Ante-Bellum Southern Plantations," *Explorations in Economic History,* XII (April, 1975), 123–50; Drew Gilpin Faust, *James Henry Hammond and the Old South: A Design for Mastery* (Baton Rouge: Louisiana State University Press, 1982), Chaps. 5–6 (pp. 69–134).

ket in regional life. Within the self-sufficient South, markets and surrounding commercial structures remained severely limited in impact, even though income data do not—and cannot—reflect this important reality. Thus Woodman has suggested that new quantitative evidence about southern prosperity and self-sufficiency does not necessarily challenge Genovese's broad view of the South's political economy.[14]

The econometricians' explanation of the slow growth of southern manufacturing as the result of agriculture's comparative advantage has also been subjected to recent criticism. In *A Deplorable Scarcity* (1981), Fred Bateman and Thomas Weiss by no means embraced Genovese's view of southern society as precapitalist. But on the basis of a new collection of industrial data, they have concluded that southern manufacturing profits were high enough to have made industrial investment a rational choice for southern planters. Yet only 6 percent of slaveholders owning twenty or more slaves placed capital in manufacturing in 1860. The southern elite was so slow to seize such opportunities that Bateman and Weiss were compelled to invoke peculiar regional values as an explanatory variable. "To the extent that theoretical or applied economic analysis can imply something about the subtleties of human behavior, this study suggests that southerners indeed were different from their Yankee brethren." In spite of their disavowals of Genovesean leanings, Bateman and Weiss have depicted a "conservative, cautious, and slow-moving southerner" averse to the risk taking that is the foundation of capitalist entrepreneurship.[15]

14. Woodman, "Economic History and Economic Theory," 340. For studies of southern markets, see Woodman, *King Cotton & His Retainers;* Morton Rothstein, "Antebellum Wheat and Cotton Exports: A Contrast in Marketing Organization and Economic Development," *Agricultural History,* XL (April, 1966), 91–100, and "The Antebellum South as a Dual Economy: A Tentative Hypothesis," *Agricultural History,* XLI (October, 1967), 373–82; Bayly Ellen Marks, "Economics and Society in a Staple Plantation System: St. Marys County, Maryland, 1790–1840" (Ph.D. dissertation, University of Maryland, 1979); John R. Killick, "The Cotton Operations of Alexander Brown and Sons in the Deep South, 1820–1860," *Journal of Southern History,* XLIII (May, 1977), 169–94.

15. Fred Bateman and Thomas Weiss, *A Deplorable Scarcity: The Failure of Industrialization in the Slave Economy* (Chapel Hill: University of North Carolina Press, 1981), 163. See also Fred Bateman, James Foust, and Thomas Weiss, "The Participation of Planters in Manufacturing in the Antebellum South," *Agricultural History,* XLVIII (April, 1974), 277–97; Thomas F. Huertas, "Damnifying Growth in the Antebellum South," *Journal of Economic History,* XXXIX (March, 1979), 87–100. Peter Wallenstein, "From Slave South to New South: Taxes and Spending in Georgia From

The South's alleged economic backwardness has traditionally been considered as closely correlated with its supposed retardation in urban development. Historians have long identified the more rapid growth of cities in the North during the nineteenth century as an important factor differentiating the two sections. And the characterization of the South as predominantly rural seemed to justify a neglect of those cities that did exist. "Urbanization in the South before 1940," one scholar explained, "was not a particularly significant activity." Not surprisingly, the recent revisions in the traditional portrait of southern economic stagnation have been accompanied by new work on southern urbanization. "It is time," as David Goldfield de-

---

1850 Through Reconstruction," *Journal of Economic History,* XXXVI (March, 1976), 287–90, finds resistance to commercialism in Georgia taxation policies, by which merchants' property was assessed at a rate higher than that for agricultural holdings.

The impact of slavery on cost and availability of labor and the potential of slaves as factory workers have been important questions within the problem of southern industrialization. See Tom E. Terrill, "Eager Hands: Labor for Southern Textiles, 1850–1860," *Journal of Economic History,* XXXVI (March, 1976), 84–99; Gavin Wright, "Cheap Labor and Southern Textiles before 1880," *Journal of Economic History,* XXXIX (September, 1979), 655–80; Philip R. P. Coelho and James F. Shepherd, "Regional Differences in Real Wages: The United States, 1851–1880," *Explorations in Economic History,* XIII (April, 1976), 203–30; Heywood Fleisig, "Slavery, the Supply of Agricultural Labor, and the Industrialization of the South," *Journal of Economic History,* XXXVI (September, 1976), 572–97; Charles B. Dew, "Disciplining Slave Ironworkers in the Antebellum South: Coercion, Conciliation, and Accommodation," *American Historical Review,* LXXIX (April, 1974), 393–418, "David Ross and the Oxford Iron Works: A Study of Industrial Slavery in the Early Nineteenth-Century South," *William and Mary Quarterly,* 3rd Ser., XXXI (April, 1974), 189–224, and "Black Ironworkers and the Slave Insurrection Panic of 1856," *Journal of Southern History,* XLI (August, 1975), 321–38; Ronald L. Lewis, *Coal, Iron, and Slaves: Industrial Slavery in Maryland and Virginia, 1715–1865* (Westport, Conn.: Greenwood Press, 1979); Robert S. Starobin, *Industrial Slavery in the Old South* (New York: Oxford University Press, 1970). Recent microstudies of southern industry include: Percival Perry, "The Naval-Stores Industry in the Old South, 1790–1860," *Journal of Southern History,* XXXIV (November, 1968), 509–26; Dale Evans Swan, *The Structure and Profitability of the Antebellum Rice Industry, 1859* (New York: Arno Press, 1975); Ernest McPherson Lander, Jr., *The Textile Industry in Antebellum South Carolina* (Baton Rouge: Louisiana State University Press, 1969); Randall Martin Miller, "The Cotton Mill Movement in Antebellum Alabama" (Ph.D. dissertation, Ohio State University, 1971), and "Daniel Pratt's Industrial Urbanism: The Cotton Mill Town in Antebellum Alabama," *Alabama Historical Quarterly,* XXXIV (Spring, 1972), 5–35; John Hebron Moore, *Andrew Brown and Cypress Lumbering in the Old Southwest* (Baton Rouge: Louisiana State University Press, 1967); John Edmund Stealey III, "Slavery and the Western Virginia Salt Industry," *Journal of Negro History,* LIX (April, 1974), 105–31.

Recent studies of particular aspects of southern agriculture include James C. Bon-

clared, "to place the magnolias on Main Street and to develop an urban view of southern history."[16]

Exploring southern cities from the wider comparative perspectives of the new urban history, Blaine Brownell, Leonard Curry, and others have suggested that the pre–Civil War South showed "substantial urbanization" in comparison with the rest of the world and even, if border-state cities were included, with the highly advanced North. Curry went so far as to argue that the South urbanized more rapidly than the North and West between 1800 and 1850.[17] In the work of many scholars, the influences of this spreading urbanism seem to have transcended and even subsumed North-South differences: cities have appeared in this literature to be remarkably similar regardless of their regional location. In the Virginia of the 1850s, David Goldfield argued, the lure of the urban commercial economy brought even

ner, *A History of Georgia Agriculture, 1732–1860* (Athens: University of Georgia Press, 1964); Julia Floyd Smith, *Slavery and Plantation Growth in Antebellum Florida, 1821–1860* (Gainesville: University Presses of Florida, 1973); Mark Daniel Schmitz, "Economic Analysis of Antebellum Sugar Plantations in Louisiana" (Ph.D. dissertation, University of North Carolina, 1974); Susan Previant Lee, *The Westward Movement of the Cotton Economy, 1840–1860: Perceived Interests and Economic Realities* (New York: Arno Press, 1977); James D. Foust, *The Yeoman Farmer and Westward Expansion of U. S. Cotton Production* (New York: Arno Press, 1975); John Thomas Schlotterbeck, "Plantation and Farm: Social and Economic Change in Orange and Greene Counties, Virginia, 1716 to 1860" (Ph.D. dissertation, Johns Hopkins University, 1980). Stephen J. Goldfarb, "A Note on Limits to the Growth of the Cotton-Textile Industry in the Old South," *Journal of Southern History,* XLVIII (November, 1982), 547*n,* has pointed out that the significance of the 6 percent figure depends upon the definition of a high rate of participation. He also sees the limits on investment, in textiles at least, as constraints of opportunity rather than ideology.

16. Leonard Reissman, "Urbanization in the South," in John C. McKinney and Edgar T. Thompson (eds.), *The South in Continuity and Change* (Durham: Duke University Press, 1965), 79. Anne Firor Scott's review of the literature on southern cities in 1966 is a striking reminder of how the field has grown since that time. See Scott, "The Study of Southern Urbanization," *Urban Affairs Quarterly,* I (March, 1966), 5–14. David R. Goldfield, *Urban Growth in the Age of Sectionalism: Virginia, 1847–1861* (Baton Rouge: Louisiana State University Press, 1977), 283.

17. Blaine A. Brownell, "Introduction: Urban Themes in the American South," *Journal of Urban History,* II (February, 1976), 139; Leonard P. Curry, "Urbanization and Urbanism in the Old South: A Comparative View," *Journal of Southern History,* XL (February, 1974), 43–60; Blaine A. Brownell, "Urbanization in the South: A Unique Experience?" *Mississippi Quarterly,* XXVI (Spring, 1973), 105–20; Lyle W. Dorsett and Arthur H. Schaffer, "Was the Antebellum South Antiurban? A Suggestion," *Journal of Southern History,* XXXVIII (February, 1972), 93–100; Edward Pessen, "The Social Configuration of the Antebellum City: An Historical and Theoretical Inquiry," *Journal of Urban History,* II (May, 1976), 267–306.

rural southerners into closer contacts and sympathy with the North. Partly through the influence of cities, southerners became less and less distinct, increasingly "part of a national pattern" that included commercialization and "rapid urban growth." Southern urbanization seemed to Goldfield to make North and South objectively more alike, yet ironically at the same time to strengthen sectionalism by enabling the South to compete more effectively and thus contemplate freeing itself from the North entirely. Urbanization bred not just similarity but equality. Cities North and South contributed to railroad expansion, witnessed the growth of urban elites, and encouraged development of urban services such as police and fire protection, street lighting, and almshouses and hospitals.[18]

The traditional assumption that cities were anomalous within the Old South had curiously never produced a general examination of the urban version of the region's peculiar institution until Richard C. Wade published *Slavery in the Cities* in 1964. Important because of its treatment of a previously neglected dimension of the slave system, Wade's study also contained significant implications for understanding southern urbanism. Slavery and cities, he concluded, were incompatible. The freedoms urban life allowed threatened the control necessary to the maintenance of slavery. As a result, by the 1850s the number of urban slaves had declined dramatically. Cities were, Wade's research suggested, at odds with the labor system on which the southern economy was based and thus ill-suited to southern civiliza-

18. Brownell, "Urbanization in the South"; Richard J. Hopkins, "Are Southern Cities Unique? Persistence as a Clue," *Mississippi Quarterly*, XXVI (Spring, 1973), 121–41; David R. Goldfield, "Urban-Rural Relations in the Old South: The Example of Virginia," *Journal of Urban History*, II (February, 1976), 146–68 (quotations on p. 163), *Urban Growth in the Age of Sectionalism*, and "Pursuing the American Urban Dream: Cities in the Old South," in Blaine A. Brownell and Goldfield (eds.), *The City in Southern History: The Growth of Urban Civilization in the South* (Port Washington, N.Y.: Kennikat Press, 1977), 52–91. Studies emphasizing the particularly "modern" aspects of Old South cities include Laylon Wayne Jordan, "Police Power and Public Safety in Antebellum Charleston: The Emergence of a New Police, 1800–1860," *South Atlantic Urban Studies*, III (1979), 122–40; Thomas Field Armstrong, "Urban Vision in Virginia: A Comparative Study of Ante-Bellum Fredericksburg, Lynchburg, and Staunton" (Ph.D. dissertation, University of Virginia, 1974); Christopher Silver, "A New Look at Old South Urbanization: The Irish Worker in Charleston, South Carolina, 1840–1860," *South Atlantic Urban Studies*, III (1979), 141–72. Gregory Allen Greb, "Charleston, South Carolina, Merchants, 1815–1860: Urban Leadership in the Antebellum South" (Ph.D. dissertation, University of California, San Diego, 1978), stresses modern aspects of the Charleston merchant elite but also sees them bound tightly to the plantation system.

tion. In 1976, Claudia Dale Goldin challenged Wade's conclusions, citing quantitative data to show that the decline in the number of urban slaves was caused by the high cotton prices of the 1850s, which encouraged masters to increase the number of workers in the cotton fields. The issue of urban slave control was never central; slavery and urban life were, she concluded, entirely compatible.[19] Goldin's conclusions served as an important reinforcement for those who were striving to demonstrate the flexibility of the slave economy and to establish southern cities as equal participants in broader patterns of urban development and growth. Slavery, her work implied, was functionally interchangeable with free urban labor; cities should have been able to grow and develop equally well North and South; southern urban development needed not await emancipation.

Harold Woodman has dissented from this representation of the relationship between slavery and cities, saying Goldin focused on minor fluctuations in absolute numbers of urban slaves while ignoring the steady decline in the percentage of unfree workers in urban areas. Woodman has insisted that free and slave labor cannot be viewed as interchangeable because of the differing context of political and economic power relations that each engendered. Slavery, he has concluded, inhibited urban growth just as it inhibited the economic development so often associated with the rise of cities. Urbanism remained limited in the South because it represented a contradiction within the prevailing economic and social system.[20]

The questions Woodman raised about the context of urbanism in the South suggest other difficulties in the recent scholarly emphasis on the dynamism and growth of southern cities. While the attention the work of these historians has drawn to the study of this previously neglected dimension of the Old South is certainly to be commended, the replacement of the rural vision of the Old South with a bustling network of metropolitan centers is surely an overcompensation.

19. Richard C. Wade, *Slavery in the Cities: The South, 1820–1860* (New York: Oxford University Press, 1964); Claudia Dale Goldin, *Urban Slavery in the American South, 1820–1860: A Quantitative History* (Chicago: University of Chicago Press, 1976), and "Urbanization and Slavery: The Issue of Compatibility," in Leo F. Schnore (ed.), *The New Urban History: Quantitative Explorations by American Historians* (Princeton: Princeton University Press, 1975), 231–46.

20. Harold D. Woodman, "Comment," in Stanley L. Engerman and Eugene D. Genovese (eds.), *Race and Slavery in the Western Hemisphere: Quantitative Studies* (Princeton: Princeton University Press, 1975), 451–54; Stanley L. Engerman, "Comments on the Study of Race and Slavery," in Engerman and Genovese (eds.), *Race and Slavery,* 518–23.

Curry's zealous claim that the South was urbanizing at a faster rate than the North has been effectively challenged.[21] Recently, David Goldfield has offered thoughtful new reflections that seem to call for a reconsideration of some of the implications of his earlier work, as well as that of other historians. The scholars who found southern and northern cities essentially similar, who stressed that both were "aggressively capitalistic in pursuing growth and prosperity," Goldfield has argued, were approaching the urban past through the model of Chicago sociologist Louis Wirtz, who has stressed that urbanism is itself a way of life that leads cities to be more like one another than their non-urban surroundings. Goldfield has suggested an alternative model, one that sees the city primarily within its regional context and regards it as a product of surrounding ecological influences. The most prominent such factors in the South, he has suggested, were ruralism, race, and economic colonialism. From an analysis of the impact of these variables, Goldfield has found that southern cities were very different from those of the North, for they were characterized by low population density, low land values, and a dependence on staple-

21. Pessen, "How Different from Each Other Were the Antebellum North and South?," 1121*n*. For studies of particular cities, see Kenneth W. Wheeler, *To Wear a City's Crown: The Beginnings of Urban Growth in Texas, 1836–1865* (Cambridge: Harvard University Press, 1968); Gary Lawson Browne, *Baltimore in the Nation, 1789–1861* (Chapel Hill: University of North Carolina Press, 1980); D. Clayton James, *Antebellum Natchez* (Baton Rouge: Louisiana State University Press, 1968); Robert C. Reinders, *End of an Era: New Orleans, 1850–1860* (New Orleans: Pelican Publishing Co., 1964); James C. Bonner, *Milledgeville: Georgia's Antebellum Capital* (Athens: University of Georgia Press, 1978); Harriet Elizabeth Amos, "Social Life in an Antebellum Cotton Port: Mobile, Alabama, 1820–1860" (Ph.D. dissertation, Emory University, 1976), published as *Cotton City: Urban Development in Antebellum Mobile* (University: University of Alabama Press, 1985); Alan Smith Thompson, "Mobile, Alabama, 1850–1861: Economic, Political, Physical, and Population Characteristics" (Ph.D. dissertation, University of Alabama, 1979); Carl Edward Kramer, "The City-Building Process: Urbanization in Central and Southern Louisville, 1772–1932" (Ph.D. dissertation, University of Toledo, 1980); Armstrong, "Urban Vision in Virginia"; James Michael Russell, "Atlanta, Gate City of the South, 1847 to 1885" (Ph.D. dissertation, Princeton University, 1972); Richard Herbert Haunton, "Savannah in the 1850's" (Ph.D. dissertation, Emory University, 1968); William Joel Ernst III, "Urban Leaders and Social Change: The Urbanization Process in Richmond, Virginia, 1840–1880" (Ph.D. dissertation, University of Virginia, 1978); David G. McComb, *Houston: A History* (Rev. ed.; Austin: University of Texas Press, 1981); Merl E. Reed, *New Orleans and the Railroads: The Struggle for Commercial Empire, 1830–1860* (Baton Rouge: Louisiana State University Press, 1966); Richard C. Wade, *The Urban Frontier: Pioneer Life in Early Pittsburgh, Cincinnati, Lexington, Louisville, and St. Louis* (Chicago: University of Chicago Press, 1964).

crop production and marketing that sharply limited their size. Large metropolises, his work has concluded, were incompatible with the southern economy; in fact only three appeared in the cotton belt before the Civil War. Antebellum southern urban areas were chiefly small towns. "It was," as he wrote, "urbanization without cities."[22]

Limited urbanization has traditionally been regarded as a major factor in the comparative underdevelopment of formal social institutions in the Old South. The plantation, the argument has run, remained the focus of southern social life and services, thus hindering the growth of public welfare and benevolence. The enormous interest in northern reform movements among scholars of the past two decades has spawned some new exploration of comparable southern efforts, the very existence of which has represented an implicit refutation of earlier assumptions. Many of these studies, however, have taken the view that even if certain movements or institutions were present North and South, their differing cultural contexts distinguished them in important ways.

Scholars have shown that the evangelicalism that motivated much of the reform crusade in the North was also central to the southern world view. But within the slave region, evangelical impulses remained focused on personal rather than social improvement, on piety rather than good works. "The South disdained social activism because of its theology, which was linked to a hands-off policy concerning slavery, while northern revivalism saw social reform as Christian business," Samuel S. Hill, Jr., recently summarized.[23] Such reform as did occur was therefore often more conservative than progressive in

22. David R. Goldfield, "The Urban South: A Regional Framework," *American Historical Review*, LXXXVI (December, 1981), 1009, 1016, and *Cotton Fields and Skyscrapers: Southern City and Region, 1607–1980* (Baton Rouge: Louisiana State University Press, 1982). Carville Earle and Ronald Hoffman take a similar perspective on the colonial South in "Urban Development in the Eighteenth-Century South," *Perspectives in American History*, X (1976), 27–78. Michael P. Johnson, "Planters and Patriarchy: Charleston, 1800–1860," *Journal of Southern History*, XLVI (February, 1980), 45–72; and John Radford, "The Charleston Planters in 1860," *South Carolina Historical Magazine*, LXXVII (October, 1976), 227–35, both demonstrate the permeation of the city by rural values. See also Frank J. Huffman, Jr., "Town and Country in the South, 1850–1880: A Comparison of Urban and Rural Social Structures," *South Atlantic Quarterly*, LXXVI (Summer, 1977), 366–81.

23. Samuel S. Hill, Jr., *The South and the North in American Religion* (Athens: University of Georgia Press, 1980), 70; Donald G. Mathews, *Religion in the Old South* (Chicago: University of Chicago Press, 1977); John B. Boles, *The Great Revival, 1787–1805: The Origins of the Southern Evangelical Mind* (Lexington: University Press of Kentucky, 1972); Anne C. Loveland, *Southern Evangelicals and the Social*

intent, for institutional change seemed all too readily to imply possible alterations in the central and peculiar institution of the South. Certainly the preoccupation of northern reform movements with abolition made this connection very real.[24] The southern reform impulse therefore expressed itself most strongly in personal crusades such as temperance.

Douglas Wiley Carson found active temperance movements in at least four southern states and identified these as evidence of important commonalities between northern and southern culture. Ian R. Tyrrell, however, regarded the southern temperance impulse as comparatively weak; the sector of society most naturally attracted to the reform effort remained underdeveloped below the Mason-Dixon Line. In contrast to the North, Tyrrell concluded, the South had not come to the point in the transition to modern urban industrialism where temperance would thrive.[25]

Similarly, the prevention and treatment of disease remained an es-

---

Order, 1800–1860 (Baton Rouge: Louisiana State University Press, 1980). See Boles's more complete discussion of southern religion in this volume.

24. On the conservative thrust of the southern reform impulse, see Craig Michael Simpson, "Henry A. Wise in Antebellum Politics, 1850–1861" (Ph.D. dissertation, Stanford University, 1973), published as *A Good Southerner: The Life of Henry A. Wise of Virginia* (Chapel Hill: University of North Carolina Press, 1985); Drew Gilpin Faust, *A Sacred Circle: The Dilemma of the Intellectual in the Old South, 1840–1860* (Baltimore: Johns Hopkins University Press, 1977), Chap. 5 (pp. 87–111); Bertram Wyatt-Brown, "Modernizing Southern Slavery: The Proslavery Argument Reinterpreted," in J. Morgan Kousser and James M. McPherson (eds.), *Region, Race, and Reconstruction: Essays in Honor of C. Vann Woodward* (New York: Oxford University Press, 1982), 27–49. On agricultural reform, a focus of southern improvement efforts, see Drew Gilpin Faust, "The Rhetoric and Ritual of Agriculture in Antebellum South Carolina," *Journal of Southern History,* XLV (November, 1979), 541–68; William Warren Rogers, Jr., "'The Husbandman That Laboureth Must Be First Partaker of the Fruits' (2 Timothy 2:6): Agricultural Reform in Ante Bellum Alabama," *Alabama Historical Quarterly,* XL (Spring and Summer, 1978), 37–50; David W. Francis, "Antebellum Agricultural Reform in *DeBow's Review,*" *Louisiana History,* XIV (Spring, 1973), 165–77. On southern reform more generally, see John Christie Dann, "Humanitarian Reform and Organized Benevolence in the Southern United States, 1780–1830" (Ph.D. dissertation, College of William and Mary, 1975); Joanne Varner Hawks, "Social Reform in the Cotton Kingdom, 1830–60" (Ph.D. dissertation, University of Mississippi, 1970).

25. Douglas Wiley Carson, "Temperance Reform in the Cotton Kingdom" (Ph.D. dissertation, University of Illinois, 1982); Ian R. Tyrrell, "Drink and Temperance in the Antebellum South: An Overview and Interpretation," *Journal of Southern History,* XLVIII (November, 1982), 485–510. See also William Graham Davis, "Attacking 'The Matchless Evil': Temperance and Prohibition in Mississippi, 1817–1908" (Ph.D. dissertation, Mississippi State University, 1975).

sentially private concern in the Old South. The growth of public health facilities taking place in the North in this period was not matched in Dixie. In part, this was because of the smaller number of cities, whose congestion made them particularly susceptible to the epidemics that demanded public action. But even in southern urban areas, where warmer weather made disease a greater problem than it was in the North, southerners proved reluctant to take actions essential to community safety. In a comparison of New York and New Orleans, John Duffy found an appalling lack of responsibility among southern leaders in regard to disease control.[26] David Goldfield documented a similar absence of public spirit among an "aggressive commercial elite" ruling southern urban centers, who always permitted "wealth [to triumph] over health." Because of slavery, he concluded, there was no articulate urban white working class, such as existed in the North, to demand public health services.[27]

Slavery had its impact on private medical practice and education as well as on public health. Southern sectionalism contributed to a body of medical thought that insisted not only upon the distinctiveness of blacks' diseases but also on the peculiarity of regional morbidity patterns.[28] In the eyes of southern practitioners of the nineteenth century,

26. John Duffy, "Nineteenth Century Public Health in New York and New Orleans: A Comparison," *Louisiana History,* XV (Fall, 1974), 325–37; and *Sword of Pestilence: The New Orleans Yellow Fever Epidemic of 1853* (Baton Rouge: Louisiana State University Press, 1966). See also John H. Ellis, "Businessmen and Public Health in the Urban South During the Nineteenth Century: New Orleans, Memphis, and Atlanta," *Bulletin of the History of Medicine,* XLIV (May-June, 1970), 197–212, (July-August, 1970), 346–71; and Flora Bassett Hildreth, "The Howard Association of New Orleans, 1837–1878" (Ph.D. dissertation, University of California, Los Angeles, 1975).

27. David R. Goldfield, "The Business of Health Planning: Disease Prevention in the Old South," *Journal of Southern History,* XLII (November, 1976), 569. See also M. Foster Farley, "The Mighty Monarch of the South: Yellow Fever in Charleston and Savannah," *Georgia Review,* XXVII (Spring, 1973), 56–70.

28. James O. Breeden, "States Rights Medicine in the Old South," *Bulletin of the New York Academy of Medicine,* LII (1968–69), 29–45; John Duffy, "A Note on Ante-Bellum Southern Nationalism and Medical Practice," *Journal of Southern History,* XXXIV (May, 1968), 266–76; James Denny Guillory, "Southern Nationalism and the Louisiana Medical Profession, 1840–1860" (M.A. thesis, Louisiana State University, 1965); John Harley Warner, "Southern Medical Reform: The Meaning of the Argument for Southern Medical Education" (Paper presented at the Convention of the American Association for the History of Medicine, Bethesda, Md., May, 1982), and "The Idea of Southern Medical Distinctiveness: Medical Knowledge and Practice in the Old South" (Paper presented at the Second Barnard-Millington Symposium on Southern Science and Medicine, Jackson, Miss., March, 1983). I have not addressed

as well as historians in the twentieth century, antebellum southern and northern medicine differed significantly.

Reform in the treatment of criminals, a central component of northern benevolence, also played a role in the South. But as Edward L. Ayers has demonstrated, the penitentiary movement, like temperance, evangelicalism, or public health, developed a particular southern accent. Penitentiaries, Ayers acknowledged, seem in their embodiment of rational control "to typify the emerging capitalist system." Yet their appearance in every southern state but the Carolinas and Florida by the time of the Civil War was not, in Ayers' view, evidence of a thriving bourgeois culture within the South. Although part of a liberal reform movement in the North, prisons in the South fit within the prevailing conservative paternalistic ideology. One important function of the prisons, which were populated largely by whites, was to free their inmates from the onus of physical punishment, identified as a hallmark of slave status. Prisons, moreover, underlined the legitimacy of elite hegemony and of the status quo by demonstrating that power was exercised in a rational and benevolent manner. But southern penitentiary spokesmen lacked the "moral energy" of their northern counterparts and never expected the same degree of benefit from incarceration as did Yankee advocates of rehabilitation. Southern penitentiaries remained outposts of bourgeois values within a context of cultural traditionalism. Prisons, Ayers concluded, thus represented the contradiction central to southern culture.[29]

---

the growing literature on medical treatment of blacks. On southern medical education and practice generally, see Joseph I. Waring, *A History of Medicine in South Carolina, 1825–1900* (Columbia: University of South Carolina Press, 1967); John H. Ellis, *Medicine in Kentucky* (Lexington: University Press of Kentucky, 1977); Gerald Lee Cates, "A Medical History of Georgia: The First Hundred Years, 1733–1833" (Ph.D. dissertation, University of Georgia, 1976); Charles Stephen Gurr, "Social Leadership and the Medical Profession in Antebellum Georgia" (Ph. D. dissertation, University of Georgia, 1973); James O. Breeden, "Body Snatchers and Anatomy Professors: Medical Education in Nineteenth-Century Virginia," *Virginia Magazine of History and Biography,* LXXXIII (July, 1975), 321–45, and "Thomsonianism in Virginia," *Virginia Magazine of History and Biography,* LXXXII (April, 1974), 150–80. Barbara Bellows offers a case study of the failure of public provision for mental health in "'Insanity is the Disease of Civilization': The Founding of the South Carolina Lunatic Asylum," *South Carolina Historical Magazine,* LXXXII (July, 1981), 263–72. See also Norman Dain, *Disordered Minds: The First Century of Eastern State Hospital in Williamsburg, Virginia, 1766–1866* (Charlottesville: University Press of Virginia, 1971).

29. Edward Lynn Ayers, "Crime and Society in the Nineteenth-Century South" (Ph.D. dissertation, Yale University, 1980), 1, 29, published as *Vengeance and Justice: Crime and Punishment in the 19th-Century American South* (New York: Oxford Uni-

Contrasting patterns of punishment North and South were closely related to contrasting configurations of crime in the two sections. Ayers' investigations confirmed Michael Hindus' earlier arguments that southern lawlessness was far more likely to involve crimes of violence than crimes against property. In the North the situation was just the reverse. To both scholars, these differences seemed symbolic of wider cultural contrasts between a traditional society where control was based in personalism and notions of honor and an emergent dynamic commercial order. The resulting systems of justice were likewise dissimilar, with the South restricting the impact of courts and law in a variety of ways. The work of both Ayers and Hindus pointed toward the reality of sharply divergent structures of authority in the two sections and toward a southern legal system designed not to interfere with the autonomous power of a ruling planter class. "The 'inefficiency' of Southern courts," Ayers has suggested, "may well have been willed by many Southerners." Southern violence was no aberration, but functional, learned behavior specifically suited to the premodern configuration of human relationships in the Old South.[30]

---

versity Press, 1984). On penitentiaries, see also James C. Bonner, "The Georgia Penitentiary at Milledgeville, 1817–1874," *Georgia Historical Quarterly,* LV (Fall, 1971), 303–28; Mark T. Carleton, *Politics and Punishment: The History of the Louisiana State Penal System* (Baton Rouge: Louisiana State University Press, 1971).

30. Michael Stephen Hindus, *Prison and Plantation: Crime, Justice, and Authority in Massachusetts and South Carolina, 1767–1878* (Chapel Hill: University of North Carolina Press, 1980), "The Contours of Crime and Justice in Massachusetts and South Carolina, 1767–1878," *American Journal of Legal History,* XXI (July, 1977), 212–37, and "Black Justice Under White Law: Criminal Prosecutions of Blacks in Antebellum South Carolina," *Journal of American History,* LXIII (December, 1976), 575–99; Ayers, "Crime and Society," 197–98. See also Robert M. Ireland, "Law and Disorder in Nineteenth-Century Kentucky," *Vanderbilt Law Review,* XXXII (January, 1979), 281–304; Robert M. Saunders, "Crime and Punishment in Early National America: Richmond, Virginia, 1784–1820," *Virginia Magazine of History and Biography,* LXXXVI (January, 1978), 33–44. On southern violence as a central component of southern culture, see also Dickson D. Bruce, Jr., *Violence and Culture in the Antebellum South* (Austin: University of Texas Press, 1979). Bruce relates violence to the same southern pessimism about human nature that made the region skeptical about the perfectionism implicit in much of northern reform. See also Jack K. Williams, *Dueling in the Old South: Vignettes of Social History* (College Station: Texas A&M University Press, 1980); Arthur F. Howington, "Violence in Alabama: A Study of Late Ante-Bellum Montgomery," *Alabama Review,* XXVII (July, 1974), 213–31; Robert M. Weir, "The South Carolinian as Extremist," *South Atlantic Quarterly,* LXXIV (Winter, 1975), 86–103; and Bertram Wyatt-Brown, *Southern Honor: Ethics and Behavior in the Old South* (New York: Oxford University Press, 1982). On specifically military traditions and the South, see Robert E. May, "Dixie's Martial Image: A Continuing Historiographical Enigma," *Historian,* XL (February, 1978),

Much recent interest in the southern legal system has focused on slave law, not just as a window into the black experience but as an important reflection of white values and self-images. A number of scholars have stressed the surprising "fairness" of criminal procedures against slaves.[31] As Mark Tushnet has pointed out, this equitableness was evident chiefly at the appeals level, where judges had to offer explanations of their actions and where such statements became ritual assertions of the morality of the slave regime. Tushnet has accordingly characterized the law of slavery as an act of southern self-definition, an embodiment of the paternalistic ethos intended to dem-

---

213–34; and Marcus Cunliffe, *Soldiers and Civilians: The Martial Spirit in America, 1775–1865* (Boston: Little, Brown, 1968), Chap. 10 (pp. 335–84), both of which question the existence of a markedly stronger military heritage in Dixie. Morton J. Horwitz, *The Transformation of American Law, 1780–1860* (Cambridge: Harvard University Press, 1977), has stressed the lack of development of commercial law in the legal systems of southern states, suggesting the validity in the legal realm of contentions of slower bourgeois development in the South. By contrast, Jane Turner Censer, "'Smiling Through Her Tears': Ante-Bellum Southern Women and Divorce," *American Journal of Legal History*, XXV (January, 1981), 24–47, has found that despite prevailing beliefs about a far less liberal and modern legal system in the Old South than in the North, law pertaining to women and divorce was not markedly different in the two regions.

31. A. E. Keir Nash, "Fairness and Formalism in the Trials of Blacks in the State Supreme Courts of the Old South," *Virginia Law Review*, LVI (February, 1970), 64–100, "The Texas Supreme Court and Trial Rights of Blacks, 1845–1860," *Journal of American History*, LVIII (December, 1971), 622–42, "Negro Rights, Unionism, and Greatness on the South Carolina Court of Appeals: The Extraordinary Chief Justice John Belton O'Neall," *South Carolina Law Review*, XXI (Spring, 1969), 141–90, "A More Equitable Past? Southern Supreme Courts and the Protection of the Antebellum Negro," *North Carolina Law Review*, XLVIII (February, 1970), 197–242, and "Reason of Slavery: Understanding the Judicial Role in the Peculiar Institution," *Vanderbilt Law Review*, XXXII (January, 1979), 7–218; Daniel J. Flanigan, "Criminal Procedure in Slave Trials in the Antebellum South," *Journal of Southern History*, XL (November, 1974), 537–64, and "The Criminal Law of Slavery and Freedom, 1800–1868" (Ph.D. dissertation, Rice University, 1973); Meredith Lang, *Defender of the Faith: The High Court of Mississippi, 1817–1875* (Jackson: University Press of Mississippi, 1977); Eugene D. Genovese, "The Hegemonic Function of the Law," in *Roll, Jordan, Roll*, 25–49. By contrast, Hindus found blacks treated harshly at lower judicial levels. For additional studies of slave treatment under the law, see Royce Gordon Shingleton, "The Trial and Punishment of Slaves in Baldwin County, Georgia, 1812–1826," *Southern Humanities Review*, VIII (Winter, 1974), 67–73; John C. Edwards, "Slave Justice in Four Middle Georgia Counties," *Georgia Historical Quarterly*, LVII (Summer, 1973), 265–73; Don Higginbotham and William S. Price, Jr., "Was It Murder for a White Man to Kill a Slave? Chief Justice Martin Howard Condemns the Peculiar Institution in North Carolina," *William and Mary Quarterly*, 3rd Ser., XXXVI (October, 1979), 593–601.

onstrate the ethical legitimacy of the slaveholders' regime. Tushnet's explicitly Marxist analysis stressed the distinctiveness of the southern legal system, which, he contended, embodied the profound contradictions engendered by the situation of the precapitalist South within a bourgeois world. Torn between considerations of paternalist humanity and capitalist interest, southern judges sought during the antebellum period to segregate slaves within a special category of law whose peculiar principles would thus be prevented from structuring white class relations. Although southerners sought to resolve the contradictions between slavery and their conflicting bourgeois leanings in the realm of law as in other dimensions of southern life, they were doomed to failure. Such an enterprise, Tushnet has concluded, was incompatible with the logic of slavery.[32]

The inescapable contradictions Tushnet and Genovese have identified as central to southern culture were perhaps most tellingly manifested in southern thought. Law, as an embodiment of southern ideology, was but one representation of this system of belief. Genovese's growing interest in the critical role of planter hegemony in structuring southern society has served as an important impetus to the exploration of the various minds of the South by those seeking either to support or to refute his overall interpretation of southern life. But Genovese's work has by no means been the only encouragement to a fuller consideration of southern thought. The growing interest of historians generally in *mentalité*, in systems of meaning embedded in the structures of everyday life, has transformed the history of ideas. No longer concerned only with the products of great minds, historians have directed their attention to the beliefs that order and influence common experience. Such an emphasis has cast the intellectual life of the Old South in fresh light, making it a newly attractive field of inquiry. While previous historical canons had led much of southern

---

32. Mark Tushnet, "Approaches to the Study of the Law of Slavery," *Civil War History*, XXV (December, 1979), 329–38, and *The American Law of Slavery, 1810–1860: Considerations of Humanity and Interest* (Princeton: Princeton University Press, 1981). In a review of Tushnet's book, William W. Freehling seized upon the author's description of this process of legal segregation as evidence that slavery and its premodern influences could be quarantined within a broader, modernizing legal system, one determined by bourgeois values. But in his effort to label Tushnet an opponent rather than a supporter of Genovese, Freehling has mistaken intention for achievement. Tushnet's point is that southern judges tried to create a system without contradictions introduced by slavery but did not succeed. Freehling, Review of Tushnet's *The American Law of Slavery*, in *Journal of Southern History*, XLVIII (November, 1982), 581–82.

thought to be either neglected entirely or examined as a species of pathology, recent works have transcended the traditional exercise of studying southern thinkers simply to underline their quaint inferiority to northern men of letters. Southern intellectual culture has become a window upon broader patterns and values; popular expressions of belief have gained attention and importance as keys to the ever-elusive southern *mentalité*.

Previously dismissed as shallowly conceived and narrowly obsessed with slavery, southern intellectual life has recently been allowed, in the words of historian Michael O'Brien, "to define its own terms." The judgmental—even condemnatory—approach in many earlier explorations of southern thought has been replaced by an effort to trace the connections between expressed beliefs and the regional way of life. As Robert Brugger has put it, this generation's scholars are dedicated to trying to understand how southern thought was "thinkable" instead of simply dismissing it as "astonishing" or "irrational." Embracing some of the cultural relativism of the anthropologist, southern historians have begun to explore the meaning of ideas within their broader social and cultural context. Many scholars of southern literature have similarly retreated from belletristic and New Critical perspectives, concerning themselves less with building Simms into an aesthetic rival to James Fenimore Cooper and more with exploring the role of the author within structures of southern life and belief.[33]

33. See O'Brien's introduction to Michael O'Brien (ed.), *All Clever Men Who Make Their Way: Critical Discourse in the Old South* (Fayetteville: University of Arkansas Press, 1982), 11. "Astonishing" is David Donald's word, although of course his treatment of southern ideas goes well beyond dismissal. Donald, "The Proslavery Argument Reconsidered," *Journal of Southern History,* XXXVII (February, 1971), 3. "Irrational" is from Steven Channing, quoted in Robert J. Brugger, "The Mind of the Old South: New Views," *Virginia Quarterly Review,* LVI (Spring, 1980), 277.

On literature, see Lewis P. Simpson, *The Man of Letters in New England and the South: Essays on the History of the Literary Vocation in America* (Baton Rouge: Louisiana State University Press, 1973); Jon L. Wakelyn, *The Politics of a Literary Man: William Gilmore Simms* (Westport, Conn.: Greenwood Press, 1973); C. Hugh Holman, *The Roots of Southern Writing: Essays on the Literature of the American South* (Athens: University of Georgia Press, 1972); Lewis P. Simpson, "Slavery and the Culture of Alienation," in *The Dispossessed Garden: Pastoral and History in Southern Literature* (Athens: University of Georgia Press, 1975), 34–64; J. V. Ridgely, *Nineteenth-Century Southern Literature* (Lexington: University Press of Kentucky, 1980), *John Pendleton Kennedy* (New York: Twayne Publishers, 1966), and *William Gilmore Simms* (New York: Twayne Publishers, 1962); Faust, *A Sacred Circle;* John McCardell, *The Idea of a Southern Nation: Southern Nationalists and Southern Nationalism, 1830–1860* (New York: Norton, 1979), 141–76; Louis D. Rubin, Jr., *The*

Interest in thought that has no pretensions to the "greatness" of the work of a Plato—or even an Emerson—has led southern historians to investigate previously neglected products of southern intellectual life. In a collection of pieces by antebellum southern essayists, Michael O'Brien has, for example, suggested some of the rich materials available for a new investigation of southern thought. Periodicals promise to be a particularly useful source for exploring the nature of the southern mind, as does public oratory, which addressed subjects from agriculture to morality and was often transcribed and published in pamphlets for wider popular dissemination.[34]

Writer in the South: Studies in a Literary Community (Athens: University of Georgia Press, 1972), 1–33. Richard Beale Davis' work tends to be more traditional in approach. See his *Intellectual Life in Jefferson's Virginia, 1790–1830* (Chapel Hill: University of North Carolina Press, 1964), which is encyclopedic but not analytical, and *Literature and Society in Early Virginia, 1608–1840* (Baton Rouge: Louisiana State University Press, 1973), which claims that the South rivaled New England in this golden age of intellectual life.

It is significant that Simms's current biographer, John McCardell, is a historian, rather than a literary scholar, as was his most recent student, Jon L. Wakelyn. But I do not mean to suggest that Simms hagiography is by any means ended. See the recent editions of his works by the Southern Studies Program, University of South Carolina.

On popular oratory, see Elgiva Dundas Watson, "The Pursuit of Pride: Cultural Attitudes in North Carolina, 1830–1861" (Ph.D. dissertation, University of North Carolina, 1972); Faust, "The Rhetoric and Ritual of Agriculture"; Waldo W. Braden (ed.), *Oratory in the Old South, 1828–1860* (Baton Rouge: Louisiana State University Press, 1970); Wyatt-Brown, *Southern Honor;* Bruce, *Violence and Culture,* Chap. 8 (pp. 178–95).

On the relationship of agriculture and the southern world view, see James Tice Moore, "Majority and Morality: John Taylor's Agrarianism," *Agricultural History,* L (April, 1976), 351–61; C. William Hill, Jr., *The Political Theory of John Taylor of Caroline* (Rutherford, N.J.: Fairleigh Dickinson University Press, 1977); Robert E. Shalhope, *John Taylor of Caroline: Pastoral Republican* (Columbia: University of South Carolina Press, 1980); and Theodore R. Marmor, "Anti-Industrialism and the Old South: The Agrarian Perspective of John C. Calhoun," *Comparative Studies in Society and History,* IX (July, 1967), 377–406.

34. O'Brien (ed.), *All Clever Men.* In his introduction, however, he has gone beyond his concern with the cultural role of these writings to assert the equality of southern intellectual achievement with that of the North. Such a claim marks a return to older ways of viewing thought and abandons the relativistic approach of recent scholarship, which has concentrated on the meaning rather than the "quality" of southern letters (Introduction, pp. 1–25).

On periodicals, see the series of articles on individual magazines in *Southern Literary Journal,* Fall, 1969–Fall, 1975; Paul F. Paskoff and Daniel J. Wilson (eds.), *The Cause of the South: Selections from "DeBow's Review," 1846–1867* (Baton Rouge: Louisiana State University Press, 1982); Diffee William Standard, "DeBow's Review, 1846–1880: A Magazine of Southern Opinion" (Ph.D. dissertation, University of

Recent work on southern science, religion, and the proslavery argument has transformed their earlier characterization as curious evidence of regional intellectual failure and isolation. Scholars have emphasized how, in each of these areas, southerners seized upon ideas current within the mainstream of western European and northern thought and adapted them to the peculiarities of southern culture. As Theodore Dwight Bozeman has shown, southerners imparted a special meaning to both natural and social science. Southern invocation of Baconian "inductive" principles was intended at once to make the region a legitimate participant in the modern scientific enterprise and to protect the South from the social dangers inherent in abstract "deductive" thought.[35] The prestige of "scientific" analysis attracted

North Carolina, 1970); Edd Winfield Parks, *Ante-Bellum Southern Literary Critics* (Athens: University of Georgia Press, 1962); Gerald M. Garmon, *John Reuben Thompson* (Boston: Twayne Publishers, 1979).

35. Theodore Dwight Bozeman, "Joseph LeConte: Organic Science and a 'Sociology for the South,'" *Journal of Southern History*, XXXIX (November, 1973), 565–82, and *Protestants in an Age of Science: The Baconian Ideal and Antebellum Religious Thought* (Chapel Hill: University of North Carolina Press, 1977); Ronald L. Numbers and Janet S. Numbers, "Science in the Old South: A Reappraisal," *Journal of Southern History*, XLVIII (May, 1982), 163–84; William Henry Longton, "The Carolina Ideal World: Natural Science and Social Thought in Ante Bellum South Carolina," *Civil War History*, XX (June, 1974), 118–34, and "Some Aspects of Intellectual Activity in Ante-Bellum South Carolina, 1830–1860: An Introductory Study" (Ph.D. dissertation, University of North Carolina, 1969); Eric H. Christianson, "The Conditions for Science in the Academic Department of Transylvania University, 1799–1857," *Register of the Kentucky Historical Society*, LXXIX (Autumn, 1981), 305–25; James X. Corgan (ed.), *The Geological Sciences in the Antebellum South* (University: University of Alabama Press, 1982). For studies of particular scientists, see James O. Breeden, *Joseph Jones, M.D.: Scientist of the Old South* (Lexington: University Press of Kentucky, 1975); Lester D. Stephens, *Joseph LeConte: Gentle Prophet of Evolution* (Baton Rouge: Louisiana State University Press, 1982).

On religion in this context, see Mathews, *Religion in the Old South;* and Neal C. Gillespie, "The Spiritual Odyssey of George Frederick Holmes: A Study of Religious Conservatism in the Old South," *Journal of Southern History*, XXXII (August, 1966), 291–307. See also Donald G. Mathews' comparison and contrast of Charles Colcock Jones and William Lloyd Garrison in "Charles Colcock Jones and the Southern Evangelical Crusade to Form a Biracial Community," *Journal of Southern History*, XLI (August, 1975), 299–320. E. Brooks Holifield dissents from the prevailing emphasis on evangelicalism and on the differences between northern and southern religion in *The Gentlemen Theologians: American Theology in Southern Culture, 1795–1860* (Durham: Duke University Press, 1978). He points to the rationalistic orthodoxy of the urban clergy as evidence that religion did not speak only for the plantation elite or the poor white masses. His association of this impulse with cities, however, is indicative of how limited its impact was.

southern as well as northern thinkers; intellectuals in both sections cast their social ideas within the legitimating context of this would-be empiricism. Yet the urge to be identified with a modern, rational, scientific world view took different shape in the two sections, Bozeman, Neal Gillespie, and others have argued.[36] The southern urge for scientism remained peculiarly conservative, embracing an organicist view of social order that proscribed intervention in existing social processes and institutions. Like the contrasting interpretations of evangelicalism in the two sections, southern and northern approaches to newly "scientific" social thought differed sharply in their implications for action and in their view of the proper sources and the desirability of social change.

Although recent work in southern intellectual history has consistently attempted to widen the perception of southern letters to include more than defenses of slavery, the examination of the proslavery argument has continued to occupy a central place in scholarly literature on the mind of the South. But the portrait of the proslavery argument has been affected by changed understanding of other dimensions of southern culture and society.

In *The World the Slaveholders Made,* Eugene Genovese portrayed George Fitzhugh's proslavery essays as the "logical outcome of the slaveholders' philosophy." Fitzhugh's critique of capitalism, his insistence that the ultimate justification for the slave system transcended race, appeared to Genovese as an important manifestation of the fundamentally noncapitalist nature of antebellum southern society. The conflicts inherent in Fitzhugh's thought represented the irrepressible contradictions of a prebourgeois society located within a larger capitalist world. The defense of slavery became in Genovese's view an index to—and proof of—the premodern essence of the Old South.[37]

Such a characterization of southern ideology directly challenged a long-standing interpretation of proslavery thought as southerners' nervous and guilt-ridden reaction to the abandonment of America's democratic creed implied by their effort to retain their profitable and peculiar institution. While Genovese regarded the proslavery argument as a basic expression of southern culture, the traditional view cast it as an idiosyncratic gesture at odds with the more fundamental nature of southern life.[38]

36. Neal C. Gillespie, *The Collapse of Orthodoxy: The Intellectual Ordeal of George Frederick Holmes* (Charlottesville: University Press of Virginia, 1972).

37. Genovese, *The World the Slaveholders Made,* v.

38. Robert E. Shalhope, "Race, Class, Slavery, and the Antebellum Southern

At issue here is the old perennial: to what extent was the Old South like or unlike the rest of the nation? To what degree did southerners really "mean it" when they defended slavery? To what extent were they compelled to adopt these distasteful views by economic interest and political necessity? Was slavery an essential and formative part of an entire regional culture and world view, as Genovese would maintain, or was it just an embarrassing appendage to a society with basic values little different from those of the North?

This confrontation between the "guiltomania" and the Genovesean interpretations of proslavery thought has produced work on southern ideology that has moved away from the tendency to regard proslavery as a defensive gesture of little meaningful substance. Instead of focusing on its seemingly anomalous, bewildering character, scholars have in recent years directed renewed attention to the ideas and symbols the tracts contain and have related these to the context of regional culture and society. This work has found in the very repetitiveness and tediousness of slavery's defenses evidence for their value as an embodiment of widely shared beliefs. Similarly, recent scholars have emphasized that the active defense of slavery was not restricted to a brief era between nullification and the Civil War but emerged in the colonial period and grew up with the Old South itself. By characterizing the proslavery argument as a fundamental and long-lived aspect of antebellum regional culture, historians have justified their treatment of it as a uniquely valuable window upon the world the slaveholders made.[39]

Mind," *Journal of Southern History*, XXXVII (November, 1971), 559. For proponents of this viewpoint, see Charles G. Sellers, Jr., "The Travail of Slavery," in Sellers (ed.), *The Southerner as American* (Chapel Hill: University of North Carolina Press, 1960), 40–71; W. J. Cash, *The Mind of the South* (New York: Knopf, 1941); Taylor, *Cavalier and Yankee*; William W. Freehling, *Prelude to Civil War: The Nullification Controversy in South Carolina, 1816–1836* (New York: Harper & Row, 1966); James M. McPherson, "Slavery and Race," *Perspectives in American History*, III (1969), 460–73; and Oakes, *The Ruling Race*.

39. On the long-lived nature of proslavery thought, see Robert McColley, *Slavery and Jeffersonian Virginia* (Urbana: University of Illinois Press, 1964; 2nd ed., 1973); and my discussion of this issue in "The Proslavery Argument in History," in Faust (ed.), *The Ideology of Slavery: Proslavery Thought in the Antebellum South, 1830–1860* (Baton Rouge: Louisiana State University Press, 1981), 3. This historiographical essay provides a fuller treatment than is possible here, and the volume also contains a lengthy bibliography of secondary works.

Such treatment of ideology as meaningful substance rather than delusive mask has been influenced both by Genovese's Gramscian views and by the different but largely consistent perspectives of Clifford Geertz, whose "Ideology as a Cultural System" has

Interest in the role of western European and northern frameworks of belief within southern culture has had an important impact, revealing the way in which proslavery thought became intellectually central to the South's definition of itself in relation to the rest of the world. Defenders of slavery invoked systems of ideas current North and South in an effort to legitimate the peculiar institution—to make it, in fact, seem not so very peculiar. Evangelicalism, Baconianism, racism, romanticism, federalism, and republicanism have all been identified as influential components of the South's defense of its peculiar institution. But scholars have differed in their evaluation of the extent to which these common strains assumed different meanings within each section. Those disposed to see North and South as a single culture have tended to stress the way values were shared by both sections; scholars more sympathetic to Genovese's views have emphasized that the concepts on which proslavery ideology was founded were, like the ideas of evangelicalism or scientism, profoundly transformed in their southern setting.[40]

One important argument by historians adhering to the belief in a single national culture has been to cast racism as a fundamental motivation and theme in proslavery thought—as well as in southern life more generally. As we have come to acknowledge the long-lived influence of racism in the North and the South, we have established a context in which racism can serve as an explanation of proslavery ideology that does not sharply differentiate southern values from those of the nation as a whole. Within the framework of northern political life, these prejudices expressed themselves in a free-soil movement; in the South, they became the proslavery argument. Such a view also permits the reconciliation of the southern outlook with fundamental American democratic values. Southerners could defend the racial

---

been widely cited in recent historical literature (*The Interpretation of Cultures: Selected Essays* [New York: Basic Books, 1973], 193–233).

40. See Larry Edward Tise, "Proslavery Ideology: A Social and Intellectual History of the Defense of Slavery in America, 1790–1840" (Ph.D. dissertation, University of North Carolina, 1975); Robert J. Brugger, *Beverley Tucker: Heart over Head in the Old South* (Baltimore: Johns Hopkins University Press, 1978); Faust, *A Sacred Circle,* Chap. 6 (pp. 112–31), and "Evangelicalism and the Meaning of the Proslavery Argument: The Reverend Thornton Stringfellow of Virginia," *Virginia Magazine of History and Biography,* LXXXV (January, 1977), 3–17; Larry E. Tise, "The Interregional Appeal of Proslavery Thought: An Ideological Profile of the Antebellum American Clergy," *Plantation Society in the Americas,* I (February, 1979), 58–72; Mathews, *Religion in the Old South.*

status quo, yet still subscribe to the notion of equality among all white male citizens.[41]

At the same time that scholars have placed the substance of the proslavery argument within a wider intellectual framework, they have also explored in new depth its social context by directing attention to the social location of slavery's defenders and to the broader structures of southern intellectual life. David Donald inaugurated this trend more than a decade ago by inquiring into the social and psychological motivations of a group of proslavery theorists. Larry Tise has associated proslavery with the clergy in a study of 275 ministers, and Drew Gilpin Faust has also examined the significance of the social role of slavery's defenders. The proslavery argument, she has concluded, was essentially the product of the marginality of men of mind within the southern social order. Biographies of a number of prominent advocates have explored these questions of social and psychological motivations within the texture of individual lives.[42]

Increased recognition of the complexity both of southern intellectuals and of regional intellectual life has made consensus on the nature of southern thought elusive. While Genovese has regarded southern beliefs as evidence for his wider interpretation of the Old South, other scholars would join Michael O'Brien in his contrasting conclusion that the mind of the South was remarkably "modern." In O'Brien's view, the "South's peculiar institution did not doom the region to anachronism." The inability to disentangle fully these threads of modernity and anachronism—or bourgeois and prebourgeois tendencies—should not detract from the important advances of the past two decades in the understanding of southern belief systems. The dissension is itself testimony to the heightened awareness of the depth

41. For interpretations stressing the role of race, see George M. Fredrickson, *The Black Image in the White Mind: The Debate on Afro-American Character and Destiny, 1817–1914* (New York: Harper & Row, 1971), and "Masters and Mudsills: The Role of Race in the Planter Ideology of South Carolina," *South Atlantic Urban Studies*, II (1978), 34–48; Winthrop D. Jordan, *White over Black: American Attitudes Toward the Negro, 1550–1812* (Chapel Hill: University of North Carolina Press, 1968); McPherson, "Slavery and Race"; Degler, *Place Over Time;* and Ronald T. Takaki, *Iron Cages: Race and Culture in Nineteenth-Century America* (New York: Knopf, 1979).

42. Donald, "The Proslavery Argument Reconsidered"; Tise, "Proslavery Ideology"; Faust, *A Sacred Circle;* Brugger, *Beverley Tucker;* Gillespie, *The Collapse of Orthodoxy;* Betty L. Mitchell, *Edmund Ruffin: A Biography* (Bloomington: Indiana University Press, 1981); Faust, *James Henry Hammond;* Wakelyn, *The Politics of a Literary Man.* See also William Kauffman Scarborough (ed.), *The Diary of Edmund Ruffin* (2 vols.; Baton Rouge: Louisiana State University Press, 1972, 1976).

and diversity of the mind of the Old South. And this new appreciation naturally embodies an enhanced sense of the rich needs and opportunities for future research.[43]

An expanded investigation of less elite manifestations of southern beliefs constitutes one such area of opportunity. In its search for the mind of the South, most recent scholarship has not gone beyond analyses of readily accessible products of southern "high culture" to explore a more popular, broadly based *mentalité*. The comparative neglect of southern education is one aspect of this failure, though work in both law and religion has made important contributions toward an understanding of the mind of the South that is not restricted to a privileged, highly literate elite.[44] But the study that has come closest to achieving a detailed and comprehensive presentation of the southern world view has treated all these dimensions of southern culture within a broader interpretive theme. Bertram Wyatt-Brown has defined the notion of honor as the element that bound all classes of southern society together, underlying southern peculiarity in family

43. O'Brien (ed.), *All Clever Men*, 24, and O'Brien, "The Nineteenth-Century American South," *Historical Journal*, XXIV (September, 1981), 751–63. Clement Eaton's *The Mind of the Old South* (Baton Rouge: Louisiana State University Press, 1964) might be seen as an introduction to the new emphasis on southern intellectual diversity. C. Vann Woodward questioned the assumption of a unified "mind of the South" in "W. J. Cash Reconsidered," in *American Counterpoint*, and Carl N. Degler explored some of this diversity in *The Other South: Southern Dissenters in the Nineteenth Century* (New York: Harper & Row, 1974). See also J. Stephen Knight, Jr., "Discontent, Disunity, and Dissent in the Antebellum South: Virginia as a Test Case, 1844–1846," *Virginia Magazine of History and Biography*, LXXXI (October, 1973), 437–56.

44. On education, however, see William R. Taylor, "Toward a Definition of Orthodoxy: The Patrician South and the Common Schools," *Harvard Educational Review*, XXXVI (Fall, 1966), 412–26; Laylon Wayne Jordan, "Education for the Community: C. G. Memminger and the Origination of Common Schools in Antebellum Charleston," *South Carolina Historical Magazine*, LXXXIII (April, 1982), 99–115; Elizabeth Brown Pryor, "An Anomalous Person: The Northern Tutor in Plantation Society, 1773–1860," *Journal of Southern History*, XLVII (August, 1981), 363–92; Charles Coleman Wall, Jr., "Students and Student Life at the University of Virginia, 1825 to 1861" (Ph.D. dissertation, University of Virginia, 1978); Ralph Edward Glauert, "Education and Society in Ante-Bellum Missouri" (Ph.D. dissertation, University of Missouri, Columbia, 1973); Christie Farnham Pope, "Preparation for Pedestals: North Carolina Antebellum Female Seminaries" (Ph.D. dissertation, University of Chicago, 1977); Jane G. Weyant, "The Debate Over Higher Education in the South, 1850–1860," *Mississippi Quarterly*, XXIX (Fall, 1976), 539–57. An area that promises to yield new insights is the growing field of material culture studies, where values may be inferred from artifacts, archaeology, and architecture. But little has been published yet on whites in the Old South.

and gender behavior, as well as in more public structures of law, community, and political life. Based on exhaustive research, Wyatt-Brown's book has the same sweeping range as does the work of Eugene Genovese, though his holism is the product of the influences of cultural anthropology rather than Marxism. Wyatt-Brown's characterization of antebellum culture is also like Genovese's in many important ways, for he shares the view of the antebellum South as sharply distinctive. But it is honor, rather than slavery, that Wyatt-Brown has identified as the source of southern peculiarity. "Honor existed before, during, and after slavery." But ultimately, Wyatt-Brown has admitted, "white man's honor and black man's slavery became in the public mind of the South practically indistinguishable." Although he has found leadership to be more fraternal than the style of control implied by Genovese's "planter hegemony," Wyatt-Brown has concurred in the view of a South retarded in its progress toward the sort of modern, bureaucratic, commercial, and secular order rapidly developing in the North.[45]

One of the greatest strengths of Wyatt-Brown's approach is that it has enabled him to place both public and private behavior within the same framework of explanation. Family in the Old South served as the repository of both personal and communal honor. The peculiarities of domestic life were thus not mere idiosyncracies but important cultural indexes. Wyatt-Brown's treatment of southern family has synthesized a recent proliferation of studies in this area. Written as dissertations, these works have been narrowly focused and have dealt chiefly with the more readily accessible planter elite. Nevertheless, they have provided important demographic and conceptual foundations for further explorations of the relationship between individual psychology and wider social values of the South's ruling class. As the major agency of socialization, the family was perhaps the most important institution in the creation of a southern *mentalité*.[46]

45. Wyatt-Brown, *Southern Honor*, 16.
46. Steven Mac Stowe, "All the Relations of Life: A Study in Sexuality, Family, and Social Values in the Southern Planter Class" (Ph.D. dissertation, State University of New York at Stony Brook, 1979); Russell Lindley Blake, "Ties of Intimacy: Social Values and Personal Relationships of Antebellum Slaveholders" (Ph.D. dissertation, University of Michigan, 1978); Ann Williams Boucher, "Wealthy Planter Families in Nineteenth-Century Alabama" (Ph.D. dissertation, University of Connecticut, 1978); Jan Ellen Lewis Grimmelmann, "This World and the Next: Religion, Death, Success and Love in Jefferson's Virginia" (Ph.D. dissertation, University of Michigan, 1977), now published as Jan Lewis, *The Pursuit of Happiness: Family and Values in Jefferson's Virginia* (Cambridge, England: Cambridge University Press, 1983); Dorothy Ann

Wyatt-Brown's focus on honor has also provided him with a special perspective on southern political nationalism. The symbolic concern with honor, he has argued, lay as close to the heart of the South's desire for equality in the territories as did any substantive desire to extend the slave institution. Securing national acknowledgment of the legitimacy of its way of life was as important to the South as any question of political power. Secession ultimately resulted from a determination to uphold the personal and sectional independence in which honor was necessarily based.

Such a view of politics, with its emphasis on the influence of ideas and principles, rather than parties or economic interests, fits neatly within a recent interpretive trend, one that sharply revises the direction of antebellum political studies of the late 1960s and early 1970s. The quantitative revolution had made it possible for historians to collect the data necessary for detailed analyses of voting patterns both within state and national legislatures and among the people at large. Confusions about political behavior seemed at last to be nearing solution. In fact, broader studies of national Jacksonian politics did produce data important to an understanding of the South. The congressional roll-call analyses by Joel H. Silbey and Thomas B. Alexander showed southern politics to be much more national in the 1830s and 1840s than scholars had previously assumed. Except on the rare occasions when the slavery question arose directly—and sometimes even then—southern congressmen voted consistently along party rather than sectional lines. Southern politics, these scholars suggested, was shaped by the same strong party allegiances and divisions as was politics in the rest of the nation; slavery did not create a distinctively southern political outlook until the years just prior to secession.[47]

Gay, "The Tangled Skein of Romanticism and Violence in the Old South: The Southern Response to Abolitionism and Feminism, 1830–1861" (Ph.D. dissertation, University of North Carolina, 1975); Jane Turner Censer, "Parents and Children: North Carolina Planter Families, 1800–1860" (Ph.D. dissertation, Johns Hopkins University, 1980), now published as *North Carolina Planters and Their Children, 1800–1860* (Baton Rouge: Louisiana State University Press, 1984); James Michael McReynolds, "Family Life in a Borderland Community: Nacogdoches, Texas, 1779–1861" (Ph.D. dissertation, Texas Tech University, 1978). I have not addressed the growing literature on antebellum women, which is discussed in Jacquelyn Dowd Hall and Anne Firor Scott's essay in this volume.

47. Joel H. Silbey, *The Shrine of Party: Congressional Voting Behavior, 1841–1852* (Pittsburgh: University of Pittsburgh Press, 1967); Thomas B. Alexander, *Sectional Stress and Party Strength: A Study of Roll-Call Voting Patterns in the United States*

Within this interpretive framework, the structure and operations of party became a central concern, and scholars turned their new analytical skills to an exploration of both the first and second party systems within the South. Noble Cunningham, James Broussard, and others investigated the meaning of federalism and Jeffersonianism, while Norman Risjord found in the Old Republicans the transition to Jacksonian political structures. Thomas Alexander and a group of his students joined the old search for the southern Whigs and concluded that party divisions in Alabama did not, as had so long been assumed, rest on class lines. "Whig support came predominantly from those whom environment, access to information, and temperament inclined toward an awareness of a way of life beyond their horizons of space and time. . . . In the counties more nearly in the main stream of the national and world economy, Whig party appeals were more effective."[48] Subsequent studies by other scholars showed similar influences operating in other southern states; Whigs and Democrats seemed to divide on the basis of their attitudes toward the intrusions of a new commercial order.[49]

House of Representatives, 1836–1860 (Nashville: Vanderbilt University Press, 1967); Richard P. McCormick, *The Second American Party System: Party Formation in the Jacksonian Era* (Chapel Hill: University of North Carolina Press, 1966). Silbey argues for partisan rather than sectional bases of allegiance even on some sectional issues before 1864 in "John C. Calhoun and the Limits of Southern Congressional Unity, 1841–1850," *Historian,* XXX (November, 1967), 58–71. See also Silbey, "The Southern National Democrats, 1845–1861," *Mid-America,* XLVII (July, 1965), 176–90.

48. Noble E. Cunningham, *The Jeffersonian Republicans in Power: Party Operations, 1801–1809* (Chapel Hill: University of North Carolina Press, 1963); James H. Broussard, *The Southern Federalists, 1800–1816* (Baton Rouge: Louisiana State University Press, 1978); Norman K. Risjord, *The Old Republicans: Southern Conservatism in the Age of Jefferson* (New York: Columbia University Press, 1965); Thomas B. Alexander *et al.,* "The Basis of Alabama's Ante-Bellum Two-Party System: A Case Study in Party Alignment and Voter Response in the Traditional Two-Party System of the United States by Quantitative Analysis Methods," *Alabama Review,* XIX (October, 1966), 276, 266.

49. On parties, see Harry Legare Watson II, "'Bitter Combinations of the Neighbourhood': The Second American Party System in Cumberland County, North Carolina" (Ph.D. dissertation, Northwestern University, 1976); Frank Mitchell Lowrey III, "Tennessee Voters During the Second Two-Party System, 1836–1860: A Study in Voter Constancy and in Socio-Economic and Demographic Distinctions" (Ph.D. dissertation, University of Alabama, 1973); Thomas Edward Jeffrey, "The Second Party System in North Carolina, 1836–1860" (Ph.D. dissertation, Catholic University of America, 1976); Donald Arthur Debats, "Elites and Masses: Political Structure, Communication and Behavior in Ante-Bellum Georgia" (Ph.D. dissertation, University of Wisconsin, Madison, 1973); Burton W. Folsom II, "The Politics of Elites: Prominence

These analyses sought to show the national orientation and character of southern politics and to place the region within a wider "ethnocultural" interpretation of American political life that de-emphasized the influences both of class and of ideological forces such

---

and Party in Davidson County, Tennessee, 1835–1861," *Journal of Southern History,* XXXIX (August, 1973), 359–78; Lynwood Miller Dent, Jr., "The Virginia Democratic Party, 1824–1847" (Ph.D. dissertation, Louisiana State University, 1974); Burton W. Folsom II, "Party Formation and Development in Jacksonian America: The Old South," *Journal of American Studies,* VII (December, 1973), 217–29; Jerry Lee Cross, "Political Metamorphosis: An Historical Profile of the Democratic Party in North Carolina, 1800–1892" (Ph.D. dissertation, State University of New York at Binghamton, 1976); Paul Eugene McAllister, "Missouri Voters, 1840–1856: An Analysis of Antebellum Voting Behavior and Political Parties" (Ph.D. dissertation, University of Missouri, Columbia, 1976); Oran Lonnie Sinclair, "Crossroads of Conviction: A Study of the Texas Political Mind, 1856–1861" (Ph.D. dissertation, Rice University, 1975); Harold Dean Moser, "Subtreasury Politics and the Virginia Conservative Democrats, 1835–1844" (Ph.D. dissertation, University of Wisconsin, Madison, 1977); W. Wayne Smith, "Jacksonian Democracy on the Chesapeake: The Political Institutions," *Maryland Historical Magazine,* LXII (December, 1967), 381–93; James R. Morrill, "The Presidential Election of 1852: Death Knell of the Whig Party of North Carolina," *North Carolina Historical Review,* XLIV (Autumn, 1967), 342–59; D. L. A. Hackett, "Slavery, Ethnicity, and Sugar: An Analysis of Voting Behaviour in Louisiana, 1828–1844," *Louisiana Studies,* XIII (Summer, 1974), 73–118; Thomas E. Redard, "The Election of 1844 in Louisiana: A New Look at the Ethno-cultural Approach," *Louisiana History,* XXII (Fall, 1981), 419–33; William H. Adams, *The Whig Party of Louisiana* (Lafayette: University of Southwestern Louisiana, 1973), and "The Louisiana Whigs," *Louisiana History,* XV (Summer, 1974), 213–28; Jean H. Baker, *Ambivalent Americans: The Know-Nothing Party in Maryland* (Baltimore: Johns Hopkins University Press, 1977); Waymon L. McClellan, "1855: The Know-Nothing Challenge in East Texas," *East Texas Historical Journal,* XII (Fall, 1974), 32–44; Ralph A. Wooster, "An Analysis of the Texas Know Nothings," *Southwestern Historical Quarterly,* LXX (January, 1967), 414–23; Thomas E. Jeffrey, "Internal Improvements and Political Parties in Antebellum North Carolina, 1836–1860," *North Carolina Historical Review,* LV (Spring, 1978), 111–56.

On early appearances of party, see Lance Banning, *The Jeffersonian Persuasion: Evolution of a Party Ideology* (Ithaca: Cornell University Press, 1978); Broussard, *The Southern Federalists,* "Party and Partisanship in American Legislatures: The South Atlantic States, 1800–1812," *Journal of Southern History,* XLIII (February, 1977), 39–58, and "The Federalist Party in the South Atlantic States, 1800–1812" (Ph.D. dissertation, Duke University, 1968); Norman K. Risjord, "The Virginia Federalists," *Journal of Southern History,* XXXIII (November, 1967), 486–517, and *The Old Republicans;* Whitman H. Ridgway, *Community Leadership in Maryland, 1790–1840: A Comparative Analysis of Power in Society* (Chapel Hill: University of North Carolina Press, 1979). The application of the term *party* to this so-called first-party system has been widely questioned. See Ronald P. Formisano, "Deferential-Participant Politics: The Early Republic's Political Culture, 1789–1840," *American Political Science Review,* LXVIII (June, 1974), 473–87.

as proslavery or abolitionism. Yet this interpretation had certain problems as it applied to the South. Most strikingly, its preoccupation with the Americanness of southern politics diverted it from any satisfactory explanation of why the South ultimately rejected the national party system and decided to secede. Not coincidentally, its overwhelming concern with behavioral and particularly quantitative data seemed to neglect important dimensions of southern political culture: the values and assumptions that to many scholars seemed to differentiate the attitudes, if not always the actions, of southerners from citizens of the rest of the nation.[50]

Scholarship emphasizing such ideological and sectional currents has been a countertheme within southern political history in the past two decades. An early representation of this point of view was William W. Freehling's *Prelude to Civil War: The Nullification Controversy in South Carolina* (1965), which argued that slavery, not economic concerns, was the essential issue in the tariff controversy.[51] Two important more recent studies have similarly emphasized the role of slavery in southern political life, but have broadened the meaning of the term *slavery* from a narrowly conceived preoccupation with racial fear or economic interest to a metaphorical understanding that simultaneously encompassed and embodied values of honor, independence, and republicanism. Focusing on political rhetoric, William J. Cooper, Jr., has argued for the centrality of slavery in southern political life from as early as 1828. Jacksonian politics, he insisted, were not defined by finance or the bank question but showed a remarkable consistency with later sectional and secessionist issues. The South could participate in national parties not be-

---

50. Lee Benson, *Toward the Scientific Study of History: Selected Essays of Lee Benson* (Philadelphia: Lippincott, 1972).

51. Freehling, *Prelude to Civil War*. See also Major L. Wilson, "A Preview of Irrepressible Conflict: The Issue of Slavery During the Nullification Controversy," *Mississippi Quarterly*, XIX (Fall, 1966), 184–93. But Paul H. Bergeron has found that slavery was simply not an issue in Tennessee during the nullification era. Bergeron, "Tennessee's Response to the Nullification Crisis," *Journal of Southern History*, XXXIX (February, 1973), 23–44, and "The Nullification Controversy Revisited," *Tennessee Historical Quarterly*, XXXV (Fall, 1976), 263–75. J. P. Ochenkowski has shown in a recent study that Freehling's evidence for the role of slavery in South Carolina is unconvincing, but he does not offer an alternative explanation ("The Origins of Nullification in South Carolina," *South Carolina Historical Magazine*, LXXXIII [April, 1982], 121–53). On the early appearance and persistence of slavery in American politics, see Donald L. Robinson, *Slavery in the Structure of American Politics, 1765–1820* (New York: Harcourt Brace Jovanovich, 1971).

cause it had abandoned its distinctive concerns but because it was able until the 1850s to define the terms of its involvement. Most southerners, in fact, saw national party allegiance as the best means of defending their sectional interests, because parties seemed to offer the best protection for slavery, John C. Calhoun and South Carolina's opinions to the contrary notwithstanding. "National parties," Cooper concluded, "fostered and nourished sectional politics in the South."[52]

What the South required of parties—and what parties had by the 1850s ceased to provide—was defense of southern honor and interests. And interest and honor converged inextricably in the protection of slavery. Slavery seemed to guarantee southerners the freedom, independence, and control of their destiny essential to the maintenance of their honor; they contended that they had to have slaves or be slaves. Slavery became a compelling metaphor within a much broader view of social and political order. Although Cooper did not use the term, other scholars have described this particular vision of society and politics as "republicanism."

Focusing on a single state, rather than on national issues confronting the region as a whole, J. Mills Thornton III found a similar outlook at the heart of southern politics. In *Politics and Power in a Slave Society: Alabama, 1800–1860* (1978), Thornton too characterized Jacksonianism as fundamentally preoccupied with slavery, which Alabamians saw as the foundation of their cherished republican "independence." Although Thornton differed sharply from Cooper in arguing that states' rights concerns became significant only at the very end of the antebellum period, the approach of the two studies to the re-creation of past political reality was similar in important ways. Like Cooper, Thornton was more interested in exploring people's perceptions and conceptualizations than in simply describing political behavior or structures. One wonders if the two historians' contrasting conclusions about when southern politics became "sectionalized" might have arisen at least in part from their different emphases on state or local versus regional or national sources, for the books share an underlying concern with the role of beliefs in what Thornton called the South's "political culture." In exploring Alabamians' world

52. William J. Cooper, Jr., *The South and the Politics of Slavery, 1828–1856* (Baton Rouge: Louisiana State University Press, 1978), 373; J. Mills Thornton III, *Politics and Power in a Slave Society: Alabama, 1800–1860* (Baton Rouge: Louisiana State University Press, 1978). For a useful overview of the role of ideology in southern politics, see McCardell, *The Idea of a Southern Nation.*

view, Thornton discovered them to have been "obsessed with the *idea of* slavery"—not so much with protecting the slave investment of the planter class as with preserving the republican status quo that seemingly prevented the political enslavement of whites.[53]

The role that both Cooper and Thornton attributed to republican ideology implied the persistence of traditional political values in the South from the Revolution to the Civil War period. Cooper underlined his belief in the continuity between Jeffersonian and Jacksonian politics, as well as Jacksonian and secessionist politics. Thornton has stressed, in turn, the way in which the world view he attributed to antebellum Alabamians was essentially backward-looking, devoted to the preservation of older values and the protection of the state against encroaching commercialism and modernization. Such emphases on continuity run counter to earlier scholarly insistence upon a major political shift in the early 1830s with the emergence of the second party system. And at the same time they challenge the notion of an ideological "Great Reaction" by positing the continuing influence of republican ideas from the Revolution to 1860. John Randolph and the Old Republicans become critical transitional figures in transmitting these values to the Jacksonian South, where they appeared in propaganda for nullification, in proslavery essays, in tracts supporting colonization, in both Whig and Democratic rhetoric, and ultimately in the justification of secession itself.[54]

53. Thornton, *Politics and Power in a Slave Society,* xviii (my italics). In this discussion of politics, I have not addressed the issue of class relations and internal distribution of power. These questions, central in the recent literature, are considered by Randolph Campbell in this volume.

54. Risjord, *The Old Republicans;* Robert Dawidoff, *The Education of John Randolph* (New York: Norton, 1979); Brugger, *Beverley Tucker;* Shalhope, *John Taylor of Caroline;* Richard B. Latner, "The Nullification Crisis and Republican Subversion," *Journal of Southern History,* XLIII (February, 1977), 19–38; Major L. Wilson, "'Liberty and Union': An Analysis of Three Concepts Involved in the Nullification Controversy," *Journal of Southern History,* XXXIII (August, 1967), 331–55; David M. Streifford, "The American Colonization Society: An Application of Republican Ideology to Early Antebellum Reform," *Journal of Southern History,* XLV (May, 1979), 201–20; Kenneth S. Greenberg, "Revolutionary Ideology and the Proslavery Argument: The Abolition of Slavery in Antebellum South Carolina," *Journal of Southern History,* XLII (August 1976), 365–84; Thomas Brown, "The Southern Whigs and Economic Development," *Southern Studies,* XX (Spring, 1981), 20–38, and "Southern Whigs and the Politics of Statesmanship, 1833–1841," *Journal of Southern History,* XLVI (August, 1980), 361–80; Daniel Walker Howe, *The Political Culture of the American Whigs* (Chicago: University of Chicago Press, 1979); Kenneth S. Greenberg, "Representation and the Isolation of South Carolina, 1776–1860," *Journal of Ameri-*

DREW GILPIN FAUST

The identification of republicanism as the motive force behind antebellum southern politics might appear as an implicit assertion of the Americanness of the region, for recent scholarship has placed republican ideology at the center of the national political faith. But as Robert Shalhope has noted, work during the past ten years on republicanism has discovered regional variations. Like other national systems of belief adopted in the South, republicanism developed a peculiar southern accent, in particular emphasizing the close relationship between white independence and black slavery.[55] Republicanism warned against the corruptions of commercialism, emphasized the dangers of change, and underlined the importance of the personal autonomy inseparable from notions of honor. It was a political creed particularly appropriate to a South involved in a politics of cultural survival, defending itself against the onrush of modernity.

Within such a view of the republican ethos lies the source of Mills Thornton's interpretation of the origins of secession. Like Genovese, he has characterized disunion as arising from the threats of modern culture to the cherished social order of the Old South. But in Thornton's view, these challenges arose most forcefully not from the North but from the adoption of Yankee ways and values by planters within Alabama society. Like Thornton's study, recent work on secession has presented a complex portrait of both the social and geographical location, as well as the character of the stresses producing disunion. A number of scholars have emphasized that fears and tensions within regional society pushed southerners toward involvement in what

can History, LXIV (December, 1977), 723–43, and "The Second American Revolution: South Carolina Politics, Society, and Secession, 1776–1860" (Ph.D. dissertation, University of Wisconsin, Madison, 1976); John William Harris, Jr., "A Slaveholding Republic: Augusta's Hinterlands Before the Civil War" (Ph.D. dissertation, Johns Hopkins University, 1982); William W. Freehling, "Spoilsmen and Interests in the Thought and Career of John C. Calhoun," Journal of American History, LII (June, 1965), 25–42; Michael F. Holt, The Political Crisis of the 1850s (New York: John Wiley & Sons, 1978); Robert E. Shalhope, "Thomas Jefferson's Republicanism and Antebellum Southern Thought," Journal of Southern History, XLII (November, 1976), 529–56.

55. Robert E. Shalhope, "Republicanism and Early American Historiography," William and Mary Quarterly, 3rd Ser., XXXIX (April, 1982), 334–56, and "Toward a Republican Synthesis: The Emergence of an Understanding of Republicanism in American Historiography," William and Mary Quarterly, 3rd Ser., XXIX (January, 1972), 49–80. See also Eric Foner, Politics and Ideology in the Age of the Civil War (New York: Oxford University Press, 1980). On republicanism and the yeoman, see Steven Hahn, The Roots of Southern Populism: Yeoman Farmers and the Transformation of the Georgia Upcountry, 1850–1890 (New York: Oxford University Press, 1983).

many hoped would be a cathartic external conflict. Michael Johnson has argued that Georgian independence was motivated in part by class strains between yeomen and slaveholders; Steven Channing has portrayed South Carolinians impelled by racial fears; William Barney has identified internal economic anxieties that led Alabama and Mississippi to regard the territorial expansion of slavery as a necessity; William W. Freehling has pointed to Virginia secessionists' fears of internal opposition to slavery as a force pushing them toward disunion. Although these historians differ in important ways in their analyses of the exact shape of the crisis, they all have portrayed a South fearful of its own internal conflicts and weaknesses. In these interpretations, southerners seem beset by anxieties about internal subversion of their way of life. The threat was not so much that of direct northern interference with slavery, the argument follows, as a more covert, insidious infiltration of northern values and way of life.[56]

56. Michael P. Johnson, *Toward a Patriarchal Republic: The Secession of Georgia* (Baton Rouge: Louisiana State University Press, 1977); Steven A. Channing, *Crisis of Fear: Secession in South Carolina* (New York: Simon & Schuster, 1970); William L. Barney, *The Secessionist Impulse: Alabama and Mississippi in 1860* (Princeton: Princeton University Press, 1974); William W. Freehling, "The Editorial Revolution, Virginia, and the Coming of the Civil War: A Review Essay," *Civil War History*, XVI (March, 1970), 64–72. See also Donald Cleveland Butts, "A Challenge to Planter Rule: The Controversy over the Ad Valorem Taxation of Slaves in North Carolina: 1858–1862" (Ph.D. dissertation, Duke University, 1978); Richard G. Lowe, "The Republican Party in Antebellum Virginia, 1856–1860," *Virginia Magazine of History and Biography*, LXXXI (July, 1973), 259–79; Fred Siegel, "Artisans and Immigrants in the Politics of Late Antebellum Georgia," *Civil War History*, XXVII (September, 1981), 221–30; Billy Don Ledbetter, "Slavery, Fear, and Disunion in the Lone Star State: Texans' Attitudes Toward Secession and the Union, 1846–1861" (Ph.D. dissertation, North Texas State University, 1972); Walter L. Buenger, *Secession and the Union in Texas* (Austin: University of Texas Press, 1984); Luke Fain Crutcher III, "Disunity and Dissolution: The Georgia Parties and the Crisis of the Union, 1859–1861" (Ph.D. dissertation, University of California, Los Angeles, 1974); Marshall J. Rachleff, "Racial Fear and Political Factionalism: A Study of the Secession Movement in Alabama, 1819–1861" (Ph.D. dissertation, University of Massachusetts, 1974). For considerations of why Maryland did not secede, see William J. Evitts, *A Matter of Allegiances: Maryland from 1850 to 1861* (Baltimore: Johns Hopkins University Press, 1974); and Jean H. Baker, *The Politics of Continuity: Maryland Political Parties from 1850 to 1870* (Baltimore: Johns Hopkins University Press, 1973).

Useful recent studies of particular aspects of the sectional crisis include Don E. Fehrenbacher, "The Missouri Controversy and the Sources of Southern Separatism," *Southern Review*, XIV (Autumn, 1978), 653–67; Alison Goodyear Freehling, *Drift Toward Dissolution: The Virginia Slavery Debate of 1831–1832* (Baton Rouge: Louisiana State University Press, 1982); Frederick Merk, *Slavery and the Annexation of*

Although only Barney's interpretation is consistent with Eugene Genovese's earlier discussions of the causes of disunion, each of these studies seems to share a perception that has in recent years come to occupy an increasingly important place in Genovese's vision of the Old South. The conflict between modern and premodern tendencies did not take place exclusively across the Mason-Dixon Line. Participation in a capitalist world economy placed the South in a fundamentally contradictory situation. Genovese's growing attention to these internal conflicts—as they were manifested in individual planters as well as in southern thought and society—has given his work an increased complexity and made it reconcilable with the views of many historians who would never consider themselves Marxists and

---

Texas (New York: Knopf, 1972); Chaplain W. Morrison, *Democratic Politics and Sectionalism: The Wilmot Proviso Controversy* (Chapel Hill: University of North Carolina Press, 1967); Thelma Jennings, *The Nashville Convention: Southern Movement for Unity, 1848–1851* (Memphis: Memphis State University Press, 1980); Craig Simpson, "Political Compromise and the Protection of Slavery: Henry A. Wise and the Virginia Constitutional Convention of 1850–1851," *Virginia Magazine of History and Biography,* LXXXIII (October, 1975), 387–405; John McCardell, "John A. Quitman and the Compromise of 1850 in Mississippi," *Journal of Mississippi History,* XXXVII (August, 1975), 239–66; John T. Hubbell, "Three Georgia Unionists and the Compromise of 1850," *Georgia Historical Quarterly,* LI (September, 1967), 307–23; John Barnwell, *Love of Order: South Carolina's First Secession Crisis* (Chapel Hill: University of North Carolina Press, 1982); Ronald T. Takaki, *A Pro-Slavery Crusade: The Agitation to Reopen the African Slave Trade* (New York: Free Press, 1971); Gerald W. Wolff, *The Kansas-Nebraska Bill: Party, Section, and the Coming of the Civil War* (New York: Revisionist Press, 1977); Don E. Fehrenbacher, *The South and Three Sectional Crises* (Baton Rouge: Louisiana State University Press, 1980); Gerald Wolff, "The Slavocracy and the Homestead Problem of 1854," *Agricultural History,* XL (April, 1966), 101–11; William S. Hitchcock, "Southern Moderates and Secession: Senator Robert M. T. Hunter's Call for Union," *Journal of American History,* LIX (March, 1973), 871–84. Biographies of prominent political figures include Roger P. Leemhuis, *James L. Orr and the Sectional Conflict* (Washington, D.C.: University Press of America, 1979); Robert W. Johannsen, *Stephen A. Douglas* (New York: Oxford University Press, 1973); William Y. Thompson, *Robert Toombs of Georgia* (Baton Rouge: Louisiana State University Press, 1966); Robert W. Dubay, *John Jones Pettus, Mississippi Fire-Eater: His Life and Times, 1813–1867* (Jackson: University Press of Mississippi, 1975); John Eddins Simpson, *Howell Cobb: The Politics of Ambition* (Chicago: Adams Press, 1973); William C. Davis, *Breckinridge: Statesman, Soldier, Symbol* (Baton Rouge: Louisiana State University Press, 1974); Faust, *James Henry Hammond;* C. M. Simpson, "Henry A. Wise in Antebellum Politics"; Alvy L. King, *Louis T. Wigfall: Southern Fire-eater* (Baton Rouge: Louisiana State University Press, 1970); Thomas Edwin Schott, "Alexander H. Stephens: Antebellum Statesman" (Ph.D. dissertation, Louisiana State University, 1978). The best recent overview of the sectional crisis is Potter, *The Impending Crisis.*

who would in many cases even dissent from the view of the South as "premodern." The notions of southern internal conflict and weakness that informed the interpretations of secession offered by Barney, Johnson, Thornton, Freehling, and Channing are in this sense entirely consistent with Genovese's wider view of structural contradictions within antebellum southern society.

The softening in the lines of Genovese's portrait of a precapitalist South has enhanced the sophistication of our generation's entire debate over the essence of antebellum southern culture. Increased methodological skill in retrieving historical detail and growing awareness of the theoretical issues that provide a broad interpretive context have led scholars to a far richer understanding of both the reality and the meaning of the antebellum southern past. Within such a framework of knowledge, the effort rigidly to classify the South as either "distinctive" or "American," as "traditional" or "modern" is perhaps becoming an anachronistic oversimplification—especially as our expanding understanding of the North has shown it to have been far less uniformly progressive and advanced than historians once thought. Change appears more as a continuum, on which different scholars would choose different spots to locate the antebellum South and North.[57] The growing interest in comparing United States slave society with other unfree labor systems certainly demonstrates that an insistence upon the "uniqueness" of the Old South is no longer appropriate. David Potter's 1967 definition of the southern historian's task now seems obsolete. The way that the same data have so often been used during the past twenty years by those arguing both for and against southern distinctiveness suggests, moreover, that the issue may largely be one of emphasis—are the bottles half empty or half full? As Stanley Engerman wrote in 1980, "All societies are diverse, and in comparing any two it will be possible . . . to emphasize either

---

57. For a discussion of the continuum of change that suggests modernization theory as the best explanation of the relationship of North and South, see O'Brien, "The Nineteenth-Century American South." O'Brien acknowledges the widespread criticism of modernization theory but does not refute it. Also on modernization as applied to the South, see Raimondo Luraghi, "The Civil War and the Modernization of American Society: Social Structure and Industrial Revolution in the Old South before and during the War," *Civil War History,* XVIII (September, 1972), 230–50.

In *The Ruling Race,* James Oakes's challenge to Eugene Genovese suffers from a sort of anachronism, for it addresses the more rigid classifications that Genovese and others have long since abandoned. In its effort to label slaveholders' behavior, it greatly oversimplifies it—at the same time, ironically, that it argues for diversity within the slave-owning class.

similarities or differences. And, even if we concluded that in only one out of the multitude of characteristics did two societies differ, that one—if important enough—might justify an emphasis upon difference, not similarity." [58]

The traditional interest of southern historians in a "central theme" that promises the key to the regional experience also shows signs of change. Under the separate influences of Marxism and of cultural anthropology, scholars have increasingly focused on the Old South as a cultural system of interlocking parts, and they have as a result succeeded in showing how each "theme" is integrally related to all the others. Within such a seamless web of influences, it becomes difficult to identify an obvious center. Genovese would argue that it was the master-slave relationship; Wyatt-Brown would name honor; McDonald and McWhiney would emphasize white southerners' Celtic heritage; Degler would point to racism. On one level, we are again confronted with differences of emphasis that seem to some degree reconcilable. Wyatt-Brown has found honor partly Celtic in origin and has admitted that it became inseparably entangled with slavery; Genovese has acknowledged that racism introduced contradictions into the southern class system and "gave shape to class hegemony." Yet for those advocating these positions, the contrasts certainly seem more important than the commonalities; emphasis is all. [59]

The past twenty years have yielded an enormous increase in substantive knowledge about the Old South. But this body of commonly accepted fact has not produced a consensus. In an important sense, we have learned that facts are not enough. Significant differences in theoretical assumptions and outlook have led such scholars as Deg-

---

58. Stanley L. Engerman, "Antebellum North and South in Comparative Perspective: A Discussion," *American Historical Review*, LXXXV (December, 1980), 1155.

59. Wyatt-Brown, *Southern Honor*; Forrest McDonald and Grady McWhiney, "The Antebellum Southern Herdsman: A Reinterpretation," *Journal of Southern History*, XLI (May, 1975), 147–66, and "The South from Self-Sufficiency to Peonage: An Interpretation," *American Historical Review*, LXXXV (December, 1980), 1095–1118; Grady McWhiney and Perry D. Jamieson, *Attack and Die: Civil War Military Tactics and the Southern Heritage* (University: University of Alabama Press, 1982); Grady McWhiney, "The Revolution in Nineteenth-Century Alabama Agriculture," *Alabama Review*, XXXI (January, 1978), 3–32; Forrest McDonald, "The Ethnic Factor in Alabama History: A Neglected Dimension," *Alabama Review*, XXXI (October, 1978), 256–65; Forrest McDonald and Ellen Shapiro McDonald, "The Ethnic Origins of the American People, 1790," *William and Mary Quarterly*, 3rd Ser., XXXVII (April, 1980), 179–99; Degler, *Place Over Time*; Genovese, *The World the Slaveholders Made*, 238.

ler, Wyatt-Brown, and Genovese to embrace ultimately quite different visions of the Old South. Only when historians begin more explicitly to address these larger issues will the lingering puzzles begin to yield solutions. The choice between alternative interpretations of a body of data is often a theoretical rather than an empirical problem. Only if we are able to agree upon the proper framework of analysis—or at least upon the standards for building such a framework—will we be able to assess the real meaning of the facts we have been so assiduously collecting. I have little faith we will ever actually arrive at such agreement. But at least we will be talking to instead of past each other. Only through such dialogue can we enter into a useful structure of confrontation.[60]

The Old South still attracts our interest as a dark reflection of our own time, as a historical counterpoint to our own identity as Americans. In the 1960s and 1970s we as a nation began to doubt the American myths of inexorable progress and inevitable success. Under the twin shadows of the failure in Vietnam and the discovery of northern racism, we as historians started to look at the past with new eyes and to recognize in the antebellum period some of the new complexity we had found in our own. With such a burden of understanding, neither life nor southern history will ever seem simple again.

60. Genovese, of course, does deal explicitly with theoretical questions. But his critics have generally failed to grapple effectively with his interpretation because they do not confront this theoretical framework and address the assumptions on which his analysis is based.

The Slavery Experience

CHARLES B. DEW

Slavery is an area of southern historical scholarship that seems to be in a perpetual state of reinterpretation and renewal. During the past two decades, prominent historians have, on more than one occasion, pronounced the subject exhausted, but the scholarly community has paid little heed to these observations. In an essay published in 1967, David M. Potter wrote that slavery was one of those topics that had "been worked to a point where diminishing returns now seem about to set in." During the ten years that followed Potter's remark, a veritable avalanche of pathbreaking studies on various aspects of the American slave system appeared. Even a partial listing of the most notable works published between 1967 and 1977 is mind-boggling: Winthrop Jordan's *White over Black* (1968), Philip Curtin's *The Atlantic Slave Trade* (1969), Robert Starobin's *Industrial Slavery in the Old South* (1970), C. Vann Woodward's *American Counterpoint* (1971), George Rawick's *From Sundown to Sunup* (1972), John Blassingame's *The Slave Community* (1972), Gerald Mullin's *Flight and Rebellion* (1972), Peter Wood's *Black Majority* (1974), Eugene Genovese's *Roll, Jordan, Roll* (1974), Robert Fogel and Stanley Engerman's *Time on the Cross* (1974), Ira Berlin's *Slaves Without Masters* (1974), Edmund Morgan's *American Slavery—American Freedom* (1975), David Brion Davis' *The Problem of Slavery in the Age of Revolution* (1975), Herbert Gutman's *The Black Family in Slavery and Freedom* (1976), Nathan Huggins' *Black Odyssey* (1977), and Lawrence Levine's *Black Culture and Black Consciousness* (1977). Little wonder that in 1977, Orlando Patterson noted, in an echo of Potter's 1967 pronouncement, that slavery in the United States "is rapidly approaching the point of being overstudied." [1] The evidence is

1. David M. Potter, "Depletion and Renewal in Southern History," in Edgar T. Thompson (ed.), *Perspectives on the South: Agenda for Research* (Durham: Duke University Press, 1967), 78; Orlando Patterson, "Slavery," *Annual Review of Sociology*, III (1977), 438. All books listed here are cited completely elsewhere in this essay.

already in, however, that students of southern history intend to pay no more attention to Patterson's admonition than they did to Potter's.

The reasons behind this extraordinary outpouring of scholarship are not difficult to find. Certainly the emergence of the civil rights movement as a major force in American political, social, and cultural life during the 1950s and 1960s brought the subject of slavery to the fore. As scholars sought to understand the origins of racial inequality in the United States, they inevitably turned back to the era when that inequality was most blatantly institutionalized and oppressive.

Investigation moved forward on several fronts. Historians started searching for new sources of information on black life in bondage, and their efforts paid off in the publication of important collections of documentary material. In a string of impressive social and cultural histories published largely in the 1970s, the slave community, the black family, and the religious and secular elements of Afro-American culture emerged as the dominant forces molding slave life in the Old South. Taken together, these major works—especially those by Blassingame, Rawick, Genovese, Gutman, and Levine—offered a sweeping reinterpretation of slavery during the decades leading up to the Civil War. Equally important, scholars began looking beyond the plantations of the nineteenth century, back to the colonial, revolutionary, and early national periods. In books and, often, in highly suggestive articles, students of the seventeenth- and eighteenth-century South extended our understanding of the origins of American slavery and revealed an institution maturing and solidifying well before the era of the Cotton Kingdom. And finally, historians applied the tools of the social sciences to slavery. New theoretical approaches brought the South's slave system into comparative, demographic, quantitative, anthropological, and psychological perspective, and acrimonious debate was spawned by a number of these innovative works. But, on balance, it is no exaggeration to say that the scholarship produced during the past two decades has broadened and immeasurably enriched our understanding of slavery.

Although the civil rights movement unquestionably sparked a revival of interest in slavery, one seminal work largely determined the direction many of these studies would take. Stanley M. Elkins' *Slavery*, first published in 1959, asked a series of important questions about life in the quarters. What was the nature of the institution when viewed from the perspective of the individual slave? How did living in what Elkins called the "closed" system of North American plantation slavery affect the personality development of those born and raised in bondage? How did slavery in the American South compare with other slave systems, particularly those of Latin America, and what accounted for the differences? His comparative analysis seemed to reveal a harsher system of slavery in the Old South and a pervasive slave personality unique to that region. That basic personality type he described in terms of the stock antebellum white caricature of the black "Sambo." The typical North American slave, Elkins insisted, was a man-child; his personality was characterized by "loyalty, docility, humility, cheerfulness, and (under supervision) diligence" and could include "such additional qualities as irresponsibility, playfulness, silliness, laziness, and (quite possibly) tendencies to lying and stealing." Using theories drawn from social psychology and analogies based on the experience of inmates in Nazi concentration camps, Elkins advanced what would soon become known as the "Sambo" thesis. "It will be assumed that there were elements in the very structure of the plantation system—its 'closed' character—that could sustain infantilism as a normal feature of behavior," he wrote. "It will be assumed that the sanctions of the system were in themselves sufficient to produce a recognizable personality type." [2]

These were very large assumptions indeed, and most historians would eventually reject both the Sambo thesis and Elkins' description of North American slavery as a closed system and a more rigorous form of servitude than that which had existed in Latin America. [3]

2. Stanley M. Elkins, *Slavery: A Problem in American Institutional and Intellectual Life* (Chicago: University of Chicago Press, 1959; 2nd ed., 1968), 131, 86 (quotations from the 1959 edition).

3. Ann J. Lane (ed.), *The Debate over Slavery: Stanley Elkins and His Critics* (Urbana: University of Illinois Press, 1971); David Brion Davis, *The Problem of Slavery in Western Culture* (Ithaca: Cornell University Press, 1966), and "Slavery," in C. Vann Woodward (ed.), *The Comparative Approach to American History* (New York: Basic Books, 1968), 121–34; Herbert S. Klein, *Slavery in the Americas: A Comparative Study of Virginia and Cuba* (Chicago: University of Chicago Press, 1967); Kenneth M. Stampp, "Rebels and Sambos: The Search for the Negro's Personality in Slavery," *Journal of Southern History*, XXXVII (August, 1971), 367–92; Vincent P. Franklin, "Slavery, Personality, and Black Culture—Some Theoretical Issues," *Phylon*, XXXV (March, 1974), 54–63; Robert H. McKenzie, "The Shelby Iron Company: A Note on Slave Personality after the Civil War," *Journal of Negro History*, LVIII (July, 1973), 341–48; Marvin Harris, *Patterns of Race in the Americas* (New York: Walker, 1964); Magnus Mörner, *Race Mixture in the History of Latin America* (Boston: Little, Brown, 1967); Carl N. Degler, *Neither Black Nor White: Slavery and Race Relations in Brazil and the United States* (New York: Macmillan, 1971); H. Hoetink, *Slavery and Race Relations in the Americas: Comparative Notes on Their Nature and Nexus* (New York: Harper & Row, 1973); Laura Foner and Eugene D. Genovese (eds.), *Slavery in the New World: A Reader in Comparative History* (Englewood Cliffs, N.J.: Prentice-

But his insistence that slavery should be seen from the vantage point of the slave and his utilization of the social sciences and the techniques of comparative history were to have a profound impact on subsequent scholarship.

Nowhere was Elkins' influence more evident than in the social and cultural histories of slavery published over the past two decades. These works almost universally took issue, either directly or indirectly, with Elkins' interpretation, but the fact that they probed deeply into subjects like the slave personality and emphasized the critical role of internal factors—the black family, community, religion, and folk culture—in shaping that personality could be attributed in large measure to Elkins' book.

Two social histories published in 1972 were harbingers of the new era in slavery studies. Both stressed the formative and creative role of elements indigenous to the quarters in determining many of the important aspects of slave life; both relied extensively on sources largely neglected by previous historians; and both were highly critical of Elkins' work. In his landmark study of the slave community, John W. Blassingame drew heavily on published fugitive accounts—autobiographies and memoirs written by former slaves—and painted a picture of slavery that showed individuals struggling to carve out decent and autonomous lives for themselves despite the cruelties and restrictions imposed on them by their servitude. He found many black men and women succeeding in these efforts in part because the system was much more open than Elkins had admitted. Blassingame asserted that "the slave quarters, religion, and family helped to shape behavior." And, as a result, the slave "held onto many remnants of his African culture, gained a sense of worth in the quarters, spent most of his time free from surveillance by whites, controlled important aspects of his life, and did some personally meaningful things on his own volition." Instead of a dominant Sambo personality, Blassingame insisted "that there were many different slave personality types." [4] It was a portrait of life under bondage that was light-years removed from the one Elkins had offered.

Hall, 1969); Robin W. Winks (ed.), *Slavery: A Comparative Perspective: Readings on Slavery from Ancient Times to the Present* (New York: New York University Press, 1972).

4. John W. Blassingame, *The Slave Community: Plantation Life in the Antebellum South* (New York: Oxford University Press, 1972; 2nd ed., 1979), viii (quotation from the 1972 edition). See also Al-Tony Gilmore (ed.), *Revisiting Blassingame's "The Slave Community": The Scholars Respond* (Westport, Conn.: Greenwood Press, 1978).

The same thing held true in the other broad interpretation of slave life published in 1972. George P. Rawick's *From Sundown to Sunup* was actually the introductory volume in an ambitious documentary project—the publication of the interviews with former slaves conducted under the auspices of Fisk and Southern universities in the 1920s and the much more extensive Slave Narrative Collection assembled by Federal Writers' Project personnel during the 1930s. Making this massive body of evidence more accessible to historians was, in itself, a major contribution to slave scholarship, but Rawick made the series even more valuable when he decided to preface the original eighteen-volume edition of interviews with an extended discussion of what they told us about American slaves and slavery. In chapters on African cultural survivals, religion, the black family, and slave treatment and resistance, Rawick outlined a portrait of life under slavery that bore a striking resemblance to that presented by Blassingame. Room for maneuver existed under slavery, Rawick insisted, and slaves, "while oppressed and exploited, were not turned into brutalized victims, but found enough social living space to allow them to survive as whole human beings." The slaves' religion was critical to this process of survival, Rawick pointed out, and the family was equally important. He dismissed as a myth the notion that "the slaves had no normal, significant family life." The interviews showed a much different situation. Many slaves lived in stable families with a strong male figure present, and, in addition, the slave community itself "acted like a generalized extended kinship system in which all adults looked after all children." The world revealed in the testimony of former slaves was a cruel mix of maltreatment, degradation, and exploitation on one hand and Christian faith, resistance, and mutual support on the other. The part of the slave's world that counted for most was clearly the one which existed, as Rawick's title indicated, between sundown and sunup.[5]

The historiographical trends launched by Elkins' *Slavery* gathered momentum rapidly in the mid-1970s. In the space of four years, three major social and cultural histories of antebellum slavery appeared, Genovese's *Roll, Jordan, Roll,* Gutman's study of the black family, and Levine's examination of black culture during and after slavery.[6]

5. George P. Rawick, *From Sundown to Sunup: The Making of the Black Community* (Westport, Conn.: Greenwood Publishing Corp., 1972), 55, 78, 93. See also his "The Historical Roots of Black Liberation," *Radical America,* II (January, 1968), 1–13.

6. Eugene D. Genovese, *Roll, Jordan, Roll: The World the Slaves Made* (New York:

The primary concerns of each work were different, and each made a distinctive contribution to our understanding of life in servitude. Genovese found a complex web of paternalistic relationships binding master and slave together, but he ultimately placed religion at the center of the slaves' universe; Gutman demonstrated the pervasiveness of the nuclear family under slavery and showed the critical role it played; and Levine opened to us the cultural world of the slaves more fully and skillfully than any scholar before him had been able to do.

"The practical question facing the slaves was not whether slavery itself was a proper relation but how to survive it with the greatest degree of self-determination," Genovese wrote. Although he paid homage to the rebels who, individually and collectively, challenged the system, the primary thrust of his investigation was a search for the mechanisms that helped achieve a balance between the demands of the master and the desires of the slave. According to Genovese's analysis, paternalism and Christianity were the keys to understanding the viability and longevity of southern slavery. In the masters' view, paternalism meant shouldering what they perceived to be the duties and burdens of being a slaveholder: providing what they considered to be an adequate level of physical maintenance; respecting the slaves' family arrangements, unless disobedience, financial stringency, or the settling of an estate "forced" a division; and inflicting punishment only when the slaves' failure to sustain satisfactory levels of work, order, and discipline required them to do so. But Genovese claimed that from the slaves' perspective, paternalism meant something quite different. Material support, protection, and kindness the slaves considered "their due," he maintained, "payment, as it were, for services loyally rendered." To the master's conception of "reciprocal duties" the slaves thus "added their own doctrine of reciprocal rights." They really had little choice but to accept the paternalism of the master, even though such an act, as Genovese put it, "signaled acceptance of an imposed white domination" as well. Yet slaves simultaneously "drew their own lines, asserted rights, and preserved their self-respect."[7]

In the end, however, religion proved to be a more powerful force

---

Pantheon, 1974); Herbert G. Gutman, *The Black Family in Slavery and Freedom, 1750–1925* (New York: Pantheon, 1976); Lawrence W. Levine, *Black Culture and Black Consciousness: Afro-American Folk Thought from Slavery to Freedom* (New York: Oxford University Press, 1977).

7. Genovese, *Roll, Jordan, Roll*, 125 (first quotation), 146 (second and third quotations), 91 (fourth and fifth quotations), 147 (final two quotations).

than paternalism in shaping the world the slaves made. Black Christianity, like paternalism, had a dual effect, Genovese insisted. "The religion practiced in the quarters gave the slaves the one thing they absolutely had to have if they were to resist being transformed into the Sambos they had been programmed to become," he wrote. "It fired them with a sense of their own worth before God and man." But Christianity, while offering "profound spiritual strength to a people at bay," also taught that everyone, black or white, was a sinner in the eyes of God and would be subject to the same stern tests on judgment day; all men, in short, were brothers in Christ. Their religion thus left the slaves "free to hate slavery but not necessarily their individual masters." As Genovese aptly noted, it was difficult to forge a revolutionary impulse from such a view, "and even harder to raise a cry for holy war." Black Christianity permitted slaves to fight the ideology of the masters, but only from inside the system; "offensively, it proved a poor instrument." [8]

Genovese's picture of the institution of slavery was subtle and complicated. Paternalism and black Christianity, as Genovese defined them, meant that slaves simultaneously accommodated themselves to their enslavement and fought the spiritual, psychological, and physical shackles that bound them. Indeed, the bright thread of the Hegelian dialectic was interwoven throughout Genovese's tapestry of slavery. Accommodation flowed into resistance, subordination was coupled with self-respect. In his view, nothing was ever really simple inside the inner recesses of slavery.

Since Genovese's goal was "to tell the story of slave life as carefully and accurately as possible," he attempted to cover most aspects of slavery as the institution stood in the late antebellum era. His vivid descriptions of a wide variety of slave figures—preachers, drivers, house servants, and mammies, for example—are some of the best and most sensitive portraits we have of blacks who filled these special roles. He provided excellent material on such topics as diet, clothing, housing, holidays, and the rhythms of time and work through which slaves moved. And his discussion of slave family life once again took us farther away from the world according to Elkins. "Many men and women resisted the 'infantilization,' 'emasculation,' and 'dehumanization' inherent in the system's aggression against the slave family," Genovese stated, and he concluded that "probably a majority" of

8. *Ibid.*, 283 (first, second, and fifth quotations), 284 (third and sixth quotations), 282 (fourth quotation).

slave men "overcame all obstacles and provided a positive male image for their wives and children."[9]

Herbert G. Gutman's monumental study of the slave family both complemented and challenged Genovese's interpretation of slavery. Using plantation birth registers, Freedmen's Bureau records, and postwar state marriage certificates, Gutman traced the evolution of the black family from the mid-eighteenth century until the era of the Civil War, and beyond. He found overwhelming evidence of stable, long-lasting marriages wherever he looked. Slaves named children after their kinfolk, exhibited a pervasive taboo against blood-cousin marriage, and extended the principles of the family to embrace the broader slave community. "The obligations to a brother or a niece were transformed into the obligations toward a fellow slave or a fellow slave's child," he noted, "and behavior first determined by familial and kin obligation became enlarged social obligation." In Gutman's view, the development of the slave family had little to do with paternalism, and he charged that Genovese's analysis of black family life, and of slavery itself, was seriously flawed. "Failure to study the development of an adaptive Afro-American slave culture prior to the spread of paternalist ideology" during the two or three decades leading up to the Civil War "impairs the detailed description and explanation of slave belief and behavior in *Roll, Jordan, Roll*," Gutman charged. Genovese had simply not traced "the long and painful process by which Africans became Afro-Americans, a process that included the development of slave standards and rules of conduct." Thus "the 'living space' within which slaves—individually and collectively—asserted their identity and acted upon their beliefs existed before any 'paternalistic compromise' could have occurred," Gutman insisted.[10]

Gutman's hope that slave culture would be studied in greater depth and over a longer span of generations than Genovese had done was partially fulfilled by Lawrence W. Levine's *Black Culture and Black Consciousness*. Although Levine focused primarily on the late antebellum era, his sensitive and imaginative probing of black culture added a significant new dimension to our understanding of slave life. He examined the slaves' spirituals and work songs, their tales of Br'er Rabbit and Br'er Fox, their humor, their traditions of folk medicine,

9. *Ibid.*, xvi (first quotation), 491 (second quotation), 492 (last two quotations).
10. Gutman, *The Black Family*, 220 (first quotation), 311 (second and third quotations), 316 (last two quotations).

and their beliefs concerning conjuring and magic, witchcraft and ghostlore. "The slaves' expressive arts and sacred beliefs were more than merely a series of outlets or strategies; they were instruments of life, of sanity, of health, and of self-respect," he argued. "Slave music, slave religion, slave folk beliefs—the entire sacred world of the black slaves—created the necessary space between the slaves and their owners and were the means of preventing legal slavery from becoming spiritual slavery."[11]

Levine, like Blassingame, Rawick, and Gutman, saw a more autonomous slave existence than the one outlined in Genovese's paternalistic interpretation. The Br'er Rabbit stories, for example, contained a number of subtle and not-so-subtle messages for a people held in bondage, and all of these tales pointed in one direction. "They encouraged trickery and guile; they stimulated the search for ways out of the system; they inbred a contempt for the powerful and an admiration for the perseverance and even the wisdom of the undermen; they constituted an intragroup lore which must have intensified feelings of distance from the world of the slaveholder," Levine wrote. He recognized that slave culture was a "syncretic blend of the old and the new, of the African and the Euro-American," but the end result of this blending was a distinctive black "cultural style . . . which in its totality was uniquely the slaves' own and defined their expressive culture and their world view at the time of emancipation."[12]

Gutman's challenge to present-day students of slavery to push their investigations back beyond the antebellum era was already being answered at the time his book was published. This scholarship, and the increasing trend toward the comparative study of slavery, would be profoundly influenced by Philip D. Curtin's numerical analysis of the Atlantic slave trade. In his brief discussion of the trade between Africa and North America, Curtin pointed out that only a very small percentage of the Africans carried across the Atlantic had ended up in areas that later became part of the United States; adding together 399,000 brought into British North America and a total of 28,000 taken into French and Spanish Louisiana, Curtin estimated that the territory of the United States received only 427,000 souls directly from Africa—approximately 4.5 percent of the Atlantic slave trade, which he placed at 9,566,000. These figures revealed "one of the

11. Levine, *Black Culture and Black Consciousness*, 80.
12. *Ibid.*, 132–33 (first quotation), 135 (last two quotations).

most striking contrasts in New World demographic history," Curtin wrote. "Rather than sustaining the regular excess of deaths over births typical of tropical America, the North American colonies developed a pattern of natural growth among the slaves." By the late 1700s, "North American slave populations were growing at nearly the same rate as that of the settler populations from Europe." Nineteenth-century demographers had noted this astounding trend, Curtin pointed out, which made it "all the more curious that historians have neglected it almost completely, even though it has an obvious and important bearing on such recent historical problems as the comparative history of slavery in the New World."[13]

After reading an advance copy of Curtin's study, C. Vann Woodward called *The Atlantic Slave Trade* "a book of prime importance and incalculable consequences." Woodward added that the history of southern slavery, and indeed the history of slavery in the entire Western Hemisphere, "is now up for reinterpretation." How could it be otherwise, Woodward later observed in *American Counterpoint*, when one knew that small islands in the Caribbean—Barbados, Martinique, Guadaloupe, and the Leeward Islands, with "a land area less than twice that of Hinds County, Mississippi"—had imported 1,390,000 slaves, well over three times the entire number of Africans brought into North America. Yet, on the eve of the Civil War, the slave population of the South stood at almost 4,000,000. This long-term growth rate was "unique among the African diaspora in all the nations of the New World," Woodward noted, and he confirmed Curtin's view that the rapid rate of natural increase among North American slaves started "early in the eighteenth century and continued throughout the period of enslavement."[14]

The scholarly waves that spread in the wake of Curtin's figures washed up on a number of historical shores. Interest quickened in subjects as diverse as slavery during the colonial, revolutionary, and early national periods, the demographics of slavery, the history of the black family, questions of miscegenation and slave breeding, slave

13. Philip D. Curtin, *The Atlantic Slave Trade: A Census* (Madison: University of Wisconsin Press, 1969), Table 24 (pp. 88–89), 73. See also Curtin, "Measuring the Atlantic Slave Trade," in Stanley L. Engerman and Eugene D. Genovese (eds.), *Race and Slavery in the Western Hemisphere: Quantitative Studies* (Princeton: Princeton University Press, 1975), 107–28.

14. Woodward's assessment quoted on *The Atlantic Slave Trade* jacket; C. Vann Woodward, *American Counterpoint: Slavery and Racism in the North-South Dialogue* (Boston: Little, Brown, 1971), 83, 84.

diet, health, and medicine, the domestic and foreign slave trades, and, of course, the comparative history of slavery. Inevitably, many of these studies took a quantitative approach, since numbers and counting were often a crucial concern. The end result was similar to the effect Elkins' *Slavery* had on the field: an outpouring of new and frequently controversial works which, ultimately, added greatly to our knowledge of slavery in a number of critical areas.

The Chesapeake region served as a focus for much of the most imaginative work on colonial slavery. Building on pioneering work done by Wesley Frank Craven, Edmund S. Morgan offered a brilliant analysis of the evolution of the twin institutions of slavery and indentured servitude in seventeenth-century Virginia. A key factor in the emergence of slavery as the dominant labor system grew out of changing mortality rates, Morgan showed. Once death rates began to decline and life expectancy rose, the slave simply "became a better buy than the servant," he observed.[15] Morgan thus largely brushed aside an extended debate which had been going on since the late 1940s over which came first, slavery or racism.[16] His analysis did not

15. Wesley Frank Craven, *White, Red, and Black: The Seventeenth-Century Virginian* (Charlottesville: University Press of Virginia, 1971); Edmund S. Morgan, *American Slavery—American Freedom: The Ordeal of Colonial Virginia* (New York: Norton, 1975), 299. See also David W. Galenson, "White Servitude and the Growth of Black Slavery in Colonial America," *Journal of Economic History*, XLI (March, 1981), 39–52, and *White Servitude in Colonial America: An Economic Analysis* (New York: Cambridge University Press, 1981).

16. Wesley Frank Craven, *The Southern Colonies in the Seventeenth Century, 1607–1689* (Baton Rouge: Louisiana State University Press, 1949), 217–19, 401–403; Oscar Handlin and Mary F. Handlin, "Origins of the Southern Labor System," *William and Mary Quarterly*, 3rd Ser., VII (April, 1950), 199–222; Carl N. Degler, "Slavery and the Genesis of American Race Prejudice," *Comparative Studies in Society and History*, II (October, 1959), 49–66; Winthrop D. Jordan, "Modern Tensions and the Origins of American Slavery," *Journal of Southern History*, XXVIII (February, 1962), 18–30, and *White over Black: American Attitudes Toward the Negro, 1550–1812* (Chapel Hill: University of North Carolina Press, 1968). See also Paul C. Palmer, "Servant into Slave: The Evolution of the Legal Status of the Negro Laborer in Colonial Virginia," *South Atlantic Quarterly*, LXV (Summer, 1966), 355–70; Alden T. Vaughan, "Blacks in Virginia: A Note on the First Decade," *William and Mary Quarterly*, 3rd Ser., XXIX (July, 1972), 469–78; Warren M. Billings, "The Cases of Fernando and Elizabeth Key: A Note on the Status of Blacks in Seventeenth-Century Virginia," *William and Mary Quarterly*, 3rd Ser., XXX (July, 1973), 467–74; Joseph Boskin, *Into Slavery: Racial Decisions in the Virginia Colony* (Philadelphia: Lippincott, 1976); William McKee Evans, "From the Land of Canaan to the Land of Guinea: The Strange Odyssey of the 'Sons of Ham,'" *American Historical Review*, LXXXV (February, 1980), 15–43. On Maryland, see Jonathan L. Alpert, "The Origin of Slavery in the United States—The Maryland Precedent," *American Journal of Legal His-*

ignore race; "it *was* an ingredient," he wrote. Virginia's white settlers considered blacks "'a brutish sort of people,'" and the only human beings they enslaved "belonged to alien races from the English." [17] But his emphasis clearly lay on the demography of seventeenth-century Virginia and the impact it had on the emergence of slavery as the chief form of labor in the colony.

Morgan's work came in the midst of a significant revival of interest in the history of slavery in the Chesapeake area. Thad W. Tate's largely descriptive *The Negro in Eighteenth-Century Williamsburg* (1965) and Gerald W. Mullin's *Flight and Rebellion* (1972) were two important studies that signaled the onset of this scholarly trend. [18] Mullin's investigation was particularly valuable for its discussion of the assimilation of African-born slaves into the plantation world of colonial Virginia and its analysis, through an imaginative use of advertisements for runaways in the *Virginia Gazette*, of who the rebellious slaves were during the eighteenth century.

This early trickle of work on Chesapeake slavery soon turned into a torrent. The acculturation of the growing number of slaves in the region, the establishment of the black family there, and the development of a slave social order during the late seventeenth and early eighteenth centuries became clearer, thanks to a group of historians who were willing to dig deeply into local records in Virginia and Maryland. In a series of pathbreaking articles, scholars like Allan Kulikoff, Russell R. Menard, and Ira Berlin looked behind the demographic statistics in order to probe their social and cultural significance. [19] In the process, they went a long way toward fulfilling Gut-

---

tory, XIV (July, 1970), 189–221; Ross M. Kimmel, "Free Blacks in Seventeenth-Century Maryland," *Maryland Historical Magazine*, LXXI (Spring, 1976), 19–25; and Whittington B. Johnson, "The Origin and Nature of African Slavery in Seventeenth-Century Maryland," *Maryland Historical Magazine*, LXXIII (Fall, 1978), 236–45.

17. Morgan, *American Slavery—American Freedom*, 315.

18. Thad W. Tate, *The Negro in Eighteenth-Century Williamsburg* (Williamsburg: Colonial Williamsburg Foundation, 1965); Gerald W. Mullin, *Flight and Rebellion: Slave Resistance in Eighteenth-Century Virginia* (New York: Oxford University Press, 1972). See also Mullin, "Rethinking American Negro Slavery from the Vantage Point of the Colonial Era," *Louisiana Studies*, XII (Summer, 1973), 398–422.

19. Allan Kulikoff, "Black Society and the Economics of Slavery," *Maryland Historical Magazine*, LXX (Summer, 1975), 203–10, "The Beginnings of the Afro-American Family in Maryland," in Aubrey C. Land, Lois G. Carr, and Edward C. Papenfuse (eds.), *Law, Society, and Politics in Early Maryland* (Baltimore: Johns Hopkins University Press, 1977), 171–96, "A 'Prolifick' People: Black Population Growth in the Chesapeake Colonies, 1700–1790," *Southern Studies*, XVI (Winter,

man's wish that the formative period of black family life receive close scrutiny. It is no exaggeration to say that the Chesapeake historians have made some of the most important and imaginative contributions to American slave historiography over the past two decades.

Peter H. Wood's *Black Majority* did for slavery in colonial South Carolina what Edmund Morgan's *American Slavery—American Freedom* did for slavery in colonial Virginia; it provided an important interpretative statement that all subsequent studies would have to consider. Wood's book went farther than Morgan's, however, in trying to penetrate the interior life of the slave. He examined black contributions to South Carolina's colonial economy, particularly rice culture and cattle raising; he traced the role of black pioneers in pushing back the frontier; and he investigated the Gullah dialect and its role in binding South Carolina's slaves together. Like the Chesapeake scholarship, his work was soundly rooted in a careful demographic analysis of the colony's population, a particularly important topic in a region that, because of its black majority, seemed "'more like a negro country'" to newly arriving white settlers in the eighteenth century. Wood's impressive study concluded with a close look at the mounting tensions between blacks and whites that culminated in the Stono Rebellion of 1739.[20]

1977), 391–428, "The Origins of Afro-American Society in Tidewater Maryland and Virginia, 1700–1790," *William and Mary Quarterly*, 3rd Ser., XXXV (April, 1978), 226–59, and "The Colonial Chesapeake: Seedbed of Antebellum Southern Culture?" *Journal of Southern History*, XLV (November, 1979), 513–40; Russell R. Menard, "The Maryland Slave Population, 1658 to 1730: A Demographic Profile of Blacks in Four Counties," *William and Mary Quarterly*, 3rd Ser., XXXII (January, 1975), 29–54, and "From Servants to Slaves: The Transformation of the Chesapeake Labor System," *Southern Studies*, XVI (Winter, 1977), 355–90; Ira Berlin, "The Slave Trade and the Development of Afro-American Society in English Mainland North America, 1619–1775," *Southern Studies*, XX (Summer, 1981), 122–36, and "Time, Space, and the Evolution of Afro-American Society in British Mainland North America," *American Historical Review*, LXXXV (February, 1980), 44–78. See also Douglas Grant, *The Fortunate Slave: An Illustration of African Slavery in the Early Eighteenth Century* (London: Oxford University Press, 1968); T. H. Breen and Stephen Innes, *"Myne Owne Ground": Race and Freedom on Virginia's Eastern Shore, 1640–1676* (New York: Oxford University Press, 1980); Timothy H. Breen, "A Changing Labor Force and Race Relations in Virginia, 1670–1710," *Journal of Social History*, VII (Fall, 1973), 3–25; and Gloria Main, *Tobacco Colony: Life in Early Maryland, 1650–1720* (Princeton: Princeton University Press, 1982).

20. Peter H. Wood, *Black Majority: Negroes in Colonial South Carolina from 1670 through the Stono Rebellion* (New York: Knopf, 1974), 132. See also Wood, "'More Like a Negro Country': Demographic Patterns in Colonial South Carolina, 1700–1740," in Engerman and Genovese (eds.), *Race and Slavery*, 131–71.

Unlike Morgan's *American Slavery—American Freedom,* Wood's *Black Majority* did not enter a booming area of scholarly inquiry. Slavery in the lower southern colonies has not drawn anything approaching the attention that Chesapeake slavery has received over the past fifteen or twenty years. Some very suggestive work has been done recently, particularly by Daniel C. Littlefield and Philip D. Morgan, and more is on the way.[21] But when compared to the well-plowed historiographical fields of the Chesapeake, slavery in the more distant reaches of the colonial South seems almost like virgin scholarly territory.[22]

Until recently, much the same thing could be said about slavery

21. Daniel C. Littlefield, *Rice and Slaves: Ethnicity and the Slave Trade in Colonial South Carolina* (Baton Rouge: Louisiana State University Press, 1981); Philip D. Morgan and George D. Terry, "Slavery in Microcosm: A Conspiracy Scare in Colonial South Carolina," *Southern Studies,* XXI (Summer, 1982), 121–45; Morgan, "Work and Culture: The Task System and the World of Lowcountry Blacks, 1770 to 1880," *William and Mary Quarterly,* 3rd Ser., XXXIX (July, 1982), 563–99, and "Black Society in the Lowcountry, 1760–1810," in Ira Berlin and Ronald Hoffman (eds.), *Slavery and Freedom in the Age of the American Revolution* (Charlottesville: University Press of Virginia, 1983), 83–141; see also his "The Ownership of Property by Slaves in the Mid-Nineteenth-Century Low Country," *Journal of Southern History,* XLIX (August, 1983), 399–420; W. Robert Higgins, "The Geographical Origins of Negro Slaves in Colonial South Carolina," *South Atlantic Quarterly,* LXX (Winter, 1971), 34–47; Darold D. Wax, "Preferences for Slaves in Colonial America," *Journal of Negro History,* LVIII (October, 1973), 371–401, and "'The Great Risque We Run': The Aftermath of Slave Rebellion at Stono, South Carolina, 1739–1745," *Journal of Negro History,* LXVII (Summer, 1982), 136–47.

22. Betty Wood, *Slavery in Colonial Georgia, 1730–1775* (Athens: University of Georgia Press, 1984), and "Thomas Stephens and the Introduction of Black Slavery in Georgia," *Georgia Historical Quarterly,* LVIII (Spring, 1974), 24–40; Ralph Gray and Betty Wood, "The Transition from Indentured to Involuntary Servitude in Colonial Georgia," *Explorations in Economic History,* XIII (October, 1976), 353–70; Darold D. Wax, "Georgia and the Negro Before the American Revolution," *Georgia Historical Quarterly,* LI (March, 1967), 63–77; Harvey H. Jackson, "The Darien Antislavery Petition of 1739 and the Georgia Plan," *William and Mary Quarterly,* 3rd Ser., XXXIV (October, 1977), 618–31; John J. TePaske, "The Fugitive Slave: Intercolonial Rivalry and Spanish Slave Policy, 1687–1764," in Samuel Proctor (ed.), *Eighteenth-Century Florida and Its Borderlands* (Gainesville: University Presses of Florida, 1975), 1–12; J. Leitch Wright, Jr., "Blacks in British East Florida," *Florida Historical Quarterly,* LIV (April, 1976), 425–42; Jack D. L. Holmes, "The Role of Blacks in Spanish Alabama: The Mobile District, 1780–1813," *Alabama Historical Quarterly,* XXXVII (Spring, 1975), 5–18; Gilbert C. Din, "*Cimarrones* and the San Malo Band in Spanish Louisiana," *Louisiana History,* XXI (Summer, 1980), 237–62; Daniel H. Unser, Jr., "From African Captivity to American Slavery: The Introduction of Black Laborers to Colonial Louisiana," *Louisiana History,* XX (Winter, 1979), 25–48; Carl A. Brasseaux, "The Administration of Slave Regulations in French Louisi-

during the revolutionary and postrevolutionary eras. The publication of Benjamin Quarles's *The Negro in the American Revolution* and Robert McColley's *Slavery and Jeffersonian Virginia* in the early 1960s seemed to indicate a new interest in late-eighteenth- and early-nineteenth-century slavery. Both books were solid, well-researched studies, and McColley's investigation went a long way toward dispelling the notion that slavery was dying before the invention of the cotton gin and that the Founding Fathers were well on their way to rooting out the institution before Eli Whitney worked his magic in 1793. Most Virginia slave owners were simply convinced "that they could be wealthy and happy more easily with slaves than without," McColley correctly observed, and since the state's political leaders "all agreed that Negroes, if freed, must be removed"—a patent impossibility—"they effectively supported the continued existence of slavery." [23]

In the aftermath of McColley's book, however, the Jeffersonian theme, not the system itself, dominated much of the writing about slavery. Interest moved primarily in two directions, neither of which added very much to our knowledge of how the slaves themselves lived and worked. The first question was how the Founding Fathers really felt about slavery and how to assess their action, or inaction, toward the institution.[24] The second was whether or not Thomas Jefferson had cohabited with one of his slave women and sired a sizable number of children by her.[25] No clear-cut answer to either query emerged,

ana, 1724–1766," *Louisiana History,* XXI (Spring, 1980), 139–58; Mathé Allain, "Slave Policies in French Louisiana," *Louisiana History,* XXI (Spring, 1980), 127–37.

23. Benjamin Quarles, *The Negro in the American Revolution* (Chapel Hill: University of North Carolina Press, 1961); Robert McColley, *Slavery and Jeffersonian Virginia* (Urbana: University of Illinois Press, 1964; 2nd ed., 1973), 183, 186 (quotations from the 1964 edition).

24. Jordan, *White over Black;* William Cohen, "Thomas Jefferson and the Problem of Slavery," *Journal of American History,* LVI (December, 1969), 503–26; Donald L. Robinson, *Slavery in the Structure of American Politics, 1765–1820* (New York: Harcourt Brace Jovanovich, 1971); William W. Freehling, "The Founding Fathers and Slavery," *American Historical Review,* LXXVII (February, 1972), 81–93; Duncan J. MacLeod, *Slavery, Race and the American Revolution* (Cambridge, England: Cambridge University Press, 1974); David Brion Davis, *The Problem of Slavery in the Age of Revolution, 1770–1823* (Ithaca: Cornell University Press, 1975); John Chester Miller, *The Wolf by the Ears: Thomas Jefferson and Slavery* (New York: Free Press, 1977); John P. Diggins, "Slavery, Race, and Equality: Jefferson and the Pathos of the Enlightenment," *American Quarterly,* XXVIII (Summer, 1976), 206–28; F. Nwabueze Okoye, "Chattel Slavery as the Nightmare of the American Revolutionaries," *William and Mary Quarterly,* 3rd Ser., XXXVII (January, 1980), 3–28.

25. Fawn M. Brodie, *Thomas Jefferson: An Intimate History* (New York: Norton,

but the search for the former was a good bit more productive than was the flapping about over the latter. Fortunately in more recent years the subject of slavery during the revolutionary and postrevolutionary periods seems to have come into its own. Serious scholarship is under way on a number of fronts, and the publication in 1983 of a superb collection of essays emphasizing the social and cultural history of slavery during this era suggests that we are on the brink of a new historiographical era in this area of slavery studies. If the pieces in this collection are any indication, the revolutionary South may well be in for the same sort of detailed investigation that the colonial Chesapeake has received. Many of the essays in this volume are demographically sophisticated treatments of their topics and exhibit the unmistakable traits of the best of the post-Curtin scholarship.[26]

1974); Miller, *The Wolf by the Ears;* Dumas Malone and Steven H. Hochman, "A Note on Evidence: The Personal History of Madison Hemmings," *Journal of Southern History,* XLI (November, 1975), 523–28; Virginius Dabney, *The Jefferson Scandals: A Rebuttal* (New York: Dodd, Mead, 1981).

26. Richard S. Dunn, "Black Society in the Chesapeake, 1776–1810," Morgan, "Black Society in the Lowcountry, 1760–1810," Allan Kulikoff, "Uprooted Peoples: Black Migrants in the Age of the American Revolution, 1790–1820," and Mary Beth Norton, Herbert G. Gutman, and Ira Berlin, "The Afro-American Family in the Age of Revolution," all in Berlin and Hoffman (eds.), *Slavery and Freedom in the Age of the American Revolution,* 49–191. See also Sylvia R. Frey, "The British and the Black: A New Perspective," *Historian,* XXXVIII (February, 1976), 225–38, and "Between Slavery and Freedom: Virginia Blacks in the American Revolution," *Journal of Southern History,* XLIX (August, 1983), 375–98; Pete Maslowski, "National Policy Toward the Use of Black Troops in the Revolution," *South Carolina Historical Magazine,* LXXIII (January, 1972), 1–17; Alan D. Watson, "Impulse Toward Independence: Resistance and Rebellion among North Carolina Slaves, 1750–1775," *Journal of Negro History,* LXIII (Fall, 1978), 317–28; Jeffrey J. Crow, "Slave Rebelliousness and Social Conflict in North Carolina, 1775 to 1802," *William and Mary Quarterly,* 3rd Ser., XXXVII (January, 1980), 79–102; Peter H. Wood, " 'Taking Care of Business' in Revolutionary South Carolina: Republicanism and the Slave Society," *South Atlantic Urban Studies,* II (1978), 49–72; M. Foster Farley, "The South Carolina Negro in the American Revolution, 1775–1783," *South Carolina Historical Magazine,* LXXIX (April, 1978), 75–86; Mary Beth Norton, "The Fate of Some Black Loyalists of the American Revolution," *Journal of Negro History,* LVIII (October, 1973), 402–26; James W. St. G. Walker, *The Black Loyalists: The Search for a Promised Land in Nova Scotia and Sierra Leone, 1783–1870* (New York: Africana Publishing Co., 1976), and "Blacks as American Loyalists: The Slaves' War for Independence," *Historical Reflections/Réflexions Historiques,* II (Summer, 1975), 51–67; Ellen Gibson Wilson, *The Loyal Blacks* (New York: G. P. Putnam's Sons, 1976); Michael Mullin, "British Caribbean and North American Slaves in an Era of War and Revolution, 1775–1807," in Jeffrey J. Crow and Larry E. Tise (eds.), *The Southern Experience in the American Revolution* (Chapel Hill: University of North Carolina Press, 1978), 235–67; Ira Berlin, "The Revolution in Black Life," in Alfred F. Young (ed.), *The American Revolution: Explo-*

The quantitative study of slavery appeared to take a quantum leap forward with the appearance in 1974 of Robert William Fogel and Stanley L. Engerman's *Time on the Cross*. Prior to the publication of their study, economic historians, beginning with Alfred H. Conrad and John R. Meyer in the 1950s, had aimed the theoretical and analytical tools of their trade on the slave South, but their attention had largely been focused on a fairly narrow range of topics. Was slavery profitable? Did slavery hinder southern industrial development? Did slavery retard southern economic growth? Was the cotton economy self-sufficient in terms of food production? All of these questions were important and all received extended discussion and vigorous debate in the 1960s and 1970s.[27] Fogel and Engerman addressed

rations in the History of American Radicalism (DeKalb: Northern Illinois University Press, 1976), 349–82; Sarah S. Hughes, "Slaves for Hire: The Allocation of Black Labor in Elizabeth City County, Virginia, 1782 to 1810," *William and Mary Quarterly,* 3rd Ser., XXXV (April, 1978), 260–86; and Frank A. Cassell, "Slaves of the Chesapeake Bay Area and the War of 1812," *Journal of Negro History,* LVII (April, 1972), 144–55.

27. Robert William Fogel and Stanley L. Engerman, *Time on the Cross* (2 vols.; Boston: Little, Brown, 1974); Alfred H. Conrad and John R. Meyer, "The Economics of Slavery in the Ante Bellum South," *Journal of Political Economy,* LXVI (April, 1958), 95–130, and *The Economics of Slavery and Other Studies in Econometric History* (Chicago: Aldine, 1964); Harold D. Woodman (ed.), *Slavery and the Southern Economy: Sources and Reading* (New York: Harcourt, Brace & World, 1966), and Woodman, "The Profitability of Slavery: A Historical Perennial," *Journal of Southern History,* XXIX (August, 1963), 303–25; David O. Whitten, "Sugar Slavery: A Profitability Model for Slave Investment in the Antebellum Louisiana Sugar Industry," *Louisiana Studies,* XII (Summer, 1973), 423–42; Edward Saraydar, "A Note on the Profitability of Ante Bellum Slavery," *Southern Economic Journal,* XXX (April, 1964), 325–32; Richard Sutch and Edward Saraydar, "The Profitability of Ante Bellum Slavery: Comment and Reply" *Southern Economic Journal,* XXXI (April, 1965), 365–83; Eugene D. Genovese, *The Political Economy of Slavery: Studies in the Economy & Society of the Slave South* (New York: Pantheon, 1965); Alfred H. Conrad *et al.,* "Slavery as an Obstacle to Economic Growth in the United States: A Panel Discussion," *Journal of Economic History,* XXVII (December, 1967), 518–60; Stanley L. Engerman, "The Effects of Slavery Upon the Southern Economy: A Review of the Recent Debate," *Explorations in Entrepreneurial History,* 2nd Ser., IV (Winter, 1967), 71–97; Marvin Fischbaum and Julius Rubin, "Slavery and the Economic Development of the American South," *Explorations in Entrepreneurial History,* 2nd Ser., VI (Fall, 1968), 116–27; William N. Parker (ed.), *The Structure of the Cotton Economy of the Antebellum South,* a special issue of *Agricultural History,* XLIV (January, 1970); Hugh Aitken (ed.), *Did Slavery Pay? Readings in the Economics of Black Slavery in the United States* (Boston: Houghton Mifflin, 1971); Robert W. Fogel and Stanley L. Engerman (eds.), *The Reinterpretation of American Economic History* (New York: Harper & Row, 1971); Gavin Wright, "New and Old Views on the Economics of Slavery," *Journal of Economic History,* XXXIII (June, 1973), 452–66, and

these same issues in *Time on the Cross*, but their investigation of slavery took on much, much more. How frequently were slaves whipped? they asked. How often were slave families broken by sale? What was the extent of slave sexual exploitation by the masters? Were slaves bred for the auction block like cattle? Were slave diet, clothing, housing, and medical care adequate or inadequate? Which was more efficient, slave labor or free labor? How much of the income slaves produced was expropriated? What was the extent of the interstate slave trade? Since their answers in every case came down on the benign side of the issue, they provoked a storm of controversy among scholars who believed they had painted much too rosy a picture of slave life. Fogel and Engerman's methodology, evidence, and conclusions were subjected to rigorous examination, and their study was, in effect, taken apart piece by piece, analyzed, sometimes ridiculed, almost universally challenged, and, in the end, rejected by most of their critics.[28] Rarely had a serious, scholarly treatment of slavery provoked such a swift and strident reaction.

The conclusions reached in *Time on the Cross* were seriously flawed in a number of major places, but the critics sometimes failed

---

The Political Economy of the Cotton South: Households, Markets, and Wealth in the Nineteenth Century (New York: Norton, 1978). See also Fred Bateman and Thomas Weiss, *A Deplorable Scarcity: The Failure of Industrialization in the Slave Economy* (Chapel Hill: University of North Carolina Press, 1981).

28. Thomas L. Haskell, "The True & Tragical History of 'Time on the Cross,'" *New York Review of Books*, October 2, 1975, pp. 33–39; Herbert G. Gutman, "The World Two Cliometricians Made," *Journal of Negro History*, LX (January, 1975), 53–227, reprinted as *Slavery and the Numbers Game: A Critique of "Time on the Cross"* (Urbana: University of Illinois Press, 1975); Richard Sutch, "The Treatment Received by American Slaves: A Critical Review of the Evidence Presented in *Time on the Cross*," Gavin Wright, "Slavery and the Cotton Boom," and Richard K. Vedder, "The Slave Exploitation (Expropriation) Rate," all in *Explorations in Economic History*, XII (October, 1975), 335–457; Paul A. David *et al.*, *Reckoning with Slavery: A Critical Study in the Quantitative History of American Negro Slavery* (New York: Oxford University Press, 1976). See also Kenneth M. Stampp, "Introduction: A Humanistic Perspective," in David *et al.*, *Reckoning with Slavery*, 1–30. The spirited debate between Fogel and Engerman and their critics continued in the late 1970s; see Fogel and Engerman, "Explaining the Relative Efficiency of Slave Agriculture in the Antebellum South," *American Economic Review*, LXVII (June, 1977), 275–96; Thomas L. Haskell, "Explaining the Relative Efficiency of Slave Agriculture in the Antebellum South: A Reply to Fogel-Engerman," Donald F. Schaefer and Mark D. Schmitz, "The Relative Efficiency of Slave Agriculture: A Comment," Paul A. David and Peter Temin, "Explaining the Relative Efficiency of Slave Agriculture in the Antebellum South: Comment," and Gavin Wright, "The Efficiency of Slavery: Another Interpretation," all in *American Economic Review*, LXIX (March, 1979), 206–26.

to give the authors credit for the things they did right. Fogel and Engerman's insistence that slavery was a very profitable business investment in mid-nineteenth-century America, that the institution "was not economically moribund on the eve of the Civil War," that slave owners were optimistic about the future of the system during the 1850s, that slave breeding was a myth, and that the decline of slavery in the cities during the 1850s had not been properly explained were all points worth making. The problem was that these same points had by and large been made by other historians, of both the quantitative and nonquantitative persuasion. The profitability of slavery, for example, had been well established by a number of econometric historians during the late 1950s and the 1960s; Fogel and Engerman simply added to the impressive body of evidence that already existed. The single most important fresh contribution in their book was probably their insight into urban slavery. "In the rural areas there were no close substitutes for slave labor," they wrote. "In the cities, however, free labor, particularly immigrant labor, proved to be a very effective substitute." In short, "slaves were shifted from the cities to the countryside not because the cities didn't want slaves, but because as slave prices rose, it was easier for the cities than the countryside to find acceptable, lower-cost alternatives to slave labor." They were right when they called this "a discovery of major importance," and their analysis was confirmed when Claudia Dale Goldin published her quantitative study of urban slavery in 1976.[29]

Perhaps the greatest single historiographical contribution of *Time on the Cross* was to accelerate the movement that Curtin's study of the Atlantic slave trade had launched. Slave birth and death statistics and infant mortality rates came under careful investigation.[30] Indeed,

29. Fogel and Engerman, *Time on the Cross*, I, 4–5, 102; Claudia Dale Goldin, *Urban Slavery in the American South, 1820–1860: A Quantitative History* (Chicago: University of Chicago Press, 1976). See also her "A Model to Explain the Relative Decline of Urban Slavery: Empirical Results," in Engerman and Genovese (eds.), *Race and Slavery*, 427–50.

30. Kenneth F. Kiple and Virginia H. Kiple, "Slave Child Mortality: Some Nutritional Answers to a Perennial Puzzle," *Journal of Social History*, X (March, 1977), 284–309; Cheryll Ann Cody, "A Note on Changing Patterns of Slave Fertility in the South Carolina Rice Belt, 1735–1865," *Southern Studies*, XVI (Winter, 1977), 457–63; Herbert S. Klein and Stanley L. Engerman, "Fertility Differentials between Slaves in the United States and the British West Indies: A Note on Lactation Practices and Their Possible Implications," *William and Mary Quarterly*, 3rd Ser., XXXV (April, 1978), 357–74; James Trussell and Richard Steckel, "The Age of Slaves at Menarche and Their First Birth," *Journal of Interdisciplinary History*, VIII (Winter, 1978),

the close publication of *Time on the Cross* and Gutman's *The Black Family* brought the slave family in all its dimensions into the forefront of historical interest.[31] The extent to which imbalances and vitamin deficiencies in the slave diet might have contributed to malnutrition, disease, and death received a fruitful new examination, with Leslie Howard Owens' *This Species of Property* (1976) offering particularly valuable insights into this area of slave life.[32] The entire

477–505; Richard H. Steckel, "Slave Mortality: Analysis of Evidence from Plantation Records," *Social Science History,* III (January, 1979), 86–114.

31. Herbert G. Gutman, "Persistent Myths About the Afro-American Family," *Journal of Interdisciplinary History,* V (Autumn, 1975), 181–210, and "Slave Culture and Slave Family and Kin Network: The Importance of Time," *South Atlantic Urban Studies,* II (1978), 73–88; John Modell, Stephen Gundeman, and Warren C. Sanderson, "A Colloquium on Herbert Gutman's *The Black Family in Slavery and Freedom, 1750–1925,*" *Social Science History,* III (January, 1979), 45–85; A. J. R. Russell-Wood, "The Black Family in the Americas," *Societas,* VIII (Winter, 1978), 1–38; Michael J. Cassity, "Slave Families and 'Living Space': A Note on Evidence and Historical Context," *Southern Studies,* XVII (Summer, 1978), 209–15; Charles Wetherell, "Slave Kinship: A Case Study of the South Carolina Good Hope Plantation, 1835–1856," *Journal of Family History,* VI (Fall, 1981), 294–308; Steven E. Brown, "Sexuality and the Slave Community," *Phylon,* XLII (Spring, 1981), 1–10; Cheryll Ann Cody, "Naming, Kinship, and Estate Dispersal: Notes on Slave Family Life on a South Carolina Plantation, 1786 to 1833," *William and Mary Quarterly,* 3rd Ser., XXXIX (January, 1982), 192–211; Shepard Krech III, "Black Family Organization in the Nineteenth Century: An Ethnological Perspective," *Journal of Interdisciplinary History,* XII (Winter, 1982), 429–52; Herbert J. Foster, "African Patterns in the Afro-American Family," *Journal of Black Studies,* XIII (December, 1983), 201–32; John C. Inscoe, "Carolina Slave Names: An Index to Acculturation," *Journal of Southern History,* XLIX (November, 1983), 527–54. On the question of miscegenation and slave "breeding," see James Hugo Johnston, *Race Relations in Virginia and Miscegenation in the South, 1776–1860* (Amherst: University of Massachusetts Press, 1970); Joel Williamson, *New People: Miscegenation and Mulattoes in the United States* (New York: Free Press, 1980); Richard Sutch, "The Breeding of Slaves for Sale and the Westward Expansion of Slavery, 1850–1860," in Engerman and Genovese (eds.), *Race and Slavery,* 173–210; Richard G. Lowe and Randolph B. Campbell, "The Slave-Breeding Hypothesis: A Demographic Comment on the 'Buying' and 'Selling' States," *Journal of Southern History,* XLII (August, 1976), 401–12; Richard H. Steckel, "Miscegenation and the American Slave Schedules," *Journal of Interdisciplinary History,* XI (Autumn, 1980), 251–63.

32. Leslie Howard Owens, *This Species of Property: Slave Life and Culture in the Old South* (New York: Oxford University Press, 1976); Kenneth F. Kiple and Virginia Himmelsteib King, *Another Dimension to the Black Diaspora: Diet, Disease, and Racism* (Cambridge, England: Cambridge University Press, 1981), Kiple and Kiple, "Slave Child Mortality," and "Black Tongue and Black Men: Pellagra and Slavery in the Antebellum South," *Journal of Southern History,* XLIII (August, 1977), 411–28; Robert W. Twyman, "The Clay Eater: A New Look at an Old Southern Enigma," *Jour-*

subject of slave health was discussed more fully and carefully than ever before; Todd L. Savitt's *Medicine and Slavery* (1978) was a model study in this field and set the standard by which other works would be measured.[33] The domestic slave trade, long a topic fraught with emotional overtones and imprecise scholarship, received new and informative attention.[34] The same held true for the foreign slave

nal of Southern History, XXXVII (August, 1971), 439–48; Tyson Gibbs *et al.*, "Nutrition in a Slave Population: An Anthropological Examination," *Medical Anthropology*, IV (Spring, 1980), 175–262; John Solomon Otto and Augustus Marion Burns III, "Black Folks and Poor Buckras: Archeological Evidence of Slave and Overseer Living Conditions on an Antebellum Plantation," *Journal of Black Studies*, XIII (December, 1983), 185–200; Nicholas Scott Cardell and Mark Myron Hopkins, "The Effect of Milk Intolerance on the Consumption of Milk by Slaves in 1860," *Journal of Interdisciplinary History*, VIII (Winter, 1978), 507–13; Richard H. Steckel, "Slave Height Profiles from Coastwise Manifests," *Explorations in Economic History*, XVI (October, 1979), 363–80; David Eltis, "Nutritional Trends in Africa and the Americas: Heights of Africans, 1819–1839," *Journal of Interdisciplinary History*, XII (Winter, 1982), 453–75; Sam Bowers Hilliard, *Hog Meat and Hoecake: Food Supply in the Old South, 1840–1860* (Carbondale: Southern Illinois University Press, 1972), and *Atlas of Antebellum Southern Agriculture* (Baton Rouge: Louisiana State University Press, 1984).

33. Todd L. Savitt, *Medicine and Slavery: The Diseases and Health Care of Blacks in Antebellum Virginia* (Urbana: University of Illinois Press, 1978), "The Invisible Malady: Sickle Cell Anemia in America, 1910–1970," *Journal of the National Medical Association*, LXXIII (August, 1981), 739–46, "The Use of Blacks for Medical Experimentation and Demonstration in the Old South," *Journal of Southern History*, XLVIII (August, 1982), 331–48, "Slave Life Insurance in Virginia and North Carolina," *Journal of Southern History*, XLIII (November, 1977), 583–600, and "Smothering and Overlaying of Virginia Slave Children: A Suggested Explanation," *Bulletin of the History of Medicine*, XLIX (Fall, 1975), 400–404; Michael P. Johnson, "Smothered Slave Infants: Were Slave Mothers at Fault?" *Journal of Southern History*, XLVII (November, 1981), 493–520; Walter Fisher, "Physicians and Slavery in the Antebellum Southern Medical Journal," *Journal of the History of Medicine and Allied Sciences*, XXIII (January, 1968), 36–49; David O. Whitten, "Medical Care of Slaves: Louisiana Sugar Region and South Carolina Rice District," *Southern Studies*, XVI (Summer, 1977), 153–80; Anne S. Lee and Everett S. Lee, "The Health of Slaves and the Health of Freedmen: A Savannah Study," *Phylon*, XXXVIII (June, 1977), 170–80; Kenneth Kiple and Virginia Kiple, "The African Connection: Slavery, Disease and Racism," *Phylon*, XLI (Fall, 1980), 211–22, and "Black Yellow Fever Immunities, Innate and Acquired, as Revealed in the American South," *Social Science History*, I (Fall, 1977), 419–36; Gary Puckrein, "Climate, Health and Black Labor in the English Americas," *Journal of American Studies*, XIII (August, 1979), 179–93.

34. William Calderhead, "How Extensive Was the Border State Slave Trade? A New Look," *Civil War History*, XVIII (March, 1972), 42–55, and "The Role of the Professional Slave Trader in a Slave Economy: Austin Woolfolk, a Case Study," *Civil War History*, XXIII (September, 1977), 195–211; Robert Evans, Jr., "Some Economic Aspects of the Domestic Slave Trade, 1830–1860," *Southern Economic Journal*, XXVII

trade, as might be expected since Curtin and Fogel and Engerman covered this field in some detail and came to similar conclusions.[35]

The historiographical trends launched by Elkins, Curtin, and Fogel

(April, 1961), 329–37; William L. Miller, "A Note on the Importance of the Interstate Slave Trade of the Ante Bellum South," *Journal of Political Economy*, LXXIII (April, 1965), 181–87; Michael Tadman, "Slave Trading in the Ante-Bellum South: An Estimate of the Extent of the Inter-Regional Slave Trade," *Journal of American Studies*, XIII (August, 1979), 195–220; Donald M. Sweig, "Reassessing the Human Dimension of the Interstate Slave Trade," *Prologue*, XII (Spring, 1980), 5–21; Julia F. Smith, "Slavetrading in Antebellum Florida," *Florida Historical Quarterly*, LI (January, 1972), 252–61; Richard Tansey, "Bernard Kendig and the New Orleans Slave Trade," *Louisiana History*, XXIII (Spring, 1982), 159–78; James William McGettigan, Jr., "Boone County Slaves: Sales, Estate Divisions and Families, 1820–1865," *Missouri Historical Review*, LXXII (January and April, 1978), 176–97, 271–95. See also the essays by Sutch and by Lowe and Campbell cited in note 31.

35. See the essays by Roger Anstey, Johannes Postma, E. Phillip LeVeen, and K. G. Davies, in Engerman and Genovese (eds.), *Race and Slavery*, 3–98; Herbert S. Klein, *The Middle Passage: Comparative Studies in the Atlantic Slave Trade* (Princeton: Princeton University Press, 1978), "Slaves and Shipping in Eighteenth-Century Virginia," *Journal of Interdisciplinary History*, V (Winter, 1975), 383–412, and "North American Competition and the Characteristics of the African Slave Trade to Cuba, 1790–1794," *William and Mary Quarterly*, 3rd Ser., XXVIII (January, 1971), 86–102; Roger Anstey, *The Atlantic Slave Trade and British Abolition, 1760–1810* (Atlantic Highlands, N.J.: Humanities Press, 1975); Wax, "Preferences for Slaves in Colonial America," and "Black Immigrants: The Slave Trade in Colonial Maryland," *Maryland Historical Magazine*, LXXIII (Spring, 1978), 30–45; Higgins, "The Geographical Origins of Negro Slaves in Colonial South Carolina"; Littlefield, *Rice and Slaves*; Henry A. Gemery and Jan S. Hogendorn (eds.), *The Uncommon Market: Essays in the Economic History of the Atlantic Slave Trade* (New York: Academic Press, 1979); David Eltis and James Walvin (eds.), *The Abolition of the Atlantic Slave Trade: Origins and Effects in Europe, Africa, and the Americas* (Madison: University of Wisconsin Press, 1981); James A. Rawley, *The Transatlantic Slave Trade: A History* (New York: Norton, 1981); Jay Coughtry, *The Notorious Triangle: Rhode Island and the African Slave Trade, 1700–1807* (Philadelphia: Temple University Press, 1981); Colin A. Palmer, *Human Cargoes: The British Slave Trade to Spanish America, 1700–1739* (Urbana: University of Illinois Press, 1981); Walter E. Minchinton, Celia King, and Peter Waite (eds.), *Virginia Slave-Trade Statistics, 1698–1775* (Richmond: Virginia State Library, 1984); Philip D. Curtin, "Epidemiology and the Slave Trade," *Political Science Quarterly*, LXXXIII (June, 1968), 190–216; Joseph C. Miller, "Mortality in the Atlantic Slave Trade: Statistical Evidence on Causality," *Journal of Interdisciplinary History*, XI (Winter, 1981), 385–423; Raymond L. Cohn and Richard A. Jensen, "The Determinants of Slave Mortality Rates on the Middle Passage," *Explorations in Economic History*, XIX (July, 1982), 269–82. On the late antebellum movement to reopen the slave trade, see Ronald T. Takaki, *A Pro-Slavery Crusade: The Agitation to Reopen the African Slave Trade* (New York: Free Press, 1971); and James P. Hendrix, Jr., "The Efforts to Reopen the African Slave Trade in Louisiana," *Louisiana History*, X (Spring, 1969), 97–123.

and Engerman all came together in the comparative study of slavery. Elkins' insistence that servitude in Latin America had, in almost every respect, been a milder form of bondage than that which had existed in the Old South crumbled under the weight of scholars' objections. Curtin's statistics, confirmed by Fogel and Engerman, on the relatively small slave importations and subsequent population growth in North America versus the huge importations and subsequent decline in the slave population in South America and the Caribbean were the starting points for a significant reexamination of slavery in the Western Hemisphere.[36] Eugene Genovese made a very useful contribution to this debate when he spelled out three distinct meanings of what constituted slave "treatment." The first category was the condition of the day-to-day existence—diet, housing, clothing, health care, and the general work regimen, for example. The second Genovese called the "conditions of life": the security of the family and the possibility for an autonomous social, cultural, and religious life were the key factors in this area. Genovese's third category was self-explanatory: "access to freedom and citizenship."[37]

In terms of day-to-day living conditions, there was little disagree-

---

36. In addition to the works cited in note 3, see C. Vann Woodward, "Protestant Slavery in a Catholic World" and "Southern Slaves in the World of Thomas Malthus," in *American Counterpoint*, 47–106; Carl N. Degler, "Slavery in Brazil and the United States: An Essay in Comparative History," *American Historical Review*, LXXV (April, 1970), 1004–1028; Richard R. Beeman, "Labor Forces and Race Relations: A Comparative View of the Colonization of Brazil and Virginia," *Political Science Quarterly*, LXXXVI (December, 1971), 609–36; Stuart B. Schwartz, "Patterns of Slaveholding in the Americas: New Evidence from Brazil," *American Historical Review*, LXXXVII (February, 1982), 55–86; Richard S. Dunn, "A Tale of Two Plantations: Slave Life at Mesopotamia in Jamaica and Mount Airy in Virginia, 1799 to 1828," *William and Mary Quarterly*, 3rd Ser., XXXIV (January, 1977), 32–65, "Servants and Slaves: The Recruitment and Employment of Labor," in Jack P. Greene and J. R. Pole (eds.), *Colonial British America: Essays in the New History of the Early Modern Era* (Baltimore: Johns Hopkins University Press, 1984), 157–94, and *Sugar and Slaves: The Rise of the Planter Class in the English West Indies, 1624–1713* (Chapel Hill: University of North Carolina Press, 1972); Richard B. Sheridan, *Sugar and Slavery: An Economic History of the British West Indies, 1623–1775* (Baltimore: Johns Hopkins University Press, 1973); Gwendolyn Midlo Hall, *Social Control in Slave Plantation Societies: A Comparison of St. Domingue and Cuba* (Baltimore: Johns Hopkins University Press, 1971); Franklin W. Knight, *Slave Society in Cuba During the Nineteenth Century* (Madison: University of Wisconsin Press, 1970); Kenneth F. Kiple, *Blacks in Colonial Cuba, 1774–1899* (Gainesville: University Presses of Florida, 1976).

37. Eugene D. Genovese, "The Treatment of Slaves in Different Countries: Problems in the Applications of the Comparative Method," in Foner and Genovese (eds.), *Slavery in the New World*, 202–10 (quotations on p. 203).

ment among historians. Southern slavery was markedly superior, and the demographic figures bore this out. Scholars disagreed on the relative merits of North and South American slavery in meeting Genovese's second category, the conditions of life, but the extensive work emerging in the 1960s and 1970s generally upgraded the status of slaves in the United States in a number of critical areas. The nuclear family was a reality for most slaves in the Old South, and the social world of the slave quarters seemed to many to be much more independent of white domination and control than scholars like Elkins had previously thought.[38] In like manner, the autonomy of antebellum slave culture was more clearly established in the aftermath of work by Levine and a number of other scholars.[39] And finally, studies of slave religion in the antebellum South showed that black Christianity had a theology that, to some considerable degree, set it apart from the religion of the masters.[40] Only in Genovese's third category, access to freedom and citizenship, was there a clear-cut edge in favor of the slave populations of Latin America.

One of the most striking findings of the comparative historians concerned the paucity of slave insurrections in North America when measured against the number and duration of the rebellions that occurred to the south. Several factors seemed to be involved. The constant importation of African-born slaves into Latin America and the Caribbean, the relative weakness of the white power structure there, the sexual imbalance between male and female slaves on the sugar and coffee plantations of the New World, a more propitious terrain, be it the mountains of Jamaica or the jungles of Brazil, and, in some areas, the presence of an Islamic religious tradition all acted to facili-

38. In addition to the work by Blassingame and Rawick already cited, see Thomas L. Webber, *Deep Like the Rivers: Education in the Slave Quarter Community, 1831–1865* (New York: Norton, 1978).

39. Sterling Stuckey, "Through the Prism of Folklore: The Black Ethos in Slavery," *Massachusetts Review,* IX (Summer, 1968), 417–37; Charles Joyner, *Down by the Riverside: A South Carolina Slave Community* (Urbana: University of Illinois Press, 1984), and "Soul Food and the Sambo Stereotype: Foodlore from the Slave Narrative Collection," *Keystone Folklore Quarterly,* XVI (1971), 171–78.

40. Donald G. Mathews, *Religion in the Old South* (Chicago: University of Chicago Press, 1977); Genovese, *Roll, Jordan, Roll;* John Jentz, "A Note on Genovese's Account of the Slaves' Religion," *Civil War History,* XXIII (June, 1977), 161–69; Albert J. Raboteau, *Slave Religion: The "Invisible Institution" in the Antebellum South* (New York: Oxford University Press, 1978); Levine, *Black Culture and Black Consciousness;* Olli Alho, *The Religion of the Slaves: A Study of the Religious Tradition and Behaviour of the Plantation Slaves in the United States, 1830–1865* (Helsinki, Finland: Suomalainen Tiedeakatemia, Academia Scientiarum Fennica, 1976).

tate the spread of revolutionary activity among South American and West Indian slaves.[41] Excellent work was done on the insurrections that did occur in the South, with Gabriel's rebellion, the Denmark Vesey plot, and the revolt led by Nat Turner receiving most of the attention.[42] The insurrectionary panics that periodically gripped the region were also examined in some detail.[43] Historians were careful to

41. Genovese, "The Treatment of Slaves in Different Countries," in Foner and Genovese (eds.), *Slavery in the New World,* and *From Rebellion to Revolution: Afro-American Slave Revolts in the Making of the Modern World* (Baton Rouge: Louisiana State University Press, 1979); Jordan, *White over Black;* Bertram Wyatt-Brown, *Southern Honor: Ethics and Behavior in the Old South* (New York: Oxford University Press, 1982); Marion D. deB. Kilson, "Towards Freedom: An Analysis of Slave Revolts in the United States," *Phylon,* XXV (Summer, 1964), 175–87; Stampp, "Rebels and Sambos"; Richard Price (ed.), *Maroon Societies: Rebel Slave Communities in the Americas* (Garden City, N.Y.: Anchor Press, 1973); Michael Craton, *Testing the Chains: Resistance to Slavery in the British West Indies* (Ithaca: Cornell University Press, 1982).

42. Mullin, *Flight and Rebellion,* and "Religion, Acculturation, and American Negro Slave Rebellions: Gabriel's Insurrection," in John H. Bracey, Jr., August Meier, and Elliott Rudwick (eds.), *American Slavery: The Question of Resistance* (Belmont, Calif.: Wadsworth, 1971), 160–78; Philip J. Schwarz, "Gabriel's Challenge: Slaves and Crime in Late Eighteenth-Century Virginia," *Virginia Magazine of History and Biography,* XC (July, 1982), 283–309; Jack D. L. Holmes, "The Abortive Slave Revolt at Pointe Coupée, Louisiana, 1795," *Louisiana History,* XI (Fall, 1970), 341–62; James H. Dormon, "The Persistent Specter: Slave Rebellion in Territorial Louisiana," *Louisiana History,* XVIII (Fall, 1977), 389–404; Richard C. Wade, "The Vesey Plot: A Reconsideration," *Journal of Southern History,* XXX (May, 1964), 143–61; William W. Freehling, *Prelude to Civil War: The Nullification Controversy in South Carolina, 1816–1836* (New York: Harper & Row, 1966); Robert S. Starobin, "Denmark Vesey's Slave Conspiracy of 1822: A Study in Rebellion and Repression," in Bracey, Meier, and Rudwick (eds.), *American Slavery,* 142–57, and Starobin (ed.), *Denmark Vesey: The Slave Conspiracy of 1822* (Englewood Cliffs, N.J.: Prentice-Hall, 1970); F. Roy Johnson, *The Nat Turner Slave Insurrection* (Murfreesboro, N.C.: Johnson Publishing Co., 1966); Henry Irving Tragle, *The Southampton Slave Revolt of 1831: A Compilation of Source Material* (Amherst: University of Massachusetts Press, 1971); Herbert Aptheker, *Nat Turner's Slave Rebellion* (New York: Humanities Press, 1966); Stephen B. Oates, *The Fires of Jubilee: Nat Turner's Fierce Rebellion* (New York: Harper & Row, 1975); Thomas C. Parramore, *Southampton County, Virginia* (Charlottesville: University Press of Virginia, 1978); William C. Suttles, Jr., "African Religious Survivals as Factors in American Slave Revolts," *Journal of Negro History,* LVI (April, 1971), 97–104; Vincent Harding, "Religion and Resistance Among Antebellum Negroes, 1800–1860," in August Meier and Elliott Rudwick (eds.), *The Making of Black America: Essays in Negro Life and History* (2 vols.; New York: Atheneum, 1969), I, 179–97.

43. Wyatt-Brown, *Southern Honor;* Lynn Veach Sadler, "Dr. Stephen Graham's Narration of the 'Duplin Insurrection': Additional Evidence on the Impact of Nat Turner," *Journal of American Studies,* XII (December, 1978), 359–67; Judith Kelleher

point out that resistance was carried on constantly by North American slaves, but most scholars agreed that organized rebellions in the nineteenth-century South could be counted on the fingers of one hand.[44]

As the literature on comparative slavery grew, it embraced more and more geographic and historical areas and included a wider variety of scholarly disciplines.[45] Sociologists, anthropologists, and linguists joined historians and demographers in seeking to uncover the differences between various slave systems and the reasons behind those differences.[46] Perhaps the zenith of the comparative approach

Schafer, "The Immediate Impact of Nat Turner's Insurrection on New Orleans," *Louisiana History*, XXI (Fall, 1980), 361–76; Edwin A. Miles, "The Mississippi Slave Insurrection Scare of 1835," *Journal of Negro History*, XLII (January, 1957), 48–60; Charles B. Dew, "Black Ironworkers and the Slave Insurrection Panic of 1856," *Journal of Southern History*, XLI (August, 1975), 321–38.

44. Raymond A. Bauer and Alice H. Bauer, "Day to Day Resistance to Slavery," *Journal of Negro History*, XXVII (October, 1942), 388–419; George M. Fredrickson and Christopher Lasch, "Resistance to Slavery," *Civil War History*, XIII (December, 1967), 315–29; Michael P. Johnson, "Runaway Slaves and the Slave Communities in South Carolina, 1799 to 1830," *William and Mary Quarterly*, 3rd Ser., XXXVIII (July, 1981), 418–41; Robert E. May, "John A. Quitman and His Slaves: Reconciling Slave Resistance with the Proslavery Defense," *Journal of Southern History*, XLVI (November, 1980), 551–70.

45. Raimondo Luraghi, "Wage Labor in the 'Rice Belt' of Northern Italy and Slave Labor in the American South—A First Approach," *Southern Studies*, XVI (Summer, 1977), 109–27, and *The Rise and Fall of the Plantation South* (New York: New Viewpoints, 1978); William C. Hine, "American Slavery and Russian Serfdom: A Preliminary Comparison," *Phylon*, XXXVI (December, 1975), 378–84; Peter Kolchin, "The Process of Confrontation: Patterns of Resistance to Bondage in Nineteenth-Century Russia and the United States," *Journal of Social History*, XI (Summer, 1978), 457–90, and "Reevaluating the Antebellum Slave Community: A Comparative Perspective," *Journal of American History*, LXX (December, 1983), 579–601; George M. Fredrickson, *White Supremacy: A Comparative Study in American and South African History* (New York: Oxford University Press, 1981).

46. Sidney W. Mintz (ed.), *Slavery, Colonialism, and Racism* (New York: Norton, 1974), and Mintz, "The Origins of Reconstituted Peasantries," in *Caribbean Transformations* (Chicago: Aldine, 1974), 146–56; Mintz and Richard Price, *An Anthropological Approach to the Afro-American Past: A Caribbean Perspective* (Philadelphia: Institute for the Study of Human Issues, 1976); Mintz, "Was the Plantation Slave a Proletarian?" *Review*, II (Summer, 1978), 81–98, and "Slavery and the Rise of Peasantries," in Michael Craton (ed.), *Roots and Branches: Current Directions in Slave Studies* (Toronto: Pergamon Press, 1979), 213–42; Orlando Patterson, *The Sociology of Slavery: An Analysis of the Origins, Development and Structure of Negro Slave Society in Jamaica* (Rutherford, N.J.: Fairleigh Dickinson University Press, 1969); Ian F. Hancock, "Gullah and Barbadian—Origins and Relationships," *American Speech*, LV (1980), 17–35.

to the study of slavery was reached in 1982 with the publication of Orlando Patterson's *Slavery and Social Death*. Patterson studied no fewer than sixty-six different slave societies, ranging from those of antiquity to the modern era and embracing an equally dazzling geographic span. The slaveholding cultures of the Mediterranean, Europe, Africa, the Middle East, and the Far East all came in for detailed discussion, as did those of the Western Hemisphere. In the end Patterson found more similarities than differences in the world's slave systems. All involved what he referred to as "natal alienation." This concept went "directly to the heart of what is critical in the slave's forced alienation, the loss of ties of birth in both ascending and descending generations," he wrote. "It was this alienation of the slave from all formal, legally enforceable ties of 'blood,' and from any attachment to groups or localities other than those chosen for him by the master" that made slavery what it was in every culture in every age. And it was this "incapacity to make any claims of birth or to pass on such claims" that made the slave, in Patterson's words, a "socially dead" person. As far as Patterson was concerned, the comparative analysis of slavery, which had started out in the 1950s emphasizing the strong differences between the New World's slave systems, actually revealed an institution of oppression that was, in its essence, close to uniform throughout the world's history.[47]

While quantitative and comparative historians were applying their skills to the study of slavery, more traditional historians were also doing yeoman scholarly service. They were editing extensive bibliographies, uncovering fresh documentary sources, providing revealing studies of slavery in microcosm, opening new areas for research, reworking old areas with imagination and laborious archival searches, organizing symposia on slavery, and developing even further many of the topics that received attention in the sweeping overviews of slavery and slave culture published in the 1960s and 1970s. Historians have also been performing one of the indispensable but oft-ignored tasks of the profession: attempting to summarize the formidable new body of interpretative material on slavery in studies that would make contemporary scholarship more accessible to a wide audience.

The bibliographic interest in slavery resulted in a number of valuable books and articles. John David Smith's massive, 1,847-page in-

47. Orlando Patterson, *Slavery and Social Death: A Comparative Study* (Cambridge: Harvard University Press, 1982), 7 (first three quotations), 8 (last two quotations).

terdisciplinary bibliography *Black Slavery in the Americas* was in a class by itself, but other useful bibliographic aids emerged as well.[48] Excellent historiographical essays, by Bennett H. Wall in the 1960s and David Brion Davis and Orlando Patterson in the 1970s, to name only three outstanding efforts, helped to place the ever-increasing wealth of new scholarship in proper perspective.[49]

Documentary collections dealing with slavery and closely related topics also arrived in significant numbers during the past two decades. Particularly noteworthy contributions include Rawick's multivolume edition of the Federal Writers' Project interviews, complemented by several other collections of slave narratives plus a valuable index, but the list does not stop there.[50] The ongoing publication of the papers of Booker T. Washington, Frederick Douglass, and Frederick Law Olmsted brought first-rate editorial skills to bear on three important figures in the history of American slavery, and an extensive documentary social history of emancipation, the first volume of which appeared in 1982, promised even greater returns for slave scholarship.[51] John W. Blassingame, the principal editor of *The Fred-*

48. John David Smith (comp.), *Black Slavery in the Americas: An Interdisciplinary Bibliography, 1865–1980* (2 vols.; Westport, Conn.: Greenwood Press, 1982); James M. McPherson *et al.*, *Blacks in America: Bibliographical Essays* (Garden City, N.Y.: Doubleday, 1971); Joseph C. Miller, *Slavery: A Comparative Teaching Bibliography* (Waltham, Mass.: Crossroads Press, 1977), periodically updated since 1980 by Miller and others in *Slavery & Abolition: A Journal of Comparative Studies;* James S. Olson, *Slave Life in America: A Historiography and Selected Bibliography* (Lanham, Md.: University Press of America, 1983).

49. Bennett H. Wall, "African Slavery," in Arthur S. Link and Rembert W. Patrick (eds.), *Writing Southern History: Essays in Historiography in Honor of Fletcher M. Green* (Baton Rouge: Louisiana State University Press, 1965), 175–97; David Brion Davis, "Slavery and the Post–World War II Historians," *Daedalus*, CIII (Spring, 1974), 1–16; Patterson, "Slavery," 407–49.

50. George P. Rawick (ed.), *The American Slave: A Composite Autobiography* (41 vols.; Westport, Conn.: Greenwood Press, 1972–79); Donald M. Jacobs (ed.), *Index to "The American Slave"* (Westport, Conn.: Greenwood Press, 1981); Paul D. Escott, *Slavery Remembered: A Record of Twentieth-Century Slave Narratives* (Chapel Hill: University of North Carolina Press, 1979); Charles L. Perdue, Jr., Thomas E. Barden, and Robert K. Phillips (eds.), *Weevils in the Wheat: Interviews with Virginia Ex-Slaves* (Charlottesville: University Press of Virginia, 1976). See also Lathan A. Windley (ed.), *Runaway Slave Advertisements: A Documentary History from the 1730s to 1790* (4 vols.; Westport, Conn.: Greenwood Press, 1983).

51. Louis R. Harlan *et al.* (eds.), *The Papers of Booker T. Washington* (13 vols.; Urbana: University of Illinois Press, 1972–84); John W. Blassingame *et al.* (eds.), *The Frederick Douglass Papers* (2 vols. to date; New Haven: Yale University Press, 1979–); Charles E. Beveridge and Charles Capen McLaughlin (eds.), *Slavery and the South,*

erick Douglass Papers, resurrected the published fugitive accounts of the nineteenth century as a valuable, albeit potentially treacherous, source of information on life under slavery.[52] Robert S. Starobin and Randall M. Miller assembled valuable collections of letters written by slaves. And Willie Lee Rose and Michael Mullin published excellent compilations of primary documents relating to the institution of slavery. Rose's volume was distinguished by its excellent selection of fresh material and the author's incisive editorial comments; Mullin's collection brought together a number of documents dealing with colonial and revolutionary slavery, areas too frequently overlooked in all phases of slave scholarship.[53]

The willingness of historians to concentrate on more limited geographic areas of the South demonstrated that if the right questions were asked of a rich body of local source material, some extremely valuable insights could be gained into the nature of black life in bondage and the day-to-day operations of the slave system. James C. Bonner and Edward W. Phifer had shown in the 1940s and 1950s that the county was a potentially fruitful area of investigation, and a number of excellent county-level studies were published during the next two decades.[54] Outstanding works on slave communities also appeared,

1852–1857 (Baltimore: Johns Hopkins University Press, 1981), vol. II of *The Papers of Frederick Law Olmsted,* 12 vols. projected; Ira Berlin, Joseph P. Reidy, and Leslie S. Rowland (eds.), *Freedom: A Documentary History of Emancipation, 1861–1867. Selected from the Holdings of the National Archives of the United States,* Series II, *The Black Military Experience* (New York: Cambridge University Press, 1982).

52. Blassingame, *The Slave Community,* Blassingame (ed.), *Slave Testimony: Two Centuries of Letters, Speeches, Interviews, and Autobiographies* (Baton Rouge: Louisiana State University Press, 1977), and "Using the Testimony of Ex-Slaves: Approaches and Problems," *Journal of Southern History,* XLI (November, 1975), 473–92; David Thomas Bailey, "A Divided Prism: Two Sources of Black Testimony on Slavery," *Journal of Southern History,* XLVI (August, 1980), 381–404; Frances Smith Foster, *Witnessing Slavery: The Development of Ante-Bellum Slave Narratives* (Westport, Conn.: Greenwood Press, 1979); Charles T. Davis and Henry Lewis Gates, Jr., *The Slave's Narrative* (New York: Oxford University Press, 1984).

53. Robert S. Starobin (ed.), *Blacks in Bondage: Letters of American Slaves* (New York: New Viewpoints, 1974); Randall M. Miller (ed.), *"Dear Master": Letters of a Slave Family* (Ithaca: Cornell University Press, 1978); Willie Lee Rose (ed.), *A Documentary History of Slavery in North America* (New York: Oxford University Press, 1976); Michael Mullin (ed.), *American Negro Slavery: A Documentary History* (Columbia: University of South Carolina Press, 1976).

54. James C. Bonner, "Profile of a Late Ante Bellum Community," *American Historical Review,* XLIX (July, 1944), 663–80; Edward W. Phifer, "Slavery in Microcosm: Burke County, North Carolina," *Journal of Southern History,* XXVIII (March, 1962), 137–65; Elinor Miller and Eugene D. Genovese (eds.), *Plantation, Town, and*

and some historians were able to sharpen their focus down to the lives of individual slaves. The best of this writing—Charles Joyner's study of the Waccamaw, South Carolina, slave community, for example—bore out Bonner's contention in an essay published in 1965 that solid, imaginative studies at the local level would pay handsome scholarly dividends. His description of the grass roots as "a fertile and unworked field" of southern history still holds true today, twenty years after Bonner's insightful call for more and better work in this area.[55]

The broad subject of slavery, southern agriculture, and the organization of the plantation—topics treated at some length in ambitious works like *Roll, Jordan, Roll* and *Time on the Cross*—received additional coverage during the past two decades, but it is safe to say that this field of study is by no means exhausted. Bennett H. Wall provided an excellent starting place for any consideration of the relationship of crops, land, and climate to slavery in his excellent essay "An Epitaph for Slavery" (1975). A more theoretical discussion of the plantation and its influence was Edgar T. Thompson's *Plantation Societies, Race Relations, and the South* (1975). Drew Gilpin Faust's biography of James Henry Hammond contained two superb chapters on how one prominent planter ran his agricultural enterprises, and Julia Floyd Smith took a wider look at slave-based agriculture in Flor-

---

County: Essays on the Local History of American Slave Society (Urbana: University of Illinois Press, 1974); Clarence L. Mohr, "Slavery in Oglethorpe County, Georgia, 1773–1865," *Phylon,* XXXIII (Spring, 1972), 4–21; Randolph Campbell, "Human Property: The Negro Slave in Harrison County, 1850–1860," *Southwestern Historical Quarterly,* LXXVI (April, 1973), 384–96; Donnie D. Bellamy, "Slavery in Microcosm: Onslow County, North Carolina," *Journal of Negro History,* LXII (October, 1977), 339–50; Phillip V. Scarpino, "Slavery in Calloway County, Missouri, 1845–1855," *Missouri Historical Review,* LXXI (October, 1976), 22–43, (April, 1977), 266–83.

55. Gary B. Mills, *The Forgotten People: Cane River's Creoles of Color* (Baton Rouge: Louisiana State University Press, 1977); Janet Sharp Hermann, *The Pursuit of a Dream* (New York: Oxford University Press, 1981); Joyner, *Down by the Riverside,* and "The Creolization of Slave Folklife: All Saints Parish, South Carolina, as a Test Case," *Historical Reflections/Réflexions Historiques,* VI (Winter, 1979), 435–53; John Hebron Moore, "Simon Gray, Riverman: A Slave Who Was Almost Free," *Mississippi Valley Historical Review,* XLIX (December, 1962), 472–84; Charles B. Dew, "Sam Williams, Forgeman: The Life of an Industrial Slave in the Old South," in J. Morgan Kousser and James M. McPherson (eds.), *Region, Race, and Reconstruction: Essays in Honor of C. Vann Woodward* (New York: Oxford University Press, 1982), 199–239; James C. Bonner, "Plantation and Farm: The Agricultural South," in Link and Patrick (eds.), *Writing Southern History,* 174.

ida, a frequently overlooked region of the cotton South.[56] Some fine work on plantation management was done in documentary form, particularly James O. Breeden's *Advice Among Masters* (1980).[57]

Both quantitative and nonquantitative historians sought to unlock some of the more intriguing mysteries of the plantation South. Otto Olsen's challenging essay on the extent of slave ownership and James Oakes's equally provocative *The Ruling Race* were, in effect, extensions of Frank L. Owsley's thesis that "economic democracy" characterized rural society in the Old South: slaveholding was widespread, and the acquisition of slave property provided a ready avenue of upward economic and social mobility for southern yeomen.[58] This view should be tested against the findings of some of the recent econometric studies of southern agriculture, however. There are a staggering number of these, but the best are Gavin Wright's *The Political Economy of the Cotton South*, the essays in William N. Parker (ed.), *The Structure of the Cotton Economy of the Antebellum South*, and the excellent work on Texas by Randolph B. Campbell and Richard J. Lowe.[59] The fascinating subject of black slaveholders has received

56. Bennett H. Wall, "An Epitaph for Slavery," *Louisiana History*, XVI (Spring, 1975), 229–56; Edgar T. Thompson, *Plantation Societies, Race Relations, and the South: The Regimentation of Populations* (Durham: Duke University Press, 1975); Drew Gilpin Faust, *James Henry Hammond and the Old South: A Design for Mastery* (Baton Rouge: Louisiana State University Press, 1982); Julia Floyd Smith, *Slavery and Plantation Growth in Antebellum Florida, 1821–1860* (Gainesville: University Presses of Florida, 1973). See also Carol Bleser (ed.), *The Hammonds of Redcliffe* (New York: Oxford University Press, 1981).

57. James O. Breeden (ed.), *Advice Among Masters: The Ideal in Slave Management in the Old South* (Westport, Conn.: Greenwood Press, 1980); James M. Clifton (ed.), *Life and Labor on Argyle Island: Letters and Documents of a Savannah River Rice Plantation, 1833–1867* (Savannah: Beehive Press, 1978); Thomas F. Armstrong, "From Task Labor to Free Labor: The Transition Along Georgia's Rice Coast, 1820–1880," *Georgia Historical Quarterly*, LXIV (Winter, 1980), 432–47; Michael L. Nicholls, "'In the Light of Human Beings': Richard Eppes and His Island Plantation Code of Laws," *Virginia Magazine of History and Biography*, LXXXIX (January, 1981), 67–78; G. Melvin Herndon, "Slavery in Antebellum Virginia: William Galt, Jr., 1839–1851, a Case Study," *Southern Studies*, XVI (Fall, 1977), 309–20; R. Keith Aufhauser, "Slavery and Scientific Management," *Journal of Economic History*, XXXIII (December, 1973), 811–24.

58. Otto H. Olsen, "Historians and the Extent of Slave Ownership in the Southern United States," *Civil War History*, XVIII (June, 1972), 101–16; James Oakes, *The Ruling Race: A History of American Slaveholders* (New York: Knopf, 1982); Frank L. Owsley and Harriet C. Owsley, "The Economic Basis of Society in the Late Antebellum South," *Journal of Southern History*, VI (February, 1940), 24–45.

59. Wright, *The Political Economy of the Cotton South*; Parker (ed.), *The Struc-

some attention, but a systematic investigation of this topic has yet to be done.[60]

The white and black supervisors responsible for running a successful plantation have come in for some much-needed reexamination in recent years. William K. Scarborough's revisionist look at the overseer was an indispensable study of that frequently maligned member of the plantation structure. Slave drivers, extensively treated in *Roll, Jordan, Roll*, were more fully discussed in solid work by William L. Van Deburg and Randall M. Miller, and the status of the driver and the various other members of the black plantation hierarchy was outlined in a revealing essay by John W. Blassingame.[61]

After decades of neglect, the subject of the nonagricultural employ-

---

ture of the Cotton Economy of the Antebellum South; Randolph B. Campbell, "Planters and Plain Folk: Harrison County, Texas, as a Test Case, 1850–1860," *Journal of Southern History,* XL (August, 1974), 369–98, and "Slaveholding in Harrison County, 1850–1860: A Statistical Profile," *East Texas Historical Journal,* XI (Spring, 1973), 18–27; Campbell and Richard Lowe, "Slave Property and the Distribution of Wealth in Texas, 1860," *Journal of American History,* LXIII (September, 1976), 316–24, and *Wealth and Power in Antebellum Texas* (College Station: Texas A&M University Press, 1977). See also Eugene D. Genovese, "Yeomen Farmers in a Slaveholders' Democracy," *Agricultural History,* XLIX (April, 1975), 331–42; Forrest McDonald and Grady McWhiney, "The Antebellum Southern Herdsman: A Reinterpretation," *Journal of Southern History,* XLI (May, 1975), 147–66; Steven Hahn, *The Roots of Southern Populism: Yeoman Farmers and the Transformation of the Georgia Upcountry, 1850–1890* (New York: Oxford University Press, 1983).

60. Mills, *The Forgotten People,* and "Coincoin: An Eighteenth-Century 'Liberated' Woman," *Journal of Southern History,* XLII (May, 1976), 205–22; R. Halliburton, Jr., "Free Black Owners of Slaves: A Reappraisal of the Woodson Thesis," *South Carolina Historical Magazine,* LXXVI (July, 1975), 129–42; David C. Rankin, "Black Slaveholders: The Case of Andrew Durnford," *Southern Studies,* XXI (Fall, 1982), 343–47.

61. William Kauffman Scarborough, *The Overseer: Plantation Management in the Old South* (Baton Rouge: Louisiana State University Press, 1966); William L. Van Deburg, *The Slave Drivers: Black Agricultural Labor Supervisors in the Antebellum South* (Westport, Conn.: Greenwood Press, 1979), and "Slave Drivers and Slave Narratives: A New Look at the 'Dehumanized Elite,'" *Historian,* XXXIX (August, 1977), 717–32; Randall M. Miller, "The Man in the Middle: The Black Slave Driver," *American Heritage,* XXX (October-November, 1979), 40–49; see also James M. Clifton, "The Rice Driver: His Role in Slave Management," *South Carolina Historical Magazine,* LXXXII (October, 1981), 331–53; Charles Hoffmann and Tess Hoffmann, "The Limits of Paternalism: Driver-Master Relations on a Bryan County Plantation," *Georgia Historical Quarterly,* LXVII (Fall, 1983), 321–35; John W. Blassingame, "Status and Social Structure in the Slave Community: Evidence from New Sources," in Harry P. Owens (ed.), *Perspectives and Irony in American Slavery* (Jackson: University Press of Mississippi, 1976), 137–51.

ment of slave labor attracted the attention of historians. Robert S. Starobin's *Industrial Slavery in the Old South* (1970) provided an excellent overview of this topic, and his work was supplemented by that of Ronald L. Lewis, John Hebron Moore, James H. Brewer, Ernest McPherson Lander, Jr., Randall M. Miller, and Charles B. Dew, among others.[62] Their work challenged the interpretation of industrial slavery put forward by Eugene Genovese in *The Political Economy of Slavery* and, more briefly, in *Roll, Jordan, Roll*. Because of the nature of the detailed records kept by the managers of industrial enterprises, this area of research frequently provided insights into slavery that transcended the limits imposed by the relatively small number of slaves engaged in nonagricultural work.

The closely related field of urban slavery followed a similar historiographical career: the ground initially broken by a single book followed by extensive amplification and, in this case, considerable revisionist writing. Richard C. Wade's *Slavery in the Cities* (1964) argued that the institution was on the decline in that setting because of

62. Robert S. Starobin, *Industrial Slavery in the Old South* (New York: Oxford University Press, 1970); Ronald L. Lewis, *Coal, Iron, and Slaves: Industrial Slavery in Maryland and Virginia, 1715–1865* (Westport, Conn.: Greenwood Press, 1979); John Hebron Moore, *Andrew Brown and Cypress Lumbering in the Old Southwest* (Baton Rouge: Louisiana State University Press, 1967); James H. Brewer, *The Confederate Negro: Virginia's Craftsmen and Military Laborers, 1861–1865* (Durham: Duke University Press, 1969); Ernest McPherson Lander, Jr., *The Textile Industry in Antebellum South Carolina* (Baton Rouge: Louisiana State University Press, 1969), and "Slave Labor in South Carolina Cotton Mills," *Journal of Negro History*, XXXVIII (April, 1953), 161–73; Randall M. Miller, "The Fabric of Control: Slavery in Antebellum Southern Textile Mills," *Business History Review*, LV (Winter, 1981), 471–90; Charles B. Dew, *Ironmaker to the Confederacy: Joseph R. Anderson and the Tredegar Iron Works* (New Haven: Yale University Press, 1966), "Disciplining Slave Ironworkers in the Antebellum South: Coercion, Conciliation, and Accommodation," *American Historical Review*, LXXIX (April, 1974), 393–418, "David Ross and the Oxford Iron Works: A Study of Industrial Slavery in the Early Nineteenth-Century South," *William and Mary Quarterly*, 3rd Ser., XXXI (April, 1974), 189–224, and "Sam Williams, Forgeman." See also John T. O'Brien, "Factory, Church, and Community: Blacks in Antebellum Richmond," *Journal of Southern History*, XLIV (November, 1978), 509–36; Rodney D. Green, "Industrial Transition in the Land of Chattel Slavery: Richmond, 1820–1960," *International Journal of Urban and Regional Research*, VIII (1984), 238–53; James D. Norris, *Frontier Iron: The Maramec Iron Works, 1826–1876* (Madison: State Historical Society of Wisconsin, 1964); Barbara L. Green, "Slave Labor at the Maramec Iron Works, 1828–1850," *Missouri Historical Review*, LXXIII (January, 1979), 150–64; Ernest F. Dibble, "Slave Rentals to the Military: Pensacola and the Gulf Coast," *Civil War History*, XXIII (June, 1977), 101–13; John Edmund Stealey III, "Slavery and the Western Virginia Salt Industry," *Journal of Negro History*, LIX (April, 1974), 105–31.

the difficulties inherent in the management and control of slaves in an urban environment. As noted earlier, Fogel and Engerman and Goldin successfully challenged the Wade thesis when they uncovered the economic reasons behind the shift of slave labor from the cities to the countryside, and other scholars pointed out that slavery was not even declining numerically in several southern cities during the late antebellum decades.[63] Urban slavery, like its industrial counterpart, seems to be an area where additional research could profitably be undertaken.

The revealing nature of the fringes of slavery was also demonstrated in work done during the past two decades on the free Negro. Again, there was a landmark study that sparked new interest, fresh research, and much able scholarship. The starting point was clearly Ira Berlin's *Slaves Without Masters* (1974), a detailed investigation that revealed the vulnerable and degraded condition of free blacks in the Old South. Berlin drew an important distinction, however, between areas of the Deep South and those farther north. "The elevated status of the free people of color and the lowly condition of slaves in the Lower South allowed a three-caste system much like that of the West Indies to develop wherever free Negroes were numerous," he claimed.[64] Leonard P. Curry's important quantitative study of urban

---

63. Richard C. Wade, *Slavery in the Cities: The South, 1820–1860* (New York: Oxford University Press, 1964); Fogel and Engerman, *Time on the Cross;* Goldin, *Urban Slavery;* Miller and Genovese (eds.), *Plantation, Town, and County;* Howard N. Rabinowitz, *Race Relations in the Urban South, 1865–1890* (New York: Oxford University Press, 1978); John W. Blassingame, *Black New Orleans, 1860–1880* (Chicago: University of Chicago Press, 1973); David R. Goldfield, *Urban Growth in the Age of Sectionalism: Virginia, 1847–1861* (Baton Rouge: Louisiana State University Press, 1977); Marianne Buroff Sheldon, "Black-White Relations in Richmond, Virginia, 1782–1820," *Journal of Southern History,* XLV (February, 1979), 27–44; Robert C. Reinders, "Slavery in New Orleans in the Decade Before the Civil War," *Mid-America,* XLIV (October, 1962), 211–21; Roger A. Fischer, "Racial Segregation in Ante Bellum New Orleans," *American Historical Review,* LXXIV (February, 1969), 926–37; Judith Kelleher Schafer, "New Orleans Slavery in 1850 as Seen in Advertisements," *Journal of Southern History,* XLVII (February, 1981), 33–56; Kenneth R. Johnson, "Slavery and Racism in Florence, Alabama, 1841–1862," *Civil War History,* XXVII (June, 1981), 155–71.

64. Ira Berlin, *Slaves Without Masters: The Free Negro in the Antebellum South* (New York: Pantheon, 1974), 198, and "The Structure of the Free Negro Caste in the Antebellum United States," *Journal of Social History,* IX (Spring, 1976), 297–318. See also Laurence J. Kotlikoff and Anton J. Rupert, "The Manumission of Slaves in New Orleans, 1827–1846," *Southern Studies,* XIX (Summer, 1980), 172–81; and David C. Rankin, "The Tannenbaum Thesis Reconsidered: Slavery and Race Relations in Antebellum Louisiana," *Southern Studies,* XVIII (Spring, 1979), 5–31.

free blacks found a situation similar to that outlined by Berlin. Free Negroes faced discrimination, confinement to the lowest-paying, most menial work, poverty, disfranchisement, a prejudiced legal system, and, often, white mob violence. They were, in short, "the most deprived and destitute element in the urban population." [65] Curry also agreed with Berlin that southern free blacks in cities like Charleston and New Orleans were better off than their counterparts in the upper South. Much the same view was advanced in another extremely significant treatment of the plight of free Negroes in the antebellum South, Joel Williamson's *New People*. But Williamson went on to point out that in the heated political climate of the 1850s, even the relatively privileged free black populations of New Orleans and Charleston suffered a marked deterioration in status. South Carolina's free people of color received additional coverage in a study by Marina Wikramanayake and, most recently, in an intriguing series of letters written by the members of a Charleston free Negro family during the late antebellum era.[66] One of the glaring omissions in Berlin's overview—his failure to deal in any systematic way with free black women—was rectified in part by Suzanne Lebsock's superb study of the women of antebellum Petersburg, both black and white.[67] Her

65. Leonard P. Curry, *The Free Black in Urban America, 1800–1850: The Shadow of the Dream* (Chicago: University of Chicago Press, 1981), 135. See also Letitia Woods Brown, *Free Negroes in the District of Columbia, 1790–1846* (New York: Oxford University Press, 1972); and James Borchert, *Alley Life in Washington: Family, Community, Religion, and Folklife in the City, 1850–1970* (Urbana: University of Illinois Press, 1980).

66. Williamson, *New People*. See also Robert Brent Toplin, "Between Black and White: Attitudes Toward Southern Mulattoes, 1830–1861," *Journal of Southern History*, XLV (May, 1979), 185–200; Gary B. Mills, "Miscegenation and the Free Negro in Antebellum 'Anglo' Alabama: A Reexamination of Southern Race Relations," *Journal of American History*, LXVIII (June, 1981), 16–34. Marina Wikramanayake, *A World in Shadow: The Free Black in Antebellum South Carolina* (Columbia: University of South Carolina Press, 1973); Michael P. Johnson and James L. Roark (eds.), *No Chariot Let Down: Charleston's Free People of Color on the Eve of the Civil War* (Chapel Hill: University of North Carolina Press, 1984). See also Johnson and Roark, "'A Middle Ground': Free Mulattoes and the Friendly Moralist Society of Antebellum Charleston," *Southern Studies*, XXI (Fall, 1982), 246–65, and *Black Masters: A Free Family of Color in the Old South* (New York: Norton, 1984); and Orville Vernon Burton, "Anatomy of an Antebellum Rural Free Black Community: Social Structure and Social Interaction in Edgefield District, South Carolina, 1850–1860," *Southern Studies*, XXI (Fall, 1982), 294–325.

67. Suzanne Lebsock, *The Free Women of Petersburg: Status and Culture in a Southern Town, 1784–1860* (New York: Norton, 1984). See also Michael L. Nicholls, "Passing Through this Troublesome World: Free Blacks in the Early Southside," *Vir-*

book was a model of its kind and deserved wide emulation. Another encouraging historiographical trend was the willingness of comparative historians to use their analytical methods to study the free black population of the entire Western Hemisphere.[68]

Concern for the legal status of slaves and free Negroes—a prominent element in slave historiography in the early years of the twentieth century—enjoyed a marked resurgence during the last decade. Excellent book-length studies by A. Leon Higginbotham, Jr., Don E. Fehrenbacher, Michael Stephen Hindus, Mark V. Tushnet, and Paul Finkelman,[69] and significant essays by William M. Wiecek, Daniel J. Flanigan, and A. E. Kier Nash, and a number of other able scholars, went a long way toward reestablishing this field as an important area of slave scholarship.[70]

ginia Magazine of History and Biography, XCII (January, 1984), 50–70; and Dorothy Sterling (ed.), *We Are Your Sisters: Black Women in the Nineteenth Century* (New York: Norton, 1984).

68. David W. Cohen and Jack P. Greene (eds.), *Neither Slave nor Free: The Freedmen of African Descent in the Slave Societies of the New World* (Baltimore: Johns Hopkins University Press, 1972).

69. A. Leon Higginbotham, Jr., *In the Matter of Color: Race and the American Legal Process, The Colonial Period* (New York: Oxford University Press, 1978); Don E. Fehrenbacher, *The Dred Scott Case: Its Significance in American Law and Politics* (New York: Oxford University Press, 1978); Michael Stephen Hindus, *Prison and Plantation: Crime, Justice, and Authority in Massachusetts and South Carolina, 1767–1878* (Chapel Hill: University of North Carolina Press, 1980), and "Black Justice Under White Law: Criminal Prosecutions of Blacks in Antebellum South Carolina," *Journal of American History*, LXIII (December, 1976), 575–99; Mark V. Tushnet, *The American Law of Slavery, 1810–1860: Considerations of Humanity and Interest* (Princeton: Princeton University Press, 1981), and "Approaches to the Study of the Law of Slavery," *Civil War History*, XXV (December, 1979), 329–38; Paul Finkelman, *An Imperfect Union: Slavery, Federalism, and Comity* (Chapel Hill: University of North Carolina Press, 1981). See also Edward L. Ayers, *Vengeance and Justice: Crime and Punishment in the 19th-Century American South* (New York: Oxford University Press, 1984).

70. William M. Wiecek, "The Statutory Law of Slavery and Race in the Thirteen Mainland Colonies of British America," *William and Mary Quarterly*, 3rd Ser., XXXIV (April, 1977), 258–80, and "Slavery and Abolition Before the United States Supreme Court, 1820–1860," *Journal of American History*, LXV (July, 1978), 34–59; Daniel J. Flanigan, "Criminal Procedure in Slave Trials in the Antebellum South," *Journal of Southern History*, XL (November, 1974), 537–64; A. E. Keir Nash, "Fairness and Formalism in the Trials of Blacks in the State Supreme Courts of the Old South," *Virginia Law Review*, LVI (February, 1970), 64–100, "A More Equitable Past? Southern Supreme Courts and the Protection of the Antebellum Negro," *North Carolina Law Review*, XLVIII (February, 1970), 197–242, "Negro Rights, Unionism, and Greatness on the South Carolina Court of Appeals: The Extraordinary Chief Jus-

Much the same thing could be said about another fascinating sub-field of slave historiography, the relationship between slavery and several native American tribes, particularly the Cherokees, the Creeks, and the Seminoles. Books by Rudia Halliburton, Jr., Daniel F. Little-field, Jr., and Theda Perdue and a raft of journal articles told us a great deal about this complex subject.[71] And one of the most reveal-ing aspects of the ties between slaves and Indians, the participation of

tice John Belton O'Neall," *South Carolina Law Review,* XXI (Spring, 1969), 141–90, "Reason of Slavery: Understanding the Judicial Role in the Peculiar Institution," *Van-derbilt Law Review,* XXXII (January, 1979), 7–218, and "The Texas Supreme Court and Trial Rights of Blacks, 1845–1860," *Journal of American History,* LVIII (De-cember, 1971), 622–42; Adele Hast, "The Legal Status of the Negro in Virginia, 1705–1765," *Journal of Negro History,* LIV (July, 1969), 217–39; Edward M. Steel, Jr., "Black Monongalians: A Judicial View of Slavery and the Negro in Monongalia County, 1776–1865," *West Virginia History,* XXXIV (July, 1973), 331–59; Alan D. Watson, "North Carolina Slave Courts, 1715–1785," *North Carolina Historical Re-view,* LX (January, 1983), 24–36; Don Higginbotham and William S. Price, Jr., "Was It Murder for a White Man to Kill a Slave? Chief Justice Martin Howard Condemns the Peculiar Institution in North Carolina," *William and Mary Quarterly,* 3rd Ser., XXXVI (October, 1979), 593–601; Patrick S. Brady, "Slavery, Race and the Criminal Law in Antebellum North Carolina: A Reconsideration of the Thomas Ruffin Court," *North Carolina Central Law Journal,* X (Spring, 1979), 248–60; Arthur F. Howing-ton, "'Not in the Condition of a Horse or an Ox': *Ford v. Ford,* the Law of Testamen-tary Manumission, and the Tennessee Court's Recognition of Slave Humanity," *Ten-nessee Historical Quarterly,* XXXIV (Fall, 1975), 249–63; Randall G. Shelden, "From Slave to Caste Society: Penal Changes in Tennessee, 1830–1915," *Tennessee Historical Quarterly,* XXXVIII (Winter, 1979), 462–78; John C. Edwards, "Slave Jus-tice in Four Middle Georgia Counties," *Georgia Historical Quarterly,* LVII (Summer, 1973), 265–73.

71. R. Halliburton, Jr., *Red Over Black: Black Slavery Among the Cherokee In-dians* (Westport, Conn.: Greenwood Press, 1977); Daniel F. Littlefield, Jr., *Africans and Creeks: From the Colonial Period to the Civil War* (Westport, Conn.: Greenwood Press, 1979); Theda Perdue, *Slavery and the Evolution of Cherokee Society, 1540– 1866* (Knoxville: University of Tennessee Press, 1979); see also Charles M. Hudson (ed.), *Red, White, and Black: Symposium on Indians in the Old South* (Athens: Uni-versity of Georgia Press, 1971). Monroe Billington, "Black Slavery in Indian Territory: The Ex-Slave Narratives," *Chronicles of Oklahoma,* LX (Spring, 1982), 56–65; Janet Halliburton, "Black Slavery in the Creek Nation," *Chronicles of Oklahoma,* LVI (Fall, 1978), 298–314; Martha Condray Searcy, "The Introduction of African Slavery into the Creek Indian Nation," *Georgia Historical Quarterly,* LXVI (Spring, 1982), 21–32; R. Halliburton, Jr., "Origins of Black Slavery Among the Cherokees," *Chronicles of Oklahoma,* LII (Winter, 1974–75), 483–96; Theda Perdue, "Cherokee Planters, Black Slaves, and African Colonization," *Chronicles of Oklahoma,* LX (Fall, 1982), 322– 31; Michael Doran, "Negro Slaves of the Five Civilized Tribes," *Annals of the Asso-ciation of American Geographers,* LXVIII (September, 1978), 335–50; William G. McLoughlin, "Red Indians, Black Slavery and White Racism: America's Slaveholding Indians," *American Quarterly,* XXVI (October, 1974), 367–85.

blacks in the Seminole Wars, fortunately received excellent coverage in studies by Littlefield and John K. Mahon.[72]

As might be expected from a burgeoning area like slavery studies, a number of symposia were organized during the 1970s in order to bring scholars together to examine this rapidly changing field. These meetings resulted in the publication of several outstanding volumes, all of which contained important contributions.[73] The slavery symposium has apparently become an extinct phenomenon in the mid-1980s, but fortunately some of the best historians of slavery brought out important collections of essays. Elizabeth Fox-Genovese and Eugene Genovese's *Fruits of Merchant Capital* (1983) included some major pieces dealing with slave historiography, the expansion of slavery into the Western Hemisphere, New World slave revolts, and a number of other slavery-related topics. Like Genovese's *From Rebellion to Revolution* (1979), these essays employed a much stronger Marxist theoretical framework than did *Roll, Jordan, Roll.*[74] An even

72. Daniel F. Littlefield, Jr., *Africans and Seminoles: From Removal to Emancipation* (Westport, Conn.: Greenwood Press, 1977); John K. Mahon, *History of the Second Seminole War, 1835–1842* (Gainesville: University of Florida Press, 1967). See also John T. Sprague, *The Origin, Progress, and Conclusion of the Florida War* (Gainesville: University of Florida Press, 1964), a facsimile reprint of the 1848 edition; J. Leitch Wright, Jr., "A Note on the First Seminole War as Seen by the Indians, Negroes, and Their British Advisers," *Journal of Southern History*, XXXIV (November, 1968), 565–75.

73. Engerman and Genovese (eds.), *Race and Slavery;* Owens (ed.), *Perspectives and Irony in American Slavery;* Craton (ed.), *Roots and Branches.* In addition, several historical journals devoted entire issues to slavery-related topics. See the Chesapeake Society issue of the *William and Mary Quarterly,* 3rd Ser., XXX (January, 1973); the St. Mary's City Commission special issue, *Maryland Historical Magazine,* LXIX (Summer, 1974); the special issue on colonial slavery, *Southern Studies,* XVI (Winter, 1977); the Blacks in Early America issue of the *William and Mary Quarterly,* 3rd Ser., XXXV (April, 1978); the special issue on antebellum free blacks, *Southern Studies,* XXI (Fall, 1982); and two issues of *Agricultural History* devoted entirely to the antebellum southern economy and agricultural system, XLIV (January, 1970) and XLIX (April, 1975).

74. Elizabeth Fox-Genovese and Eugene D. Genovese, *Fruits of Merchant Capital: Slavery and Bourgeois Property in the Rise and Expansion of Capitalism* (New York: Oxford University Press, 1983). See also Genovese's two earlier collections of essays, *The World the Slaveholders Made: Two Essays in Interpretation* (New York: Pantheon, 1969), and *In Red and Black: Marxian Explorations in Southern and Afro-American History* (New York: Pantheon, 1971). Two excellent critiques of Genovese's application of Marxist theory to the antebellum South are Richard H. King, "Marxism and the Slave South," *American Quarterly,* XXIX (Spring, 1977), 117–31; and Carl N. Degler, *Place Over Time: The Continuity of Southern Distinctiveness* (Baton Rouge: Louisiana State University Press, 1977).

more important volume of essays was Willie Lee Rose's *Slavery and Freedom*. This slender book was infused with much wisdom and insight, and it charted the way for further slave studies. As Stanley Elkins pointed out, Rose's priorities were the most valuable guides for future students of slavery: her concern for time (what changes occurred in the institution over the decades and centuries) and her insistence on place and particularity—what was slavery really like for individual men, women, and children held in bondage.[75]

A number of essays in the published papers of the slavery symposia indicated another important historiographical trend. In ever-increasing numbers, historians were attempting to probe more deeply the cultural life of southern slaves. The Christianity in the quarters received detailed treatment in Albert J. Raboteau's *Slave Religion* (1978), a book that stressed the "invisible" nature of the slaves' religious practices.[76] John B. Boles's *Religion in Antebellum Kentucky* argued, however, that blacks and whites frequently shared religious experiences in organized church congregations in the Old South.[77] Much has been written about the attitudes of the major white religious denominations toward the institution of slavery,[78] and histo-

75. Willie Lee Rose, *Slavery and Freedom*, ed. William W. Freehling (New York: Oxford University Press, 1982); Stanley Elkins, "How to Understand Slavery," *New York Review of Books*, April 29, 1982, pp. 21–23. See also Kenneth M. Stampp, "Slavery—The Historian's Burden," in Owens (ed.), *Perspectives and Irony in American Slavery*, 153–70.

76. Raboteau, *Slave Religion*, "The Slave Church in the Era of the American Revolution," in Berlin and Hoffman (eds.), *Slavery and Freedom in the Age of the American Revolution*, 193–213, and "Slave Autonomy and Religion," *Journal of Religious Thought*, XXXVIII (Fall-Winter, 1982), 51–64. See also Timothy L. Smith, "Slavery and Theology: The Emergence of Black Christian Consciousness in Nineteenth-Century America," *Church History*, XLI (December, 1972), 497–512; Mechal Sobel, *Trabelin' On: The Slave Journey to an Afro-Baptist Faith* (Westport, Conn.: Greenwood Press, 1979); Eugene D. Genovese, "Black Plantation Preachers in the Slave South," *Louisiana Studies*, XI (Fall, 1972), 188–214; and David R. Roediger, "And Die in Dixie: Funerals, Death, & Heaven in the Slave Community, 1700–1865," *Massachusetts Review*, XXII (Spring, 1981), 163–83.

77. John B. Boles, *Religion in Antebellum Kentucky* (Lexington: University Press of Kentucky, 1976). See also Kenneth K. Bailey, "Protestantism and Afro-Americans in the Old South: Another Look," *Journal of Southern History*, XLI (November, 1975), 451–72.

78. Donald G. Mathews, *Slavery and Methodism: A Chapter in American Morality, 1780–1845* (Princeton: Princeton University Press, 1965), and *Religion in the Old South;* Andrew E. Murray, *Presbyterians and the Negro—A History* (Philadelphia: Presbyterian Historical Society, 1966); Denzil T. Clifton, "Anglicanism and Negro

rians have also investigated the effort by clergymen in some of these faiths to organize missionary work among the slaves.[79] The subject of voodoo was intelligently discussed in an article by Blake Touchstone.[80]

Levine's *Black Culture and Black Consciousness* was unquestionably the place to begin any serious study of slave folk practices and beliefs, but various aspects of slave cultural life came in for additional scholarly investigation. Thomas L. Webber's *Deep Like the Rivers* skillfully probed the methods by which folk wisdom was transmitted from generation to generation, and a number of articles appeared dealing with black folktales.[81] Slave secular and religious music was extensively discussed in works by Dena J. Epstein and Eileen South-

Slavery in Colonial America," *Historical Magazine of the Protestant Episcopal Church,* XXXIX (March, 1970), 29–70; Glen Jeansonne, "Southern Baptist Attitudes Toward Slavery, 1845–1861," *Georgia Historical Quarterly,* LV (Winter, 1971), 510–22; James David Essig, "A Very Wintry Season: Virginia Baptists and Slavery, 1785–1797," *Virginia Magazine of History and Biography,* LXXXVIII (April, 1980), 170–85, and *The Bonds of Wickedness: American Evangelicals Against Slavery, 1770–1808* (Philadelphia: Temple University Press, 1982); W. Harrison Daniel, "Virginia Baptists and the Negro in the Early Republic," *Virginia Magazine of History and Biography,* LXXX (January, 1972), 60–69, "Virginia Baptists and the Negro in the Antebellum Era," *Journal of Negro History,* LVI (January, 1971), 1–16, and "Southern Presbyterians and the Negro in the Early National Period," *Journal of Negro History,* LVIII (July, 1973), 291–312.

79. Donald G. Mathews, "The Methodist Mission to the Slaves, 1829–1844," *Journal of American History,* LI (March, 1965), 615–31, and "Charles Colcock Jones and the Southern Evangelical Crusade to Form a Biracial Community," *Journal of Southern History,* XLI (August, 1975), 299–320; Robert Manson Myers (ed.), *The Children of Pride: A True Story of Georgia and the Civil War* (New Haven: Yale University Press, 1972); Erskine Clarke, *Wrestlin' Jacob: A Portrait of Religion in the Old South* (Atlanta: John Knox Press, 1979); Anne C. Loveland, *Southern Evangelicals and the Social Order, 1800–1860* (Baton Rouge: Louisiana State University Press, 1980).

80. Blake Touchstone, "Voodoo in New Orleans," *Louisiana History,* XIII (Fall, 1972), 371–86. See also Liliane Crété, *Daily Life in Louisiana, 1815–1830,* trans. Patrick Gregory (Baton Rouge: Louisiana State University Press, 1981).

81. Webber, *Deep Like the Rivers;* Dickson D. Bruce, Jr., "The 'John and Old Master' Stories and the World of Slavery: A Study of Folktales and History," *Phylon,* XXXV (December, 1974), 418–29; Mary Arnold Twining, "An Anthropological Look at Afro-American Folk Narrative," *CLA Journal,* XIV (September, 1970), 57–61; D. J. M. Muffett, "Uncle Remus Was a Hausaman?" *Southern Folklore Quarterly,* XXXIX (June, 1975), 151–66; John Solomon Otto, "The Case for Folk History: Slavery in the Highlands South," *Southern Studies,* XX (Summer, 1981), 167–73; Daryl Dance, "In the Beginning: A New View of Black American Etiological Tales," *Southern Folklore Quarterly,* XLI (March-June, 1977), 53–64.

ern, among others.[82] Even slave decorative arts, a subject briefly but imaginatively treated in Blassingame's *The Slave Community*, received some much-deserved study.[83]

Several historians assumed the difficult task of trying to summarize the astonishing recent outpouring of slave scholarship so that it might reach an enlarged readership. The best of these efforts were three quite different works. C. Duncan Rice's *The Rise and Fall of Black Slavery* (1975) took on the entire New World: from slave trading to slave law and the actual operation of slavery in Protestant and Catholic countries to the eventual abolition of slavery throughout the Western Hemisphere. By tying the treatment of slaves in both North and South America to the market for staple crops—the stronger the demand, the harsher the slave system—he gave his study an interpretative slant that made it more than a summary of other views. Nathan I. Huggins' *Black Odyssey* (1977), on the other hand, was an intensely personal book that attempted to look inside the mind and soul of the African carried across the Atlantic and thrust into the strange and brutal world of southern slavery. Huggins' hope, clearly, was that someone reading his story in the latter part of the twentieth century would be able to understand, and empathize with, the plight of those who came to America in chains. John B. Boles took a third tack. After an extraordinarily wide-ranging review of the current literature on slavery, he produced an overview that effectively distilled the most important new studies of the slave South into a single readable volume. His *Black Southerners* also managed to avoid the grinding of ideological or racial axes, a challenge some other recent broad-based treatments of slavery have not been able to meet.[84]

---

82. Dena J. Epstein, *Sinful Tunes and Spirituals: Black Folk Music to the Civil War* (Urbana: University of Illinois Press, 1977); Eileen Southern, *The Music of Black Americans: A History* (New York: Norton, 1971); Paul A. Cimbala, "Fortunate Bondsmen: Black 'Musicianers' and Their Role as an Antebellum Southern Plantation Slave Elite," *Southern Studies*, XVIII (Fall, 1979), 291–303. See also Lawrence W. Levine, "Slave Songs and Slave Consciousness: An Exploration in Neglected Sources," in Tamara K. Hareven (ed.), *Anonymous Americans: Explorations in Nineteenth-Century Social History* (Englewood Cliffs, N.J.: Prentice-Hall, 1971), 99–130.

83. Marcus Christian, *Negro Ironworkers of Louisiana, 1718–1900* (Gretna, La.: Pelican Publishing Co., 1972); Richard Price, "Saramaka Woodcarving: The Development of an AfroAmerican Art," *Man*, n.s., V (September, 1970), 363–78; John Michael Vlach, *The Afro-American Tradition in Decorative Arts* (Cleveland: Cleveland Museum of Art, 1978).

84. C. Duncan Rice, *The Rise and Fall of Black Slavery* (New York: Harper & Row, 1975); Nathan Irvin Huggins, *Black Odyssey: The Afro-American Ordeal in*

No review of contemporary writing on southern slavery would be complete without at least mentioning one of the most amazing cultural events of the past decade. The publication of Alex Haley's *Roots* and the subsequent television series drawn from his book brought the subject of slavery dramatically to the forefront of American popular consciousness. The phenomenon could not last, of course, and there was much questionable history in both the novel and the television production, as scholars were quick to point out.[85] But the fact remained that *Roots* forced white Americans, if only for a brief moment, to do something most had never done before: to confront slavery head on and to see it through the eyes of the slave.

In conclusion, it seems fair to say that the historical literature described in this essay has given us a fuller picture of black life under slavery than we have ever had before. Given the difficulties and potential pitfalls that will always face scholars working in this emotionally charged field, the substantial progress made in the past twenty years toward a deeper understanding of slavery must certainly rank as a historiographical accomplishment of the first magnitude.

Slavery (New York: Pantheon, 1977); John B. Boles, *Black Southerners, 1619–1869* (Lexington: University Press of Kentucky, 1983); Philip S. Foner, *History of Black Americans* (3 vols. to date; Westport, Conn.: Greenwood Press, 1975–); Vincent Harding, *There Is a River: The Black Struggle for Freedom in America* (New York: Harcourt Brace Jovanovich, 1981); Mary Frances Berry and John W. Blassingame, *Long Memory: The Black Experience in America* (New York: Oxford University Press, 1982).

85. Alex Haley, *Roots* (Garden City, N.Y.: Doubleday, 1976); Willie Lee Rose, "An American Family," *New York Review of Books,* November 11, 1976, pp. 3–4, 6; Robert D. McFadden, "Some Points of 'Roots' Questioned; Haley Stands By Book as a Symbol," New York *Times,* April 10, 1977, pp. 1, 29; Gary B. Mills and Elizabeth Shown Mills, "*Roots* and the New 'Faction': A Legitimate Tool for Clio?" *Virginia Magazine of History and Biography,* LXXXIX (January, 1981), 3–26.

The White South from Secession to Redemption

JOE GRAY TAYLOR

This essay has a large area of history to cover, and it is restricted to the "white South." However, there is no hard and fast line between white history and black history in the South that can be applied in every case. Southern blacks and southern whites were bound together inseparably, and so is their history. Therefore some overlap between this essay and that by LaWanda Cox elsewhere in this volume is probably inevitable.

Another problem arises as to what was "southern" and what was "northern" during the Civil War and Reconstruction. Certainly the secession crisis involved both sections, as did military action. But studies that are concerned solely with northern politics, economics, or society have been ignored here. Likewise, biographies of northern leaders, political and military, have been omitted. In a consideration of Reconstruction, however, it is not at all easy to say what is northern history and what is southern history. The historiography of Lincoln's approach to Reconstruction and of the events of Andrew Johnson's administration that pertained to Reconstruction have been considered here because these matters were of vital importance to the South.

Although this essay is basically concerned with the writings of the last twenty years, that time frame has been disregarded when it seemed appropriate. Since this essay was written in 1982, it cannot take account of later publications or even all those of 1982. The concern is primarily with books; articles have been discussed only when that seemed absolutely essential. This can be justified on the ground that most significant articles develop into books, but it is necessary here because there are simply too many articles to be dealt with effectively.

A student who read only what has been written on the secession crisis since 1960 might have great difficulty understanding the long controversy over the causes of the Civil War. In more recent works, slavery is unquestionably the cause. This concentration of historians' minds is no doubt a result of the civil rights controversy of the 1950s and 1960s, and it may well be that future historians will emphasize other causes. But for the present, slavery holds center stage. Nor have historians in the 1960s and 1970s been particularly concerned whether this great conflict over slavery was repressible or irrepressible.

Even Avery Craven, author of *The Repressible Conflict* (1939), who accused a blundering generation of bringing on a needless war, retreated far from that position before his death. At a conference on the Civil War held at Stanford University in March of 1963, Craven explained secession by arguing that Abraham Lincoln's election to the presidency seemed to southerners to demonstrate that northern opponents of slavery would resort to any means, legislative or violent, to make certain that slavery came to an end. Thus it seemed that the only hope southerners had of defending themselves against social, economic, and political ruin lay in placing slavery out of reach of its foes by secession. Southerners also feared loss of honor because of Republican claims of moral superiority over slave owners. No compromise was possible because the slavery issue had become one "of right versus wrong and had thereby created a situation with which the democratic process of toleration and compromise could not deal."[1]

David M. Potter, who stood against Craven and other so-called revisionists for many years, continued to contribute to understanding of the secession crisis as long as he lived. He was much concerned that the civil rights controversy's influence on the study of the past might give the slavery question more importance than it deserved. He noted that when David Donald, in his *Charles Sumner and the Coming of the Civil War* (1960), showed the warts on Sumner's pompous and arrogant personality as well as the Massachusetts senator's great leadership in the antislavery struggle, he was harshly criticized for suggesting that an antislavery man could be something less than perfect. Donald, incidentally, seems to have been correct when he said in 1960 that the causation of the Civil War was dead as a serious subject of historical analysis.[2]

1. Avery O. Craven, *The Repressible Conflict, 1830–1861* (Baton Rouge: Louisiana State University Press, 1939), and "Why the Southern States Seceded," in George Harmon Knoles (ed.), *The Crisis of the Union, 1860–1861* (Baton Rouge: Louisiana State University Press, 1965), 60–79 (quotation on p. 66). See also Craven, *An Historian and the Civil War* (Chicago: University of Chicago Press, 1964).

2. David M. Potter, *The South and the Sectional Conflict* (Baton Rouge: Louisiana State University Press, 1968), 78–79, 107–108; David H. Donald, *Charles Sumner*

A "southern" point of view on the secession crisis no longer exists among professional historians. Barrington Moore, Jr., in *Social Origins of Dictatorship and Democracy* (1966), and Eugene Genovese, in "Marxian Interpretations of the Slave South" (1968), made slavery as a cause of the Civil War secondary, in Moore's opinion, to conflict between two kinds of capitalism and, according to Genovese, to conflict between prebourgeois, not feudal, society and capitalism. Followers of these more or less Marxist writers have not been active in dealing with the secession crisis. In a paper read at the 1982 annual meeting of the Southern Historical Association, Bertram Wyatt-Brown attributed secession in part to the southern concept of honor.[3]

The last word, up to the present, seems to have been said by David M. Potter in *The Impending Crisis* (1976), a magisterial work completed by Don E. Fehrenbacher after Potter's death. Potter believed that the South did have reason for fear after Lincoln's election, not because of possible legislation, but because the "closed system of social and intellectual arrangements upon which the South relied for the perpetuation of slavery might be disrupted." Potter recognized the fact that hysteria gripped the Deep South in 1861, but he also made it clear that the secessionists even in hysteria were motivated by their determination to defend slavery. Thus we speak, correctly, of "the secession crisis," "yet all of the efforts at compromise in Congress dealt with the issue of slavery and only obliquely with the problem of secession."[4]

A number of state studies, of which more are needed, have also contributed to understanding of the secession crisis. Steven A. Channing concluded (1970) that fear for slavery as an institution, but more immediately fear of a slave insurrection, hastened secession in

---

and the Coming of the Civil War (New York: Knopf, 1960), and "American Historians and the Causes of the Civil War," *South Atlantic Quarterly*, LIX (Summer, 1960), 351–55.

3. Barrington Moore, Jr., *Social Origins of Dictatorship and Democracy: Lord and Peasant in the Making of the Modern World* (Boston: Beacon Press, 1966); Eugene D. Genovese, "Marxian Interpretations of the Slave South," in Barton J. Bernstein (ed.), *Towards a New Past: Dissenting Essays in American History* (New York: Pantheon, 1968); Bertram Wyatt-Brown, "Honor as a Cause of Southern Secession" (Paper presented at the annual meeting of the Southern Historical Association, Memphis, Tenn., November 4, 1982). See also Wyatt-Brown, *Southern Honor: Ethics and Behavior in the Old South* (New York: Oxford University Press, 1982).

4. David M. Potter, *The Impending Crisis, 1848–1861* (New York: Harper & Row, 1976), 477 (first quotation), 500–501, 529 (second quotation).

South Carolina. William L. Barney's *The Secessionist Impulse* (1974) concluded in agreement with Channing that fear was the chief factor impelling Mississippi and Alabama toward leaving the Union. The most frightened men, he found, were newly established planters who would be vulnerable to a decline in slave prices, which they expected to follow the confinement of slavery within existing geographical bounds. Michael P. Johnson, in a study of secessionist Georgia (1977), argued that two revolutions took place in that state. The first was secession, intended to protect slavery from the external threat of black Republicanism. The second revolution came when the Georgia constitutional convention of 1861 devised a constitution that would protect Georgia planters, and especially old Whig planters, against the internal threat of white democracy.[5]

Donald E. Reynolds' *Editors Make War* (1970) discussed the role of southern newspapers in the crisis. The old controversy over whether or not Lincoln deliberately provoked the crisis at Fort Sumter so as to put the onus of the first shot upon the South received detailed treatment from Richard N. Current in *Lincoln and the First Shot* (1963). Current's reasoning was that Lincoln hoped to avoid war, that no one forced Jefferson Davis to order the bombardment, but that Lincoln was determined that if war had to come, the South would start it.[6]

Thus for twenty years it has been accepted, largely without question, that whatever might have been said in earlier decades, slavery was at the very center of the secession crisis. Allan Nevins had pointed this out in 1950, noting that fear and hysteria at the time were possible only because of the existence of slavery. But, as Potter indicated, Nevins did not attribute the crisis and the war that followed to slavery alone. Much more was involved: "The main root of the conflict . . . was the problem of slavery *with its complementary problem of race-adjustment*. . . . It was a war over slavery *and* the future position of the Negro race in North America." The newest historiography

---

5. Steven A. Channing, *Crisis of Fear: Secession in South Carolina* (New York: Simon & Schuster, 1970); William L. Barney, *The Secessionist Impulse: Alabama and Mississippi in 1860* (Princeton: Princeton University Press, 1974); Michael P. Johnson, *Toward a Patriarchal Republic: The Secession of Georgia* (Baton Rouge: Louisiana State University Press, 1977); Ralph A. Wooster, *The Secession Conventions of the South* (Princeton: Princeton University Press, 1963).

6. Donald E. Reynolds, *Editors Make War: Southern Newspapers in the Secession Crisis* (Nashville: Vanderbilt University Press, 1970); Richard N. Current, *Lincoln and the First Shot* (Philadelphia: Lippincott, 1963).

of the secession crisis and Civil War causation is not too far away from the "central theme" of southern history that Ulrich B. Phillips set forth many years ago.[7]

An abundance of histories of the Confederacy was available by 1960, that of Robert S. Henry (1931) being the most readable and E. Merton Coulter's volume (1950) in *The History of the South* being the most detailed. Clement Eaton's *History of the Southern Confederacy* (1954) is definitely worth reading, as is Charles P. Roland's *The Confederacy* (1960). In 1970, Frank E. Vandiver produced *Their Tattered Flags* to high critical praise. The most recent general history of the Confederacy is Emory M. Thomas' *The Confederate Nation* (1979), a volume in the new American Nation Series. Thomas placed great emphasis on nationalism in the Confederacy. This could have been predicted, because in 1971 he had published *The Confederacy as a Revolutionary Experience,* which stressed the revolutionary nationalism of the seceded states.[8]

Three other books of the last twenty years deal with centralization and nationalism within the Civil War South. Curtis A. Amlund maintained that war forced centralization upon a South dedicated to states' rights. Paul D. Escott argued that the failure of the common people of the South to develop a sense of nationalism was a major cause of the South's losing the Civil War and that the class consciousness of the southern people inhibited the development of nationalism. He also drew a more favorable picture of Jefferson Davis than the one painted by most historians. Finally, Raimondo Luraghi, in his Marxist *The Rise and Fall of the Plantation South* (1978), devoted six chapters to the fall of the regime. Like Escott, he emphasized class consciousness and suggested that the dominant planters leaped from

7. Allan Nevins, *The Emergence of Lincoln* (2 vols.; New York: Charles Scribner's Sons, 1950), II, 468, 470; Nevins quoted in Potter, *The South and the Sectional Conflict,* 104; Ulrich B. Phillips, "The Central Theme of Southern History," *American Historical Review,* XXIV (October, 1928), 30–43.

8. Robert S. Henry, *The Story of the Confederacy* (Indianapolis: Bobbs-Merrill, 1931); E. Merton Coulter, *The Confederate States of America, 1861–1865* (Baton Rouge: Louisiana State University Press, 1950); Clement Eaton, *A History of the Southern Confederacy* (New York: Macmillan, 1954); Charles P. Roland, *The Confederacy* (Chicago: University of Chicago Press, 1960); Frank E. Vandiver, *Their Tattered Flags: The Epic of the Confederacy* (New York: Harper's Magazine Press, 1970); Emory M. Thomas, *The Confederate Nation, 1861–1865* (New York: Harper & Row, 1979), and *The Confederacy as a Revolutionary Experience* (Englewood Cliffs, N.J.: Prentice-Hall, 1971).

what he called a "seigneural civilization" to state socialism during the war in order to prevent the rise of a bourgeois class.[9]

Interest in the government of the Confederacy was strong during the period under review. W. Buck Yearns published his well-received *The Confederate Congress* in 1960. He collaborated with Ezra J. Warner to bring out a biographical register (1975) of that Congress, providing a long-needed reference work. Of more interpretive significance is Thomas B. Alexander and Richard E. Beringer's *The Anatomy of the Confederate Congress* (1972), which attempts an analysis of the voting behavior of Confederate congressmen. They discovered that neither nationalism nor commitment to states' rights was demonstrated by the votes of these representatives of the southern people. These more recent studies of the Confederate government suggest that William Ewart Gladstone erred when he believed that Jefferson Davis had built a nation. Another book that adds to understanding of the Confederate government is the study of Confederate constitutions (1963) by Charles Robert Lee.[10]

A number of newer biographies of Confederate leaders contribute to knowledge of the southern government during the Civil War. Clement Eaton's life of Jefferson Davis (1977) is popular, but the section on the war has been rather severely criticized for a superficial approach and some errors of fact. Robert Penn Warren's *Jefferson Davis Gets His Citizenship Back* (1980) deserves attention. William C. Davis' life of John Breckinridge (1974) filled a definite need and is exceptionally well written. Another biography of Breckinridge, by Frank H. Heck (1976), is short but readable. Ben H. Procter's life of John H. Reagan (1962) also adds to knowledge of wartime government in Richmond. Alvy L. King may have overstated the influence of fire-eater Louis T. Wigfall, to whom he assigned the major responsi-

9. Curtis A. Amlund, *Federalism in the Southern Confederacy* (Washington, D.C.: Public Affairs Press, 1966); Paul D. Escott, *After Secession: Jefferson Davis and the Failure of Confederate Nationalism* (Baton Rouge: Louisiana State University Press, 1978); Raimondo Luraghi, *The Rise and Fall of the Plantation South* (New York: New Viewpoints, 1978).

10. W. Buck Yearns, *The Confederate Congress* (Athens: University of Georgia Press, 1960); Ezra J. Warner and W. Buck Yearns, *Biographical Register of the Confederate Congress* (Baton Rouge: Louisiana State University Press, 1975); Thomas B. Alexander and Richard E. Beringer, *The Anatomy of the Confederate Congress: A Study of the Influences of Member Characteristics on Legislative Voting Behavior, 1861–1865* (Nashville: Vanderbilt University Press, 1972); Charles Robert Lee, *The Confederate Constitutions* (Chapel Hill: University of North Carolina Press, 1963).

bility for the southern public's loss of confidence in Jefferson Davis and the South's military leaders. Knowledge of the fire-eaters has been further increased by William K. Scarborough's two-volume edition of the diary of Edmund Ruffin (1972, 1976).[11]

Some of the important contributions to Civil War literature during the last twenty years have been state studies, studies of subregions of the South, and biographies of state leaders. May Spencer Ringold examined the state legislatures (1966), and William E. Parrish wrote an excellent monograph (1963) on the relations between Missouri and the Lincoln administration in wartime. Richard Orr Curry scrutinized West Virginia (1964) and disputed the popular view of that mountain area as overwhelmingly Unionist. Michael B. Dougan studied Arkansas during the war, emphasizing the frontier nature of that state (1976). Lowell H. Harrison produced a short study of Kentucky during the war (1975).[12]

As might be expected, a number of state studies resulted from the Civil War centennial. John E. Johns's description of wartime Florida (1963) is mainly concerned, of necessity, with nonmilitary developments. John D. Winters' excellent and unbiased monograph on the Civil War in Louisiana (1963) almost completely supersedes a previous work on the same subject by Jefferson D. Bragg (1941). John G. Barrett wrote an abundantly researched account of the war in North Carolina (1963), and this was followed by Memory F. Mitchell's study of the North Carolina Supreme Court's resistance to Confeder-

11. Clement Eaton, *Jefferson Davis: The Sphinx of the Confederacy* (New York: Free Press, 1977); Robert Penn Warren, *Jefferson Davis Gets His Citizenship Back* (Lexington: University Press of Kentucky, 1980); William C. Davis, *Breckinridge: Statesman, Soldier, Symbol* (Baton Rouge: Louisiana State University Press, 1974); Frank H. Heck, *Proud Kentuckian: John C. Breckinridge, 1821–1875* (Lexington: University Press of Kentucky, 1976); Ben H. Procter, *Not Without Honor: The Life of John H. Reagan* (Austin: University of Texas Press, 1962); Alvy L. King, *Louis T. Wigfall: Southern Fire-eater* (Baton Rouge: Louisiana State University Press, 1970); William Kauffman Scarborough (ed.), *The Diary of Edmund Ruffin*, Vol. I, *Toward Independence: October, 1856–April, 1861*, Vol. II, *The Years of Hope: April, 1861–June, 1863* (Baton Rouge: Louisiana State University Press, 1972, 1976).

12. May Spencer Ringold, *The Role of State Legislatures in the Confederacy* (Athens: University of Georgia Press, 1966); William E. Parrish, *Turbulent Partnership: Missouri and the Union, 1861–1865* (Columbia: University of Missouri Press, 1963); Richard Orr Curry, *A House Divided: A Study of Statehood Politics and the Copperhead Movement in West Virginia* (Pittsburgh: University of Pittsburgh Press, 1964); Michael B. Dougan, *Confederate Arkansas: The People and Policies of a Frontier State in Wartime* (University: University of Alabama Press, 1976); Lowell H. Harrison, *The Civil War in Kentucky* (Lexington: University Press of Kentucky, 1975).

ate conscription (1965). In 1964, James L. Nichols' monograph on the role of the quartermaster in the Trans-Mississippi Confederacy was published, and in 1972, Robert L. Kerby produced a well-organized and well-written history of the Confederacy west of the Mississippi.[13]

Jon L. Wakelyn's computerized *Biographical Dictionary of the Confederacy* (1977), though certainly not without fault, is a highly useful source of information on both political and military leaders. Frontis W. Johnston's work in editing the papers of Governor Zebulon Baird Vance of North Carolina (1963) provides information on how governors affected the course of the war. Vance is the subject of a biography by Glenn Tucker (1966). Vincent H. Cassidy and Amos E. Simpson, in their biography of Henry Watkins Allen (1964), demonstrated that Allen was an administrative genius who introduced what amounted to state socialism in order to keep that part of Louisiana still controlled by the Confederacy economically alive in 1864 and 1865. F. N. Boney's *John Letcher of Virginia* (1966) is another useful study of a Confederate governor. Joseph H. Parks has written the first full-length biography of the controversial Joseph E. Brown of Georgia (1977). Inasmuch as Brown's personal papers were destroyed not once but twice, this long and detailed work is a major accomplishment.[14]

The diplomatic history of the Civil War has received much attention during the two decades under review. It is only fair to state, how-

13. John E. Johns, *Florida During the Civil War* (Gainesville: University of Florida Press, 1963); John D. Winters, *The Civil War in Louisiana* (Baton Rouge: Louisiana State University Press, 1963); Jefferson D. Bragg, *Louisiana in the Confederacy* (Baton Rouge: Louisiana State University Press, 1941); John G. Barrett, *The Civil War in North Carolina* (Chapel Hill: University of North Carolina Press, 1963); Memory F. Mitchell, *Legal Aspects of Conscription and Exemption in North Carolina, 1861–1865* (Chapel Hill: University of North Carolina Press, 1965); James L. Nichols, *The Confederate Quartermaster in the Trans-Mississippi* (Austin: University of Texas Press, 1964); Robert L. Kerby, *Kirby Smith's Confederacy: The Trans-Mississippi South, 1863–1865* (New York: Columbia University Press, 1972).

14. Jon L. Wakelyn, *Biographical Dictionary of the Confederacy* (Westport, Conn.: Greenwood Press, 1977); Frontis W. Johnston (ed.), *The Papers of Zebulon Baird Vance*, Vol. I, *1843–1862* (Raleigh: State Department of Archives and History, 1963); Glenn Tucker, *Zeb Vance: Champion of Personal Freedom* (Indianapolis: Bobbs-Merrill, 1966); Vincent H. Cassidy and Amos E. Simpson, *Henry Watkins Allen of Louisiana* (Baton Rouge: Louisiana State University Press, 1964); F. N. Boney, *John Letcher of Virginia: The Story of Virginia's Civil War Governor* (University: University of Alabama Press, 1966); Joseph H. Parks, *Joseph E. Brown of Georgia* (Baton Rouge: Louisiana State University Press, 1977).

ever, that a student would do well to read Frank L. Owsley's *King Cotton Diplomacy* (1959) before turning to the works noted here. The Australian historian David P. Crook produced a complete and unbiased study aptly entitled *The North, the South, and the Powers, 1861–1865* (1974). An abridged version is available. Thomas David Schoonover's *Dollars Over Dominion* (1978) deals to a limited extent with Confederate relations with Mexico. A different form of diplomatic history, Harold M. Hyman's collection of reactions to and interpretations of the American Civil War by foreign leaders (1969) is an especially valuable addition to Civil War literature.[15]

Other works dealing with foreign affairs during the Civil War include Brian Jenkins' two-volume study of Great Britain and the war (1974, 1980). In the opinion of at least one reviewer, Jenkins' books are better on Confederate than on Union diplomacy. Jenkins suggested, among other things, that the failure of Great Britain to intervene in the struggle should be attributed primarily to the turmoil in Europe in the early 1860s. W. Stanley Hoole edited the wartime diary of Major Edward C. Anderson (1976), a Confederate agent in Europe. Finally, Charles P. Cullop produced a study of Confederate propaganda in France and England (1969) that concludes that Henry Hotze was by far the most successful southern propagandist.[16]

The economy of the Civil War South has received less attention than might be expected in this day of computerized studies. The books published have been the result primarily of conventional research and not of cliometrics. Angus James Johnston II's discussion of Virginia railroads appeared in 1961. A book of great value, Charles B. Dew's study of Joseph R. Anderson and the Tredegar Iron Works, appeared in 1966. Richard I. Lester's *Confederate Finance and Purchasing in Great Britain* (1975) is of importance and breaks new ground.

15. Frank L. Owsley, *King Cotton Diplomacy: Foreign Relations of the Confederate States of America* (2nd ed. rev.; Chicago: University of Chicago Press, 1959); David P. Crook, *The North, the South, and the Powers, 1861–1865* (New York: John Wiley & Sons, 1974), and *Diplomacy During the American Civil War* (New York: John Wiley & Sons, 1975); Thomas David Schoonover, *Dollars Over Dominion: The Triumph of Liberalism in Mexican–United States Relations, 1861–1867* (Baton Rouge: Louisiana State University Press, 1978); Harold M. Hyman (ed.), *Heard Round the World: The Impact Abroad of the Civil War* (New York: Knopf, 1969).

16. Brian A. Jenkins, *Britain and the War for the Union* (2 vols.; Montreal: McGill-Queens University Press, 1974, 1980); W. Stanley Hoole (ed.), *Confederate Foreign Agent: The European Diary of Major Edward C. Anderson* (University, Ala.: Confederate Publishing Co., 1976); Charles P. Cullop, *Confederate Propaganda in Europe, 1861–1865* (Coral Gables, Fla.: University of Miami Press, 1969).

Paul W. Gates's study of agriculture during the Civil War (1965), North and South, has special significance because it questions the more or less accepted belief that the South produced more food than it needed and that bad administration and bad communications alone kept Confederate soldiers hungry. It suggests that the South probably did not produce enough food to support a large army in the first place and that bad administration and faulty communications simply made a bad situation worse. Richard D. Goff's study *Confederate Supply* (1969) discusses the inefficiency of Confederate administration.[17]

Probably the most important source about the Confederate home front is C. Vann Woodward's edition (1981) of Mary Boykin Chesnut's "Diary from Dixie." This erstwhile primary source on Confederate Richmond, life behind the lines, and a woman's reaction to slavery and war has become a semi-secondary source, a literary effort by Chesnut based on a much briefer diary that she had kept during the war. Elisabeth Muhlenfeld's biography of Chesnut (1981) contributes to the understanding of this remarkable woman. Mary Elizabeth Massey made two signal contributions, *Refugee Life in the Confederacy* (1964) and *Bonnet Brigades* (1966). John Marszalek provided interesting information on life in Charleston and in the Carolina upcountry during the war in *The Diary of Miss Emma Holmes* (1979). Henry E. Sterkx's essays on Alabama women during the war (1970) are worth reading, and Bell I. Wiley's *Confederate Women* (1975), though it concentrates mainly on upper-class women, is nonetheless valuable. William J. Kimball's *Starve or Fall* (1976) is a history of Richmond and its people during the war years. Emory M. Thomas' *The Confederate State of Richmond* (1971) is a valuable work. Robert Manson Myers' edition of the letters of the Charles Colcott Jones family of Georgia (1972) before, during, and to some extent after the war is probably the most useful work on life behind the lines published in the last twenty years.[18]

17. Angus James Johnston II, *Virginia Railroads in the Civil War* (Chapel Hill: University of North Carolina Press, 1961); Charles B. Dew, *Ironmaker to the Confederacy: Joseph R. Anderson and the Tredegar Iron Works* (New Haven: Yale University Press, 1966); Richard I. Lester, *Confederate Finance and Purchasing in Great Britain* (Charlottesville: University Press of Virginia, 1975); Paul W. Gates, *Agriculture and the Civil War* (New York: Knopf, 1965); Richard D. Goff, *Confederate Supply* (Durham: Duke University Press, 1969).

18. C. Vann Woodward (ed.), *Mary Chesnut's Civil War* (New Haven: Yale University Press, 1981); Elisabeth Muhlenfeld, *Mary Boykin Chesnut: A Biography* (Baton

Some monographs on the Civil War do not fit into any convenient category, and yet they may be more valuable than many of those that do. J. Cutler Andrews' *The South Reports the Civil War* (1970) is the best book yet available on Confederate journalism. William C. Davis has produced the first two volumes (1981, 1982) of a projected six-volume pictorial history that will bear the overall title *The Image of War*. Ovid L. Futch's *History of Andersonville Prison* (1968) received high praise from professional reviewers. Paul E. Steiner's study of disease in the Civil War (1968) is a highly original work that opens a vital area to further research. Larry E. Nelson's *Bullets, Ballots, and Rhetoric* (1980) is a well-researched and well-written study of Confederate attempts to influence the United States election of 1864. Robert F. Durden's *The Gray and the Black* (1972) tells of the Confederate debate over emancipation in the last desperate days of the war. Gerald M. Capers' account of New Orleans under Federal occupation (1965) is a unique and valuable contribution to American history. Last, but not least, E. B. Long and Barbara Long have compiled a Civil War almanac (1971), a chronology of events that can be extremely useful.[19]

Rouge: Louisiana State University Press, 1981); Mary Elizabeth Massey, *Refugee Life in the Confederacy* (Baton Rouge: Louisiana State University Press, 1964), and *Bonnet Brigades* (New York: Knopf, 1966); John F. Marszalek (ed.), *The Diary of Miss Emma Holmes, 1861–1866* (Baton Rouge: Louisiana State University Press, 1979); Henry E. Sterkx, *Partners in Rebellion: Alabama Women in the Civil War* (Rutherford, N.J.: Fairleigh Dickinson University Press, 1970); Bell I. Wiley, *Confederate Women* (Westport, Conn.: Greenwood Press, 1975); William J. Kimball, *Starve or Fall: Richmond and Its People, 1861–1865* (Ann Arbor: University Microfilms International, 1976); Emory M. Thomas, *The Confederate State of Richmond: A Biography of the Capital* (Austin: University of Texas Press, 1971); Robert Manson Myers (ed.), *The Children of Pride: A True Story of Georgia and the Civil War* (New Haven: Yale University Press, 1972).

19. J. Cutler Andrews, *The South Reports the Civil War* (Princeton: Princeton University Press, 1970); William C. Davis (ed.), *The Image of War*, Vol. I, *Shadows of the Storm*, Vol. II, *The Guns of '62* (Garden City, N.Y.: Doubleday, 1981, 1982); Ovid L. Futch, *History of Andersonville Prison* (Gainesville: University of Florida Press, 1968); Paul E. Steiner, *Disease in the Civil War: Natural Biological Warfare in 1861–1865* (Springfield, Ill.: Charles C. Thomas, 1968); Larry E. Nelson, *Bullets, Ballots, and Rhetoric: Confederate Policy for the United States Presidential Contest of 1864* (University: University of Alabama Press, 1980); Robert F. Durden, *The Gray and the Black: The Confederate Debate on Emancipation* (Baton Rouge: Louisiana State University Press, 1972); Gerald M. Capers, *Occupied City: New Orleans Under the Federals, 1862–1865* (Lexington: University of Kentucky Press, 1965); E. B. Long with Barbara Long, *The Civil War Day by Day: An Almanac, 1861–1865* (Garden City, N.Y.: Doubleday, 1971).

David Donald's revision of James G. Randall's *The Civil War and Reconstruction* appeared in 1961. Despite attempts to supersede it, the book remains to this day an excellent beginning point for the study of the Civil War and its aftermath. It is revisionist in the traditional sense, but as revised it does not assert that the Civil War should have been avoided, or even that it could have been avoided. It remains balanced and objective throughout. Robert H. Jones's *Disrupted Decades* (1973) is a satisfactory synthesis basically designed for undergraduates. Peter J. Parrish's *The American Civil War* (1975) treats slavery as the central cause of the war and is highly critical of Confederate military leadership, Jefferson Davis, and Andrew Johnson. James McPherson's *Ordeal by Fire* (1982) is a new work that may rival Randall and Donald, especially in its treatment of the Reconstruction period. It undoubtedly reflects the writing of the last twenty years better than does the older work.[20]

It is interesting, especially in view of the great influence that the civil rights movement has had on Civil War historiography, that the antiwar movement that was almost exactly contemporaneous should have had so little influence. Edmund Wilson presented a Copperhead anti–United States point of view in his *Patriotic Gore* (1962), but this book may have reflected the eminent critic's disputes with the Internal Revenue Service as much as his study of the Civil War. John S. Rosenberg asserted in 1969 that the benefits that came to the freedmen as a result of the Civil War were simply not worth 600,000 lives. This led to a spirited exchange between Rosenberg and Phillip S. Paludan in the pages of *Civil War History* (1974–1975) but apparently to nothing else.[21]

The last volume of Bruce Catton's *The Centennial History of the Civil War* was completed in 1965, well within the period under re-

20. J. G. Randall and David Donald, *The Civil War and Reconstruction* (Boston: Heath, 1961); Robert H. Jones, *Disrupted Decades: The Civil War and Reconstruction Years* (New York: Charles Scribner's Sons, 1973); Peter J. Parrish, *The American Civil War* (New York: Holmes & Meier, 1975); James M. McPherson, *Ordeal by Fire: The Civil War and Reconstruction* (New York: Knopf, 1982).

21. Edmund Wilson, *Patriotic Gore: Studies in the Literature of the American Civil War* (New York: Oxford University Press, 1962); John S. Rosenberg, "Toward a New Civil War Revisionism," *American Scholar*, XXXVIII (Spring, 1969), 250–72; Phillip S. Paludan, "The American Civil War: Triumph through Tragedy," *Civil War History*, XX (September, 1974), 239–50; Rosenberg, "The American Civil War and the Problem of 'Presentism': A Reply to Phillip S. Paludan," *Civil War History*, XXI (September, 1975), 242–53; Paludan, "Taking the Benefits of the Civil War Issue Seriously: A Rejoinder to John S. Rosenberg," *Civil War History*, XXI (September, 1975), 254–60.

view, and is a major contribution to American historical writing. The completion of Shelby Foote's three-volume work (1958, 1963, 1974) on the struggle was another literary milestone. The overall subtitle of Foote's work is *A Narrative,* and that is exactly what he wrote. He gave ample attention to strategy and tactics and enough to politics and the home front, but he did not attempt a lengthy analysis of what caused the war, why the South lost, or what might have happened if half a dozen or more things had been different. Foote is a successful novelist, and his history is as gripping and as hard to put down as a good novel.[22]

The posthumous publication (1971) of the last two volumes of Allan Nevins' eight-volume history of the United States from 1847 to 1865 was a momentous event in United States history. As Robert W. Johannsen stated in his lengthy review in the *Journal of American History* (1972), Nevins has often been compared to James Ford Rhodes, but his work "exceeds Rhodes in the quality of his interpretation and in the sweep of his narrative." Furthermore, "his volumes are a strong reminder that the task of the historian is, after all, to tell a story."[23] In the long run, Nevins may be remembered most for the richness of detail, social, political, economic, and military, in his account of a period that he looked on as a triumph of healthy nationalism. It must be noted here that he looked at the Civil War with a northern and Unionist point of view.

Civil War strategy receives attention in many of the works already mentioned, and especially in the volumes by Foote and Nevins. John T. Hubbell edited a collection of articles on Civil War strategy and tactics (1975), and in 1961, *Confederate Strategy from Shiloh to Vicksburg* by Archer Jones was published. Later Jones joined with Thomas Lawrence Connelly to produce *The Politics of Command* (1973), a perceptive analysis of southern strategy. These authors gave Jefferson Davis credit for a successful early strategy in the West, and they wrote that Robert E. Lee's pro-Virginia influence on Davis had

22. Bruce Catton, *Never Call Retreat* (New York: Doubleday, 1965), vol. III of *The Centennial History of the Civil War;* Shelby Foote, *The Civil War: A Narrative,* Vol. I, *Fort Sumter to Perryville,* Vol. II, *Fredericksburg to Meridian,* Vol. III, *Red River to Appomattox* (New York: Random House, 1958, 1963, 1974).

23. Allan Nevins, *The War for the Union,* Vol. III, *The Organized War, 1863– 1864,* Vol. IV, *The Organized War to Victory, 1864–1865* (New York: Charles Scribner's Sons, 1971); Robert W. Johannsen, Review of Nevins' *The War for the Union,* III, IV, in *Journal of American History,* LIX (September, 1972), 426–32 (quotations on pp. 430, 431).

to be countered by western leaders. Michael C. C. Adams' *Our Masters the Rebels* (1978) is not a study of strategy, but it advances the interesting thesis that the Union generals in the East, before Grant, were overcome, not by strategy or tactics, but by the "mystique" of the victorious Army of Northern Virginia. In a recent and intriguing volume, *Attack and Die* (1982), Grady McWhiney and Perry D. Jamieson asserted that Confederate leaders were so imbued with the doctrine of the offensive, derived from the Mexican War experience and directly or indirectly from the writings of Baron Antoine Henri Jomini, that they bled the South to death in useless and strategically unnecessary offensives, attacks, and counterattacks. The last chapters of this work suggest that this suicidal bent toward the offensive was in part a result of the Celtic background of most white southerners.[24]

Thomas Lawrence Connelly, mentioned above, made a major addition to Civil War history with his two-volume history of the Army of Tennessee (1967, 1971), a work that completely supersedes Stanley F. Horn's *Army of Tennessee* (1941), published more than forty years ago. Connelly did prodigious research, and it is unlikely that any significant additional information concerning this army will become available in the future. If Connelly is vulnerable to criticism, it is because of his almost totally negative attitude. He has almost nothing good to say about Braxton Bragg, Joseph E. Johnston, John B. Hood, or any of their most important subordinates.[25]

Histories of battles and campaigns are abundant. Among useful books on the war in the West is James J. Hamilton's study of the Battle of Fort Donelson (1968), that early manifestation of U. S. Grant's pugnacity and determination. Wiley Sword's account of the bloody two days at Shiloh (1974) has been well received, but it can be con-

---

24. John T. Hubbell (ed.), *Battles Lost and Won: Essays from Civil War History* (Westport, Conn.: Greenwood Press, 1975); Archer Jones, *Confederate Strategy from Shiloh to Vicksburg* (Baton Rouge: Louisiana State University Press, 1961); Thomas Lawrence Connelly and Archer Jones, *The Politics of Command: Factions and Ideas in Confederate Strategy* (Baton Rouge: Louisiana State University Press, 1973); Michael C. C. Adams, *Our Masters the Rebels: A Speculation on Union Military Failure in the East* (Cambridge: Harvard University Press, 1978); Grady McWhiney and Perry D. Jamieson, *Attack and Die: Civil War Military Tactics and the Southern Heritage* (University: University of Alabama Press, 1982).

25. Thomas Lawrence Connelly, *Army of the Heartland: The Army of Tennessee, 1861–1862* (Baton Rouge: Louisiana State University Press, 1967), and *Autumn of Glory: The Army of Tennessee, 1862–1865* (Baton Rouge: Louisiana State University Press, 1971); Stanley F. Horn, *The Army of Tennessee: A Military History* (Indianapolis: Bobbs-Merrill, 1941).

fusing for the careless reader. James Lee McDonough has written *Shiloh: In Hell Before Night* (1968) and an excellent narrative of the Battle of Murfreesboro (1980). Two new books deal with Vicksburg, one a collection of contemporary accounts edited by Richard Wheeler (1978), the other Samuel Carter III's *The Final Fortress* (1980). Edwin C. Bearss, in *Forrest at Brice's Cross Roads* (1979), dared to be critical of the "swift and terrible" Nathan Bedford Forrest. Samuel Carter also produced a book on the siege of Atlanta (1973). Sherman's march has attracted the attention of two historians—Burke Davis, with a popular account (1980), and Richard Wheeler, who edited *Sherman's March* (1978). James Pickett Jones's story of Wilson's cavalry raid through Alabama and Georgia (1976) is probably the last account of that operation that will be needed. Finally, Marion B. Lucas has almost certainly said the last scholarly word on that controversial subject, the burning of Columbia after its occupation by Sherman (1976).[26]

As in the past, the East received more attention than the West. William C. Davis prepared a highly readable history of the first Bull Run campaign (1977). Joseph P. Cullen's story of the peninsula campaign (1973) is equally readable, but it provides no new information or interpretations. Robert G. Tanner described Stonewall Jackson's marches and battles in the Shenandoah Valley (1976), and in *The Gleam of Bayonets* (1965), James V. Murfin told of that bloody September day at Antietam. Gettysburg, as might be expected, received more attention than did any other engagement. Warren W. Hassler, Jr., wrote on the first day at Gettysburg (1970); William A. Frassanito studied the photographs taken during the three days (1975); James Warner Bellah wrote a conventional study of the battle (1962); Ed-

26. James J. Hamilton, *The Battle of Fort Donelson* (New York: Thomas Yoseloff, 1968); Wiley Sword, *Shiloh: Bloody April* (New York: Morrow, 1974); James Lee McDonough, *Shiloh: In Hell Before Night* (Knoxville: University of Tennessee Press, 1968), and *Stones River: Bloody Winter in Tennessee* (Knoxville: University of Tennessee Press, 1980); Richard Wheeler (ed.), *The Siege of Vicksburg* (New York: Thomas Y. Crowell, 1978); Samuel Carter III, *The Final Fortress: The Campaign for Vicksburg* (New York: St. Martin's Press, 1980); Edwin C. Bearss, *Forrest at Brice's Cross Roads and in North Mississippi in 1864* (Dayton, Ohio: Press of Morningside Bookshop, 1979); Samuel Carter III, *The Siege of Atlanta* (New York: St. Martin's Press, 1973); Burke Davis, *Sherman's March* (New York: Random House, 1980); Richard Wheeler (ed.), *Sherman's March: An Eyewitness History* (New York: Thomas Y. Crowell, 1978); James Pickett Jones, *Yankee Blitzkrieg: Wilson's Raid Through Alabama and Georgia* (Athens: University of Georgia Press, 1976); Marion B. Lucas, *Sherman and the Burning of Columbia*, foreword by Bell I. Wiley (College Station: Texas A&M University Press, 1976).

win B. Coddington used the campaign as a setting for a study in command (1968). This last monograph is in great detail and is especially useful as a reference. Three other battle or campaign histories worth noting are William C. Davis' story of the Battle of New Market (1975), Marshall Moore Brice's account of the Union conquest of the Shenandoah Valley (1965), and Richard J. Sommers' somewhat misleadingly titled *Richmond Redeemed* (1981), dealing with the siege of Petersburg. Benjamin Franklin Cooling told of the defense of Washington throughout the war (1975), and E. Milby Burton described the siege of Charleston (1970).[27]

The cavalry in the Civil War received attention in addition to Jones's *Yankee Blitzkrieg* and Bearss's *Forrest at Brice's Cross Roads.* Samuel Carter III's *The Last Cavaliers* (1979) is a popular account of the mounted army of both sides. Edward G. Longacre's *Mounted Raids of the Civil War* (1975) received good reviews. Stephen Z. Starr has published two volumes (1979, 1981) of a projected three-volume history of the Union cavalry. This work promises to be the definitive history of the subject.[28]

The last two decades have seen a number of new books on Confed-

27. William C. Davis, *Battle at Bull Run: A History of the First Major Campaign of the Civil War* (Garden City, N.Y.: Doubleday, 1977); Joseph P. Cullen, *The Peninsula Campaign, 1862: McClellan and Lee Struggle for Richmond* (Harrisburg, Pa.: Stackpole Books, 1973); Robert G. Tanner, *Stonewall in the Valley: Thomas J. "Stonewall" Jackson's Shenandoah Valley Campaign, Spring 1862* (Garden City, N.Y.: Doubleday, 1976); James V. Murfin, *The Gleam of Bayonets: The Battle of Antietam and the Maryland Campaign of 1862* (New York: Thomas Yoseloff, 1965); Warren W. Hassler, Jr., *Crisis at the Crossroads: The First Day at Gettysburg* (University: University of Alabama Press, 1970); William A. Frassanito, *Gettysburg: A Journey in Time* (New York: Charles Scribner's Sons, 1975); James Warner Bellah, *Soldier's Battle: Gettysburg* (New York: David McKay, 1962); Edwin B. Coddington, *The Gettysburg Campaign: A Study in Command* (New York: Charles Scribner's Sons, 1968); William C. Davis, *The Battle of New Market* (Garden City, N.Y.: Doubleday, 1975); Marshall Moore Brice, *Conquest of a Valley* (Charlottesville: University Press of Virginia, 1965); Richard J. Sommers, *Richmond Redeemed: The Siege at Petersburg* (Garden City, N.Y.: Doubleday, 1981); Benjamin Franklin Cooling, *Symbol, Sword, and Shield: Defending Washington During the Civil War* (Hamden, Conn.: Archon Books, 1975); E. Milby Burton, *The Siege of Charleston, 1861–1865* (Columbia: University of South Carolina Press, 1970).

28. Samuel Carter III, *The Last Cavaliers and Union Cavalry in the Civil War* (New York: St. Martin's Press, 1979); Edward G. Longacre, *Mounted Raids of the Civil War* (South Brunswick, N.J.: A. S. Barnes & Co., 1975); Stephen Z. Starr, *The Union Cavalry in the Civil War*, Vol. I, *From Fort Sumter to Gettysburg, 1861–1863*, Vol. II, *The War in the East, from Gettysburg to Appomattox, 1863–1865* (Baton Rouge: Louisiana State University Press, 1979, 1981). Volume III, *The War in the West, 1861–1865*, was published in 1985.

erate naval topics. Myron J. Smith compiled a bibliography of sources (1972), and the United States Department of the Navy provided a chronology of Civil War naval events (1971). Howard P. Nash wrote a relatively brief naval history (1972). Tom Henderson Wells's posthumous *The Confederate Navy: A Study in Organization* (1971) is exactly what the title says and not in any sense a history of naval operations. Wells's book received mixed reviews; it differs from previous studies in that it is rather critical of Confederate Secretary of the Navy Stephen R. Mallory. James M. Merrill wrote *Battle Flags South* (1970), a study of naval action on western rivers. Frank J. Merli's *Great Britain and the Confederate Navy* (1970) is a thorough study of British policy toward the southern navy.[29]

Two historians have written new accounts of the prophetic battle between the *Merrimac* and the *Monitor*. William C. Davis' *Duel Between the First Ironclads* (1975) offered a history of the two ships as well as an account of the battle, and A. A. Hoehling, in *Thunder at Hampton Roads* (1976), presented a popular account. David R. Smith compiled a bibliography (1968) on this one naval encounter. Confederate armored ships as a whole are the subject of Maurice Melton's *The Confederate Ironclads* (1968) and of William N. Still, Jr.'s *Iron Afloat* (1971). Still asserted that armored Rebel ships made a much more important contribution to naval operations than some previous histories have indicated. Notice must also be taken of Milton F. Perry's history of Confederate mine and submarine warfare (1965). At least five new books deal with Confederate raiders, and they present new details of raider operations, but it is doubtful that they necessitate any significant change in estimates of the raiders' overall effectiveness.[30]

29. Myron J. Smith, *American Civil War Navies: A Bibliography* (New York: Scarecrow Press, 1972); United States Department of the Navy, Naval Historical Division, *Civil War Naval Chronology, 1861–1865* (Washington, D.C.: U.S. Government Printing Office, 1971); Howard P. Nash, *A Naval History of the Civil War* (South Brunswick, N.J.: A. S. Barnes & Co., 1972); Tom Henderson Wells, *The Confederate Navy: A Study in Organization* (University: University of Alabama Press, 1971); James M. Merrill, *Battle Flags South: The Story of the Civil War Navies on Western Waters* (Rutherford, N.J.: Fairleigh Dickinson University Press, 1970); Frank J. Merli, *Great Britain and the Confederate Navy, 1861–1865* (Bloomington: Indiana University Press, 1970).

30. William C. Davis, *Duel Between the First Ironclads* (Garden City, N.Y.: Doubleday, 1975); A. A. Hoehling, *Thunder at Hampton Roads* (Englewood Cliffs, N.J.: Prentice-Hall, 1976); David R. Smith, *The Monitor & the Merrimac: A Bibliography* (Los Angeles: University of Southern California Library, 1968); Maurice

Another noticeable feature of Civil War history over the last twenty years has been the appearance of a large number of biographical works, some of which have been noted earlier. Undoubtedly Thomas L. Connelly's *The Marble Man* (1977) is the most controversial biography. Connelly attempted a limited and somewhat unfavorable psychological analysis of Robert E. Lee, but in the main his book is a study in mythmaking. The author maintained that during and after the Civil War, Lee's staff and other Virginians deliberately built up the image of an almost superhuman Lee and emphasized Lee and the war in Virginia at the expense of other leaders and other areas of warfare. Peter Earle wrote a biography of Lee for the general reader (1974), as did Clifford Dowdey (1965). Marshall W. Fishwick recounted Lee's life after the war (1963), as did Charles B. Flood in a more recent work (1981). Finally, Charles P. Roland defended Lee (1964) against scholarly detractors and heaped high praise upon him. The only other significant biography of an eastern leader is John Selby's study of Stonewall Jackson's military career (1968), and it is probably inferior to G. F. R. Henderson's, Lenoir Chambers', and Frank E. Vandiver's work on the same subject.[31]

Melton, *The Confederate Ironclads* (South Brunswick, N.J.: Thomas Yoseloff, 1968); William N. Still, Jr., *Iron Afloat: The Story of the Confederate Armorclads* (Nashville: Vanderbilt University Press, 1971); Milton F. Perry, *Infernal Machines: The Story of Confederate Submarine and Mine Warfare* (Baton Rouge: Louisiana State University Press, 1965); Charles G. Summersell, *The Cruise of C.S.S. Sumter* (Tuscaloosa, Ala.: Confederate Publishing Co., 1965); Norman C. Delaney, *John McIntosh Kell of the Raider Alabama* (University: University of Alabama Press, 1973); Royce G. Shingleton, *John Taylor Wood: Sea Ghost of the Confederacy* (Athens: University of Georgia Press, 1977); William Stanley Hoole, *Four Years in the Confederate Navy: The Career of Captain John Low on the C.S.S. Fingal, Florida, Alabama, Tuscaloosa, and Ajax* (Athens: University of Georgia Press, 1964); Charles G. Summersell (ed.), *The Journal of George Townley Fullam: Boarding Officer of the Confederate Sea Raider Alabama* (University: University of Alabama Press, 1973).

31. Thomas L. Connelly, *The Marble Man: Robert E. Lee and His Image in American Society* (New York: Knopf, 1977); Peter Earle, *Robert E. Lee* (New York: Saturday Review Press, 1974); Clifford Dowdey, *Lee* (Boston: Little, Brown, 1965); Marshall W. Fishwick, *Lee After the War* (New York: Dodd, Mead, 1963); Charles B. Flood, *Lee: The Last Years* (Boston: Houghton Mifflin, 1981); Bruce Catton *et al.*, *Grant, Lee, Lincoln, and the Radicals: Essays on Civil War Leadership*, ed. Grady McWhiney (Evanston, Ill.: Northwestern University Press, 1964); John M. Selby, *Stonewall Jackson as Military Commander* (London: B. T. Batsford Ltd.; Princeton: Van Nostrand, 1968); G. F. R. Henderson, *Stonewall Jackson and the American Civil War* (London and New York: Longmans, 1937); Lenoir Chambers, *Stonewall Jackson* (2 vols.; New York: Morrow, 1959); Frank E. Vandiver, *Mighty Stonewall* (New York: McGraw-Hill, 1957).

Symptomatic of increased interest in the western Confederacy is
the appearance of a number of biographies of leaders in that area.
John Bell Hood, the subject of a book by Richard M. McMurry
(1982), served both in the East and in the West. Charles P. Roland
wrote an excellent biography of Albert Sidney Johnston (1964),
which, of necessity, pays more attention to Johnston's earlier years than
to his brief Civil War career. Howell Purdue and Elizabeth Purdue
wrote on Patrick Cleburne (1973), and Nathaniel Cheairs Hughes, Jr.,
on General William J. Hardee (1965). Herman Hattaway produced a
good life of General Stephen D. Lee (1976), who had a distinguished
postwar career. Another good and probably definitive biography is
Robert G. Hartje's treatment of General Earl Van Dorn (1967). Although Sterling Price was hardly a major figure, he has been the subject of two biographies, one by Albert Castel in 1968, the other by
Robert E. Shalhope in 1971. Grady McWhiney's first volume on
Braxton Bragg (1969) was a fine piece of work that makes one wonder when and if the second volume will appear.[32]

What trends can be detected in Civil War historiography over the
last two decades? Obviously, interest in the conflict remains strong
among historians and the reading public. As the number of books
dealing with the subject increases, and by now the number must be in
the tens of thousands, historians tend to write about smaller and
smaller segments, but the interest is still there. The antiwar movement of the 1960s seems to have had no effect at all on the fascination this bloodiest of all American wars has for Americans. The
American Epic seems an ever more justified description. Even though
it is agreed now that the purpose of the war, intentional or not, was
to free the slaves, the officers and men of the Confederate armies have

---

32. Richard M. McMurry, *John Bell Hood and the War for Southern Independence*
(Lexington: University Press of Kentucky, 1982); Charles P. Roland, *Albert Sidney
Johnston: Soldier of Three Republics* (Austin: University of Texas Press, 1964); Howell
Purdue and Elizabeth Purdue, *Patrick Cleburne: Confederate General* (Hillsboro, Tex.:
Hill Junior College Press, 1973); Nathaniel Cheairs Hughes, Jr., *General William J.
Hardee: Old Reliable* (Baton Rouge: Louisiana State University Press, 1965); Herman
Hattaway, *General Stephen D. Lee* (Jackson: University Press of Mississippi, 1976);
Robert G. Hartje, *Van Dorn: The Life and Times of a Confederate General* (Nashville:
Vanderbilt University Press, 1967); Albert E. Castel, *General Sterling Price and the
Civil War in the West* (Baton Rouge: Louisiana State University Press, 1968); Robert E.
Shalhope, *Sterling Price: Portrait of a Southerner* (Columbia: University of Missouri
Press, 1971); Grady McWhiney, *Braxton Bragg and Confederate Defeat*, Vol. I, *Field
Command* (New York: Columbia University Press, 1969).

somehow managed to escape identification with a bad cause. The men contending on both sides were heroes all.

Interest in the West has increased, but one wonders if this did not result to a considerable degree from the fact that more topics in the West were available to aspiring historians. Previous scholarly generations had searched the East rather thoroughly. One other notable fact is that the application of cliometrics to the Civil War has been slight.

One possible historiographical trend exists, but it is too early to define it precisely. In 1976, John Keegan of the Royal Military College, Sandhurst, published *The Face of Battle,* an essay on military historiography and an examination of three battles from the point of view of British participants. It is Keegan's contention, somewhat oversimplified here, that the study of military history from the perspective of the individual and the small unit will tell more about the "face of battle" than do conventional studies of command, strategy, and tactics. He chooses to call this the "inquisitorial approach," and this method certainly brings his narratives to life.[33]

Bell I. Wiley, in his studies of the private soldier North and South, was interested in their motivations and their reactions to battle as well as other aspects of their lives. Both Bruce Catton and Shelby Foote let the individual soldier speak often in their narratives, so it might be said that a beginning has been made in this direction. Marvin R. Cain called for more of this approach in "A 'Face of Battle' Needed," an article published in *Civil War History* early in 1982. If there is such a trend, it should become apparent during the next twenty years.[34]

Limiting this essay to the "white South" becomes something of a handicap in dealing with the events that followed the war. Some of the most significant publications concerning Reconstruction over the last twenty years have been devoted to the black South. These are discussed elsewhere in this volume. Even so, the black South and the white South were often inseparable. What one historian has called "the new orthodoxy" of Reconstruction history is the contention

33. John Keegan, *The Face of Battle* (New York: Viking, 1976).
34. Bell I. Wiley, *The Life of Johnny Reb: The Common Soldier of the Confederacy* (Indianapolis: Bobbs-Merrill, 1943), and *The Life of Billy Yank: The Common Soldier of the Union* (Indianapolis: Bobbs-Merrill, 1952); Catton, *The Centennial History of the Civil War;* Foote, *The Civil War;* Marvin R. Cain, "A 'Face of Battle' Needed: An Assessment of Motives and Men in Civil War Historiography," *Civil War History,* XXVIII (March, 1982), 5–27.

that the great failure of the Civil War was that the victors did not break up the plantations and distribute the land among the freed-men.[35] Obviously such an idea cannot be ignored here because it is primarily concerned with black people. The land that presumably should have been redistributed belonged, after all, to southern whites. Attention will be given here, also, to some aspects of the historiography of Reconstruction from the national point of view, because events in the South did not take place in a vacuum.

No centennial of Reconstruction was ever proclaimed, but the last two decades have seen a great outpouring of articles and monographs on the years that followed the Civil War. Undoubtedly the "second Reconstruction" of the 1950s and 1960s aroused an interest in the first. In some cases, the attitude of historians toward the civil rights movement was probably influential in determining their attitude toward events of the 1860s and 1870s. This is certainly not surprising, but neither should it be ignored.

In 1947, E. Merton Coulter published *The South During Reconstruction*, a book crammed with information but unhesitating in its adherence to the Dunning school of Reconstruction historiography, disapproving of Radical Republicans North and South, siding with President Andrew Johnson, and generally asserting the views that white southerners began to proclaim even while Reconstruction was in progress. The real significance of Coulter's volume is not so much what he said but that it was the last major work on Reconstruction to set forth that particular point of view.[36]

Another approach to Reconstruction once much in vogue was the non-Marxist economic determinism typified by the views of Howard K. Beale. These ideas are probably best expressed in Beale's 1930 work, *The Critical Year: A Study of Andrew Johnson and Reconstruction*. Whereas historians of the Dunning school believed that northern Radical leaders were motivated by a desire to punish the South and to maintain the dominance of the Republican party, Beale believed that their primary motivation was economic interest—their own and their constituents'. Both groups of historians identified Andrew Johnson with the forces of light and the Radicals with the forces of darkness.[37] During the last two decades, neither the Dun-

---

35. Herman Belz, "The New Orthodoxy in Reconstruction Historiography," *Reviews in American History*, I (March, 1973), 106–13.

36. E. Merton Coulter, *The South During Reconstruction, 1865–1877* (Baton Rouge: Louisiana State University Press, 1947).

37. Howard K. Beale, *The Critical Year: A Study of Andrew Johnson and Recon-*

ning nor the Beale approach to Reconstruction has had any significant support.

Revisionism is a word so overworked that it is in danger of becoming meaningless. It is used here to mean an approach to Reconstruction history that does not automatically assume that the Radicals
were wicked, that the Radical state governments in the South were
corrupt and extravagant beyond compare, and that Andrew Johnson
was a man of principle resisting the attacks of rascals. Revisionism
might be said to have begun with W. E. B. Du Bois, who read a paper,
"Reconstruction and Its Benefits," before the American Historical
Association in 1909. In 1922, John R. Lynch, a black participant in
Mississippi Reconstruction, published *Some Historical Errors of
James Ford Rhodes,* arguing that the picture of black Republicans in
the Reconstruction South presented by Rhodes was inaccurate and
unfair. In 1932, Francis B. Simkins and Robert H. Woody published
South Carolina During Reconstruction, challenging some of the veri-
ties of the Dunning school. Six years later, Simkins read "New Viewpoints of Southern Reconstruction" before the Southern Historical
Association, demanding an explanation of the events of Reconstruction based on some ground other than black racial inferiority. In
1935, already embittered and a convert to Marxism, Du Bois published his *Black Reconstruction,* as much polemic as history, which
called attention to many existing errors of interpretation and fact
concerning the role of blacks during Reconstruction. Beale's "On Rewriting Reconstruction History" went even farther than Simkins'
paper in declaring that earlier accounts of Reconstruction were at
best grossly oversimplified and in demanding new and unbiased studies. These and other early works on Reconstruction are discussed in
Vernon L. Wharton's pathbreaking essay in Arthur S. Link and Rembert W. Patrick (eds.), *Writing Southern History* (1965).[38]

---

struction (New York: Harcourt, Brace, 1930). See also Beale, "On Rewriting Reconstruction History," *American Historical Review,* XLV (July, 1940), 807–27.

38. W. E. Burghardt Du Bois, "Reconstruction and Its Benefits," *American Histori-
cal Review,* XV (July, 1910), 781–99; John R. Lynch, *Some Historical Errors of James
Ford Rhodes* (New York: Cornhill Publishing Co., 1922); Francis B. Simkins and
Robert H. Woody, *South Carolina During Reconstruction* (Chapel Hill: University of
North Carolina Press, 1932); Simkins, "New Viewpoints of Southern Reconstruc-
tion," *Journal of Southern History,* V (February, 1939), 49–61; W. E. Burghardt Du
Bois, *Black Reconstruction: An Essay Toward a History of the Part Which Black Folk
Played in the Attempt to Reconstruct Democracy in America, 1860–1880* (New York:
Harcourt, Brace, 1935); Beale, "On Rewriting Reconstruction History"; Vernon L.
Wharton, "Reconstruction," in Arthur S. Link and Rembert W. Patrick (eds.), *Writing

For whatever reasons, there was little response to these demands for new approaches until the last twenty or twenty-five years. J. G. Randall's *The Civil War and Reconstruction* (1937) was the text in most graduate and undergraduate classes, and it fully reflected traditional attitudes. After Randall's death, this text was thoroughly revised by David Donald (1961) and included new points of view in the discussion of Reconstruction. By this time, however, historians had broken out of conventional approaches and revisionist Reconstruction history was on its way.[39]

In the 1960s, four new overall accounts of Reconstruction were published. The first was John Hope Franklin's *Reconstruction After the Civil War*, published in 1961. Franklin's work was thoroughly revisionist, but perhaps because it was brief and undocumented or perhaps because Franklin was black, it had little impact. The same could not be said of Kenneth M. Stampp's *The Era of Reconstruction*, which came out in 1965. Stampp had already made it clear in *The Peculiar Institution* (1956) that he rejected the prevailing view of black inferiority. He said that he regarded Negroes as white men in black skins, for which some blacks criticized him in the 1960s. Naturally his treatment of Reconstruction was revisionist, and it set the stage for works to follow. Rembert Patrick's *The Reconstruction of the Nation* (1967) was likewise revisionist, but Patrick saw Andrew Johnson as a principled Jeffersonian rather than as a villain. Equally revisionist was Avery Craven's *Reconstruction: The Ending of the Civil War* (1969), but it added little if anything to the works of Franklin, Stampp, and Patrick. The same can be said of Jones's *Disrupted Decades*. McPherson's *Ordeal by Fire*, a definite synthesis, is nonetheless revisionist in its treatment of Reconstruction.[40]

In 1906 and 1907, Walter Lynwood Fleming brought out the two-volume *Documentary History of Reconstruction*. Fleming was anti-northern, anti-Radical, and anti-Negro. In an earlier work he had

---

Southern History: Essays in Historiography in Honor of Fletcher M. Green (Baton Rouge: Louisiana State University Press, 1965), 295–315.

39. J. G. Randall, *The Civil War and Reconstruction* (Boston: Heath, 1937); Randall and Donald, *The Civil War and Reconstruction.*

40. John Hope Franklin, *Reconstruction After the Civil War* (Chicago: University of Chicago Press, 1961); Kenneth M. Stampp, *The Era of Reconstruction, 1865–1877* (New York: Knopf, 1965), and *The Peculiar Institution: Slavery in the Antebellum South* (New York: Knopf, 1956); Rembert W. Patrick, *The Reconstruction of the Nation* (New York: Oxford University Press, 1967); Avery O. Craven, *Reconstruction: The Ending of the Civil War* (New York: Holt, Rinehart & Winston, 1969).

demonstrated "lack of sympathy for . . . the Negro," had emphasized black "ignorance, irresponsibility, and criminality," and had at one and the same time denied but also justified "the use of terrorism and violence" against Republicans. He chose for inclusion in his *Documentary History* "slivers of information which one man chose to regard as significant." These were the only printed documents available to most students for more than fifty years. The nature of Fleming's work, and no doubt academic pressure for publication, has led to the appearance over the last twenty years of a number of collections of documents, giving students a wide choice of printed sources.[41]

Reconstruction is a historical era that excites passions even in historiography; even the titles of essays tend to be vivid. Bernard A. Weisberger's "The Dark and Bloody Ground of Reconstruction Historiography," published in 1959, is an example. Others are Eric McKitrick, "Reconstruction: Ultraconservative Revolution" (1968); Gerald Grob, "Reconstruction: An American Morality Play" (1971); Larry Kincaid, "Victims of Circumstance" (1970); Herman Belz, "The New Orthodoxy in Reconstruction Historiography" (1973); Michael Les Benedict, "Equality and Expediency in the Reconstruction Era" (1977); and Richard O. Curry, "The Abolitionists and Reconstruction" (1968). Robert F. Durden's "Civil War and Reconstruction, 1861–1877" (1973) deserves notice as a quiet and thorough study of Civil War and Reconstruction historiography from approximately 1960 through the middle 1970s; it is designed primarily for teachers. Staughton Lynd expresses what was once the "new left" point of view in "Rethinking Slavery and Reconstruction" (1965). Almost forgotten is Thomas J. Pressly's "Racial Attitudes, Scholarship, and Reconstruction: A Review Essay" (1966), in which the author warns modern historians of Reconstruction that their own

---

41. Walter L. Fleming (ed.), *Documentary History of Reconstruction: Political, Military, Social, Religious, Educational, & Industrial, 1865 to the Present Time* (2 vols.; Cleveland: A. H. Clark Co., 1906, 1907); Wharton, "Reconstruction," in Link and Patrick (eds.), *Writing Southern History*, 300, 301 (last two quotations); James P. Shenton (ed.), *The Reconstruction: A Documentary History of the South After the War, 1865–1877* (New York: G. P. Putnam's Sons, 1963); Richard N. Current (ed.), *Reconstruction, 1865–1877* (Englewood Cliffs, N.J.: Prentice-Hall, 1965); Staughton Lynd (ed.), *Reconstruction* (New York: Harper & Row, 1967); Robert W. Johannsen (ed.), *Reconstruction, 1865–1877* (New York: Free Press, 1970); Michael Les Benedict, *The Fruits of Victory: Alternatives in Restoring the Union* (Philadelphia: Lippincott, 1975); Hans L. Trefousse, *Reconstruction: America's First Effort at Racial Democracy* (Huntington, N.Y.: R. E. Krieger Publishing Co., 1979).

equalitarian attitudes could affect the history they write, just as racist attitudes had affected the work by earlier authors.[42]

The traditional view of Abraham Lincoln and the Radical Republicans has been that they were adversaries, a moderate, even conservative, president being pushed by the Radicals and by events into taking steps against slavery and in support of freedmen's rights that he would have preferred to delay or not to take at all. Now historians who specialize in the area of presidential Reconstruction take a decidedly different view. David Donald, in a series of lectures delivered at Louisiana State University in 1965, presented a statistical analysis of the votes of so-called Radicals in Congress and concluded that the traditional view of them was incorrect. He was not at all sure, in fact, that any distinction could be made between the "moderate" Republicans with whom Lincoln agreed and the "Radicals" with whom he supposedly disagreed. That same year, in a review of Stampp's *The Era of Reconstruction,* Harold M. Hyman stated his "estimate" that Lincoln at the time of his death was well on his way to becoming a Radical.[43]

This trend soon went farther. Herman Belz emphasized the nearness of Lincoln's position to that of the Radicals in *Reconstructing the Union* (1969). Hans L. Trefousse, in *The Radical Republicans*

42. Bernard A. Weisberger, "The Dark and Bloody Ground of Reconstruction Historiography," *Journal of Southern History,* XXV (November, 1959), 427–47; Eric McKitrick, "Reconstruction: Ultraconservative Revolution," in C. Vann Woodward (ed.), *The Comparative Approach to American History* (New York: Basic Books, 1968), 146–59; Gerald Grob, "Reconstruction: An American Morality Play," in George A. Billias and Gerald N. Grob (eds.), *American History: Retrospect and Prospect* (New York: Free Press, 1971), 191–231; Larry Kincaid, "Victims of Circumstance: An Interpretation of Changing Attitudes Toward Republican Policy Makers and Reconstruction," *Journal of American History,* LVII (June, 1970), 48–66; Belz, "The New Orthodoxy in Reconstruction Historiography"; Michael Les Benedict, "Equality and Expediency in the Reconstruction Era: A Review Essay," *Civil War History,* XXIII (December, 1977), 322–35; Richard O. Curry, "The Abolitionists and Reconstruction: A Critical Appraisal," *Journal of Southern History,* XXXIV (November, 1968), 527–45; Robert F. Durden, "Civil War and Reconstruction, 1861–1877," in William H. Cartwright and Richard L. Watson, Jr. (eds.), *The Reinterpretation of American History and Culture* (Washington, D.C.: National Council for the Social Studies, 1973), 357–75; Staughton Lynd, "Rethinking Slavery and Reconstruction," *Journal of Negro History,* L (July, 1965), 198–209; Thomas J. Pressly, "Racial Attitudes, Scholarship, and Reconstruction: A Review Essay," *Journal of Southern History,* XXXII (February, 1966), 88–93.

43. David H. Donald, *The Politics of Reconstruction, 1863–1867* (Baton Rouge: Louisiana State University Press, 1965); Harold M. Hyman, Review of Stampp's *The Era of Reconstruction,* in *Journal of American History,* LII (September, 1965), 401.

(1969), also emphasized the area of agreement and suggested that at the time he was killed, Lincoln was coming around to favoring black suffrage. Peyton McCrary, in *Abraham Lincoln and Reconstruction: The Louisiana Experiment* (1978), concluded that Lincoln planned to extend suffrage to Louisiana blacks but was thwarted by General Nathaniel P. Banks. When a reviewer who had fallen behind in his reading suggested that no reputable historian agreed with McCrary, Harold M. Hyman wrote a letter of reprimand to the *American Historical Review* stating that he agreed with McCrary and that he did not feel lonely. In 1981, LaWanda Cox published *Lincoln and Black Freedom*, in which she asserted, in effect, that Lincoln was a Radical, or almost a Radical, all the time. He made moderate statements, even racist statements, because he was a politician who understood the art of the possible.[44]

These studies are all well researched and scholarly in every sense. Yet, in regard to Lincoln, the conclusions are based not so much on new evidence as on new interpretations of old evidence. There is nothing wrong with this; historians have been doing it for centuries. But it is doubtful that this particular interpretation could have come about at this particular time had it not been for the overwhelmingly problack reactions of historians to the civil rights controversy. Lincoln was the greatest of presidents, and we find it difficult to see him as insensitive to the aspirations of people with whom we are so much in sympathy. But does this mean that we can soon expect a scholarly work that makes Lincoln a champion of women's rights and then another that reveals that he was secretly a pacifist?

The Reconstruction scholars of the past two decades have not only rehabilitated the once-despised Radical Republicans, they have toppled Andrew Johnson from the pinnacle upon which he was placed by Howard K. Beale and others. In 1963, LaWanda F. Cox and John H. Cox published *Politics, Principle, and Prejudice*, wherein they presented a Radical Reconstruction program based on principle, not on hate, political expediency, or economic interests. The

---

44. Herman Belz, *Reconstructing the Union: Theory and Policy During the Civil War* (Ithaca: Cornell University Press for the American Historical Association, 1969); Hans L. Trefousse, *The Radical Republicans: Lincoln's Vanguard for Racial Justice* (New York: Knopf, 1969); Peyton McCrary, *Abraham Lincoln and Reconstruction: The Louisiana Experiment* (Princeton: Princeton University Press, 1978); Harold M. Hyman, in "Communications," *American Historical Review*, LXXXV (April, 1980), 504–505; LaWanda F. Cox, *Lincoln and Black Freedom: A Study in Presidential Leadership* (Columbia: University of South Carolina Press, 1981).

moderate Republicans, according to the Coxes, were driven to support the Radicals by Andrew Johnson's shrewdly calculated efforts to take complete control of the government. Also in 1963, W. R. Brock's *An American Crisis* appeared. Brock, a British historian, concluded that by the end of the war, there was a vague consensus in the North that a more nationalistic state, government encouragement of capitalistic enterprise, and some means of protecting the freedmen should come out of the struggle. It was these goals that the Radicals sought to achieve, but the United States Constitution, with its requirement of periodic elections and its emphasis on separation of powers, made it impossible to institutionalize all the reforms the Radicals wanted and doomed Reconstruction to failure insofar as the rights of the freedmen were concerned.[45]

Other books have dealt with this theme. Martin E. Mantell suggested (1973) that Johnson, through the power of the presidency, was in control of Reconstruction until his impeachment and that Grant was working behind the scenes to bring about congressional control. Mantell agrees with the Coxes and McCrary that the Radicals really believed in black equality, even for the northern states. Michael Les Benedict, who has been praised for his combination of cliometrics and conventional historical methods, does not disagree, but he did point out that the Radicals were never very radical (1974). Glenn M. Linden, in *Politics or Principle* (1976), analyzed congressional voting on the Civil War amendments and measures intended to help the freedmen and concluded that principle did indeed play a role in Radical behavior. In 1979, Patrick W. Riddleberger produced *1866: The Critical Year Revisited* and found himself largely in agreement with Eric McKitrick, the Coxes, and Brock that Andrew Johnson was the great obstacle to a successful Reconstruction. Riddleberger did not find the Radicals particularly attractive, however, and he concluded that Johnson's obstinacy was based as much on consistent states' rights principles as upon racism. J. Michael Quill was somewhat out of step with other writers of the period. Quill, in *Prelude to the Radicals* (1980), concluded that the assassination of Abraham Lincoln brought a northern demand that the South be punished and that southern ac-

45. LaWanda F. Cox and John H. Cox, *Politics, Principle, and Prejudice, 1865–1866: Dilemma of Reconstruction America* (New York: Free Press, 1963); W. R. Brock, *An American Crisis: Congress and Reconstruction, 1865–1867* (New York: St. Martin's Press, 1963).

tions after the war ended made northern public opinion even more antisouthern. Thus the Radicals responded to popular will.[46]

Eric McKitrick began the modern criticism of Andrew Johnson with *Andrew Johnson and Reconstruction*, published in 1960. It is to be hoped that the publication of Johnson's papers, now brought up to 1864, will make possible a more completely satisfactory evaluation of this Tennessean than now seems practicable. McKitrick could find little good in the bigoted, stubborn, somewhat deceitful, states' rightist politician. Albert Castel's *The Presidency of Andrew Johnson* (1979) was highly critical of the racism that made it impossible for the president to accept Radical measures, but Castel gave him credit for realism in warning that sooner or later southern blacks would have to come to terms with southern whites. James E. Sefton, in *Andrew Johnson and the Uses of Constitutional Power* (1980), maintained that whatever his drawbacks, Johnson was a states' rights Democrat who was consistent in his view of the Constitution and of presidential and congressional power under the Constitution.[47]

Except for state and local studies, which will be discussed later, and studies of the freedmen, which are outside the scope of this essay, little has been done on the South during presidential Reconstruction. In 1965, Theodore Wilson published *The Black Codes of the South*, and he concluded that however unwise these statutes might have been, they were much milder than might have been expected under the circumstances. Of much more consequence was Michael Perman's *Reunion Without Compromise* (1973). Perman is far from a friend of white southerners of the nineteenth century, but he argued correctly

46. Martin E. Mantell, *Johnson, Grant, and the Politics of Reconstruction* (New York: Columbia University Press, 1973); Michael Les Benedict, *A Compromise of Principle: Congressional Republicans and Reconstruction, 1863–1869* (New York: Norton, 1974); Glenn M. Linden, *Politics or Principle: Congressional Voting on the Civil War Amendments and Pro-Negro Measures, 1838–1869* (Seattle: University of Washington Press, 1976); Patrick W. Riddleberger, *1866: The Critical Year Revisited* (Carbondale: Southern Illinois University Press, 1979); J. Michael Quill, *Prelude to the Radicals: The North and Reconstruction During 1865* (Washington, D.C.: University Press of America, 1980).

47. Eric L. McKitrick, *Andrew Johnson and Reconstruction* (Chicago: University of Chicago Press, 1960); LeRoy P. Graf *et al.* (eds.), *The Papers of Andrew Johnson*, Vol. IV, *1860–1861*, Vol. V, *1861–1862*, Vol. VI, *1862–1864* (Knoxville: University of Tennessee Press, 1976, 1978, 1983); Albert Castel, *The Presidency of Andrew Johnson* (Lawrence: Regents Press of Kansas, 1979); James E. Sefton, *Andrew Johnson and the Uses of Constitutional Power* (Boston: Little, Brown, 1980).

that these southerners never gave an inch on the race question during Reconstruction. He carries his analysis only through 1868, but it is obvious that his conclusions would apply through 1877. Perman believes that draconian methods might have been applied successfully on behalf of the freedmen. This is might-have-been rather than history, but an answer of sorts seems appropriate. Certainly these draconian measures would have had to be applied at the end of the war, and if southerners had known that northern war aims included black equality, the war might have lasted much longer. Despite occasional attempts to make it go away, the fact remains that the most strongly Unionist people of the South were also in general the most racist. Furthermore, Perman himself makes it clear that the southern whites were far more united *against* black equality than the northern Republicans (not to mention the northern Democrats) were united *in favor* of it.[48]

The Ku Klux Klan of Reconstruction has always excited interest, but by its very nature it was an organization that left few records. Two recent books have attempted to deal with this slippery subject. Only the first chapter of David M. Chalmers' *Hooded Americanism* (1965) tells of the Klan of the Reconstruction era, but Allen W. Trelease's *White Terror* (1971) is the best work yet on these hooded terrorists of the late 1860s and early 1870s. Any heroic imagery that remained should have been erased by this monograph. Trelease also made the point that southerners of all classes were involved in Klan activities.[49]

Some of the monographs already discussed deal with the constitutional issues of Reconstruction to a greater or lesser extent, but three deal explicitly with such issues. Stanley I. Kutler, in a collection of essays published in 1968, rejected the idea that Congress and the courts were hostile to one another until the Supreme Court surrendered. Kutler asserted that the power and prestige of the courts increased during the years the Radicals dominated Congress. Herman

48. Theodore Brantner Wilson, *The Black Codes of the South* (University: University of Alabama Press, 1965); Michael Perman, *Reunion Without Compromise: The South and Reconstruction, 1865–1868* (New York: Cambridge University Press, 1973). See also Joel H. Silbey, *A Respectable Minority: The Democratic Party in the Civil War Era, 1860–1868* (New York: Norton, 1977).

49. David M. Chalmers, *Hooded Americanism: The First Century of the Ku Klux Klan, 1865–1965* (Garden City, N.Y.: Doubleday, 1965); Allen W. Trelease, *White Terror: The Ku Klux Klan Conspiracy and Southern Reconstruction* (New York: Harper & Row, 1971).

Belz summarized the political and constitutional questions that concerned the Republicans during the Civil War and Reconstruction in *Emancipation and Equal Rights* (1978). He concluded that the Radicals accomplished as much as they could have accomplished within the federalist constitutional framework to which they confined themselves. Harold M. Hyman, in *A More Perfect Union* (1973), likewise stressed the essential conservatism of the Radicals. Like Kutler, he emphasized the cooperation of Congress and the courts. Hyman, who is perhaps more radical than the Radicals, agrees with Michael Les Benedict that impeachment of the president was the appropriate action for the Radicals to take under the circumstances. Hyman and William M. Wiecek argue, in *Equal Justice Under Law* (1982), that the Supreme Court during Reconstruction was aware of minority rights and that the Court firmly maintained its independence. Phillip S. Paludan, author of *A Covenant with Death* (1975), examined the ideas of five leading lawyers of the mid-nineteenth century and concluded that the Union they wanted to reconstruct was one that would maintain the pre–Civil War federal-state relationship. This meant that the rights of blacks could not be fully guaranteed and therefore that the failure of Reconstruction resulted from Radical adherence to the Constitution.[50]

Economic studies of the Reconstruction period, including those dealing with the South, have been fairly numerous. Walter T. K. Nugent's *The Money Question During Reconstruction* (1967) is concerned with the nation as a whole. Three books treat mainly the economic situation of the freedmen, but it must be remembered that the freedmen and white landowners were willy-nilly bound together by economic circumstances. Carl R. Osthaus' *Freedmen, Philanthropy, and Fraud* (1976) is a history of the Freedman's Savings Bank, but the bank is not related to other aspects of Reconstruction. Roger L. Ransom and Richard Sutch's *One Kind of Freedom* (1977) looks on the South's failure to give land to the freedmen as the great tragedy of Reconstruction and damns the general store without suggesting what

50. Stanley I. Kutler, *Judicial Power and Reconstruction Politics* (Chicago: University of Chicago Press, 1968); Herman Belz, *Emancipation and Equal Rights: Politics and Constitutionalism in the Civil War Era* (New York: Norton, 1978); Harold M. Hyman, *A More Perfect Union: The Impact of the Civil War and Reconstruction on the Constitution* (New York: Knopf, 1973); Hyman and William M. Wiecek, *Equal Justice Under Law: Constitutional Development, 1835–1875* (New York: Harper & Row, 1982); Phillip S. Paludan, *A Covenant with Death: The Constitution, Law, and Equality in the Civil War Era* (Urbana: University of Illinois Press, 1975).

might have carried out the store's economic function if it had not come into being. Finally, in a Marxist study, *The Roots of Black Poverty* (1978), Jay R. Mandle maintained that the southern plantation substituted economic coercion for slavery and that the poverty of black people in the modern world results from this fact.[51]

Three specialized studies deal particularly with economic Reconstruction in the South. James P. Baughman's *Charles Morgan and the Development of Southern Transportation* (1968) is a good business history, much concerned with Morgan's holdings in Texas and Louisiana. Claude F. Oubre's *Forty Acres and a Mule* (1978) is a study of black land ownership during Reconstruction. Of special value is Lawrence N. Powell's *New Masters* (1980), a study of those northerners who came South and became planters during the war or soon afterward. These entrepreneurs failed almost universally, defeated by the hostility of the old master class, bad crops, and the highly un-Yankee work ethic of the freedmen. The freedmen so exasperated their new employers that these Yankees quickly developed the racial attitudes of their predecessors.[52]

Three good books treat southern agriculture during Reconstruction. The second half of Harold D. Woodman's *King Cotton & His Retainers* (1968) discusses the Civil War and afterward, down to 1925. Woodman is primarily interested in the financing and marketing of the staple. Stephen J. DeCanio, in *Agriculture in the Postbellum South* (1974), concluded that cotton was the best crop for the South and that there was no discernible difference between white and black productivity in the cotton fields. Finally, Gavin Wright's *The*

---

51. Walter T. K. Nugent, *The Money Question During Reconstruction* (New York: Norton, 1967); Carl R. Osthaus, *Freedmen, Philanthropy, and Fraud: A History of the Freedman's Savings Bank* (Urbana: University of Illinois Press, 1976); Roger L. Ransom and Richard Sutch, *One Kind of Freedom: The Economic Consequences of Emancipation* (Cambridge, England: Cambridge University Press, 1977); Jay R. Mandle, *The Roots of Black Poverty: The Southern Plantation Economy After the Civil War* (Durham: Duke University Press, 1978).

52. James P. Baughman, *Charles Morgan and the Development of Southern Transportation* (Nashville: Vanderbilt University Press, 1968); Claude F. Oubre, *Forty Acres and a Mule: The Freedmen's Bureau and Black Land Ownership* (Baton Rouge: Louisiana State University Press, 1978); Lawrence N. Powell, *New Masters: Northern Planters During the Civil War and Reconstruction* (New Haven: Yale University Press, 1980). See also William S. McFeely, *Yankee Stepfather: General O. O. Howard and the Freedmen* (New Haven: Yale University Press, 1968); and LaWanda Cox, "The Promise of Land for the Freedmen," *Mississippi Valley Historical Review*, XLV (December, 1958), 413–40.

Political Economy of the Cotton South (1978) is concerned mainly with the antebellum period, but the last chapter deals with cotton after the war. Wright provided a particularly lucid account of the origins of sharecropping and the crop lien and the resulting decline in self-sufficiency on southern lands.[53]

Most recent works on the social history of Reconstruction focus on the freedmen, but some are part of the history of the white South. One phenomenon that often impressses those who study this period of southern life is how little attention literate southerners paid to political Reconstruction. This is manifest again in two collections of correspondence published during the 1970s, G. Ray Mathis' edition of *College Life in the Reconstruction South* and Betsy Fleet's *Green Mount After the War*. James L. Roark's *Masters Without Slaves* (1977) is a good study of the frustration, despair, and opportunism of planters during the war and after. Jonathan M. Wiener's *Social Origins of the New South* (1978) and Dwight B. Billings, Jr.'s *Planters and the Making of a "New South"* (1979) are Marxist studies that argue that the old planter elite remained in control throughout Reconstruction and the "New South" period. Thus they challenge C. Vann Woodward's *Origins of the New South* (1951).[54]

During the past twenty years, biographies have added to knowledge of Reconstruction. Two biographies of national rather than southern figures are essential: David Donald's *Charles Sumner and the Rights of Man* (1970) and William S. McFeely's *Grant: A Biog-*

---

53. Harold D. Woodman, *King Cotton & His Retainers: Financing & Marketing the Cotton Crop of the South, 1800–1925* (Lexington: University of Kentucky Press, 1968); Stephen J. DeCanio, *Agriculture in the Postbellum South: The Economics of Production and Supply* (Cambridge: M.I.T. Press, 1974); Gavin Wright, *The Political Economy of the Cotton South: Households, Markets, and Wealth in the Nineteenth Century* (New York: Norton, 1978).

54. G. Ray Mathis (ed.), *College Life in the Reconstruction South: Walter B. Hill's Student Correspondence, University of Georgia, 1869–1871* (Athens: University of Georgia Libraries, 1974); Betsy Fleet (ed.), *Green Mount After the War: The Correspondence of Maria Louisa Wacker Fleet and Her Family, 1865–1900* (Charlottesville: University Press of Virginia, 1978); James L. Roark, *Masters Without Slaves: Southern Planters in the Civil War and Reconstruction* (New York: Norton, 1977); Jonathan M. Wiener, *Social Origins of the New South: Alabama, 1860–1885* (Baton Rouge: Louisiana State University Press, 1978); Dwight B. Billings, Jr., *Planters and the Making of a "New South": Class, Politics, and Development in North Carolina, 1865–1900* (Chapel Hill: University of North Carolina Press, 1979); C. Vann Woodward, *Origins of the New South, 1877–1913* (Baton Rouge: Louisiana State University Press, 1951).

raphy (1981). McFeely is far more interested in Grant the Reconstruction president than in Grant the military savior of the Union. A biography of Adelbert Ames (1964), carpetbagger governor of Mississippi, is a far better book than one might expect from the pen of Ames's octogenarian daughter. Lillian A. Pereyra's life of James Lusk Alcorn (1966), scalawag governor of Mississippi, is highly useful. Joseph H. Parks's already-mentioned *Joseph E. Brown* is as helpful for the Reconstruction period as for the Civil War. Three other serviceable biographical works are John L. Weller's *Colonel Hamilton of Texas* (1968), James B. Murphy's *L. Q. C. Lamar* (1973), and Jack P. Maddex, Jr.'s *The Reconstruction of Edward A. Pollard* (1974).[55]

More studies of the carpetbaggers and scalawags of the Reconstruction period are needed, but few such works are forthcoming. Blanche Ames's biography of her father has been mentioned. Richard N. Current's *Three Carpetbag Governors* (1968) discusses Harrison Reed of Florida, Henry Clay Warmoth of Louisiana, and Adelbert Ames. Otto H. Olsen's *Carpetbagger's Crusade* (1965) is a biography of Albion Tourgée, a notable North Carolina carpetbagger and a national literary figure. One article, Richard L. Hume's "Carpetbaggers in the Reconstruction South" (1977), is a study of northerners in the "Radical" southern state conventions and is especially useful.[56]

The scalawags are even more difficult to pin down for examination. Pereyra's life of Alcorn and Weller's biography of Andrew Jackson Hamilton are the only recent biographies of major scalawag leaders, though it should be noted that Joseph E. Brown was a Republican for

55. David H. Donald, *Charles Sumner and the Rights of Man* (New York: Knopf, 1970); William S. McFeely, *Grant: A Biography* (New York: Norton, 1981); Blanche Ames Ames, *Adelbert Ames, 1835–1933: General, Senator, Governor . . .* (New York: Argosy-Antiquarian, 1964); Lillian A. Pereyra, *James Lusk Alcorn: Persistent Whig* (Baton Rouge: Louisiana State University Press, 1966); J. H. Parks, *Joseph E. Brown*; John L. Weller, *Colonel Hamilton of Texas: A Biography of Andrew Jackson Hamilton, Militant Unionist and Reconstruction Governor* (El Paso: Texas Western Press, 1968); James B. Murphy, *L. Q. C. Lamar: Pragmatic Patriot* (Baton Rouge: Louisiana State University Press, 1973); Jack P. Maddex, Jr., *The Reconstruction of Edward A. Pollard: A Rebel's Conversion to Postbellum Unionism* (Chapel Hill: University of North Carolina Press, 1974).

56. Richard N. Current, *Three Carpetbag Governors* (Baton Rouge: Louisiana State University Press, 1968); Otto H. Olsen, *Carpetbagger's Crusade: The Life of Albion Winegar Tourgée* (Baltimore: Johns Hopkins Press, 1965); Richard L. Hume, "Carpetbaggers in the Reconstruction South: A Group Portrait of Outside Whites in the 'Black and Tan' Constitutional Conventions," *Journal of American History*, LXIV (September, 1977), 313–30.

a season. Whether the scalawags were persistent Whigs, opportunists, or lower-class whites expressing antagonism toward their betters has not been determined. Five articles by noted scholars touch on this problem to some extent, but only one monograph has yet appeared. Sarah Woolfolk Wiggins, author of *The Scalawag in Alabama Politics* (1977), found that the native Republicans in Alabama included prominent men from the Black Belt as well as poor men from northern Alabama and that the Black Belt dominated scalawag leadership. The question remaining is whether Alabama was typical or whether other patterns existed in other states.[57]

In his essay in *Writing Southern History*, the late Vernon L. Wharton called for more local studies of Reconstruction. That call has been abundantly answered. For border areas, note should be taken of Dean Sprague's analysis (1965) of Lincoln's dealing with dissent in the loyal border states and of M. Thomas Bailey's *Reconstruction in Indian Territory* (1972). Richard O. Curry edited a collection of nine articles (1969) concerned with political parties in the border states. The reader of these articles is forced to the conclusion that the Republican party, identified as it was with the demise of slavery and efforts to achieve black equality, had no chance of maintaining power in the border states. William E. Parrish wrote *Missouri Under Radical Rule* (1965), giving a definitely unfavorable view of the Missouri Radicals, and Ross A. Webb published *Kentucky in the Reconstruction Era* (1979).[58]

The two decades under review have seen the publication of a number of state studies of high quality. They include Jack P. Maddex, Jr.'s

---

57. Thomas B. Alexander, "Persistent Whiggery in the Confederate South, 1860–1877," *Journal of Southern History*, XXVII (August, 1961), 305–29; David H. Donald, "The Scalawag in Mississippi Reconstruction," *Journal of Southern History*, X (November, 1944), 447–60; Allen W. Trelease, "Who Were the Scalawags?" *Journal of Southern History*, XXIX (November, 1963), 445–68; Otto H. Olsen, "Reconsidering the Scalawags," *Civil War History*, XII (December, 1966), 304–20; Warren A. Ellem, "Who Were the Mississippi Scalawags?" *Journal of Southern History*, XXXVIII (May, 1972), 217–40; Sarah Woolfolk Wiggins, *The Scalawag in Alabama Politics, 1865–1881* (University: University of Alabama Press, 1977).

58. Dean Sprague, *Freedom Under Lincoln* (Boston: Houghton Mifflin, 1965); M. Thomas Bailey, *Reconstruction in Indian Territory: A Story of Avarice, Discrimination, and Opportunism* (Port Washington, N.Y.: Kennikat Press, 1972); Richard O. Curry (ed.), *Radicalism, Racism, and Party Realignment: The Border States During Reconstruction* (Baltimore: Johns Hopkins Press, 1969); William E. Parrish, *Missouri Under Radical Rule, 1865–1870* (Columbia: University of Missouri Press, 1965); Ross A. Webb, *Kentucky in the Reconstruction Era* (Lexington: University Press of Kentucky, 1979).

examination (1970) of the conservatives in Virginia from the end of the Civil War until 1879, Elizabeth Studley Nathans' history (1968) of the Republicans in Georgia until the "redemption" of that state, and Carl H. Moneyhon's monograph (1980) on the Republicans in Texas. Two excellent studies of the Freedmen's Bureau are Martin Abbott's review of that agency in South Carolina (1967) and Howard White's study of Louisiana (1970). If any vestige remained of the onetime conception of the bureau as primarily an agency of Radicalism, these monographs should put an end to it. Alan Conway published a history of Reconstruction in Georgia in 1966, the first of a series of highly revisionist works of some quality. William C. Harris wrote two volumes on Mississippi, *Presidential Reconstruction* (1967) and *The Day of the Carpetbagger* (1979). Louisiana and Florida were described in Joe Gray Taylor's *Louisiana Reconstructed* (1974) and Jerrell H. Shofner's *Nor Is It Over Yet* (1974). These last four works not only recount the political developments in the states examined but also give full attention to social and economic developments. All reflect the latest scholarship at time of publication and fill a most definite need.[59]

Two works deserving attention in any historiographical review of Reconstruction are James E. Sefton's *The United States Army and Reconstruction* (1967) and William Gillette's *The Right to Vote* (1965). It is appropriate that they be considered together because both are somewhat at odds with the dominant historical opinion of this era. Sefton, probably influenced by the generally conservative opinions of the military officers whose work he studied, showed little sympathy, indeed some contempt, for the Radical Republican regimes in the

---

59. Jack P. Maddex, Jr., *The Virginia Conservatives, 1867–1879: A Study in Reconstruction Politics* (Chapel Hill: University of North Carolina Press, 1970); Elizabeth Studley Nathans, *Losing the Peace: Georgia Republicans and Reconstruction, 1865–1871* (Baton Rouge: Louisiana State University Press, 1968); Carl H. Moneyhon, *Republicanism in Reconstruction Texas* (Austin: University of Texas Press, 1980); Martin Abbott, *The Freedmen's Bureau in South Carolina, 1865–1872* (Chapel Hill: University of North Carolina Press, 1967); Howard Ashley White, *The Freedmen's Bureau in Louisiana* (Baton Rouge: Louisiana State University Press, 1970); Alan Conway, *The Reconstruction of Georgia* (Minneapolis: University of Minnesota Press, 1966); William C. Harris, *Presidential Reconstruction in Mississippi* (Baton Rouge: Louisiana State University Press, 1967), and *The Day of the Carpetbagger: Republican Reconstruction in Mississippi* (Baton Rouge: Louisiana State University Press, 1979); Joe Gray Taylor, *Louisiana Reconstructed, 1863–1877* (Baton Rouge: Louisiana State University Press, 1974); Jerrell H. Shofner, *Nor Is It Over Yet: Florida in the Era of Reconstruction, 1863–1877* (Gainesville: University Presses of Florida, 1974).

southern states. It might be mentioned that Joseph G. Dawson III's *Army Generals and Reconstruction: Louisiana* (1982) is scrupulously neutral toward the Radicals but does not in any way discredit Sefton. Gillette concluded that the primary purpose of congressional Radicals in promoting the Fifteenth Amendment to the Constitution was to enfranchise *northern* blacks. Both Sefton and Gillette were castigated by those who believed that the Radicals were motivated primarily by principle.[60]

Most of the historical thought devoted to the ending of Reconstruction revolves around C. Vann Woodward's *Reunion and Reaction,* first published in 1951. In 1973, Allen Peskin argued in the *Journal of American History* that there had been no Compromise of 1877 and was answered by Woodward. The debate has not ended. James Tice Moore, in "Redeemers Reconsidered" (1978), argued that the Redeemers were far more agrarian than Woodward had pictured them, and Michael Les Benedict published another assault on *Reunion and Reaction* in 1980. Keith Ian Polakoff's thoroughly researched account of the election of 1876 was published in 1973. William Gillette's *Retreat from Reconstruction* (1979) accused the Radicals of not having been completely resolute in their program for the South. He argued that if Radical Reconstruction ever had a chance, it was after Grant took office, thus giving the Radicals full control of the White House and both houses of Congress. When they failed to take advantage of this opportunity, it became necessary to sacrifice the Republican party in the South in order to save it in the North. Finally, *Reconstruction and Redemption in the South,* a collection of esssays edited by Otto H. Olsen in 1980, leads to the conclusion that from the very beginning, Radical Reconstruction really never had a chance of success.[61]

60. James E. Sefton, *The United States Army and Reconstruction, 1865–1877* (Baton Rouge: Louisiana State University Press, 1967); William Gillette, *The Right to Vote: Politics and the Passage of the Fifteenth Amendment* (Baltimore: Johns Hopkins Press, 1965); Joseph G. Dawson III, *Army Generals and Reconstruction: Louisiana, 1862–1877* (Baton Rouge: Louisiana State University Press, 1982).

61. C. Vann Woodward, *Reunion and Reaction: The Compromise of 1877 and the End of Reconstruction* (Boston: Little, Brown, 1951); Allen Peskin, "Was There a Compromise of 1877?" *Journal of American History,* LX (June, 1973), 63–73; Woodward, "Yes, There Was a Compromise of 1877," *Journal of American History,* LX (June, 1973), 215–23; James Tice Moore, "Redeemers Reconsidered: Change and Continuity in the Democratic South, 1870–1900," *Journal of Southern History,* XLIV (August, 1978), 357–78; Michael Les Benedict, "Southern Democrats in the Crisis of 1876–1877: A Reconsideration of *Reunion and Reaction," Journal of South-*

Thus ends, for the time being, this far-from-simple story. The works considered have been mentioned because the author, sometimes with the advice of colleagues, decided that they should be reviewed. Some works first included were later omitted in order to meet requirements as to the length of the essay. It may well be that some have been left out as a result of the author's ignorance. Undoubtedly many good books dealing with the Civil War and Reconstruction will come off the press before this essay does, but that is the way of historiography.

---

ern History, XLVI (November, 1980), 489–524; Keith Ian Polakoff, *The Politics of Inertia: The Election of 1876 and the End of Reconstruction* (Baton Rouge: Louisiana State University Press, 1973); William Gillette, *Retreat from Reconstruction, 1869–1879* (Baton Rouge: Louisiana State University Press, 1979); Otto H. Olsen (ed.), *Reconstruction and Redemption in the South* (Baton Rouge: Louisiana State University Press, 1980).

From Emancipation to Segregation
National Policy and Southern Blacks

LaWANDA COX

In the early 1960s, the point of departure for this accounting of the state of writings on southern history, two revolutions were approaching a climax—the revolution in Reconstruction historiography and the revolution in black civil rights. Only yesterday the nation had been aroused and challenged by the historic school desegregation decision of the Supreme Court, by the Montgomery bus boycott, the sit-ins, the freedom rides, Little Rock, the electric cattle prods of Birmingham, the march on Washington inspired by Martin Luther King, Jr. Just ahead lay the wide-ranging Civil Rights Act of 1964, the biracial march from Selma (joined before it reached Montgomery by a contingent of historians),[1] and the crucial Voting Rights Act of 1965. Then came Watts, followed by similar black explosions in other cities of the West and North. Added to all this during the last half of the 1960s were the angry proud cries of "black power."

In its own way, the revolution in Reconstruction historiography was equally dramatic. It shattered generally accepted stereotypes long considered authenticated by the impressive research of the Dunning school historians.[2] This revolution, like the civil rights movement, had been in process for some time. In 1940 when Howard K. Beale challenged established views, he could cite for support the work of W. E. B.

1. Walter Johnson, "Historians Join the March on Montgomery," *South Atlantic Quarterly*, LXXIX (Spring, 1980), 158–74.

2. Dunning's own work is presented as being less racist, and also less scholarly, than his reputation by Philip R. Muller in "Look Back without Anger: A Reappraisal of William A. Dunning," *Journal of American History*, LXI (September, 1974), 325–38.

Black historians, lacking a white supremacist bias and concerned to undermine the denigration of blacks, were revisionist from the start of their participation in American historical scholarship. See Daniel Savage Gray, "Bibliographical Essay: Black Views on Reconstruction," *Journal of Negro History*, LVIII (January, 1973), 73–85; Rayford W. Logan, "Carter G. Woodson: Mirror and Molder of His Time, 1875–1950," *Journal of Negro History*, LVIII (January, 1973), 1–17; and *Negro History Bulletin*, XIII (May, 1950), especially the tribute to Woodson by John Hope Franklin.

Du Bois, Vernon L. Wharton, Horace Mann Bond, Francis B. Simkins, and others. Nearly two decades later, in 1959, Bernard A. Weisberger's influential appraisal "The Dark and Bloody Ground of Reconstruction Historiography" appeared in the *Journal of Southern History*. After its publication the denigration of "carpetbaggers," "scalawags," Negro freedmen, and the work of the Reconstruction legislators in the southern states no longer would carry unquestioned scholarly authority. The changing climate of Reconstruction historiography was confirmed by John Hope Franklin's *Reconstruction After the Civil War* and David Donald's revision of J. G. Randall's *The Civil War and Reconstruction*, both published in 1961. The two books consolidated the victory of revisionism in dealing with events in the South and foreshadowed major reinterpretations of northern policy.[3]

By the early 1960s, the racial assumptions that had girded the older view of Reconstruction, though apparently still pervasive among white southerners generally, no longer bound the historians who were writing and reviewing southern history.[4] For them, the old orthodoxy had been discredited; the scholarly revolution, however, was suspect. The effect of the civil rights movement was both to accelerate and to compromise the new historiography. Shaken by the demolition of a structure of interpretation long accepted as sound, historians feared that revisionists were replacing the old construct with another equally vulnerable. To the shock of destruction was added unease over the moral implications of the new viewpoint, as if value judgments were inappropriate to the historian's task and somehow escapable, even in the midst of a great national struggle to right racial injustice. Thus Vernon Wharton, from whom commendation and en-

---

3. Howard K. Beale, "On Rewriting Reconstruction History," *American Historical Review*, XLV (July, 1940), 807–27; Bernard A. Weisberger, "The Dark and Bloody Ground of Reconstruction Historiography," *Journal of Southern History*, XXV (November, 1959), 427–47; John Hope Franklin, *Reconstruction After the Civil War* (Chicago: University of Chicago Press, 1961); J. G. Randall and David Donald, *The Civil War and Reconstruction* (Boston: Heath, 1961).

4. Although not without exception, the generalization is based upon an examination of the articles and reviews in the *Journal of Southern History*, 1963–65; Carl N. Degler, "The South in Southern History Textbooks," *Journal of Southern History*, XXX (February, 1964), 52–53; and other evidence. The last major work on Reconstruction to be totally unreconstructed was E. Merton Coulter, *The South During Reconstruction, 1865–1877* (Baton Rouge: Louisiana State University Press, 1947). For comment on its generally favorable reception and a critique, see John Hope Franklin, "Whither Reconstruction Historiography?" *Journal of Negro Education*, XVII (Fall, 1948), 446–61.

couragement might have been expected in view of his own early revisionist study, *The Negro in Mississippi* (1947), gave only grudging recognition to the new views in his examination of Reconstruction historiography for *Writing Southern History* (1965). Wharton emphasized the paucity of basic research since 1940 and the danger that reinterpretation was becoming a simplistic reversal of the role of saints and sinners, villains and heroes. The following year, Thomas J. Pressly was cautioning those historians who opposed racial discrimination to examine with particular rigor findings that coincided with their convictions. In 1970, Larry Kincaid rendered a blanket indictment of recent writings on Reconstruction politics as "Republican apologias." Shortly thereafter, David Donald, several of whose essays had been seminal for the reconstruction of Reconstruction politics, expressed concern that "bleeding-heart liberalism" was afflicting "too many historians . . . [with] the delusion that good causes can only be advocated by good men with good motives."[5]

The civil rights and black power movements, together with the changed perception of race from which they drew strength, did have significant influence upon historiography, upon its perspective, the subject matter with which it dealt, and the conclusions at which it arrived. However, the interplay of events and historical writing was not so obvious as first appearance might suggest. The timeliness of some influential studies was little more than coincidence. The mood and central concerns of the contemporary scene were varied and changing—from civil rights to Vietnam, Watergate, the economy,

5. Vernon L. Wharton, *The Negro in Mississippi, 1865–1890* (Chapel Hill: University of North Carolina Press, 1947), and "Reconstruction," in Arthur S. Link and Rembert W. Patrick (eds.), *Writing Southern History: Essays in Historiography in Honor of Fletcher M. Green* (Baton Rouge: Louisiana State University Press, 1965), 295–315; Thomas J. Pressly, "Racial Attitudes, Scholarship, and Reconstruction: A Review Essay," *Journal of Southern History*, XXXII (February, 1966), 92–93; Larry Kincaid, "Victims of Circumstance: An Interpretation of Changing Attitudes Toward Republican Policy Makers and Reconstruction," *Journal of American History*, LVII (June, 1970), 62; David Donald, Review of Bonadio's *North of Reconstruction*, in *Journal of American History*, LVIII (September, 1971), 472–73. For Donald's early revisionism, see his "The Scalawag in Mississippi Reconstruction," *Journal of Southern History*, X (November, 1944), 447–60, "The Radicals and Lincoln," in his *Lincoln Reconsidered: Essays on the Civil War Era* (New York: Knopf, 1956), 103–27, "Why They Impeached Andrew Johnson," *American Heritage*, VIII (December, 1956), 20–25, 102–103, and "Devils Facing Zionwards," in Grady McWhiney (ed.), *Grant, Lee, Lincoln, and the Radicals: Essays on Civil War Leadership* (Evanston, Ill.: Northwestern University Press, 1964), 72–91.

from hope and exhilaration to disillusionment, reproach, bitterness, uncertainty. This did not make for a new orthodoxy, nor was it conducive to beatification. As early as 1960 the most likely candidates for sainthood, the Radicals, were charged with abandonment of the Negro; before the end of the decade, the pejorative term *betrayal* attained the status of common currency in the vocabulary of Reconstruction.[6] Moreover, there were more fundamental, though unarticulated, reassurances against the dire forebodings about the course of revisionism. An acute awareness that discredited concepts of race had distorted the old synthesis did not in fact constitute reverse bias. And historians engaged in reexamining the record continued to honor the traditional canons of their profession that underscored complexity and enjoined integrity, as well as diligence, in the pursuit and use of evidence. Their major works were well received by the profession. Revisionist essays and articles aroused more dissent, but the controversies they stirred were generally accepted as a necessary and constructive part of the process of pursuing an understandable and undistorted past.

Moreover, historians dealing with the politics and consequences of emancipation were responsive to developments within their craft, particularly those that seemed to promise immunization against subjectivity. In an effort to find answers to intractable questions of politics, power, and intent, they turned to quantitative techniques, impersonal data, and collective biography.[7] They were numbered among

6. Patrick W. Riddleberger, "The Radicals' Abandonment of the Negro During Reconstruction," *Journal of Negro History,* XLV (April, 1960), 88–102; August Meier, "Negroes in the First and Second Reconstructions of the South," *Civil War History,* XIII (June, 1967), 114–30.

7. For early examples, David Donald, *The Politics of Reconstruction, 1863–1867* (Baton Rouge: Louisiana State University Press, 1965); and Edward L. Gambill, "Who Were the Senate Radicals?" *Civil War History,* XI (September, 1965), 237–44; for later, more sophisticated usage, J. Morgan Kousser, "Progressivism—For Middle-Class Whites Only: North Carolina Education, 1880–1910," *Journal of Southern History,* XLVI (May, 1980), 169–94; and Allan G. Bogue, *The Earnest Men: Republicans of the Civil War Senate* (Ithaca: Cornell University Press, 1981). A monumental undertaking is that of Richard L. Hume to analyze the delegate composition and voting record of all the state constitutional conventions of congressional Reconstruction. See his articles in *Florida Historical Quarterly,* especially "Membership of the Florida Constitutional Convention of 1868: A Case Study of Republican Factionalism in the Reconstruction South," *Florida Historical Quarterly,* LI (July, 1972), 1–21, "The Arkansas Constitutional Convention of 1868: A Case Study in the Politics of Reconstruction," *Journal of Southern History,* XXXIX (May, 1973), 183–206, "Carpetbaggers in the Reconstruction South: A Group Portrait of Outside Whites in

the pioneers of the "new political history" with its emphasis upon ethnicity, localism, and party systems.[8] They made use of social science concepts, undertook sophisticated community and urban studies, and sought a comparative perspective.[9] Their efforts contributed to the flowering of black history with its focus on blacks as active shapers of history.[10] The "historiographical whirlwind" of the 1970s

---

the 'Black and Tan' Constitutional Conventions," *Journal of American History,* LXIV (September, 1977), 313–30, "The Membership of the Virginia Constitutional Convention of 1867–1868: A Study of the Beginnings of Congressional Reconstruction in the Upper South," *Virginia Magazine of History and Biography,* LXXXVI (October, 1978), 461–84, and "Negro Delegates to the State Constitutional Conventions of 1867–69," in Howard N. Rabinowitz (ed.), *Southern Black Leaders of the Reconstruction Era* (Urbana: University of Illinois Press, 1982), 129–53. For a lucid, informed plea for a quantitative approach to black history, Thomas Holt, "On the Cross: The Role of Quantitative Methods in the Reconstruction of the Afro-American Experience," *Journal of Negro History,* LXI (April, 1976), 158–72.

8. See Robert P. Swierenga (ed.), *Beyond the Civil War Synthesis: Political Essays of the Civil War Era* (Westport, Conn.: Greenwood Press, 1975), especially the editor's introduction (xi–xx) and the essay by Joel H. Silbey, "The Civil War Synthesis in American Political History" (3–13).

9. For an example of effective use of a theoretical concept, J. William Harris, "Plantations and Power: Emancipation on the David Barrow Plantations," in Orville Vernon Burton and Robert C. McMath, Jr. (eds.), *Toward a New South? Studies in Post–Civil War Southern Communities* (Westport, Conn.: Greenwood Press, 1982), 246–64. For innovative nonpolitical urban studies, John W. Blassingame, *Black New Orleans, 1860–1880* (Chicago: University of Chicago Press, 1973); and James Borchert, *Alley Life in Washington: Family, Community, Religion, and Folklife in the City, 1850–1970* (Urbana: University of Illinois Press, 1980). For the comparative approach to postemancipation, C. Vann Woodward, "The Price of Freedom," in David G. Sansing (ed.), *What Was Freedom's Price?* (Jackson: University Press of Mississippi, 1978), 93–113; George M. Fredrickson, "After Emancipation," in Sansing (ed.), *What Was Freedom's Price?,* 71–92, and *White Supremacy: A Comparative Study in American and South African History* (New York: Oxford University Press, 1981); Thomas C. Holt, "'An Empire Over the Mind': Emancipation, Race, and Ideology in the British West Indies and the American South," in J. Morgan Kousser and James M. McPherson (eds.), *Region, Race, and Reconstruction: Essays in Honor of C. Vann Woodward* (New York: Oxford University Press, 1982), 283–313; and Eric Foner, *Nothing But Freedom: Emancipation and Its Legacy* (Baton Rouge: Louisiana State University Press, 1983).

10. Two studies that have received critical acclaim are Thomas Holt, *Black Over White: Negro Political Leadership in South Carolina during Reconstruction* (Urbana: University of Illinois Press, 1977); and Leon F. Litwack, *Been in the Storm So Long: The Aftermath of Slavery* (New York: Knopf, 1979). Recognition is also due August Meier for his contributions to black history not only as productive scholar but as editor of the University of Illinois Press series Blacks in the New World. His major special study within the time span of this essay appeared in 1963, *Negro Thought in America,*

did not pass them by, though a contrary conclusion might be inferred from the account of contemporary historical writing undertaken for the American Historical Association and published in 1980. That volume found no place in its table of contents or even in its index for Civil Rights, Civil War, Emancipation, Freedmen, Race or Racism, Radical Republicans, Reconstruction, Redemption, or Segregation.[11] For all their receptivity to new approaches and techniques, historians of the emancipation and postemancipation decades continued to affirm rather than repudiate the centrality of politics and law as elements of power. They concerned themselves with related ideology, interests, issues, motives, and leadership.[12] They helped reinvigorate constitutional-legal history and pursued justice at the local level in order to determine the bounds of the former slave's freedom. Not even the contentious reexamination of the postemancipation economy has ignored political power implemented through courthouse and statehouse or abdicated at the national level.[13] And while the "presidential synthesis" was presumably discredited as superficial, revisionist historians of Reconstruction were establishing the importance of President Andrew Johnson's role in obstructing social change.

A handful of books published from 1960 through 1964 shifted the focus of the revisionist revolution from the South to the nation's capital and further north.[14] They linked Reconstruction to the antislavery

---

1880–1915: Racial Ideologies in the Age of Booker T. Washington (Ann Arbor: University of Michigan Press).

11. The footnotes are somewhat more generous in recognizing work in the field. Michael Kammen (ed.), *The Past Before Us: Contemporary Historical Writing in the United States* (Ithaca: Cornell University Press, 1980).

12. The affirmation is implicit in their work; for an explicit statement, see Eric Foner, *Politics and Ideology in the Age of the Civil War* (New York: Oxford University Press, 1980), 3–12.

13. Harold M. Hyman, *A More Perfect Union: The Impact of the Civil War and Reconstruction on the Constitution* (New York: Knopf, 1973), and "Law and the Impact of the Civil War: A Review Essay," *Civil War History*, XIV (March, 1968), 51–59; William Cohen, "Negro Involuntary Servitude in the South, 1865–1940: A Preliminary Analysis," *Journal of Southern History*, XLII (February, 1976), 31–60; Harold D. Woodman, "Post–Civil War Southern Agriculture and the Law," *Agricultural History*, LIII (January, 1979), 319–37; and see Harold D. Woodman's essay in this volume.

14. Eric L. McKitrick, *Andrew Johnson and Reconstruction* (Chicago: University of Chicago Press, 1960); LaWanda F. Cox and John H. Cox, *Politics, Principle, and Prejudice, 1865–1866: Dilemma of Reconstruction America* (New York: Free Press, 1963); W. R. Brock, *An American Crisis: Congress and Reconstruction, 1865–1867* (New York: St. Martin's Press, 1963); James M. McPherson, *The Struggle for Equality:*

movement and pushed back its chronological beginning to the first years of the Civil War. Previously, the generally accepted view of the conflict over national policy toward the seceded South had been one of Radicals as vindictive conspirators, of Andrew Johnson as a flawed but genuine statesman, and of identity between his policy—and his enemies (*i.e.,* the Radicals)—and those of Lincoln. Except for conceding sincere concern on the part of a few righteous impractical idealists, the historiography still dominant in the 1950s had reduced to a nonissue, a mere rhetorical cover for other objectives, the question of the emancipated Negro's status as a free man.[15]

The composite picture derived much of its strength from Howard K. Beale's *The Critical Year* (1930). His work supplemented rather than discredited that of the Dunningites, for Beale had not yet questioned their view of a postwar South prostrate under military rule and "negro supremacy." With impressive scholarship, he had extended

---

Abolitionists and the Negro in the Civil War and Reconstruction (Princeton: Princeton University Press, 1964); Willie Lee Rose, *Rehearsal for Reconstruction: The Port Royal Experiment* (Indianapolis: Bobbs-Merrill, 1964).

An important link between revisionism facing North and the earlier revisionism facing South was John Hope Franklin's concept of developments under Johnson ("Reconstruction: Confederate Style," Chap. 3 of *Reconstruction After the Civil War*). David Donald's essays on impeachment and on Lincoln and the Radicals (see note 5) were seminal, as were the Coxes' articles published in the 1950s on O. O. Howard and the Freedmen's Bureau and on the promise of land for the freedmen (see notes 47, 53).

15. The most important dissent, W. E. Burghardt Du Bois, *Black Reconstruction: An Essay Toward a History of the Part Which Black Folk Played in the Attempt to Reconstruct Democracy in America, 1860–1880* (New York: Harcourt, Brace, 1935), had little impact on white historiography in part because of its Marxist orientation. Analyses of writings on Reconstruction have been numerous. In addition to those by Weisberger, Wharton, Pressly, and Kincaid, see T. Harry Williams, "An Analysis of Some Reconstruction Attitudes," *Journal of Southern History,* XII (November, 1946), 469–86; Willard Hays, "Andrew Johnson's Reputation," *East Tennessee Historical Society Publications,* XXXI (1959), 1–31, XXXII (1960), 18–50; Albert Castel, "Andrew Johnson: His Historiographical Rise and Fall," *Mid-America,* XLV (July, 1963), 175–84; Staughton Lynd, "Rethinking Slavery and Reconstruction," *Journal of Negro History,* L (July, 1965), 198–209; B. P. Gallaway, "Economic Determinism in Reconstruction Historiography," *Southwestern Social Science Quarterly,* XLVI (December, 1965), 244–54; Harold M. Hyman (ed.), *The Radical Republicans and Reconstruction, 1861–1870* (Indianapolis: Bobbs-Merrill, 1967), xvii–lxviii; James E. Sefton, "The Impeachment of Andrew Johnson: A Century of Writing," *Civil War History,* XIV (June, 1968), 120–47; Eric L. McKitrick (ed.), *Andrew Johnson: A Profile* (New York: Hill & Wang, 1969), vii–xxii; Richard O. Curry, "The Civil War and Reconstruction, 1861–1877: A Critical Overview of Recent Trends and Interpretations," *Civil War History,* XX (September, 1974), 215–38; and Albert Castel, *The Presidency of Andrew Johnson* (Lawrence: Regents Press of Kansas, 1979), 218–30.

the Beardian concept of the Civil War as economic revolution to the postwar struggle between Johnson and Congress. In the election of 1866 he saw the triumph of northern business interests through campaign techniques that made the democratic process a mockery. Radical Republicans had skillfully used "claptrap" and emotion to obscure the real (*i.e.,* economic) issues; as a result, it had been impossible for the electorate to know the truth or to vote wisely. The result ushered in the Age of Big Business. Reinforcing the hostile portrait of the Radicals were four books published from 1928 to 1930 that brightened Andrew Johnson's image. Two were sympathetic biographies, and the others were dramatic accounts of the period as an era of tragedy and hate. Of similar effect was T. Harry Williams' *Lincoln and the Radicals,* which appeared a decade later.[16]

The first part of the composite picture to be discredited was Beale's economic interpretation. Three historians who cannot be classified as Reconstruction revisionists, Robert P. Sharkey, Stanley Coben, and Irwin Unger, each published studies in 1959 that collectively destroyed Beale's assumption of a community of interest among northern businessmen and between them and the Radicals. Moreover, President Johnson was found to have enjoyed substantial support from the North's economic elite and the Radicals among the leaders of organized labor. Only by implication did one of the three, Stanley Coben, call for a fresh examination of the motivation and aims of Radical Reconstruction, and even he did not hazard an interpretation to replace the one he helped shatter.[17] The Beard-Beale thesis never regained respectability, but there has been a remarkable power of persistence in the assumption that economic interests or forces

16. Howard K. Beale, *The Critical Year: A Study of Andrew Johnson and Reconstruction* (New York: Harcourt, Brace, 1930), esp. 1–9; Robert W. Winston, *Andrew Johnson: Plebeian and Patriot* (New York: H. Holt & Co., 1928); Lloyd P. Stryker, *Andrew Johnson: A Study in Courage* (New York: Macmillan, 1929); Claude G. Bowers, *The Tragic Era: The Revolution after Lincoln* (New York: Blue Ribbon Books, 1929); George Fort Milton, *The Age of Hate: Andrew Johnson and the Radicals* (New York: Coward-McCann, 1930); T. Harry Williams, *Lincoln and the Radicals* (Madison: University of Wisconsin Press, 1941).

17. Robert P. Sharkey, *Money, Class, and Party: An Economic Study of Civil War and Reconstruction* (Baltimore: Johns Hopkins Press, 1959), esp. 279–82, 287–311; Stanley Coben, "Northeastern Business and Radical Reconstruction: A Reexamination," *Mississippi Valley Historical Review,* XLVI (June, 1959), 67–90; Irwin Unger, "Business Men and Specie Resumption," *Political Science Quarterly,* LXXIV (March, 1959), 46–70, and *The Greenback Era: A Social and Political History of American Finance, 1865–1879* (Princeton: Princeton University Press, 1964), esp. 3–9. See also Gallaway, "Economic Determinism in Reconstruction Historiography."

must somehow constitute the primary explanatory element in accounting for what the nation did, and omitted to do, in respect to former slaves.[18]

The revisionists of the early 1960s did major damage to the Beard-Beale explanation by supplanting it. They provided an answer to Coben's implicit query: if the Reconstruction conflict was not over economic interests, what was it all about? The answer that their work suggested coincided with the spirit of the times: at stake in the political contention over readmission of the seceded states had been the status of the freedmen and, by racial identity, the status of all Afro-Americans. The revisionists brought back to center stage in the drama of Reconstruction the issue of the future of the slave—his release from bondage and the nature of his freedom. Involvement in that issue, as some of their work suggested and later studies confirmed, had not been confined to the few but had extended to the electorate of the free states, both North and West.[19] The claim to civil rights and human dignity for—and by—blacks in the name of justice and a more perfect Union linked the 1860s and the 1960s. A changed conception of the past became evident as the terms *First Reconstruction* and *Second Reconstruction* gained wide usage to denote two great national efforts on behalf of black rights. And for a fleeting moment, both past and present seemed to dispel disillusion with the democratic process, a disillusionment Beale had voiced and the Dunningites had implied.

While the Coxes and Brock had been explicit in identifying the rights of blacks as central to the conflict between the president and the Republican Congress, McKitrick's account, with its delineation of Andrew Johnson as "outsider," its emphasis upon the importance of symbolism, and its suggestion of a moderate compromise, was more ambiguous. Indeed, a hostile critic could commend McKitrick

18. Patrick W. Riddleberger attempted to synthesize Beale's work and that of the revisionists in *1866: The Critical Year Revisited* (Carbondale: Southern Illinois University Press, 1979). See also August Meier, "An Epitaph for the Writing of Reconstruction History?" *Reviews in American History,* IX (March, 1981), 82–87; and my discussion later of the army, the Freedmen's Bureau, education for freedmen, the land question, and the various class interpretations of the "failure" of Reconstruction.

19. A recent study that strikingly illustrates the point is Eugene H. Berwanger, *The West and Reconstruction* (Urbana: University of Illinois Press, 1981), esp. 3–12. See also James C. Mohr, *The Radical Republicans and Reform in New York during Reconstruction* (Ithaca: Cornell University Press, 1973), and Mohr (ed.), *Radical Republicans in the North: State Politics During Reconstruction* (Baltimore: Johns Hopkins University Press, 1976).

"for not bleeding at the pores over phony moralities or beating his breast in the modern manner about democracy." Yet appearing as it did in the midst of the civil rights revolution, *Andrew Johnson and Reconstruction* became identified with the thesis "the true issue . . . of Reconstruction was the status of the Negro in American society."[20] Both James McPherson, in *The Struggle for Equality,* and Willie Lee Rose, in *Rehearsal for Reconstruction,* revealed the integrity and continuing vitality of the antislavery commitment to black freedom and black advancement. The Coxes had arrived at the conclusion that the unnegotiable issue between President Johnson and the Republican leadership was citizenship for blacks, with immediate recognition of equal civil rights except suffrage.

In a review of the Rose and McPherson volumes, David Brion Davis accepted in respect to the abolitionists an implication of the revisionists' work not confined to the antislavery vanguard, namely, that a revolution had been attempted. And he identified a key problem. He held it "imperative for us to know what went wrong."[21] Explanations already had been offered and many more were to follow, yet almost two decades later, no answer commanded consensus among historians. Indeed, by then, there were those who held that no revolution had been intended. A second question emerged, similarly intractable and at this writing but partially resolved. With the publication of Leon Litwack's *North of Slavery* in 1961, it was evident that scholarship had demolished the illusion, if ever it existed, of an antebellum North free of race prejudice. During the 1960s and 1970s an outpouring of historical writing on white racial attitudes and race relations, quantitatively the most verifiable impact of contemporary concerns upon historical inquiry, kept that reality highly visible.[22] In

---

20. Cox and Cox, *Politics, Principle, and Prejudice,* 195–232; Brock, *An American Crisis,* 14, 18–23, 85–92, 248–49; McKitrick, *Andrew Johnson and Reconstruction,* 21–41, 334–35, 409–10, 421, 442–43; William B. Hesseltine, Review of McKitrick's *Andrew Johnson and Reconstruction,* in *Journal of Southern History,* XXVII (February, 1961), 111; Castel, *The Presidency of Andrew Johnson,* 222.

21. David Brion Davis, "Abolitionists and the Freedmen: An Essay Review," *Journal of Southern History,* XXXI (May, 1965), 167.

22. A pathbreaking article was Leslie H. Fishel, Jr. "Northern Prejudice and Negro Suffrage, 1865–1870," *Journal of Negro History,* XXXIX (January, 1954), 8–26. The most influential general works were Leon F. Litwack, *North of Slavery: The Negro in the Free States, 1790–1860* (Chicago: University of Chicago Press, 1961); Winthrop D. Jordan, *White over Black: American Attitudes Toward the Negro, 1550–1812* (Chapel Hill: University of North Carolina Press, 1968); and George M. Fredrickson, *The Black Image in the White Mind: The Debate on Afro-American*

this context the complementary question to What went wrong? was How did it happen that a race-conscious white North, where (to use Lincoln's words) "not a single man of your [the black] race is made the equal of a single man of ours," set black slaves free and then made all blacks the equal of whites before the law and at the ballot box? The difficulty of this critical question has been compounded by semantics. In the terminology of the 1960s, the aim of the revolution attempted in the 1860s became "racial equality" rather than equality of civil rights irrespective of race. All white racial attitudes falling short of the 1960s' standard tended to become homogenized under the undifferentiated label of "racism."

The northward direction of revisionist writings stimulated investigation of an apparently more manageable set of queries centering on the congressional Radicals and their relationship to fellow Republicans. In the discredited orthodoxy, Radicals had been the policy makers, using conspiracy and manipulation. McKitrick, the Coxes, and Brock all gave to moderates the critical role in the break with President Johnson. Meanwhile, Harold Hyman had called attention to the influence of army generals who had become radicalized, and David Donald had pointed out the near unanimity of the Republican vote on Reconstruction measures.[23] The new tool of roll-call analysis seemed to offer the possibility of settling once and for all who the Radicals were, their motives and interests, their divergence and convergence with other Republicans, and whether party had been more important than faction or geographic bloc in determining policy.

The first major reexamination of the Radicals was not based upon the new methodology. In *The Radical Republicans* (1969), Hans Trefousse reestablished their critical importance, at least through the

Character and Destiny, 1817–1914 (New York: Harper & Row, 1971). Other studies of special import for the Civil War era included Eugene H. Berwanger, *The Frontier Against Slavery: Western Anti-Negro Prejudice and the Slavery Extension Controversy* (Urbana: University of Illinois Press, 1967); V. Jacque Voegeli, *Free but Not Equal: The Midwest and the Negro During the Civil War* (Chicago: University of Chicago Press, 1967); James A. Rawley, *Race & Politics: "Bleeding Kansas" and the Coming of the Civil War* (Philadelphia: Lippincott, 1969); Forrest G. Wood, *Black Scare: The Racist Response to Emancipation and Reconstruction* (Berkeley: University of California Press, 1968); and David A. Gerber's fine state study, *Black Ohio and the Color Line, 1860–1915* (Urbana: University of Illinois Press, 1976).

23. Harold M. Hyman, "Johnson, Stanton, and Grant: A Reconsideration of the Army's Role in the Events Leading to Impeachment," *American Historical Review*, LXVI (October, 1960), 85–100; Donald, "Devils Facing Zionwards," in McWhiney (ed.), *Grant, Lee, Lincoln, and the Radicals*, 79–80.

war years, in moving the Republican party toward the elimination of slavery and the recognition of civil rights for blacks. He saw these goals as shared by President Lincoln, who was politically astute enough to implement them. In the face of President Johnson's opposition and the magnitude of the postwar problem, their influence diminished and was finally lost when the Senate failed to convict in the impeachment trial. As in his earlier biography of Benjamin Wade, Trefousse exposed race prejudice among friends of the Negro without painting them as hypocrites or diminishing their achievements. A notable reinterpretation of Edwin M. Stanton and a growing number of biographies of Republican congressional leaders provided an additional dimension to revisionism.[24]

Roll-call analysis found impressive application in Michael Les Benedict's detailed legislative study, *A Compromise of Principle* (1974). As a synthesis and extension of revisionism, as well as a fusion of traditional and new research methods, Benedict's work commanded universal respect. However, his identification and classification of Radicals and other Republicans did not settle that problem once and for all. Of greater significance in the development of Reconstruction historiography was a different question Benedict raised: Was congressional Reconstruction policy "in any true sense radical"? His

24. Hans L. Trefousse, *The Radicals Republicans: Lincoln's Vanguard for Racial Justice* (New York: Knopf, 1969), *Ben Butler: The South Called Him BEAST!* (New York: Twayne Publishers, 1957), *Benjamin Franklin Wade: Radical Republican from Ohio* (New York: Twayne Publishers, 1963), and *Carl Schurz: A Biography* (Knoxville: University of Tennessee Press, 1982); Fawn M. Brodie, *Thaddeus Stevens: Scourge of the South* (New York: Norton, 1959); Benjamin P. Thomas and Harold M. Hyman, *Stanton: The Life and Times of Lincoln's Secretary of War* (New York: Knopf, 1962); Charles A. Jellison, *Fessenden of Maine: Civil War Senator* (Binghamton, N.Y.: Syracuse University Press, 1962); Norma L. Peterson, *Freedom and Franchise: The Political Career of B. Gratz Brown* (Columbia: University of Missouri Press, 1965); Mark M. Krug, *Lyman Trumbull: Conservative Radical* (New York: A. S. Barnes & Co., 1965); Richard S. West, Jr., *Lincoln's Scapegoat General: A Life of Benjamin F. Butler, 1818–1893* (Boston: Houghton Mifflin, 1965); David Donald, *Charles Sumner and the Rights of Man* (New York: Knopf, 1970); Ernest McKay, *Henry Wilson: Practical Radical, A Portrait of a Politician* (Port Washington, N.Y.: Kennikat Press, 1971); Richard H. Abbott, *Cobbler in Congress: The Life of Henry Wilson, 1812–1875* (Lexington: University Press of Kentucky, 1972); Gerald S. Henig, *Henry Winter Davis: Antebellum and Civil War Congressman from Maryland* (New York: Twayne Publishers, 1973); Robert F. Horowitz, *The Great Impeacher: A Political Biography of James M. Ashley* (New York: Brooklyn College Press, 1979); James Pickett Jones, *John A. Logan: Stalwart Republican from Illinois* (Tallahassee: University Presses of Florida, 1982).

work was read as answering the question in the negative. Benedict effectively demonstrated that Reconstruction legislation and amendments were the result of compromise, compromise that rejected the more extreme, or radical, proposals. He implied much more, but not unambiguously. His study, he warned, by concentrating on differences *among* Republicans offered "a somewhat distorted picture," for it directed attention away from the "immense" difference between Republicans and their adversaries, President Johnson and the Democrats. The latter involved a difference in principle which the former did not.[25] The warning was little heeded. By the mid-1970s the view that Radical Reconstruction had not been radical, with the implication that it should have been, appeared dominant, though not without challenge.[26] And by then, in-depth study of the nature and extent of the societal change that followed upon emancipation was only beginning.

In 1975, Richard N. Current observed that categorizing Reconstruction congressmen by roll-call analysis had reached the point of diminishing returns. Yet there was to be one more major effort, Allan Bogue's *The Earnest Men* (1981), the culmination of work begun much earlier. It is an exhaustive, technically sophisticated study of voting and rhetoric in the Civil War Senate, but its findings are limited. They indicate that Radicals in the Senate were less racist, less scrupulous about constitutional restraints, and more vengeful than their Republican colleagues. Bogue believes such distinctions within the party important, taking issue with historians who emphasize the basic agreement among Republicans. Yet he does not deny a Republican consensus on goals, or the importance of party, or the difference between parties. Nor does his division of all Republicans into two categories, radical and nonradical (he uses the small *r*), settle the question of Radical identity. A faint echo of Beard and Beale is evident in his observation that the Radicals' readiness to extend national at the expense of state power was "certainly such as to gratify the industrialist interested in untrammeled development of the nation's economic potential." And by focusing on a problem that arose out of the old orthodoxy, Bogue appears to sound a retreat from the

25. Michael Les Benedict, *A Compromise of Principle: Congressional Republicans and Reconstruction, 1863–1869* (New York: Norton, 1974), 14. See also his "Racism and Equality in America," *Reviews in American History*, VI (March, 1978), 18–20.

26. See Peter Kolchin, "The Myth of Radical Reconstruction," *Reviews in American History*, III (June, 1975), 228–35.

centrality in historical writing since the early 1960s of race attitudes and the black man's status.[27]

Since roll-call analysis could not definitely settle the question of who were the Radicals or deal with the problem of whether Republican party unity or intraparty differences were of greater historical significance, it is not surprising that the new technique proved incapable of establishing the motivation of Republican congressmen generally. It did, however, show conclusively a high degree of Republican consistency toward legislation favorable to blacks.[28]

Historical writings, both traditional and methodologically innovative, made increasingly apparent a significant divergence in respect to race issues and attitudes between Republicans and northern Democrats. The racist stigma so readily attached to Republicans of the 1860s by scholars writing in the midst of the civil rights struggles of the 1960s has been significantly qualified in light of divergent party behavior. The degree of Republican support for emancipation, and then for the protection and rights of blacks, contrasted sharply with the record of their political opponents at the state as well as the national level. Recognition of this party difference relates to the basic riddle—how had race-prejudiced northern whites come to make blacks their equals in both the law and the franchise? Sophisticated quantitative techniques applied to election returns at the local level when fused with other types of evidence and analysis, including the ethnocultural, have made it possible to explore with remarkable subtlety and precision the interrelations between party and constituency on issues affecting the status of blacks. To date, the outstanding example is Phyllis F. Field's *The Politics of Race in New York* (1982). Her work and that of Robert Dykstra, John Rozett, and Michael McManus, when combined with other recent studies less technical in their approach, have clarified important components of the riddle.[29]

27. Except as a technical achievement, the place of the book in the mainstream of Reconstruction historiography is unclear, for Bogue's caveats are numerous and his conclusions guarded. Bogue, *The Earnest Men*, esp. 98–124, 296–341 (quotation on p. 333).

28. Glenn M. Linden, "A Note on Negro Suffrage and Republican Politics," *Journal of Southern History*, XXXVI (August, 1970), 411–20, and *Politics or Principle: Congressional Voting on the Civil War Amendments and Pro-Negro Measures, 1838–1869* (Seattle: University of Washington Press, 1976).

29. Phyllis F. Field, *The Politics of Race in New York: The Struggle for Black Suffrage in the Civil War Era* (Ithaca: Cornell University Press, 1982), and "Republicans and Black Suffrage in New York State: The Grass Roots Response," *Civil War History*, XXI (June, 1975), 136–47; Robert R. Dykstra, "Iowa: 'Bright Radical Star,'" in

The riddle itself has many dimensions. Not surprisingly, in the writings of the past two decades, there has been disagreement, major but often latent, over the question of whether Republicans during the war and the postwar years had used blacks for party (or national) advantage or had used party (and national policy) to advance the condition of blacks.[30] Debate crystallized over one aspect of the disagreement, the issue of why Republicans supported equal suffrage. The view that they did so in order to maintain the party's political power, shorn of its Beard-Beale economic component, appeared credible. Few would dispute the basic assumption that the purpose of a major party was to obtain or retain political power. The history of the Republican party, though brief, conformed to that norm; and by the 1960s, historians had unearthed convincing evidence that made Republican action suspect—a pervasive race prejudice in the free

---

Mohr (ed.), *Radical Republicans in the North*, 167–93; John M. Rozett, "Racism and Republican Emergence in Illinois, 1848–1860: A Re-Evaluation of Republican Negrophobia," *Civil War History*, XXII (June, 1976), 101–15; Michael J. McManus, "Wisconsin Republicans and Negro Suffrage: Attitudes and Behavior, 1857," *Civil War History*, XXV (March, 1979), 36–54. Through a sophisticated statistical analysis of voting behavior, Dale Baum, *The Civil War Party System: The Case of Massachusetts, 1848–1876* (Chapel Hill: University of North Carolina Press, 1984), has established the primary importance of antislavery together with "middling" wealth in forging and sustaining the Republican majority in Massachusetts until the mid-1870s. For more traditional accounts, Cox and Cox, *Politics, Principle, and Prejudice*, 211–28; Eric Foner, *Free Soil, Free Labor, Free Men: The Ideology of the Republican Party Before the Civil War* (New York: Oxford University Press, 1970), 261–300, 333; Mohr, *The Radical Republicans and Reform in New York*, 202–70; Richard H. Sewell, *Ballots for Freedom: Antislavery Politics in the United States, 1837–1860* (New York: Oxford University Press, 1976), esp. viii, 321–42; Richard Paul Fuke, "Hugh Lennox Bond and Radical Republican Ideology," *Journal of Southern History*, XLV (November, 1979), 569–86; Berwanger, *The West and Reconstruction*, esp. 5–6, 102–84, 202–208; LaWanda F. Cox, *Lincoln and Black Freedom: A Study in Presidential Leadership* (Columbia: University of South Carolina Press, 1981), 161–64.

For fresh perspectives on the Democratic party that take into account racial attitudes and tactics, Jean H. Baker, *Affairs of Party: The Political Culture of Northern Democrats in the Mid-Nineteenth Century* (Ithaca: Cornell University Press, 1983); Joel H. Silbey, *A Respectable Minority: The Democratic Party in the Civil War Era, 1860–1868* (New York: Norton, 1977); Lawrence Grossman, *The Democratic Party and the Negro: Northern and National Politics, 1868–92* (Urbana: University of Illinois Press, 1976). See also Edward L. Gambill, *Conservative Ordeal: Northern Democrats and Reconstruction, 1865–1868* (Ames: Iowa State University Press, 1981); and Jerome Mushkat, *The Reconstruction of the New York Democracy, 1861–1874* (Rutherford, N.J.: Fairleigh Dickinson University Press, 1981).

30. The sharp dichotomy is, of course, an overstatement, but even when viewed as a matter of emphasis, the disagreement is fundamental.

states and its existence within the party's leadership and ranks. Yet the interest-of-party view was open to challenge. Advocacy of equal suffrage in the face of pervasive prejudice could be presumed to carry immediate political risk, and the potential ultimate gain for Republicans from impartial suffrage was not obvious and assured.[31] Although the studies cited here bear upon the disagreement over motivation, particularly as to the extension of suffrage, their conclusions are tentative and qualified.

A consensus appears to be emerging, however, in respect to certain aspects of the riddle of black advancement and white prejudice—the importance of party, of national issues at the state level, and of the dynamics of party attitude toward race issues. Through the 1860s, Republican sentiment became progressively more well disposed; static analysis cannot explain Republican behavior. While Democrats, with only minor deviation, were united against problack legislation, the Republican party was divided sufficiently to jeopardize its political fortunes. In advancing the cause of blacks, Republican political leaders safeguarded the interest of party by a variety of strategies. They manipulated the timing and wording of issues and justified the party's commitment to blacks by uniting it with patriotism, with animosity toward slavery and the South, and with loyalty to party. It now appears that party identification with efforts to improve the status of blacks was indispensable, though not always sufficient, for their success. This evolving historiographic recognition of the critical role of party carries no necessary corollary as to motive. Neither does it establish a greater influence of party on constituency than of constituency on party, since hazard to party on issues of black status lay not in a majority but in a minority of northern Republican voters. In short, the role of party illuminates but cannot solve the riddle if viewed solely as an instrument for formulating strategy and evoking loyalty.

31. The challenge was made in LaWanda Cox and John H. Cox, "Negro Suffrage and Republican Politics: The Problem of Motivation in Reconstruction Historiography," *Journal of Southern History*, XXXIII (August, 1967), 303–30. See also Cox and Cox (eds.), *Reconstruction, the Negro, and the New South* (Columbia: University of South Carolina Press, 1973), xiv–xix. For the most authoritative conflicting view, William Gillette, *The Right to Vote: Politics and the Passage of the Fifteenth Amendment* (Baltimore: Johns Hopkins Press, 1965), and in the 1969 paperback edition, the added epilogue (166–90). For comment, Curry, "The Civil War and Reconstruction," 227.

The significance of state studies that examine the relationship between party and constituency on race issues does not diminish the importance of the national arena. Three books by Herman Belz, sharply focused upon congressional action and constitutional theory, added significantly to revisionism. They linked Reconstruction to emancipation and in doing so offered a distinctive explanation for the Republican party's identification with black rights. In *Reconstructing the Union* (1969), Belz pushed back the chronological beginning of Reconstruction to 1861 by showing that Congress deliberately refrained from pledging noninterference with the institution. He also highlighted Lincoln's commitment to emancipation in his Reconstruction Proclamation and confirmed the contention that Lincoln and the Radicals were in basic agreement, capable of jointly resolving the Reconstruction dilemma. In *A New Birth of Freedom* (1976), Belz started with the assumption that congressional emancipation began as a measure of military expediency. He then followed the process and reasoning through which emancipation became a commitment beyond expediency, culminating in the guarantees of citizenship and civil rights embodied in the Civil Rights Act of 1866 and the Fourteenth Amendment. His third book, *Emancipation and Equal Rights* (1978), argued that Republicans held a constitutional concept of republicanism as a nonmonarchical government based upon popular consent and participation, a concept incompatible with slavery that led to emancipation and equal citizenship for blacks.[32] In other words, Belz presented an inherently logical explanation for the Republican party commitment to black civil equality. It had resulted from a process of interaction between events from 1861 through 1866 and basic political concepts, those of self-government and of the inherent natural rights of free persons.

In upholding black civil rights during the Second Reconstruction, the Supreme Court both utilized constitutional-political scholarship and ensured continuing attention to the constitutional amendments

32. Herman Belz, *Reconstructing the Union: Theory and Policy During the Civil War* (Ithaca: Cornell University Press for the American Historical Association, 1969), *A New Birth of Freedom: The Republican Party and Freedmen's Rights, 1861 to 1866* (Westport, Conn.: Greenwood Press, 1976), and *Emancipation and Equal Rights: Politics and Constitutionalism in the Civil War Era* (New York: Norton, 1978). See also the Belz revision of *The American Constitution: Its Origin and Development*, by Alfred H. Kelly and Winfred A. Harbison (6th ed.; New York: Norton, 1983), 299–371.

of the 1860s and their judicial interpretation during the posteman-cipation decades.[33] Attack on segregation was paramount in the mid-twentieth-century civil rights movement in and out of court, but the issues, both historical and contemporary, went beyond Jim Crow. Segregation by the 1950s had become intolerable as a "badge of ser-vitude," the blatant symbol of the distance between reality and the equal citizenship and human rights of free men that the Republican party had sought to secure by legislation and constitutional amend-ment in the 1860s.

Ironically, while the law Republicans had framed became the basis for the Court's belated defense of black rights, the dominant view of their work as interpreted by constitutional historians during the 1960s and 1970s was one of fundamental inadequacy because it had failed to revolutionize the federal structure of American government. First presented briefly but brilliantly by Alfred H. Kelly in comments during a 1965 conference on Reconstruction, the thesis was incorpo-rated by Harold Hyman in his impressive examination of the impact of war and Reconstruction upon the Constitution, and ably developed by Michael Les Benedict and Phillip Paludan.[34] The criticism may have arisen from apprehension over the outcome of the Second Re-construction as much as from the thicket of constitutional argument over the intent and scope of the emancipation amendments. Even as they were being cleared of the old charge of flagrant disregard for Constitution and courts,[35] Republican congressional leaders stood

33. See Alfred H. Kelly, Review of H. J. Graham's *Everyman's Constitution,* in *Journal of Southern History,* XXXV (May, 1969), 290–92; and Charles R. Black, Jr., *Brief for Appellants: Brown v. Board of Education of Topeka* . . . (rpr. New York: Supreme Printing, 1954), foreword and Pt. 2 (pp. 67–188). For citations to relevant historical and legal scholarship, see Harold M. Hyman and William M. Wiecek, *Equal Justice Under Law: Constitutional Development, 1835–1875* (New York: Harper & Row, 1982), 552–53; Belz, *Emancipation and Equal Rights,* 160–61; Kelly, Har-bison, and Belz, *The American Constitution,* 799–800; and footnotes in Michael Les Benedict, "Preserving Federalism: Reconstruction and the Waite Court," *Supreme Court Review,* 1978, pp. 39–79.

34. See Alfred H. Kelly's comments on Hyman's paper in Harold M. Hyman (ed.), *New Frontiers of the American Reconstruction* (Urbana: University of Illinois Press, 1966), 51–57; Hyman, *A More Perfect Union,* 438–41, 447–49; Michael Les Bene-dict, "Preserving the Constitution: The Conservative Basis of Radical Reconstruc-tion," *Journal of American History,* LXI (June, 1974), 65–90; Phillip S. Paludan, *A Covenant with Death: The Constitution, Law, and Equality in the Civil War Era* (Urbana: University of Illinois Press, 1975), 1–60, 274–82.

35. Stanley I. Kutler, "Reconstruction and the Supreme Court: The Numbers

reindicted for the offense of a constitutional conservatism so devoted to traditional state-oriented federalism as to have foredoomed the former slaves' rights as free men and citizens. There were dissenting voices, none more insistent among younger scholars in the field than that of Robert Kaczorowski, who characterized constitutional change as indeed revolutionary. He held that legal authority under the Thirteenth and Fourteenth amendments was sufficient for national action to protect civil rights, that such authority was intended, exercised, and generally recognized until the Supreme Court's 1873 decision in the Slaughterhouse cases.[36]

The charge of constitutional conservatism, with its emphasis upon continuity, fed a negative judgment on the Republican Reconstruction effort reached on a number of other counts by historians writing in the late 1960s and 1970s. Yet disparagement met resistance from constitutional historians, including those identified with the criticism of Republicans as constitutional conservatives. Thus it was Paludan who answered the most scathing historical verdict on the war and emancipation to appear in print during the two decades under review. Despite the constricting effect of federalism, Benedict has shown that the Waite Court of the 1870s and 1880s recognized that power to protect civil rights had been given to Congress under the postwar amendments. According to his analysis, the justices in their *dicta* left a heritage that preserved, rather than repudiated, that power. And Hyman, in a fresh synthesis of mid-nineteenth-century constitutional development written in collaboration with William Wiecek, presented the Thirteenth Amendment as a sufficient constitutional base for national authority to make secure an expansive concept of civil rights. The work of Belz has generally emphasized the positive in

---

Game Reconsidered," *Journal of Southern History*, XXXII (February, 1966), 42–58, and *Judicial Power and Reconstruction Politics* (Chicago: University of Chicago Press, 1968).

36. Robert J. Kaczorowski, *The Politics of Judicial Interpretation: The Federal Courts, Department of Justice and Civil Rights, 1866–1876* (New York: Oceana Publications, 1985), "Searching for the Intent of the Framers of the Fourteenth Amendment," *Connecticut Law Review*, V (Winter, 1972–73), 368–98, and two papers on civil rights during Reconstruction presented at the annual meetings of the Southern Historical Association, Atlanta Ga., November, 1973, and the Organization of American Historians, Boston, April, 1975. From a different perspective, Peyton McCrary, like Kaczorowski, presents emancipation-postemancipation developments as revolutionary ("The Party of Revolution: Republican Ideas About Politics and Social Change, 1862–1867," *Civil War History*, XXX [December, 1984], 328–50).

terms of the magnitude of the constitutional change that transformed the legal status of blacks and nationalized civil rights.[37]

Ambivalence and outright clash of attitude mark historical writings dealing with the origin, nature, and execution of national policy toward southern blacks. Rehabilitation of Republican policy makers at the hands of revisionists of the early 1960s was eclipsed but not obliterated. With the climax of the civil rights and the historiographic revolutions coinciding in time, attention naturally focused on the problem of What went wrong? And as study after study exposed the pervasiveness of northern race prejudice in the Civil War era and the failure even of antislavery men to meet the standard of "full" equality for blacks, the inference that "racism" had been the fatal contaminant of the nation's first civil rights effort found wide acceptance. Within the work of a single historian, the most striking example of ambivalence and the darkening historiographic mood can be found in two widely read essays. C. Vann Woodward, in "Equality: The Deferred Commitment," identified equality as a third aim that emerged during the Civil War and became a formal commitment in the Civil Rights Act of 1866. Some years later, he repudiated "the third war aim" and, in "Seeds of Failure in Radical Race Policy," reduced the impetus for the Civil Rights Act of 1866 to little more than a desire to prevent southern blacks from bursting in hordes upon the North. Yet he concluded: "It is, nevertheless, impossible to account fully for such limited successes as the Second Reconstruction can claim without acknowledging its profound indebtedness to the First."[38]

---

37. John S. Rosenberg, "Toward a New Civil War Revisionism," *American Scholar,* XXXVIII (Spring, 1969), 250–72; the response of Phillip S. Paludan, "The American Civil War: Triumph through Tragedy," *Civil War History,* XX (September, 1974), 239–50; Rosenberg, "The American Civil War and the Problem of 'Presentism': A Reply to Phillip S. Paludan," *Civil War History,* XXI (September, 1975), 242–53; Paludan, "Taking the Benefits of the Civil War Issue Seriously: A Rejoinder to John S. Rosenberg," *Civil War History,* XXI (September, 1975), 254–60; Benedict, "Preserving Federalism"; Hyman and Wiecek, *Equal Justice Under Law,* 386–438; Kelly, Harbison, and Belz, *The American Constitution,* 328–44, 362–71. For another way in which Reconstruction legislators strengthened federal jurisdiction in the interest of civil rights, see William M. Wiecek, "The Great Writ and Reconstruction: The Habeas Corpus Act of 1867," *Journal of Southern History,* XXXVI (November, 1970), 530–48.

38. C. Vann Woodward, "Equality: The Deferred Commitment," in *The Burden of Southern History* (Baton Rouge: Louisiana State University Press, 1960), 69–87, and "Seeds of Failure in Radical Race Policy," in *American Counterpoint: Slavery and Rac-*

The revisionists of the early 1960s focused attention on Andrew Johnson, leaving unchallenged for a time the interpretation of Lincoln then generally accepted by academic scholars. In contrast to the "Lincoln legend," it portrayed a reluctant emancipator, forced by the pressure of political and military necessity into issuing an Emancipation Proclamation that set no slave free. Lincoln's Reconstruction policy was applauded for its generosity to the (white) South, its opposition to the harsh and revolutionary designs of the Radicals, and its aim of restoring the Union quickly with "the Southern people [allowed] to solve their own race problem."[39] Most authorities did not discount as mere politics Lincoln's moral stance against slavery; Fehrenbacher's 1962 study of Lincoln in the 1850s was notably persuasive. Yet Richard Hofstadter's searing prose retained its corrosive force, particularly his assertion that the Emancipation Proclamation "had all the moral grandeur of a bill of lading." Scholarship had un-

---

ism in the North-South Dialogue (Boston: Little, Brown, 1971), 159–60, 163–83 (quotation on p. 183).

39. J. G. Randall, *The Civil War and Reconstruction* (Boston: Heath, 1937), 483–96, 498, 507–508, 706–707, *Lincoln, the President: Springfield to Gettysburg* (2 vols.; New York: Dodd, Mead, 1946), II, 126, 130–32, 137–39, 141–42, 150, 157–58, 164–65, 181–82; Randall and Richard N. Current, *Lincoln, the President: Last Full Measure* (New York: Dodd, Mead, 1955), 2–6, 27–28, 33; Randall, *Lincoln and the South* (Baton Rouge: Louisiana State University Press, 1946), 81–161; Benjamin P. Thomas, *Abraham Lincoln: A Biography* (New York: Knopf, 1953), 333, 356–57, 359, 405–407, 438 (quotation on p. 407). For a more positive assessment by Randall of Lincoln as emancipator, see his *Lincoln: The Liberal Statesman* (New York: Dodd, Mead, 1947), 192–97.

For two decades Randall was recognized as the leading Lincoln authority in academe, and for an even longer period Thomas' book, which owed much to Randall, was characterized as the best one-volume biography of Lincoln. Randall's views were challenged largely by those outside the ranks of professional historians. In keeping with what appeared the paramount problem of Randall's time, he saw greatness in Lincoln's design for a generous peace. On the peacemaker image, see also Frank L. Owsley, "A Southerner's View of Abraham Lincoln," in Harriet Chappell Owsley (ed.), *The South: Old and New Frontiers: Selected Essays of Frank Lawrence Owsley* (Athens: University of Georgia Press, 1969), 223–34. For comment on Randall's place in historiography, Benjamin P. Thomas, *Portrait for Posterity: Lincoln and His Biographers* (New Brunswick, N.J.: Rutgers University Press, 1947), 275–84; David M. Potter, *The Lincoln Theme and American National Historiography, an Inaugural Lecture Delivered Before the University of Oxford . . .* (Oxford: Clarendon Press, 1948), 22–24; Don E. Fehrenbacher, *The Changing Image of Lincoln in American Historiography* (Oxford: Clarendon Press, 1968), 17–18; and Mark E. Neely, Jr., "The Lincoln Theme Since Randall's Call: The Promises and Perils of Professionalism," *Papers of the Abraham Lincoln Association*, I (1979), 10–18, 23–29, 59.

dermined Lincoln as emancipator and friend of freedom despite the fact that Richard Current had emphasized Lincoln's role in the passage of the Thirteenth Amendment and his ability to outgrow racial prejudices, and Benjamin Quarles, in his evenhanded *Lincoln and the Negro,* had added convincing evidence that in personal relations with blacks Lincoln respected their dignity as persons. It is not surprising that one of the earliest syntheses of Reconstruction revisionism, and undoubtedly the most influential, presented a wartime president who never transcended race prejudice, an enemy of slavery but "not quite the friend of the Negro," a man who embraced his destiny as liberator with reluctance, a skillful politician looking to build a Republican party in the South although that meant white southerners would be free to govern black men subject only "to certain minimum requirements of fair play." [40]

The temper of the civil rights movement, its acute racial sensitivities, its celebration of the "clean, straight tracks of radical reform," its "scorn for the devious ways of statecraft" further darkened Lincoln's already tarnished image. As historians continued to uncover the shocking extent and power of white race prejudice in the Civil War generation and as White Citizens Councils invoked the authority of Lincoln in defense of segregation, Lincoln's denials in the 1850s that he intended or favored political and social equality between the races became familiar and damning quotations. They threatened to transform the image of Lincoln the emancipator into Lincoln the symbol of white America's injustice to black America. Fanned by the defiant spirit of the black power movement, the charge of "white supremacist" made by Lerone Bennett, Jr., in *Ebony* caught fire. The accusation evoked scholarly, thoughtful scrutiny from white historians. Significantly, the response most sympathetic and sensitive to Lincoln left him only a "stepfather," faulted for want of moral indignation in the face of systematic discrimination against free Negroes. In the 1960s and 1970s it was difficult for white historians to recon-

40. Don E. Fehrenbacher, *Prelude to Greatness: Lincoln in the 1850s* (Stanford: Stanford University Press, 1962); Richard Hofstadter, *The American Political Tradition and the Men Who Made It* (New York: Knopf, 1948), 92–134 (quotation on p. 131); Richard N. Current, *The Lincoln Nobody Knows* (New York: Hill & Wang, 1958), 214–36; Benjamin Quarles, *The Negro in the Civil War* (Boston: Little, Brown, 1953), 134–36, 140, 251–55, and *Lincoln and the Negro* (New York: Oxford University Press, 1962), 194–208, 217–24; Kenneth M. Stampp, *The Era of Reconstruction, 1865–1877* (New York: Knopf, 1965), 24–49 (quotations on pp. 35, 48).

cile Lincoln's role "with our own consciences" (to use the words of Robert Johannsen) or to ignore the challenge as ahistorical.[41]

Ironically, what first appeared conclusive documentary proof that Lincoln by 1864 did in fact wish a reconstruction based "upon the principle of civil and political equality of both races," a letter to James S. Wadsworth included in the authoritative *Collected Works of Abraham Lincoln,* proved vulnerable, a suspect document that could not be authenticated. Although its exposure was countered by other evidence that Lincoln was tending toward the Radical position on black suffrage, the long-dominant view of Lincoln's conservatism in

41. Fehrenbacher, *The Changing Image of Lincoln,* 21–22 (quotations on p. 21); Ludwell H. Johnson and Fawn M. Brodie, letters to the editor, *New York Times Book Review,* September 23, 1962, pp. 50–51; Lerone Bennett, Jr., "Was Abe Lincoln a White Supremacist?" *Ebony,* XXIII (February, 1968), 35–38; Herbert Mitgang, "Was Lincoln Just a Honkie?" *New York Times Magazine,* February 11, 1968, p. 35; Robert F. Durden, "A. Lincoln: Honkie or Equalitarian?" *South Atlantic Quarterly,* LXXI (Summer, 1972), 281–91.

For restrained but negative references to Lincoln's position on black rights in scholarly literature, Litwack, *North of Slavery,* 276–77; McPherson, *The Struggle for Equality,* 23–25, 241; Voegeli, *Free but Not Equal,* 169; Berwanger, *The Frontier Against Slavery,* 136–37; James A. Rawley, *Turning Points of the Civil War* (Lincoln: University of Nebraska Press, 1966), 132–33, 139, 143, and *Race & Politics,* 197–99, 255–56, 258, 268–69; Fredrickson, *The Black Image,* 91, 165–67; Don E. Fehrenbacher, "Lincoln and the Constitution," in Cullom Davis *et al.* (eds.), *The Public and the Private Lincoln: Contemporary Perspectives* (Carbondale: Southern Illinois University Press, 1979).

For careful consideration of Lincoln's racial attitudes, Don E. Fehrenbacher, "Only His Stepchildren: Lincoln and the Negro," *Civil War History,* XX (December, 1974), 293–310; George M. Fredrickson, "A Man But Not a Brother: Abraham Lincoln and Racial Equality," *Journal of Southern History,* XLI (February, 1975), 39–58, and his comment in Davis *et al.* (eds.), *The Public and the Private Lincoln,* 95–98. See also Robert W. Johannsen, "In Search of the Real Lincoln, Or Lincoln at the Crossroads," *Journal of the Illinois State Historical Society,* LXI (Autumn, 1968), 229–47 (quotation on p. 237); Christopher N. Breiseth, "Lincoln and Frederick Douglass: Another Debate," *Journal of the Illinois State Historical Society,* LXVIII (February, 1975), 9–26; Richard K. Fleischman, "The Devil's Advocate: A Defense of Lincoln's Attitude Toward the Negro, 1837–1863," *Lincoln Herald,* LXXXI (Fall, 1979), 172–86; Richard N. Current, "Lincoln, the Civil War, and the American Mission," in Davis *et al.* (eds.), *The Public and the Private Lincoln,* 143–46; and Curry, "The Civil War and Reconstruction," 220–24.

Otto H. Olsen has presented Lincoln as revolutionary, risking war for an ideal, but the ideal at stake he identifies as the free-labor ideology and structure of an expanding capitalism, holding that slavery's violation of the "rights of the enslaved was of secondary concern to Lincoln" ("Abraham Lincoln as Revolutionary," *Civil War History,* XXIV [September, 1978], 213–24 [quotation on p. 217]).

respect to Reconstruction and race issues was reinforced. Indeed, as late as 1979, in appraising Peyton McCrary's careful study of wartime Reconstruction in Louisiana in which he concluded that Lincoln at the time of his death was moving to align himself with Radical policy, one reviewer objected that "this contradicts the conclusion of all other reputable scholars." One "other reputable scholar" immediately took exception.[42]

In fact, by the end of the 1970s a strong crosscurrent was evident in Lincoln historiography. Originating in David Donald's essays challenging the adversarial relationship between Lincoln and the Radicals, later confirmed in his biography of Charles Sumner, the new perspective was effectively developed by Hans Trefousse. His study of the Radicals, subtitled *Lincoln's Vanguard for Racial Justice*, made a strong case for similarity of basic aim and mutual reinforcement without glossing over the strains that surfaced between Lincoln and the Republican vanguard. It was Herman Belz who identified Lincoln's marginal notations on proposed new legislation that would have substantially enacted the provisions of the vetoed Wade-Davis reconstruction bill adding recognition of Louisiana and black suf-

---

42. Ludwell H. Johnson, "Lincoln and Equal Rights: The Authenticity of the Wadsworth Letter," *Journal of Southern History*, XXXII (February, 1966), 83–87 (quotation on p. 84), and "Lincoln's Solution to the Problem of Peace Terms, 1864–1865," *Journal of Southern History*, XXXIV (November, 1968), 576–86; Harold M. Hyman, "Lincoln and Equal Rights for Negroes: The Irrelevancy of the 'Wadsworth Letter,'" *Civil War History*, XII (September, 1966), 258–66; Johnson, "Lincoln and Equal Rights: A Reply," *Civil War History*, XIII (March, 1967), 66–73; Peyton McCrary, *Abraham Lincoln and Reconstruction: The Louisiana Experiment* (Princeton: Princeton University Press, 1978); Joe Gray Taylor, Review of McCrary's *Abraham Lincoln and Reconstruction*, in *American Historical Review*, LXXXIV (October, 1979), 1161–62; Harold M. Hyman, in "Communications," *American Historical Review*, LXXXV (April, 1980), 504–505.

A related area of historical controversy is Lincoln on colonization, how long he favored it and the degree to which his support was a strategy to counter opposition to emancipation rather than a solution of the race problem. See Voegeli, *Free but Not Equal*, 45; Fehrenbacher, "Only His Stepchildren," 307–308; G. S. Boritt, "The Voyage to the Colony of Lincolnia: The Sixteenth President, Black Colonization, and the Defense Mechanism of Avoidance," *Historian*, XXXVII (August, 1975), 619–32; Mark E. Neely, Jr., "Abraham Lincoln and Black Colonization: Benjamin Butler's Spurious Testimony," *Civil War History*, XXV (March, 1979), 77–83; Gary R. Planck, "Abraham Lincoln and Black Colonization: Theory and Practice," *Lincoln Herald*, LXXII (Summer, 1970), 61–77; Jason H. Silverman, "'In Isles Beyond the Main': Abraham Lincoln's Philosophy on Black Colonization," *Lincoln Herald*, LXXX (Fall, 1978), 115–22. For additional writings on the subject, see citations in the Silverman article.

frage. He concluded that Lincoln agreed, though reluctant to accept universal as distinct from limited suffrage. David Donald also found evidence of Lincoln's readiness to accept the compromise proposal, including the requirement that voting be without racial discrimination. In *With Malice Toward None*, the first book to challenge the preeminence of Benjamin Thomas' 1952 life as a one-volume biography of Lincoln, Stephen Oates incorporated these fresh perspectives and findings. In subsequent essays he explicitly stated and expanded the sympathetic view of Lincoln's emancipation and Reconstruction policies suggested in the biography.[43] Then in *Lincoln and Black Freedom* (1981), LaWanda Cox reexamined the presidential role, its exercise and the limits of its potential in the destruction of slavery and the attempt to establish equal citizenship. Lincoln emerged as a determined, though circumspect, emancipator and friend of black civil and political rights, consistently striving to obtain what was possible in the face of constitutional restraints, political realities, and white prejudice. Whether the crosscurrent becomes the mainstream remains with future historical writings.[44]

By the mid-1970s the negative thrust of racially sensitive accounts

43. Trefousse, *The Radical Republicans*, and see also his *Lincoln's Decision for Emancipation* (Philadelphia: Lippincott, 1975); Belz, *Reconstructing the Union*, 252–55, and "Origins of Negro Suffrage During the Civil War," *Southern Studies*, XVII (Summer, 1978), 115–30; Donald, *Charles Sumner and the Rights of Man*, 196–97; cf. Cox, *Lincoln and Black Freedom*, 36–37, 119–21; Stephen B. Oates, *With Malice Toward None: The Life of Abraham Lincoln* (New York: Harper & Row, 1977), *Our Fiery Trial: Abraham Lincoln, John Brown, and the Civil War Era* (Amherst: University of Massachusetts Press, 1979), 61–85, "Toward a New Birth of Freedom: Abraham Lincoln and Reconstruction, 1854–1865," *Lincoln Herald*, LXXXII (Spring, 1980), 287–96, and *Abraham Lincoln: The Man Behind the Myths* (New York: Harper & Row, 1984), 93–119, 136–47. See also David Lightner, "Abraham Lincoln and the Ideal of Equality," *Journal of the Illinois State Historical Society*, LXXV (Winter, 1982), 289–307; and Eugene H. Berwanger, "Lincoln's Constitutional Dilemma: Emancipation and Black Suffrage," *Papers of the Abraham Lincoln Association*, V (1983), 25–38.

44. Cox, *Lincoln and Black Freedom*, 3–43, 142–84. Other recent historiographic developments may reinforce the negative image. The important and basically valid view of blacks as active shapers rather than passive recipients of history has sometimes been used to overemphasize the need for black manpower as the explanation for the emancipation proclamations and to fault Lincoln as friend of freedom because as such he became a symbol that robbed blacks of credit for "setting themselves free" (Vincent Harding, *There Is a River: The Black Struggle for Freedom in America* [New York: Harcourt Brace Jovanovich, 1981], 214, 231–37, 254–57 [quotation on p. 236]).

A sharply different perspective, one in which the impersonal forces of moderniza-

challenged not only the image of Lincoln as friend of freedom but the very concept of emancipation as a meaningful reality. Federal policy toward southern blacks as implemented by the army and the Freedmen's Bureau was presented as irreparably flawed and counterrevolutionary in intent. The indictment went far beyond the too frequent incidence of harsh, prejudiced, or unfeeling treatment of blacks by Union officers and men. It charged a deliberate purpose to prevent fundamental social and economic change and to ensure instead continuity of white control, black subordination, and a functioning plantation economy. The yearly contract-labor system introduced by the army and inherited by the Freedmen's Bureau was seen as precluding a radical postwar change in the status of former slaves. This view, first presented in a 1971 article by J. Thomas May, gained wide acceptance, strengthened by the publication two years later of Louis Gerteis' book on federal policy toward southern blacks and by the work of William Messner and C. Peter Ripley.[45] Evidence to support the

---

tion doom slavery, carries a hazard of reducing to insignificance the way in which the institution was legally destroyed and the role of Lincoln in that process.

A third approach that can carry negative implications is that of putting Lincoln "on the analyst's couch" (to borrow a title from Richard O. Curry). In seeking explanations for Lincoln's actions in respect to the Union and slavery in his subconscious filiopiety, filial rebellion, or narcissistic search for immortality, psychohistorians demean both the public man and the issues of slavery and black freedom. George B. Forgie, *Patricide in the House Divided: A Psychological Interpretation of Lincoln and His Age* (New York: Norton, 1979); Charles B. Strozier, *Lincoln's Quest for Union: Public and Private Meanings* (New York: Basic Books, 1982); Dwight G. Anderson, *Abraham Lincoln: The Quest for Immortality* (New York: Knopf, 1982).

Two preeminent Lincoln authorities appear ambivalent toward the newer scholarship that presents as positive Lincoln's record on race and Reconstruction. Don E. Fehrenbacher, "The Anti-Lincoln Tradition," *Papers of the Abraham Lincoln Association*, IV (1982), 20–28; Richard N. Current, "Lincoln the Southerner," in *Speaking of Abraham Lincoln: The Man and His Meaning for Our Times* (Urbana: University of Illinois Press, 1983), 150–52, 164–66. See also Current, *Northernizing the South* (Athens: University of Georgia Press, 1983), 52–53.

In a remarkable explication of his changing views on Lincoln, Stampp has repudiated his earlier judgment of Lincoln as a reluctant emancipator. That the negative assessment still carries credence, however, is evident in the Fortenbaugh Memorial Lecture delivered at Gettysburg in November, 1983, by David Brion Davis. Kenneth M. Stampp, *My Life with Lincoln*, Bernard Moses Memorial Lecture, March 1, 1983 (Berkeley: Graduate Division, University of California, 1983); Davis, *The Emancipation Movement* (Gettysburg: Gettysburg College, 1983), 20–21.

45. J. Thomas May, "Continuity and Change in the Labor Program of the Union Army and the Freedmen's Bureau," *Civil War History*, XVII (September, 1971), 245–54; Louis S. Gerteis, *From Contraband to Freedman: Federal Policy Toward Southern Blacks, 1861–1865* (Westport, Conn.: Greenwood Press, 1973); William F.

argument was drawn primarily from army policy in the Mississippi Valley and especially in occupied Louisiana.[46]

The army as such, especially its professional nucleus, never enjoyed a reputation as the black man's friend and champion. On the other hand, the Freedmen's Bureau, though essentially a military organization, was so regarded for a brief historiographic interlude. The availability to scholars of the manuscript records of the Freedmen's Bureau, made possible by the establishment of the National Archives in the 1930s, opened a rich resource with almost unlimited potential for the study of emancipation and the early postwar South. By the mid-1950s the first fruits of research in the records included several articles and a general history of the bureau that remains the standard account, though reflecting Beale's view of the Radicals using the Negro and the bureau for political and economic exploitation of the South. The more revisionist of the articles challenged the characteri-

---

Messner, "Black Violence and White Response: Louisiana, 1862," *Journal of Southern History*, XLI (February, 1975), 19–38, "Black Education in Louisiana, 1863–1865," *Civil War History*, XXII (March, 1976), 41–59, and *Freedmen and the Ideology of Free Labor: Louisiana, 1862–1865* (Lafayette: University of Southwestern Louisiana, 1978); C. Peter Ripley, *Slaves and Freedmen in Civil War Louisiana* (Baton Rouge: Louisiana State University Press, 1976). A similar view, but one sympathetic to the white South, can be found in Theodore Brantner Wilson, *The Black Codes of the South* (University: University of Alabama Press, 1965), esp. 57–60, 142, 145, 147, 149.

46. For an evenhanded treatment of the labor system in wartime Louisiana under General Nathaniel P. Banks, see McCrary, *Abraham Lincoln and Reconstruction*, 135–58; see also Cox, *Lincoln and Black Freedom*, 131–34. Important for an evaluation of federal policy is the role of John Eaton and his assistant, Samuel Thomas, in the establishment of a black community at Davis Bend, Mississippi. *Cf.* accounts by Gerteis, *From Contraband to Freedman*, 175–81; Steven Joseph Ross, "Freed Soil, Freed Labor, Freed Men: John Eaton and the Davis Bend Experiment," *Journal of Southern History*, XLIV (May, 1978), 213–32; James T. Currie, *Enclave: Vicksburg and Her Plantations, 1863–1870* (Jackson: University Press of Mississippi, 1980), 83–144; and Janet Sharp Hermann, *The Pursuit of a Dream* (New York: Oxford University Press, 1981), 37–105.

Broader studies of the army's role during and after the war are suggestive, especially that of Joseph G. Dawson III, *Army Generals and Reconstruction: Louisiana, 1862–1877* (Baton Rouge: Louisiana State University Press, 1982). See also his "General Phil Sheridan and Military Reconstruction in Louisiana," *Civil War History*, XXIV (June, 1978), esp. 150–51; Marvin R. Cain, "A 'Face of Battle' Needed: An Assessment of Motives and Men in Civil War Historiography," *Civil War History*, XXVIII (March, 1982), esp. 22–25; Kenneth E. St. Clair, "Military Justice in North Carolina, 1865: A Microcosm of Reconstruction," *Civil War History*, XI (December, 1965), 341–50; and James E. Sefton, *The United States Army and Reconstruction, 1865–1877* (Baton Rouge: Louisiana State University Press, 1967), which has been characterized as anti-revisionist in perspective.

zation of bureau operations in the older orthodoxy as partisan, corrupt, oppressive of white southerners, the source of racial antagonism and labor unrest. And O. O. Howard, the bureau's head, was portrayed as conscientiously striving, in the face of President Johnson's covert opposition and the hostility of southern whites, to safeguard the freedmen and to bring into being a genuine freedom that upset the established norm of race relationships. Support for the more sympathetic evaluation of the bureau found reinforcement in two major studies of the 1960s, John A. Carpenter's biography of O. O. Howard and Martin Abbott's examination of bureau activities in South Carolina.[47]

The Freedmen's Bureau was no sooner redeemed from old hostile stereotypes than it was subjected to the demanding racial standards of the late 1960s and found wanting. The most influential voice in discrediting Howard and the bureau was that of William McFeely. He presented Howard as a man of self-deceptive piety who, out of concern for his future as a professional army officer, followed the directives of President Johnson rather than resign his post to help the political opposition expose the president's proplanter, antiblack policy. According to McFeely, General Howard had for a time the power and resources to achieve a fundamental change in the status of blacks but instead capitulated to the president (his commander in chief) and delivered black labor into the hands of the planters. The effect was "to preclude rather than promote Negro freedom." Howard alone was not at fault. McFeely saw the ultimate source of the bureau's failure to effect social change in the South in the unwillingness of northerners "to prescribe similarly for the nation as a whole," that is, to create the prerequisites for mobility of the poor, both white and black, North and South.[48]

---

47. George R. Bentley, *A History of the Freedmen's Bureau* (Philadelphia: University of Pennsylvania Press, 1955), viewed the bureau as arousing white racial hostility that seriously hurt the freedmen; W. A. Low, "The Freedman's Bureau and Civil Rights in Maryland," *Journal of Negro History*, XXXVII (July, 1952), 221–47; John Cox and LaWanda Cox, "General O. O. Howard and the 'Misrepresented Bureau,'" *Journal of Southern History*, XIX (November, 1953), 427–56; John A. Carpenter, *Sword and Olive Branch: Oliver Otis Howard* (Pittsburgh: University of Pittsburgh Press, 1964); Martin Abbott, "Free Land, Free Labor, and the Freedmen's Bureau," *Agricultural History*, XXX (October, 1956), 150–56, and *The Freedmen's Bureau in South Carolina, 1865–1872* (Chapel Hill: University of North Carolina Press, 1967).

48. William S. McFeely, *Yankee Stepfather: General O. O. Howard and the Freedmen* (New Haven: Yale University Press, 1968), 5, and "Unfinished Business: The Freedmen's Bureau and Federal Action in Race Relations," in Nathan I. Huggins, Mar-

The stern and sweeping judgments pronounced against army, Freedmen's Bureau, and national policy have evoked reappraisals more subtle and more charitable than those conditioned by the temper of the 1960s. Although these voices are not dominant, there is a growing recognition that even as the immediate aims of the bureau and of southern planters coincided, their long-range goals in respect to the status of the freedmen fundamentally differed. And with increasing challenge to the concept of continuity in the social pattern of southern agriculture and recognition of the freedmen's role in initiating family share tenancy or sharecropping, the conclusion at which Ronald Davis arrived for the Natchez district could prove to have more than local validity. He found that "army and bureau policy enabled district freedmen to resist gang labor and planter determination of their working conditions." [49] Despite contradictory instances often cited, the presence of a bureau agent may have served to erode

tin Kilson, and Daniel M. Fox (eds.), *Key Issues in the Afro-American Experience* (2 vols.; New York: Harcourt Brace Jovanovich, 1971), II, 5–25 (quotation on p. 23). For other generally unfavorable accounts of the bureau's work, see Kenneth B. White, "Wager Swayne: Racist or Realist?" *Alabama Review,* XXXI (April, 1978), 92–109; James Oakes, "A Failure of Vision: The Collapse of the Freedmen's Bureau Courts," *Civil War History,* XXV (March, 1979), 66–76; Todd L. Savitt, "Politics in Medicine: The Georgia Freedmen's Bureau and the Organization of Health Care, 1865–1866," *Civil War History,* XXVIII (March, 1982), 45–64; Gaines M. Foster, "The Limitations of Federal Health Care for Freedmen, 1862–1868," *Journal of Southern History,* XLVIII (August, 1982), 349–72; and Thomas D. Morris, "Equality, 'Extraordinary Law,' and Criminal Justice: The South Carolina Experience, 1865–1866," *South Carolina Historical Magazine,* LXXXIII (January, 1982), 15–33. See also Howard Ashley White, *The Freedmen's Bureau in Louisiana* (Baton Rouge: Louisiana State University Press, 1970).

49. Foner, *Politics and Ideology,* 100–112; Richard Paul Fuke, "A Reform Mentality: Federal Policy Toward Black Marylanders, 1864–1868," *Civil War History,* XXII (September, 1976), 214–35; Paul A. Cimbala, "The 'Talisman Power': Davis Tillson, the Freedmen's Bureau, and Free Labor in Reconstruction Georgia, 1865–1866," *Civil War History,* XXVIII (June, 1982), 153–71; Harris, "Plantations and Power," and Ralph Shlomowitz, "The Squad System on Postbellum Cotton Plantations," both in Burton and McMath (eds.), *Toward a New South?,* 246–80; Shlomowitz, "'Bound' or 'Free'? Black Labor in Cotton and Sugarcane Farming, 1865–1880," *Journal of Southern History,* L (November, 1984), 569–96; Ronald L. F. Davis, *Good and Faithful Labor: From Slavery to Sharecropping in the Natchez District, 1860–1890* (Westport, Conn.: Greenwood Press, 1982), 58–83, 105–106, 192–96 (quotation on p. 192), and "Labor Dependency Among Freedmen, 1865–1880," in Walter J. Fraser, Jr., and Winfred B. Moore, Jr. (eds.), *From the Old South to the New: Essays on the Transitional South* (Westport, Conn.: Greenwood Press, 1981), 155–65; and William Cohen, *Black Mobility and the Transformation of the Southern Labor System* (forthcoming).

planter control and nourish black assertiveness more often than has been recognized. No consensus is in sight, but Donald Nieman's careful study of bureau efforts, and failures, to provide security for blacks against white violence, oppressive employers, and unequal treatment before the law makes clear that a fair judgment on the work of the bureau must take account of the constraints under which it labored and the wide range of responses from its state officers and local agents.[50] Fair judgment will also require an ability to stand aside from twentieth-century repugnance toward assumptions prevalent in nineteenth-century benevolence, namely, that blacks emerging from slavery required tutelage in diligence, thrift, and family responsibility if they were to act responsibly as free men in a free society and garner the fruits thereof. And fair judgment cannot be based upon an unexamined assumption of the inherent conservatism, in the sense of hostility to social change, of the effort to bring stability and renewed productivity to a society disorganized by war, defeat, and the destruction of its "peculiar institution."

Impatience with white paternalism and the ideology of free labor has affected no aspect of recent writings on emancipation more negatively than that dealing with the education of freedmen, once considered the most constructive legacy of the northern effort to refashion southern society. In this field the darker mood of Reconstruction revisionism has been intensified by a parallel revisionism in educational history generally, one that sees American education as "shaped by cultural homogeneity" and functioning to service, and to secure acquiescence in, "an inegalitarian social structure." Varying in tone

50. Donald G. Nieman, *To Set the Law in Motion: The Freedmen's Bureau and the Legal Rights of Blacks, 1865–1868* (Millwood, N.Y.: KTO Press, 1979). See also Barry A. Crouch, "The Freedmen's Bureau and the 30th Sub-District in Texas: Smith County and Its Environs During Reconstruction," *Chronicles of Smith County, Texas,* XI (Spring, 1972), 15–30; Rebecca Scott, "The Battle Over the Child: Child Apprenticeship and the Freedmen's Bureau in North Carolina," *Prologue,* X (Summer, 1978), 101–13; James Smallwood, "Charles E. Culver, a Reconstruction Agent in Texas: The Work of Local Freedmen's Bureau Agents and the Black Community," *Civil War History,* XXVII (December, 1981), 350–61; and William Cohen, "Black Immobility and Free Labor: The Freedmen's Bureau and the Relocation of Black Labor, 1865–1868," *Civil War History,* XXX (September, 1984), 221–34.

John A. Carpenter before his death had identified 2,441 agents of the Freedmen's Bureau and compiled for each a data sheet consisting of forty-five categories pertaining to the man's background, bureau assignment, attitudes, and performance. These data, when made available to the profession, as is Mrs. Carpenter's intent, will be an invaluable resource for many purposes, not the least of which is a more comprehensive understanding of the bureau's functioning in the field.

from restraint to stridency, four books published from 1978 through 1981 exemplify the dominant trend. Their criticism includes accommodation by northern teachers to southern white racism, insensitivity to black desire for independence from all white control, cultural imperialism, use of education to discipline and subjugate black labor, and betrayal of black freedom by choosing the "placebo" of education over the option of "direct means to black power . . . confiscation, expanded military protection, social planning, and an abandonment of laissez-faire social theory."[51] Although not in the ascendancy, the more sympathetic view of earlier revisionism must still be reckoned with, especially as presented in James McPherson's scholarly, racially sensitive account of the continuing effort of abolitionists and their offspring to assist blacks in the struggle for equality, *The Abolitionist Legacy* (1975).[52] While there is no dispute as to the

51. Marvin Lazerson, Review of Nasaw's *Schooled to Order*, in *American Historical Review*, LXXXVI (October, 1981), 909; Donald Spivey, *Schooling for the New Slavery: Black Industrial Education, 1868–1915* (Westport, Conn.: Greenwood Press, 1978), ix–x, 3–44; Jacqueline Jones, *Soldiers of Light and Love: Northern Teachers and Georgia Blacks, 1865–1873* (Chapel Hill: University of North Carolina Press, 1980); Ronald E. Butchart, *Northern Schools, Southern Blacks, and Reconstruction: Freedmen's Education, 1862–1875* (Westport, Conn.: Greenwood Press, 1980), quotations on pp. 74, 202; Robert C. Morris, *Reading, 'Riting, and Reconstruction: The Education of Freedmen in the South, 1861–1870* (Chicago: University of Chicago Press, 1981). See also Keith Wilson, "Education as a Vehicle of Racial Control: Major General N. P. Banks in Louisiana, 1863–64," *Journal of Negro Education*, L (Spring, 1981), 156–70; and Lois E. Horton and James Oliver Horton, "Race, Occupation, and Literacy in Reconstruction Washington, D.C.," in Burton and McMath (eds.), *Toward a New South?*, 135–51.

52. James M. McPherson, *The Abolitionist Legacy: From Reconstruction to the NAACP* (Princeton: Princeton University Press, 1975), and "White Liberals and Black Power in Negro Education, 1865–1915," *American Historical Review*, LXXV (June, 1970), 1357–86. See also John W. Blassingame, "The Union Army as an Educational Institution for Negroes, 1862–1865," *Journal of Negro Education*, XXXIV (Spring, 1965), 152–59; Howard N. Rabinowitz, "Half a Loaf: The Shift from White to Black Teachers in the Negro Schools of the Urban South, 1865–1890," *Journal of Southern History*, XL (November, 1974), 565–94; Sandra E. Small, "The Yankee Schoolmarm in Freedmen's Schools: An Analysis of Attitudes," *Journal of Southern History*, XLV (August, 1979), 381–402; and William Preston Vaughn, *Schools for All: The Blacks & Public Education in the South, 1865–1877* (Lexington: University Press of Kentucky, 1974), a major study concerned primarily with the issue of integration.

Northern and bureau efforts to promote black education in the upper South have generally been treated with sympathy. See W. A. Low, "The Freedmen's Bureau in the Border States," in Richard O. Curry (ed.), *Radicalism, Racism, and Party Realignment: The Border States During Reconstruction* (Baltimore: Johns Hopkins Press, 1969), 245–64; Larry Wesley Pearce, "The American Missionary Association and the

short-term failure of schooling to revolutionize race relations or to achieve widespread social mobility for blacks and while other areas of agreement exist as well, the difference in the two perspectives is fundamental. Northern support for freedmen's education is seen by the one as expanding, by the other as constricting, black freedom.

By the early 1970s, one judgment on Reconstruction policy was so generally accepted that Herman Belz challenged it as the "new orthodoxy," with little more effect than Don Quixote's assault upon the windmill. It holds that Reconstruction failed because it did not provide land for the freedmen. The assumptions usually present, explicit or implied, are that confiscation with land redistribution to freedmen was a policy option and that landownership would have provided a basis for black well-being, equality, and power more sturdy than the grant of suffrage and equality before the law. Unlike the attribution of Reconstruction failure to northern racism, this explanation took firm root without anything comparable to the outpouring of scholarship on mid-nineteenth-century white racial attitudes and race relations. The desire of freedmen for land, however, was well established as was the reasonableness of their expectation of a supportive government policy. Since Belz's challenge, grounds for skepticism have found their way into print, but there have been no comprehensive studies of how contemporaries, particularly Republicans, saw the issue of confiscation and land grants, why no land program was put in place, or what economic and political consequences could have

---

Freedmen in Arkansas, 1863–1878," *Arkansas Historical Quarterly*, XXX (Summer, 1971), 123–44, 242–59; Richard Paul Fuke, "The Baltimore Association for the Moral and Educational Improvement of the Colored People, 1864–1870," *Maryland Historical Magazine*, LXVI (Winter, 1971), 369–404; Joe M. Richardson, "The American Missionary Association and Black Education in Civil War Missouri," *Missouri Historical Review*, LXIX (July, 1975), 433–48; Roberta Sue Alexander, "Hostility and Hope: Black Education in North Carolina during Presidential Reconstruction, 1865–1867," *North Carolina Historical Review*, LIII (April, 1976), 113–32; and Philip Clyde Kimball, "Freedom's Harvest: Freedmen's Schools in Kentucky After the Civil War," *Filson Club Historical Quarterly*, LIV (July, 1980), 272–88.

Ironically, a recent theme in the "revisionist" class-emphasis historiography of education, namely, that the self-activity of former slaves deserves major credit for the origin and development of freedmen's education, may inadvertently undermine the education-for-subordination thesis. See James D. Anderson, "Ex-Slaves and the Rise of Universal Education in the New South, 1860–1880," in Ronald K. Goodenow and Arthur O. White (eds.), *Education and the Rise of the New South* (Boston: G. K. Hall, 1981), 1–25. For educational historiography, see Harvey Neufeldt and Clinton Allison, "Education and the Rise of the New South: An Historiographical Essay," in Goodenow and White (eds.), *Education and the Rise of the New South*, 250–93.

been expected.[53] Comparisons have been made with postemancipation in other agrarian areas, and some southern communities with a high degree of black proprietorship have been studied. Such measuring rods, by their very nature, can be only suggestive, but they do raise serious doubt that the effect of landownership in alleviating rural black poverty in the South would have been more than minimal. Nor is it clear, except for the pride of ownership, that the psychological and social satisfactions associated with black communities derived from title to the land rather than from a racial separateness that permitted some degree of escape from white dominance.[54]

53. Herman Belz, "The New Orthodoxy in Reconstruction Historiography," *Reviews in American History*, I (March, 1973), 106–13; Cox and Cox (eds.), *Reconstruction, the Negro, and the New South*, xxviii–xxx; Willie Lee Rose, "Jubilee & Beyond: What Was Freedom?" in Sansing (ed.), *What Was Freedom's Price?*, 12–14; Manning Marable, "The Politics of Black Land Tenure, 1877–1915," *Agricultural History*, LIII (January, 1979), 142–52; Cox, *Lincoln and Black Freedom*, 175–78.

Attention had been directed to national land policy affecting the South and the freedmen by Paul Wallace Gates, "Federal Land Policy in the South, 1866–1888," *Journal of Southern History*, VI (August, 1940), 303–30; LaWanda Cox, "The Promise of Land for the Freedmen," *Mississippi Valley Historical Review*, XLV (December, 1958), 413–40; Rose, *Rehearsal for Reconstruction;* and McPherson, *The Struggle for Equality.* Subsequent special studies: Carol K. Rothrock Bleser, *The Promised Land: The History of the South Carolina Land Commission, 1869–1890* (Columbia: University of South Carolina Press, 1969); Christie Farnham Pope, "Southern Homesteads for Negroes," *Agricultural History*, XLIV (April, 1970), 201–12; Warren Hoffnagle, "The Southern Homestead Act: Its Origins and Operation," *Historian*, XXXII (August, 1970), 612–29; Herman Belz, "The Freedmen's Bureau Act of 1865 and the Principle of No Discrimination According to Color," *Civil War History*, XXI (September, 1975), 197–217; Lawrence N. Powell, "The American Land Company and Agency: John A. Andrew and the Northernization of the South," *Civil War History*, XXI (December, 1975), 293–308; Robert F. Horowitz, "Land to the Freedmen: A Vision of Reconstruction," *Ohio History*, LXXXVI (Summer, 1977), 187–99; Claude F. Oubre, *Forty Acres and a Mule: The Freedmen's Bureau and Black Land Ownership* (Baton Rouge: Louisiana State University Press, 1978).

54. J. W. Cooke, "Stoney Point, 1866–1969," *Filson Club Historical Quarterly*, L (October, 1976), 337–52; Charles Nesbitt, "Rural Acreage in Promise Land, Tennessee: A Case Study," in Leo McGee and Robert Boone (eds.), *The Black Rural Landowner—Endangered Species: Social, Political, and Economic Implications* (Westport, Conn.: Greenwood Press, 1979), 67–81; Norman L. Crockett, *The Black Towns* (Lawrence: Regents Press of Kansas, 1979); Hermann, *The Pursuit of a Dream,* esp. 219–45; Elizabeth Rauh Bethel, *Promiseland: A Century of Life in a Negro Community* (Philadelphia: Temple University Press, 1981); Crandall A. Shifflett, *Patronage and Poverty in the Tobacco South: Louisa County, Virginia, 1860–1900* (Knoxville: University of Tennessee Press, 1982). By 1900 an amazing 88 percent of all black heads of household in Louisa County owned land, but Shifflett sees landownership as bringing neither economic well-being nor independence from white dominance. For cita-

One redoubt on the battleground of Reconstruction historiography captured by the revisionists of the early 1960s appears to be firmly held. White violence against blacks has been stripped of justification and recognized as a causal factor of immense importance in delimiting postwar freedom for southern blacks. The manuscript records of the Freedmen's Bureau yielded the evidence that destroyed the older orthodoxy. In a telling article published in 1962, John Carpenter established from reports of bureau agents the reality of numerous atrocities in 1865 and 1866, before freedmen were enfranchised. He saw the outrages as impetus for congressional Reconstruction policy. Drawing upon the manuscript records and published reports of the attorney general's office, Everette Swinney discredited the prevailing view that the Enforcement Acts of 1870–1871 were unwarranted, harsh, and iniquitous. These fresh directions culminated in Allen Trelease's comprehensive *White Terror* (1971), a study of Klan violence in the Reconstruction years from 1866 through 1872.[55] National policy decisions to protect southern blacks stand justified. Tragically, effective protection did not follow upon legislative decision. No historical accounting for that failure has yet been convincingly comprehensive, evenhanded, and discerning.[56]

---

tions to earlier accounts of black communities, see Bethel, *Promiseland,* 273*n*1, 274*n*12.

55. John A. Carpenter, "Atrocities in the Reconstruction Period," *Journal of Negro History,* XLVII (October, 1962), 234–47; Everette Swinney, "Enforcing the Fifteenth Amendment, 1870–1877," *Journal of Southern History,* XXVIII (May, 1962), 202–18; Allen W. Trelease, *White Terror: The Ku Klux Klan Conspiracy and Southern Reconstruction* (New York: Harper & Row, 1971). William Gillette, *Retreat from Reconstruction, 1869–1879* (Baton Rouge: Louisiana State University Press, 1979), deals with enforcement efforts during the Grant administration. See also Herbert Shapiro, "Afro-American Responses to Race Violence During Reconstruction," *Science and Society,* XXXVI (Summer, 1972), 158–70. Episodes of violence have been examined in a number of articles published after *White Terror,* most recently, Barry A. Crouch, "A Spirit of Lawlessness: White Violence; Texas Blacks, 1865–1868," *Journal of Social History,* XVIII (Winter, 1984), 217–32. And a comprehensive study of violence as an instrument of southern counterrevolution has recently appeared, George C. Rable, *But There Was No Peace: The Role of Violence in the Politics of Reconstruction* (Athens: University of Georgia Press, 1984). The Federal Elections Bill of 1890, the so-called Force Bill, was rescued from unmerited opprobrium by Richard E. Welch, Jr., "The Federal Elections Bill of 1890: Postscript and Prelude," *Journal of American History,* LII (December, 1965), 511–26.

56. Cox, *Lincoln and Black Freedom,* 165–71, has suggested that coercion alone, without a substantial degree of consent from southern whites, was an inadequate means to secure black civil and political rights in view of the national tradition of government based upon consent and of opposition to military authority. See also Wilbert

A major though not necessarily an ultimate responsibility for protecting the freedmen rested with the three postwar presidents. Historians have tended, at least in their generalizations, to favor more impersonal factors as explanation, yet Johnson, Grant, and Hayes have each been found wanting. C. Vann Woodward's study of the settlement of the disputed election of 1876, *Reunion and Reaction,* continues to be the centerpiece for interpretation of Hayes's southern policy, one that ended the use of military force to uphold Republican regimes. Although Woodward himself stated that Grant, not Hayes, deserved whatever "of the credit or blame" attached to the new policy and that it came as a response to widespread public sentiment in the North, *Reunion and Reaction* has appeared a damning confirmation of a shabby bargain to exchange political and economic favors at the expense of southern blacks, the epitome of abandonment and betrayal. William Gillette, in *Retreat from Reconstruction,* developed the case against Grant; he also disclosed the magnitude of difficulty inherent in the task Grant attempted. Calling for a reconsideration of President Grant's role, Richard Current has characterized Grant as "in a certain respect, one of the greatest, if not the greatest of all presidents. . . . None of the others carried on such a determined struggle, against such hopeless odds," to protect all citizens and give reality to the Fourteenth and Fifteenth amendments.[57] As for Andrew Johnson, the revisionists of the early 1960s indicated his opposition to equal citizenship for blacks and suggested that not only states' rights principles but ineptness of political leadership, ambition, and

---

H. Ahern, "Laissez Faire vs. Equal Rights: Liberal Republicans and Limits to Reconstruction," *Phylon,* XL (March, 1979), 52–65; and George C. Rable, "Bourbonism, Reconstruction, and the Persistence of Southern Distinctiveness," *Civil War History,* XXIX (June, 1983), 135–53, and *But There Was No Peace.* Further light on the problem can be expected from Michael Les Benedict's *Let Us Have Peace: Republicans and Reconstruction, 1869–1880* (New York: Norton, forthcoming).

57. C. Vann Woodward, *Reunion and Reaction: The Compromise of 1877 and the End of Reconstruction* (Boston: Little, Brown, 1951), 9–10 (quotation on p. 10); Introduction and Vincent P. De Santis, "Rutherford B. Hayes and the Removal of the Troops and the End of Reconstruction," both in Kousser and McPherson (eds.), *Region, Race, and Reconstruction,* xxvii–xxviii, 417–50, challenge Woodward's interpretation; Richard N. Current, "President Grant and the Continuing Civil War," in David L. Wilson and John Y. Simon (eds.), *Ulysses S. Grant: Essays and Documents* (Carbondale: Southern Illinois University Press, 1981), 8. William S. McFeely, in *Grant: A Biography* (New York: Norton, 1981), deals only briefly with Grant's southern policy (416–25). See also George Rable, "Republican Albatross: The Louisiana Question, National Politics, and the Failure of Reconstruction," *Louisiana History,* XXIII (Spring, 1982), 109–30.

race prejudice affected his course as president. It remained for Hans Trefousse and Michael Les Benedict in their studies of impeachment to show Johnson's deliberate obstruction of Republican Reconstruction. Trefousse argues that the president's opposition was effective, so weakening the congressional program that the result was defeat of the Reconstruction effort and victory for white supremacy in the South.[58]

In criticizing national policy and its implementation, historians have seen southern blacks as victims, which indeed they were; but blacks were not only victims. They were also active participants and shapers, and to some extent winners, in the history of emancipation and its aftermath. A vigorous and challenging aspect of present historiography is the retrieval and interpretation of the black or Afro-American experience from the early years of the Civil War, through the period of Republican party control in southern states, and beyond. This effort, while gathering momentum from the black power and black studies movements, has built upon a sturdy foundation of early scholarship by black historians and a few whites.[59] For ex-

---

58. Hans L. Trefousse, *Impeachment of a President: Andrew Johnson, the Blacks, and Reconstruction* (Knoxville: University of Tennessee Press, 1975); Michael Les Benedict, *The Impeachment and Trial of Andrew Johnson* (New York: Norton, 1973). On Johnson's obstructionism, see also Donald G. Nieman, "Andrew Johnson, the Freedmen's Bureau, and the Problem of Equal Rights, 1865–1866," *Journal of Southern History*, XLIV (August, 1978), 399–420, and *To Set the Law in Motion.* For the way in which southern leaders took advantage of Johnson's policy, see Michael Perman, *Reunion Without Compromise: The South and Reconstruction, 1865–1868* (New York: Cambridge University Press, 1973).

Two recent brief volumes on Andrew Johnson tend to avoid or minimize the question of his impact as president upon the quality of freedom for southern blacks. Castel, *The Presidency of Andrew Johnson;* James E. Sefton, *Andrew Johnson and the Uses of Constitutional Power* (Boston: Little, Brown, 1980). LeRoy P. Graf and Ralph W. Haskins, as editors of *The Papers of Andrew Johnson* (6 vols. to date; Knoxville: University of Tennessee Press, 1967–), present in their introductions the most informed and convincing analysis of Andrew Johnson now available, but the series has not yet reached the years of his presidency.

59. For black historiography, see note 2; and George B. Tindall, "Southern Negroes Since Reconstruction: Dissolving the Static Image," in Arthur S. Link and Rembert W. Patrick (eds.), *Writing Southern History: Essays in Historiography in Honor of Fletcher M. Green* (Baton Rouge: Louisiana State University Press, 1965), 337–61; John Hope Franklin, "Reconstruction and the Negro," and August Meier, "Comment on John Hope Franklin's Paper," both in Hyman (ed.), *New Frontiers,* 59–86; I. A. Newby, "Historians and Negroes," *Journal of Negro History,* LIV (January, 1969), 32–47; Eugene D. Genovese, "The Influence of the Black Power Movement on Historical Scholarship: Reflections of a White Historian," *Daedalus,* IC (Spring, 1970), 473–94; August Meier, "Benjamin Quarles and the Historiography of Black America," *Civil War History,* XXVI (June, 1980), 101–16, and "Review Essay: Whither

ample, state studies of Negroes during Reconstruction and after, pioneered by the black historian Alrutheus A. Taylor and followed by the more widely noted volumes by Vernon Wharton in 1947 and George Tindall in 1952, had emphasized the positive role of blacks in the economy and in politics. The early works had also called attention to black life and developing institutions, to education, the church, the black press, the Freedman's Savings Bank, associations for mutual support and sociability, even to black geographic mobility. More recent state accounts continue the pattern they set, and these aspects of black life have received further attention in both state and special studies.[60] Innovative, and particularly noteworthy, is the ex-

the Black Perspective in Afro-American Historiography?" *Journal of American History,* LXX (June, 1983), 101–105; Willie Lee Rose, *Slavery and Freedom,* ed. William W. Freehling (New York: Oxford University Press, 1982), 90–111; August Meier and Elliott Rudwick, "J. Franklin Jameson, Carter G. Woodson, and the Foundations of Black Historiography," *American Historical Review,* LXXXIX (October, 1984), 1005–15, and *Black History and the Historical Profession* (Urbana: University of Illinois Press, 1986).

60. Alrutheus A. Taylor, *The Negro in South Carolina During the Reconstruction* (Washington, D.C.: Association for the Study of Negro Life and History, 1924), *The Negro in the Reconstruction of Virginia* (Washington, D.C.: Association for the Study of Negro Life and History, 1926), and *The Negro in Tennessee, 1865–1880* (Washington, D.C.: Associated Publishers, 1941); Wharton, *The Negro in Mississippi;* George Brown Tindall, *South Carolina Negroes, 1877–1900* (Columbia: University of South Carolina Press, 1952); Joel Williamson, *After Slavery: The Negro in South Carolina During Reconstruction, 1861–1877* (Chapel Hill: University of North Carolina Press, 1965); Joe M. Richardson, *The Negro in the Reconstruction of Florida, 1865–1877* (Tallahassee: Florida State University, 1965). See also Frenise A. Logan, *The Negro in North Carolina, 1876–1894* (Chapel Hill: University of North Carolina Press, 1964); Margaret Law Callcott, *The Negro in Maryland Politics, 1870–1912* (Baltimore: Johns Hopkins Press, 1969); Lawrence D. Rice, *The Negro in Texas, 1874–1900* (Baton Rouge: Louisiana State University Press, 1971); and James M. Smallwood, *Time of Hope, Time of Despair: Black Texans During Reconstruction* (Port Washington, N.Y.: Kennikat Press, 1981).

Special studies include Clarence E. Walker, *A Rock in a Weary Land: The African Methodist Episcopal Church During the Civil War and Reconstruction* (Baton Rouge: Louisiana State University Press, 1982); W. Harrison Daniel, "Virginia Baptists and the Negro, 1865–1902," *Virginia Magazine of History and Biography,* LXXVI (July, 1968), 340–63; Robert L. Hall, "Tallahassee's Black Churches, 1865–1885," *Florida Historical Quarterly,* LVIII (October, 1979), 185–96; Daniel F. Littlefield, Jr., and Patricia Washington McGraw, "The Arkansas Freeman, 1869–1870—Birth of the Black Press in Arkansas," *Phylon,* XL (March, 1979), 75–85; Allen W. Jones, "The Black Press in the 'New South': Jesse C. Duke's Struggle for Justice and Equality," *Journal of Negro History,* LXIV (Summer, 1979), 215–28; Carl R. Osthaus, *Freedmen, Philanthropy, and Fraud: A History of the Freedman's Savings Bank* (Urbana: University of Illinois Press, 1976); Nell Irvin Painter, *Exodusters: Black Migration to*

tensive research published since the 1960s on the black family. This work exemplifies the increased use of manuscript census returns and related sources for aggregate data that illuminate the lives of the inarticulate. Other innovations in black history are the mapping of urban geography, the use of twentieth-century slave narratives and contemporary oral recollections, and the perceptive analysis of folklore expressed in tales and song. Although additional investigation can be expected, the result to date is a positive picture of black initiative and achievement in building institutions that provided autonomy, support, and opportunity for leadership, in short, a community infrastructure far more developed and varied than was possible under slavery.[61]

Kansas after Reconstruction (New York: Knopf, 1977); Robert G. Athearn, _In Search of Canaan: Black Migration to Kansas, 1879–80_ (Lawrence: Regents Press of Kansas, 1978); and Anne S. Lee and Everett S. Lee, "The Health of Slaves and the Health of Freedmen: A Savannah Study," _Phylon,_ XXXVIII (June, 1977), 170–80.

61. John W. Blassingame, "Before the Ghetto: The Making of the Black Community in Savannah, Georgia, 1865–1880," _Journal of Social History,_ VI (Summer, 1973), 463–88; Armstead L. Robinson, "Plans Dat Comed from God: Institution Building and the Emergence of Black Leadership in Reconstruction Memphis," in Burton and McMath (eds.), _Toward a New South?,_ 71–102. On the black family, see Peter Kolchin, _First Freedom: The Responses of Alabama's Blacks to Emancipation and Reconstruction_ (Westport, Conn.: Greenwood Press, 1972), 56–78; Blassingame, _Black New Orleans,_ 79–105, 236–41; Elaine C. Everly, "Marriage Registers of Freedmen," _Prologue,_ V (Fall, 1973), 150–54; C. Peter Ripley, "The Black Family in Transition: Louisiana, 1860–1865," _Journal of Southern History,_ XLI (August, 1975), 369–80; Herbert G. Gutman, _The Black Family in Slavery and Freedom, 1750–1925_ (New York: Pantheon, 1976), 363–450; William Harris, "Work and the Family in Black Atlanta, 1880," _Journal of Social History,_ IX (Spring, 1976), 319–30; James Smallwood, "Emancipation and the Black Family: A Case Study in Texas," _Social Science Quarterly,_ LVII (March, 1977), 849–57; Edmund L. Drago, "Sources at the National Archives for Genealogical and Local History Research: The Black Household in Dougherty County, Georgia, 1870–1900," _Prologue,_ XIV (Summer 1982), 81–88; Davis, _Good and Faithful Labor,_ 169–84; Shifflett, _Patronage and Poverty,_ 84–98. Of closely related interest, Claudia Goldin, "Female Labor Force Participation: The Origin of Black and White Differences, 1870 and 1880," _Journal of Economic History,_ XXXVII (March, 1977), 87–108. The history of black women in the South during the postemancipation decades has received only incidental attention, but more can be expected. See Sharon Harley and Rosalyn Terborg-Penn (eds.), _The Afro-American Woman: Struggles and Images_ (Port Washington, N.Y.: Kennikat Press, 1978); and John E. Fleming, "Slavery, Civil War and Reconstruction: A Study of Black Women in Microcosm," _Negro History Bulletin,_ XXXVIII (August–September, 1975), 430–33.

Newer techniques are exemplified in John Kellogg, "The Formation of Black Residential Areas in Lexington, Kentucky, 1865–1887," _Journal of Southern History,_ XLVIII (February, 1982), 21–52; Borchert, _Alley Life in Washington;_ Paul D. Escott, _Slavery Remembered: A Record of Twentieth-Century Slave Narratives_ (Chapel Hill:

While state accounts of the Negro continue to advance our knowledge of black history and race relations, a recent historiographic trend may prove even more enlightening, namely, localized studies of city, town, county, or district. This approach has already resulted in several significant volumes: Howard Rabinowitz's comparative study of race relations in Atlanta, Montgomery, Nashville, Raleigh, and Richmond; Robert Engs's account of black Hampton, Virginia; Eric Anderson's of North Carolina's black second congressional district (a predominantly political study); and John Blassingame's *Black New Orleans*, the only one of the four that fails to include politics. The focus of Ronald Davis' study of the Natchez district and Crandall Shifflett's of Louisa County in the Virginia tobacco country is the changing economic-class structure. Only segments have been published of two comprehensive local studies, one by Vernon Burton of Edgefield, South Carolina, a predominantly though not overwhelmingly black rural county with a village, and the other by Frank Huffman of Clarke County, Georgia, with an agrarian economy, the town of Athens, and a population roughly half black and half white.[62]

University of North Carolina Press, 1979), 119–75; Lawrence W. Levine, *Black Culture and Black Consciousness: Afro-American Folk Thought from Slavery to Freedom* (New York: Oxford University Press, 1977).

62. Howard N. Rabinowitz, *Race Relations in the Urban South, 1865–1890* (New York: Oxford University Press, 1978), contains a good deal more on black life than the title suggests; Robert Francis Engs, *Freedom's First Generation: Black Hampton, Virginia, 1861–1890* (Philadelphia: University of Pennsylvania Press, 1979); Eric Anderson, *Race and Politics in North Carolina, 1872–1910: The Black Second* (Baton Rouge: Louisiana State University Press, 1981); Davis, *Good and Faithful Labor;* and for the Natchez district, see also Michael Wayne, *The Reshaping of Plantation Society: The Natchez District, 1860–1880* (Baton Rouge: Louisiana State University Press, 1983); Shifflett, *Patronage and Poverty;* Orville Vernon Burton, "The Rise and Fall of Afro-American Town Life: Town and Country in Reconstruction Edgefield, South Carolina," in Burton and McMath (eds.), *Toward a New South?*, 152–92, and "Race and Reconstruction: Edgefield County, South Carolina," in Edward Magdol and Jon L. Wakelyn (eds.), *The Southern Common People: Studies in Nineteenth-Century Social History* (Westport, Conn.: Greenwood Press, 1980), 211–37; Frank J. Huffman, Jr., "Town and Country in the South, 1850–1880: A Comparison of Urban and Rural Social Structures," in Magdol and Wakelyn (eds.), *The Southern Common People,* 239–51. The intersection of urban and black studies promises to be continuingly fruitful; see Steven W. Engerrand, "Black and Mulatto Mobility and Stability in Dallas, Texas, 1880–1910," *Phylon*, XXXIX (September, 1978), 203–15; and Joanne Wheeler, "Together in Egypt: A Pattern of Race Relations in Cairo, Illinois, 1865–1915," in Burton and McMath (eds.), *Toward a New South?*, 103–34. On the other hand, several outstanding area studies give disappointingly little attention to blacks: David L. Carlton, *Mill and Town in South Carolina, 1880–1920* (Baton Rouge: Louisiana State University Press, 1982); Steven Hahn, *The Roots of Southern Populism:*

Since the South, the black South as well as the white, was not monolithic, more such investigations are needed. Localized studies can lead
to important generalizations, a notable example being Rabinowitz's
conclusion that in many areas of black urban life, segregation constituted an improvement over previous exclusion. But a focus upon
locality, as on state or institution, carries the hazard of fragmentation, the challenge to create a dynamic synthesis. The black encounter with freedom in the South during the half century from emancipation to the great exodus had a coherence and drama yet to be
captured by the historian. The conventional time span of Reconstruction is inhibiting, as is the "static image" of blacks during the decades
that followed, an image fractured since George Tindall criticized it
twenty years ago, but not replaced.[63]

Economic aspects of the black postemancipation experience fall
outside the bounds of this essay, but the division of labor in this volume should not be interpreted to reflect the trend in historical literature. On the contrary, recent work increasingly recognizes and
pursues the intimate relationship between political and economic
condition, between each and the nature of black institutions and
black identity. Thus important treatments of the black family and
household can be found in the essentially economic studies by Ronald
Davis and Crandall Shifflett. Harold Woodman's interest in the transformation of the southern economy has led him to examine state law,
while Donald Nieman's concern with law and local justice has necessitated close attention to the conditions of labor. J. Morgan Kousser,
in reexamining southern politics, has linked the legalized suffrage restrictions of the 1890s and 1900s to the curtailed availability for
blacks of educational facilities and leadership roles. And Eric Foner's

Yeoman Farmers and the Transformation of the Georgia Upcountry, 1850–1890
(New York: Oxford University Press, 1983); Lacy K. Ford, "Rednecks and Merchants:
Economic Development and Social Tensions in the South Carolina Upcountry, 1865–
1900," *Journal of American History*, LXXI (September, 1984), 294–318. Two impor-
tant state studies have appeared too late for comment. Barbara Jeanne Fields, *Slavery
and Freedom on the Middle Ground: Maryland during the Nineteenth Century* (New
Haven: Yale University Press, 1985); and Roberta Sue Alexander, *North Carolina
Faces the Freedmen: Race Relations During Presidential Reconstruction, 1865–67*
(Durham: Duke University Press, 1985).

63. Tindall, "Southern Negroes Since Reconstruction," in Link and Patrick (eds.),
Writing Southern History, 338–39. A topically fragmented but useful general account
of postemancipation southern blacks is Arnold H. Taylor, *Travail and Triumph: Black
Life and Culture in the South Since the Civil War* (Westport, Conn.: Greenwood Press,
1976).

account of strikes by the rice workers of South Carolina indicates an intimate relationship between black participation in politics and black labor militancy, or at least its chance for some degree of success.[64]

Emancipation was a central dynamic of southern history, forcing a reconstruction of southern society of which Reconstruction after the Civil War was but an episode. The destruction of slavery, indeed the very prospect of its destruction, was momentous for southerners, both white and black. The consequences for the class structure and the economy of the South are matters of lively dispute, dealt with elsewhere in this volume. The immediate impact of emancipation upon those caught in the experience has been first of all a challenge to historical discovery. To a degree that would have appeared impossible only two decades ago, the response of the presumed mute, the former slaves—their acts, their thoughts, their words—are being recaptured with dramatic vividness. Leon Litwack's widely acclaimed success in doing so in his *Been in the Storm So Long* (1979) was based upon the sensitive, perceptive use of a wide array of primary sources, but most especially the interviews with former slaves conducted principally by WPA workers in the 1930s. Made readily available in several series totaling forty-one volumes edited by George P. Rawick, *The American Slave: A Composite Autobiography,* these recollections include many references to events during and after the war.[65]

64. Woodman, "Post–Civil War Southern Agriculture and the Law," 319–37; Nieman, *To Set the Law in Motion,* 33–71; J. Morgan Kousser, *The Shaping of Southern Politics: Suffrage Restriction and the Establishment of the One-Party South, 1880–1910* (New Haven: Yale University Press, 1974), 228–29, 248–50, "A Black Protest in the 'Era of Accommodation': Documents," *Arkansas Historical Quarterly,* XXXIV (Summer, 1975), 155, "Progressivism—For Middle-Class Whites Only," and "Making Separate Equal: Integration of Black and White School Funds in Kentucky," *Journal of Interdisciplinary History,* X (Winter, 1980), 399–428; Foner, *Nothing But Freedom,* Chap. 3. See also Jerrell H. Shofner, "Militant Negro Laborers in Reconstruction Florida," *Journal of Southern History,* XXXIX (August, 1973), 397–408; and Charles L. Flynn, Jr., *White Land, Black Labor: Caste and Class in Late Nineteenth-Century Georgia* (Baton Rouge: Louisiana State University Press, 1983), esp. 84–114 on the role of law. Mark W. Summers, *Railroads, Reconstruction, and the Gospel of Prosperity: Aid under the Radical Republicans, 1865–1877* (Princeton: Princeton University Press, 1984), links southern railroad development to the political fortunes of southern Republicanism. On the recent revival of interest in the economic and class aspects of Reconstruction, see Michael Les Benedict, "The Politics of Prosperity in the Reconstruction South," *Reviews in American History,* XII (December, 1984), 507–14.

65. Litwack, *Been in the Storm So Long,* xiii; George P. Rawick, *From Sundown to*

Sources in the National Archives contemporary with the emancipation experience, and too extensive for the capacity of the individual researcher or editor, have been thoroughly canvassed by the Freedmen and Southern Society Project. Under the direction of Ira Berlin and his associates, forty thousand documents illuminating black life during the early years of freedom (1861 through 1867) have been culled from twenty-two record groups, including those of the Freedmen's Bureau. A substantial proportion preserves the words of former slaves, in letters often dictated, in depositions, testimony, and joint statements. An extensive selection will be printed in *Freedom: A Documentary History of Emancipation,* the first volume published being *The Black Military Experience* (1982), and the entire collection will be made available on microfilm. Introductory essays designed to indicate the historical context of the published documents also include fresh and challenging interpretations of the black experience. The series as a whole seeks to examine how black men and women sought "to enlarge their freedom and secure their independence from those who would dominate their lives."[66]

From these works and others focused on the early years of emancipation some conclusions are emerging. As Peter Kolchin was the first to argue, this period, though overshadowed in historiography by the years of Republican control in the South, significantly affected the shape of a new social order for blacks. Litwack eschewed overt generalization but made convincing the diversity of individual black response, and the editors of *Freedom* similarly are alert to variations, especially those related to time and place. While the myth of the loyal slave was laid to rest in the 1930s by Bell I. Wiley, recent writings underscore the eagerness for freedom and establish the former slave's ability to recognize and assert the rights of free men against arbitrary authority and injustice through protest, appeal, and use of those legal channels available to him. At the same time most slaves appear

---

Sunup: The Making of the Black Community (Westport, Conn.: Greenwood Publishing Corp., 1972), xv–xviii. Use of the forty-one volumes edited by Rawick has been facilitated by the publication of Donald M. Jacobs (ed.), *Index to "The American Slave"* (Westport, Conn.: Greenwood Press, 1981).

66. Ira Berlin, Joseph P. Reidy, and Leslie S. Rowland (eds.), *Freedom: A Documentary History of Emancipation, 1861–1867. Selected from the Holdings of the National Archives of the United States,* Series II, *The Black Military Experience* (New York: Cambridge University Press, 1982), quotation on p. xxii. On the Freedmen's Bureau records, see Barry A. Crouch, "Hidden Sources of Black History: The Texas Freedmen's Bureau Records as a Case Study," *Southwestern Historical Quarterly,* LXXXIII (January, 1980), 211–26.

to have embraced freedom with pragmatic caution and wariness of whites. The active role taken by those who joined the ranks of the Union army or fled from bondage as the army advanced made them parties to their own liberation and to that of their fellows. Black men in blue uniforms saw themselves as liberators.[67]

Attention to early emancipation and to black institutions has not diminished the interest in black politics and black political leaders. Indeed, the editors of *Freedom* argue that the war years politicized former slaves who served in the military, and the call for suffrage by blacks in the South as well as in the North before Congress acted suggests a continuum of black political activity. Biographical studies of political leaders, individual and collective, as books and as articles, have multiplied since 1970.[68]

67. Kolchin, *First Freedom*, xix; Berlin, Reidy, and Rowland (eds.), *The Black Military Experience*, esp. 1–34, 183–97, 433–42; Escott, *Slavery Remembered*, 119–44; Barry A. Crouch, "Black Dreams and White Justice," *Prologue*, VI (Winter, 1974), 255–65; Robert H. McKenzie, "The Shelby Iron Company: A Note on Slave Personality after the Civil War," *Journal of Negro History*, LVIII (July, 1973), 341–48; Bobby L. Lovett, "The Negro's Civil War in Tennessee, 1861–1865," *Journal of Negro History*, LXI (January, 1976), 36–50; Martin Abbott, "Voice of Freedom: The Response of Southern Freedmen to Liberty," *Phylon*, XXXIV (December, 1973), 399–405; Edmund L. Drago, "How Sherman's March Through Georgia Affected the Slaves," *Georgia Historical Quarterly*, LVII (Fall, 1973), 361–75; Paul D. Escott, "The Context of Freedom: Georgia's Slaves During the Civil War," *Georgia Historical Quarterly*, LVIII (Spring, 1974), 79–104; William C. Hine, "The 1867 Charleston Streetcar Sit-ins: A Case of Successful Black Protest," *South Carolina Historical Magazine*, LXXVII (April, 1976), 110–14; Clarence L. Mohr, "Before Sherman: Georgia Blacks and the Union War Effort, 1861–1864," *Journal of Southern History*, XLV (August, 1979), 331–52; John T. O'Brien, "Reconstruction in Richmond: White Restoration and Black Protest, April–June 1865," *Virginia Magazine of History and Biography*, LXXXIX (July, 1981), 259–81; Victor B. Howard, *Black Liberation in Kentucky: Emancipation and Freedom, 1862–1884* (Lexington: University Press of Kentucky, 1983).

68. Okon Edet Uya, *From Slavery to Public Service: Robert Smalls, 1839–1915* (New York: Oxford University Press, 1971); Victor Ullman, *Martin R. Delany: The Beginnings of Black Nationalism* (Boston: Beacon Press, 1971); Edwin S. Redkey (comp. and ed.), *Respect Black: The Writings and Speeches of Henry McNeal Turner* (New York: Arno Press, 1971); James Haskins, *Pinckney Benton Stewart Pinchback* (New York: Macmillan, 1973); Peggy Lamson, *The Glorious Failure: Black Congressman Robert Brown Elliott and the Reconstruction in South Carolina* (New York: Norton, 1973); Peter D. Klingman, *Josiah Walls: Florida's Black Congressman of Reconstruction* (Gainesville: University Presses of Florida, 1976); Loren Schweninger, *James T. Rapier and Reconstruction* (Chicago: University of Chicago Press, 1978); Charles Vincent, *Black Legislators in Louisiana During Reconstruction* (Baton Rouge: Louisiana State University Press, 1976).

Articles are an important supplement to book-length studies: David C. Rankin,

The outstanding biography of a southern black leader of the poste-mancipation decades, the only one to leave an extensive collection of private papers, might at first glance appear an exception to the pre-dominantly political focus, for its subject concentrated his effort on black education and at least publicly renounced black politics. Yet Booker T. Washington, as presented by Louis Harlan, his biographer and the editor of his papers, as well as by August Meier in his study of Negro social thought, was a profoundly political figure, seeking and

---

"The Origins of Black Leadership in New Orleans During Reconstruction," *Journal of Southern History,* XL (August, 1974), 417–40; Walter J. Fraser, Jr., "Black Recon-structionists in Tennessee," *Tennessee Historical Quarterly,* XXXIV (Winter, 1975), 362–82; Barry A. Crouch, "Self-Determination and Local Black Leaders in Texas," *Phylon,* XXXIX (December, 1978), 344–55; Joe M. Richardson, "Jonathan C. Gibbs: Florida's Only Negro Cabinet Member," *Florida Historical Quarterly,* XLII (April, 1964), 363–68, and "Francis L. Cardozo: Black Educator During Reconstruction," *Journal of Negro Education,* XLVIII (Winter, 1979), 73–83; Edwin S. Redkey, "Bishop Turner's African Dream," *Journal of American History,* LIV (September, 1967), 270–90; William C. Harris, "James Lynch: Black Leader in Southern Reconstruction," *Historian,* XXXIV (November, 1971), 40–61; Kenneth Eugene Mann, "Blanche Kelso Bruce: United States Senator Without a Constituency," *Journal of Mississippi History,* XXXVIII (May, 1976), 183–98; James W. Leslie, "Ferd Havis: Jefferson County's Black Republican Leader," *Arkansas Historical Quarterly,* XXXVII (Autumn, 1978), 240–51; Charles E. Wynes, "T. McCants Stewart: Peripatetic Black South Carolin-ian," *South Carolina Historical Magazine,* LXXX (October, 1979), 311–17; Bess Beatty, "John Willis Menard: A Progressive Black in Post–Civil War Florida," *Florida Historical Quarterly,* LIX (October, 1980), 123–43; Charles Vincent, "Aspects of the Family and Public Life of Antoine Dubuclet: Louisiana's Black State Treasurer, 1868–1878," *Journal of Negro History,* LXVI (February, 1981), 26–36; Samuel Shapiro, "A Black Senator from Mississippi: Blanche K. Bruce," *Review of Politics,* XLIV (January, 1982), 83–109; William C. Hine, "Black Politicians in Reconstruc-tion Charleston, South Carolina: A Collective Study," *Journal of Southern History,* XLIX (November, 1983), 555–84.

Black political leaders also figure in state histories of Reconstruction, of the Republi-can party, and of the Negro (see note 62; and citations in the essay by Joe Gray Taylor in this volume). A useful collection by authorities on state politics of the period is Otto H. Olsen (ed.), *Reconstruction and Redemption in the South* (Baton Rouge: Louisiana State University Press, 1980). They shift the focus of explanation for the failure of southern Republicanism to the South. So does Loren Schweninger, "Black Citizenship and the Republican Party in Reconstruction Alabama," *Alabama Review,* XXIX (April, 1976), 83–103. On the other hand, in a defense of southern Republican con-gressmen, Terry L. Seip has added yet another charge against northern Republicans, namely, that they failed to give their southern colleagues the political and economic support essential to sustain them and southern Republicanism in power. See his *The South Returns to Congress: Men, Economic Measures, and Intersectional Relation-ships, 1868–1879* (Baton Rouge: Louisiana State University Press, 1983).

wielding power including that of political patronage.[69] Washington was also a complex and elusive character, both as a personality and as a leader of his race. Scholars continue to write about him and to disagree.[70] One of the most interesting, and perhaps unanswerable, questions recent differences raise is whether Washington diminished or enhanced racial pride and solidarity. However judged as a race leader, this man who came "up from slavery" attained extraordinary influence during a period when white resistance had drastically narrowed the opening for black talent in the South created by national policy in the 1860s.

The subjects of most biographical treatment are black political leaders in the obvious sense, those who held national, state, or local office or who exerted influence within the party. A significant beginning has been made in extending black political history into the post-Reconstruction years, although most writings center on the period of Republican control when blacks exercised a substantial degree of direct political power throughout the former Confederacy. The main thrust of biography has continued to liberate blacks in politics from the defamation and distortion of the old orthodoxy that pictured them as ignorant, propertyless, venal men, lording it over former

69. Louis R. Harlan, *Booker T. Washington: The Making of a Black Leader, 1856–1901*, and *Booker T. Washington: The Wizard of Tuskegee, 1901–1915* (New York: Oxford University Press, 1972, 1983); Harlan *et al.* (eds.), *The Papers of Booker T. Washington* (13 vols.; Urbana: University of Illinois Press, 1972–84); Harlan, "Booker T. Washington in Biographical Perspective," *American Historical Review*, LXXV (October, 1970), 1581–99, "The Secret Life of Booker T. Washington," *Journal of Southern History*, XXXVII (August, 1971), 393–416, and "Booker T. Washington and the *Voice of the Negro*, 1904–1907," *Journal of Southern History*, XLV (February, 1979), 45–62; Meier, *Negro Thought*, 100–18. See also Willard B. Gatewood, "William D. Crum: A Negro in Politics," *Journal of Negro History*, LIII (October, 1968), 301–20; and Emma Lou Thornbrough, *T. Thomas Fortune: Militant Journalist* (Chicago: University of Chicago Press, 1972).

70. See Arvarh E. Strickland, "Booker T. Washington: The Myth and the Man," *Reviews in American History*, I (December, 1973), 559–64; Lawrence J. Friedman, "Life 'in the Lion's Mouth': Another Look at Booker T. Washington," *Journal of Negro History*, LIX (October, 1974), 337–51; Allen W. Jones, "The Role of Tuskegee Institute in the Education of Black Farmers," *Journal of Negro History*, LX (April, 1975), 252–67; Alfred Young, "The Educational Philosophy of Booker T. Washington: A Perspective for Black Liberation," *Phylon*, XXXVII (September, 1976), 224–35; Don Quinn Kelley, "Ideology and Education: Uplifting the Masses in Nineteenth Century Alabama," *Phylon*, XL (June, 1979), 147–58, and "The Political Economy of Booker T. Washington: A Bibliographic Essay," *Journal of Negro Education*, XLVI (Fall, 1977), 403–18.

masters or manipulated by self-serving white carpetbaggers and scalawags. So completely have these misconceptions been destroyed that biography, especially collective biography, has now become an instrument of political analysis. The identification of local leaders is serving not primarily to rescue them from obscurity but to illuminate the political process. Recent writings include some sharp criticism of individual and collective black leadership and of historians for having lavished praise without examining achievements.[71]

The most challenging study of black politics during Reconstruction is Thomas Holt's *Black Over White* (1977). Combining quantitative analysis and traditional research, Holt established the predominance of black political power in the Republican party and legislature of South Carolina and then held blacks accountable for the failure of Republicanism and Reconstruction, at least in the state. He argued that division among black legislators had been fatal. Using correlations between voting record and social origins, he concluded that the most important reasons for intraracial cleavage were color and social class. Propertied mulattoes, some freeborn and others skilled former slaves, who constituted a bourgeois elite with over-representation among legislators, lacked the perception to meet the urgent needs of darker-skinned agricultural workers. With this thesis of black class-color responsibility for failure, though foreshadowed by August Meier, Holt presented a distinctive and provocative class interpretation.[72] There has been increasing emphasis during the 1970s upon class rather than race as an explanation for "what went wrong," but historians who favor class have been largely concerned with conflict of interest between planter and agrarian worker, or between

71. John Hosmer and Joseph Fineman, "Black Congressmen in Reconstruction Historiography," *Phylon*, XXXIX (June, 1978), 97–107; Euline W. Brock, "Thomas W. Cardozo: Fallible Black Reconstruction Leader," *Journal of Southern History*, XLVII (May, 1981), 183–206; Holt, *Black Over White*, and "Negro State Legislators in South Carolina during Reconstruction," in Rabinowitz (ed.), *Southern Black Leaders*, 223–46.

72. For Louisiana a similar, though weaker, case has been made for the political relevance of intraracial class differences. David C. Rankin, "The Impact of the Civil War on the Free Colored Community of New Orleans," *Perspectives in American History*, XI (1977–78), 379–416, and "The Origins of Negro Leadership in New Orleans during Reconstruction," in Rabinowitz (ed.), *Southern Black Leaders*, 162, 169–73; Ted Tunnell, "Free Negroes and the Freedmen: Black Politics in New Orleans During the Civil War," *Southern Studies*, XIX (Spring, 1980), 5–28. Meier, "Negroes in the First and Second Reconstructions," 119–20, argued that the Negro elite was most concerned with civil rights and the franchise; the black masses with landownership.

planter and southern merchant or industrialist. Interestingly, the major critique of Holt's conclusions has come from another young black historian, Armstead Robinson, whose own views center on conflict of class interest within each race, across racial lines, and between what he sees as the equalitarianism of the Republican party in the South and its subservience to economic conservatism in the North.[73]

Holt's bold thesis constitutes a challenge to historians who accept the primacy of white class interests, to those who give greater weight to white racism, and to all who attribute major responsibility to northern rather than to southern wielders of power. However, in other respects, Holt's work is in the mainstream of scholarship in that it seeks to determine the social characteristics of southern black leaders, their relationship with their constituencies, and the reasons for the excessive factionalism within southern Republicanism. Distinctions of color can be expected to figure in future writings, perhaps even more importantly, in view of the arresting studies of miscegenation and mulattoes by Joel Williamson and Gary Mills.[74]

Using Holt's social analysis as a basis of comparison, Edmund Drago in a study of Georgia black politicians has found a markedly different leadership in that state, less affluent, less well educated, with fewer mulattoes and fewer free men than freedmen. Like South Carolina's black leaders, they failed to use the full potential of their political power but for different reasons. According to Drago, Georgia's blacks turned to black ministers for political leadership, and their religious conviction led them to be unduly conciliatory and deferential, although they later learned from bitter experience to be more aggressive and black oriented. Another distinctive perspective on the

---

73. The latter assumption apparently reflects the influence of David Montgomery, who argues in *Beyond Equality: Labor and the Radical Republicans, 1862–1872* (New York: Knopf, 1967) that southern Republicanism was an indirect casualty of northern industrialists' concern for controlling northern labor. Armstead L. Robinson, "Explaining the Failure of Democratic Reform in Reconstruction South Carolina," *Reviews in American History,* VIII (December, 1980), 521–30, "Beyond the Realm of Social Consensus: New Meanings of Reconstruction for American History," *Journal of American History,* LXVIII (September, 1981), 276–97, and "Plans Dat Comed from God," in Burton and McMath (eds.), *Toward a New South?,* 88–99. For a fresh distinctive explanation of Republican factionalism, see Lawrence N. Powell, "The Politics of Livelihood: Carpetbaggers in the Deep South," in Kousser and McPherson (eds.), *Region, Race, and Reconstruction,* 315–47.

74. Joel Williamson, *New People: Miscegenation and Mulattoes in the United States* (New York: Free Press, 1980), esp. 75–91; Gary B. Mills, "Miscegenation and the Free Negro in Antebellum 'Anglo' Alabama: A Reexamination of Southern Race Relations," *Journal of American History,* LXVIII (June, 1981), 16–34.

collapse of Republicanism is offered by John Matthews for Georgia and Ted Tunnell for Louisiana. Each holds that disillusionment of blacks with Republican performance, not intimidation and terrorism, explains the Democratic victories. This reflects discredit upon white Republicans rather than black. Euline Brock has gone further than any other revisionist historian in criticism of a black leader. She sees Thomas W. Cardozo, Mississippi's black superintendent of education, as a gifted man who failed his race because of his class arrogance, his ambition, and his lack of scruple in increasing his personal fortune.[75]

Howard Rabinowitz, in editing *Southern Black Leaders of the Reconstruction Era* (1982), has undertaken "to examine how blacks gained, maintained, and finally lost power." Five congressmen, five state or local leaders, and four collective biographies are included in the volume. Fortunately several essays outrun the chronological boundaries of Reconstruction, of which the most provocative are by Michael Chesson on Richmond's black councilmen from 1871 to 1896 and by Eric Anderson on James O'Hara of North Carolina, a congressman in the 1880s but, more important, chairman of his county board of commissioners from 1874 to 1878 (in North Carolina, redemption is dated from 1870 or 1874). In the "Afterword," August Meier undertakes the difficult assignment of formulating "tentative conclusions." To more obvious generalizations about origin and diversity of the leadership group he adds the judgment that for black political leaders, a base in the black community was essential but not sufficient. To exercise significant influence or hold high office, they needed the cooperation of whites in general or an alliance with a particular white leader or faction. On the ground that present knowledge is inadequate for generalization, Meier sidesteps an answer to the critical question of whether a gulf in social origins between leaders and their black constituencies compromised the interest of the latter. He does, however, point out that blacks operating in

75. Edmund L. Drago, *Black Politicians and Reconstruction in Georgia: A Splendid Failure* (Baton Rouge: Louisiana State University Press, 1982); John M. Matthews, "Negro Republicans in the Reconstruction of Georgia," *Georgia Historical Quarterly,* LX (Summer, 1976), 145–64; T. B. Tunnell, Jr., "The Negro, the Republican Party, and the Election of 1876 in Louisiana," *Louisiana History,* VII (Spring, 1966), 101–16 (he has repudiated that conclusion in Ted Tunnell, *Crucible of Reconstruction: War, Radicalism, and Race in Louisiana, 1862–1877* [Baton Rouge: Louisiana State University Press, 1984], 212n4); Brock, "Thomas W. Cardozo."

a white-dominated world were under more than the usual constraints of American politics, which of themselves necessitated compromise.[76]

August Meier's caution is understandable, yet these studies and others separately published suggest a more positive evaluation of black political leaders even while acknowledging "ambiguities" (to use Meier's term) between their personal ambitions, or class status, and service to the race. More often than not, they were able, practical men, skillful in the art of politics, or soon becoming so. Within the limits open to them, most of these black leaders established creditable and meaningful records in terms of the interests of their black constituencies. It is undoubtedly true that some leaders served primarily as symbols, but a symbol of status and acceptance is not inconsequential to a people subjected to insult and intent on guarding their dignity. In legislative bodies, some served by articulating protest against white discrimination and injustice, offering remedial proposals and fighting repressive measures. Again, protest and proposals are not to be dismissed as irrelevant. Others, especially local leaders, obtained results insignificant in terms of the large issues of race and economic structure but of immediate consequence to their people. Richmond's black councilmen stopped the practice of grave robbing in black cemeteries; those of Atlanta obtained a sidewalk in front of the AME church and prevented Atlanta University from being bisected by a thoroughfare; those of Jacksonville, Florida, secured the appointment of a black police commissioner; Tennessee black legislators gained an annual appropriation for training black teachers and opened to Negroes state institutions for the blind and the deaf.[77]

---

76. Rabinowitz (ed.), *Southern Black Leaders*, esp. xi–xx, 393–405 (quotations on pp. xviii, 393).

77. *Ibid.*, 212–13, 318–19; Edward N. Akin, "When a Minority Becomes the Majority: Blacks in Jacksonville Politics, 1887–1907," *Florida Historical Quarterly*, LIII (October, 1974), 123–45; Joseph H. Cartwright, "Black Legislators in Tennessee in the 1880's: A Case Study in Black Political Leadership," *Tennessee Historical Quarterly*, XXXII (Fall, 1973), 265–84. See also Elizabeth Balanoff, "Negro Legislators in the North Carolina General Assembly, July 1868–Feb. 1872," *North Carolina Historical Quarterly*, XLIX (Winter, 1972), 22–55; Ruth Currie McDaniel, "Black Power in Georgia: William A. Pledger and the Takeover of the Republican Party," *Georgia Historical Quarterly*, LXII (Fall, 1978), 225–39; James T. Moore, "Black Militancy in Readjuster Virginia, 1879–1883," *Journal of Southern History*, XLI (May, 1975), 167–86; Allen W. Trelease, "Republican Reconstruction in North Carolina: A Roll-Call Analysis of the State House of Representatives, 1868–1870," *Journal of Southern History*, XLII (August, 1976), 330, 341; George W. Reid, "Four in Black: North Caro-

On the basis of what is known of black politics in the 1880s and 1890s, it appears that members of the second generation of black political leaders were sufficiently effective to have helped trigger their own undoing, the white racist reaction that led to the displacement of partial by total disfranchisement and the hardening of de facto into legal segregation. Nor can the functioning of blacks in politics be determined without considering their behavior as voters. For a people without prior political experience, their response in the years immediately following enfranchisement was remarkable—in extent of participation, in courage when faced with physical or economic hazard, in independence asserted against the advice of former masters and, on occasion, against a deeply felt loyalty to the party of emancipation. Like most of their leaders, the black electorate seem generally to have been "their own men." Where black leaders continued to exercise political influence in the 1880s, it suggests that black voters, rather than lapsing into confusion and apathy after redemption, responded whenever an avenue remained open to some measure of power or meaningful self-assertion.[78]

J. Morgan Kousser has made striking contributions and ventured further than any historian since C. Vann Woodward in generalizing about post-Reconstruction or New South politics. At least in its first fruits, his work was not primarily concerned with blacks and Republican politics; yet it carries important implications for both. Kousser holds invalid several widely accepted concepts, the idea of a solid South after 1877, white Republican betrayal of blacks, black passivity after Hayes's inaugural, and lower-class-white responsibility for

---

lina's Black Congressmen, 1874–1901," *Journal of Negro History,* LXIV (Summer, 1979), 229–43; and note 68.

78. See Holt, *Black Over White,* 4, 206; Joseph H. Cartwright, *The Triumph of Jim Crow: Tennessee Race Relations in the 1880s* (Knoxville: University of Tennessee Press, 1976); William F. Cheek, "A Negro Runs for Congress: John Mercer Langston and the Virginia Campaign of 1888," *Journal of Negro History,* LII (January, 1967), 14–34; Eugene J. Watts, "Black Political Progress in Atlanta: 1868–95," *Journal of Negro History,* LIX (July, 1974), 268–86; William Warren Rogers and Robert David Ward, " 'Jack Turnerism': A Political Phenomenon of the Deep South," *Journal of Negro History,* LVII (October, 1972), 313–32; William J. Cooper, Jr., "Economics or Race: An Analysis of the Gubernatorial Election of 1890 in South Carolina," *South Carolina Historical Magazine,* LXXIII (October, 1972), 209–19; Peter D. Klingman and David T. Geithman, "Negro Dissidence and the Republican Party, 1864–1872," *Phylon,* XL (June, 1979), 172–82; Loren Schweninger, "Alabama Blacks and the Congressional Reconstruction Acts of 1867," *Alabama Review,* XXXI (July, 1978), 182–98. I have not attempted to review here the literature on populism as it relates to blacks; see the essay in this volume by Harold D. Woodman.

black disfranchisement. He sees black progress in the 1880s and 1890s as having threatened white and Democratic party supremacy, thereby helping to precipitate Jim Crow legislation and to complete black disfranchisement. In demonstrating the major impact of the last round of voting restrictions, he has also shown that blacks and their white allies had made a significant difference in southern politics after redemption. The conclusion of his 1980 article on the Kentucky school-fund referendum is a challenge to those "historians who have neglected to distinguish degrees of racism among southern whites or failed to note that, outside the Deep South at least, blacks in the post-Reconstruction era were neither powerless nor friendless." The substance of the article deals with the approval in 1882 by Kentucky voters of a substantial increase in property taxes for whites in order to finance a 300 percent increase in state expenditures for the education of black children.[79]

For the earlier period, Eric Foner has raised related challenging issues. He has called attention to the unique, dramatic quality of postemancipationism in America as the only instance where blacks soon after freedom exercised a real measure of political power. Unlike the sequel to slavery in other countries, in the South during Reconstruction he sees the polity as the scene of battle between former master and former slave to determine the degree of economic and social autonomy for the freed.[80] These fresh perspectives can be expected to relieve the bleak historiographic outlook dominant since the late 1960s that saw only the limits of northern action and the

79. Kousser, *The Shaping of Southern Politics*, 11, 14–29, 36–37, 43–44, 228–29, "Post-Reconstruction Suffrage Restrictions in Tennessee: A New Look at the V. O. Key Thesis," *Political Science Quarterly*, LXXXVIII (December, 1973), 655–83, "Separate but *not* Equal: The Supreme Court's First Decision on Racial Discrimination in Schools," *Journal of Southern History*, XLVI (February, 1980), 17–44, "A Black Protest in the 'Era of Accommodation,'" "Progressivism—For Middle Class Whites Only," "Making Separate Equal," quotation on p. 424, and Review of Anderson's *Race and Politics in North Carolina*, in *Journal of Southern History*, XLVIII (February, 1982), 123–25. See also Gordon B. McKinney, "Southern Mountain Republicans and the Negro, 1865–1900," *Journal of Southern History*, XLI (November, 1975), 493–516.

80. Eric Foner, "Reconstruction Revisited," *Reviews in American History*, X (December, 1982), 91–92. The emergence of southern legal history as a distinctive field of scholarship also promises new insight into postemancipation developments. See Edward L. Ayers, *Vengeance and Justice: Crime and Punishment in the 19th-Century American South* (New York: Oxford University Press, 1984), 141–84; and David J. Bodenhamer and James W. Ely, Jr. (eds.), *Ambivalent Legacy: A Legal History of the South* (Jackson: University Press of Mississippi, 1984), 3–29, 80–86.

dismal continuities between black slavery and black freedom. There are other indications as well, some mentioned earlier, that the writings of the next decade will find less imbalance between the negatives and the positives of emancipation, both as black experience and as national policy. A straw in the wind is the reappearance of the term *revolution* in scholarly writings on the postemancipation South for purposes other than to deny its existence.

By the turn of the century, or shortly thereafter, the southern states by law had closed and bolted the door to political influence and publicly acknowledged dignity opened to blacks through emancipation and Reconstruction. A half century later, even as the civil rights revolution was gathering momentum, disfranchisement and segregation seemed to most southerners part of a natural immutable order. The first target of revolt was Jim Crow. In *The Strange Career of Jim Crow,* a series of lectures delivered at the University of Virginia in 1954, published in 1955, and reissued in a revised edition in 1966, C. Vann Woodward produced a tract for the times that was also a history of such quality as to remain for three decades the point of departure for scholarly discourse, controversy, and research on the origins and history of segregation. To convince his fellow southerners that "proscription, segregation and disfranchisement" were not immutable, he showed that for more than two decades after Reconstruction, there had existed a degree of fluidity and tolerance in relations between the races unthinkable for later generations. He implied that an alternate pattern to Jim Crow might have developed and explained the South's "capitulation to racism" in the 1890s by a concurrent decline of restraints both external (northern) and internal (southern), by aggression arising from frustration, and by a general crescendo of white racism.[81]

The extent to which *The Strange Career* helped undermine southern white resistance to change is a question impossible to answer, but it can be said with some assurance that its result for historical writing was remarkably fruitful. Woodward accepted much of the new scholarship it stimulated, even where it modified his own. Investigation centered upon the origins of segregation, the impact of emancipation, and the reality of an alternative racial solution.[82] An addi-

---

81. C. Vann Woodward, *The Strange Career of Jim Crow* (2nd rev. ed.; New York: Oxford University Press, 1966), 64, 67 (chapter title).

82. For Woodward's response to subsequent scholarship, see his *The Strange Career of Jim Crow,* "The Strange Career of a Historical Controversy," in *American Counterpoint,* 234–60, Review of Rabinowitz's *Race Relations in the Urban*

tional dimension was added when Rabinowitz showed that in terms of some social services, segregation was a distinct advance over total exclusion and had black support. He also shifted attention to the question of why southern whites in the 1890s felt it necessary to substitute *de jure* for the widespread de facto segregation, and he offered a tentative hypothesis. A new generation of blacks unconditioned by slavery was sufficiently aggressive, especially in resisting local white policemen, to arouse white fears. More recently, David Donald has argued the inadequacy of all previous explanations for the deterioration of race relations in the 1890s and presented a white generational theory. Southern whites who as young men had experienced the dual traumas of the Civil War with defeat and of emancipation with the conduct of former slaves seen as betrayal had reordered their lives and their social order on the basis of sharecropping, Democratic party supremacy, and the subordination of blacks. Fearful that their successors would not perpetuate their achievements, in their fifties they sought to ensure the future by codifying into law racial segregation and disfranchisement.[83]

South, in *Journal of Southern History,* XLIV (August, 1978), 476–78, and foreword to Howard N. Rabinowitz, *Race Relations in the Urban South* (Urbana: University of Illinois Press, 1980), ix–x. For other evaluations of the literature on segregation, see Joel Williamson (ed.), *The Origins of Segregation* (Boston: Heath, 1968); August Meier and Elliott Rudwick, "A Strange Chapter in the Career of 'Jim Crow,'" in Meier and Rudwick (eds.), *The Making of Black America: Essays in Negro Life and History,* Vol. II, *The Black Community in Modern America* (New York: Atheneum, 1969), 14–19; Howard N. Rabinowitz, "From Exclusion to Segregation: Southern Race Relations, 1865–1890," *Journal of American History,* LXIII (September, 1976), 325–50, and *Race Relations* (1980), 331; Kousser and McPherson (eds.), *Region, Race, and Reconstruction,* xxv–xxvii. For the continuing vitality of *The Strange Career* as a stimulus, see John W. Cell, *The Highest Stage of White Supremacy: The Origins of Segregation in South Africa and the American South* (Cambridge, England: Cambridge University Press, 1982). Delaware's race relations, at least as to disfranchisement, apparently were not typical. See Amy M. Hiller, "The Disfranchisement of Delaware Negroes in the Late Nineteenth Century," *Delaware History,* XIII (October, 1968), 124–53.

83. Rabinowitz, *Race Relations* (1980), esp. 332–39; David Herbert Donald, "A Generation of Defeat," in Fraser and Moore (eds.), *From the Old South to the New,* 3–20.

Even more recently, Joel Williamson has linked *de jure* disfranchisement and segregation to southern white male sexual appetites and attitudes toward white womanhood. Under the explosive pressure of economic depression, white men set in motion a vicious scapegoating of the black male by racist radicals. This was expressed in restrictive legislation as well as in racial violence. According to Williamson, the laws found support from racist conservatives who sought to protect blacks, from Democrats who

Although Donald dismissed out of hand the possibility that black restiveness and self-assertion triggered the change, the work of historians dealing with black political activity in the 1880s suggests a need to develop and test the black generational thesis. However generational explanations, white or black, may fare in the give and take of scholarly exchange, they seem less likely to replace than to supplement Woodward's analysis. More vulnerable is the implication in *The Strange Career* that southern whites of their own volition might have reversed the course of race relations. Before the 1890s, the de facto segregation prevalent in many areas indicated a broadly based white determination to keep the Negro "in his place." Nonetheless, Woodward's central argument, that there was a relative openness in the post-Reconstruction decades as compared with what followed, remains valid and has been strengthened by Kousser's analysis of southern politics.

Like revisionist writings on Reconstruction, the historiographic consequences of *The Strange Career* indicate how exaggerated were fears that emotional commitment to the civil rights revolution would result in simplistic history, merely a role reversal of saints and sinners. It is true that the presentism of a generation of scholars fostered some distortions. While elevating few to sainthood, it found a superabundance of sinners. In seeking explanation, it tended to diminish the role of the South and to exaggerate that of the North.[84] And by con-

---

desired to disenfranchise their political opponents, and from a reforming impulse that would purify de facto disfranchisement by eliminating the necessity for fraud and intimidation. They completed a cultural separation between blacks and whites (*The Crucible of Race: Black-White Relations in the American South Since Emancipation* [New York: Oxford University Press, 1984], 115–18, 134–35, 224–58, 305–23, 513–17).

84. A shift of attention from North to South appears to be accelerating. In a strikingly original analysis of southern politics, Michael Perman finds the white South moving to accept the essentials of Reconstruction until the Republican victory of 1872 led their opponents to embrace the politics of race and blacks to increased assertiveness within the Republican party. Ted Tunnell highlights the inescapable contradictions facing a Republican party that sought both its own survival and a biracial society but also faults Louisiana's white Republican leaders for lack of the commitment and daring needed to mobilize blacks in militant resistance to white terrorism. Dan Carter's account of the failure of southern white conservative leaders during presidential Reconstruction, without absolving them from responsibility, implies that failure was inevitable, given the chaos of the postwar South, the confusion of politics, the obsessive white fears rooted in racial assumptions of the proslavery argument, and the persistence of the southern sense of honor. Michael Perman, *The Road to Redemption: Southern Politics, 1869–1879* (Chapel Hill: University of North Carolina Press, 1984), esp. Chaps. 5–6; Tunnell, *Crucible of Reconstruction*, 160–72, 212–18; Dan

centrating on Jim Crow, the priority of their own generation, historians both diverted attention from the political substance of power and gave undue weight to integration as a criterion for moral judgment upon white allies of blacks in the mid nineteenth century. Fortunately the historical profession is self-healing.

This is not to imply that specific issues still very much in contention, and key questions for which there are no satisfactory answers, will be readily resolved. Nor is reconciliation in sight for major elements of explanation that too often contend as adversaries: race versus class, continuity versus change, individualism versus community. In addition, there is increasing evidence of significant variation associated with locality. The repeated calls for a grand new synthesis to replace the discredited Dunningite-Beard-Beale orthodoxy may reflect a yearning for the impossible. The racial bias that falsified but unified old accounts of "The Tragic Era" is gone. Nostalgia for a return of the Beard-Beale thesis in modernized garb is evident and may be answered, but universal acceptance cannot be expected for a holistic economic interpretation. Reconstruction itself, as time period or as concept, is an obstacle to effective synthesis. As the former, it has burst the boundaries that once contained its beginning and its end. As a concept, it invites disunity, for it can as reasonably be interpreted as reconstruction of the Union or as reconstruction of southern society. Finally, Reconstruction has so long reflected white perspectives that it will be difficult to transform it into a vehicle of history that fulfills John Hope Franklin's call for a synthesis that includes "the whole range of the freedmen's experience." [85] Perhaps the time has come to discard Reconstruction as an organizational category in favor of emancipation—its anticipation, its complexity, and its consequences.

T. Carter, *When the War Was Over: The Failure of Self-Reconstruction in the South, 1865–1867* (Baton Rouge: Louisiana State University Press, 1985).

85. John Hope Franklin, "Mirror for Americans: A Century of Reconstruction History," *American Historical Review*, LXXXV (February, 1980), 11.

Economic Reconstruction and the Rise of the New South, 1865–1900

HAROLD D. WOODMAN

W. E. B. Du Bois concluded his massive study *Black Reconstruction* with an angry denunciation of the state of scholarship, calling the racist writings of the time "lies" and "propaganda." Few historians listened to Du Bois when he wrote in 1935, but two decades later a change was clearly under way as members of a group labeled "revisionists" were rewriting Reconstruction history and beginning to rewrite the history of blacks. The revisionists seldom accepted Du Bois's interpretation, and, indeed, few even directly acknowledged his work, but because they began with new assumptions and found new evidence, they produced interpretations that came closer to those by Du Bois than to those being revised.[1]

Du Bois also condemned the elitist bias and the excessively political emphasis in Reconstruction historiography. Historians depicted blacks as fools or scoundrels, and ignored the nonslaveholding whites as if they "left no history and had no descendants." A major problem, he concluded, was the narrow, exclusively political approach: "The whole development of Reconstruction was primarily an economic development, but no economic history or proper material for it has been written. It has been regarded as a purely political matter, and of politics most naturally divorced from industry."[2]

Few responded to Du Bois's challenge to write the economic and social history of Reconstruction. Revisionists glossed over social and economic changes, viewing them as background or influences on

1. W. E. Burghardt Du Bois, *Black Reconstruction: An Essay Toward a History of the Part Which Black Folk Played in the Attempt to Reconstruct Democracy in America, 1860–1880* (New York: Harcourt, Brace, 1935), Chap. 17, "The Propaganda of History." The state of revisionist scholarship by the mid-1960s may be found in Arthur S. Link and Rembert W. Patrick (eds.), *Writing Southern History: Essays in Historiography in Honor of Fletcher M. Green* (Baton Rouge: Louisiana State University Press, 1965), particularly Chap. 12, "Reconstruction," by Vernon L. Wharton (pp. 295–315), and Chap. 14, "Southern Negroes Since Reconstruction: Dissolving the Static Image," by George B. Tindall (pp. 337–61).

2. Du Bois, *Black Reconstruction*, 721–22.

politics and race relations. Obviously, political Reconstruction deserved the attention it received and continues to receive. Rebuilding the Union following a civil war precipitated by southern attempts to create a separate nation and deciding upon such matters as citizenship and voting rights were momentous political tasks. But equally important was the task of rebuilding the southern economy. The destruction of southern separatism also destroyed slavery, wiping out the section's most important source of movable wealth and ending the legal and physical means to mobilize a major portion of its work force. Surely, therefore, as Du Bois insisted, economic and social reconstruction—replacing the slave system with a free-labor system—is a significant part of the Reconstruction story.

Where Du Bois erred was in his implied assumption that economic and social reconstruction could be adequately considered within the time limits traditionally assigned to Reconstruction, limits that are primarily political, beginning with Federal occupation and the creation of Republican governments in the southern states and concluding with the overthrow of these governments and the withdrawal of troops. Nowhere did political Reconstruction extend beyond 1877, and in most states it ended even earlier. But economic and social changes, by their very nature, occurred more slowly, sometimes even imperceptibly, so that those affected were not always fully aware of the changes in which they were participating. Forcing economic and social reconstruction into the traditional time period of political Reconstruction inevitably subordinated it to politics and truncated a story that often extended beyond 1877.

Of course historians did not completely ignore long-run postbellum economic and social change. They considered the crop-lien system and its effects, the rise and expansion of tenancy and sharecropping, the cotton mill campaign and other efforts to "yankeeize" the South after the Civil War. But the amount of such work was meager, and historians usually subordinated economics to New South politics or populism or, later, New Deal agricultural reforms.[3]

---

3. An indication of the lack of work in this area as well as its subordination to politics as late as the mid-1960s may be seen in Link and Patrick (eds.), *Writing Southern History*. The index contains no reference to sharecropping; the two references to tenancy lead the reader to the chapter on the twentieth century. Chapter 15, "The Agrarian Revolt," by Allen J. Going, refers to some studies of economic matters as they relate to populism and concludes: "Usually included in the general and state studies of Populism are discussions of the agricultural background, but postbellum agriculture itself is a neglected field" (p. 369), a point that C. Vann Woodward had made in 1951 ("Critical

Thus, the political emphasis that dominated Reconstruction historiography continued into the later years as well. In 1971, when Charles B. Dew appended his 112-page "Critical Essay on Recent Works" to a new edition of C. Vann Woodward's *Origins of the New South, 1877–1913*, he had to devote many more pages to politics and government than to economic and social history. "The economic history of the New South remains an underdeveloped area of scholarship," Dew concluded. A year later, when Sheldon Hackney reviewed the scholarship that had appeared after the publication of Woodward's book, he found it "remarkable" that there had been "so little fundamental challenge" to its main arguments. But he noted that the durability of Woodward's interpretation of economic and social developments rested less on its ability to survive challenges of new scholarship than on the lack of such work. "We are still in need of detailed studies of landownership, rural mobility patterns, and local economies and politics before we can be certain as to the effects of the Civil War upon southern social structures," he concluded.[4]

Yet, even as Dew and Hackney wrote, change was under way. The trickle of works they had considered proved to be the beginning of a flood of books and articles dealing with the economic and social history of the postwar South. Some of this new work attempts to supply the information and details that Dew and Hackney called for. Much of it reflects Woodward's influence as it explicitly attempts to support, extend, or modify his general interpretation, although, as will be shown, a significant proportion rejects his major contention that a fundamental discontinuity separated the postbellum from the antebellum South. And, finally, many recent studies take the long view, seeking to understand the social and economic changes in the late-nineteenth-century South as results of the Civil War and emancipation, that is, as part of the history of economic and social reconstruction.[5]

Essay on Authorities," *Origins of the New South, 1877–1913* [Baton Rouge: Louisiana State University Press, 1951], 507) and Charles B. Dew repeated twenty years later when he wrote "Critical Essay on Recent Works," in Woodward, *Origins of the New South, 1877–1913* (Baton Rouge: Louisiana State University Press, 1971), 591.

4. Dew, "Critical Essay," in Woodward, *Origins of the New South* (1971), 596–97. See also Gerald D. Nash, "Research Opportunities in the Economic History of the South After 1880," *Journal of Southern History*, XXXII (August, 1966), 308–24. Sheldon Hackney, "*Origins of the New South* in Retrospect," *Journal of Southern History*, XXXVIII (May, 1972), 191–216 (first and second quotations on p. 191; third quotation on p. 203).

5. One sign of the extent (and significance) of the new work was the appearance of

The defeat of the South and the emancipation of the slaves created enormous political and constitutional problems, vexing contemporary politicians and creating political turmoil. But most southerners had to subordinate politics to the more immediate problem of supporting themselves and their families, a formidable task in the face of wartime destruction and neglect, military occupation, and the uncertain political climate. Recent scholarship, examining this task from new perspectives, provides fresh insights into social and economic problems contributing to the turmoil and conflict of the postwar years. The immediate need was to return to work, but emancipation destroyed the traditional means to that end. The new ways southerners found to replace the old shaped the postwar economy and society.

But historians sharply disagree about the extent of the changes and their significance. Some argue that the Civil War and emancipation marked a basic discontinuity in southern history, bringing significant, even revolutionary change to the region. For others, continuity is the theme of nineteenth-century southern history. Thus, some disagreements stem from very different evaluations of the antebellum South.[6] Although this division of opinion is the source of some of the debate, many of the sharpest disagreements appear among those who agree on continuity (or discontinuity) but then disagree on other issues.

Continuity is the prevailing point of view, as C. Vann Woodward noted in a 1983 review: "In the last few years an emphasis on continuity has threatened to regain ascendancy over the theme of change in the interpretation of Southern history." Continuity, he explained, "had always been the preferred and predominant emphasis among writers of Southern history . . . down to the middle of the present century. Then for twenty years or so the emphasis swung to change and discontinuity," a change in emphasis for which he takes some credit but assigns more influence to the great changes that were

a rash of historiographic essays surveying it. See Harold D. Woodman, "Sequel to Slavery: The New History Views the Postbellum South," *Journal of Southern History,* XLIII (November, 1977), 523–54; Peter Kolchin, "Race, Class, and Poverty in the Post–Civil War South," *Reviews in American History,* VII (December, 1979), 515–26; William N. Parker, "The South in the National Economy, 1865–1970," *Southern Economic Journal,* XLVI (April, 1980), 1019–48; Carl N. Degler, "Rethinking Post–Civil War History," *Virginia Quarterly Review,* LVII (Spring, 1981), 250–67.

6. An excellent discussion of the problem and its complexity is Barbara Jeanne Fields, "The Nineteenth-Century American South: History and Theory," *Plantation Society in the Americas,* II (April, 1983), 7–27.

taking place in the South at the time, which, he suggests, influenced how historians viewed the past.[7]

Woodward did not identify the work of those two decades in which change replaced continuity, but, presumably, he was referring to the flood of revisionist studies. To be sure, this work presented an interpretation of events and particularly of the role of blacks that differed sharply from that of the so-called orthodox or Dunning school historians.[8] But the emphasis usually did not shift to discontinuity. If the traditionalists viewed Radical rule as potentially revolutionary, so too did the revisionists. Where the traditionalists greeted redemption as the return to honest government and an end to the danger of revolutionary changes, the revisionists saw redemption as a return of rule to the prewar elite and the failure to institute needed reforms. Both, then, could see Reconstruction as a tragedy, the first for what it might have done but luckily did not, the second for what it might have done but unfortunately did not. In either case, the period of Radical con-

7. Woodward, Review of Fraser and Moore (eds.), *From the Old South to the New*, in *American Historical Review*, LXXXVIII (February, 1983), 187–89 (quotation on p. 187). Woodward, of course, sharply disagrees with the continuity interpretations. Continuity also prevails in more general studies taking a national perspective. In the years following World War II, American historians began to express doubts about the validity of the progressive synthesis, with its emphasis on conflict and discontinuity. Charles A. Beard and Mary R. Beard had described the Civil War as "the second American revolution," marking the victory of industrialism over agrarianism (*The Rise of American Civilization* [New York: Macmillan, 1927], Chap. 18), but so-called consensus historians such as Daniel J. Boorstin doubted that the conflict revealed as fundamental a clash as the term *revolution* suggested (*The Genius of American Politics* [Chicago: University of Chicago Press, 1953]). Others, focusing more narrowly on economic change, tended to agree with the critics of the Beards. Douglass North and W. W. Rostow dated the nation's industrial revolution from the prewar years and found that the Civil War interrupted rather than stimulated industrial development, a point that business historian Thomas C. Cochran supported with detailed figures on the output of various industries before, during, and after the war (North, *The Economic Growth of the United States, 1790–1860* [Englewood Cliffs, N.J.: Prentice-Hall, 1961]; W. W. Rostow, *The Stages of Economic Growth: A Non-Communist Manifesto* [Cambridge, England: Cambridge University Press, 1960]; Thomas C. Cochran, "Did the Civil War Retard Industrialization?" *Mississippi Valley Historical Review*, XLVIII [September, 1961], 197–210). When a group of economic and business historians met to consider the effect of the war on economic institutions, they found little change except in the area of banking (David T. Gilchrist and W. David Lewis [eds.], *Economic Change in the Civil War Era* [Greenville, Del.: Eleutherian Mills–Hagley Foundation, 1965]).

8. A good survey of the Dunning school and the work of the early revisionists is Wharton, "Reconstruction," in Link and Patrick (eds.), *Writing Southern History*, 295–315. Surveys of recent work are in Cox's and Taylor's chapters herein.

trol was brief; once ended, continuity prevailed. More recent work, which Eric Foner labels "postrevisionist," questions even the momentary radicalism found by traditionalists and revisionists by emphasizing the essential conservatism of all parties: "Postrevisionist writers insisted the impact of the Civil War upon American life was less pervasive than had once been believed."[9] In short, then, the prevailing emphasis on continuity is less a *return* to an older interpretation than a *continuation* of an older emphasis.

Agreement on continuity does not signify consensus among historians. On the contrary, recent work reveals sharply different pictures of the nature and extent of continuity. Put simply, the debate arises over what continued and why. Because those who emphasize continuity either implicitly or explicitly begin with different interpretations of antebellum society, they evaluate postbellum society differently.

It is possible to identify three approaches or schools. Although lines separating them are not sharp and considerable differences exist within each school, each has enough in common to set it apart from the other two. All attempt to explain the rise and effects of economic institutions such as tenancy, sharecropping, and the crop-lien system, and all offer explanations for postbellum poverty in the South. Each assesses the extent of change brought by the Civil War and emancipation, but in the end, despite important differences, continuity rather than change is the underlying theme in all.

One school emphasizes race, what Ulrich B. Phillips in 1928 called the "central theme of southern history," the agreement among all white southerners "that [the South] shall be and remain a white man's country." According to this interpretation, white southerners united in their efforts to control and subordinate blacks in their midst. Slavery, sharecropping, Jim Crow segregation, and violence were merely variations on that single goal of race control. Whites always subordinated differences among themselves based on wealth, class, status, and political power whenever these differences threat-

---

9. Eric Foner, "Reconstruction Revisited," *Reviews in American History*, X (December, 1982), 82–100 (quotation on p. 84). In all cases, the result is the same: If radical change was happily thwarted, tragically avoided, or never seriously considered, continuity remains the underlying theme. It should be noted that postrevisionism, which Foner finds to be a product of the 1970s and a reaction to revisionism, is in many ways a return to the consensus view of the 1950s. See also Dan T. Carter, "From the Old South to the New: Another Look at the Theme of Change and Continuity," in Walter J. Fraser, Jr., and Winfred B. Moore, Jr. (eds.), *From the Old South to the New: Essays on the Transitional South* (Westport, Conn.: Greenwood Press, 1981), 23–32.

ened to undermine white domination over blacks. In Carl Degler's words, "Race in the South, as in the nation, has always overwhelmed class."[10]

The evidence to support this interpretation seems overwhelming. The United States has always been a racist society. Until recently, few whites bothered to hide their racist views; indeed, even so-called moderates or liberals on the race question usually accepted racist assumptions. Politicians and others regularly trotted out the race issue to win support, damage opponents, head off reform, break strikes or build unity to win strikes, and, in general, to divert attention from other issues. Racism, then, often becomes an explanation for the failure of the Republicans and the success of the Redeemers and for the development of the lien laws, discriminatory wage rates, coercion, peonage, and the persisting poverty among southern blacks. It also explains why blacks and poor whites with similar problems failed to achieve lasting unity; racism caused people to behave in ways contrary to their best interests. The explanation is potent, ubiquitous, and timeless.

But it is just this universality that some insist weakens racism's explanatory power; anything that explains everything in the end explains nothing. No one denies the existence of racism in the form of a consistent set of racist ideas and attitudes.[11] But critics argue that these attitudes and ideas cannot bear the interpretive burden placed upon them by those who insist on the primacy of race and racism. The racism that breaks up black-white coalitions apparently did not prevent the coalitions from forming in the first place. Moreover, racism has been manifested in a variety of different ways and with varying degrees of intensity.[12] Barbara J. Fields has suggested that rac-

10. Ulrich B. Phillips, "The Central Theme of Southern History," *American Historical Review*, XXIV (October, 1928), 30–43 (quotation on p. 31); Carl N. Degler, "Racism in the United States: An Essay Review," *Journal of Southern History*, XXXVIII (February, 1972), 101–108 (quotation on p. 102). Degler's fuller and more recent discussion is *Place Over Time: The Continuity of Southern Distinctiveness* (Baton Rouge: Louisiana State University Press, 1977). Other influential statements that emphasize this theme are W. J. Cash, *The Mind of the South* (New York: Knopf, 1941); and V. O. Key, Jr., *Southern Politics in State and Nation* (New York: Knopf, 1949).

11. Enlightening discussions may be found in George M. Fredrickson, *The Black Image in the White Mind: The Debate on Afro-American Character and Destiny, 1817–1914* (New York: Harper & Row, 1971); and Claude H. Nolen, *The Negro's Image in the South: The Anatomy of White Supremacy* (Lexington: University of Kentucky Press, 1967).

12. See the perceptive discussion of this point as it relates to Reconstruction poli-

ism—and, indeed, the very existence of race itself—cannot be understood apart from the particular social context in which it appears. Many historians, she observes, "tend to accord race a transhistorical, almost metaphysical, status that removes it from all possibility of analysis and understanding." Fields's largely theoretical discussion requires further elaboration, which a number of comparative analyses have begun to provide by showing how race and racism took particular forms when used by particular classes or groups for particular purposes.[13] This approach gives racism the explanatory power it lacks when viewed simply as a set of unchanging attitudes.

Race and discrimination play secondary roles in the work of the new economic historians or cliometricians, a second school that emphasizes continuity. Although they often disagree, the cliometricians apply a common method or approach. In Robert Higgs's words, "This approach, which employs modern economic theory to derive refutable hypotheses and submits these hypotheses to statistical and other empirical tests, squarely confronts the facts in all of their diversity." We may pass over the hyperbole about confronting the facts in all their diversity. Historians have not developed any method that could do that; they confront a certain set of facts that for various reasons they deem important. The cliometricians in particular confront those facts that modern neoclassical economic theory—more precisely, price theory—posits as essential in order to understand the workings of the market.[14] Nevertheless, the cliometricians have con-

tics and attitudes toward blacks in LaWanda F. Cox, *Lincoln and Black Freedom: A Study in Presidential Leadership* (Columbia: University of South Carolina Press, 1981), Chap. 5.

13. Barbara J. Fields, "Ideology and Race in American History," in J. Morgan Kousser and James M. McPherson (eds.), *Region, Race, and Reconstruction: Essays in Honor of C. Vann Woodward* (New York: Oxford University Press, 1982), 143–77 (quotation on p. 144). See Thomas C. Holt, "'An Empire Over the Mind': Emancipation, Race, and Ideology in the British West Indies and the American South," in Kousser and McPherson (eds.), *Region, Race, and Reconstruction*, 283–313; Pierre L. van den Berghe, *Race and Racism: A Comparative Perspective* (New York: John Wiley & Sons, 1967); Robert Brent Toplin, *Freedom and Prejudice: The Legacy of Slavery in the United States and Brazil* (Westport, Conn.: Greenwood Press, 1981); John W. Cell, *The Highest Stage of White Supremacy: The Origins of Segregation in South Africa and the American South* (Cambridge, England: Cambridge University Press, 1982); and George M. Fredrickson, *White Supremacy: A Comparative Study in American and South African History* (New York: Oxford University Press, 1981).

14. Robert Higgs, "Comment" on Jonathan M. Wiener, "Class Structure and Economic Development in the American South, 1865–1955," *American Historical Review*, LXXXIV (October, 1979), 993–97 (quotation on p. 996). There is a vast

fronted many of the most vexing and important problems in postbellum southern history: the region's persisting poverty, the origins,
development, and effects of sharecropping, tenancy, and the lien system, the role of storekeepers and merchants, and the effects of racism, discrimination, and coercion on the economy.

The cliometricians who study the antebellum South have attempted
to alter the terms of the debate over slavery that have dominated the
discussion by historians for more than a century. Most historians had
tried to explain the causes of antebellum southern economic backwardness, poverty, and slow growth and development; they had disagreed over whether slavery caused these problems. The cliometricians, however, questioned the initial assumption, insisting instead
that the antebellum South was neither backward nor poor, that its
per capita income, if lower than that of the Northeast, exceeded that
of the Midwest and, even more important, was growing at a faster
rate than that of the nation as a whole, indicating rapid, not slow,
economic growth and development.[15]

The income figures for the postbellum South seemed to reveal a
very different picture.[16] Southern per capita income fell precipitously
after the Civil War and remained low and far behind that of the
North for the remainder of the nineteenth century and well into the
twentieth. (Even today the South's per capita income lags behind that
of the rest of the nation.) The task, it appears, was to explain the persistence of southern poverty and economic stagnation for at least
seven or eight decades after the Civil War, years in which the rest of
the nation experienced rapid economic development. It was necessary to discover the origins as well as the persistence of southern eco-

and controversial literature concerning this approach and its scientific claims. I have
surveyed some of it in "Economic History and Economic Theory: The New Economic
History in America," *Journal of Interdisciplinary History*, III (Autumn, 1972), 323–50.

15. The fullest statement is Robert William Fogel and Stanley L. Engerman, *Time
on the Cross* (2 vols.; Boston: Little, Brown, 1974). This book is controversial and
some of its severest critics have been other cliometricians. But the argument that
the South was not poor and lagging in growth was not questioned by the cliometri-
cian critics.

16. The basic per capita income data for both the antebellum and postbellum periods come from Richard A. Easterlin, "Regional Income Trends, 1840–1950," in Seymour E. Harris (ed.), *American Economic History* (New York: McGraw-Hill, 1961),
525–47, and "Interregional Differences in Per Capita Income, Population, and Total
Income, 1840–1950," in Conference on Research in Income and Wealth, *Trends in
the American Economy in the Nineteenth Century* (Princeton: Princeton University

nomic problems. If the findings of those who had studied the ante-bellum South were accepted—that is, if the slave South was neither poor nor stagnating and if antebellum southerners, like northerners, responded in a rational economic way to market signals—it followed that the source of postbellum poverty and stagnation could not simply be a direct legacy of slavery or other antebellum institutions. Moreover, if southern poverty and lagging economic growth per-sisted, some interference with the free market had to be found. In a free market, regional income disparities should disappear; if they did not, then monopoly power, government interference, or some other form of barrier had to be discovered to account for the persistence of income disparities over the long run. The cliometricians approached their task with energy and inventiveness and produced results that are innovative and important, if controversial.

Robert Higgs, Stanley L. Engerman, and Stephen J. DeCanio be-gan the work in the early 1970s. They neither rejected the income data that pointed to persisting southern poverty nor abandoned the model of the free market but instead found an ingenious way to rec-oncile the two. As a result of the Civil War and its immediate after-math, they argued, the South suffered a massive but onetime loss of income-producing wealth. This loss caused the South's per capita in-come, which had almost equaled the national average in 1860, to fall to 51 percent of the national average in 1880. This explained the ori-gins of the poverty, but not its persistence given free-market condi-tions. But, once again, the income figures provided answers. In 1900 the South's per capita income remained at 51 percent of the national average and by 1920 it had risen to 62 percent. This meant, they con-cluded, that the South grew at the same rate as the nation as a whole between 1880 and 1900, because it retained its relative position, and at a faster rate between 1900 and 1920, because it improved its rela-tive standing. Thus, the South's poverty resulted from massive losses brought by war. But, despite these losses, the region's economy was neither stagnant nor debilitated by inhibiting institutions or attitudes inasmuch as its economic growth either equaled or exceeded the na-tional rate. The free market, which had produced an efficient and rapidly growing antebellum economy, had the same result after the

Press, 1960), 73–140. More recent work makes some adjustments in these data, but the changes are relatively minor and do not alter the general picture presented by Easterlin.

war. In this sense, these cliometricians found continuity. The onetime massive interference with the market's operation—the war and its immediate aftermath—only momentarily broke the continuity.[17]

With this much firmly established and supported by the income data, other matters could be solved by a simple matter of deduction. If the South grew at the national rate or even exceeded it, then postwar economic institutions could not have been inefficient. Neither these institutions nor other social factors such as discrimination, violence, and coercion blocked the optimal allocation of resources. These were indeed the conclusions many cliometricians reached, but to their credit they did not rely on deduction but studied these matters in detail. The general propositions arising from their analysis of the income figures served as working hypotheses.

In a second book and a series of articles, Higgs presented extensive empirical evidence that supported and extended his general propositions.[18] After weighing the relative importance of competition and coercion to the economic progress and well-being of southern blacks after the Civil War, Higgs concluded that competition, that is, the re-

17. Robert Higgs, *The Transformation of the American Economy, 1865–1914: An Essay in Interpretation* (New York: John Wiley & Sons, 1971); Stanley L. Engerman, "Some Economic Factors in Southern Backwardness in the Nineteenth Century," in John F. Kain and John R. Meyer (eds.), *Essays in Regional Economics* (Cambridge: Harvard University Press, 1971), 279–306; Stephen J. DeCanio, *Agriculture in the Postbellum South: The Economics of Production and Supply* (Cambridge: M.I.T. Press, 1974). These scholars do not deny the long-term effects of the onetime loss. The South fell far behind the North and had to grow as fast as the northern economy merely to maintain its relative position. Inasmuch as the northern economy was growing at a very rapid rate, this meant that the southern economy was growing rapidly also. Catching up required an even faster growth rate, which the South managed to achieve after 1880. But there simply was not enough time for the South to close the gap completely.

18. Robert Higgs, *Competition and Coercion: Blacks in the American Economy, 1865–1914* (Cambridge, England: Cambridge University Press, 1977), "Race, Tenure, and Resource Allocation in Southern Agriculture, 1910," *Journal of Economic History,* XXXIII (March, 1973), 149–69, "Did Southern Farmers Discriminate?" *Agricultural History,* XLVI (April, 1972), 325–28, "Did Southern Farmers Discriminate? An Exchange—Interpretive Problems and Further Evidence," *Agricultural History,* XLIX (April, 1975), 445–47, "Patterns of Farm Rental in the Georgia Cotton Belt, 1880–1900," *Journal of Economic History,* XXXIV (June, 1974), 468–82, "Racial Wage Differentials in Agriculture: Evidence from North Carolina in 1887," *Agricultural History,* LII (April, 1978), 308–11, "Firm-Specific Evidence on Racial Wage Differentials and Workforce Segregation," *American Economic Review,* LXVII (March, 1977), 236–45, and "Accumulation of Property by Southern Blacks Before World War I," *American Economic Review,* LXXII (September, 1982), 725–37.

source allocation dictated by the free market, prevailed. Employers and merchants competed for labor and business and were unwilling to pay the costs of racism by giving preferential treatment to whites.[19] Thus competition prevented discrimination against blacks in wage payments, in the sale of lands and goods, and in the allocation of land and equipment for tenant and sharecrop production. Most of the observed differences between blacks and whites in these areas, Higgs insists, reflected differences in skills, credit worthiness, and experience, not overt racial discrimination.

Higgs does not deny the existence of coercion; indeed, he suggests that racial differences in skills, credit worthiness, and experience may have resulted from discrimination that blocked access to opportunities: "As long as hostile whites controlled the legal machinery the blacks—poor, ignorant, and powerless—were bound to be exploited." [20] In short, the most important forms of discrimination were those that occurred before the final market transactions that Higgs analyzes, but unfortunately he does not pursue this important point.[21] Gavin Wright provides some insight into this matter by noting that

19. The influential theoretical discussion upon which Higgs and others rely is Gary S. Becker, *The Economics of Discrimination* (Chicago: University of Chicago Press, 1957). For a different theoretical model, see Ray Marshall, "The Economics of Racial Discrimination: A Survey," *Journal of Economic Literature,* XII (September, 1974), 849–71.

20. Higgs, *Competition and Coercion,* 58–59. DeCanio implies a similar argument. Although he denies that blacks were exploited, he, unlike Higgs in the sentence quoted, uses that term in a technical sense: black croppers and tenants did not receive less than the value of their marginal product, and therefore they were not exploited. "The various repressive laws and acts of violence perpetrated against blacks were indeed widespread but were not instruments of economic exploitation in the labor market." Black incomes were lower than white incomes because blacks were poor, because they owned less of the "nonhuman factors of production" than did whites (*Agriculture in the Postbellum South,* 13, 14). DeCanio considers this matter explicitly and in more detail in "Accumulation and Discrimination in the Postbellum South," *Explorations in Economic History,* XVI (April, 1979), 182–206. A theoretical discussion using data from a later period is Wallace E. Huffman, "Black-White Human Capital Differences: Impact on Agricultural Productivity in the U.S. South," *American Economic Review,* LXXI (March, 1981), 94–107.

21. Determining whether blacks and whites were receiving equal pay for equal work is fraught with difficulties that Higgs does not consider. Recent experiences with wage discrimination against women seem to confirm a point made by Monroe N. Work almost half a century ago. He argued that whites often received higher wages than blacks when both had the same duties, but their *reported* occupations were different ("Problems of Adjustment of Race and Class in the South," *Social Forces,* XVI [October, 1937], 108–16, esp. p. 112).

wages for both blacks and whites in the South were below the national level and sectional wages showed no tendency to converge, indicating "the isolation of southern labor markets from national labor markets" that, in turn, suggests southern employers used the race issue to divide workers and drive wages of whites to the low level paid blacks.[22]

Joseph D. Reid, Jr., examines the question of exploitation from a different perspective and, like Higgs, emphasizes the force of the free market. Reid studies land tenure and the effects of sharecropping and tenancy on the well-being of the people and on the economic development of the South. He denies that tenancy and sharecropping resulted from discrimination and coercion and that these tenure forms signaled a misallocation of resources. Both tenants and landlords gained from the tenure arrangements. Tenants received the benefits of the landlords' superior managerial expertise; tenants and landlords shared an interest in the output, thereby increasing efficiency and decreasing supervision costs; mutual interests facilitated risk reduction and lowered transaction costs in contract negotiations.[23]

Higgs, DeCanio, and Reid should not be dismissed as southern apologists or Pollyannaish supporters of free enterprise.[24] They nei-

---

22. Gavin Wright, "The Strange Career of the New Southern Economic History," *Reviews in American History*, X (December, 1982), 164–80 (quotation on p. 176), and "Black and White Labor in the Old New South," in Fred Bateman (ed.), *Business in the New South: A Historical Perspective* (Sewanee, Tenn.: University Press, 1981), 35–50. Wright's conclusions do not directly contradict Higgs's contention that blacks and whites received equal pay for equal work. But when Wright argues that the southern labor markets were isolated from the national labor markets, he implies interference with the free movement of workers out of the South into higher-wage areas elsewhere. As will be noted below, other scholars emphasize this interference with the free market.

23. Joseph D. Reid, Jr., "Sharecropping as an Understandable Market Response: The Post-Bellum South," *Journal of Economic History*, XXXIII (March, 1973), 106–30, "Antebellum Southern Rental Contracts," *Explorations in Economic History*, XIII (January, 1976), 69–83, "White Land, Black Labor, and Agricultural Stagnation: The Causes and Effects of Sharecropping in the Postbellum South," *Explorations in Economic History*, XVI (January, 1979), 31–55, "Sharecropping and Agricultural Uncertainty," *Economic Development and Cultural Change*, XXIV (April, 1976), 549–76, "Sharecropping in History and Theory," *Agricultural History*, XLIX (April, 1975), 426–40, "Progress on Credit: Comment," *Agricultural History*, L (January, 1976), 117–24, and "The Theory of Share Tenancy Revisited—Again," *Journal of Political Economy*, LXXXV (April, 1977), 403–407.

24. Jonathan M. Wiener suggests otherwise. The cliometricians, he writes, "have an ideological commitment to the notion that competitive capitalism, if left alone, maximizes benefits for everyone in society," and this, in turn, carries the "political im-

ther deny the coercion of blacks nor maintain that economic conditions in the postbellum South were good. They argue merely that given postwar circumstances, the free market created economic institutions that produced optimal economic results. Postbellum southern poverty arose from war-induced interference with the free market, exacting massive economic losses on the South.[25] But the South was not economically stagnant. By 1880, free-market conditions once again predominated, and the economy grew apace.

For these cliometricians, then, war and emancipation did not break the continuity of bourgeois or capitalist social relations. They maintain that the slave South was a capitalist society and therefore the Civil War did not bring revolutionary social change. This belief in the continuity of bourgeois social relations unites those cliometricians who emphasize the significance of free-market competition in shaping institutions and determining economic behavior with cliometricians Roger L. Ransom and Richard Sutch, who deny that a competitive market prevailed in the postwar South. In a series of articles and, most fully, in *One Kind of Freedom*, Ransom and Sutch argue that the postwar southern economy was marred by "institutional flaws"—sharecropping and the merchant monopoly—that resulted in the misallocation of resources, the stifling of incentive, the prevention of economic diversification with consequent overproduction of cotton, and the blocking of improvements in land and equipment—all of which slowed economic growth and perpetuated poverty.[26]

---

plication . . . that government intervention reduced the capacity of the economy to bring progress and prosperity to blacks" ("Class Structure and Economic Development in the American South," 973). For historians to have an ideological commitment is hardly a criticism; the political implication, true or not, is beside the point. Higgs, in his "Comment," 993–97, accuses Wiener of having an ideological commitment of another kind, and bad manners besides, though Higgs's manners seem equally bad.

25. Cliometricians have debated the nature and extent of these losses. For varying views, see Roger Ransom and Richard Sutch, "The Impact of the Civil War and of Emancipation on Southern Agriculture," *Explorations in Economic History*, XII (January, 1975), 1–28; and Claudia D. Goldin and Frank D. Lewis, "The Economic Cost of the American Civil War: Estimates and Implications," *Journal of Economic History*, XXXV (June, 1975), 299–326. Peter Temin, "The Post-Bellum Recovery of the South and the Cost of the Civil War," *Journal of Economic History*, XXXVI (December, 1976), 898–907, reviews the debate and attempts to resolve it.

26. Roger L. Ransom and Richard Sutch, *One Kind of Freedom: The Economic Consequences of Emancipation* (Cambridge, England: Cambridge University Press, 1977), 176, "Debt Peonage in the Cotton South After the Civil War," *Journal of Economic History*, XXXII (September, 1972), 641–69, "The Ex-Slave in the Post-Bellum South: A Study of the Economic Impact of Racism in a Market Environment," *Journal*

Ransom and Sutch argue that because emancipation left blacks without property and with few skills, they had little bargaining power in the marketplace. Although they successfully resisted efforts to return them to gang labor on plantations, they had no choice but to return to work as sharecroppers on the lands of their former owners and had to turn to merchants for the credit necessary to support production and family maintenance. Merchants established local monopolies, allowing them to charge high interest rates that kept the croppers in debt and dependent. They forced the croppers to concentrate on cotton production, the only crop for which there was a ready market, leading to overproduction and low prices and the necessity for croppers to buy food from the merchants at inflated prices, food they might have grown themselves had the merchants allowed it.

Not surprisingly, other cliometricians have been sharply critical of Ransom and Sutch, insisting, among other things, that high interest rates reflected high risk, not merchant monopoly power, that sharecropping was not exploitative but mutually beneficial to both croppers and landlords, and that croppers were not forced to overproduce cotton at the expense of food but rather chose the most profitable mix.[27] Much of this debate centers on technical issues of data manipulation and considers neither methods nor their underlying assumptions.[28] Both Ransom and Sutch and their critics agree that a capi-

---

of Economic History, XXXIII (March, 1973), 131–48, and "The 'Lock-in' Mechanism and Overproduction of Cotton in the Postbellum South," *Agricultural History,* XLIX (April, 1975), 405–25.

27. Ransom and Sutch's book was the subject of a Duke University Symposium in February 1978. Several of the papers presented were later published in *Explorations in Economic History,* XVI: Claudia Goldin, " 'N' Kinds of Freedom: An Introduction to the Issues" (January, 1979), 8–30; Reid, "White Land, Black Labor, and Agricultural Stagnation"; Peter Temin, "Freedom and Coercion: Notes on the Analysis of Debt Peonage in *One Kind of Freedom*" (January, 1979), 56–63; Gavin Wright, "Freedom and the Southern Economy" (January, 1979), 90–108; DeCanio, "Accumulation and Discrimination in the Postbellum South." Ransom and Sutch replied to their critics in two articles in the same volume: "Credit Merchandising in the Post-Emancipation South: Structure, Conduct, and Performance" (January, 1979), 64–89, and "Growth and Welfare in the American South of the Nineteenth Century" (April, 1979), 207–36. Stanley L. Engerman included his contribution to the discussion in a longer article published separately: "Economic Adjustments to Emancipation in the United States and British West Indies," *Journal of Interdisciplinary History,* XIII (Autumn, 1982), 191–220.

28. The exception is the essay by Gavin Wright, "Freedom and the Southern Economy," 90–91, in which he raised doubts about "many of the analytical distinctions and working presuppositions" of the neoclassical economic theory that both Ransom

talist South survived the Civil War and emancipation, and both agree that the new postwar world was peopled by profit-maximizing planters, merchants, and black and white farmers. But where Higgs, De-Canio, and Reid find that the free market, under existing circumstances, produced optimal results, Ransom and Sutch insist that the market allowed planters and merchants to utilize their wealth, power, and the racist ideology that was a legacy of slavery to build an economic monopoly that hindered economic growth.

The differences between Ransom and Sutch and the other cliometricians are significant, for they result in sharply contrasting pictures of the nature of the postbellum economy. Nevertheless, beneath these sharp differences lies their common acceptance of the continuity of bourgeois institutions. They differ over the effects of these institutions.

Some of the most ardent critics of the cliometricians constitute a third school of historians who emphasize continuity. Primarily social historians, many in this group find even less change than do the cliometricians, concluding that the economic losses brought by war and emancipation had little significant effect on the social and political structure of the South. But where the cliometricians find continuity in bourgeois social relations, members of this school find it in pre-bourgeois social relations. They argue that despite its loss of wealth as a result of emancipation and the steep postwar decline in land values, the prewar ruling class, the planter elite, continued to dominate the postwar South and to perpetuate the slave South's precapitalist social relations.

---

and Sutch and their critics employ. Wright maintains that many of the postbellum South's economic problems stemmed from the declining worldwide demand for cotton, which lowered prices and created a class of farmers who gambled by concentrating on cotton production in hopes of achieving an economic competence and self-sufficiency, a gamble that continually failed to pay off because of falling cotton prices. See Wright, "Cotton Competition and the Post-Bellum Recovery of the American South," *Journal of Economic History*, XXXIV (September, 1974), 610–35; Wright and Howard Kunreuther, "Cotton, Corn, and Risk in the Nineteenth Century," *Journal of Economic History*, XXXV (September, 1975), 526–51; the criticism by Robert McGuire and Robert Higgs, "Cotton, Corn, and Risk in the Nineteenth Century: Another View," *Explorations in Economic History*, XIV (April, 1977), 167–82; and Wright and Kunreuther's reply, "Cotton, Corn, and Risk in the Nineteenth Century: A Reply," *Explorations in Economic History*, XIV (April, 1977), 183–95. For other evidence of a declining demand for cotton, see Marvin Fischbaum and Julius Rubin, "Slavery and the Economic Development of the American South," *Explorations in Entrepreneurial History*, 2nd Ser., VI (Fall, 1968), 116–27.

A number of scholars, using methods developed by students of social mobility, have attempted to assess the social and economic effects of the Civil War by measuring the "persistence" of the planter elite, that is, the extent to which the wealthiest planters remained in their prewar counties in the postwar decade and retained their relative elite status. Although their methods differ somewhat and their data are not strictly comparable, most come to similar conclusions: the wealthiest antebellum planters in the areas studied tended to persist geographically and to retain their top-wealth-holding position in the postwar decade.[29] If their absolute wealth declined because of emancipation and the decline in land values, their relative wealth did not; they remained the dominant economic class.

From this it follows, first, that the persisting antebellum elite dominated the new South as they had the old and, second, that political, social, and economic domination also signaled ideological domination.[30] Thus not only did individual members of the antebellum landed elite (or their descendants) retain their power and influence,

29. A convenient discussion and assessment of mobility studies is Howard P. Chudacoff, "Success and Security: The Meaning of Social Mobility in America," *Reviews in American History*, X (December, 1982), 101–12. Jonathan M. Wiener, "Planter Persistence and Social Change: Alabama, 1850–1870," *Journal of Interdisciplinary History*, VII (Autumn, 1976), 235–60, and *Social Origins of the New South: Alabama, 1860–1885* (Baton Rouge: Louisiana State University Press, 1978), Chap. 1; Randolph B. Campbell, "Population Persistence and Social Change in Nineteenth-Century Texas: Harrison County, 1850–1880," *Journal of Southern History*, XLVIII (May, 1982), 185–204; Lee W. Formwalt, "Antebellum Planter Persistence: Southwest Georgia—A Case Study," *Plantation Society in the Americas*, I (October, 1981), 410–29; A. Jane Townes, "The Effect of Emancipation on Large Landholdings, Nelson and Goochland Counties, Virginia," *Journal of Southern History*, XLV (August, 1979), 403–12; Kenneth S. Greenberg, "The Civil War and the Redistribution of Land: Adams County, Mississippi, 1860–1870," *Agricultural History*, LII (April, 1978), 292–307; Gail W. O'Brien, "Power and Influence in Mecklenburg County, 1850–1880," *North Carolina Historical Review*, LIV (Spring, 1977), 120–44; Michael Wayne, *The Reshaping of Plantation Society: The Natchez District, 1860–1880* (Baton Rouge: Louisiana State University Press, 1983), Chap. 4; Dwight B. Billings, Jr., *Planters and the Making of a "New South": Class, Politics, and Development in North Carolina, 1865–1900* (Chapel Hill: University of North Carolina Press, 1979). James Tice Moore and Numan V. Bartley, using different methods and concentrating on politics, come to similar conclusions. See Moore, "Redeemers Reconsidered: Change and Continuity in the Democratic South, 1870–1900," *Journal of Southern History*, XLIV (August, 1978), 357–78; and Bartley, "Another New South?" *Georgia Historical Quarterly*, LXV (Summer, 1981), 119–37.

30. Wayne, *The Reshaping of Plantation Society*, explicitly disagrees. Although he agrees that the planter elite persisted, he finds "a profound break between the plantation regime of the old order and the plantation regime of the new" (p. 203). Thus

they also retained and imposed upon the new South their antebellum prebourgeois ideas and attitudes.[31]

The persisting planter elite faced challenges to their economic and ideological hegemony. An early challenge came from local merchants who began to deal directly with the freedmen, thus threatening planter control. Jonathan M. Wiener argues that in Alabama the planters used their political power to get legal changes that increased the risk of merchant loans to freedmen, thereby driving most merchants out of the plantation areas and into the uplands. Industrialism posed a more persistent threat to planter domination. Initially, Wiener argues, Alabama planters used political roadblocks to prevent industrialization, but later, no longer able to stop industrial development, they reluctantly accepted it. Dwight B. Billings, Jr., however, finds North Carolina planters embracing industry and making it a variant of the agricultural plantation: "The slaveholders' hegemony, far from dying out, persisted as the paternalism of the plantation was translated into mill villages." In the end, both Wiener and Billings conclude, the agrarian and industrial elites united, and the South, a latecomer to industrialization and dominated by a reactionary agrarian elite, took the "Prussian road" to capitalism, creating a repressive and coercive society rather than the liberal society of the nations that industrialized earlier and took the "classic" road.[32]

Continuity, persistence, and illiberalism are also themes in the

---

Wayne does not really belong in the continuity school, despite his agreement on the matter of planter persistence.

31. Strictly speaking, *prebourgeois* is not the proper term to apply to Billings' description of the antebellum South. He draws upon the ideas of Immanuel Wallerstein, who insists that capitalism became a "world economy" in the sixteenth century. Therefore the South, a part of the "periphery," differed from the North, rapidly becoming a part of the core, but both were capitalistic. See Wallerstein, *The Modern World System: Capitalist Agriculture and the Origins of the European World Economy in the Sixteenth Century* (New York: Academic Press, 1974), and *The Capitalist World Economy* (Cambridge, England: Cambridge University Press, 1979). Nevertheless, Wiener and Billings agree on the characteristics of the antebellum ideology—agrarian, communal, paternalistic, and illiberal—even if they might disagree over the name to give it.

32. In addition to Wiener's works already cited, see Wiener, "Planter-Merchant Conflict in Reconstruction Alabama," *Past and Present*, LXVIII (April, 1975), 73–94. Billings, *Planters and the Making of a "New South*," 130. David L. Carlton, *Mill and Town in South Carolina, 1880–1920* (Baton Rouge: Louisiana State University Press, 1982), sharply disagrees with Billings' view of the mills and their owners. The concept of the "Prussian road" and the "classic" comes from Barrington Moore, Jr., *Social Origins of Dictatorship and Democracy: Lord and Peasant in the Making of the Modern World* (Boston: Beacon Press, 1966).

work of Jay R. Mandle, who argues that the South both before and after the Civil War, in common with other societies in the Caribbean and elsewhere, had a distinct "mode of production" that he calls the "plantation economy." Drawing on the works of Eugene D. Genovese, Immanuel Wallerstein, and Edgar T. Thompson, Mandle argues that the plantation economy was—and is, in those areas where it continues to exist—characterized by market-oriented, profit-maximizing landowners producing a single staple crop mainly for export and using laborers forced to accept wages below what they could earn in a free-labor market. Emancipation merely changed the form of worker coercion but not its substance.[33]

Thus, according to Wiener, Billings, and Mandle, slavery continued in a new guise. Emancipation destroyed the legal basis for slavery, but in its place new forms of coercive labor controls continued to hold blacks in thralldom and perpetuated planter rule of the South. Violence and threats, legal restraints, and economic coercion are central to their interpretations and to those of others who agree that emancipation had little real meaning for blacks. Pete Daniel, William Cohen, Daniel A. Novak, and others describe the legal, extralegal, and often illegal means used by landlords to prevent blacks from freely moving about in order to escape debt peonage and/or improve their working conditions and income. As a result, blacks, in Daniel's words, occupied a "vague twilight zone between freedom and slavery."[34]

33. Jay R. Mandle, *The Roots of Black Poverty: The Southern Plantation Economy After the Civil War* (Durham: Duke University Press, 1978), "The Plantation Economy: An Essay in Definition," *Science and Society*, XXXVI (Spring, 1972), 49–62, "The Re-establishment of the Plantation Economy in the South, 1865–1910," *Review of Black Political Economy*, III (Winter, 1973), 68–88, "The Plantation States as a Sub-Region of the Post-Bellum South," *Journal of Economic History*, XXXIV (September, 1974), 732–38, and "The Plantation Economy and Its Aftermath," *Review of Radical Political Economics*, VI (Spring, 1974), 32–48. In his discussion of his theoretical approach in the first chapter of *The Roots of Black Poverty*, Mandle discusses and cites these authors. See Eugene D. Genovese, *Roll, Jordan, Roll: The World the Slaves Made* (New York: Pantheon, 1974), and *The World the Slaveholders Made: Two Essays in Interpretation* (New York: Pantheon, 1969); Wallerstein, *The Modern World System;* Edgar T. Thompson, "The Plantation: The Physical Basis of Traditional Race Relations," in Thompson (ed.), *Race Relations and the Race Problem: A Definition and an Analysis* (Durham: Duke University Press, 1939), 180–218, and Thompson, *Plantation Societies, Race Relations, and the South: The Regimentation of Populations* (Durham: Duke University Press, 1975).

34. Pete Daniel, *The Shadow of Slavery: Peonage in the South, 1901–1969* (Urbana: University of Illinois Press, 1972), and "The Metamorphosis of Slavery, 1865–

Implicit in all analyses that find the perpetuation of slavery or slavelike conditions is the assumption that blacks lacked the power to give real meaning to their freedom. Some scholars have found the source of this powerlessness in the failure to distribute land to the freedmen. This view, which Herman Belz in 1973 called an emerging "new orthodoxy," is questioned by others who insist that land-ownership would provide no guarantees of equality and economic power unless backed up by political rights. A full discussion of this debate properly belongs elsewhere, but it should be noted that both sides in the controversy agree that Reconstruction failed—for whatever reasons—to provide blacks with the power necessary to give real substance to their freedom.[35]

The three schools that in such different and often contradictory ways emphasize continuity from the old to the new South also tend to find relatively little significant change over time. Once the adjustment to emancipation had been made and once the disruption and uncertainty of war and Reconstruction had ended, social and economic relations in the South remained stable for some three-quarters of a century. When significant change finally occurred, its impetus came from outside the South. Depression-bred New Deal reforms, war-induced demand for labor in the North, perfection of cotton-picking machinery, and civil rights legislation and court decisions finally, and variously, depending upon the scholars' interpretation of the source(s) of continuity, destroyed the plantation system, undermined landlord or merchant hegemony, diversified agriculture and

---

1900," *Journal of American History*, LXVI (June, 1979), 88–99 (quotation on p. 98); William Cohen, "Negro Involuntary Servitude in the South, 1865–1940: A Preliminary Analysis," *Journal of Southern History*, XLII (February, 1976), 31–60; Daniel A. Novak, *The Wheel of Servitude: Black Forced Labor after Slavery* (Lexington: University Press of Kentucky, 1978); N. Gordon Carper, "Slavery Revisited: Peonage in the South," *Phylon*, XXXVII (March, 1976), 85–99; Randall G. Shelden, "From Slave to Caste Society: Penal Changes in Tennessee, 1830–1915," *Tennessee Historical Quarterly*, XXXVIII (Winter, 1979), 462–78; James Smallwood, "Perpetuation of Caste: Black Agricultural Workers in Reconstruction Texas," *Mid-America*, LXI (January, 1979), 5–23; Robert J. Haws and Michael V. Namorato, "Race, Property Rights, and the Economic Consequences of Reconstruction: A Case Study [of Mississippi]," *Vanderbilt Law Review*, XXXII (January, 1979), 305–26; William F. Holmes, "Labor Agents and the Georgia Exodus, 1899–1900," *South Atlantic Quarterly*, LXXIX (Autumn, 1980), 436–48.

35. Herman Belz, "The New Orthodoxy in Reconstruction Historiography," *Reviews in American History*, I (March, 1973), 106–13. See the essay by LaWanda Cox, in this volume, for a full discussion of the debate, and *Lincoln and Black Freedom*, Chap. 5.

transformed it from a labor- to a capital-intensive industry, and ended the legal and extralegal supports for racism. The discontinuity that war, invasion, military occupation, the confiscation of slave property, and state and national legislation failed to bring in the mid nineteenth century finally arrived in the second third of the twentieth century. A "second reconstruction" created a real New South or, in Numan V. Bartley's words, "a new New South," in contrast to an old New South that was not really new at all.[36]

Of course, the three schools I have described as in one way or another emphasizing continuity do not ignore all change. Indeed, the central concern of all of the scholars in each of the schools is to describe, assess, and explain the changes that occurred. Nevertheless, their underlying theme is continuity, which, despite their differences in both method and conclusions, they find to be far more significant than the changes they describe. In this, they differ markedly from another smaller group of scholars who stress discontinuity and insist that the Civil War marked a major turning point in southern history.

The theme of discontinuity was implicit in Charles Beard and Mary Beard's description of the Civil War as "the second American revolution," during which industrial capitalists established their domination by defeating and subordinating the South. Revisionists such as William B. Hesseltine and Howard K. Beale provided support for this interpretation, but their emphasis was on national politics and the ways in which it influenced Reconstruction policy.[37] It remained for C. Vann Woodward to apply the Beardian insights specifically to the history of the postbellum South.

In his *Origins of the New South,* Woodward abandoned the Beards' rigid economic determinism but retained and applied their thesis to the South. The Civil War and emancipation, Woodward argued, destroyed the planter class; the builders of the New South were new men, business oriented and thoroughly bourgeois in their ideology, unlike the slave-owning planter class they replaced. In *Reunion and*

36. Bartley, "Another New South?," 132.
37. William B. Hesseltine, "Economic Factors in the Abandonment of Reconstruction," *Mississippi Valley Historical Review,* XXII (September, 1935), 191–220; Howard K. Beale, *The Critical Year: A Study of Andrew Johnson and Reconstruction* (New York: Harcourt, Brace, 1930). A more general study that adopted the Beardian approach in a more overtly Marxian guise but retained the northern and national focus is Louis M. Hacker, *The Triumph of American Capitalism: The Development of Forces in American History to the End of the Nineteenth Century* (New York: Columbia University Press, 1940).

Reaction, he described the economic arrangements behind the Compromise of 1877, and in *The Strange Career of Jim Crow,* he argued that Jim Crow segregation was a post–Civil War innovation and not a legacy of the Old South.[38] Although Woodward's interpretations of postwar southern history have had enormous influence and surprising longevity, his central thesis, that the Civil War and emancipation marked a sharp discontinuity in nineteenth-century southern history, has been disputed by those I have identified as members of the various continuity schools.[39]

There is no general study of the social and economic history of the postwar era that stresses discontinuity. But a number of recent studies, usually dealing with particular localities or industries and often specifically designed to be case-study tests of one or another of Woodward's arguments, present interpretations that emphasize change rather than continuity.

Ronald L. F. Davis and Michael Wayne both studied the Natchez district. Although they differ in their estimates of planter persistence in the area, Wayne finding far greater persistence than does Davis, both agree that emancipation significantly transformed social and economic relations. For Davis, emancipation gave blacks the power to refuse to work in gangs as they had during slavery times, but not enough power to rise above the status of sharecroppers. Landowners first opposed, then reluctantly accepted, and finally adapted to the cropping arrangement. In the process, the plantation as a unit of land tenure remained, though many former planters lost their land to merchants. But both landlords and merchants became businessmen, rather than planters in the antebellum sense, directing "an unusual form of farming that involved neither the cash nexus of wages be-

---

38. C. Vann Woodward, *Reunion and Reaction: The Compromise of 1877 and the End of Reconstruction* (Rev. ed.; Boston: Little, Brown, 1966), and *The Strange Career of Jim Crow* (3rd rev. ed.; New York: Oxford University Press, 1974), first published in 1955. See also his *American Counterpoint: Slavery and Racism in the North-South Dialogue* (Boston: Little, Brown, 1971), and *The Burden of Southern History* (Rev. ed.; Baton Rouge: Louisiana State University Press, 1968). Woodward puts his interpretation in a comparative perspective in "The Price of Freedom," in David G. Sansing (ed.), *What Was Freedom's Price?* (Jackson: University Press of Mississippi, 1978), 93–113.

39. Some of these scholars seem unaware that they are disagreeing with Woodward, often citing him approvingly, albeit selectively. A conspicuous exception is Carl N. Degler, whose discussion of some of the new work clearly shows how his views and those of others in the continuity schools differ from Woodward on this issue. See "Rethinking Post–Civil War History."

tween labor and capital nor the landed security of a peasant tenancy."
Wayne finds discontinuity of a somewhat different kind. He argues
that emancipation radically transformed the plantation and the antebellum planter ruling class, producing "a fundamentally new and different plantation order" in which "a cash nexus now intervened between planter and laborer," replacing the paternalistic relations of
the antebellum era: "The road to the New South plantation ran
through the marketplace."[40]

George C. Rogers, Jr., discovered substantial change in Georgetown
County, South Carolina. By the 1880s, he writes, the old planter elite
had been replaced by a "new economic leadership," drawn from the
"middle ranks" of antebellum society or from newcomers to the
county. When Justin Fuller studied late-nineteenth-century Alabama
business leaders, he found that fewer than a third of them had fathers
whose occupation was in agriculture, but over half were descended
from fathers in business or the professions. Like those who have studied the national business elite, he found that those who reached elite
status in business were from families of upper or middle economic
and social status. Fuller was not specifically concerned with the question of planter persistence, but his evidence that most business leaders came from nonagricultural backgrounds suggests a significant al-
teration in the class structure and social relations in postbellum
Alabama.[41]

40. Ronald L. F. Davis, *Good and Faithful Labor: From Slavery to Sharecropping
in the Natchez District, 1860–1890* (Westport, Conn.: Greenwood Press, 1982), 5;
Wayne, *The Reshaping of Plantation Society,* 111 (first quotation), 149 (second and
third quotations). Mandle's "plantation economy," it will be recalled, had similar characteristics, but Mandle, unlike Davis, finds it to be an economic arrangement that continued from the antebellum period and not a new social formation. Wiener insists that
his approach emphasizes "class" while that of the cliometricians emphasizes the "market" ("Class Structure and Economic Development in the American South," 970).
Wright argues that this is not a meaningful distinction: "'Class' and 'market' should
not be viewed as incompatible opposites" ("The Strange Career of the New Southern
Economic History," 164). Wayne seems to agree, for he finds class relations and class
conflicts operating at least in part through the marketplace.

41. George C. Rogers, Jr., *The History of Georgetown County, South Carolina*
(Columbia: University of South Carolina Press, 1970), 464; Justin Fuller, "Alabama
Business Leaders: 1865–1900," *Alabama Review,* XVI (October, 1963), 279–86,
XVII (January, 1964), 63–75. See also Robert H. McKenzie, Warner O. Moore, and
Jerry C. Oldshue, "Business Success and Leadership in Alabama: A Preliminary In-
quiry," *Alabama Historical Quarterly,* XLIII (Winter, 1981), 259–87, for brief bio-
graphical sketches of the lives of twenty-six Alabamians elected to the Alabama Busi-
ness Hall of Fame.

The extent of planter persistence remains unclear in part, at least, because scholars (such as Davis and Wayne, for example) use different methods to measure the persistence rate. Additional studies using uniform or comparable methods might clear up some of the uncertainty. But the problems will remain. Persistence, as measured in most studies, requires that a planter or his direct descendants be listed on two consecutive manuscript census schedules and/or, depending upon the particular study, tax rolls and probate records similarly separated in time; those who do not appear, either because they were missed by the census taker or failed to pay their taxes or because they moved away, cannot be counted and their economic status remains unknown. Another problem arises from the use of land-ownership rather than other possible forms of wealth to measure elite status. The destruction of slave wealth and the precipitous decline in land values after the Civil War make absolute antebellum-postbellum comparisons impossible. Therefore, elite status is measured by land values in relative rather than absolute terms.

These problems aside, the postbellum persistence rate, for those who find persisting planters, is about 50 percent, a figure deemed high because it equals the persistence rate of the 1850s but might be considered low inasmuch as half the planters apparently did *not* persist. In any event, finding half the richest group gone and those that remained without slave wealth and with sharply diminished landed wealth should give pause to those who insist on the significance of such figures.

The 1870 terminal date used in most of the studies compounds the problem, for by that date, persisting planters could be in the process of losing their lands, to say nothing of their influence, but they might still appear on the census rolls as large landowners. The experience of the Hammond family of South Carolina may not have been typical, but it is doubtful that it was unique. Harry Hammond, the son of antebellum planter James Henry Hammond, appears to be a persisting planter in 1870 in terms of his landholding, but as Carol Bleser reveals in her volume of Hammond family correspondence, this hardly describes his real situation.[42]

Future studies of persistence must not only solve the problems of data collection and manipulation but must also recognize that Woodward's contention that the New South was led by new men does not

42. Carol Bleser (ed.), *The Hammonds of Redcliffe* (New York: Oxford University Press, 1981), Pt. 2.

stand or fall on the question of the genealogy of the South's post-bellum leaders. Histories of particular families might not provide the quantitative exactitude of available persistence studies, but such histories should give added insights into the fortunes, the ideologies, and the class status of postbellum leaders (and those who failed to maintain their leadership), which is the real point Woodward raised.

A number of studies dealing primarily with postbellum politics on the state level touch on the background, the ideology, and the policies and programs of southern political leaders in varying degrees of detail.[43] While conclusions vary, most suggest, some tentatively, others sharply, that the Redeemers were not new men with a probusiness ideology, but rather were agrarian in their outlook and tended to be antagonistic toward, or, at least, not ardent supporters of, manufacturing and other forms of nonagricultural business. Although such conclusions imply continuity between the Old and New South,[44] a continuity interpretation does not fully explain the sources of the conflicts that led to the Alliance and Populist movements.

William J. Cooper, Jr., for example, argues that the conservative leaders of the New South came from the ranks of the agrarian aristocracy of the Old South. Their opponents, the Tillmanites, came from the same class background but from a different generation; the younger men were merely the political "outs" who wanted a larger say in political affairs. Both groups, Cooper concludes, ignored the tenants and sharecroppers. But tenants and sharecroppers were also agrarians and farmers and, it seems, had interests and needs that differed from those of both the conservative leaders and the Tillmanites. Roger L. Hart writes that the middling farmers who joined the Tennessee Alliance felt that "they were not given the respect they deserved" and objected to their "dependence on merchants." Similarly,

43. See Jack P. Maddex, Jr., *The Virginia Conservatives, 1867–1879: A Study in Reconstruction Politics* (Chapel Hill: University of North Carolina Press, 1970); Sheldon Hackney, *Populism to Progressivism in Alabama* (Princeton: Princeton University Press, 1969); William J. Cooper, Jr., *The Conservative Regime: South Carolina, 1877–1890* (Baltimore: Johns Hopkins Press, 1968); William Ivy Hair, *Bourbonism and Agrarian Protest: Louisiana Politics, 1877–1900* (Baton Rouge: Louisiana State University Press, 1969); William Warren Rogers, *One-Gallused Rebellion: Agrarianism in Alabama, 1865–1896* (Baton Rouge: Louisiana State University Press, 1970); Roger L. Hart, *Redeemers, Bourbons, and Populists: Tennessee, 1870–1896* (Baton Rouge: Louisiana State University Press, 1975); Edward C. Williamson, *Florida Politics in the Gilded Age, 1877–1893* (Gainesville: University Presses of Florida, 1976).

44. Such is the conclusion of Moore, in "Redeemers Reconsidered," after surveying this literature.

Sheldon Hackney found that protesting Alabama farmers resented their loss of the power necessary to control their lives.[45]

Such interpretations suggest that the debate that begins with the assumption that postbellum southern society was divided between farmers (or, more vaguely, agrarians) and businessmen or between the rural and the urban oriented may not capture the reality of social class divisions. In a predominantly rural and agricultural society, we would expect that many of the political leaders and members of the wealthy elite would have agricultural origins and rural ties. Moore wisely notes that residence and occupation may not determine ideology: "Some of the 'urban-oriented' Redeemer leaders may have emerged from the old plantation elite and borne its impress on their personal values and intellectual heritage."[46] But this perceptive observation can be altered without losing its force: some of the Redeemer leaders may have emerged from the old plantation elite, but their postbellum experiences may have significantly changed their personal values and ideology. My altered statement suggests that a more meaningful social differentiation might be between businessman (agricultural, mercantile, or industrial) and worker (both industrial and agricultural, the latter including farm workers, tenants, sharecroppers, and even small landowners).

Recent studies of the Farmers' Alliance and the southern Populists by Lawrence Goodwyn, Bruce Palmer, Robert C. McMath, Jr., and Michael Schwartz use this distinction. Despite their differences, these historians conclude that the farm protest movements in the South in the late nineteenth century presented a truly radical alternative to the way in which the economy and society had evolved since the Civil War.[47]

According to these scholars, the southern world had changed in the decades following the Civil War. If it remained agrarian, largely rural, and dominated by staple-crop production, it had also become a bourgeois world, one led by landlords and merchants and bankers

45. Cooper, *The Conservative Regime*, 132, 204; Hart, *Redeemers, Bourbons, and Populists*, 115, 117; Hackney, *Populism to Progressivism*, Chap. 4 and pp. 326–27.

46. Moore, "Redeemers Reconsidered," 362.

47. Lawrence Goodwyn, *Democratic Promise: The Populist Moment in America* (New York: Oxford University Press, 1976); Bruce Palmer, *"Man Over Money": The Southern Populist Critique of American Capitalism* (Chapel Hill: University of North Carolina Press, 1980); Robert C. McMath, Jr., *Populist Vanguard: A History of the Southern Farmers' Alliance* (Chapel Hill: University of North Carolina Press, 1975); Michael Schwartz, *Radical Protest and Social Structure: The Southern Farmers' Alliance and Cotton Tenancy, 1880–1890* (New York: Academic Press, 1976).

with an outlook and an ideology that closely resembled those of northern businessmen. For many farmers—tenants, sharecroppers, and small (and a few large) landowners—the concrete and immediate manifestations of this new world were the crop lien, high interest rates, low prices for crops grown, and high prices for supplies purchased. They felt themselves caught in a system they could not control, a system in which the most important decisions, those that affected their lives and well-being, were no longer made by producers in a local community but by forces beyond the reach of the people. Behind their specific reform proposals designed to solve these problems lay a vision of a path to the future for the nation to follow, one that veered radically from the direction the country was following.[48]

Thus, these recent historians of southern populism find massive social and economic changes in the South during the two decades following the Civil War. The Redeemer leadership, whatever their social origins, their means of livelihood, or their place of residence, had become bourgeois businessmen on the northern pattern and had led their section down the road being followed in the North toward modern, centralized industrial capitalism. Members of the Alliance and the Populists resisted the change because it had such devastating effects on their lives, but their failure to change the course of southern development confirmed the control of the South's new elite by removing a serious challenge to their control.

Steven Hahn argues that the forces that transformed the southern elite also radically altered the status of the white farmers who pro-

---

48. These scholars differ as to how radical the Alliance and Populist solutions were. Palmer argues that the Populists stopped short of a truly radical solution, their understanding limited by their small-producer outlook. McMath finds similar contradictions in the understanding of the Alliance members. Goodwyn insists that the Alliance, and especially its local members and leaders, had a clear radical perception and understanding, but others, especially the Populist party leaders, had little understanding or interest in the truly radical solutions. He dismisses this group as a "shadow movement" (Chap. 13 and *passim*). Schwartz comes to similar conclusions, arguing that the party leaders sold out the real movement. James Turner provides a perceptive survey of Populist historiography and his own interpretation based on an analysis of Texas populism. He argues that populism was strongest in the most isolated areas. Feeling the economic distress and failing fully to understand and to accept the changes they observed, rural, isolated Texans opposed them. When their isolation ended, so too did their opposition ("Understanding the Populists," *Journal of American History*, LXVII [September, 1980], 354–73). E. James Hindman, "A Mirror's Image: Anti-Populist Sentiment in Texas—A Sampling of Business Attitudes," *East Texas Historical Journal*, XIV (Fall, 1976), 37–51, concludes that businessmen opposed the Populists out of fear of the latter's radicalism.

vided the strongest support for the Alliance and the Populists. In his studies of the Georgia upcountry, Hahn traces the area's economic problems to the transformation of the white yeomanry from near self-sufficiency in the antebellum era to commercial production in the decades following the Civil War. He argues that business-oriented, profit-hungry merchants and landlords succeeded in getting legislation passed concerning fencing, grazing, hunting, and other matters that undermined yeoman society and forced the upcountry farmers into commercial production.[49]

Forrest McDonald and Grady McWhiney emphasize the destruction of the open-range livestock industry in explaining the transformation of the self-sufficient antebellum yeomen into commercial farmers. Wartime destruction of cattle began the process, but the ability of merchants and planters to get southern legislatures to enact fence laws prevented the plain folk from rebuilding their herds, which, in turn, destroyed the economic basis of their antebellum self-sufficiency and forced them to turn to staple-crop commercial production.[50]

If many of the antebellum planters had been transformed into thoroughly bourgeois businessmen and if their thinning ranks had been filled by "new men" with a similar business outlook and if this new business class became a new southern ruling class, then it becomes apparent why southern separation died so quickly and com-

49. Steven Hahn, *The Roots of Southern Populism: Yeoman Farmers and the Transformation of the Georgia Upcountry, 1850–1890* (New York: Oxford University Press, 1983), "Common Right and Commonwealth: The Stock-Law Struggle and the Roots of Southern Populism," in Kousser and McPherson (eds.), *Region, Race, and Reconstruction*, 51–88, and "Hunting, Fishing, and Foraging: Common Rights and Class Relations in the Postbellum South," *Radical History Review*, XXVI (1982), 37–64.

50. Forrest McDonald and Grady McWhiney, "The South from Self-Sufficiency to Peonage: An Interpretation," *American Historical Review*, LXXXV (December, 1980), 1095–1118, and "The Antebellum Southern Herdsman: A Reinterpretation," *Journal of Southern History*, XLI (May, 1975), 147–66; McWhiney, "The Revolution in Nineteenth-Century Alabama Agriculture," *Alabama Review*, XXXI (January, 1978), 3–32. See also J. Crawford King, Jr., "The Closing of the Southern Range: An Exploratory Study," *Journal of Southern History*, XLVIII (February, 1982), 53–70. J. Mills Thornton III argues that the Radical Reconstruction state governments' taxation policies bore heavily on the hill folk, increasing their debt load, which had already risen sharply during the war. Thornton sees this as an explanation for the plain folks' desertion of the Republicans, but his work also shows how their financial position was weakened, making them vulnerable to the pressures from merchants ("Fiscal Policy and the Failure of Radical Reconstruction in the Lower South," in Kousser and McPherson [eds.], *Region, Race, and Reconstruction*, 349–94).

pletely following the defeat of the Confederacy: the leaders of the New South accepted the ideology of the northern victors.[51]

This describes the discontinuity but does not fully explain it. The recent studies of the Populists and upcountry plain folk explain discontinuity by tracing the destruction of the antebellum yeomanry. As they moved from near self-sufficiency to commercial production the yeomanry did not simply suffer a decline in living standards or change the crops they grew; their entire way of life, their ideology, their class status, and their relationship to other classes in society altered fundamentally. Central to all these studies is force or coercion. The plain folk, or at least some of them, clung to older ways and opposed the changes, but their struggle failed. Coercion explains their transformation.

Missing from this equation is an analysis of the source of the coercion. To find this in an altered market structure, or in the designs of profit-maximizing businessmen who were junior partners of Yankee capitalism, merely names a source but does not explain it. Those who argue that the New South was fundamentally different from the Old and that the rulers of the New South were new men or transformed members of the Old South elite must explain why and how the change took place.

Explaining *why* seems easy enough. Emancipation destroyed the

---

51. Woodward argued that although they became partners of the northern capitalists, they accepted a junior partnership, making the postbellum South "a colonial economy" (*Origins of the New South* [1951], Chap. 11). The notion of the South as a colony of the North has a long tradition in southern historiography. It predates Woodward's discussion, and scholars continue to apply it to present-day North-South economic relations. Some point to northern ownership and control of southern industries and natural resources, others to discriminatory pricing and railroad rates that benefited the North to the detriment of the South. Two influential early statements are B. B. Kendrick, "The Colonial Status of the South," *Journal of Southern History*, VIII (February, 1942), 3–22; and A. B. Moore, "One Hundred Years of Reconstruction of the South," *Journal of Southern History*, IX (May, 1943), 153–80. George Brown Tindall, *The Emergence of the New South, 1913–1945* (Baton Rouge: Louisiana State University Press, 1967), devotes a chapter to the "dilemmas of a colonial economy" for the period he covers. A more recent argument is Joe Persky, "Regional Colonialism and the Southern Economy," *Review of Radical Political Economics*, IV (Fall, 1972), 70–79. Charles P. Roland concluded in his 1981 presidential address to the Southern Historical Association that the southern economy "is still very much a colonial economy" ("The Ever-Vanishing South," *Journal of Southern History*, XLVIII [February, 1982], 3–20 [quotation on p. 6]). A perceptive survey of the literature on the question is Robert H. McKenzie, "Postbellum Economic Development in the South: Consequences of Belief," *Southern Studies*, XXI (Spring, 1982), 27–60 (discussion on pp. 27–36).

social and economic basis of the slave society (termed, variously, pre-bourgeois, premodern, traditional, agrarian). Explaining *how* proves more difficult. Although some studies have described the influx of northerners into the postbellum south,[52] no one has suggested that the antebellum rulers were simply pushed aside and replaced by northerners. The problem, then, is to describe and explain their adjustment to the new free-labor system, that is, the process that transformed them from a prebourgeois aristocracy into a modern business class.

Woodward and others found part of the explanation in the ability of antebellum Whigs after the war to move into positions of political power, which enabled them to bring changes they had long favored but could not achieve because of their weaker position in the antebellum era. Thus, this persisting-Whigs thesis suggests that the slave society nurtured within itself a bourgeois or modern group that managed to gain control after emancipation. Some critics insist that this explanation is flawed because the data fail to support it; they argue that the Redeemer governments were not dominated by former Whigs.[53] But even if the data are found to be consistent with the thesis, the explanation leads in directions that its advocates do not seem to be fully aware of. The largest and richest slave-owning planters tended to be Whigs in the antebellum South. If these are the persisting Whigs, then the persisting-Whigs thesis becomes a variant of the persisting-planters thesis, but a peculiar variant that finds persisting planters with a bourgeois or modern ideology.[54] The Civil War, therefore, brings discontinuity by increasing the influence of the Whigs. Ironically, their loss of wealth increased their influence.[55] A form of

52. See Lawrence N. Powell, "The Politics of Livelihood: Carpetbaggers in the Deep South," in Kousser and McPherson (eds.), *Region, Race, and Reconstruction,* 315–47, and the works cited therein. Powell argues that carpetbaggers moved into politics after they had failed in the economic enterprises that first drew them into the South.

53. See Woodward, *Origins of the New South* (1951), Chap. 1, and *Reunion and Reaction.* The debate may be followed in Thomas B. Alexander, "Persistent Whiggery in the Confederate South, 1860–1877," *Journal of Southern History,* XXVII (August, 1961), 305–29; John Vollmer Mering, "Persistent Whiggery in the Confederate South: A Reconsideration," *South Atlantic Quarterly,* LXIX (Winter, 1970), 124–43; and Moore, "Redeemers Reconsidered."

54. The persisting-Whigs argument therefore comes far closer to the position of Fogel and Engerman, *Time on the Cross,* than its supporters realize and would care to admit.

55. This argument, it should be noted, has important implications for interpreting

discontinuity remains, but emancipation is no longer a source of that discontinuity.

Some recent work suggests a much different interpretation by exploring the deep ideological differences among the various groups involved in the postwar settlement. These studies suggest that the slave society ideology created perceptions and expectations that departed radically from those of the free-labor society in the North, leading to conflicts and misunderstandings even when people were using the same language to describe and explain their actions.

Eric Foner, David Montgomery, and Daniel T. Rodgers have described a pervasive free-labor ideology in the mid-nineteenth-century North, an outlook that emphasized the dignity of labor and equality of opportunity. Such ideas denied a harsh and lasting conflict between employers and employees—today's workers could become tomorrow's businessmen—and emphasized the importance of hard and faithful work as the means to individual success and community progress. By the mid nineteenth century, these ideas were rapidly becoming anachronistic and conservative, for they failed to describe the harsh realities of class relations in an expanding industrial society and denied the need for unions, shorter working hours, and similar reforms that might alleviate some of the hardships. In short, the ideology of free labor was fast becoming primarily a middle- and upper-class outlook that workers did not fully accept, or, at least, they interpreted it in a vastly different way from their employees. Nevertheless, the ideology remained potent and profoundly affected the programs, the policies, and the expectations brought to the South by victorious northerners.[56]

the antebellum period. It denies that the planter aristocracy constituted the antebellum ruling class and supports the argument that secession was the work of the yeomanry who feared that if the growing influence of the planters, tied closely to northern business, went unchecked, the upcountry, yeoman way of life would be destroyed. For examples of this interpretation, see J. Mills Thornton III, *Politics and Power in a Slave Society: Alabama, 1800–1860* (Baton Rouge: Louisiana State University Press, 1978); and William L. Barney, *The Secessionist Impulse: Alabama and Mississippi in 1860* (Princeton: Princeton University Press, 1974). This interpretation would not be inconsistent with that of Hahn and of McDonald and McWhiney. Indeed, McDonald and McWhiney would probably agree, though they do not make the connection as explicit as does King, one of their students. Hahn, however, would disagree. See note 50.

56. Eric Foner, *Free Soil, Free Labor, Free Men: The Ideology of the Republican Party Before the Civil War* (New York: Oxford University Press, 1970), and "Reconstruction and the Crisis of Free Labor," in Foner, *Politics and Ideology in the Age of the Civil War* (New York: Oxford University Press, 1980), 97–127; David Montgomery, *Beyond Equality: Labor and the Radical Republicans, 1862–1872* (New York:

In her perceptive study of the Southern Homestead Act, Christie Farnham Pope concludes that its failure and ultimate repeal in 1876 can be explained by the "erroneous assumptions" upon which the law was based: that antebellum southern institutions could easily be remade in the northern image because free black landowners would behave like northern whites. She quotes one of the bill's ardent supporters, Indiana radical congressman George W. Julian, who looked forward to the creation of little Indianas in the South once blacks became independent farmers on their homesteads. Julian's Jeffersonian vision may have been anachronistically romantic by 1865, but in its acceptance of the traditional work ethic the vision was not "radical," at least for Indiana and other northern states.[57]

Yet the northern free-labor ideology could also support other visions. If Julian envisioned independent, hardworking, small commercial farmers on the romanticized pattern of his native Indiana, other northerners envisioned free blacks contracting to work on plantations to produce the South's traditional staple crops, particularly cotton. In this case, very practical considerations combined nicely with the free-labor ideology. If blacks were to work as free people, they had to take those jobs that were available, which meant work on the plantations for some form of wage. The alternative was rations (or what today we would call welfare), which were not only costly but, worse, debilitating and contrary to the work ethic. That work on the cotton plantations would also please speculators, merchants, and cotton-hungry textile manufacturers at home and abroad merely grounded ideological concerns in practical economics.[58]

But the South was not Indiana or New England. Southerners had been brought up quite differently from northerners and they responded to their new situation in ways northerners did not expect. Former slaveholders might applaud northerners' efforts to get the

---

Knopf, 1967); Daniel T. Rodgers, *The Work Ethic in Industrial America, 1850–1920* (Chicago: University of Chicago Press, 1978). The prevalence of these ideas among northerners helps to explain their behavior. Issues such as the treatment of blacks by the army and the Freedmen's Bureau agents and aspects of the land question—matters that have been and continue to be hotly debated by historians—might be more productively considered from the free-labor ideological perspective of the actors themselves.

57. Christie Farnham Pope, "Southern Homesteads for Negroes," *Agricultural History*, XLIV (April, 1970), 201–12 (quotation on p. 211).

58. See William F. Messner, *Freedmen and the Ideology of Free Labor: Louisiana, 1862–1865* (Lafayette: University of Southwestern Louisiana, 1978); and Davis, *Good and Faithful Labor*, Chap. 3.

freedmen to contract to work on the plantations; there was no other way to get the labor to work their lands. But they were firmly convinced that blacks would not work except under compulsion, which to them meant the compulsion of the lash, not of the market. James L. Roark, in his *Masters Without Slaves*, examines the difficulties former slave-owners had in adjusting to emancipation, to bargaining with their former chattel over wages and working conditions, and especially to discovering that they really did not know the people with whom they had long dealt and claimed to know and understand. They had little faith in the free-labor ideology and little experience in dealing with free labor.[59]

Beyond the day-to-day accommodations to his new condition, the planter had to make deeper, more profound adjustments. As Willie Lee Rose has noted, the planter had "endorsed the antebellum polemicist's view of the slaveholder as benevolent paternalist, the Biblical patriarch at the center of a stable and orderly agrarian world." But now that world was gone, and all the relationships the planter had always taken for granted had to be rethought. "Nothing less than his own significance in the only world he knew was at stake."[60]

The world that most blacks had known was gone as well. They were no longer slaves—that was clear enough. But what freedom actually meant was not so clear. Leon F. Litwack describes in detail, and often in the words of the freedmen themselves, the varied responses of blacks to emancipation—both the excitement and enthusiasm as well as the confusion and uncertainty.[61] Simple experience gave freedom an obvious, if negatively defined, meaning. It meant the absence of slavery with all its coercion, restraints, and humiliations. Blacks knew that if freedom was to have any meaning, they could not allow these features of slavery to be reimposed under a new guise. Freedom

59. James L. Roark, *Masters Without Slaves: Southern Planters in the Civil War and Reconstruction* (New York: Norton, 1977). Discussions concerning the Freedmen's Bureau and its agents tend to be concerned with debates over whether the agents sided with planters or with freedmen or whether they were racists or not. The debates might be more enlightening if the agents were seen as northerners, imbued with the free-labor ideology, who sought to deal with planters and blacks with quite different outlooks toward the future.

60. Willie Lee Rose, "Masters without Slaves," in Rose, *Slavery and Freedom*, ed. William W. Freehling (New York: Oxford University Press, 1982), 73–89 (quotations on p. 76).

61. Leon F. Litwack, *Been in the Storm So Long: The Aftermath of Slavery* (New York: Knopf, 1979).

offered them powerful weapons—the ability to refuse to accept a job and the right to leave a job—and they used those weapons, much to the disgust and chagrin of their former owners. Therefore, when planters insisted that the blacks would not work except under the compulsion of the lash, they were not altogether wrong, though they misunderstood what motivated the blacks. Blacks would not work like slaves or under conditions they associated with slavery unless compelled to by force. Freedom had little meaning if work regimes remained unchanged and if meager pay merely sufficed to buy those bare necessities that had been provided under slavery. Freedmen did not have to hear radical talk about wage slavery to understand its meaning for their own lives.[62]

Those who emphasize ideology and the expectations and perceptions it engendered seek to understand the varying motives of the actors in the immediate postemancipation period as a means to explain the resulting conflict, sometimes overtly physical, sometimes political, usually both.[63] If ideological differences stemmed from antebellum experiences in a slave society, then the creation of new institutions necessary for the functioning of a free-labor system required an ideological transformation, and this, in turn, suggests the need to study the process of change over time.

Implicit in this approach would be the recognition that changes would occur gradually, some quickly, some much more slowly. The variety of tenure arrangements, the changing laws, the varying nature and extent of violence and coercion, and the recurring attempts at reform would become more understandable if seen in the context of the gradual building of a new business society and ideology on the ruins of a destroyed slave society. This approach would reveal significant changes over time and variations from place to place, pro-

62. Blacks quickly disabused northerners of their expectations that the compulsion of the marketplace would be a welcome replacement for the lash. The experiences of northerners who went south expecting to apply the principles of free labor to growing cotton are discussed in Lawrence N. Powell, *New Masters: Northern Planters During the Civil War and Reconstruction* (New Haven: Yale University Press, 1980). Willie Lee Rose considers experiences on the Sea Islands in *Rehearsal for Reconstruction: The Port Royal Experiment* (Indianapolis: Bobbs-Merrill, 1964).

63. In recent years, this emphasis on ideology has become a major feature in historical scholarship. For an interesting survey of this development as a means to create a new synthesis in American history, see Daniel Singal, "Beyond Consensus: Richard Hofstadter and American Historiography," *American Historical Review*, LXXIX (October, 1984), 976–1004.

ducing a fuller, more dynamic picture of the social and economic history of the South in the half century following the Civil War. Differences between those who would emphasize continuity and those who would emphasize discontinuity would remain, but the insights of both groups might be used to extend our understanding and thereby put the change/continuity debate on a new and more productive level.[64]

In recent years, a number of studies have appeared that show the potential value of this dynamic approach. Some directly confront the continuity-discontinuity question, but others relate to it only indirectly. Taken together, they suggest that the transformation of the slave society was far more gradual than many seem to think, that the late nineteenth century was neither monolithic nor unchanging, and that the inevitable conflicts that arose in the course of the creation of a black working class and a white ruling class helped to shape and

64. This long-run and dynamic approach should provide equally productive insights into the history of southern blacks in the half century following emancipation. If former planters and newcomers became bourgeois businessmen, former slaves became free workers, a class transformation that necessarily included ideological, social, and legal as well as economic changes. But much of the work concerning blacks by those in both the continuity and the discontinuity camps tends to find economic and social patterns solidly established within a decade of the end of the Civil War and changing little until the third or fourth decade of the twentieth century. Histories of blacks, including the recent revisionist state studies, also present a static picture. Although they provide a wealth of detail concerning black life in the postwar decades including efforts at self-improvement and although they assess the extent of progress achieved by blacks, they find little change in the social and economic institutions, especially those in the rural, plantation areas. Peter Kolchin's view is typical: "In general, by 1869 the nature of the new system which the overthrow of slavery made possible was fairly clear. Developments after that date more often consisted of variations on themes already suggested than radical new departures" (*First Freedom: The Responses of Alabama's Blacks to Emancipation and Reconstruction* [Westport, Conn.: Greenwood Press, 1972], 187). See also Frenise A. Logan, *The Negro in North Carolina, 1876–1894* (Chapel Hill: University of North Carolina Press, 1964); Vernon L. Wharton, *The Negro in Mississippi, 1865–1890* (Chapel Hill: University of North Carolina Press, 1947); Joel Williamson, *After Slavery: The Negro in South Carolina During Reconstruction, 1861–1877* (Chapel Hill: University of North Carolina Press, 1965); George Brown Tindall, *South Carolina Negroes, 1877–1900* (Columbia: University of South Carolina Press, 1952); I. A. Newby, *Black Carolinians: A History of Blacks in South Carolina from 1895 to 1968* (Columbia: University of South Carolina Press, 1973); James M. Smallwood, *Time of Hope, Time of Despair: Black Texans During Reconstruction* (Port Washington, N.Y.: Kennikat Press, 1981); Lawrence D. Rice, *The Negro in Texas, 1874–1900* (Baton Rouge: Louisiana State University Press, 1971). A survey of prerevisionist and early revisionist work is Tindall, "Southern

define both groups in particular ways and to place both in particular relationships to the former yeomanry. This approach avoids making dichotomies of race or class and class or market, allowing a more useful investigation of their interaction.

Recent studies of the origins of sharecropping and tenancy among blacks provide a valuable beginning for this dynamic approach. Ralph Shlomowitz's investigation of contracts between planters and freedmen in the first decade after the Civil War reveals extensive variation in the amount and method of payment, the size of land allotments, tenure arrangements, and work rules. These variations lasted through the 1870s, only gradually becoming standardized in the sharecropping arrangement. Shlomowitz argues that the original scheme proposed by the landowners was to hire their former slaves to work in gangs on the plantation under the supervision of an overseer, a plan that the landlords favored because it approximated the antebellum arrangements they were familiar with and freedmen opposed for precisely the same reason. Landlords next tried what Shlomowitz calls the "squad system," wherein they divided their land into large tracts that were rented to self-organized groups of freedmen, the leader of each group or squad being responsible for overseeing the work, dividing the workers' shares of the product among the workers, and paying the landlord for use of the land. Dissension among members of the squads led to a further division of the land, creating the sharecropping pattern in which families received allotments of land. Shlomowitz attributes the changes he describes to experimentation by both planters and freedmen searching for "optimal" arrangements under new conditions.[65]

Shlomowitz's picture of planters and freedmen searching for mutually advantageous arrangements appears rather benign when compared to Orville Vernon Burton's view of similar developments in Edgefield County, South Carolina. Burton describes sharp political and class conflict during the transition, with the balance tipping in favor of the blacks during Radical Reconstruction and then in favor

Negroes Since Reconstruction," in Link and Patrick (eds.), *Writing Southern History,* 337–61.

65. Ralph Shlomowitz, "The Origins of Southern Sharecropping," *Agricultural History,* LIII (July, 1979), 557–75, and "The Squad System on Postbellum Cotton Plantations," in Orville Vernon Burton and Robert C. McMath, Jr. (eds.), *Toward a New South? Studies in Post–Civil War Southern Communities* (Westport, Conn.: Greenwood Press, 1982), 265–80.

of the landlords after the Redeemers took control. He traces changes in the laws and in their enforcement and assesses the nature and extent of extralegal activities to support his interpretation.[66]

Despite their differences, Shlomowitz and Burton, as well as others who have begun to consider this matter, describe a period of uncertainty and experimentation.[67] Like other cliometricians, Schlomowitz finds marketplace competition creating mutually advantageous results. Burton, by giving more attention to politics, shows how each side at different times influenced the market. Taken together, they reveal that market and class are not mutually exclusive. Class conflict took place in the market, but the course of the conflict influenced the nature of the market. Neither extends his discussion beyond the first decade or so after the war and therefore neither describes any continuing changes that might have occurred.

If the experimentation and ensuing conflicts described by these scholars were seen as part of a continuing process of education, transforming slave owners and slaves into businessmen and workers, we would gain additional insights into this process. One promising approach would be to follow changes in the law, both statutory and judicial, in all the states of the former Confederacy over several decades. Given their importance, it is surprising that there is no full study of the legal history of liens and sharecropping and tenancy. The information we have from a number of brief surveys or from investigations of the law in particular states reveals a consistent pattern. The lien laws, first passed during Radical Reconstruction, were to provide security for necessary credit and, because they gave freedmen a laborers' lien superior to all other liens on the crop produced, to

66. Orville Vernon Burton, "Race and Reconstruction: Edgefield County, South Carolina," *Journal of Social History*, XII (Fall, 1978), 31–56.

67. For other areas and other crops, see J. William Harris, "Plantations and Power: Emancipation on the David Barrow Plantations," in Burton and McMath (eds.), *Toward a New South?*, 246–64; Thomas F. Armstrong, "From Task Labor to Free Labor: The Transition Along Georgia's Rice Coast, 1820–1880," *Georgia Historical Quarterly*, LXIV (Winter, 1980), 432–47; Mark Schmitz, "The Transformation of the Southern Sugar Cane Sector, 1860–1930," *Agricultural History*, LIII (January, 1979), 270–85; Richard J. Amundson, "Oakley Plantation: A Post–Civil War Venture in Louisiana Sugar," *Louisiana History*, IX (Winter, 1968), 21–42; James M. Clifton, "A Half-Century of a Georgia Rice Plantation," *North Carolina Historical Review*, XLVII (October, 1970), 388–415; Henry C. Dethloff, "Rice Revolution in the Southwest, 1880–1910," *Arkansas Historical Quarterly*, XXIX (Spring, 1970), 66–75; and Louis Ferleger, "Farm Mechanization in the Southern Sugar Sector After the Civil War," *Louisiana History*, XXIII (Winter, 1982), 21–34. A considerable amount of work on this subject is under way but has not yet been published.

guarantee that freedmen would receive their wages. Redeemer legislatures changed the law to give the landlord the primary lien for rent
and also a lien superior to that of merchants for supplies advanced to
tenants. At the same time, statutes and court rulings made a clear distinction between tenants and sharecroppers, designating the latter
workers paid in kind rather than tenants.[68]

The legal changes clearly subordinated croppers to their landlord-
employers, not by returning them to a position of servitude but by
transforming them into a form of wage labor. The laws also defined
another relationship, that of landlord and tenant, and provided safe-
guards, via the crop liens, for those who made loans (or "advances,"
as they were called) both to tenants and to landowners based upon a
crop to be grown in the future. These differences suggest differences
in farm organization, but unfortunately we have only sketchy information about the process of change in the organization of plantations
and other farming units. Evidence from the courts provides some information as do the bitter complaints by Populists. Further evidence,
generally more suggestive than definitive, comes from recent studies
of the Colored Farmers' Alliance.

Little is known about the Colored National Farmers' Alliance and
Cooperative Union. Organized in Houston County, Texas, in 1886 by
a group of black farmers, it was led from the start by R. M. Humphrey,
a white minister-farmer in the area. Its demands often paralleled
those of the southern Alliance (which excluded blacks), leading to
some cooperation between the two organizations. Woodward, in his
biography of Georgia Populist leader Tom Watson, emphasized this
cooperation, arguing that Watson and the Populists favored black-
white unity in their struggles. Some later studies support Woodward,[69] but others sharply disagree, pointing to the racist views of
leaders of the white Alliance, and in particular to those of Watson,

68. I have briefly sketched these changes and some of their effects in "Post–Civil
War Southern Agriculture and the Law," *Agricultural History*, LIII (January, 1979),
319–37, and "Postbellum Social Change and Its Effects on Marketing the South's
Cotton Crop," *Agricultural History*, LVI (January, 1982), 215–30. An important
older study is Oscar Zeichner, "The Legal Status of the Agricultural Laborer in the
South," *Political Science Quarterly*, LV (September, 1940), 412–28. The end result of
the changes (but unfortunately with little discussion of the process that brought this
result) is considered in great detail in Charles S. Mangum, Jr., *The Legal Status of the
Tenant Farmer in the Southeast* (Chapel Hill: University of North Carolina Press,
1952). Some of the state studies mentioned earlier consider the law but do not relate it
to general trends.

69. C. Vann Woodward, *Tom Watson: Agrarian Rebel* (New York: Macmillan,

and arguing that the failure by white leaders to mount a campaign against racism meant that cooperation between the two groups was meager and sporadic at best and quickly and easily degenerated into violent hostility.[70] Often this debate turns on definitions and emphasis and tends to be anachronistic, measuring Watson and the Alliance and Populist leaders by modern standards.

Other historians, without ignoring the potency of racism as a divisive element, emphasize other differences that sometimes divided the black and white Alliances and, indeed, sometimes created divisions that crossed race lines. These historians note that the two organizations did cooperate on a number of issues and the white Alliancemen often expressed support for the blacks. The black Alliance, however, was never a mere appendage of the white. It often took stands that the white Alliance did not support and, indeed, strenuously opposed. Interestingly enough, some members of the black Alliance also opposed these actions by their leaders.

Thus, in 1891 when Humphrey, at the urging of some members of the Colored Alliance, sought support for a cotton pickers' strike, the white Alliance refused and actively opposed the effort; many of the black Alliance leaders also opposed the strike. The attempt to raise pickers' wages appealed to landless black tenants and black wage workers (some of whom belonged to the Colored Alliance) but outraged many landowners (some of whom belonged to the white or the black Alliance) who feared that higher wages for pickers would raise production costs at a time when they were already suffering eco-

---

1938); Jack Abramowitz, "The Negro in the Agrarian Revolt," *Agricultural History,* XXIV (April, 1950), 89–95, and "The Negro in the Populist Movement," *Journal of Negro History,* XXXVIII (July, 1953), 257–89; William W. Rogers, "The Negro Alliance in Alabama," *Journal of Negro History,* XLV (January, 1960), 38–44.

70. Robert Saunders, "Southern Populists and the Negro, 1893–1895," *Journal of Negro History,* LIV (July, 1969), 240–61; Herbert Shapiro, "The Populists and the Negro: A Reconsideration," in August Meier and Elliott Rudwick (eds.), *The Making of Black America: Essays in Negro Life and History* (2 vols.; New York: Atheneum, 1969), II, 27–36; Charles Crowe, "Tom Watson, Populists, and Blacks Reconsidered," *Journal of Negro History,* LV (April, 1970), 99–116; Floyd J. Miller, "Black Protest and White Leadership: A Note on the Colored Farmers' Alliance," *Phylon,* XXXIII (Summer, 1972), 169–74; Eugene R. Fingerhut, "Tom Watson, Blacks, and Southern Reform," *Georgia Historical Quarterly,* LX (Winter, 1976), 324–43; Robert L. Allen, *Reluctant Reformers: Racism and Social Reform Movements in the United States* (Washington, D.C.: Howard University Press, 1974), Chap. 3 (pp. 51–84); Francis M. Wilhoit, "An Interpretation of Populism's Impact on the Georgia Negro," *Journal of Negro History,* LII (April, 1967), 116–27. Miller finds Humphrey, the leader of the Colored Alliance, as racist as the leaders of the white Alliance.

nomic hardship. When such economic or class differences divided farmers and when these class differences paralleled (even when they did not exactly coincide with) race differences, racism became an important means to mobilize the whites in opposition to the blacks.[71]

Unfortunately, only a sprinkling of work attempts to study the evolution of social class differences among blacks after the Civil War. Robert Higgs notes the increase in landownership among blacks—by 1910, about 20 percent of black farmers owned land—which he rightly considers a sign of progress. But others have noted that 1910 was the high point in black landownership; it declined sharply in the years that followed. Others have argued that blacks usually owned inferior land and often owned parcels too small to support themselves. There is also evidence of instability in black landownership, suggesting that figures showing aggregate increases in black landownership might hide the fact that blacks were moving in and out of the ranks of owners.[72] Nevertheless, some blacks did become land-

71. William F. Holmes, "The Leflore County Massacre and the Demise of the Colored Farmers' Alliance," *Phylon*, XXXIV (September, 1973), 267–74, "The Arkansas Cotton Pickers Strike of 1891 and the Demise of the Colored Farmers' Alliance," *Arkansas Historical Quarterly*, XXXII (Summer, 1973), 107–19, and "The Demise of the Colored Farmers' Alliance," *Journal of Southern History*, XLI (May, 1975), 187–200; Martin Dann, "Black Populism: A Study of the Colored Farmers' Alliance through 1891," *Journal of Ethnic Studies*, II (Fall, 1974), 58–71; William Edward Spiggs, "The Virginia Colored Farmers' Alliance: A Case Study of Race and Class Identity," *Journal of Negro History*, LXIV (Summer, 1979), 191–204; Gerald Gaither, "Blacks and the Southern Farmers' Alliance Movement," *East Texas Historical Journal*, XIV (Spring, 1976), 24–38, and *Blacks and the Populist Revolt: Ballots and Bigotry in the "New South"* (University: University of Alabama Press, 1977); Thomas W. Kremm and Diane Neal, "Challenges to Subordination: Organized Black Agricultural Protest in South Carolina, 1865–1895," *South Atlantic Quarterly*, LXXVII (Winter, 1978), 98–112, and "Clandestine Black Labor Societies and White Fear: Hiram F. Hoover and the 'Cooperative Workers of America' in the South," *Labor History*, XIX (Spring, 1978), 226–37; Robert C. McMath, Jr., "Southern White Farmers and the Organization of Black Farm Workers: A North Carolina Document," *Labor History*, XVIII (Winter, 1977), 115–19. Similar efforts at black-white cooperation that met with similar problems after the Populist era are considered in H. L. Meredith, "Agrarian Socialism and the Negro in Oklahoma, 1900–1918," *Labor History*, XI (Summer, 1970), 277–84; and Rick Gregory, "Robertson County and the Black Patch War, 1904–1909," *Tennessee Historical Quarterly*, XXXIX (Fall, 1980), 341–58.

72. Higgs, *Competition and Coercion*; Leo McGee and Robert Boone (eds.), *The Black Rural Landowner—Endangered Species: Social, Political, and Economic Implications* (Westport, Conn.: Greenwood Press, 1979); Edward Magdol, *A Right to the Land: Essays on the Freedmen's Community* (Westport, Conn.: Greenwood Press, 1977); Edward H. Bonekemper III, "Negro Ownership of Real Property in Hampton and Elizabeth City County, Virginia, 1860–1870," *Journal of Negro History*, LV (July,

owning farmers. Several studies recount the efforts of Tuskegee Institute and the Department of Agriculture to aid these farmers.[73]

The sources of class differentiation in the black community remain largely unexplored. Armstead L. Robinson, in a study of black leaders in Reconstruction Memphis, finds two groups of leaders—one largely slave born and poor and mainly concerned with "religious/benevolent functions" and the other coming from an emerging middle class of artisans and primarily concerned with "political activity."[74] Additional work on the sources of class differentiation and changing ideologies remains to be done.

The scattered evidence of the development of significant class differences that sometimes paralleled and sometimes crossed racial lines suggests potentially important areas for new work. Farmers of both races, either owning land or renting it, could feel the squeeze of low prices and high costs and join the Alliances in hopes of improving their condition. These same farmers could hire workers or use croppers on their lands and resent efforts by either to improve their condition because such improvements would add to their already burdensome costs. Additional work that would provide a fuller picture of farm organization and tenancy and sharecropping patterns in the late nineteenth century is needed.[75] We also need more detailed stud-

---

1970), 165–81; Theodore Rosengarten, *All God's Dangers: The Life of Nate Shaw* (New York: Knopf, 1974); Ransom and Sutch, *One Kind of Freedom*, 81–87; A. Lee Coleman and Larry D. Hall, "Black Farm Operators and Farm Population, 1900–1970: Alabama and Kentucky," *Phylon*, XL (December, 1979), 387–402; James S. Fisher, "Negro Farm Ownership in the South," *Annals of the Association of American Geographers*, LXIII (December, 1973), 478–89.

73. Allen W. Jones, "The Role of Tuskegee Institute in the Education of Black Farmers," *Journal of Negro History*, LX (April, 1975), 252–67, and "The South's First Black Farm Agents," *Agricultural History*, L (October, 1976), 636–44; Donnie D. Bellamy, "Henry A. Hunt and Black Agricultural Leadership in the New South," *Journal of Negro History*, LX (October, 1975), 464–79; Joel Schor, *Agriculture in the Black Land-Grant System to 1930* (Tallahassee: Florida A&M University, 1982).

74. Armstead L. Robinson, "Plans Dat Comed from God: Institution Building and the Emergence of Black Leadership in Reconstruction Memphis," in Burton and McMath (eds.), *Toward a New South?*, 71–102. See also Robinson, "Beyond the Realm of Social Consensus: New Meanings of Reconstruction for American History," *Journal of American History*, LXVIII (September, 1981), 276–97.

75. We know far more about these matters as they existed in the 1930s, when the system came under the strains of depression leading to the New Deal reforms. Both the contemporary literature—government studies, reformist polemics, scholarly analyses, and popular descriptions—and later studies by historians and other scholars are extensive. Examples of recent work that uses such literature and provides patterns that would be fruitful if applied to the earlier years are Pete Daniel, "The Transformation of

ies of black leaders and their backgrounds, of black business enterprise, and of black artisanship.[76]

Surprisingly little work has been done in labor history where a potentially valuable approach would be to use the methods and perspectives of the new labor history. Most work on southern labor in the years before the 1930s has concentrated on nonagricultural labor and on trade unions, with race relations being a primary theme. The Knights of Labor's official policy was to organize all workers without regard to color, but in the South, the Knights' organizers often ignored black workers. Nevertheless, the Knights did attempt to organize blacks, most of whom, according to Melton Alonza McLaurin, were rural workers. McLaurin does not make it clear whether those blacks who joined the Knights were tenants, sharecroppers, or wage workers—or all of these groups—but he argues that "the Knights encountered their most violent opposition from white planters and large farmers, who saw the organization of Blacks as a threat to their labor supply."[77]

---

the Rural South 1930 to the Present," *Agricultural History*, LV (July, 1981), 231–48, and *Breaking the Land: The Transformation of Cotton, Tobacco, and Rice Cultures since 1880* (Urbana: University of Illinois Press, 1985); Lawrence J. Nelson, "Welfare Capitalism on a Mississippi Plantation in the Great Depression," *Journal of Southern History*, L (May, 1984), 225–50.

76. We know little about the role of antebellum free blacks in the postwar era. Ira Berlin devotes a few pages to their fate (*Slaves Without Masters: The Free Negro in the Antebellum South* [New York: Pantheon, 1974], 381–95). See also David C. Rankin, "The Impact of the Civil War on the Free Colored Community of New Orleans," *Perspectives in American History*, XI (1977–78), 379–416. There is some work on black political leaders but very little on businessmen and artisans. On the clearly exceptional but important experiences of the Montgomery family, see James T. Currie, "Benjamin Montgomery and the Davis Bend Colony," *Prologue*, X (Spring, 1978), 5–21; Steven Joseph Ross, "Freed Soil, Freed Labor, Freed Men: John Eaton and the Davis Bend Experiment," *Journal of Southern History*, XLIV (May, 1978), 213–32; and Janet Sharp Hermann, *The Pursuit of a Dream* (New York: Oxford University Press, 1981).

77. Melton Alonza McLaurin, "The Racial Policies of the Knights of Labor and the Organization of Southern Black Workers," *Labor History*, XVII (Fall, 1976), 568–85 (quotation on p. 577). See also Irvin M. Marcus, "The Southern Negro and the Knights of Labor," *Negro History Bulletin*, XXX (March, 1967), 5–7; Leon Fink, "'Irrespective of Party, Color or Social Standing': The Knights of Labor and Opposition Politics in Richmond, Virginia," *Labor History*, XIX (Summer, 1978), 325–49; Kenneth Kann, "The Knights of Labor and the Southern Black Worker," *Labor History*, XVIII (Winter, 1977), 49–70; Philip S. Foner, "The IWW and the Black Worker," *Journal of Negro History*, LV (January, 1970), 45–64; Ray Marshall, "The Negro in Southern Unions," in Julius Jacobson (ed.), *The Negro and the American Labor Movement* (Garden City, N.Y.: Anchor Books, 1968), 128–54; William Warren Rogers, "Negro Knights of Labor in Arkansas: A Case Study of the 'Miscellaneous'

In two books dealing primarily with white mill workers, McLaurin argues that the workers organized into the Knights showed great militancy in their struggles but were defeated by a combination of iron-fisted employer opposition and a lack of true trade union consciousness among the workers. The workers, he argues, were interested in more than improved working conditions and wages; they were fighting the discipline of a new industrial system their employers were forcing upon them. Inasmuch as most of the mill workers were former yeomen, McLaurin's work provides another dimension to the class and social transformation of the antebellum yeomen in the postwar South.[78]

In recent years, urban history has provided fresh insights into postbellum social and economic change. Historians had long neglected the history of the nineteenth-century South's cities and towns. The southern population throughout the century remained overwhelmingly rural and the economy primarily agricultural, and therefore it is hardly surprising that historians devoted most of their attention to the countryside. Cities and towns entered the picture primarily as negative evidence: the lagging development of southern cities at a time when the rest of the nation was experiencing massive urban growth became another sign of the South's economic problems. But the growth of the new urban and new social history in the last couple of decades has increased historians' interest in southern cities and urban communities. The quantitative methods used to capture details about the lives of the inarticulate, to measure social and geographic mobility, to study the family and the role of women all stimulated interest in towns, cities, and communities including those in the South. Another stimulus for the study of the urban South came from developments in the field of Afro-American history. The structure of the black family, the rise of urban ghettos and their effects on

---

Strike," *Labor History,* X (Summer, 1969), 498–505; and Paul B. Worthman and James R. Green, "Black Workers in the New South, 1865–1915," in Nathan I. Huggins, Martin Kilson, and Daniel M. Fox (eds.), *Key Issues in the Afro-American Experience* (2 vols.; New York: Harcourt Brace Jovanovich, 1971), II, 47–69. The ambivalent and changing attitudes of black leaders toward the trade union movement are analyzed by August Meier and Elliott Rudwick, "Attitudes of Negro Leaders Toward the American Labor Movement from the Civil War to World War I," in Jacobson (ed.), *The Negro and the American Labor Movement,* 27–48.

78. Melton Alonza McLaurin, *Paternalism and Protest: Southern Cotton Mill Workers and Organized Labor, 1875–1905* (Westport, Conn.: Greenwood Publishing Corp., 1971), and *The Knights of Labor in the South* (Westport, Conn.: Greenwood Press, 1978).

blacks, and discrimination and its effects were problems that had to be addressed not only for northern cities in the twentieth century but also for nineteenth-century southern cities from which so many of the black migrants to the North came.[79]

An immediate impetus for the increased attention to southern urban history, like so much of the work on the postwar South, came from the pen of C. Vann Woodward. In 1955 Woodward published *The Strange Career of Jim Crow*. What was "strange" about Jim Crow's career, according to Woodward, was that the laws that fastened segregation on the South were of relatively recent vintage. Coming a year after the Brown decision and in the midst of the civil rights movement to end segregation, Woodward's argument that the Jim Crow laws originated not with emancipation or even with the end of Radical Reconstruction but entered the lawbooks in the South beginning in the last decade of the nineteenth century was startling. It suggested that segregation was not "traditional" as its supporters insisted but was a new development; southerners had lived without legal segregation for decades after emancipation. Woodward's findings began a lively debate among historians. Because Jim Crow's most obvious manifestations were in the towns and cities, much of the debate and the evidence used centered on urban areas.[80]

Howard N. Rabinowitz's investigation of Atlanta, Montgomery, Nashville, Raleigh, and Richmond added a significantly new dimension to the debate. He found that in the postwar years, blacks usually faced the alternatives not of segregation or integration but of exclu-

79. Some of the early work compared northern and southern cities and found that though southern cities tended to be fewer in number and smaller in size than their northern counterparts, both exhibited similar characteristics when such matters as geographic mobility, urban services, and urban problems were compared. See Blaine A. Brownell, "Urbanization in the South: A Unique Experience?" *Mississippi Quarterly*, XXVI (Spring, 1973), 105–20; and Richard J. Hopkins, "Are Southern Cities Unique? Persistence as a Clue," *Mississippi Quarterly*, XXVI (Spring, 1973), 121–41. David R. Goldfield, "The Urban South: A Regional Framework," *American Historical Review*, LXXXVI (December, 1981), 1009–34, found similarities but concluded that "ruralism, race, and colonialism have always characterized a distinctive region and its cities" (p. 1033). A collection of interpretive essays with discussions of the scholarship to date is Blaine A. Brownell and David R. Goldfield (eds.), *The City in Southern History: The Growth of Urban Civilization in the South* (Port Washington, N.Y.: Kennikat Press, 1977). The essay by Howard N. Rabinowitz, "Continuity and Change: Southern Urban Development, 1860–1900," in the Brownell and Goldfield volume (pp. 92–122) covers the post–Civil War decades.

80. The views of his critics and Woodward's response may be seen in *The Strange Career of Jim Crow* (1974).

sion or segregation. The Confederate leaders who took office immediately after the war continued the antebellum practice of excluding
blacks from most areas of public accommodations. During Radical
Reconstruction federal legislation and the demands of blacks ended
this policy of exclusion, but, Rabinowitz argues, replaced it with a
policy of segregation. Blacks, with the support of their white allies,
fought for and accepted the doctrine of separate but equal facilities
as a significant improvement over exclusion. The Redeemers continued the policy of segregation but, once in control, abandoned any
semblance of equality. Rabinowitz notes that though some blacks objected to segregation, most did not, focusing instead on the demand
that the segregated facilities be equal. Many blacks began to provide
facilities for their own people rather than insist on integration when
the quality of public accommodations deteriorated. In this manner,
segregation became characteristic of race relations in the South by
1890 and was accomplished, Rabinowitz concludes, without legal
sanction. By 1890, however, a new generation of younger, more aggressive blacks, angered by the complete absence of any semblance of
equality in accommodations, challenged the de facto arrangement,
and this challenge led whites to replace custom with law.[81]

Neither exclusion nor segregation (de facto or *de jure*) fully explains housing patterns in the urban South after the Civil War. Studies of urban residential patterns in southern cities have attempted to
determine if the pattern of black ghettoization, so familiar in northern cities after the great migrations of blacks to the North in the
twentieth century, was characteristic of southern cities that had large
and growing black populations soon after the Civil War. These studies
reveal a tendency toward the "clustering" of blacks and whites within
the cities, but they also show wide variation. Some nineteenth-century
southern cities tended toward ghettoization on the later northern
pattern, but in others, clusters of black residences were found throughout the city within larger white communities. These two patterns persisted well into the twentieth century.[82]

81. Howard N. Rabinowitz, "From Exclusion to Segregation: Southern Race Relations, 1865–1890," *Journal of American History*, LXIII (September, 1976), 325–50,
and "From Reconstruction to Redemption in the Urban South," *Journal of Urban
History*, II (February, 1976), 169–94. These points and more are spelled out in greater
detail in Rabinowitz's *Race Relations in the Urban South, 1865–1890* (New York:
Oxford University Press, 1978). See also Woodward's "Introduction" to the paperback
edition (Urbana: University of Illinois Press, 1980) in which he enthusiastically recognizes Rabinowitz's work as an extension rather than a criticism of his work.
82. Leo F. Schnore and Philip C. Evenson, "Segregation in Southern Cities,"

Scholars have identified a number of factors to explain these differences: the age of the city and its antebellum experience; the size, extent of growth, and economic base and resulting occupational structure of the city; and the timing of the city's growth. Older antebellum cities that had a relatively large free black and slave servant population and those that did not grow rapidly and lacked a strong industrial base did not develop ghettos on the northern pattern; newer, industrial cities developed housing patterns much closer to those of northern cities.[83]

The considerable attention given to residential patterns is not matched by detailed studies of the black urban work force and the effects of the urban living and work experience on blacks. John Blassingame concluded from his studies of Savannah and New Orleans that urban experiences allowed blacks to shed "ante-bellum customs perpetuated in the countryside and . . . to develop a variety of social, intellectual and creative talents . . . denied to them as slaves

---

American Journal of Sociology, LXXXII (July, 1966), 58–67; Karl E. Taeuber and Alma F. Taeuber, *Negroes in Cities: Residential Segregation and Neighborhood Change* (Chicago: Aldine, 1965). This pattern had been noted by Gunnar Myrdal, *An American Dilemma: The Negro Problem and Modern Democracy* (2 vols.; New York: Harper & Brothers, 1944), I, 618–22; and E. Franklin Frazier, *The Negro in the United States* (Rev. ed.; New York: Macmillan, 1957), 237.

83. John Kellogg, "Negro Urban Clusters in the Postbellum South," *Geographical Review,* LXVII (July, 1977), 310–21, and "The Formation of Black Residential Areas in Lexington, Kentucky, 1865–1887," *Journal of Southern History,* XLVIII (February, 1982), 21–52; Geraldine McTigue, "Patterns of Residence: Housing Distribution by Color in Two Louisiana Towns, 1860–1880," *Louisiana Studies,* XV (Winter, 1976), 345–88; John W. Blassingame, "Before the Ghetto: The Making of the Black Community in Savannah, Georgia, 1865–1880," *Journal of Social History,* VI (Summer, 1973), 463–88, and *Black New Orleans, 1860–1880* (Chicago: University of Chicago Press, 1973); Herbert A. Thomas, "Victims of Circumstance: Negroes in a Southern Town, 1865–1880," *Register of the Kentucky Historical Society,* LXXI (July, 1973), 253–71; Paul A. Groves and Edward K. Muller, "The Evolution of Black Residential Areas in Late Nineteenth-Century Cities," *Journal of Historical Geography,* I (April, 1975), 169–91; John P. Radford, "Race, Residence and Ideology: Charleston, South Carolina, in the Mid-Nineteenth Century," *Journal of Historical Geography,* II (October, 1976), 329–46; Paul B. Worthman, "Working Class Mobility in Birmingham, Alabama, 1880–1914," in Tamara K. Hareven (ed.), *Anonymous Americans: Explorations in Nineteenth-Century Social History* (Englewood Cliffs, N.J.: Prentice-Hall, 1971), 172–213; Zane L. Miller, "Urban Blacks in the South, 1865–1920: The Richmond, Savannah, New Orleans, Louisville, and Birmingham Experience," in Leo F. Schnore (ed.), *The New Urban History: Quantitative Explorations by American Historians* (Princeton: Princeton University Press, 1975), 184–204; Michael B. Chesson, *Richmond After the War, 1865–1890* (Richmond: Virginia State Library, 1981), Chap. 5.

and as quasifree men."[84] Blassingame and Rabinowitz discuss the political, social, and cultural organizations in the black community and the emergence of a new class of leaders, and they provide some information about the jobs held by blacks. But their discussion is more descriptive than analytical.

Studies of social and geographical mobility and of black family structure in southern cities provide some additional information. All such studies tend to agree that blacks were poorer than whites, that they predominated in the low-skill manual-labor occupations, that they experienced far less social mobility than did whites, that they were more likely to remain in the same place for longer periods than were whites, and that black women were more likely to be in the work force than were white women, both married and single. They also find that the urban experience did not destroy or significantly weaken the "traditional" nuclear, male-headed family structure.[85]

Together, these studies show that despite restrictions, urban blacks had opportunities that were absent in the countryside. Ironically, these opportunities arose in part, at least, from the greater impact in the urban areas of Jim Crow and segregation, which opened a market for black business and tradespeople who provided services to the black community. The precise ways in which urban experiences affected the ideology and outlook of the black community and the

84. Blassingame, "Before the Ghetto," 463, and *Black New Orleans*.

85. Blassingame, "Before the Ghetto," and *Black New Orleans*, Chap. 4; William Harris, "Work and the Family in Black Atlanta, 1880," *Journal of Social History*, IX (Spring, 1976), 319–30; Steven W. Engerrand, "Black and Mulatto Mobility and Stability in Dallas, Texas, 1880–1910," *Phylon*, XXXIX (September, 1978), 203–15; Richard J. Hopkins, "Occupational and Geographic Mobility in Atlanta, 1870–1896," *Journal of Southern History*, XXXIV (May, 1968), 200–213; Worthman, "Working Class Mobility in Birmingham"; Robert Francis Engs, *Freedom's First Generation: Black Hampton, Virginia, 1861–1890* (Philadelphia: University of Pennsylvania Press, 1979). James Smallwood studied three Texas rural counties and found that the same pattern existed in 1870: blacks were poorer than whites but their family structures were almost identical, except that a much larger proportion of black women than white worked outside of their homes (*Time of Hope, Time of Despair*, Chap. 3 [pp. 109–27]). Rural-urban comparisons may be found in Barbara F. Agresti, "Town and Country in a Florida Rural County in the Late 19th Century: Some Population and Household Comparisons," *Rural Sociology*, XLII (Winter, 1977), 556–68; Frank J. Huffman, Jr., "Town and Country in the South, 1850–1880: A Comparison of Urban and Rural Social Structures," *South Atlantic Quarterly*, LXXVI (Summer, 1977), 366–81; and Orville Vernon Burton, "The Rise and Fall of Afro-American Town Life: Town and Country in Reconstruction Edgefield, South Carolina," in Burton and McMath (eds.), *Toward a New South?*, 152–92.

ways in which urban attitudes affected rural views remain to be studied.[86]

We must also learn more about the kinds and amounts of work available to blacks in the cities. Census data provide information about jobs people held but give little information about the extent of unemployment and virtually nothing about underemployment; research to date has not gone significantly beyond such data. It appears that there was significant underemployment among blacks in the urban areas, for during periods when labor was needed in the fields, especially at harvest time, large numbers of workers could be recruited from the cities.[87]

The role of women in the postbellum South remains almost completely unexplored. Ransom and Sutch argue that there was a withdrawal of black women and children from field work immediately after emancipation. But this withdrawal was temporary, for, as we have seen, studies of later years show that the labor force participation rate of black women in rural areas as well as in the cities far exceeded that of white women.[88] Nevertheless, black urban migration after emancipation meant that a smaller proportion was available for field work. But we know little about the precise effects of this urban

86. We know relatively little about the development of the black middle class and its relations with the black and white communities. Some of the studies already mentioned insist that members of the black middle class came primarily from the ranks of antebellum free Negroes, but others suggest that they were newcomers, either former slaves or northerners. Although black political leaders have received some attention, new work on nineteenth-century black business leaders is virtually nonexistent. The major general work remains E. Franklin Frazier, *Black Bourgeoisie* (Glencoe, Ill.: Free Press, 1957). A valuable insight into the ideology of at least a portion of the black middle class may be found in Norman L. Crockett's *The Black Towns* (Lawrence: Regents Press of Kansas, 1979), a discussion of the leadership in the all-black towns in Kansas, Oklahoma, and Mississippi that he studied.

87. Cohen, "Negro Involuntary Servitude in the South," finds the cooperation of local police in rounding up workers when needed in the fields to be a sign of the continuation of forms of "involuntary servitude" after emancipation. One might assume that if such people were working steadily, their white employers would object to police activities that deprived them of their employees for the benefit of others.

88. Ransom and Sutch, *One Kind of Freedom*, 44–47, 232–34. In addition to studies already cited, see Claudia Goldin, "Female Labor Force Participation: The Origin of Black and White Differences, 1870 and 1880," *Journal of Economic History*, XXXVII (March, 1977), 87–108; Minnie Miller Brown, "Black Women in American Agriculture," *Agricultural History*, L (January, 1976), 202–12; John E. Fleming, "Slavery, Civil War and Reconstruction: A Study of Black Women in Microcosm," *Negro History Bulletin*, XXXVIII (August-September, 1975), 430–33.

migration. Population figures suggest that women without husbands were more likely to move to the urban areas where jobs as domestics were available. Under slavery women were valued as workers but also for their reproductive functions, while after emancipation a woman with young children was a costly burden. Such women, finding it difficult to get work in the rural areas, may have moved to the cities in large numbers. Without further investigation, however, this can only be conjecture.[89]

Given the recent attention to women's history, it is surprising that studies of white women in the postbellum South are also lacking. Anne Firor Scott has surveyed the changes in their lives following the Civil War as women joined their returning men—or replaced those who did not return—in rebuilding their farms; many took advantage of new opportunities in teaching and other work outside the home. Carol Bleser provides a vivid picture of members of the South Carolina Hammond family women through their letters, but leaves conclusions and analysis to her readers. Suzanne D. Lebsock points to a significant link between wartime destruction and postwar disruption and the new state constitutions that provided greater property rights to southern women. These changes, she argues, were primarily designed to protect family property from being lost to debtors. Most scholars see the farm protest movement as a solely male activity, but Julie Roy Jeffrey's study of women in the North Carolina Farmers' Alliance shows that women often participated in meetings, wrote letters to newspapers, and sometimes even held minor office.[90] These studies merely hint at the range of problems still to be explored.

Health and welfare is another important problem that has received little attention. Historians have noted the existence of endemic and dietary diseases but have provided little sustained analysis of their effects on the economy and the society.[91]

89. Gerda Lerner (ed.), *Black Women in White America: A Documentary History* (New York: Pantheon, 1972), is a splendid collection of documents, many of which concern the South.

90. Anne Firor Scott, *The Southern Lady: From Pedestal to Politics, 1830–1930* (Chicago: University of Chicago Press, 1970), Pt. 2; Bleser (ed.), *The Hammonds of Redcliffe;* Suzanne D. Lebsock, "Radical Reconstruction and the Property Rights of Southern Women," *Journal of Southern History,* XLIII (May, 1977), 195–216; Julie Roy Jeffrey, "Women in the Southern Farmers' Alliance: A Reconsideration of the Role and Status of Women in the Late Nineteenth-Century South," *Feminist Studies,* III (Fall, 1975), 72–91. A view of the day-to-day life of a farm woman may be found in Margaret Jones Bolsterli (ed.), *Vinegar Pie and Chicken Bread: A Woman's Diary of Life in the Rural South, 1890–1891* (Fayetteville: University of Arkansas Press, 1982).

91. Robert W. Twyman, "The Clay Eater: A New Look at an Old Southern

It is clear that scholars are now heeding W. E. B. Du Bois's call to write the social and economic history of the postbellum South. In describing recent work, I have deliberately placed it in one of two camps—that of change or of continuity. Although this does not distort the themes of the work, I do not mean to suggest that the two camps are mutually exclusive, each having nothing to offer the other. By combining them, or, more precisely, by finding a synthesis that uses insights from both camps, we cannot erase sharp differences, but we may arrive at fresh insights.

A synthesis must consider the process of change over time as blacks and whites accommodated and adapted to the new free-labor system. It would be foolish to ignore the legacy of slavery in shaping postwar institutions and ideology; 250 years of history cannot be washed away even by the rivers of blood that flowed from 1861 to 1865. At the same time, it would be equally foolish to contend that emancipation made no difference if for no other reason than that those who experienced its results, black and white, northerners and southerners, knew better. True, they did not always fully understand what was happening and had little notion of what the future would bring. Indeed, their confusion was a result of their attempting to understand the changing new world by viewing it through lenses that remained focused on the old.

Changed circumstances demanded adjustment. Those with land to till could no longer buy the laborers they needed; they had to promise some form of payment to entice laborers to work for them. If these potential workers had no choice other than some form of employment or starvation, they did have the freedom to bargain with potential employers, and if they lacked experience with such bargaining, they had strong ideas, albeit of a negative kind, about what their newly acquired freedom meant. A return to conditions resem-

Enigma," *Journal of Southern History*, XXXVII (August, 1971), 439–48; Alan Raphael, "Health and Social Welfare of Kentucky Black People, 1865–1870," *Societas*, II (Spring, 1972), 143–57; J. Thomas May, "A 19th Century Medical Care Program for Blacks: The Case of the Freedmen's Bureau," *Anthropological Quarterly*, XLVI (July, 1973), 160–71; Edward Meeker, "Mortality Trends of Southern Blacks, 1850–1910: Some Preliminary Findings," *Explorations in Economic History*, XIII (January, 1976), 13–42; Anne S. Lee and Everett S. Lee, "The Health of Slaves and the Health of Freedmen: A Savannah Study," *Phylon*, XXXVIII (June, 1977), 170–80; Marshall Scott Legan, "Disease and the Freedmen in Mississippi during Reconstruction," *Journal of the History of Medicine and Allied Sciences*, XXVIII (July, 1973), 257–67; D. Clayton Brown, "Health of Farm Children in the South, 1900–1950," *Agricultural History*, LIII (January, 1979), 170–87.

bling those of slavery was unacceptable. Freedmen quickly learned that they could avoid starvation and increase their bargaining power by doing some work and then leaving or threatening to leave before the entire job was completed, a tactic that seemed to be a reasonable right of free people even if it appeared to their employers as a sign of laziness, irresponsibility, or unfaithfulness and proof that blacks would not work except under compulsion.

Creating a free-labor market (and the necessary discipline to make it work) in a population with little experience with it, indeed, with 250 years of contrary experience, took time and was inevitably marked by confusion and conflict.[92] Their new experiences educated both employers and employees. Many of these experiences were of the most mundane kind—arriving at some kind of agreement concerning rights and duties when contracting for work or learning to deal with merchants or, for that matter, learning to be merchants.[93]

Formal education also played a part. The desire of blacks for education and the failure of whites to provide adequate funding for black schools have been amply demonstrated and evoke little debate. But the significance of inadequate education has not been fully appreciated by economic historians. Even in the absence of other restraints on blacks, the inadequate education closed most of the doors leading to economic and social progress. Scholars disagree about the content of that education that was available to blacks. Some insist that Yankee teachers inculcated northern ideas among blacks to help them achieve true independence; others insist that the goal of both north-

92. Historians have examined this process in other times and places, but their insights have not been used in trying to examine the process in the South. See, for example, E. P. Thompson, *The Making of the English Working Class* (New York: Pantheon, 1964); and Herbert G. Gutman, *Work, Culture, and Society in Industrializing America: Essays in American Working Class and Social History* (New York: Knopf, 1976).

93. Scholars have investigated the role of the army and the Freedmen's Bureau in establishing schools, setting rules, and, in the case of the army, providing black recruits with a special form of educational experience. See John W. Blassingame, "The Union Army as an Educational Institution for Negroes, 1862–1865," *Journal of Negro Education,* XXXIV (Spring, 1965), 152–59; Ronald L. F. Davis, "The U.S. Army and the Origins of Sharecropping in the Natchez District—A Case Study," *Journal of Negro History,* LXII (January, 1977), 60–80; and Ira Berlin, Joseph P. Reidy, and Leslie S. Rowland (eds.), *Freedom: A Documentary History of Emancipation, 1861–1867. Selected from the Holdings of the National Archives of the United States,* Series II, *The Black Military Experience* (New York: Cambridge University Press, 1982). The efforts of planters and merchants to adjust to new conditions are clearly shown in their papers and in court records and newspapers.

ern and southern teachers was social control, aiming to promote docility among blacks; and still others insist that black teachers, within the constraints imposed on them, sought to improve the lot of their people.[94]

Interestingly enough, the debate often centers on the interpretation of much the same evidence. Teaching promptness, responsibility, honesty, industry, and other such "middle-class" virtues and emphasizing industrial and other forms of practical education may be seen as efforts at social control as well as efforts to equip people to survive in the world in which they lived. Comparisons of the content of education given to working-class and immigrant children in the North with the content of education provided for blacks in the South would, of course, reveal the inferiority of southern educational facilities, but would also reveal striking similarities.

The new relationships and new institutions that began to emerge reflected the education, both formal and informal, and, of course, were affected by many of the relationships surviving from the old system. The relative strength of each group or class as it sought to define and achieve its goals helped to determine the kind of institutions that evolved.

Understanding the process requires avoiding a static view that sees the Redeemers' victory resolving conflicts. That victory tipped the

94. These differing views may be seen in Henry Allen Bullock, *A History of Negro Education in the South From 1619 to the Present* (Cambridge: Harvard University Press, 1967); William Preston Vaughn, *Schools for All: The Blacks & Public Education in the South, 1865–1877* (Lexington: University Press of Kentucky, 1974); William F. Messner, "Black Education in Louisiana, 1863–1865," *Civil War History,* XXII (March, 1976), 41–59; Robert G. Sherer, *Subordination or Liberation? The Development and Conflicting Theories of Black Education in Nineteenth Century Alabama* (University: University of Alabama Press, 1977); F. Bruce Rosen, "The Influence of the Peabody Fund on Education in Reconstruction Florida," *Florida Historical Quarterly,* LV (January, 1977), 310–20; Donald Spivey, *Schooling for the New Slavery: Black Industrial Education, 1868–1915* (Westport, Conn.: Greenwood Press, 1978); Sandra E. Small, "The Yankee Schoolmarm in Freedmen's Schools: An Analysis of Attitudes," *Journal of Southern History,* XLV (August, 1979), 381–402; Ronald E. Butchart, *Northern Schools, Southern Blacks, and Reconstruction: Freedmen's Education, 1862–1875* (Westport, Conn.: Greenwood Press, 1980); Keith Wilson, "Education as a Vehicle of Racial Control: Major General N. P. Banks in Louisiana, 1863–64," *Journal of Negro Education,* L (Spring, 1981), 156–70; Robert C. Morris, *Reading, 'Riting, and Reconstruction: The Education of Freedmen in the South, 1861–1870* (Chicago: University of Chicago Press, 1981); Kenneth B. White, "The Alabama Freedmen's Bureau and Black Education: The Myth of Opportunity," *Alabama Review,* XXXIV (April, 1981), 107–24.

balance of power to the side of the employers, but neither ended conflict nor stopped the process of change. The defeat of the Alliance and Populist challenges and the disfranchisement of blacks and many whites[95] gave employers additional power to impose their ways. But future work must not merely note the hegemony of the landlords, merchants, and industrialists; it must investigate the goals they sought and the means they adopted to achieve these goals.

Comparative histories of emancipation will continue to offer useful insights, but future work should give more attention to sectional—North-South—comparisons. The cliometricians rightly point to the existence of bourgeois social relations in the postbellum South, but they do not carry their argument beyond the level of market transactions. Most of the other studies of the social and economic history of the South view the region in curious isolation from the North. A fuller investigation of the similarities as well as the differences should provide revealing insights into southern developments.

Historians no longer date the start of the Industrial Revolution in the United States with the Civil War; nevertheless, the postwar decades were marked by massive industrial expansion. The South did not share fully in that industrial development, though the growth of the steel, tobacco, textile, lumber, and other industries shows that industrial development did not completely bypass the South. Historians have rightly noted the southern lag, but few make explicit comparisons.[96] And most have failed to notice a number of important

95. J. Morgan Kousser, *The Shaping of Southern Politics: Suffrage Restriction and the Establishment of the One-Party South, 1880–1910* (New Haven: Yale University Press, 1974).

96. On banking, see John A. James, "The Development of the National Money Market, 1893–1911," *Journal of Economic History*, XXXVI (December, 1976), 878–97, "Cost Functions of Postbellum National Banks," *Explorations in Economic History*, XV (April, 1978), 184–95, and "Financial Underdevelopment in the Postbellum South," *Journal of Interdisciplinary History*, XI (Winter, 1981), 443–54; and William E. Laird and James R. Rinehart, "Deflation, Agriculture, and Southern Development," *Agricultural History*, XLII (April, 1968), 115–24. On manufacturing, see Albert W. Niemi, Jr., "Structural Shifts in Southern Manufacturing, 1849–1899," *Business History Review*, XLV (Spring, 1971), 79–84; and Patrick J. Hearden, *Independence and Empire: The New South's Cotton Mill Campaign, 1865–1901* (DeKalb: Northern Illinois University Press, 1982). On trade, see J. R. Killick, "The Transformation of Cotton Marketing in the Late Nineteenth Century: Alexander Sprunt and Son of Wilmington, N.C., 1884–1956," *Business History Review*, LV (Summer, 1981), 143–69; and Harold D. Woodman, *King Cotton & His Retainers: Financing & Marketing the Cotton Crop of the South, 1800–1925* (Lexington: University of Kentucky Press, 1968), Pts. 5, 6.

similarities. Robet Wiebe, Alfred D. Chandler, Jr., and others who have developed the so-called organization synthesis stress important social and economic changes associated with the development of big business. They point to the development of national markets, the growing centralization of production and distribution, the professionalization and specialization of business leadership, and the use of government to achieve the interbusiness cooperation necessary to organize planning, research, and market control. Agricultural historians, while noting that agricultural production remained far more dispersed and competitive than did manufacturing, note similar developments including increases in the size of productive units, in the use of machinery, in the dependence upon banks, distributors, and big business consumers of farm products, and in the use of scientific methods—all leading toward what later would be termed "agribusiness." [97]

Many of these same developments occurred in the South. As we have seen, recent studies of the southern Alliance and Populist movements agree it was just such trends that farmers opposed. The development in the Delta and elsewhere of large-scale, professionally managed business plantations; the increasing use of sharecroppers, who were given no voice in production decisions; the growing reliance on scientific methods, with the cooperation of state and national agricultural agencies; the centralization of ginning and especially of buyers—are all signs of changes in the rural South that paralleled those in the North. To recognize these important similarities is not to dismiss southern distinctiveness but merely to see that distinctiveness within the context of the development of modern American capitalism.

97. Robert H. Wiebe, *The Search for Order, 1877–1920* (New York: Hill & Wang, 1967); Alfred D. Chandler, Jr., *Strategy and Structure: Chapters in the History of the Industrial Enterprise* (Cambridge: M.I.T. Press, 1962), and *The Visible Hand: The Managerial Revolution in American Business* (Cambridge: Harvard University Press, 1977); Chandler and Louis Galambos, "The Development of Large-Scale Economic Organizations in Modern America," *Journal of Economic History,* XXX (March, 1970), 201–17; Galambos, "The Emerging Organizational Synthesis in Modern American History," *Business History Review,* XLIV (Autumn, 1970), 279–90; Harold D. Woodman, "Agriculture in the Postbellum South: The Transformation of a Slave Society," in Bateman (ed.), *Business in the New South,* 51–61. Tom G. Hall, "Agricultural History and the 'Organizational Synthesis': A Review Essay," *Agricultural History,* XLVIII (April, 1974), 313–25, raises a number of questions concerning the validity of the organizational synthesis for agricultural history.

From Populism Through the New Deal
Southern Political History

RICHARD L. WATSON, JR.

In the early 1960s, when Dewey Grantham wrote "The Twentieth-Century South" for *Writing Southern History,* historical writing, particularly about the twentieth century, was at a crossroads. Historians were de-emphasizing the class struggle and emphasizing continuities and agreements. Richard Hofstadter is mentioned in *Writing Southern History,* but it was too early to prophesy the number of books and articles that the concept of the status revolt would inspire.[1] In 1957, Lee Benson had launched his fight for using the social sciences in historical research. Four years later, his *The Concept of Jacksonian Democracy* appeared, and reviewers cited it as a landmark in the writing of ethnocultural history. In the meantime, Samuel P. Hays had been developing similar interests, but his name does not appear in the index of *Writing Southern History.* Yet that fertile mind was to be one of the most important influences in shaping future directions of historical research. Indeed, he and others who thought like him made writing an essay such as this one an almost impossible task because of his insistence that "traditional distinctions between political history on the one hand and ideological, economic, social, and cultural history on the other are artificial."[2]

1. Dewey W. Grantham, Jr., "The Twentieth-Century South," in Arthur S. Link and Rembert W. Patrick (eds.), *Writing Southern History: Essays in Historiography in Honor of Fletcher M. Green* (Baton Rouge: Louisiana State University Press, 1965), 410–44. Perhaps the first article inspired by Hofstadter's concept of status revolt was E. Daniel Potts, "The Progressive Profile in Iowa," *Mid-America,* XLVII (October, 1965), 257–68. A general criticism was David P. Thelen, "Social Tensions and the Origins of Progressivism," *Journal of American History,* LVI (September, 1969), 323–41.

2. Lee Benson, "Research Problems in American Political Historiography," in Mirra Komarovsky (ed.), *Common Frontiers of the Social Sciences* (Glencoe, Ill.: Free Press, 1957), 113–83, and *The Concept of Jacksonian Democracy: New York as a Test Case* (Princeton: Princeton University Press, 1961); Samuel P. Hays, "The Social Analysis of American Political History, 1880–1920," and "New Possibilities for American Political History: The Social Analysis of Political Life," both in Hays, *American Political History as Social Analysis: Essays by Samuel P. Hays* (Knoxville: University of Tennessee Press, 1980), 66–132 (quotation on p. 98).

By the mid-1960s, other elements were being added. Benson, Allan Bogue, Hays, and others were working to accumulate election data at the Inter-University Consortium for Political and Social Research at the University of Michigan's Center for Political Studies; the controversy over "that Bitch-goddess QUANTIFICATION," as Carl Bridenbaugh called it, was warming up; *Studies on the Left,* an early manifestation of the New Left, had been coming out since 1959; Gabriel Kolko would soon shake up progressive historiography by describing that era as the "triumph of Conservatism"; and Barton Bernstein and others would criticize the New Deal in similar terms.[3] Invasions from abroad combined with changing interests here were rejuvenating the field of social history and challenging historians, in Jesse Lemisch's words, to view history "from the bottom up."[4]

Although no clear-cut pattern of historical writing about the South emerged between 1963 and 1983, these various approaches have made a significant impact. J. Morgan Kousser and James M. McPherson have argued that "a Southern 'consensus school' long predated its national counterpart, and [that] the Dixie branch was at the height of its influence in the 1930s and 1940s." They referred in part to the

---

3. Lee Benson, "Quotation, Scientific History, and Scholarly Innovation," *AHA Newsletter,* IV (June, 1966), 12; Allan G. Bogue, *The Earnest Men: Republicans of the Civil War Senate* (Ithaca: Cornell University Press, 1981), and *Clio and the Bitch Goddess: Quantification in American Political History* (Beverly Hills, Ca.: Sage Publications, 1983). The consortium was organized in 1962, and the first seminar was in 1966. See also Samuel P. Hays, "Quantification in History: The Implications and Challenges for Graduate Training," *AHA Newsletter,* IV (June, 1966), 8–11, "New Possibilities for American Political History," 130, and "A Systematic Social History," in Hays, *American Political History,* 141; and William O. Aydelotte, "Quantification in History," *American Historical Review,* LXXI (April, 1966), 803–25; Carl Bridenbaugh, "The Great Mutation," *American Historical Review,* LXVIII (January, 1963), 326; Barton J. Bernstein (ed.), *Towards a New Past: Dissenting Essays in American History* (New York: Pantheon, 1968), x; Gabriel Kolko, *The Triumph of Conservatism: A Reinterpretation of American History, 1900–1916* (New York: Free Press of Glencoe, 1963); Bernstein, "The New Deal: The Conservative Achievements of Liberal Reform," in Bernstein (ed.), *Towards a New Past,* 263–88; Paul Conkin, *The New Deal* (New York: Harlan Davidson, 1967); introduction to Howard Zinn (ed.), *New Deal Thought* (Indianapolis: Bobbs-Merrill, 1966).

4. Jesse Lemisch, "The American Revolution Seen from the Bottom Up," in Bernstein (ed.), *Towards a New Past,* 3–45; Grantham, "The Twentieth-Century South," in Link and Patrick (eds.), *Writing Southern History,* 430–40. Grantham also pointed to the importance of the social sciences for research in southern history in his presidential address to the Southern Historical Association, "The Regional Imagination: Social Scientists and the American South," *Journal of Southern History,* XXXIV (February, 1968), 3–32.

seemingly widespread acceptance of W. J. Cash's conclusions that after the Civil War only "superficial and unrevolutionary" changes took place in the southern mind and that even such limited changes took "place within the ancient framework."[5]

Although dissent from this kind of consensus was muted in the historical profession before the 1960s, graduate students were showing an interest in populism, a topic that did not jibe with the idea of a happy southern unity. Then in 1946, Arthur S. Link published an article that argued that the South had as much right to claim credit for the reforms of the Progressive Era as did any other section.[6]

By this time, the most effective revisionist had raised his voice. In 1938, C. Vann Woodward's biography of Tom Watson, described as "an attack on the myth of an everlastingly solid south," was published. Three years later, in reviewing *The Mind of the South*, Woodward took exception to Cash's thesis of the "continuity of the southern mind and to a lesser extent its unity."[7] Then in 1951 came *Origins of the New South*, a book written with such scholarly care that its essential ingredients—the neo-Beardianism of class conflict brought about by the emergence of a new class of businessmen and

5. J. Morgan Kousser and James M. McPherson (eds.), *Region, Race, and Reconstruction: Essays in Honor of C. Vann Woodward* (New York: Oxford University Press, 1982), xvii; W. J. Cash, *The Mind of the South* (New York: Knopf, 1941), 219; Horace H. Cunningham, "The Southern Mind Since the Civil War," in Link and Patrick (eds.), *Writing Southern History*, 384. Paul M. Gaston showed how early-twentieth-century writers believed that "one partyism, white supremacy, patriotism, morality in government and the industrial revolution" added up to the Solid South ("The 'New South,'" in Link and Patrick [eds.], *Writing Southern History*, 326).

6. Grantham, "The Twentieth-Century South," in Link and Patrick (eds.), *Writing Southern History*, 412–13, 431; Arthur S. Link, "The Progressive Movement in the South, 1870–1914," *North Carolina Historical Review*, XXIII (April, 1946), 172–95.

7. Quotation in Kousser and McPherson (eds.), *Region, Race, and Reconstruction*, xviii; C. Vann Woodward, *Tom Watson: Agrarian Rebel* (New York: Macmillan, 1938), and Review of Cash's *The Mind of the South*, in *Journal of Southern History*, VII (August, 1941), 400. Woodward made a more sweeping indictment of *The Mind of the South* in "The Elusive Mind of the South," in Woodward, *American Counterpoint: Slavery and Racism in the North-South Dialogue* (Boston: Little, Brown, 1971), a revision of an essay originally published in the *New York Review of Books*, December 4, 1969, pp. 28–34. For a more sympathetic treatment of Cash, see Joseph L. Morrison, "W. J. Cash: The Summing Up," *South Atlantic Quarterly*, LXX (Autumn, 1971), 477–86, reprinted in the Autumn, 1977, issue (LXXVI, 508–17). Michael O'Brien adds that "*The Mind of the South*, though weak as an assessment of current knowledge about the Old South, was better as a guide to the New South than one could have found in most studies by professional historians in the 1930s" ("W. J. Cash, Hegel, and the South," *Journal of Southern History*, XLIV [August, 1978], 381).

individuals, the venality of the Redeemers, the pervasiveness of race, and the concept of "progressivism for whites only"—still survive. *Origins* became a model against which any new interpretation of the South of the late nineteenth century and the Progressive Era would be measured.[8]

As important for the period between the two world wars as *Origins of the New South* is for the earlier period, V. O. Key's *Southern Politics in State and Nation* (1949) is a study that found wide variations in political experiences among the southern states. Key concluded, however, that "the politics of the South revolves around the position of the Negro," "that the fundamental explanation of southern politics is that the black-belt whites succeeded in imposing their will on their states and thereby presented a solid regional front in national politics on the race issue," that "consistent and unquestioning attachment . . . to the Democratic party nationally has meant that the politics within the southern states . . . has had to be conducted without the benefit of political parties," and that "by yielding to their black belts in their desire for solidarity in national politics, the states of the South condemned themselves internally to a chaotic factional politics."[9]

8. C. Vann Woodward, *Origins of the New South, 1877–1913* (Baton Rouge: Louisiana State University Press, 1951); Sheldon Hackney, "*Origins of the New South* in Retrospect," *Journal of Southern History,* XXXVIII (May, 1972), 191–216; David M. Potter, "C. Vann Woodward and the Uses of History," in Don E. Fehrenbacher (ed.), *History and American Society: Essays of David M. Potter* (New York: Oxford University Press, 1973), Chap. 7; see especially "Introduction" in Kousser and McPherson (eds.), *Region, Race, and Reconstruction,* xx; Michael O'Brien, "C. Vann Woodward and the Burden of Southern Liberalism," *American Historical Review,* LXXVIII (June, 1973), 589–604; Robert B. Westbrook, "C. Vann Woodward: The Southerner as Liberal Realist," *South Atlantic Quarterly,* LXXVII (Winter, 1978), 54–71. The 1971 edition of *Origins of the New South* is revised only in that it includes a comprehensive, 112-page critical bibliographical essay by Charles B. Dew. Other dissenters are mentioned in Gaston, "The 'New South,'" and Grantham, "The Twentieth-Century South," both in Link and Patrick (eds.), *Writing Southern History,* 328–29, 415–16. John W. Cell has provided a refreshing historiographical study in his *The Highest Stage of White Supremacy: The Origins of Segregation in South Africa and the American South* (Cambridge, England: Cambridge University Press, 1982).

9. V. O. Key, Jr., *Southern Politics in State and Nation* (New York: Knopf, 1949), 5 (first quotation), 11 (second and third quotations), 11–12 (fourth quotation); Grantham, "The Twentieth-Century South," in Link and Patrick (eds.), *Writing Southern History,* 437–38; see also Grantham, "The Regional Imagination," 20–21; Gary C. Ness, "The *Southern Politics* Project and the Writing of Recent Southern History," *South Atlantic Quarterly,* LXXVI (Winter, 1977), 58–72; "Symposium: The Legacy

Both Woodward and Key emphasized the theme of the changing South, a theme that continues to be hotly debated. Some of the South's most distinguished scholars, including Clement Eaton, Charles P. Roland, who revised Francis Butler Simkins' text in 1972, Thomas D. Clark and Albert D. Kirwan, and Monroe Lee Billington, have treated that theme in different ways.[10] More recently, I. A. Newby

---

of V. O. Key's 'Southern Politics,'" *South Atlantic Urban Studies,* III (1979), 257–92, with articles or comments by Jack R. Censer, Jack Bass, Hugh Davis Graham, William C. Havard, Jr., and George B. Tindall. A significant essay on different types of southern politicians is William C. Havard, Jr., "Southern Politics: Old and New Style," in Louis D. Rubin, Jr. (ed.), *The American South: Portrait of a Culture* (Baton Rouge: Louisiana State University Press, 1980), 38–58.

10. David M. Potter, "On Understanding the South: A Review Article," *Journal of Southern History,* XXX (November, 1964), 460, 457–58; Clement Eaton, *The Waning of the Old South Civilization, 1860's–1880's* (Athens: University of Georgia Press, 1968); Francis Butler Simkins and Charles Pierce Roland, *A History of the South* (New York: Knopf, 1972); Roland, "The Ever-Vanishing South," *Journal of Southern History,* XLVIII (February, 1982), 3–20, and "The South, America's Will-o-the-Wisp Eden," *Louisiana History,* XI (Spring, 1970), 101–19. For some support for the belief that the South will continue to be different, see James McBride Dabbs, *Who Speaks for the South?* (New York: Funk & Wagnalls, 1964); and Dudley L. Poston, Jr., and Robert H. Weller (eds.), *The Population of the South: Structure and Change in Social Demographic Context* (Austin: University of Texas Press, 1981). But note Howard Zinn, who says that "the South is but a distorted mirror image of the North" (*The Southern Mystique* [New York: Knopf, 1964], 13). David L. Smiley insists that the American South is an idea and suggests that students should study not "*what* the South is or has been, but *why* the idea of the South began" ("The Quest for the Central Theme in Southern History," *South Atlantic Quarterly,* LXXI [Summer, 1972], 324–25). See also Michael O'Brien, *The Idea of the American South: 1920–1941* (Baltimore: Johns Hopkins University Press, 1979); cf. William C. Havard, Jr., "The Distinctive South: Fading or Reviving?" in *Why the South Will Survive by Fifteen Southerners* (Athens: University of Georgia Press, 1981), 35–44. A different perspective is Jack Temple Kirby, *Media-Made Dixie: The South in the American Imagination* (Baton Rouge: Louisiana State University Press, 1978). Grantham, "The Twentieth-Century South," in Link and Patrick (eds.), *Writing Southern History,* 416; Thomas D. Clark and Albert D. Kirwan, *The South Since Appomattox: A Century of Regional Change* (New York: Oxford University Press, 1967), 7, 117; John Hope Franklin, "The Great Confrontation: The South and the Problem of Change," *Journal of Southern History,* XXXVIII (February, 1972), 20; Thomas D. Clark, *The Emerging South* (New York: Oxford University Press, 1961), and *Three Paths to the Modern South: Education, Agriculture, and Conservation* (Athens: University of Georgia Press, 1965). Clark emphasized particularly such factors leading to change as industrialism, education, agriculture, the breakdown of the agricultural economy, and conservation ("The Changing Emphases in the Writing of Southern History," *Filson Club Historical Quarterly,* XLV [April, 1971], 145–57). Monroe Lee Billington emphasized progressivism, opposition to participation of the Negro in politics, and the New Deal as factors contributing to change and dividing the Solid South (*The American South: A Brief His-*

prophesied that changes in the twentieth century have been so great that the South itself would disappear. He saw the "final triumph of the Solid South" in the failure of populism in the 1890s. He warned that the concept of the "Solid South" is misleading if interpreted as meaning agreement on political issues yet useful if understood to show that divisions on specific issues were kept "within the larger unity demanded by white supremacy." [11]

While Woodward and Key provided controversial ideas for later historians to question, Dewey Grantham and George B. Tindall are the two historians who have in the past twenty years most comprehensively tested these ideas. Grantham, drawing largely from his understanding of the Progressive Era, insisted that political alternatives have been available in the South in spite of the one-party system. In short, he argued, unlike V. O. Key, that the conservatism characteristic of so much southern thought has obscured the factions that have frequently divided the Democratic party along liberal and conservative lines. Moreover, while emphasizing the appropriateness of regional research, he noted the disappearance of other regional distinctions and concluded that it is "increasingly difficult to write about the South as a clearly defined entity." [12]

---

tory [New York: Charles Scribner's Sons, 1971], and *The Political South in the Twentieth Century* [New York: Charles Scribner's Sons, 1975]). John Samuel Ezell, another of Billington's teachers, published *The South Since 1865* (New York: Macmillan, 1963). See also John Hope Franklin, *From Slavery to Freedom: A History of Negro Americans* (4th rev. ed.; New York: Knopf, 1974).

11. I. A. Newby, *The South: A History* (New York: Holt, Rinehart & Winston, 1978), 342. Although the works of Carl Degler, David Potter, and George Mowry do not concentrate upon southern political history of the twentieth century, the insights that they bring are essential ingredients for understanding southern history in general. See especially Carl N. Degler, *Place Over Time: The Continuity of Southern Distinctiveness* (Baton Rouge: Louisiana State University Press, 1977), and "The Foundations of Southern Distinctiveness," *Southern Review*, XIII (Spring, 1977), 225–39; Sheldon Hackney, Review of Degler's *The Other South*, in *Journal of Southern History*, XL (November, 1974), 634; Potter, "On Understanding the South," 460; and *The South and the Concurrent Majority*, ed. Don E. Fehrenbacher and Carl N. Degler (Baton Rouge: Louisiana State University Press, 1972), 6. A statistical study that helps show the relationship of the South to the relative strength of the political parties is Paul T. David, *Party Strength in the United States, 1872–1970* (Charlottesville: University Press of Virginia, 1972). George E. Mowry, *Another Look at the Twentieth-Century South* (Baton Rouge: Louisiana State University Press, 1973). Mowry's first lecture (pp. 3–32), in raising a question of why there is so much interest in southern history, compares the South with the Midwest.

12. Dewey W. Grantham, Jr., *The Democratic South* (Athens: University of Georgia Press, 1963), and "Interpreters of the Modern South," *South Atlantic Quarterly*,

In 1967, Grantham attempted "to create an organizational framework for the study of the South's political history since Reconstruction." He found a South solid at the end of the nineteenth century, yet he pointed to continuing factionalism in the twentieth. He showed how "the one-party system was supported by the most powerful economic and social interests in the region" as well as by southern politicians, and concluded that "despite internal conflicts and nationalizing pressures, sectionalism has been and remains a significant factor in southern politics." [13]

George Tindall's *The Emergence of the New South* (1967) in *A History of the South* has become a classic and suitable sequel to Woodward's *Origins of the New South*. Chapters are devoted to political, social, economic, and intellectual topics, but the integration is skillful. Following Arthur Link's interpretation of Woodrow Wilson's first administration, Tindall blazed a new trail in his coverage of World War I in which southern congressional committee chairmen contributed significantly to managing the war. He coined the term *business progressivism* in treating the 1920s and produced a brilliant synthesis of the New Deal, showing the love-hate relationship between Roosevelt and the South and bringing out both accomplishments and inconsistencies. As David Potter put it, Tindall "has placed his stamp upon a segment of Southern history which embraces one-sixth of the period since the founding of the Republic, and has done this with force, effectiveness, and authority, despite the fact that no other segment has presented such complexities, such contradictions, such multiplicity of significant developments, and such immeasurable sweep of change." [14]

Woven into the almost overwhelming detail were numerous ideas, several of which Tindall later developed as separate studies. In 1972, for example, in *The Disruption of the Solid South,* he discussed the rise of the Republican party in the South. Although emphasizing de-

---

LXIII (Autumn, 1964), 521–29 (quotation on p. 529). See also Grantham, "The South to Posterity!" *Midwest Quarterly,* VIII (Autumn, 1966), 59–65, and "The Regional Imagination."

13. Dewey W. Grantham, Jr., "The South and the Politics of Sectionalism," in Grantham, *The Regional Imagination: The South and Recent American History* (Nashville: Vanderbilt University Press, 1979), 1–22 (quotations on pp. 1, 2).

14. George Brown Tindall, *The Emergence of the New South, 1913–1945* (Baton Rouge: Louisiana State University Press, 1967). See also Tindall's comments in Edgar T. Thompson (ed.), *Perspectives on the South: Agenda for Research* (Durham: Duke University Press, 1967), 92. David M. Potter, "The Emergence of the New South: An Essay Review," *Journal of Southern History,* XXXIV (August, 1968), 423–24.

velopments since 1952, he grappled with the earlier failure of the Republican party to take advantage of Democratic factionalism, thus allowing the one-party South to persist until the Dixiecrat revolt of 1948. Then three years later, in *The Persistent Tradition in New South Politics*, he proposed perhaps his most thought-provoking thesis. "The persistent tradition" Tindall defined as a concept of community that had developed as "a process of dialectic": "the Bourbons supplied a thesis, the Populists set up an antithesis, and the Progressives worked out a synthesis which governed southern politics through the first half of the twentieth century." The Bourbons had reconciled "tradition with innovation"; the Populists posed a threat to that sense of community. But their defeat led to the triumph of the Solid South when the Progressives were able to borrow from the Populists while keeping the persistent tradition of southern community intact.[15]

In the meantime, the students of Samuel P. Hays, Lee Benson, and others had added the ethnocultural dimension to those of race, class, and party in interpreting late-nineteenth-century politics. Their efforts had largely been focused on the Midwest and the Northeast, but in 1974, George Tindall, in his presidential address to the Southern Historical Association, issued a challenge to southern historians to study the significance of the ethnic differences peculiar to their own region, and two years later appeared a formidable effort by Numan V. Bartley to deal with questions of race, class, sectionalism, and culture in searching for a central theme in southern history. Bartley, while finding "a muted form of class conflict . . . relatively common," came down on the side of "the centrality of ethnocultural values" in tracing the history of five party systems.[16]

15. George B. Tindall, *The Disruption of the Solid South* (Athens: University of Georgia Press, 1972), and *The Persistent Tradition in New South Politics* (Baton Rouge: Louisiana State University Press, 1975), xii. For an essay that comments on Key, Grantham, and Tindall, see Monroe Billington, "Recent Southern Political History: A Review Essay," *Red River Valley Historical Review*, III (Summer, 1978), 89–99.

16. George B. Tindall, "Beyond the Mainstream: The Ethnic Southerners," *Journal of Southern History*, XL (February, 1974), 3–18, and *The Ethnic Southerners* (Baton Rouge: Louisiana State University Press, 1976); Numan V. Bartley, "The South and Sectionalism in American Politics," *Journal of Politics*, XXXVIII (August, 1976), 239–57 (quotations on p. 257). See also Robert Kelley, "Ideology and Political Culture from Jefferson to Nixon," *American Historical Review*, LXXXII (June, 1977), 531–82, with comments by Ronald P. Formisano. Some of the early ethnocultural studies—such as Paul Kleppner, *The Cross of Culture: A Social Analysis of Midwestern Politics, 1850–1900* (New York: Free Press, 1970); and Samuel T. McSeveney, *The Politics of Depression: Political Behavior in the Northeast, 1893–1896* (New

Nonetheless, with regard to the history of southern politics of the late nineteenth century, the most important influence has undoubtedly been C. Vann Woodward's clear invitation in *Origins of the New South* to analyze the tensions of race and class in the agrarian revolt.[17] By the end of the 1960s, historians for many southern states had responded.[18] Yet in spite of the number and variety of state studies, no study encompassing the region was published in the 1960s. Robert Durden's *The Climax of Populism,* however, came close, with its study of the national election of 1896 and the factional struggle between the North Carolina Populist Marion Butler and the Georgia Populist Tom Watson. Durden concluded that the Populist party was not radical in ideology but was made up of farmers angry about legiti-

---

York: Oxford University Press, 1972)—are criticized in Richard L. McCormick, "Ethno-Cultural Interpretations of Nineteenth-Century American Voting Behavior," *Political Science Quarterly,* LXXXIX (June, 1974), 351–77; and J. Morgan Kousser, "The 'New Political History': A Methodological Critique," *Reviews in American History,* IV (March, 1976), 1–14.

17. A convenient summary is Patrick E. McLear, "The Agrarian Revolt in the South: A Historiographical Essay," *Louisiana Studies,* XII (Summer, 1973), 443–63.

18. H. L. Meredith, "The 'Middle Way': The Farmers' Alliance in Indian Territory, 1889–1896," *Chronicles of Oklahoma,* XLVII (Winter, 1969–70), 377–87; Donald K. Pickens, "Oklahoma Populism and Historical Interpretation," *Chronicles of Oklahoma,* XLIII (Autumn, 1965), 275–83; Terry Paul Wilson, "The Demise of Populism in Oklahoma Territory," *Chronicles of Oklahoma,* XLIII (Autumn, 1965), 265–74; Leah R. Atkins, "Populism in Alabama: Reuben F. Kolb and the Appeals to Minority Groups," *Alabama Historical Quarterly,* XXXII (Fall and Winter, 1970), 167–80; William F. Holmes, "Whitecapping in Mississippi: Agrarian Violence in the Populist Era," *Mid-America,* LV (April, 1973), 134–48; William Warren Rogers, "The Agricultural Wheel in Alabama," *Alabama Review,* XX (January, 1967), 5–16; F. Clark Elkins, "The Agricultural Wheel: County Politics and Consolidation, 1884–1885," *Arkansas Historical Quarterly,* XXIX (Summer, 1970), 152–75, and "State Politics and the Agricultural Wheel," *Arkansas Historical Quarterly,* XXXVIII (Autumn, 1979), 248–58; Clifton Paisley, "The Political Wheelers and Arkansas' Election of 1888," *Arkansas Historical Quarterly,* XXV (Spring, 1966), 3–21; Henry C. Dethloff, "The Alliance and the Lottery: Farmers Try for the Sweepstakes," *Louisiana History,* VI (Spring, 1965), 141–59; Robert Saunders, "Southern Populists and the Negro, 1893–1895," *Journal of Negro History,* LIV (July, 1969), 240–61; Joseph F. Steelman, "Vicissitudes of Republican Party Politics: The Campaign of 1892 in North Carolina," *North Carolina Historical Review,* XLIII (Autumn, 1966), 430–32, and "Republican Party Strategists and the Issue of Fusion with Populists in North Carolina, 1893–1894," *North Carolina Historical Review,* XLVII (Summer, 1970), 244–69; H. Larry Ingle, "A Southern Democrat at Large: William Hodge Kitchin and the Populist Party," *North Carolina Historical Review,* XLV (Spring, 1968), 178–94; Frederick A. Bode, "Religion and Class Hegemony: A Populist Critique in North Carolina," *Journal of Southern History,* XXXVII (August, 1971), 417–38.

mate grievances, that fusion between Democrats and Populists was a logical expedient rather than a kind of conspiracy, as Woodward considered it, and that the election was, indeed, the climax of populism.[19]

In any case, by the end of the 1960s, the numerous state studies had provided overwhelming evidence in support of Woodward's attack upon consensus history as applied to the late nineteenth century. The 1970s added to that evidence. By that time, a new generation of students was responding to the challenges to look at history from the bottom up, to be sensitive to questions of race and ethnicity, and to make use of theory and statistics. One of the most significant of the new studies is Lawrence Goodwyn's *Democratic Promise* (1976).[20] This stalwart volume is significant not only because it is the first scholarly history to study populism in its entirety since the classic work by John D. Hicks in 1931 but also because Goodwyn insisted that Hicks's work, partly because of its emphasis on what Goodwyn calls "the shadow movement" of free silver, has had a crippling influence on subsequent scholarship. Among Goodwyn's main points are that populism grew out of the Southern Farmers' Alliance, which started in Texas, that the heart of the efforts of the Alliance was in the cooperatives and the lecture program, that the free-silver drive culminating in the nomination of Bryan was a "shadow movement," and

19. Robert F. Durden, *The Climax of Populism: The Election of 1896* (Lexington: University of Kentucky Press, 1965). Durden had pointed out the logic of Bryan's nomination and denied that free-silverites conspired to bring about a fusion with the Populists ("The 'Cow-bird' Grounded: The Populist Nomination of Bryan and Tom Watson in 1896," *Mississippi Valley Historical Review,* L [December, 1963], 397–423).

20. Lawrence Goodwyn, *Democratic Promise: The Populist Moment in America* (New York: Oxford University Press, 1976), and subsequently revised in paperback as *The Populist Moment* (1978). The importance of this book was telegraphed in advance by a significant article in which oral history was imaginatively used. Goodwyn, "Populist Dreams and Negro Rights: East Texas as a Case Study," *American Historical Review,* LXXVI (December, 1971), 1435–56. Two other volumes came out within a year of Goodwyn's. Robert C. McMath, Jr., *Populist Vanguard: A History of the Southern Farmers' Alliance* (Chapel Hill: University of North Carolina Press, 1975), is a careful study of the Alliance in Texas, its spread through the South and the West, the failure of the cooperatives, the political structure that remained, and the Populist party balanced on an insecure economic structure. Michael Schwartz's *Radical Protest and Social Structure: The Southern Farmers' Alliance and Cotton Tenancy, 1880–1890* (New York: Academic Press, 1976) is a controversial study that advances stimulating ideas not always with convincing evidence. It is useful in pointing out the class struggle within the Alliance. William F. Holmes has pointed to the variety of Alliancemen and concluded that most of them in Georgia were relatively conservative ("The Southern Farmers' Alliance and the Georgia Senatorial Election of 1890," *Journal of Southern History,* L [May, 1984], 195–224).

that true populism was a democratic ideology, the defeat of which led to the triumph of corporate capitalism.[21]

Another general study, Bruce Palmer's "*Man Over Money*" (1980), develops a number of the themes Goodwyn advanced. Palmer seemed less willing than Goodwyn, however, to see populism as the "Democratic promise." The Populists did, Palmer suggested, launch a strong rhetorical attack against the capitalist system, but southern Populists "all" believed in the benefits of private property and the market economy; "they wanted black support without relinquishing white dominance"; and they wanted to correct disparities "between the way the world was and the way it should be."[22]

As important as *Democratic Promise* in throwing new light on late-nineteenth-century politics is J. Morgan Kousser's *The Shaping of Southern Politics* (1974). Using extensive printed sources and election statistics analyzed in part by ecological regression, Kousser, like Woodward, showed that the South was not solid in the late nine-

---

21. Woodward enthusiastically endorsed these findings. Populism, he wrote in reviewing Goodwyn, "constituted the largest and most powerful movement attempting the structural reform of the American economic and political system in the nineteenth century" ("The Promise of Populism," *New York Review of Books,* October 28, 1976, p. 28). Some reviewers have been less favorable. David Montgomery argued that Goodwyn "is at a loss to understand the relationship of industrial workers to Populism" and that he "offers no class analysis of rural America" ("On Goodwyn's Populists," *Marxist Perspectives,* I [Spring, 1978], 169, 171). William F. Holmes questioned Goodwyn's notion of "Alliance radicalism" and also pointed out that there is inconsistency between his argument that "the Populists attempted to form a political union between black and white farmers" and his thesis that populism emerged from the Southern Alliance, which "adhered" to a strong racist position ("Lawrence Goodwyn's *Democratic Promise:* An Essay-Review," *Georgia Historical Quarterly,* LXI [Summer, 1977], 173–74, 174–75). James Turner, in his important historiographical article "Understanding the Populists," *Journal of American History,* LXVII (September, 1980), 354–73, praises Goodwyn but says that the latter accepted "the historiographic tradition" that "economic hardship made Populists" (p. 357). Turner suggested tentatively that economic distress did not in itself create Populists but that "the primary cause of Populism was the impact of economic distress on socially isolated farmers" (p. 367) "on the fringe of" an increasingly predominant "metropolitan culture" (p. 371). Stanley B. Parsons *et al.* take more serious exception to Goodwyn's work. They argue "(1) that massive numbers of cooperatives did not exist in the Populist states; (2) that in the relatively few instances when they did exist, coops, a radical monetary policy, and politics often occurred simultaneously, not in the sequence of coop to ideology to political revolt that the Goodwyn hypothesis demands" ("The Role of Cooperatives in the Development of the Movement Culture of Populism," *Journal of American History,* LXIX [March, 1983], 868).

22. Bruce Palmer, "*Man Over Money*": *The Southern Populist Critique of American Capitalism* (Chapel Hill: University of North Carolina Press, 1980), xvii, 217.

teenth century and, like V. O. Key, pointed to Black Belt southerners rather than those of the uplands as the strongest supporters of
disfranchisement. Unlike Key, however, and more like Woodward,
Kousser argued that the actual disfranchisement laws as well as earlier intimidation and restrictive devices were important in the disfranchising process. Among Kousser's most important, yet debatable,
conclusions were that disfranchisement was political rather than racial in motive, designed to keep the Democrats in power, and that the
white primary, rather than being racial in its motivation, was designed to contain differences within the Democratic party and to prevent the strengthening of a second party.[23]

Kousser's research led him to be sympathetic with one of Woodward's most controversial suggestions in *The Strange Career of Jim
Crow* that black and white Populists had cooperated in a relatively
friendly fashion against common enemies. Indeed this suggestion
proved so controversial that within a few years after its publication,
Woodward found himself caught in what he described as an adver-
sary procedure and, hoping to end the controversy, he summarized in
a typically judicious essay the literature on the subject.[24] A number of
studies continued to question, however, whether real racial harmony
existed. Robert Saunders, for example, found that blacks held a few
token offices in the upper levels of the Populist party but that they
had little influence with the rank and file, save possibly in Virginia.
Gerald H. Gaither put relationships among black and white Populists
somewhere between sweetness and light on one hand and confrontive
hostility on the other. He saw the whites as having cocked a wary eye

23. J. Morgan Kousser, *The Shaping of Southern Politics: Suffrage Restriction and
the Establishment of the One-Party South, 1880–1910* (New Haven: Yale University
Press, 1974). Although the secret ballot has usually been considered a reform, Kousser
showed how it actually disfranchised illiterate voters. For a preview of *The Shaping of
Southern Politics*, see Kousser, "Post-Reconstruction Suffrage Restrictions in Tennessee: A New Look at the V. O. Key Thesis," *Political Science Quarterly*, LXXXVIII
(December, 1973), 678–79. See also L. E. Fredman, *The Australian Ballot: The Story
of an American Reform* (East Lansing: Michigan State University Press, 1968). James H.
Stone concluded that "the Mississippi Understanding Clause" was administered more
equitably than usually assumed ("A Note on Voter Registration Under the Mississippi
Understanding Clause, 1892," *Journal of Southern History*, XXXVIII [May, 1972],
293–96).

24. Kousser and McPherson (eds.), "Introduction," *Region, Race, and Reconstruction*, xxvii; Woodward, "The Strange Career of a Historical Controversy," in *American
Counterpoint*, 237, "The Southern Ethic in a Puritan World," in *American Counterpoint*, 45, and *The Strange Career of Jim Crow* (2nd rev. ed; New York: Oxford University Press, 1966), 78–80.

on their black fellow farmers and forged a coalition with them to get the votes necessary for a viable third party. Certain black leaders, equally wary, saw in white Populists possible support against the constant threat of racial violence. Attempts at coalition warfare had, however, failed by 1892, and the goal of disfranchisement began to replace that of coalition.[25]

It is, however, impossible to make a generalization universally applicable to southern Populists, as studies of individual states make clear. In Virginia, for example, Charles E. Wynes supported the Woodward thesis that race relations, while relatively favorable immediately after the Civil War, degenerated dramatically in the 1890s. Allen W. Moger added that the conservative leadership that usually prevailed in Virginia was not characterized by the corruption and demagogy that appeared in some states. And Robert M. Saunders, while sympathetic to Woodward's thesis about the relationship between black and white Populists, criticized historians such as Moger and Woodward for exaggerating the farmers' economic grievances as a cause for their revolt. Saunders found a blurring of differences between farmers and businessmen and stressed psychological factors such as loss of status and a power struggle between rural and urban politicians as decisive factors in Virginia.[26]

Maryland's political experience in the late nineteenth century was

25. Saunders, "Southern Populists and the Negro"; Gerald H. Gaither, *Blacks and the Populist Revolt: Ballots and Bigotry in the "New South"* (University: University of Alabama Press, 1977). Although reviewers have generally praised Gaither for his research, serious questions have been raised about the usefulness of the sixty-page statistical appendix. Carl V. Harris, Review of Gaither's *Blacks and the Populist Revolt,* in *Journal of Southern History,* XLIV (August, 1978), 479–80. Howard N. Rabinowitz provides another amplification of the Woodward thesis. Using Nashville, Atlanta, Montgomery, Raleigh, and Richmond as examples, he finds discriminatory practices, continuous and virtually complete, from the 1870s on. Black and white Republicans instituted these practices, however, on the basis of "separate but equal" in order to prevent exclusion. When blacks began to resist these practices, laws were passed to enforce them (*Race Relations in the Urban South, 1865–1890* [New York: Oxford University Press, 1978]). An unduly brief study is Daniel M. Johnson and Rex R. Campbell, *Black Migration in America: A Social Demographic History* (Durham: Duke University Press, 1981).

26. Charles E. Wynes, *Race Relations in Virginia, 1870–1902* (Charlottesville: University of Virginia Press, 1961), 149–50; Allen W. Moger, *Virginia: Bourbonism to Byrd, 1870–1925* (Charlottesville: University Press of Virginia, 1968); Robert M. Saunders, "Progressive Historians and the Late Nineteenth-Century Agrarian Revolt: Virginia as a Historiographical Test Case," *Virginia Magazine of History and Biography,* LXXIX (October, 1971), 484–92. See Saunders, "Southern Populists and the Negro."

unique in that black people were not deprived of the right to vote or to hold office. A two-party system continued to exist there, as Margaret Law Callcott pointed out, with the Republicans' being a coalition of mountain whites and southern Maryland blacks. Compared to other states, Maryland did not have a sizable black population, and few blacks were tenants. Moreover, the white population, being much more ethnically diverse than in other southern states, included elements opposed to disfranchisement.[27]

In Tennessee the rise of populism made a complicated political situation more intricate. Factional rivalries were intense; the Republicans were always a threat; and there were differences between the Bourbons, who were similar to pre–Civil War Democrats, and the Democrats of the New South, who were involved in industry. In this complicated situation, all factions tried to obtain black support, but then the threat of black political power, according to Joseph H. Cartwright, caused paternalism to degenerate into racism, which in turn led to restrictions on black voting. Indeed, Tennessee, as J. Morgan Kousser pointed out, preceded Mississippi in disfranchising the blacks. To this complex picture Roger L. Hart added a psychological dimension, consciously drawing on the status-anxiety theory of Richard Hofstadter. The Populists, he found, were just as racist as the Bourbons, but rural elements were frustrated by their lack of power and wished to elect to public office men from their own group. Hart used literary sources and election statistics persuasively, but the evidence for status anxiety is certainly not conclusive.[28]

Georgia's Populists have drawn considerable historical attention, perhaps because Georgia was the home of Woodward's Tom Watson. Eugene R. Fingerhut has added a practical note to the Woodward thesis of the alliance between black and white Populists by suggesting that the "southern black was . . . a prospective ally in the 1890s" to achieve the goals of populism but that "when the blacks were no longer useful, Watson discarded them." Francis M. Wilhoit introduced a slightly different dimension—that white Populists in that state first cooperated with blacks but after 1892, fearing that blacks

27. Margaret Law Callcott, *The Negro in Maryland Politics, 1870–1912* (Baltimore: Johns Hopkins Press, 1969).

28. Joseph H. Cartwright, *The Triumph of Jim Crow: Tennessee Race Relations in the 1880s* (Knoxville: University of Tennessee Press, 1976); Kousser, "Post-Reconstruction Suffrage Restrictions in Tennessee," 682; Roger L. Hart, *Redeemers, Bourbons, and Populists: Tennessee, 1870–1896* (Baton Rouge: Louisiana State University Press, 1975).

were gaining too much power, supported disfranchisement. Charles Crowe, contradicting Woodward, denied that Watson had any interest in promoting the well-being of blacks or ever had any radical aspirations for his class. On the other hand, John Dittmer, in an excellent monograph, described Watson as an opportunist who saw Georgia politics as a class struggle; Democrats successfully used race to preserve their power; and "white Populists then made the black man scapegoat for their defeat." [29]

Subtle distinctions in interpretation are brought out in the treatment of blacks' and Populists' relations in Alabama. Sheldon Hackney, in an innovative study, for example, found that the Populists were pragmatically inclined toward black people in that state. They "made a major effort to secure Negro votes," but they were "less successful . . . than were their opponents." They opposed disfranchisement only because they realized that poor whites might be disfranchised too. In short, concluded Hackney, "there was . . . no objective difference" between Populists and Democrats on racial policy. Coming to this question from the perspective of the Farmers' Alliance, William Warren Rogers came to a somewhat different conclusion: "To ascribe

29. Eugene R. Fingerhut, "Tom Watson, Blacks, and Southern Reform," *Georgia Historical Quarterly,* LX (Winter, 1976), 324–43 (quotation on p. 342); *cf.* Alfred E. Hicks, "Tom Watson and the Arthur Glover Case in Georgia Politics," *Georgia Historical Quarterly,* LIII (September, 1969), 265–86; Francis M. Wilhoit, "An Interpretation of Populism's Impact on the Georgia Negro," *Journal of Negro History,* LII (April, 1967), 116–27; Charles Crowe, "Tom Watson, Populists, and Blacks Reconsidered," *Journal of Negro History,* LV (April, 1970), 99–116; John Dittmer, *Black Georgia in the Progressive Era, 1900–1920* (Urbana: University of Illinois Press, 1977), 6–7. Steven Hahn, "Common Right and Commonwealth: The Stock-Law Struggle and the Roots of Southern Populism," in Kousser and McPherson (eds.), *Region, Race, and Reconstruction,* 74–77, showed how the stock law created differences among farmers. Like Goodwyn, however, he saw a "cooperative commonwealth" as a principal goal of populism. Hahn developed these points in depth and breadth in *The Roots of Southern Populism: Yeoman Farmers and the Transformation of the Georgia Upcountry, 1850–1890* (New York: Oxford University Press, 1983). See also Olive Hall Shadgett, *The Republican Party in Georgia: From Reconstruction through 1900* (Athens: University of Georgia Press, 1964). Lawrence J. Friedman presents a thought-provoking but controversial thesis of the need of white people for Negro servility. Friedman with undue harshness takes issue with Woodward in *The White Savage: Racial Fantasies in the Postbellum South* (Englewood Cliffs, N. J.: Prentice-Hall, 1970). A better-documented study of late-nineteenth-century southern thought is Paul M. Gaston, *The New South Creed: A Study in Southern Mythmaking* (New York: Knopf, 1970). Gaston sees the New South program as being one of economic development and cooperative race relations. The myth was the belief that by 1890 the program had been achieved, thus disguising the need for further reform.

to the Populists a sustained and righteous desire to correct the wrongs done to the Negroes in Alabama is to overstate the case," he wrote. "Yet the Populists promoted the cause of the Negroes, admitted them to their councils, and advocated their political and economic advancement. To ignore these efforts is to miss an important part of the agrarian movement." [30]

Jeffrey Crow issued a reminder that relationships between populism and progressivism were not the same in every state. The case of North Carolina is particularly significant because only in that state did a successful fusion of Republicans and Populists temporarily oust the Democratic party. As in other states, according to Alan Bromberg, the Farmers' Alliance created a "muddle" in North Carolina politics. Previous campaigns had turned on personality and service to party or to the Confederacy; now serious economic issues raised emotions. Still, Joseph Steelman argued, party strategy and racial questions were as important as the economic issues associated with populism, and much of the argument over strategy involved the best way to use Negro votes. Indeed, Larry Ingle took issue with those (and he specifically mentioned Woodward) who associated populism with radicals wishing to overturn the system. Ingle used William Hodge Kitchin to illustrate how an essentially conservative white supremacist joined the Populist party for personal reasons. [31]

30. Sheldon Hackney, *Populism to Progressivism in Alabama* (Princeton: Princeton University Press, 1969), 39, 47. Except for mild questions about the depth of Hackney's research on the Progressive Era, reviewers seemed enthusiastic until 1975. See George B. Tindall, Review of Hackney's *Populism to Progressivism*, in *American Historical Review*, LXXV (June, 1970), 1537–38; Dewey W. Grantham, Jr., Review of Hackney's *Populism to Progressivism*, in *Journal of Southern History*, XXXVI (February, 1970), 115–17; and Allen J. Going, Review of Hackney's *Populism to Progressivism*, in *Journal of American History*, LVI (March, 1970), 928–29. Then J. Morgan Kousser opened fire not only at Hackney but at two of the pillars of ethnocultural history, Ronald Formisano and Paul Kleppner. He asked them why they did not employ a "more sophisticated multivariate technique" such as multiple regression analysis and "why Hackney and Kleppner often substitute rank order for Pearsonian correlations" ("The 'New Political History,'" 9). William Warren Rogers, *The One-Gallused Rebellion: Agrarianism in Alabama, 1865–1896* (Baton Rouge: Louisiana State University Press, 1970), 333. See also Atkins, "Populism in Alabama," 167–80.

31. Using railroad regulation as a specific example, Jeffrey J. Crow concluded that in North Carolina "Tar Heel populists and progressives shared similar, if not identical, goals" ("'Populism to Progressivism' in North Carolina: Governor Daniel Russell and His War on the Southern Railway Company," *Historian*, XXXVII [August, 1975], 649–67 [quotation on p. 666]). Alan B. Bromberg, "'The Worst Muddle Ever Seen in N. C. Politics': The Farmers' Alliance, the Subtreasury, and Zeb Vance," *North Caro-*

Were there basic differences among the political parties in North Carolina? Frederick A. Bode suggested that "*interest* (and perhaps a rudimentary form of class consciousness) was beginning to take precedence over old social and cultural restraints." He pointed to the effectiveness of Populist attacks on clergymen who were opposing economic reform. Having attacked white supremacy, they were attacking "'pure religion' [which was] still another part of a hegemonic and consensual ethos that the Democratic oligarchy relied upon to remain in power."[32] Yet, as Allen Trelease has shown, in a careful voting analysis of the state legislatures of 1895 and 1897, it would be difficult to pin an overruling ideological label on any one of the three political parties in the North Carolina of the 1890s.[33]

The election that returned a majority of Republicans and Populists to the North Carolina legislature also chose Daniel Russell as governor, the only Republican governor of the state between Reconstruction and the 1970s. Jeffrey Crow and Robert Durden said Russell was characterized by a "unique blend of Old South paternalism toward blacks with New South Radicalism concerning currency and railway reform." They saw his administration as offering a "viable alternative to the racial and economic dicta of the Bourbon Democrats." Endorsing a radical Populist program in the midterm of his governorship, he saw the opportunity blasted away in the vicious white supremacy campaign of 1898, which returned the legislature to Democratic control.[34]

---

lina Historical Review, LVI (Winter, 1979), 19–40; Steelman, "Vicissitudes of Republican Party Politics," and "Republican Party Strategists"; Ingle, "A Southern Democrat at Large."

32. Bode, "Religion and Class Hegemony," 438.

33. The Republicans were more apt to support electoral reform, more responsive to the blacks and the rights of women, more supportive of business, and least supportive of welfare and penal institutions. The Populists were the most supportive of anti-business legislation, the parity of silver, and restriction on the sale of liquor, and favored the public schools rather than "higher education." The Democrats were, perhaps, not quite so favorable to business as were the Republicans, favored the party of silver as much as the Populists did, and had the worst record on the rights of women and blacks. Allen W. Trelease, "The Fusion Legislatures of 1895 and 1897: A Roll-Call Analysis of the North Carolina House of Representatives," *North Carolina Historical Review*, LVII (Summer, 1980), 280–309.

34. Jeffrey J. Crow and Robert F. Durden, *Maverick Republican in the Old North State: A Political Biography of Daniel L. Russell* (Baton Rouge: Louisiana State University Press, 1977), xv. Durden has also shown how Russell in 1904 tried to embarrass the Democrats by a complicated plan by which another state would sue North Carolina for the payment of Reconstruction bonds. See his *Reconstruction Bonds &*

Robert Dean Pope, in a survey of political biographies, concluded that "in the early twentieth century it was almost impossible to find an influential Southern white man who did not want blacks removed from the political process." Russell's position was different. He endorsed Negro political participation "firmly superintended by upper-class whites."[35]

Throughout this period, it appears, blacks were pawns in the political maneuvers of all the political parties. As long as blacks had the vote, however, whites, regardless of party, looked upon them as a potential threat. White politicians sometimes minimized the influence of blacks, most of whom were Republicans, by concentrating as many of them as possible in particular districts. Eric Anderson, in a history of such a district in North Carolina, developed the theme of the paradox of black economic, social, and political progress and the degeneration of race relations.[36]

In Texas, as in North Carolina, the elements for successful fusion existed. In *Democratic Promise,* Goodwyn pointed out how white Populists made strong efforts to persuade black farmers to join the third party. Lawrence D. Rice added that blacks probably dominated the Republican party in Texas "more thoroughly" than in any other southern state and that fusion threatened Democratic control and thus brought the rallying cry "Negro domination" and the demand for disfranchisement. Essentially the same story was told by Alwyn Barr, except that he brought out more explicitly the double-talk, threats, violence, and murder perpetrated against the blacks.[37]

A particularly complicated situation existed in Louisiana, as William Ivy Hair has demonstrated in an excellent study. With findings that generally agree with Woodward and Key, Hair showed a clear dichotomy between the conservative Democrats on one hand and wage laborers and less well off farmers on the other. Alliances at-

Twentieth-Century Politics: South Dakota v. North Carolina (1904) (Durham: Duke University Press, 1962).

35. Robert Dean Pope, "Of the Man at the Center: Biographies of Southern Politicians from the Age of Segregation," in Kousser and McPherson (eds.), *Region, Race, and Reconstruction,* 101; Crow and Durden, *Maverick Republican,* 147.

36. Eric Anderson, *Race and Politics in North Carolina, 1872–1901: The Black Second* (Baton Rouge: Louisiana State University Press, 1981).

37. Lawrence D. Rice, *The Negro in Texas, 1874–1900* (Baton Rouge: Louisiana State University Press, 1971); Alwyn Barr, *Reconstruction to Reform: Texas Politics, 1876–1906* (Austin: University of Texas Press, 1971).

tempted between black and white Populists led to an attempt on the part of a ruthless Bourbon Oligarchy to disfranchise the poor of both races. Religious and ethnic differences made an already complicated situation worse. Disfranchisement occurred, and though it temporarily reduced the number of white voters, it created "havoc" with black voters. The Bourbon oligarchy won out and prevented even the kind of progressivism that was to surface in other states. The way was paved for Huey Long.[38]

Although Republicans in no other state had success as in North Carolina, Gordon B. McKinney found that between 1865 and 1900 a competitive two-party system existed in the mountain sections of Virginia, West Virginia, North Carolina, Kentucky, and Tennessee. There, Republican leaders were more effective in adapting to the needs of their constituents, glorifying their role in the Civil War, and de-emphasizing the racial issue. The Republicans, moreover, were more willing than the Democrats to support education, fight the use of convict labor, support institutions for the handicapped, and solicit government support for opening the region.[39]

Although Woodward viewed "the continued proliferation of monographs" on Jim Crow rather unhappily, the evidence is clear that no generalization about how white and black Populists worked together is safe. Perhaps the safest is that by Herbert Shapiro, who concluded that "the Populists sought Negro support but failed to make the commitments that would assure future equality between the races."[40] In the meantime, new challenges have been made to another thesis that has been associated with Woodward—that political and economic

38. William Ivy Hair, *Bourbonism and Agrarian Protest: Louisiana Politics, 1877–1900* (Baton Rouge: Louisiana State University Press, 1969). Matthew J. Schott has cautioned against putting too much emphasis upon class conflict in explaining the course of Louisiana history in the late nineteenth and twentieth centuries and urges attention to "sectional economic and cultural differences between the northern Protestant and the southern Catholic parishes" ("Class Conflict in Louisiana Voting Since 1877: Some New Perspectives," *Louisiana History*, XII [Spring, 1971], 149–65 [quotation on p. 150]).

39. Gordon B. McKinney, *Southern Mountain Republicans, 1865–1900: Politics and the Appalachian Community* (Chapel Hill: University of North Carolina Press, 1978), esp. 201–204.

40. "Introduction," in Kousser and McPherson (eds.), *Region, Race, and Reconstruction*, xxv–xxvii, xxx; Woodward, "The Strange Career of a Historical Controversy," 242; Herbert Shapiro, "The Populists and the Negro: A Reconsideration," in August Meier and Elliott Rudwick (eds.), *The Making of Black America: Essays in Negro Life and History* (2 vols.; New York: Atheneum, 1969), II, 32. See also Robert

power in the New South was dominated not by prewar planters but by men "of middle class, industrialist, capitalist outlook." This is not the place to comment in detail on the specialized studies that have treated the economy of the post-Reconstruction South.[41] It is difficult, however, to separate the economy of the South from its political economy. William J. Cooper, Jr., has, in fact, demonstrated their interrelationship while attempting to revise Woodward's concepts of the close relationship between the new Redeemer class and prewar leadership and between the Redeemers and northern capital. Cooper's study is carefully researched and persuasively argued, though some of the revisions suggested appear as much like politely offered alternatives to as deviations from Woodward's model. Jonathan Wiener has also argued that studies of southern economic development have been too much separated from politics. His connection is what Barrington Moore, Jr., called the "Prussian road to modern society," a concept implying economic development "that preserves and intensifies authoritarian, repressive social relations." Applying this concept to the South, Wiener found that the combination of poverty and the conscious political oppression of the laboring class by a continuing planter class "posed a major obstacle not only to the development of a classically capitalist growth economy, but also to liberal democracy as well."[42]

Wiener's conclusions were based principally upon a study of Alabama that appeared to show that the planter class played a strong role in the New South as well as in the Old. Wiener argued that in the New South, industrialists were fighting with planters for control, that the planters generally won out but that the threat of the Populists "finally brought the planters and industrialists together." Although Wiener made a strong case, Harold Woodman found inconsistency in the concept of the continuing planter class and of the merging of the planters and industrialists at the end of the century. By that time,

---

L. Allen, *Reluctant Reformers: Racism and Social Reform Movements in the United States* (Washington, D.C.: Howard University Press, 1974), 49–79.

41. Woodward, *Origins of the New South* (1951), 20. Harold D. Woodman has analyzed the significant economic work elsewhere and has also done so in this volume; see his "Sequel to Slavery: The New History Views the Postbellum South," *Journal of Southern History*, XLIII (November, 1977), 523–24.

42. William J. Cooper, Jr., *The Conservative Regime: South Carolina, 1877–1890* (Baltimore: Johns Hopkins Press, 1968); Jonathan M. Wiener, "Class Structure and Economic Development in the American South, 1865–1955," *American Historical Review*, LXXXIV (October, 1979), 970–92 (quotations on pp. 985, 992).

Woodman suggested, the planters were no longer pure and not necessarily "fighting to maintain their prebourgeois society."[43]

The concept of the "Prussian road" was also adopted by Dwight B. Billings, Jr., a sociologist-turned-historian.[44] Billings de-emphasized the Civil War as a significant turning point for the South and, like Wiener, found evidence that the prewar planter class continued to provide leadership in the New South. Billings' picture of populism includes a scenario of well-to-do farmers competing for political office and differs significantly from Goodwyn's class-conscious variety. The ideas are thought-provoking, but differences in origin between the textile and tobacco leadership are overlooked, and there appears to be an assumption that no fundamental differences existed between a society based on slave labor and one based on free labor.[45]

The difficulty of coming to ultimate conclusions when historians differ is shown in a review article by Numan Bartley. Bartley concluded that a fundamental ingredient in the southern economy was labor control and that labor control both before and after the Civil War was a question of race. In short, "defense of white supremacy [was] the overriding issue in southern politics." Although sympathetic to arguments of Billings and Wiener that there was a continuity of leadership between the Old and the New South, Bartley drew a fine line against Wiener, who had seen industrialists of the New South in a battle with the planters for "hegemony." In Georgia, Bart-

43. Jonathan M. Wiener, *Social Origins of the New South: Alabama, 1860–1885* (Baton Rouge: Louisiana State University Press, 1978), 5; Woodman, "Sequel to Slavery," 546–47. Woodman cites several articles by Wiener that preceded the book.

44. Whereas Wiener added a dimension of Antonio Gramsci and Eugene Genovese to Barrington Moore, Billings adds a dimension of Immanual Wallerstein and defines the South as an "economically peripheral region within the American economy" (Dwight B. Billings, Jr., *Planters and the Making of a "New South": Class, Politics, and Development in North Carolina, 1865–1900* [Chapel Hill: University of North Carolina Press, 1979], 34). Billings has developed his thesis in broad terms in a review essay in which he says, "Following Woodward, conventional accounts of southern history have interpreted the industrial 'New South' as resulting from the decline of the anti-industrial planter class and the rise of middle-class entrepreneurs and enterprises to positions of prominence. A revised model of southern development, however, contends that one cannot understand postbellum modernization apart from the centrally important class relations between planters and tenants" ("New Ways of Telling the New South Story: Numan Bartley on the Creation of Modern Georgia," *Georgia Historical Quarterly,* LXVII [Winter, 1983], 481).

45. Carl N. Degler has concluded, however, in "Rethinking Post–Civil War History," *Virginia Quarterly Review,* LVII (Spring, 1981), 250–67, that Wiener and Billings have presented enough evidence to modify significantly Woodward's thesis of discontinuity.

ley did not find "hard-driving" modernizers or serious differences between planters and industrialists; both supported the social structure
based upon segregation, a single party, and disfranchisement.[46]

For those who accept the argument of Lawrence Goodwyn, the defeat of the Populists in the 1890s was a crucial turning point. It sig-
nified the end of a promising attempt to create a truly democratic
society. McKinley's victory represented a victory of corporate capitalism, and liberals, entrapped in that culture, did little more than
tinker with the weaknesses in the system from then on. That case is
strong if the goal is some unidentified but quite different political and
economic system. Historians agree that between 1900 and 1940 a
great deal of tinkering was done. The question is whether the tinkering led to significant change, a question that is the basis of considerable historical controversy. Indeed, some historians have seriously
considered abolishing the name "Progressive Era," a name given to
the period from the 1890s to World War I by its participants. The
South has been involved in these controversies at least since Arthur
Link pointed out that the South had its progressivism too. The explo-
sion of works on southern progressivism, however, did not occur until Woodward, in *Origins of the New South,* elaborated on a theme of
Link's article "Progressivism for Whites Only." Even then the reaction was delayed, and in 1965, Dewey Grantham could cite fewer
than a dozen significant books on southern progressivism.

Between 1960 and the 1980s, however, the output was tremendous. The influence of Woodward, Key, and Link is still significant,
but George Tindall and Dewey Grantham are increasingly associated
with the subject. Tindall, in *The Emergence of the New South* (1967),
provided another prizewinning mark to shoot at and, in *The Persistent
Tradition* (1975), produced a most thought-provoking historiographical treatment. He warned of the danger of becoming ideologically involved in interpreting progressivism; found little justification for the
status-anxiety concept in the South, since most Progressive leaders

46. In the differences between Woodward and Carl Harris over the "Right Fork–
Left Fork Alliance," Bartley came down on the side of Woodward. Carl V. Harris,
"Right Fork or Left Fork? The Section-Party Alignments of Southern Democrats in
Congress, 1873–1897," *Journal of Southern History,* XLII (November, 1976), 506;
Numan V. Bartley, "Another New South?" *Georgia Historical Quarterly,* LXV (Sum-
mer, 1981), 119–37 (quotation on p. 127). I do not see, however, that Bartley has
actually refuted Harris' roll-call analysis, and James Tice Moore strongly supports
Harris in "Redeemers Reconsidered: Change and Continuity in the Democratic South,
1870–1900," *Journal of Southern History,* XLIV (August, 1978), 357–78.

"came from elements of upward mobility"; found even less evidence of progressivism being inspired by intellectual leaders; but showed more sympathy for Robert Wiebe's concept of "the search for order" in an atmosphere of "growing specialization" by a developing urban middle class inspired by "the values of 'continuity and regularity, functionality and rationality, administration and management.'"[47]

Dewey Grantham has been exploring the Progressive Era in the South from the time that he wrote a biography of Hoke Smith of Georgia in 1958. His extensive research, published in numerous thoughtful books and articles, has led him to the thesis that southern progressivism resulted from the reconciliation of progress and tradition, a thesis he then incorporated in the most important book yet published with a focus on the South in the Progressive Era. In *Southern Progressivism* (1983), he concluded that progressivism was inspired by dynamic factors such as industrialization, urbanization, otherwise-minded individuals, and the southern church. He wrestled with the paradox that there was progressivism, but no typical Progressive, and concluded that Progressives were reformers who shared interrelated values of humanitarianism, efficiency, and a morality that included a "democratic propensity" circumscribed by one-party politics and black disfranchisement. He traced the way in which these values manifested themselves in subregional and state politics. He showed how each state dealt with such topics as state regulation, prohibition, urbanization, education, and social justice and carried the theme into the 1920s. Although Grantham is fully aware of negative assessments of progressivism in recent years, his assessment is refreshingly positive. He considered that Progressives were reformers who were willing to make use of government for the general good. On the race issue, he concluded that "progressives shared the widespread convictions among white southerners that disfranchisement, segregation, and black proscription" were basically desirable. Although he gave no indication that he himself accepts such a conclusion, he might perhaps have given more weight to such arguments as those by J. Morgan Kousser or Leon Prather that southern progressivism was designed for middle-class whites only. At the same time, he properly has refused to apply late-twentieth-century standards to early-twentieth-century society. Grantham's synthesis overlaps with George Tindall's treatment of Wilson's administrations in

47. Tindall, *The Persistent Tradition*, 52–56 (first quotation on p. 52; others on p. 54).

The Emergence of the New South. Both described the legislation during those administrations, stressed the importance of southerners, and sought to explain the paradox of conservative southern congressmen providing the entering wedge for increased national power. Both saw progressivism as a "synthesis of the antithetical approaches of the Bourbons and populists." "The progressives," as Grantham put it, "were able to function both as agents of modernization and as guardians of Southern tradition."[48]

Although Grantham has provided the most comprehensive account of southern progressivism, there have been several other approaches to the general subject. Hugh Bailey, for example, described the careers of George Washington Cable, Alexander J. McKelway, Booker T. Washington, T. Thomas Fortune, Walter Hines Page, and Edgar Gardner Murphy, putting them in the setting of the issues of race relations, public education, child labor, and national politics. Bailey acknowledged that most Deep South reformers accepted race repression and that southern Progressive politicians "sustained themselves by its exploitation." But, he added, a later generation has too frequently used attitudes on race as the single measure of the reformer and has "not realized that many of the Southern social reformers were for their time and place liberal in racial matters." This is a generalization that Tindall seems not to have accepted,[49] but it could well be applied to Walter Hines Page, who has been blessed with a splendid biography by John Milton Cooper, Jr. Cooper succeeded in showing how Page throughout his years as a southern expatriate retained his "engagement" with the South and indeed played a significant role in promoting Progressive reforms while developing a rather ambivalent attitude toward race. John Cell, in a comparative

48. Dewey W. Grantham, *Southern Progressivism: The Reconciliation of Progress and Tradition* (Knoxville: University of Tennessee Press, 1983), 10, 126. In a thoughtful essay, Grantham provided a framework for what he developed in the book. See his "Review Essay: The Contours of Southern Progressivism," *American Historical Review,* LXXXVI (December, 1981), 1035–59 (quotations on pp. 1055–56).

49. Hugh C. Bailey, *Liberalism in the New South: Southern Social Reformers and the Progressive Movement* (Coral Gables: University of Miami Press, 1969), 12; see also Bailey, *Edgar Gardner Murphy: Gentle Progressive* (Coral Gables: University of Miami Press, 1968). *Cf.* Tindall, *The Persistent Tradition,* 53; and especially George M. Fredrickson, who argued that "the Southern Progressive alternative . . . constituted no real break with the fundamentals of racist ideology but attempted rather to bring the ideology into harmony with such conservative goals as law and order, social harmony, and rule by a benevolent elite" (*White Supremacy: A Comparative Study in American and South African History* [New York: Oxford University Press, 1981], 296).

study of the origins of segregation in South Africa and the American South, looked at what he called "moderate segregationists" and argued persuasively that they could insist that "if they didn't regulate the South's order of race relations," extremists would, and that, indeed, no system of white supremacy could have functioned at all "on the basis of the unyielding fanaticism of a Tillman or a Vardaman." [50]

Jack Temple Kirby provided an all-too-brief synthesis of progressivism in the South, one which Tindall in 1975 called "the best . . . that we have." Happily, Kirby understands that definitions of terms such as *progressive* and *reform* are relative matters and that the substantive content of progressivism was infinitely complex. Yet he argued that "reform ran deeper and broader in the South than in other regions . . . simply because there was so much more to do in the impoverished South." Then, he concluded, apparently not ironically, that black disfranchisement and segregation together constituted "the seminal 'progressive' reform of the era," and that with blacks controlled, other reforms, "from building better schools to closing the saloons," became possible. Thus "the darkness at the dawning," a dawning that was one of social control, of order, and of sustaining traditional values. [51]

J. Morgan Kousser, in *The Shaping of Southern Politics* (1974), takes issue with Kirby and other southern historians on this point. Kousser insisted that the Progressive Era was one of reaction and a self-serving struggle for power and that "discrimination in voting paralleled discrimination in government services." Indeed, Peter Argersinger suggested that "Kousser's Progressive South corresponds . . . with the conclusion of Gabriel Kolko and Robert Wiebe regarding the larger society: Suffrage restriction helped rationalize a chaotic political system, replace informal practices with legal regulations, and produce reforms that secured the status quo and weakened radical opposition." [52]

---

50. John Milton Cooper, Jr., *Walter Hines Page: The Southerner as American, 1855–1918* (Chapel Hill: University of North Carolina Press, 1977); Cell, *The Highest Stage of White Supremacy*, 190–91.

51. Tindall, *The Persistent Tradition*, 55; Jack Temple Kirby, *Darkness at the Dawning: Race and Reform in the Progressive South* (Philadelphia: Lippincott, 1972), 2–4. See also Allen, *Reluctant Reformers*, 81–119.

52. Kousser, *The Shaping of Southern Politics*, 229; Peter H. Argersinger, "The Southern Search for Order," *Reviews in American History*, III (June, 1975), 239. A further undergirding to the network of ideas that complicated the progressive South is Bruce Clayton, *The Savage Ideal: Intolerance and Intellectual Leadership in the South 1890–1914* (Baltimore: Johns Hopkins University Press, 1972). This is an incisive

While the Democratic party was disfranchising black people, Republicans could not agree as to the role of blacks in their party. Paul Casdorph illuminated this issue by a study of the conflict between Roosevelt and Taft forces in the South between 1912 and 1916. Roosevelt, whose personal attitude toward black people was somewhat more pragmatic than those of the typical white supremacist of the early twentieth century, by 1912 favored a lily-white southern party. Taft went along with the traditional black-and-tan participation. In a series of detailed studies of the scramble for state delegates to the Republican convention, Casdorph showed how Taft won most of the battles but concluded that Roosevelt had a legitimate complaint when only ten of the contested sixteen positions were awarded to him. Casdorph's work, though based on prodigious research, contributed little in the way of voting analysis.[53]

In state politics the Republicans were most successful in North

---

treatment of a generation of men (some of whom were treated by Bailey) who had advanced ideas on virtually all matters of social justice—save race. Indeed, their own racial prejudice and belief in segregation "helped to increase the gap between blacks and whites . . . [and] helped nourish the Savage Ideal" (p. 181). For another approach, see Milton D. Speizman, "The Movement of the Settlement House Idea into the South," *Southwestern Social Science Quarterly*, XLIV (December, 1963), 237–46.

Southern historians of the era contributed their share to nursing the Savage Ideal. According to John David Smith, they resurrected "the fundamentals of the old proslavery argument," thus justifying discrimination against black people and giving "a timely boost to southern Progressives who believed that their region would advance materially once the 'Negro problem' was settled" ("An Old Creed for the New South: Southern Historians and the Revival of the Proslavery Argument, 1890–1920," *Southern Studies*, XVIII [Spring, 1979], 76, 87).

53. Paul D. Casdorph, *Republicans, Negroes, and Progressives in the South, 1912–1916* (University: University of Alabama Press, 1981); see also Casdorph, "The 1912 Republican Presidential Campaign in Mississippi," *Journal of Mississippi History*, XXXIII (February, 1971), 1–19. As a fine example of what can be done with the same data, see Lewis L. Gould, "Theodore Roosevelt, William Howard Taft, and the Disputed Delegates in 1912: Texas as a Test Case," *Southwestern Historical Quarterly*, LXXX (July, 1976), 33–56. For a broader coverage of the relationship between blacks and the Republican party, see Richard B. Sherman, *The Republican Party and Black America: From McKinley to Hoover, 1896–1933* (Charlottesville: University Press of Virginia, 1973). For specific studies, see G. N. Green, "Republicans, Bull Moose, and Negroes in Florida, 1912," *Florida Historical Quarterly*, XLIII (October, 1964), 153–64; William F. Mugleston, "An Attempt to Break the 'Solid South,'" *Alabama Historical Quarterly*, XXXVIII (Summer, 1976), 126–36, and "The 1912 Progressive Campaign in Georgia," *Georgia Historical Quarterly*, LXI (Fall, 1977), 233–45. A little-known episode is described by Harlan Hahn in "The Republican Party Convention of 1912 and the Role of Herbert S. Hadley in National Politics," *Missouri Historical Review*, LIX (July, 1965), 407–23.

Carolina. Only there was fusion successful when it elected not only Daniel Russell as governor in 1896 but Marion Butler, a Populist, and John Pritchard, a Republican, as U.S. senators. Even though the Democrats by a skillful use of the racial issue were able to undermine the Populists and defeat the Republicans in 1898 and 1900, the Republicans, as Joseph F. Steelman pointed out in a series of articles, continued to be a threat.[54]

In the rest of the South, only in Tennessee did the Republicans meet with significant success. Paul Isaac treated the governorship of Ben Hooper, the only Republican governor between 1880 and 1920 who, owing no doubt to fusion with independent Democrats, made a record between 1910 and 1914 of prison reform, improved education, enforcement of prohibition, and regulation of business. Willard B. Gatewood, Jr., described the problems of the Republican party in Arkansas and South Carolina. In both states, the principal issue was not whether the Republicans could win elections but how to choose and control delegates who would attend party conventions.[55]

Even though the Republicans here and there made their pressure felt in the South, the real excitement during the Progressive years came from within the Democratic party. Woodward's explanation of this ferment was that the collapse of populism "brought back into the old party its disaffected left wing." The Populists brought along with

54. Joseph F. Steelman, "Jonathan Elwood Cox and North Carolina's Gubernatorial Campaign of 1908," *North Carolina Historical Review*, XLI (Autumn, 1964), 436–47, "Republicanism in North Carolina: John Motley Morehead's Campaign to Revive a Moribund Party, 1908–1910," *North Carolina Historical Review*, XLII (Spring, 1965), 153–68, "The Trials of a Republican State Chairman: John Motley Morehead and North Carolina Politics, 1910–1912," *North Carolina Historical Review*, XLIII (Winter, 1966), 31–42, and "Richmond Pearson, Roosevelt Republicans, and the Campaign of 1912 in North Carolina," *North Carolina Historical Review*, XLIII (Spring, 1966), 122–39. See also David C. Roller, "Republican Factionalism in North Carolina, 1904–1906," *North Carolina Historical Review*, XLI (Winter, 1964), 62–73.

55. Paul E. Isaac, "The Problems of a Republican Governor in a Southern State: Ben Hooper of Tennessee, 1910–1914," *Tennessee Historical Quarterly*, XXVII (Fall, 1968), 229–48; Willard B. Gatewood, Jr., "Theodore Roosevelt and Arkansas, 1901–1912," *Arkansas Historical Quarterly*, XXXII (Spring, 1973), 3–24, and "Theodore Roosevelt and Southern Republicans: The Case of South Carolina, 1901–1904," *South Carolina Historical Magazine*, LXX (October, 1969), 251–66. Richard H. Collin described the enthusiasm that still existed for Roosevelt in Louisiana before the off-year elections of 1914 but argued that he had run out of steam and did not provide effective leadership. Collin, "Theodore Roosevelt's Visit to New Orleans and the Progressive Campaign of 1914," *Louisiana History*, XII (Winter, 1971), 5–19.

them "their ideological baggage," and in hard times, according to Woodward, forged an alliance with small businessmen and an urban middle class. Their enemy was "the plutocracy of the Northeast" allied with local machines and party bosses. Such reforms as the direct primary system, then, became a means of undermining entrenched power. Woodward's interpretation remains the classic, but from one state to another, there are variations.[56]

In Alabama, for example, Sheldon Hackney insisted that "there was no continuity between Populism and Progressivism." Braxton Bragg Comer, a planter who became a merchant, businessman, and cotton manufacturer, won the governorship in 1906 largely because of his campaign to regulate the railroads. Like many other southern industrialists, he was unhappy about child-labor legislation, but he fought the machine, supported conservation and statewide prohibition, promoted government services and a tax system that shifted the tax burden to "those most able to pay." Hackney made a strong point that Alabama progressivism was *sui generis.*[57]

A hero quite different from Comer, the demagogue type, emerged from the Arkansas of the Progressive Era. Jeff Davis, a practicing lawyer with a law degree who was elected governor in 1900, was a virulent racist who constantly appealed to class interests. Richard Niswonger, using Davis as an example, argued that the southern demagogue "despite limitations and bigotry, served a useful purpose" in rallying "the common white man . . . to storm the battlements of the Conservatives." Cal R. Ledbetter, Jr., added a psychological dimension in describing Davis as a campaigner who had no peer in the use of invective, ridicule, and character assassination yet as a governor promoted schools for the deaf and the blind, hospitals for the mentally ill, and railroad regulation.[58]

56. Woodward, *Origins of the New South* (1951), 371–72.

57. Hackney, *Populism to Progressivism,* 278 (first quotation), 312 (second quotation), 329–32. But see Kousser, "The 'New Political History,'" 1–14. See also Tennant S. McWilliams, *Hannis Taylor: The New Southerner as an American* (University: University of Alabama Press, 1978); Allen W. Jones, "Political Reforms of the Progressive Era," *Alabama Review,* XXI (July, 1968), 173–94, and "Political Reform and Party Factionalism in the Deep South: Alabama's 'Dead Shoes' Senatorial Primary of 1906," *Alabama Review,* XXVI (January, 1973), 3–32.

58. Cal R. Ledbetter, Jr., "Jeff Davis and the Politics of Combat," *Arkansas Historical Quarterly,* XXXIII (Spring, 1974), 16–37, and "The Constitutional Convention of 1917–1918," *Arkansas Historical Quarterly,* XXXIV (Spring, 1975), 3–40; Richard L. Niswonger, "A Study in Southern Demagoguery: Jeff Davis of Arkansas," *Arkansas*

Florida in the Progressive Era had a combination of demagoguery and statesmanship. Two of its governors came from backgrounds quite different from those of either Comer or Davis. Napoleon Bonaparte Broward, a sailor, riverfront man, and onetime filibuster, was elected governor in 1904, fought the railroads, and defended the public lands in a relatively dignified fashion. The demagogue Sidney J. Catts had an equally bizarre background. Owner of a large plantation, a fundamentalist minister with a law degree from Cumberland University, and a traveling insurance salesman, he was elected governor in 1916. He took a strong position in favor of labor unions (not characteristic of southern governors), supported penal reforms, public health programs, increased funds for education, and woman suffrage. The state ratified the Eighteenth Amendment with his blessing. This paradoxical character remained a disturbing factor in Florida's political life by combining racism and bigotry largely directed against Roman Catholics. Wayne Flynt, in a detailed, carefully researched biography, saw Catts as the "clerical messiah" symbolizing "an entire genre of 'reform' . . . the enigmatic demagogue who voices the frustrations of inarticulate white Protestants."[59]

Flynt has written another informative biography of a different type of southern politician—Duncan U. Fletcher, "a reluctant Progressive," who served as U.S. senator from Florida from 1919 until his death in 1936. A law graduate of Vanderbilt University and a practicing lawyer with a "compassion for the underdog," Fletcher went so far as to promote coalitions including blacks and union members. He distrusted the Populists, however, and became a "straight out" Democrat favoring the regulation of railroads and corporations. As a senator he supported Wilson's New Freedom, was a conservative in the 1920s, but turned New Dealer in the 1930s.[60]

Historical Quarterly, XXXIX (Summer, 1980), 114; Rod Farmer, "Direct Democracy in Arkansas, 1910–1918," *Arkansas Historical Quarterly*, XL (Summer, 1981), 99–118. Davis later was an ineffective U.S. senator.

59. Samuel Proctor, *Napoleon Bonaparte Broward: Florida's Fighting Democrat* (Gainesville: University of Florida Press, 1950); Wayne Flynt, *Cracker Messiah: Governor Sidney J. Catts of Florida* (Baton Rouge: Louisiana State University Press, 1977), xiii, 341. See also Flynt (ed.), "William V. Knott and the Gubernatorial Campaign of 1916," *Florida Historical Quarterly*, LI (April, 1973), 423–30.

60. Wayne Flynt, *Duncan Upshaw Fletcher: Dixie's Reluctant Progressive* (Tallahassee: Florida State University Press, 1971). Flynt has also pointed out the strengths of labor unions in the urban areas in "Pensacola Labor Problems and Political Radicalism, 1908," *Florida Historical Quarterly*, XLIII (April, 1965), 315–32.

While most of the seminal writing on southern progressivism came after 1965, in Georgia the lines had already been clearly drawn by Woodward's *Tom Watson* (1938) and Grantham's *Hoke Smith* (1958). Although their interpretations are unlikely to be changed significantly, gaps are being filled. Alton D. Jones suggested that in the brilliance of the careers of Watson and Hoke Smith, it is possible to overlook a perfectly respectable governor whose record was mildly progressive. He pointed to the governorship of Joseph M. Terrell, whom Smith succeeded. Jones performed the astonishing feat of not mentioning Negroes in a twenty-page article on a period when blacks were very active indeed. The blacks of the period have in fact received a first-rate study by John Dittmer, whose research was exhaustive and included personal interviews. With few exceptions, studies of southern progressivism describe blacks only as victims of white oppression. Victims they were, but Dittmer pointed out that of the one million blacks in Georgia in 1900, many were property owners, literate, and courageous. Horribly persecuted, "they fought back at all levels."[61]

Although West Virginia was a state topographically and demographically different from the other southern states, many of the same conditions that inspired the Progressive reformers elsewhere existed there. In two articles, Nicholas C. Burckel described how the state was controlled by conservative political and business interests and how tension developed between two moderately Progressive governors, Albert B. White and William M. O. Dawson (both previously journalists), and Senator Stephen B. Elkins (closely associated with mines, banks, and railroads).[62]

Burckel managed to write about these two governors without becoming entangled with labor problems, which must have been boiling beneath the surface, since their successors, William E. Glasscock and Henry D. Hatfield, confronted what David A. Corbin has described in a prizewinning article as "one of the more violent labor wars in American history." While rather incidentally bringing out the antilabor policies of the two governors, Corbin concentrated his at-

---

61. Alton DuMar Jones, "The Administration of Governor Joseph M. Terrell Viewed in the Light of the Progressive Movement," *Georgia Historical Quarterly*, XLVIII (September, 1964), 271–90; *cf.* Charles Crowe, "Racial Violence and Social Reform—Origins of the Atlanta Riot of 1906," *Journal of Negro History*, LIII (July, 1968), 234–56; Dittmer, *Black Georgia in the Progressive Era*, xi.

62. Nicholas C. Burckel, "Governor Albert B. White and the Beginning of Progressive Reform, 1901–05," *West Virginia History*, XL (Fall, 1978), 1–12, and "Publiciz-

tention on the role of Eugene V. Debs in the strike and concluded that Debs sold out the strikers and the local socialists.[63]

Burckel also wrote a series of articles on Kentucky during the Progressive Era. He found that "progressive reformers did not emerge . . . until the fear of free silver, the specter of black political control, and the anti-immigrant agitation of the nativists dissipated." From 1911 to 1919, however, Governor James B. McCreary and Augustus O. Stanley fought the American Tobacco Company and the United States Steel Corporation and endorsed programs that embodied the direct primary, workman's compensation, improved education, regulation of industry and railroads, and antilobby laws.[64]

A particularly complicated political situation, typical of the state,

---

ing Progressivism: William M. O. Dawson," *West Virginia History,* XLII (Spring-Summer, 1981), 222–48.

63. David A. Corbin, "Betrayed in the West Virginia Coal Fields: Eugene V. Debs and the Socialist Party of America, 1912–1914," *Journal of American History,* LXIV (March, 1978), 987–1009 (quotation on p. 990). See also Gary J. Tucker, "William E. Glasscock and the West Virginia Election of 1910," *West Virginia History,* XL (Spring, 1979), 254–67. The problem of interpretation is suggested by Carolyn Karr, who concluded, in referring to Henry Hatfield, that "with the exception of Charles Evans Hughes, Robert LaFollette, and Woodrow Wilson, few governors have achieved as much in so little time" ("A Political Biography of Henry Hatfield," *West Virginia History,* XXVIII [October, 1966], 35–63, and [January, 1967], 137–70 [quotation on p. 158]). See also Lucy Lee Fisher, "John J. Cornwell, Governor of West Virginia, 1917–1921," *West Virginia History,* XXIV (April, 1963), 258–88, and (July, 1963), 370–89.

64. Nicholas C. Burckel, "William Goebel and the Campaign for Railroad Regulation in Kentucky, 1888–1900," *Filson Club Historical Quarterly,* XLVIII (January, 1974), 43–60, "From Beckham to McCreary: The Progressive Record of Kentucky Governors," *Register of the Kentucky Historical Society,* LXXVI (October, 1978), 285–306 (quotation on p. 286), and "A. O. Stanley and Progressive Reform, 1902–1919," *Register of the Kentucky Historical Society,* LXXIX (Spring, 1981), 136–61. See also Gerald S. Grinde, "Politics and Scandal in the Progressive Era: Alben W. Barkley and the McCracken County Campaign of 1909," *Filson Club Historical Quarterly,* L (April, 1976), 36–51. Burckel has written on progressivism in Maryland, how it came gradually to the Old Line State, appearing first in Baltimore, then expanding to the state, and beginning with the minority Republican party, then capturing a significant portion of the Democratic party. Austin Lane Crothers, farmer, teacher, graduate of the law school at the University of Maryland, practicing lawyer, and public official, "more than any other governor succeeded in achieving the progressive reforms for which individuals and groups had unsuccessfully agitated in the past" ("Governor Austin Lane Crothers and Progressive Reform in Maryland, 1908–1912," *Maryland Historical Magazine,* LXXVI [Summer, 1981], 184–201 [quotation on p. 184]). Burckel's articles are carefully researched and tell clearly what happened, though they lack analysis as to why things happened the way they did.

characterized Louisiana during the Progressive Era. Although there has been no full-scale treatment of that period, Matthew J. Schott has made an excellent beginning. He found himself in theoretical agreement with Samuel P. Hays's thesis of reform by the upper classes largely for their own benefit and in partial agreement with J. Morgan Kousser's thesis, which Schott described as "electoral reform . . . motivated and influenced by upper-class, elite reformers with undemocratic attitudes and goals." Schott showed how John M. Parker, businessman, governor in 1920, and "the man most prominently associated with Louisiana progressivism," endorsed political reforms that might have been intended both to eliminate corruption and inefficiency and to undermine the influence of the "lower classes." Although Parker's moralistic attitude was clearly undemocratic, he and his business friends "did not generally advocate racial disfranchisement." The Democratic machine centered in New Orleans, on the other hand, wanted "to protect the voting rights of the white poor and illiterates, a substantial number of whom were Italian immigrants." [65]

A historical framework for Mississippi progressivism was drawn early by A. D. Kirwan's *Revolt of the Rednecks*. Published in 1951, the same year as *Origins of the New South,* and described by Dewey Grantham in 1965 as a model for other state studies, Kirwan's book treated the governorships of James K. Vardaman and Theodore G. Bilbo—both extreme racists distinguished by the uninhibited violence of their public utterances. Vardaman continued to challenge biographers because of the way in which he shifted political alliances. In the late nineteenth century, he was part of the Bourbon establishment and fought the Populists; then he broke with the establishment and as governor supported regulation of railroads, increased state support for schools, roads, and charitable institutions, and penal reform. Admitting that lynching was demoralizing, he advocated it in the case of Negro men who were believed to have raped white

65. Matthew J. Schott, "Progressives Against Democracy: Electoral Reform in Louisiana, 1894–1912," *Louisiana History*, XX (Summer, 1979), 247–60 (quotation on p. 253). Schott further develops the theme of the complexity of progressivism in New Orleans and argues that "the sinister aspects of the city machine and its role as part of an oligarchy" have been exaggerated ("The New Orleans Machine and Progressivism," *Louisiana History*, XXIV [Spring, 1983], 142). A somewhat different point is made by Adam Fairclough, who described a comfortable relationship between the business elite of New Orleans and the Democratic politicians ("The Public Utilities Industry in New Orleans: A Study in Capital, Labor and Government, 1894–1929," *Louisiana History*, XXII [Winter, 1981], 45–65).

women—so long as the mobs lynched their victims as quickly and simply as possible. William F. Holmes has gone far toward meeting the biographical challenge while making the complexities of Mississippi politics understandable. His thesis is simple: the "great white chief" used those issues of southern progressivism that appealed to the rural whites of northeastern and southern Mississippi. Although Vardaman sought political power, Holmes concluded that he was sincere even in his most extreme views.[66]

More unpleasant than Vardaman as an individual was Theodore Bilbo, about whom George Tindall commented that "no other leader of the plebeian masses in the teens had either a program or a record to equal his." The principal biography (since Kirwan's) is that by A. Wigfall Green, *The Man Bilbo* (1963), a lively, short study that clearly brings out the extremism of Bilbo's racism but does not put it in context or make clear why Mississippi voters kept electing him to office. In 1981, Vincent A. Giroux, Jr., partly answered that question. While admitting a constructive first session as governor, Giroux claimed that Bilbo gained popular support by playing on fears and prejudices and "providing scapegoats." Moreover, Giroux concluded, "during his twelve years as governor or lieutenant governor, the state government had accomplished little."[67]

North Carolina's governors have not had the same reputation for

66. Albert D. Kirwan, *Revolt of the Rednecks: Mississippi Politics, 1876–1925* (Lexington: University of Kentucky Press, 1951); William F. Holmes, "James K. Vardaman and Prison Reform in Mississippi," *Journal of Mississippi History,* XXVII (August, 1965), 229–48, "James K. Vardaman: From Bourbon to Agrarian Reformer," *Journal of Mississippi History,* XXXI (May, 1969), 97–115, and *The White Chief: James Kimble Vardaman* (Baton Rouge: Louisiana State University Press, 1970). See also Holmes, "Whitecapping: Agrarian Violence in Mississippi, 1902–1906," *Journal of Southern History,* XXXV (May, 1969), 165–85; and Nannie Pitts McLemore, "James K. Vardaman: A Mississippi Progressive," *Journal of Mississippi History,* XXIX (February, 1967), 1–11.

67. Tindall, *The Emergence of the New South,* 25; A. Wigfall Green, *The Man Bilbo* (Baton Rouge: Louisiana State University Press, 1963); Vincent A. Giroux, Jr., "The Rise of Theodore G. Bilbo (1908–1932)," *Journal of Mississippi History,* XLIII (August, 1981), 180–209 (quotations on pp. 180, 205); William D. McCain, "Theodore Gilmore Bilbo and the Mississippi Delta," *Journal of Mississippi History,* XXXI (February, 1969), 1–27; Wilmuth Saunders Rutledge, "The John J. Henry–Theodore G. Bilbo Encounter, 1911," *Journal of Mississippi History,* XXXIV (November, 1972), 357–72; John R. Skates, Jr., "Journalist vs. Politician: Fred Sullens and Theodore G. Bilbo," *Southern Quarterly,* VIII (April, 1970), 273–86. Martha Bigelow suggested that Governor Edmund F. Noel deserves more attention ("Mississippi Progressivism," *Journal of Mississippi History,* XXIX [August, 1967], 202–209).

violent racism as those of Mississippi, but appearances can be deceiving. Although V. O. Key concluded that "an economic oligarchy has held sway" in the first fifty years of the century, his assessment of North Carolina progressivism was favorable. He added that "the modern era dates from the administration of . . . Charles Brantley Aycock" as governor in 1900 and that, though Aycock stood for disfranchisement, "he and North Carolina did not exclude the black man from the universe." Aycock's reputation, however, has slipped. Oliver H. Orr, Jr., Aycock's skillful biographer, made clear that Aycock was a white supremacist who believed that political progress was possible only by eliminating the Negro from politics, and Joseph Steelman showed that efforts for constitutional reform were flavored with racism; in 1914, moreover, conservative Democrats quashed an extraordinary movement within the party for extensive reforms.[68] Even more persuasively, J. Morgan Kousser, in a brilliant article, questioned even the much-touted education reform: "School taxes for whites were higher among blacks than whites." "In North Carolina education at least," he concluded, "'progressivism' was, as a consequence of disfranchisement, for middle-class whites only."[69]

Kousser's pessimistic assessment is even more sweepingly stated by H. Leon Prather, Jr. Prather too insisted that "in several ways, southern progressivism was a myth" and that "reform measures benefited the middle classes most." He described Aycock as "more a friend to the 'tax dodging corporations' than to public education" and ac-

---

68. Key, *Southern Politics*, 211, 208. Oliver H. Orr, Jr., *Charles Brantley Aycock* (Chapel Hill: University of North Carolina Press, 1961). Joseph L. Morrison's two books on Josephus Daniels portray another example of the southern Progressive who preached white supremacy (*Josephus Daniels says . . . : An Editor's Political Odyssey From Bryan to Wilson and F.D.R., 1894–1913* [Chapel Hill: University of North Carolina Press, 1962], and *Josephus Daniels: The Small-d Democrat* [Chapel Hill: University of North Carolina Press, 1966]). Joseph F. Steelman, "The Progressive Democratic Convention of 1914 in North Carolina," *North Carolina Historical Review*, XLVI (Spring, 1969), 83–104, "Edward J. Justice: Profile of a Progressive Legislator, 1899–1913," *North Carolina Historical Review*, XLVIII (Spring, 1971), 148–60, and "Origins of the Campaign for Constitutional Reform in North Carolina, 1912–1913," *North Carolina Historical Review*, LVI (Autumn, 1979), 396–418.

69. J. Morgan Kousser, "Progressivism—For Middle-Class Whites Only: North Carolina Education, 1880–1910," *Journal of Southern History*, XLVI (May, 1980), 169–94 (quotation on p. 192). Steelman finds some agitation for legal reform in North Carolina, but he questioned whether there was any overwhelming demand for reform within the legal profession. Steelman, "Progressivism and Agitation for Legal Reform in North Carolina, 1897–1917," *East Carolina College Publications in History*, I (1964), 77–93.

cused the Democrats of failing "miserably" in providing education to the white illiterates and of trying to ignore the blacks. Yet, while denouncing the politicians, Prather praised the educational leaders Charles D. McIver, James Y. Joyner, Eugene C. Brooks, and Charles Coon, who "laid a solid foundation" for a "democratic school system" and provided "the most discernible and outstanding achievement of southern progressivism."[70]

Frederick A. Bode added a religious dimension to Key's concept of the "economic oligarchy" behind progressivism in North Carolina. Using Antonio Gramsci's concept of hegemony, Bode argued that certain elements in the churches, personified by Josiah W. Bailey, editor of the *Baptist Biblical Recorder,* and John Carlisle Kilgo, president of (Methodist) Trinity College, were "proposing an important ideological shift for the churches: the severing of certain ties to pre-industrial society and the securing of others to the progressive capitalism of the New South."[71]

South Carolina in the Progressive Era produced the two types of southern Progressive governors. Coleman L. Blease could be compared to Vardaman and Bilbo in the vitriol of his rhetoric but not in the record of positive accomplishment of either of the Mississippians. Indeed, Blease fought against those backing Progressive causes, perhaps because, as Clarence Stone reminded us, he believed that child-labor laws, compulsory education, and other so-called reforms would deprive many poor white families of badly needed income. Blease has earned few plaudits from historians, but Robert Milton Burts, in a scholarly biography, showed how another South Carolina governor, Richard I. Manning, a scion of a planter family and a successful lawyer and businessman, made a record that George Tindall described as "an almost complete muster roll of progressive reforms." In the pro-

---

70. H. Leon Prather, Jr., *Resurgent Politics and Educational Progressivism in the New South: North Carolina, 1890–1913* (Rutherford, N.J.: Fairleigh Dickinson University Press, 1979), quotations on pp. 277–83. For a defense of Aycock, see John Herbert Roper, "Charles Brantley Aycock: A Study in Limitation and Possibility," *Southern Studies,* XVI (Fall, 1977), 277–91.

71. Frederick A. Bode, *Protestantism and the New South: North Carolina Baptists and Methodists in Political Crisis, 1894–1903* (Charlottesville: University Press of Virginia, 1975), esp. 1–2, 6–7, 67, 159. A different approach to the "governing class" is found in Samuel M. Kipp III, "Old Notables and Newcomers: The Economic and Political Elite of Greensboro, North Carolina, 1880–1920," *Journal of Southern History,* XLIII (August, 1977), 373–94. Kipp sees "a new, relatively unified local elite" (p. 394) resulting from the rapid urbanization of small towns, such as Greensboro, and dominating politics, business, religion, and in general other social functions.

cess, Manning rarely resorted to white supremacy to rouse his supporters, a point that Burts passed over rather casually.[72]

The case of Oklahoma during the Progressive Era is unique and has been blessed with thoughtful historical investigation. Not a state until 1907, by 1912 it had "the strongest Socialist state organization in the nation." Danney Goble's *Progressive Oklahoma* (1980), based almost entirely on documents available in Oklahoma, develops persuasively the two propositions that "the reform movement that ushered in the twentieth century appeared at the state level before making itself known in national affairs" and that the Oklahoma Constitution of 1907 was "a particularly lucid example of Progressive reform." Goble summarized the history of the territory and assessed the hostile responses to business that culminated in the constitutional convention.[73]

Several other excellent studies explore the emergence and rapid expansion of socialism in the first two decades of the twentieth century. Garin Burbank, for example, admitting to having been influenced by E. P. Thompson, was fascinated by "the experience of the Oklahomans who were trying to become socialists in the midst of the mobilized biases of liberal capitalism."[74] In the process, he posed the question, "Did the local socialists of Oklahoma acquire the 'proletarian perspective'?" Burbank seems to say no. Particularly when it came to landholding, he found, few Oklahoma socialists opted for a

72. Clarence N. Stone, "Bleaseism and the 1912 Election in South Carolina," *North Carolina Historical Review*, XL (Winter, 1963), 54–74; see also Daniel W. Hollis, "Samuel Chiles Mitchell, Social Reformer in Blease's South Carolina," *South Carolina Historical Magazine*, LXX (January, 1969), 20–37; Robert Milton Burts, *Richard Irvine Manning and the Progressive Movement in South Carolina* (Columbia: University of South Carolina Press, 1974); Tindall, *The Emergence of the New South*, 22.

73. James R. Green, *Grass-Roots Socialism: Radical Movements in the Southwest, 1895–1943* (Baton Rouge: Louisiana State University Press, 1978), xi; Danney Goble, *Progressive Oklahoma: The Making of a New Kind of State* (Norman: University of Oklahoma Press, 1980), ix–x. See also Charles Wayne Ellinger, "Political Obstacles Barring Oklahoma's Admission to Statehood, 1890–1906," *Great Plains Journal*, III (Spring, 1964), 60–83, and "The Drive for Statehood in Oklahoma, 1889–1906," *Chronicles of Oklahoma*, XLI (Spring, 1963), 15–37; and George O. Carney, "Oklahoma's House Delegation in the Sixty-first Congress: Progressive or Conservative?" *Chronicles of Oklahoma*, LV (Summer, 1977), 190–210.

74. Garin Burbank, *When Farmers Voted Red: The Gospel of Socialism in the Oklahoma Countryside, 1910–1924* (Westport, Conn.: Greenwood Press, 1976), xiii, 188. See also Burbank, "The Disruption and Decline of the Oklahoma Socialist Party," *Journal of American Studies*, VII (August, 1973), 133–52.

cooperative commonwealth. Nor were they persuaded by any theory of class conflict to accept racial cooperation and to abandon the conception of whites' being superior to blacks. At the same time, Burbank insisted that "impoverished farmers" were hostile to "the politics of ethnic and moral bigotry" and associated consciously with nonagricultural workers and oppressed groups.[75]

James R. Green takes a different position on the ideological purity of the Oklahoma socialists in a brilliant study of socialism in the states of Oklahoma, Texas, Louisiana, and Arkansas. Like Burbank, Green acknowledged the influence of E. P. Thompson. His work also suggested similarities and differences between the socialists and Goodwyn's Populists. He found the same enthusiasm and network of organizers but not the kind of ideological base that the Populists had in the Alliances. Green's main point is that there was "a new kind of class struggle in the Southwest . . . that united the rural producers—indebted yeomen and landless tenants—against the 'parasites' in the towns and cities" yet was also attached "firmly to the . . . principles of Marxian socialism."[76]

Although socialism made its mark also on Texas, traditional politics was more characteristic of that state. Evan Anders has shown how Progressive insurgents battled conservative Democrats for control of Texas politics during the first two decades of the twentieth century. The Texas Progressives agitated for government regulation of corporations, a fairer distribution of the tax burden, and, most important, the elimination of political corruption. Anders pointed particularly to the south Texas counties where corruption, violence, and "a loose coalition of Democratic machines dominated." Unlike Hackney in Alabama, Alwyn Barr found links between Populist and Progressive leadership. As in other southern states, Barr saw businessmen and reformers, individually and in groups, combining to promote "re-

75. Burbank, *When Farmers Voted Red*, xv, and "Agrarian Radicals and Their Opponents: Political Conflict in Southern Oklahoma, 1910–1924," *Journal of American History*, LVIII (June, 1971), 23. Another angle on the study of Oklahoma in the period is provided in articles by Keith L. Bryant, Jr., who focuses on the role of organized labor in a laboratory of progressive experimentation. See Bryant, "Kate Barnard, Organized Labor, and Social Justice in Oklahoma During the Progressive Era," *Journal of Southern History*, XXXV (May, 1969), 145–64, and "Labor in Politics: The Oklahoma State Federation of Labor During the Age of Reform," *Labor History*, XI (Summer, 1970), 259–76.

76. Green, *Grass-Roots Socialism*, xvii, xiv. See also G. Gregory Kiser, "The Socialist Party in Arkansas, 1900–1912," *Arkansas Historical Quarterly*, XL (Summer, 1981), 119–53.

form" while being equally convinced that the electoral system would be purified by disfranchising blacks, Mexicans, and landless whites. This clearly written monograph pays careful attention to racial, cultural, regional, and class issues, but it does not make use of the more esoteric statistical tools that distinguish Hackney's analysis. As in other states, at least one governor, the successful lawyer and railroad operator Thomas M. Campbell, fought the bosses and succeeded in promoting antitrust enactments, tax reforms, and electoral reforms—all, to be sure, in a context of Mexican and black disfranchisement.[77]

Political machines have likewise been the focus of much of the historiography on progressivism in Virginia. A key question is how much further than the reform of machine politics were Virginia Progressives willing to go. Raymond H. Pulley, in *Old Virginia Restored* (1968), adopts what appears to be the "consensus" approach to Virginia politics. Instead of stressing the "rancor and acrimony" that characterized the factional squabbles revolving around the organization dominated by Thomas S. Martin, Claude A. Swanson, and Henry D. Flood, Pulley pointed to the "progressive peace" given by Democrats under the flag of black disfranchisement, the one-party system, and the gentility of Old Virginia, but at a high cost to political democracy.[78]

Other writings suggest something less than "progressive peace" and give no clear indication of a statewide Progressive movement. Andrew Buni, for example, argued that many Democrats and Repub-

77. James R. Green, "Tenant Farmer Discontent and Socialist Protest in Texas, 1901–1917," *Southwestern Historical Quarterly*, LXXXI (October, 1977), 133–54; Graham Adams, Jr., "Agrarian Discontent in Progressive Texas," *East Texas Historical Journal*, VIII (March, 1970), 24–28; Evan Anders, *Boss Rule in South Texas: The Progressive Era* (Austin: University of Texas Press, 1982), and "Boss Rule and Constituent Interests: South Texas Politics During the Progressive Era," *Southwestern Historical Quarterly*, LXXXIV (January, 1981), 269–92 (quotation on p. 269); Barr, *Reconstruction to Reform*. An equally conventional and equally significant volume is Rupert N. Richardson's study of the early career of Colonel House and the Wilson movement in Texas culminating in House's emerging with most of the patronage (*Colonel Edward M. House: The Texas Years, 1858–1912*, Hardin-Simmons University Publications in History, I [Abilene, Tex., 1964]). Janet Schmelzer, "Thomas M. Campbell: Progressive Governor of Texas," *Red River Valley Historical Review*, III (Fall, 1978), 52–63.

78. Raymond H. Pulley, *Old Virginia Restored: An Interpretation of the Progressive Impulse, 1870–1930* (Charlottesville: University Press of Virginia, 1968). See also Pulley, "The May Movement of 1899: Irresolute Progressivism in the Old Dominion," *Virginia Magazine of History and Biography*, LXXV (April, 1967), 186–201; and Tindall, *The Persistent Tradition*, 55.

licans expected Negro disfranchisement to open the way to the re-establishment of the two-party system in Virginia, and he showed how race continued to be used as an issue in spite of disfranchisement. William Larsen's biography of Andrew J. Montague provides evidence for a consensus interpretation in suggesting that the Democrats rather effectively took over Populist goals without disrupting the party. Moreover, Larsen found that Montague, who had come "as close as any contestant to displacing a major leader of the machine in a direct contest," stood for a way of life redolent of the Old South. In spite of all that, however, confrontations took place, and Montague's governorship was only moderately successful because of the bitter opposition of the organization, which no doubt recognized that the principal planks in Montague's program—direct election of senators, electoral reform, and improved education—were designed to combat entrenched political leaders. Larsen put Montague in "the mainstream" of southern progressivism—beyond the mainstream, it appears, since he even looked forward to the enfranchisement of educated Negroes.[79]

Whereas Montague's background was classics and law, Westmoreland Davis' was scientific agriculture. Jack Temple Kirby, in a biography much praised for its research and analysis of the Virginia political scene, shows how Davis and his friends welded a political organization from disparate elements (planters, professionals, rural businessmen, and urban wets) to defeat the machine in 1917. He then succeeded in doing what the "business progressives" aimed at doing—creating a more efficient government around an executive budget, putting able men into office, and improving the prison system.[80]

Historians have found even less evidence of a statewide Progressive movement in Tennessee than in Virginia. This lack of a statewide movement may be explained by the way in which the best-known ma-

79. Andrew Buni, *The Negro in Virginia Politics, 1902–1965* (Charlottesville: University Press of Virginia, 1967), 254–55. See also Wythe W. Holt, Jr., "The Virginia Constitutional Convention of 1901–1902: A Reform Movement Which Lacked Substance," *Virginia Magazine of History and Biography*, LXXVI (January, 1968), 67–102, for a fine analysis of the Daniels-Martin-Flood relationship. William E. Larsen, *Montague of Virginia: The Making of a Southern Progressive* (Baton Rouge: Louisiana State University Press, 1965), 289, 298.

80. Jack Temple Kirby, *Westmoreland Davis: Virginia Planter-Politician, 1859–1942* (Charlottesville: University Press of Virginia, 1968), and "Alcohol and Irony: The Campaign of Westmoreland Davis for Governor, 1909–1917," *Virginia Magazine of History and Biography*, LXXIII (July, 1965), 259–79.

chine in the South, that of Edward H. Crump, confused the issue by its relationship to the city of Memphis. William D. Miller clarified the confusion somewhat not only in a history of progressivism in Memphis but in a biography of Crump. Like so many other political figures of the day, Crump had a somewhat anomalous relationship to progressivism. He first came into office as mayor in 1909 on a platform of eliminating corruption in city government and developing public power, thus earning the hostility of private utilities. His influence in Memphis continued until his death in 1954. Miller described him as a kind of benevolent despot, and Allen Kitchens went even further, asserting that "Crump turned Memphis from an uncongealed mass of confusion, political disorder, chaos, waste, and corruption into a proud, clean, modern, healthy, and well-run city." J. Joseph Huthmacher, on the other hand, described the Crump organization as "one of the most repressive urban machines in recent American history."[81]

This state-by-state survey of the historical writings about southern progressivism since 1965 has so far ignored one of the principal breakthroughs of that period—the acceptance of prohibition by historians as a legitimate facet of the Progressive Era. As George Tindall put it in 1967, "For the better part of three decades prohibition and progressivism usually traveled the same road." David E. Kyvig later added, "The legal ban on alcoholic beverages represented one of the most significant measures adopted during the early-twentieth-

81. J. M. Shahan, "The Rhetoric of Reform: The 1906 Gubernatorial Race in Tennessee," *Tennessee Historical Quarterly,* XXXV (Spring, 1976), 65–82; William R. Majors, "A Re-Examination of V. O. Key's *Southern Politics in State and Nation:* The Case of Tennessee," *East Tennessee Historical Society Publications,* XLIX (1977), 120–22, 127, 129; William D. Miller, *Memphis During the Progressive Era, 1900–1917* (Madison: American Research Center, 1957), and *Mr. Crump of Memphis* (Baton Rouge: Louisiana State University Press, 1964); Allen H. Kitchens, "Ouster of Mayor Edward H. Crump, 1915–1916," *West Tennessee Historical Society Papers,* XIX (1965), 119–20 (quotation on p. 120). Lester C. Lamon noted an exception to Woodward's generalization in "Progressivism Was Not 'For Whites Only': The Black Progressive Reformers of Nashville, Tennessee, 1906–1918," *Indiana Academy of the Social Sciences: Proceedings,* IX (1974), 103–12. J. Joseph Huthmacher, Review of Miller's *Mr. Crump of Memphis,* in *American Historical Review,* LXX (July, 1965), 1258. A thought-provoking comparative case study of an aspect of progressivism in Tennessee is Margaret Ripley Wolfe's *Lucius Polk Brown and Progressive Food and Drug Control: Tennessee and New York City, 1908–1920* (Lawrence: Regents Press of Kansas, 1978). See also Wolfe, "Lucius Polk Brown: Tennessee Pure Food and Drug Inspector, 1908–1915," *Tennessee Historical Quarterly,* XXIX (Spring, 1970), 62–78.

century outburst of reform." Several authors, in fact, have provided careful, serious treatments of the national crusade, but these authors do not agree as to the motivation of the prohibitionists. Class seemed at times to be involved, as did at other times ethnic, sectional, rural, religious, urban/rural, broadly cultural, and psychological factors. Indeed, Jack S. Blocker, Jr.'s fascinating but rather speculative conclusions find class and ethnicity as the significant factors combined with a middle-class concern about status, all presented in a tone reminiscent of the New Left's attitude toward corporate capitalism.[82]

The danger of pronouncing any generalization on prohibition that could be applied to all the states is clearly demonstrated by Lewis Gould's study of prohibitionists in Texas (1973). In a brilliantly argued work, Gould supported the proposition that prohibition was not "cranky and narrow bigotry" but a legitimate element in Progressive reform. Finding that ethnocultural pressures were essential factors in the coming of prohibition in Texas, he nonetheless showed that a strong element was rural people's fear of the cities. Texas politics during the Progressive Era had similarities to and differences from other southern states. The racism and lack of attention to rural poverty were there, and battles over corporate regulation ended early in the century. Prohibition, however, was the only significant issue dividing the Democratic party after about 1910, and the prohibitionists considered that their position made them the progressives. State, even federal, power could be justified in stamping out the evils associated with drunkenness and the saloon. Gould went beyond a mere analysis of the story of prohibition. He explained the phenomenon of James E. ("Pa") Ferguson and Miriam A. ("Ma") Ferguson and provided a base for understanding the equally complex state politics of the 1920s.[83]

---

82. Tindall, *The Emergence of the New South*, 20; David E. Kyvig, *Repealing National Prohibition* (Chicago: University of Chicago Press, 1979), xi, xii; Joseph R. Gusfield, *Symbolic Crusade: Status Politics and the American Temperance Movement* (Urbana: University of Illinois Press, 1963), and "Prohibition: The Impact of Political Utopianism," in John Braeman et al. (eds.), *Change and Continuity in Twentieth-Century America: The 1920's* (Columbus: Ohio State University Press, 1968), 257–308; James H. Timberlake, *Prohibition and the Progressive Movement, 1900–1920* (Cambridge: Harvard University Press, 1963); J. C. Burnham, "New Perspectives on the Prohibition 'Experiment' of the 1920's," *Journal of Social History*, II (Fall, 1968), 51–68; J. C. Furnas, *The Life and Times of the Late Demon Rum* (New York: G. P. Putnam's Sons, 1965), provides a jocular approach; Jack S. Blocker, Jr., *Retreat From Reform: The Prohibition Movement in the United States, 1890–1913* (Westport, Conn.: Greenwood Press, 1976).

83. Lewis L. Gould, *Progressives and Prohibitionists: Texas Democrats in the*

It is difficult to detect a connection between progressivism and prohibition in Tennessee and Oklahoma. Paul E. Isaac has contributed a conventional political study of prohibition in Tennessee that effectively points out the danger of broad generalization. He made a particular point that he found no significant connection between either religious fundamentalism or progressivism and prohibition.[84] The story of prohibition in Oklahoma is unique in that the territory actually entered the Union with prohibition on the books. The state was "born sober," and Jimmie Lewis Franklin described the complicated process by which the infant was conceived, the attempts over the years to provide sustenance, and its lingering death in 1959. He found little connection with other reform issues, since the Anti-Saloon League, with customary diligence, was concentrating on prohibition and using as an argument, to the still frontier-minded voters, the desirability of keeping ardent spirits from the red man.[85]

Prohibition became entwined in Virginia politics in various mysterious ways. It figures prominently in state histories and in biographical studies of the Progressive Era. In 1967 a general study of prohibition, based upon a manuscript written by C. C. Pearson and revised by J. Edwin Hendricks, was published. A straightforward chronicle from the colonial period to the ratification of the Eighteenth Amendment, it makes little effort to unravel the complicated relationship between prohibition and Virginia reform. Henry C. Ferrell, Jr., was more successful in showing how, as he put it, the prohibition "move-

---

Wilson Era (Austin: University of Texas Press, 1973), xii. See also Gould, "Progressives and Prohibitionists: Texas Democratic Politics, 1911–1921," *Southwestern Historical Quarterly*, LXXV (July, 1971), 5–18. Ferguson should have a scholarly biography; Gould's more recent assessment is devastating: "He had no fixed policy positions other than personal advantage, no real values save his own profit" ("The University Becomes Politicized: The War with Jim Ferguson, 1915–1918," *Southwestern Historical Quarterly*, LXXXVI [October, 1982], 261).

84. Paul E. Isaac, *Prohibition and Politics: Turbulent Decades in Tennessee, 1885–1920* (Knoxville: University of Tennessee Press, 1965). See also Eric Russell Lacy, "Tennessee Teetotalism: Social Forces and the Politics of Progressivism," *Tennessee Historical Quarterly*, XXIV (Fall, 1965), 219–40; and H. Walton, Jr., "Another Force for Disfranchisement: Blacks and the Prohibitionists in Tennessee," *Journal of Human Relations*, XVIII (First Quarter, 1970), 728–38.

85. Jimmie Lewis Franklin, *Born Sober: Prohibition in Oklahoma, 1907–1959* (Norman: University of Oklahoma Press, 1971), xii–xiii. For a carefully researched article analyzing four referenda and exploring urban/rural, ethnic, and religious factors, see G. K. Renner, "Prohibition Comes to Missouri, 1910–1919," *Missouri Historical Review*, LXII (July, 1968), 363–97. See also Thomas H. Appleton, Jr., "Prohibition and Politics in Kentucky: The Gubernatorial Campaign and Election of 1915," *Register of the Kentucky Historical Society*, LXXV (January, 1977), 28–54.

ment itself became factionalized . . . as practicing politicians sought to secure the dry sentiment for their own political profit" and how "the other reforms of the era . . . blunted the sharp edge of the temperance attack." Bishop James Cannon, Jr., played a significant role in this complex story, but he awaits a biographer who can put both his career and the prohibition issue in proper perspective. Robert Hohner made a beginning in his description of the maneuvers that led wet politicians to nominate a well-known dry for governor in 1909 and the skill with which Cannon helped promote "not only a dry Virginia, but a dry America."[86]

Another issue of perennial interest in southern historiography is child labor. Although the number of general works written on that subject between 1965 and 1982 were few, the growing interest in labor history has inspired several important conventional studies as well as some revisionism. Walter I. Trattner wrote what he called "neither an exhaustive treatment of child labor reform in America nor a complete history of the National Child Labor Committee." It is, however, a carefully researched case study of a social crusade that points to the special situation in the South, where, Trattner claims with perhaps some exaggeration, "states were controlled by Democratic party machines which invariably catered to the large mill owners who controlled a great many votes." Stephen B. Wood, in an excellent study of the constitutional controversies over child-labor legislation, looked at millowners somewhat more sympathetically. The southerners, Wood argued, contended with considerable justice that northern millowners backed child-labor legislation because the extensive use of child labor in the South gave that section a competitive advantage.[87]

86. C. C. Pearson and J. Edwin Hendricks, *Liquor and Anti-Liquor in Virginia, 1619–1919* (Durham: Duke University Press, 1967); Henry C. Ferrell, Jr., "Prohibition, Reform, and Politics in Virginia, 1895–1916," *East Carolina College Publications in History,* III (1966), 175–76; Robert A. Hohner, "Prohibition and Virginia Politics: William Hodges Mann Versus Henry St. George Tucker, 1909," *Virginia Magazine of History and Biography,* LXXIV (January, 1966), 88–107, and "Bishop Cannon's Apprenticeship in Temperance Politics, 1901–1918," *Journal of Southern History,* XXXIV (February, 1968), 33–49 (quotation on p. 49).

87. Walter I. Trattner, *Crusade for the Children: A History of the National Child Labor Committee and Child Labor Reform in America* (Chicago: Quadrangle Books, 1970), 13, 79–80; Stephen B. Wood, *Constitutional Politics in the Progressive Era: Child Labor and the Law* (Chicago: University of Chicago Press, 1968). See also Hugh C. Bailey, "Edgar Gardner Murphy and the Child Labor Movement," *Alabama Review,* XVIII (January, 1965), 47–59; Alton D. Jones, "The Child Labor Reform Movement in Georgia," *Georgia Historical Quarterly,* XLIX (December, 1965), 396–

Those two volumes are rather conventional accounts, but an increasing number of scholars, perhaps influenced by E. P. Thompson and Herbert Gutman, are taking a revisionist approach. Melton Alonza McLaurin, for example, has contributed a significant study of southern mill workers and of the relationship between problems of labor and state politics. He denied that southern textile workers in the early twentieth century were docile but found that organized labor failed to develop in the South "because management took the offensive against it and destroyed it." Of particular moment in the South, he concluded, was the extent to which both rural-controlled and industry-controlled legislators were hostile to the industrial worker. Equally revisionist is David L. Carlton's excellent book, *Mill and Town in South Carolina, 1880–1920* (1982). Carlton, a student of C. Vann Woodward's, documents the development of a new class of "town people," "composed of rising business men," the confrontation between town people and mill workers, and the way in which demagogues such as Cole Blease took advantage of this confrontation. Carlton made clear that compulsory education and restrictions on child labor have to be considered not merely as humanitarian issues but as devices for social control.[88]

Gary M Fink found a different kind of labor controversy in Missouri. The labor force included not only unorganized workers but also strong elements of the American Federation of Labor and the Socialist party. Fink concluded, however, that the majority in Missouri supported an independent labor party rather than either the business unionism of Gompers or the revolutionary goals of socialism. Yet such a party did not develop, and Fink implicitly accused historians of having failed to explain satisfactorily why a labor party has not emerged in the United States. "Too little attention has been paid," he

417; Lala Carr Steelman, "Mary Clare de Graffenried: The Saga of a Crusader for Social Reform," *East Carolina College Publications in History,* III (1966), 53–83, esp. 62–80; Howard B. Clay, "Daniel Augustus Tompkins: The Role of a New South Industrialist in Politics," *East Carolina College Publications in History,* III (1966), 85–118, esp. 96–99.

88. Melton Alonza McLaurin, *Paternalism and Protest: Southern Cotton Mill Workers and Organized Labor, 1875–1905* (Westport, Conn.: Greenwood Publishing Corp., 1971), xiv–xv, 210–11 (quotation on p. 211), and "Early Labor Union Organizational Efforts in South Carolina Cotton Mills," *South Carolina Historical Magazine,* LXXII (January, 1971), 44–59; David L. Carlton, *Mill and Town in South Carolina, 1880–1920* (Baton Rouge: Louisiana State University Press, 1982), 27. Note also Ronald D. Eller, *Miners, Millhands, and Mountaineers: Industrialization of the Appalachian South, 1880–1930* (Knoxville: University of Tennessee Press, 1982).

insisted, "to the institutional structure of the American labor move-ment and the resourcefulness with which its leaders defused and frus-trated those advocates of independent political action in the lower echelons."[89]

Another study of an economic issue during the Progressive Era is that by William Graebner on coal mining. Graebner used the prob-lem of safety in the mines as a case study to test some of the theories of Progressive reform. In sum, he questioned whether the concept of a status revolt is valid within a healthy society; he associated the safety movement with the ideal of the conservation of natural and hu-man resources, but, along with Samuel Haber and Samuel Hays, he saw the emphasis as being on efficient process rather than on goals; he discussed social control and nativism because of the number of im-migrant workers in the mines; he found businessmen much involved in the reform process, somewhat in accord with the theories of Gabriel Kolko and James Weinstein; he warned that the concept of business disunity promulgated by Robert Wiebe could be selectively applied; he concluded that the process of bureaucratic centralization described by Samuel P. Hays was thought-provoking; and to this rather materialistic composite he added "a strong element of human-itarian progressivism." In the final analysis, however, Graebner found that the federal system did not work for the strange kind of competi-tive capitalism that existed at the turn of the century. He raised con-troversial questions, his answers to which were even more controver-sial, and his arguments were skillful.[90]

The problem of states' rights in a federal system, pointed out by Graebner, became acute for the South after 1910, when southerners acquired a predominant influence in national politics. During this period the Wilson administrations made an impressive legislative

89. Gary M Fink, *Labor's Search for Political Order: The Political Behavior of the Missouri Labor Movement, 1890–1940* (Columbia: University of Missouri Press, 1973), 6 (quotation on p. 178).

90. William Graebner, *Coal-Mining Safety in the Progressive Era: The Political Economy of Reform* (Lexington: University Press of Kentucky, 1976), 163. Graebner developed his conclusion in a significant article in which he argued that "the process of reform took place within a framework that was both economic and political, within a political economy, whose major components were interstate competition and feder-alism, working at cross purposes," and that the "structural definition of progressive politics" should not be that of either the New Freedom or the New Nationalism but should employ "its own distinctive methodology, uniform state legislation" ("Feder-alism in the Progressive Era: A Structural Interpretation of Reform," *Journal of Ameri-can History*, LXIV [September, 1977], 331–57 [quotations on pp. 355, 356, 357]).

record and waged successfully the most complicated war in the nation's history to a considerable extent because of the cooperation of Congress and president. The literature on Woodrow Wilson continues to be paced by one of the most important scholarly projects of the century, *The Papers of Woodrow Wilson* (1966–), magnificently edited by Arthur S. Link and his associates. Link, in his presidential address to the Southern Historical Association in 1969, pointed out that Wilson experienced at first an inner tension over his southernness but that he concluded "that in a country as large as the United States one can love his country only by first loving the region and people with whom he identifies historically and emotionally." This recognition of his southernness undoubtedly facilitated Wilson's collaboration with congressional leaders, most of whom were southern.[91] Anne Firor Scott in 1963 pointed to the constructive record of southern congressmen when they gained this power and to the pragmatic approach to the various legislative programs followed even by ideologically conservative southerners.[92]

Since 1963, there has been considerable research in congressional organization, roll-call analysis, and collective biography. Claude Barfield, for example, showed in 1970 how once ineffective Democratic congressional delegations in the early years of the twentieth century "surprised the nation and themselves by the efficiency and good sense of their rule." The Inter-University Consortium for Political and Social Research has provided some useful analyses of voting behavior during this period. One essay, for example, concluded that Democrats, mostly southerners and westerners, were usually cohesive in supporting political reforms except when southern Democrats broke off on issues of states' rights and woman suffrage. Northeastern Republicans generally opposed political reforms while at the same time being "the strongest defenders of Negro rights."[93]

Another essay developed some of the same points on a broader

---

91. Arthur S. Link *et al.* (eds.), *The Papers of Woodrow Wilson* (44 vols. to date; Princeton: Princeton University Press, 1966–); Link, "Woodrow Wilson: The American as Southerner," *Journal of Southern History*, XXXVI (February, 1970), 3–17 (quotation on pp. 13–14). In spite of the fact that McAdoo's career intersected only indirectly with the South, his career as secretary of the treasury and director of the railroads brought him into close association with southerners. And to some, he became a hero. John J. Broesamle, *William Gibbs McAdoo: A Passion for Change, 1863–1917* (Port Washington, N.Y.: Kennikat Press, 1973).

92. Anne Firor Scott, "A Progressive Wind from the South, 1906–1913," *Journal of Southern History*, XXIX (February, 1963), 53–70.

93. Claude E. Barfield, "'Our Share of the Booty': The Democratic Party, Can-

canvas. Pointing out that little social welfare legislation was pushed through Congress in the Progressive years, Howard Allen and Jerome Clubb concluded that supporters of Progressive political reform in Congress were generally from the South and the West, where problems of immigrants, slums, and factories were comparatively unimportant. They arrived at the unoriginal conclusion that "reforms" in and out of Congress had varied goals and that no single movement or common ideology united the reformers. More significantly, they found that even though disfranchisement of black people was taking place in the South, "no group in the Senate came forth to combat actively this southern movement."[94]

Indeed, a facet of racism that has been of particular fascination to historians was the continued segregation of the offices of the federal government during the Wilson administrations. John B. Wiseman suggested in 1969, for example, that racism stood in the way of Democratic revival during the first few years of the Progressive Era because of southern paranoia about federal intervention. With Wilson elected and the South safely in the saddle, he concluded, southerners moderated their concerns about blacks and by 1916 confronted "social and economic questions without measuring" their impact on white supremacy. Even this relatively sympathetic interpretation, however, does not discount the fact that, as Morton Sosna has put it, "color consciousness was . . . a central theme of the progressive era."[95]

The importance of the South in the Wilson administrations has led to considerable interest in congressional delegations and individuals

---

nonism, and the Payne-Aldrich Tariff," *Journal of American History,* LVII (September, 1970), 308–23 (quotation on p. 323); Howard W. Allen, Aage R. Clausen, and Jerome M. Clubb, "Political Reform and Negro Rights in the Senate, 1909–1915," *Journal of Southern History,* XXXVII (May, 1971), 191–212. See also Daniel W. Crofts, "The Warner-Foraker Amendment to the Hepburn Bill: Friend or Foe of Jim Crow?" *Journal of Southern History,* XXXIX (August, 1973), 341–58.

94. Howard W. Allen and Jerome Clubb, "Progressive Reform and the Political System," *Pacific Northwest Quarterly,* LXV (July, 1974), 130–45 (quotation on p. 136).

95. John B. Wiseman, "Racism in Democratic Politics, 1904–1912," *Mid-America,* LI (January, 1969), 38–58 (quotation on p. 58); Morton Sosna, "The South in the Saddle: Racial Politics During the Wilson Years," *Wisconsin Magazine of History,* LIV (Autumn, 1970), 30–49 (quotation on p. 49). Phylis Thomas has shown the importance of white supremacy in the 1916 presidential election ("The Role of Mississippi in the Presidential Election of 1916," *Southern Quarterly,* IV [January, 1966], 207–26). Edwina C. Smith found that the opposition of southern senators to the annexation of the Philippines was due not only to racial prejudice but to their sense of national honor ("Southerners on Empire: Southern Senators and Imperialism: 1898–1899," *Mississippi Quarterly,* XXXI [Winter, 1977–78], 89–107).

who played responsible roles.[96] One of the best of the collective biographies is that of Alabama, perhaps because of the importance of Oscar W. Underwood. In one of the few full-length biographies of southern congressmen published since 1965, Evans Johnson has pointed out that Underwood, "the first man since Henry Clay" to lead his party in both houses of Congress, had been virtually ignored by historians. While warning against the use of labels, Johnson called Underwood a Bourbon, "a member of the old planter aristocracy who favored concessions to business and strict economy, and who extolled the glories of the Old South and envisioned a great industrial future for the New South." Underwood is a good example of a professional congressman who worked hard and, through seniority and character, became influential.[97] In some ways, in fact, Underwood's record reflected that of the Alabama delegation during the Wilson administration. Most of them would undoubtedly have been described as economic conservatives before 1912. However, as Jack E. Kendrick put it, they "embraced most of the progressive reforms advocated by Wilson and helped to enact a program of constructive legislation."[98]

96. See Flynt, *Duncan Upshaw Fletcher;* Holmes, *The White Chief;* Green, *The Man Bilbo;* and Monroe Lee Billington, *Thomas P. Gore: The Blind Senator from Oklahoma* (Lawrence: University of Kansas Press, 1967). Another biography of a professional politician who became influential through seniority is Ruth Warner Towne, *Senator William J. Stone and the Politics of Compromise* (Port Washington, N.Y.: Kennikat Press, 1979). For an account of the brief senatorial career of LeRoy Percy, see Lewis Baker, *The Percys of Mississippi: Politics and Literature in the New South* (Baton Rouge: Louisiana State University Press, 1983).

97. Evans C. Johnson, *Oscar W. Underwood: A Political Biography* (Baton Rouge: Louisiana State University Press, 1980), xv, 451, and "The Underwood Forces and the Democratic Nomination of 1912," *Historian,* XXXI (February, 1969), 173–93; James S. Fleming, "Reestablishing Leadership in the House of Representatives: The Case of Oscar W. Underwood," *Mid-America,* LIV (October, 1972), 234–50; Richard N. Sheldon, "Richmond Pearson Hobson as a Progressive Reformer," *Alabama Review,* XXV (October, 1972), 243–61. Underwood defeated Hobson, a supporter of woman suffrage and prohibition, in the senatorial primary in 1916 in part because Hobson was accused of being soft on the racial issue. See Evans C. Johnson, "Oscar Underwood and the Hobson Campaign," *Alabama Review,* XVI (April, 1963), 125–40.

98. Jack E. Kendrick, "Alabama Congressmen in the Wilson Administration," *Alabama Review,* XXIV (October, 1971), 243–60 (quotation on p. 260). See also Karl Rodabaugh, "Congressman Henry D. Clayton, Patriarch in Politics: A Southern Congressman During the Progressive Era," *Alabama Review,* XXXI (April, 1978), 110–20, "Congressman Henry D. Clayton and the Dothan Post Office Fight: Patronage and Politics in the Progressive Era," *Alabama Review,* XXXIII (April, 1980), 125–49, and "The Dothan Post Office Fight: A Case Study of the Conflict of Local and Translocal Forces During the Progressive Era," *Southern Studies,* XIX (Spring, 1980), 65–80.

Such a statement could be made about other southern delegations. In Virginia, for example, unusual bitterness developed between the longtime friends of Senator Thomas Martin and those of an anti-organization coalition that included Carter Glass. In spite of the bloodbath, intraparty harmony developed behind Wilson, even though the conservative Martin emerged as majority leader.[99]

The influence of the South on the national government diminished sharply with the off-year elections of 1918. Southern congressmen had played a leading role in wartime mobilization. In the Sixty-fifth Congress (1917–1919), as in the four preceding years, their skill as legislators was put to the test as they chaired most of the important committees. Considering the lack of precedent and the overwhelming nature of the crisis, they passed the test very well.[100] In 1918, however, a turnover occurred, and the Democrats lost their chairman-

---

99. Burton Ira Kaufman, "Virginia Politics and the Wilson Movement, 1910–1914," *Virginia Magazine of History and Biography,* LXXVII (January, 1969), 3–21; Wythe W. Holt, Jr., "The Senator from Virginia and the Democratic Floor Leadership: Thomas S. Martin and Conservatism in the Progressive Era," *Virginia Magazine of History and Biography,* LXXXIII (January, 1975), 3–21. See also Philip A. Grant, Jr., "Tennesseans in the 63rd Congress, 1913–1915," *Tennessee Historical Quarterly,* XXIX (Fall, 1970), 278–86. Other recent articles on southern congressmen during the first Wilson administration are: George C. Herring, Jr., "James Hay and the Preparedness Controversy, 1915–1916," *Journal of Southern History,* XXX (November, 1964), 383–404; William G. Johnson, "The Senatorial Career of Henry Algernon duPont," *Delaware History,* XIII (April, 1969), 234–51; George Q. Flynn, "A Louisiana Senator and the Underwood Tariff," *Louisiana History,* X (Winter, 1969), 5–34; Robert Hoyt Block, "Southern Congressmen and Wilson's Call for Repeal of the Panama Canal Tolls Exemption," *Southern Studies,* XVII (Spring, 1978), 91–100; Richard Leverne Niswonger, "William F. Kirby, Arkansas's Maverick Senator," *Arkansas Historical Quarterly,* XXXVII (Autumn, 1978), 252–63; Stephen Kerber, "Park Trammell and the Florida Democratic Senatorial Primary of 1916," *Florida Historical Quarterly,* LVIII (January, 1980), 255–72; Stephen A. Kambol, "Southern Congressmen and the 1912 Army Appropriations Bill," *Southern Studies,* XIX (Spring, 1980), 50–64; Alexander Graham Shanks, "Sam Rayburn in the Wilson Administrations, 1913–1921," *East Texas Historical Journal,* VI (March, 1968), 63–76; and Stuart Towns, "Joseph T. Robinson and Arkansas Politics, 1912–1913," *Arkansas Historical Quarterly,* XXIV (Winter, 1965), 291–307.

100. I. A. Newby, "States' Rights and Southern Congressmen During World War I," *Phylon,* XXIV (Spring, 1963), 34–50; Richard L. Watson, Jr., "A Testing Time for Southern Congressional Leadership: The War Crisis of 1917–1918," *Journal of Southern History,* XLIV (February, 1978), 3–40, and "Principle, Party, and Constituency: The North Carolina Congressional Delegation, 1917–1919," *North Carolina Historical Review,* LVI (Summer, 1979), 298–323; Tindall, *The Emergence of the New South,* Chap. 2 (pp. 33–69).

ships. For the next twelve years the Democrats battled once more in the political wilderness of minority status.[101] It is no longer in vogue to consider the 1920s simply a transition period between the war and the New Deal; there were too many important things going on. From the point of view of the Democratic party, however, it was a transitional period. That party was being torn apart by cultural issues while southerners in Congress were getting the seniority that after 1931 would put them and their political heirs in control of the committee structure for much of the next fifty years.

The key issues during the 1920s were economic and cultural, sometimes a combination of both. In 1959, Arthur Link described progressivism in the 1920s. In 1967, George Tindall also found that the "progressive urge" continued in southern politics during the 1920s, with some tendencies emphasized and others distorted. "The impulse for 'good government' and public services" Tindall labeled "business progressivism"; "the impulse for reform," however, he saw turning "into a drive for moral righteousness and conformity." [102] In fact, the interest of ethnocultural history found a fertile field in the

101. The literature on southerners during the First World War is scanty; some of the biographies that relate to the Progressive Era likewise relate to the war period. The best book on the politics of the period is still Seward W. Livermore, *Politics Is Adjourned: Woodrow Wilson and the War Congress, 1916–1918* (Middletown, Conn.: Wesleyan University Press, 1966). It should, however, be supplemented by David M. Kennedy, *Over Here: The First World War and American Society* (New York: Oxford University Press, 1980). See also Robert David Ward and Frederick W. Brogdon, "The Revolt Against Wilson: Southern Leadership and the Democratic Caucus of 1920," *Alabama Historical Quarterly*, XXXVIII (Summer, 1976), 144–57; and E. David Cronon (ed.), *The Cabinet Diaries of Josephus Daniels, 1913–1921* (Lincoln: University of Nebraska Press, 1963).

102. Arthur S. Link, "What Happened to the Progressive Movement in the 1920's?" *American Historical Review*, LXIV (July, 1959), 833–51; Tindall, *The Emergence of the New South*, 219, 224. See also Tindall, "Business Progressivism: Southern Politics in the Twenties," *South Atlantic Quarterly*, LXII (Winter, 1963), 92–106; cf. Don S. Kirschner, "Conflicts and Politics in the 1920's: Historiography and Prospects," *Mid-America*, XLVIII (October, 1966), 219–33. Examples of specific national issues in which southerners were involved are Sherman, *The Republican Party and Black America;* Charles M. Dollar, "The South and the Fordney-McCumber Tariff of 1922: A Study in Regional Politics," *Journal of Southern History*, XXXIX (February, 1973), 45–66; Carl G. Ryant, "The South and the Movement Against Chain Stores," *Journal of Southern History*, XXXIX (May, 1973), 207–22; Dennis E. Simmons, "Conservatism, Cooperation, and Controversy: The Establishment of Shenandoah National Park, 1924–1936," *Virginia Magazine of History and Biography*, LXXXIX (October, 1981), 387–404; Patrick G. O'Brien, "A Reexamination of the Senate Farm Bloc,

South of the 1920s. The continuing importance of prohibition, the revival of the Ku Klux Klan, controversies over the evolutionary hypothesis and biblical criticism, and the growing tension between urban and rural values rival economic issues in importance in southern politics.

Throughout the 1920s, the evangelical churches frequently became involved in these cultural issues. Kenneth K. Bailey, for example, showed how changing circumstances influenced the social thought of three white Protestant denominations: the Baptists, Methodists, and Presbyterians. About half of his study is devoted to the 1920s; in more descriptive than analytical terms, he described the fundamentalist controversy, the anti-evolution crusade, and the election of 1928. He concluded that the concept of the Lost Cause and the extreme and abject poverty of the South had "borne heavily on the churches."[103]

George M. Marsden, in a splendid study of fundamentalism, went over essentially the same ground Bailey covered but on a much broader canvas. After tracing the theological and philosophical origins of fundamentalism, Marsden saw as "the fundamentalists' most alarming experience . . . finding themselves living in a culture that by the 1920s was openly turning away from God." Moreover, without developing any "systematic political thought," they were becoming very much involved in the anti-evolution crusade, the support of prohibition, and "the general conservative Protestant opposition to Roman Catholicism."[104]

Although fundamentalism had no direct relationship to the Ku Klux Klan, the clash of cultures that led to the alienation of the fundamentalists in the 1920s was partly responsible for the reemergence of the Klan. Little of scholarly significance had been written on the Klan before the 1960s, but then with the growing interest in ethnocultural history stimulated, no doubt, by the civil rights controversies, more began to appear. David Chalmers' *Hooded Americanism* (1965) is one of several studies that looks at the country as a whole.

1921–1933," *Agricultural History*, XLVII (July, 1973), 248–63; Philip A. Grant, Jr., "Southern Congressmen and Agriculture, 1921–1932," *Agricultural History*, LIII (January, 1979), 338–51.

103. Kenneth K. Bailey, *Southern White Protestantism in the Twentieth Century* (New York: Harper & Row, 1964), 162.

104. George M. Marsden, *Fundamentalism and American Culture: The Shaping of Twentieth-Century Evangelicalism: 1870–1925* (New York: Oxford University Press, 1980), 3 (first quotation), 208 (second and third quotations).

In a state-by-state treatment, Chalmers destroyed the stereotype of the uneducated, rural, anti-Negro Klansmen. He showed the complex web of race, ethnicity, economics, religion, and morals that at one time or another inspired the members of the Klan.[105]

More revisionist is Kenneth Jackson's *The Ku Klux Klan in the City,* a book designed "to test the hypothesis that Kleagles (recruiters) were as active and successful in establishing Klans in large cities as in 'towns' of fewer than 75,000 persons." Jackson researched thoroughly the newspapers of nine large cities, including Atlanta, Memphis, Knoxville, and Dallas, and found that Louisville and New Orleans were the only "big southern cities" that effectively resisted the Klan. Jackson found the strength of the urban Klan in a lower middle class that was inspired by "fear of change, not vindictiveness or cruelty." He did not make clear, however, whether the main source of Klan strength was in the cities or in the village and town.[106]

Although the Ku Klux Klan was not a phenomenon limited to the South in the 1920s, every southern state had its Klan, and each state was torn by ethnocultural questions that were related to the Klan. A state that has attracted much historical attention since 1965 is Tennessee not only because the Klan was strong there but because the state staged the Scopes trial and had a famous political boss, Edward Crump, and a controversial and able governor, Austin Peay. David D. Lee has provided a first-rate, though disappointingly brief, survey of the decade based on both traditional documentation and roll-call analysis. Lee described how Peay built up a stable state machine and passed it on to his successors and how the state organization of Luke Lea, a Nashville publisher, became the principal power in the state while Crump was building up his power in Memphis. Lee brought out the importance of urban/rural differences but was not so suc-

105. John M. Mecklin, *The Ku Klux Klan: A Study of the American Mind* (New York: Harcourt, Brace, 1924); Emerson H. Loucks, *The Ku Klux Klan in Pennsylvania* (New York: Telegraph Press, 1936); David M. Chalmers, *Hooded Americanism: The First Century of the Ku Klux Klan, 1865–1965* (Garden City, N.Y.: Doubleday, 1965), and "The Ku Klux Klan in Politics in the 1920's," *Mississippi Quarterly,* XVIII (Fall, 1965), 234–47. A more general study is Arnold S. Rice, *The Ku Klux Klan in American Politics* (Washington, D.C.: Public Affairs Press, 1962). See also John Hope Franklin, "'Birth of a Nation'—Propaganda as History," *Massachusetts Review,* XX (Autumn, 1979), 417–34. An excellent essay is Robert Moats Miller, "The Ku Klux Klan," in Braeman *et al.* (eds.), *Change and Continuity,* 215–55.

106. Kenneth T. Jackson, *The Ku Klux Klan in the City, 1915–1930* (New York: Oxford University Press, 1967), xiv, 242; Arnold S. Rice, Review of Jackson's *The Ku Klux Klan in the City,* in *Journal of American History,* LV (June, 1968), 174–75.

cessful in clarifying the significance of cultural issues such as prohibition, the Ku Klux Klan, and evolution.[107]

Some of these same ethnocultural issues played a significant part in Missouri politics in the 1920s. Franklin D. Mitchell found the situation almost infinitely complex. As he put it, "Sectional rivalries, rural-urban antagonisms, ethnic differences, and charismatic leaders—influenced, in varying degree, Democratic politics in Missouri." At the same time, to add to the complexity, rural Anglo-Saxon Protestants and urban Catholic immigrants were on occasion completely consumed by the prohibition issue, and long before the Great Depression, partly as a result of the political skill of the Pendergast organization in Kansas City, black voters were being drawn away from an insensitive Republican party.[108]

Although ethnocultural issues, particularly prohibition, were important in Virginia also, few would question Virginius Dabney's claim that the meteoric rise of Harry Flood Byrd to a position of undisputed leadership in Virginia's Democratic party was the most impressive political phenomenon of the 1920s in that state. Henry C. Ferrell, Jr., attributed Byrd's rise "to his family influence, his past association with the ruling coalition, and his own political ability." Robert T. Hawkes, Jr., supported the favorable assessment in describing Byrd's administration as "the most significant and progressive in twentieth-century Virginia" in the building of roads and hospitals and the passage of an effective antilynching law. His passion for economy, however, undoubtedly affected his educational program. As

107. David D. Lee, *Tennessee in Turmoil: Politics in the Volunteer State, 1920–1932* (Memphis: Memphis State University Press, 1979). See also Lee, "Rural Democrats, Eastern Republicans, and Tradeoffs in Tennessee, 1922–1932," *East Tennessee Historical Society Publications,* XLVIII (1976), 104–15; Joseph T. MacPherson, "Democratic Progressivism in Tennessee: The Administrations of Governor Austin Peay, 1923–1927," *East Tennessee Historical Society Publications,* XL (1968), 50–61; Cromwell Tidwell, "Luke Lea and the American Legion," *Tennessee Historical Quarterly,* XXVIII (Spring, 1969), 70–83. For an indication of the immediate effect of woman suffrage, see Gary W. Reichard, "The Aberration of 1920: An Analysis of Harding's Victory in Tennessee," *Journal of Southern History,* XXXVI (February, 1970), 33–49. Lamar W. Bridges, "Editor Mooney versus Boss Crump," *West Tennessee Historical Society Papers,* XX (1966), 77–107; Kenneth D. Wald, "The Visible Empire: The Ku Klux Klan as an Electoral Movement," *Journal of Interdisciplinary History,* XI (Autumn, 1980), 217–34.

108. Franklin D. Mitchell, *Embattled Democracy: Missouri Democratic Politics, 1919–1932* (Columbia: University of Missouri Press, 1968), xii–xiii, 161 (quotation on p. xii). See also Fink, *Labor's Search for Political Order,* 82–127.

George Tindall pointed out, no one more consciously used business as a model for administering a state.[109]

Although North Carolina probably never had a political organization as pervasive and dominating as those of twentieth-century Virginia, the period of the 1920s was critical for North Carolina politics because it witnessed a transfer of political influence from the friends of Furnifold M. Simmons to the so-called Shelby dynasty led at first by O. Max Gardner. The three governors in the 1920s, Cameron Morrison, Angus W. McLean, and Gardner, might be considered "business Progressives."[110] They supported the building of roads, hospitals, and schools—the expansion of government services—while living within the budget. Throughout the 1920s, moreover, the issue of fundamentalism versus modernism split the churches, led Governor Morrison to ban several "evolution textbooks" in 1924, and divided the state legislature over the passage of anti-evolutionary laws. Willard Gatewood told this dramatic story, arguing that "the disturbance was caused by a collision between two states of mind," and that the protagonists chose evolution as the issue on which "to wage their major struggle."[111]

109. Virginius Dabney, *Virginia: The New Dominion* (New York: Doubleday, 1971), 480; Henry C. Ferrell, Jr., "The Role of Democratic Party Factionalism in the Rise of Harry Flood Byrd, 1917–1923," *East Carolina College Publications in History*, II (1965), 166; Robert T. Hawkes, Jr., "The Emergence of a Leader: Harry Flood Byrd, Governor of Virginia, 1926–1930," *Virginia Magazine of History and Biography*, LXXXII (July, 1974), 259–81 (quotation on p. 260); Tindall, *The Emergence of the New South*, 229. See also Joseph A. Fry, "Senior Adviser to the Democratic 'Organization': William Thomas Reed and Virginia Politics, 1925–1935," *Virginia Magazine of History and Biography*, LXXXV (October, 1977), 445–69; Fry and Brent Tarter, "The Redemption of the Fighting Ninth: The 1922 Congressional Election in the Ninth District of Virginia and the Origins of the Byrd Organization," *South Atlantic Quarterly*, LXXVII (Summer, 1978), 352–70.

110. Unfortunately only Gardner has a scholarly biography, a lively one by Joseph L. Morrison, *Governor O. Max Gardner: A Power in North Carolina and New Deal Washington* (Chapel Hill: University of North Carolina Press, 1971). Gardner tried to buck Simmons in 1920 but Simmons came out ahead, though he negotiated a treaty with Gardner in 1928. See Douglas Carl Abrams, "A Progressive-Conservative Duel: The 1920 Gubernatorial Primaries in North Carolina," *North Carolina Historical Review*, LV (Autumn, 1978), 241–43. John Robert Moore, "The Shaping of a Political Leader: Josiah W. Bailey and the Gubernatorial Campaign of 1924," *North Carolina Historical Review*, XLI (Spring, 1964), 190–213.

111. Willard B. Gatewood, Jr., "Politics and Piety in North Carolina: The Fundamentalist Crusade at High Tide, 1925–1927," *North Carolina Historical Review*, XLII (Summer, 1965), 275–90, and *Preachers, Pedagogues & Politicians: The Evolu-*

In South Carolina, Georgia, and Florida, factional politics in the 1920s, enlivened by the Ku Klux Klan, has not yet inspired significant scholarly work. Coleman Blease remained a disturbing factor in South Carolina politics throughout the decade but has found no scholarly defenders, though Daniel Hollis has suggested that Blease was determined to protect his poor white followers even to the point of defending their right to lynch and pardoning them if they were convicted.[112] Georgia, after the death of Watson and before the rise of Talmadge, was plagued by factionalism. Even the Klan, in the state where the twentieth-century Klan was launched and where until 1925 it continued to thrive, has had no definitive history.[113] In Florida, though Catts continued to be a factor in state politics, Victoria H. McDonell sees the state leaping "from its past agricultural orientation into a modern, urban-oriented future" during the governorship of John Martin. The Klan was active there but, according to David Chalmers, was divided among "a myriad of growing, active Klaverns" and not significantly involved in politics. In south Florida, however, Joseph D. Cushman, Jr., showed how the Episcopal church was tolerant about the teaching of the evolutionary hypothesis, stood for temperance but opposed prohibition, and was hostile to lynching and the Klan.[114]

---

tion Controversy in North Carolina, 1920–1927 (Chapel Hill: University of North Carolina Press, 1966), esp. 230–33 (quotations on p. 230).

112. Daniel W. Hollis, "Cole Blease: The Years Between the Governorship and the Senate, 1915–1924," *South Carolina Historical Magazine,* LXXX (January, 1979), 1–17. See also Carlton, *Mill and Town in South Carolina.* For the rising star of Congressman John McSwain, see John C. Weaver, "Lawyers, Lodges, and Kinfolk: The Workings of a South Carolina Political Organization, 1920–1936," *South Carolina Historical Magazine,* LXXVIII (October, 1977), 272–85.

113. David J. Ginzl, "Patronage, Race, and Politics: Georgia Republicans During the Hoover Administration," *Georgia Historical Quarterly,* LXIV (Fall, 1980), 280–93; Robert E. Hauser, "'The Georgia Experiment': President Warren G. Harding's Attempt to Reorganize the Republican Party in Georgia," *Georgia Historical Quarterly,* LXII (Winter, 1978), 288–303; Clement Charlton Mosely, "The Political Influence of the Ku Klux Klan in Georgia, 1915–1925," *Georgia Historical Quarterly,* LVII (Summer, 1973), 235–55; Roger K. Hux, "The Ku Klux Klan in Macon, 1919–1925," *Georgia Historical Quarterly,* LXII (Summer, 1978), 155–68.

114. Victoria H. McDonell, "Rise of the 'Businessman's Politician': The 1924 Florida Gubernatorial Race," *Florida Historical Quarterly,* LII (July, 1973), 50; David Chalmers, "The Ku Klux Klan in the Sunshine State: The 1920's," *Florida Historical Quarterly,* XLII, (January, 1964), 209; Joseph D. Cushman, Jr., *The Sound of Bells: The Episcopal Church in South Florida, 1892–1969* (Gainesville: University Presses of Florida, 1976). See also Wayne Flynt, "Florida's 1926 Senatorial Primary," *Florida Historical Quarterly,* XLII (October, 1963), 142–53.

Another combination of elements raises unique questions about Alabama in the 1920s. It had a notoriously anti-Catholic reputation, provided enthusiastic support for prohibition, yet had regularly elected Oscar Underwood, who opposed prohibition and had consistently denounced the Ku Klux Klan.[115] Alabama also claimed the Klavern that Kenneth Jackson called "perhaps the most powerful . . . in the Southeast," and one of its members was Hugo Black, who would become years later on the U.S. Supreme Court a leading champion of civil liberties. Virginia Van der Veer Hamilton confronted these contradictions in a study of Black's Alabama years. She contended that Black felt akin to those thousands in Alabama who joined the Klan, that he took the oath while knowing the excesses that Klansmen were willing to perform, but that "there is no evidence in Black's philosophy or actions to suggest that his affiliation with the Klan was other than an act of purest expediency."[116]

The paradoxical nature of the Klan is well illustrated in the southwestern states of Texas, Louisiana, Arkansas, and Oklahoma. The principal historian of the Klan in these states, Charles C. Alexander, found that though "rural-mindedness" characterized the Klan, it was also powerful in cities that had experienced rapid growth. He concluded that the "distinctive quality of the Klan" was that "its motivation . . . lay not so much in racism and nativism as in moral authoritarianism." Alexander's work complements that of Green on socialism in the Southwest, but there is still a need for a comprehensive study of Texas politics in the 1920s. This gap is only partly filled by Roger M. Olien's study of Texas Republicans, which shows how Renfro B. Creager of Brownsville used the Republican party for patronage from

115. William R. Snell, "Fiery Crosses in the Roaring Twenties: Activities of the Revised Klan in Alabama, 1915–1930," *Alabama Review*, XXIII (October, 1970), 256–76; Evans C. Johnson, "Oscar W. Underwood and the Senatorial Campaign of 1920," *Alabama Review*, XXI (January, 1968), 3–20. Organized labor fought Underwood in the primary of 1920 because of his support for returning the railroads to private enterprise after the war. Wayne Flynt, "Organized Labor, Reform, and Alabama Politics, 1920," *Alabama Review*, XXIII (July, 1970), 163–80. See also Arthur F. Howington, "John Barley Corn Subdued: The Enforcement of Prohibition in Alabama," *Alabama Review*, XXIII (July, 1970), 212–25.

116. Jackson, *The Ku Klux Klan in the City*, 82; Virginia Van der Veer Hamilton, *Hugo Black: The Alabama Years* (Baton Rouge: Louisiana State University Press, 1972), 305. Gerald T. Dunne suggested that Black joined the Klan as an attempt to control it (*Hugo Black and the Judicial Revolution* [New York: Simon & Schuster, 1977]). See also James J. Magee, *Mr. Justice Black: An Absolutist on the Court* (Charlottesville: University Press of Virginia, 1980).

the 1920s through the 1940s and then how it became a successful organization in the 1960s.[117]

In Oklahoma, though Roman Catholics were a tiny minority, anti-Catholicism became a crusade that was combated by Catholic laymen. Thomas Elton Brown has shown the impact of cultural issues on a state's society. He explained how the prohibition issue became linked with the religious issue and how this combination provided fertile ground for the appearance of the Klan in 1921 and for a battle in 1923 between the Klan, by then entrenched in the legislature, and the governor, John C. Walton.[118]

The culmination of the cultural conflicts of the 1920s came with the election of 1928. The Democratic nomination for the presidency of Alfred E. Smith, wet, Roman Catholic, urban, posed a dilemma for those southerners who saw the Democratic party as the bastion of white supremacy and to professional congressmen from the South who had used control of the party machinery to obtain influential positions in the Congress and in national conventions. Most professional Democratic politicians voted for Smith; many other voters did not. Historians and political scientists have grappled with explanations ever since and have tried to decide what issue was decisive.[119]

117. Charles C. Alexander, *The Ku Klux Klan in the Southwest* (Lexington: University of Kentucky Press, 1965), vii. See also Alexander, *Crusade for Conformity: The Ku Klux Klan in Texas, 1920–1930* (Houston: Texas Gulf Coast Historical Association, 1962), "Secrecy Bids for Power: The Ku Klux Klan in Texas Politics in the 1920's," *Mid-America*, XLVI (January, 1964), 3–28, "White Robed Reformers: The Ku Klux Klan Comes to Arkansas, 1921–1922," *Arkansas Historical Quarterly*, XXII (Spring, 1963), 8–23, "White Robes in Politics: The Ku Klux Klan in Arkansas, 1922–1924," *Arkansas Historical Quarterly*, XXII (Fall, 1963), 195–214, and "Defeat, Decline, Disintegration: The Ku Klux Klan in Arkansas, 1924 and After," *Arkansas Historical Quarterly*, XXII (Winter, 1963), 311–31; Roger M. Olien, *From Token to Triumph: The Texas Republicans Since 1920* (Dallas: Southern Methodist University Press, 1982). See also Evan Anders, "The Origins of the Parr Machine in Duval County, Texas," *Southwestern Historical Quarterly*, LXXXV (October, 1981), 119–38; and Harry Krenek, *The Power Vested: The Use of Martial Law and the National Guard in Texas Domestic Crisis . . . 1919–1932* (Austin: Presidial Press, 1980).

118. Thomas Elton Brown, *Bible Belt Catholicism: A History of the Roman Catholic Church in Oklahoma, 1905–1945* (New York: U.S. Catholic Historical Society, 1977). See also Sheldon Neuringer, "Governor Walton's War on the Ku Klux Klan: An Episode in Oklahoma History," *Chronicles of Oklahoma*, XLV (Summer, 1967), 153–79; and Franklin, *Born Sober*. Arkansas passed an anti-evolution referendum in 1928, "the only state to protect Genesis by a [direct] vote of the people" (R. Halliburton, Jr., "The Adoption of Arkansas' Anti-Evolution Law," *Arkansas Historical Quarterly*, XXIII [Autumn, 1964], 271–83 [quotation on p. 282]).

119. Tindall, *The Emergence of the New South*, 253.

Although the grappling is probably hopeless, it continues, and at times armed with statistics and the computer, the analysts have gained confidence. One of the marks that historians have shot at is the thesis of V. O. Key that "generally the whites of the black belts remained most steadfast in their loyalty to the Democratic party, while in the areas of few Negroes the shift to Hoover was most marked." Key's analysis has stood up well for Alabama and Mississippi. All the controversial issues played a part in influencing the voters of these states, it appears, but race seems to have been the essential factor in keeping them in the Democratic column.[120] Steven D. Zink argued, however, that Louisiana did not fit the Key pattern. In a careful statistical study, Zink showed that "the whites of the predominantly black parishes did not remain the . . . 'most steadfast in their loyalty to the Democratic party.'" These parishes, he pointed out, were predominantly Protestant; religion there was the primary issue. Factors peculiar to Louisiana were important too—the tendency of Louisiana sugar planters to favor a Republican tariff policy and the appeal that Herbert Hoover made to those whom he had recently aided when the Mississippi River had obligingly flooded in 1927.[121]

In Tennessee, Hoover carried the state only because of large majorities in east and middle Tennessee, and G. Michael McCarthy asked, "What impulse was powerful enough to fuse a stridently wet New York Tammany Catholic to fifteen dry, conservative, Protestant west Tennessee counties at the tail end of a decade already infamous for its social intolerance and the depth of its rural-urban antagonisms?" His answer was that though party loyalty was important, the primary factor was fear of the Republican position on race.[122]

120. Key, *Southern Politics*, 318; Hugh D. Reagan, "Race as a Factor in the Presidential Election of 1928 in Alabama," *Alabama Review*, XIX (January, 1966), 5–19; Ben G. Edmonson, "Pat Harrison and Mississippi in the Presidential Elections of 1924 and 1928," *Journal of Mississippi History*, XXXIII (November, 1971), 333–50; Donald Brooks Kelley, "Deep South Dilemma: The Mississippi Press in the Presidential Election of 1928," *Journal of Mississippi History*, XXV (April, 1963), 63–92. See also David J. Ginzl, "Lily-Whites Versus Black-and-Tans: Mississippi Republicans During the Hoover Administration," *Journal of Mississippi History*, XLII (August, 1980), 194–211.

121. Steven D. Zink, "Cultural Conflict and the 1928 Presidential Campaign in Louisiana," *Southern Studies*, XVII (Summer, 1978), 175–97 (quotation on pp. 180–81). Another excellent article essentially supports Zink's argument and adds the dimension of the emergence of Huey Long. See Barbara C. Wingo, "The 1928 Presidential Election in Louisiana," *Louisiana History*, XVIII (Fall, 1977), 405–35.

122. G. Michael McCarthy, "Smith vs. Hoover—The Politics of Race in West Ten-

One result of the emotionalism that developed over the cultural issues of the 1920s was the near destruction of the Democratic party. Robert K. Murray described how the northern and southern wings of the party tore themselves apart at the Democratic convention in 1924 and how the campaign for William G. McAdoo in the southern states brought out cultural tensions. McAdoo does not come off well in this assessment. Indeed, James C. Prude argued that the reason for the deadlocked convention was that McAdoo had the forlorn hope that the convention would abolish the two-thirds rule and that he would be nominated.[123]

In 1927, McAdoo withdrew from the campaign for the presidential nomination in an attempt to restore party unity. The withdrawal symbolized the decline of the influence of southerners within the party. At the same time, Cordell Hull, a party chairman "indifferent to the changing habits of political life," according to Judith Stanley, was offering "to the warring urban-rural wings of his party . . . pious exhortations and the healing, saving grace of an orthodox Jeffersonian faith." The election of 1928 showed how wrong he was, and so serious was the outcome to the Solid South that some thought that the damage to the Democrats was permanent. The party professionals, however, quickly recovered. In Virginia in 1929, Bishop Cannon failed to "topple the Democratic regulars" only one year after he had succeeded in doing just that. Moreover, the two most famous

---

nessee," *Phylon*, XXXIX (June, 1978), 154–68 (quotation on p. 155), and "The Brown Derby Campaign in West Tennessee: Smith, Hoover, and the Politics of Race," *West Tennessee Historical Society Papers*, XXVII (1973), 81–98. J. Winfield Qualls argued, not persuasively, that race was not "an overriding consideration," since both sides use the issue equally effectively ("The 1928 Presidential Election in West Tennessee: Was Race A Chief Factor?" *West Tennessee Historical Society Papers*, XXVII [1973], 99–107). Richard H. Bradford argued that Smith's wetness was more important than his religion in West Virginia, and that John Kennedy was aware of the fact when he chose that state for a trial of strength with Hubert Humphrey in 1960 ("Religion and Politics: Alfred E. Smith and the Elections of 1928 in West Virginia," *West Virginia History*, XXXVI [April, 1975], 213–21).

123. Robert K. Murray, *The 103rd Ballot: Democrats and the Disaster in Madison Square Garden* (New York: Harper & Row, 1976). See also James Levin, "Governor Albert Ritchie and the Democratic National Convention of 1924," *Maryland Historical Magazine*, LXVI (Summer, 1971), 101–20; Lee N. Allen, "The McAdoo Campaign for the Presidential Nomination in 1924," *Journal of Southern History*, XXIX (May, 1963), 211–28; and William H. Harbaugh, *Lawyer's Lawyer: The Life of John W. Davis* (New York: Oxford University Press, 1973). James C. Prude, "William Gibbs McAdoo and the Democratic National Convention of 1924," *Journal of Southern History*, XXXVIII (November, 1972), 621–28.

bolters, Furnifold M. Simmons, longtime Democratic leader in North Carolina, and J. Thomas Heflin, the notorious Alabama demagogue, lost their political lives for committing the unforgivable sin of working against their party's candidate in a national election.[124]

When the Democrats returned to power in 1932, the situation was comparable to what it had been twenty years before upon the election of Woodrow Wilson. Indeed, a good many Wilsonian Democrats from the South again held positions of power in Congress. Superficially the comparison does not hold so well for the two presidents, but, as Frank Freidel pointed out, Franklin D. Roosevelt secured southern support in his nominating campaign and retained it through much of his first term. Concern that he was "jeopardizing the caste system," from a racial point of view as well as a class point of view, however, divided southerners during his second administration.[125]

Attempting to understand the configurations of Congress has become a popular historical game in the last twenty years. As W. Wayne Shannon put it, since the New Deal the gray eminences in the House

124. Here is not the place to note the numerous works on the election of 1928, but see particularly Allan J. Lichtman, *Prejudice and the Old Politics: The Presidential Election of 1928* (Chapel Hill: University of North Carolina Press, 1979). Judith M. Stanley, "Cordell Hull and Democratic Party Unity," *Tennessee Historical Quarterly,* XXXII (Summer, 1973), 169–87 (quotations on pp. 170–71, 169); Alvin L. Hall, "Virginia Back in the Fold: The Gubernatorial Campaign of 1929," *Virginia Magazine of History and Biography,* LXXIII (July, 1965), 280–302; Michael S. Patterson, "The Fall of a Bishop: James Cannon, Jr., *Versus* Carter Glass, 1909–1934," *Journal of Southern History,* XXXIX (November, 1973), 517; Richard L. Watson, Jr., "A Southern Democratic Primary: Simmons vs. Bailey in 1930," *North Carolina Historical Review,* XLII (Winter, 1965), 21–46; J. Mills Thornton III, "Alabama Politics, J. Thomas Heflin, and the Expulsion Movement of 1929," *Alabama Review,* XXI (April, 1968), 83–112; Glenn T. Harper, "'Cotton Tom' Heflin and the Election of 1930: The Price of Party Disloyalty," *Historian,* XXX (May, 1968), 389–411; Ralph M. Tanner, "The Wonderful World of Tom Heflin," *Alabama Review,* XXXVI (July, 1983), 163–74.

125. Frank Freidel, *F.D.R. and the South* (Baton Rouge: Louisiana State University Press, 1965). Some unusual oral history materials came out of the New Deal. Tom E. Terrill and Jerrold Hirsh (eds.), *Such as Us: Southern Voices of the Thirties* (Chapel Hill: University of North Carolina Press, 1978); David H. Culbert, "The Infinite Variety of Mass Experience: The Great Depression, W. P. A. Interviews, and Student Family History Projects," *Louisiana History,* XIX (Winter, 1978), 43–63; Jerrold Hirsh and Tom E. Terrill, "Conceptualization and Implementation: Some Thoughts on Reading the Federal Writers' Project Southern Life Histories," *Southern Studies,* XVIII (Fall, 1979), 351–62. See also J. Christopher Schnell, "Missouri Progressives and the Nomination of F.D.R.," *Missouri Historical Review,* LXVIII (April, 1974), 269–79; Philip A. Grant, Jr., "The Presidential Election of 1932 in Missouri," *Bulletin of the Missouri Historical Society,* XXXV (April, 1979), 164–70.

of Representatives, little known as they might be, have had an enormous influence in shaping national legislation.[126] A question that harassed Democratic presidents was how to outmaneuver these gray eminences from the South. At the same time, an important question that faced the Republicans was how to form an anti–New Deal coalition with those same southerners. James T. Patterson made the principal contribution in considering the second of these questions. By 1937, he found, an actual realignment of the parties seemed possible, but local Democratic machines were too firmly entrenched and kept reelecting congressmen with the same regional philosophy and political affiliation regardless of what was going on in Washington. There was sufficient anti–New Deal sentiment in both political parties, however, to sabotage some of the goals of the later New Deal. Patterson insisted, however, that there was no firm coalition and that "southerners were seldom united." He concluded that the "coalition was composed not so much of Republicans and southern Democrats as of Republicans and rural Democrats." He found that southerners were practically solid on racial issues in Congress and that in the Senate "nearly half of the twenty-two southerners voted against the Administration on non-Agricultural economic issues." [127]

126. W. Wayne Shannon, "Revolt in Washington: The South in Congress," in William C. Havard (ed.), *The Changing Politics of the South* (Baton Rouge: Louisiana State University Press, 1972), 637–87. This volume aspires to be a kind of sequel to Key's *Southern Politics*. See also Garrison Nelson, "Partisan Patterns of House Leadership Change, 1789–1977," *American Political Science Review*, LXXI (September, 1977), 918–39; and Barbara Deckard Sinclair, "Party Realignment and the Transformation of the Political Agenda: The House of Representatives, 1925–1938," *American Political Science Review*, LXXI (September, 1977), 940–53.

127. James T. Patterson, "The Failure of Party Realignment in the South, 1937–1939," *Journal of Politics*, XXVII (August, 1965), 602–17, "A Conservative Coalition Forms in Congress, 1933–1939," *Journal of American History*, LII (March, 1966), 757–72 (quotations on pp. 761, 763), and *Congressional Conservatism and the New Deal: The Growth of the Conservative Coalition in Congress, 1933–1939* (Lexington: University of Kentucky Press, 1967), 329. See also John Robert Moore, "Senator Josiah W. Bailey and the 'Conservative Manifesto' of 1937," *Journal of Southern History*, XXXI (February, 1965), 21–39; and David W. Brady and Charles S. Bullock III, "Is There a Conservative Coalition in the House?" *Journal of Politics*, XLII (May, 1980), 549–59. David L. Porter has provided an addition to Patterson's concept of the conservative coalition by emphasizing a third stage that he said historians have usually ignored. During this stage, he argued, "Congress increased its powers in relation to the executive branch, extended several New Deal programs, enacted a few pioneering domestic measures, and reduced federal spending." Although Porter did not adequately explain his choice of legislation for analysis, he did analyze several roll calls which suggest that the usual assumptions about the influence of southern Democrats in Congress

One of the usual assumptions is that Senator Josiah Bailey of North Carolina was a key figure in the Republican–southern Democratic coalition. Yet John Robert Moore found even Bailey difficult to label. He voted for more legislation of the New Deal than he opposed, and he was not about to desert the Democratic party. Bailey had been a thorn in the flesh to Simmons and Simmons' friends and does not fit into the mold of the North Carolina economic oligarchy created by V. O. Key.[128]

Far more influential than Bailey in the Senate was Senator Byron Patton ("Pat") Harrison of Mississippi. Harrison, who was elected to the House in 1910 and to the Senate in 1919, was the most influential member of a state delegation, seven of whom would serve as chairmen of standing committees. Martha Swain, in a study of Harrison's political career, called him "a political sage" and "a master of fiscal legislation." Like many southerners, he supported the early legislation of the New Deal but began to drag his feet after 1936. He was ahead of his time, however, in supporting federal aid to education, and labor in Mississippi endorsed him.[129]

One of the most dramatic events of the 1930s was the contest in 1937 between Harrison and Alben W. Barkley of Kentucky for the post of majority leader of the Senate. Roosevelt preferred Barkley for that post, and Swain found that "Harrison was hurt that his party record of service seemed to mean little to the President." [130] The issue,

---

might have to be modified (*Congress and the Waning of the New Deal* [Port Washington, N.Y.: Kennikat Press, 1980], xi). For an analysis of the constituencies of congressmen, see George R. Boynton, "Southern Congressmen: Constituency Opinion and Congressional Voting," *Public Opinion Quarterly*, XXIX (Summer, 1965), 259–69.

128. John Robert Moore, *Senator Josiah William Bailey of North Carolina: A Political Biography* (Durham: Duke University Press, 1968). Another conservative North Carolinian, Graham Barden, had his greatest influence after the New Deal, but he served from 1935 to 1960. See Elmer L. Puryear, *Graham A. Barden: Conservative Carolina Congressman* (Buies Creek, N.C.: Campbell University Press, 1979).

129. Philip A. Grant, Jr., "Ten Mississippians Who Served in Congress, 1931– 1937," *Journal of Mississippi History*, XXXIX (August, 1977), 205–12; Martha H. Swain, *Pat Harrison: The New Deal Years* (Jackson: University Press of Mississippi, 1978), 258, 256.

130. Martha H. Swain, "The Lion and the Fox: The Relationship of President Franklin D. Roosevelt and Senator Pat Harrison," *Journal of Mississippi History*, XXXVIII (November, 1976), 333–59 (quotation on p. 359), "Pat Harrison and the Social Security Act of 1935," *Southern Quarterly*, XV (October, 1976), 1–14, and "The Harrison Education Bills, 1936–1941," *Mississippi Quarterly*, XXXI (Winter, 1977–78), 119–31; Wayne Flynt, "A Vignette in Southern Labor Politics—The 1936 Mississippi Senatorial Primary," *Mississippi Quarterly*, XXVI (Winter, 1972–73),

however, as Polly Davis pointed out, was far more significant than personal whims. Harrison clearly represented the traditional southern version of the Democratic party. Barkley had positioned himself with the developing New Deal coalition. Roosevelt's actions in supporting Barkley provided clear evidence as to where the president stood. Ironically, the new senator from Mississippi, Theodore Bilbo, voted for Barkley. Bilbo was a 100 percent New Dealer and one who, Robert J. Bailey has argued, showed that "Progressivism and Demagoguery are not necessarily mutually exclusive."[131]

Quite different from the statesmanlike Harrison and Barkley was Huey Long, and in T. Harry Williams, Long gained a worthy biographer. Using oral sources skillfully, Williams arrived at the general thesis that men of power can influence history but that in attempting to do good, they may have to do some evil. More specifically, he concluded that Long "in striving to do good . . . was led on to grasp for more and more power, until finally he could not . . . distinguish between the method and the goal, the power and the good."[132]

Although Williams' biography was widely praised, several of its conclusions are questionable. Henry C. Dethloff and George Tindall, for example, would probably give Long's predecessors, particularly Governor John M. Parker, higher marks. Williams likewise left the racial issue cloudy. Although there is general agreement that the Long movement was one based on class rather than race, Williams

---

89–99; David Porter, "Senator Pat Harrison of Mississippi and the Reciprocal Trade Act of 1940," *Journal of Mississippi History,* XXXVI (November, 1974), 363–76.

131. Polly Davis, "Court Reform and Alben W. Barkley's Election as Majority Leader," *Southern Quarterly,* XV (October, 1976), 15–31; Robert J. Bailey, "Theodore G. Bilbo and the Senatorial Election of 1934," *Southern Quarterly,* X (October, 1971), 104. See also William S. Coker, "Pat Harrison: The Formative Years," *Journal of Mississippi History,* XXV (October, 1963), 251–78, and "Pat Harrison—Strategy for Victory," *Journal of Mississippi History,* XXVIII (November, 1966), 267–85; Philip A. Grant, Jr., "Editorial Reaction to the Harrison-Barkley Senate Leadership Contest, 1937," *Journal of Mississippi History,* XXXVI (May, 1974), 127–41; George W. Robinson, "The Making of a Kentucky Senator: Alben W. Barkley and the Gubernatorial Primary of 1923," *Filson Club Historical Quarterly,* XL (April, 1966), 123–35; John Henry Hatcher, "Alben Barkley, Politics in Relief and the Hatch Act," *Filson Club Historical Quarterly,* XL (July, 1966), 249–64; Glenn Finch, "The Election of United States Senators in Kentucky: The Barkley Period," *Filson Club Historical Quarterly,* XLV (July, 1971), 286–304; Gerald S. Grinde, "The Emergence of the 'Gentle Partisan': Alben W. Barkley and Kentucky Politics, 1919," *Register of the Kentucky Historical Soiciety,* LXXVIII (Summer, 1980), 243–58.

132. T. Harry Williams, *Huey Long* (New York: Knopf, 1969), ix–x (quotation on p. x).

admitted that Long was not above making racist appeals. More specifically, Alan Brinkley questioned whether Williams' categorizing Long as the "mass leader" on the model of Eric Hoffer is accurate. Brinkley sees the Long movement as "shifting, volatile, loosely structured," with constituents showing "only conditional loyalty to their leader" on the national level. On the other hand, Robert E. Snyder and Michael Cassity concluded that the national program was an alternative to the New Deal and one that might have prevented Roosevelt's reelection in 1936.[133]

Whereas any analysis of the influence of the Louisiana congressional delegation must focus on one man, Huey Long, in the case of Texas such an analysis must focus on the delegation as a whole. That delegation included the vice-president of the United States and nine chairmen of permanent committees. Indeed, "in the modern era," concluded Lionel V. Patenaude, "no Congressional delegation had more influence." Like other southern delegations, its majority supported the New Deal as a party program in its early phases but drifted off toward the end, and two of its most liberal members were defeated in Democratic primaries.[134]

133. Charles A. Bobbitt, "Huey P. Long: The Memphis Years," *West Tennessee Historical Society Papers*, XXXII (1978), 133–39; Hugh Davis Graham, "The Enigma of Huey Long: An Essay Review," *Journal of Southern History*, XXXVI (May, 1970), 205–11; Courtney Vaughn, "The Legacy of Huey Long," *Louisiana History*, XX (Winter, 1979), 93–101; T. Harry Williams, "Huey, Lyndon, and Southern Radicalism," *Journal of American History*, LX (September, 1973), 267–93; Edward T. Jennings, "Some Policy Consequences of the Long Revolution and Bifactional Rivalry in Louisiana," *American Journal of Political Science*, XXI (May, 1977), 225–46; Henry C. Dethloff, "The Longs: Revolution or Populist Retrenchment?" *Louisiana History*, XIX (Fall, 1978), 401–12; George B. Tindall, Review of Williams' *Huey Long*, in *American Historical Review*, LXXV (October, 1970), 1792–94; Alan Brinkley, "Huey Long, The Share Our Wealth Movement, and the Limits of Depression Dissidence," *Louisiana History*, XXII (Spring, 1981), 117–34 (quotations on p. 121); Robert E. Snyder, "Huey Long and the Presidential Election of 1936," *Louisiana History*, XVI (Spring, 1975), 117–43; Michael J. Cassity, "Huey Long: Barometer of Reform in the New Deal," *South Atlantic Quarterly*, LXXII (Spring, 1973), 255–69; cf. Glen Jeansonne, "Challenge to the New Deal: Huey P. Long and the Redistribution of National Wealth," *Louisiana History*, XXI (Fall, 1980), 331–39, and "Gerald L. K. Smith and the Share Our Wealth Movement," *Red River Valley Historical Review*, III (Summer, 1978), 52–65.

134. Lionel V. Patenaude, "Garner, Sumners, and Connally: The Defeat of the Roosevelt Court Bill in 1937," *Southwestern Historical Quarterly*, LXXIV (July, 1970), 36–51, "The Garner Vote Switch to Roosevelt: 1932 Democratic Convention," *Southwestern Historical Quarterly*, LXXIX (October, 1975), 189–204, "The Texas Congressional Delegation," *Texana*, IX (1971), 3–16 (quotation on p. 3), and "Vice

Since 1965, there have been biographies of Sam Rayburn, Marvin Jones, and Maury Maverick. These three men represent different political ideologies, but all were more supportive of the New Deal than were most of their colleagues. Marvin Jones, chairman of the House Committee on Agriculture, was the most conservative of the three. Yet the drought, the farmers' depression, and his humanitarianism combined to persuade him to accept unprecedented government involvement in things agricultural. Irvin M. May, Jr., in a well-written, thoroughly researched biography, depicted Roosevelt at his best in his relationship with Jones, who was, according to May, "one of the most powerful chairmen in the House's long history." Unfortunately an even more important Texan, Sam Rayburn, chairman of the House Committee on Interstate and Foreign Commerce during the New Deal and later Speaker of the House, is yet to have an adequate biography. That by C. Dwight Dorough is an affectionate life story by a constituent. That by Alfred Steinberg is more scholarly to the extent of having footnotes. Both outline in some detail the rise of a small-town Texas farm boy and schoolteacher to the speakership of the House. Yet Steinberg's book is too long to be considered an interpretative essay and too short to be a careful analysis of the career of one of the most powerful figures in twentieth-century American politics.[135]

Far less important than Rayburn, but more colorful, was Maury Maverick. Whereas Rayburn had served in Congress since 1913 and Marvin Jones since 1916, Maverick was of the class of 1934. As Richard B. Henderson pointed out in a study based upon the extensive Maverick papers, Maverick "was truly 'unbranded.'" Perhaps the only 100 percent New Dealer in the Texas delegation, he along with Thomas R. Amlie of Wisconsin organized the thirty-five or

President John Nance Garner: A Study in the Use of Influence During the New Deal," *Texana*, XI (1973), 124–44. Patenaude sums it all up, particularly rehabilitating Garner, in *Texans, Politics and the New Deal* (New York: Garland Publishing, 1983). See also Jordan A. Schwarz, "John Nance Garner and the Sales Tax Rebellion of 1932," *Journal of Southern History*, XXX (May, 1964), 162–80.

135. Irvin M. May, Jr., *Marvin Jones: The Public Life of an Agrarian Advocate* (College Station: Texas A&M University Press, 1980), and "Marvin Jones: Agrarian and Politician," *Agricultural History*, LI (April, 1977), 421–40 (quotation on p. 421); C. Dwight Dorough, *Mr. Sam* (New York: Random House, 1962); Alfred Steinberg, *Sam Rayburn: A Biography* (New York: Hawthorn Books, 1975). See also David Porter, "The Battle of the Texas Giants: Hatton Sumners, Sam Rayburn, and the Logan-Walter Bill of 1939," *Texana*, XII (1974), 349–61; and Shanks, "Sam Rayburn in the Wilson Administrations."

more newly elected New Dealers to "serve the President as shock troops" in fighting conservatives in Congress. This stance caused Maverick's defeat in 1938 while his conservative colleagues were all being reelected.[136]

There were few exceptions to the rule that southern congressmen generally supported the New Deal during Roosevelt's first administration but became disenchanted during the second. At least two members of the Tennessee delegation, however, might be exceptions: Joseph W. Byrns, the fourteen-term congressman who became Speaker of the House in 1934 and died two years later, and Senator Kenneth D. McKellar, who, according to Robert Dean Pope, stood for organized labor, woman suffrage, and in general "bread-and-butter liberalism."[137] Fred M. Vinson of Kentucky, another exception, supported Roosevelt even on the Supreme Court plan. Ellison D. ("Cotton Ed") Smith, whom Daniel Hollis described as "a senator of ordinary ability who remained in office too long," reverted to the old pattern. A supporter in 1933, he revolted so dramatically that Roosevelt tried to purge him in 1938. Nor could FDR hold the Georgia delegation. Thomas H. Coode pointed out how economic conditions and party loyalty led to initial strong support, but it eroded gradually after the One Hundred Days.[138]

136. Richard B. Henderson, *Maury Maverick: A Political Biography* (Austin: University of Texas Press, 1970), 4; Stuart L. Weiss, "Maury Maverick and the Liberal Bloc," *Journal of American History,* LVII (March, 1971), 886. Lyndon Johnson was elected in 1937 in spite of making support of the Supreme Court plan a "major" issue. Tindall, *The Emergence of the New South,* 622; Joe B. Frantz, "Opening a Curtain: The Metamorphosis of Lyndon B. Johnson," *Journal of Southern History,* XLV (February, 1979), 3–26.

137. Eugene W. Goll, "Frank R. Kent's Opposition to Franklin D. Roosevelt and the New Deal," *Maryland Historical Magazine,* LXIII (June, 1968), 158–71; J. M. Galloway, "Speaker Joseph W. Byrns: Party Leader in the New Deal," *Tennessee Historical Quarterly,* XXV (Spring, 1966), 63–76; Robert Dean Pope, "The Senator from Tennessee," *West Tennessee Historical Society Papers,* XXII (1968), 102–22 (quotation on p. 120). See also Lamar W. Bridges, "Tennessee Representative Kenneth McKellar and the Sixty-second Congress (1911–1913)," *West Tennessee Historical Society Papers,* XXVII (1973), 63–80; Thomas H. Coode, "Tennessee Congressmen and the New Deal, 1933–1938," *West Tennessee Historical Society Papers,* XXXI (1977), 132–58.

138. James Bolner, "Fred M. Vinson: 1890–1938, the Years of Relative Obscurity," *Register of the Kentucky Historical Society,* LXIII (January, 1965), 3–16; Daniel W. Hollis, "'Cotton Ed Smith'—Showman or Statesman?" *South Carolina Historical Magazine,* LXXI (October, 1970), 235–56 (quotation on p. 256); Thomas H. Coode, "Georgia Congressmen and the First Hundred Days of the New Deal," *Georgia Historical Quarterly,* LIII (June, 1969), 129–46; Howard N. Mead, "Russell vs. Tal-

In Virginia the New Deal met its match in the organizaton of Senator Harry F. Byrd. Some have viewed Byrd, by this time in alliance with Carter Glass, as being invulnerable in Virginia; an exception was Alvin L. Hall, who concluded that had Roosevelt distributed his patronage more effectively, he could have broken the Byrd organization. On the other hand, A. Cash Koeniger argued that though FDR might have undermined Byrd in Virginia, strong-arm methods would have so alienated the friends of Byrd and Glass in the Senate that Roosevelt's influence there, already tottering by 1938, would have been destroyed. The importance of the New Deal and yet its failure to convert Virginia to a "modern progressive state" is well brought out in a fine synthesis by Ronald Heineman.[139]

Undoubtedly the most significant monographs on southern history involving the New Deal have been on agricultural policy. Throughout the 1930s, as Edward L. Schapsmeier and Frederick H. Schapsmeier have pointed out, southerners played a vital role in the formulation of major farm programs. Inspired no doubt by the interest in looking at history "from the bottom up," several monographs have explored the effect of agricultural policies upon small farmers, particularly tenants and sharecroppers. Van L. Perkins, describing the establishment of the Agricultural Adjustment Administration (AAA), provided a clear explanation for the plight of the tenants in 1933. He pointed to the

---

madge: Southern Politics and the New Deal," *Georgia Historical Quarterly*, LXV (Spring, 1981), 28–45. See also Jack Brien Key, "Henry B. Steagall: The Conservative as a Reformer," *Alabama Review*, XVII (July, 1964), 198–209.

139. Alvin L. Hall, "Politics and Patronage: Virginia's Senators and the Roosevelt Purges of 1938," *Virginia Magazine of History and Biography*, LXXXII (July, 1974), 331–50; Brent Tarter, "A Flier on the National Scene: Harry F. Byrd's Favorite-Son Presidential Candidacy of 1932," *Virginia Magazine of History and Biography*, LXXXII (July, 1974), 282–305; A. Cash Koeniger, "Carter Glass and the National Recovery Administration," *South Atlantic Quarterly*, LXXIV (Summer, 1975), 349–64, "The Politics of Independence: Carter Glass and the Elections of 1936," *South Atlantic Quarterly*, LXXX (Winter, 1981), 95–106, and "The New Deal and the States: Roosevelt Versus the Byrd Organization in Virginia," *Journal of American History*, LXVIII (March, 1982), 876–96; Ronald L. Heineman, *Depression and New Deal in Virginia: The Enduring Dominion* (Charlottesville: University Press of Virginia, 1983), 190, and "Blue Eagle or Black Buzzard? The National Recovery Administration in Virginia," *Virginia Magazine of History and Biography*, LXXXIX (January, 1981), 90–100; John Syrett, "Jim Farley and Carter Glass: Allies Against a Third Term," *Prologue*, XV (Summer, 1983), 89–102; James E. Sargent, "Clifton A. Woodrum of Virginia: A Southern Progressive in Congress, 1923–1945," *Virginia Magazine of History and Biography*, LXXXIX (July, 1981), 341–64. See also Larry Sabato, *The Democratic Party Primary in Virginia: Tantamount to Election No Longer* (Charlottesville: University Press of Virginia, 1977).

"extreme emergency of 1933" and to the long-developed notions that all elements in agrarian society would benefit from an increase in price and concluded that the plight of the tenants was partly the result of unscrupulous landlords not living up to the terms of their contracts, and that the AAA should have checked more carefully the local leaders through whom they worked. Perkins investigated further the protest that arose over very large payments to certain corporate farms and found that few of these farms received the large payments and that these payments were necessary to persuade such farmers to participate in the crop-reduction program. Lawrence J. Nelson shows that all landlords were not villains by describing the welfare capitalism of one large plantation and urging the development of a scholarly profile of the twentieth-century southern planter.[140]

From the perspective of the sharecroppers, crop reduction looked different. David Conrad explained how the AAA in concentrating on price supports increased "the misery of the tenant farmers." Although Donald Grubbs found some weaknesses in Conrad's research, the main point is that tenants suffered. The plight of the sharecropper, moreover, is supported in Louis Cantor's story of roadside demonstrations in Missouri in 1939. The story tells of the displaced croppers, an effective protest demonstration, and eventual failure because of the inability or unwillingness of the Farm Security Administration to help.[141] An even more moving story is the "tortured cry from the

140. Edward L. Schapsmeier and Frederick H. Schapsmeier, "Farm Policy From FDR to Eisenhower: Southern Democrats and the Politics of Agriculture," *Agricultural History*, LIII (January, 1979), 352–71; Van L. Perkins, *Crisis in Agriculture: The Agricultural Adjustment Administration and the New Deal, 1933* (Berkeley: University of California Press, 1969); Lawrence J. Nelson, "Welfare Capitalism on a Mississippi Plantation in the Great Depression," *Journal of Southern History*, L (May, 1984), 248, and "Oscar Johnston, the New Deal, and the Cotton Subsidy Payments Controversy, 1936–1937," *Journal of Southern History*, XL (August, 1974), 399–416. For a rather one-sided biography of the chief of the Cotton Production Section of the AAA, see Roy V. Scott and J. G. Shoalmire, *The Public Career of Cully A. Cobb: A Study in Agricultural Leadership* (Jackson: University Press of Mississippi, 1973). The origins of the New Deal farm policy are brought out in Christiana McFadyen Campbell, *The Farm Bureau and the New Deal: A Study of the Making of National Farm Policy, 1933–40* (Urbana: University of Illinois Press, 1962).

141. David Eugene Conrad, *The Forgotten Farmers: The Story of Sharecroppers in the New Deal* (Urbana: University of Illinois Press, 1965); Donald H. Grubbs, Review of Conrad's *The Forgotten Farmers*, in *Journal of Southern History*, XXXII (May, 1966), 266–67 (quotation on p. 266); Louis Cantor, *A Prologue to the Protest Movement: The Missouri Sharecropper Roadside Demonstration of 1939* (Durham: Duke University Press, 1969). See also M. S. Venkataramani, "Norman Thomas, Arkansas Sharecroppers, and the Roosevelt Agricultural Policies, 1933–1937," *Arkansas His-*

Cotton belt." This cry, described by Donald Grubbs, came from the Southern Tenant Farmers' Union; Grubbs's description is based upon interviews as well as careful research in the records. Grubbs may have exaggerated the influence of the union, but he clearly described the existence of class conflict, as well as the courage, internal bickering, and bloodshed.[142]

The New Deal's attempts to meet the needs of the tenants and sharecroppers have proved to be as controversial as the responsibility of the AAA for their plight. Sidney Baldwin, a political scientist attempting to apply theoretical concepts of administration to the Farm Security Administration and the Resettlement Administration, showed how difficult it was to make any fundamental changes in the class system of the South. This is the story of such liberal New Dealers as Rexford G. Tugwell and Will Alexander in their continuous battle with those southerners who controlled congressional purse strings. Donald Holley made an even stronger case for the needs of the sharecroppers. He described their disgraceful living conditions and studied the attempts of the Resettlement Administration and the Farm Security Administration to help them. He showed how local factors and an increasingly hostile Congress prevented significant accomplishments. Under such circumstances, he concluded, "the surprising thing is . . . that they managed to do as much as they did."[143]

Paul Mertz, in a study geographically more comprehensive than

---

torical Quarterly, XXIV (Spring, 1965), 3–28 (reprinted with permission from Mississippi Valley Historical Review, XLVII [September, 1960], 225–46).

142. Donald H. Grubbs, Cry from the Cotton: The Southern Tenant Farmers' Union and the New Deal (Chapel Hill: University of North Carolina Press, 1971), xi; Jerold S. Auerbach, "Southern Tenant Farmers: Socialist Critics of the New Deal," Labor History, VII (Winter, 1966), 3–18. Vital for an understanding of this story is H. L. Mitchell, Mean Things Happening in This Land: The Life and Times of H. L. Mitchell, Co-Founder of the Southern Tenant Farmers Union (Montclair, N.J.: Allenheld, Osmun & Co., 1979). Lowell K. Dyson described the communist attempt to get control of the STFU, "The Southern Tenant Farmers Union and Depression Politics," Political Science Quarterly, LXXXVIII (June, 1973), 230–52. Pete Daniel adds perspective to the problem of the southern tenants in "The Crossroads of Change: Cotton, Tobacco, and Rice Cultures in the Twentieth-Century South," Journal of Southern History, L (August, 1984), 429–56.

143. Sidney Baldwin, Poverty and Politics: The Rise and Decline of the Farm Security Administration (Chapel Hill: University of North Carolina Press, 1968); Donald Holley, Uncle Sam's Farmers: The New Deal Communities in the Lower Mississippi Valley (Urbana: University of Illinois Press, 1975), x–xi. See also Holley, "Trouble in Paradise: Dyess Colony and Arkansas Politics," Arkansas Historical Quarterly, XXXII (Autumn, 1973), 203–16.

Holley's, raised the same questions. Although the implications of his answers are essentially the same, he showed in greater detail how the early agencies relieved southern rural poverty and how congressional resistance together with the president's political sensitivities prevented effective legislation from being passed.[144]

Jonathan Wiener introduced another controversial element by applying to the South over a period of a hundred years after Reconstruction his concept of the "Prussian road" to modernization. In this version of the class struggle, a repressive labor-intensive system that lasted until the depression of the 1930s created such a vast labor supply that planters "could free themselves of responsibility for the year-round subsistence of their sharecroppers." Then, Wiener suggested, the planters took advantage of various farm programs of the New Deal to relieve themselves of responsibility for their tenants or croppers when convenient to do so but required them to come back when they were needed as wage laborers.[145]

Almost without exception the historians of the agricultural programs of the New Deal have been critical of the AAA. Anthony Badger, in a study of the tobacco program in North Carolina, is an exception only in the extent of his criticism. In a unique study, he accepted the tobacco program as one designed to raise prices; pointed out how the AAA maneuvered the growers into accepting policies favored by the AAA; admitted that little if any attention was paid to the tenants; but then argued that the program was successful in fulfilling its purpose in raising prices, and that, in so doing, the program caused few tenants to be displaced and the economic well-being of those who remained was improved.[146]

To be sure, other factors besides the New Deal were responsible for the plight of southern rural whites. Indeed, Theodore Saloutos, in a meticulous assessment, concluded that "with all its limitations and frustrations, the New Deal . . . constituted the greatest innovative epoch in the history of American agriculture." Wayne Flynt traced the

144. Paul E. Mertz, *New Deal Policy and Southern Rural Poverty* (Baton Rouge: Louisiana State University Press, 1978).

145. Wiener, "Class Structure and Economic Development in the American South," 988–89.

146. Anthony J. Badger, *Prosperity Road: The New Deal, Tobacco, and North Carolina* (Chapel Hill: University of North Carolina Press, 1980). The farm program had less to offer Virginia farmers. See Robert F. Hunter, "The AAA Between Neighbors: Virginia, North Carolina, and the New Deal Farm Program," *Journal of Southern History*, XLIV (November, 1978), 537–70.

deep roots of southern poverty back into the nineteenth century, hoping to undermine the stereotype of the rural southerner. Up to a point, he succeeded, for though he found "violence, racism, . . . resistance to change, and apathy," he also saw "nobility, endurance, courage, and faith." And to what they had to endure Pete Daniel added a frightening dimension, the continuing existence of peonage. Daniel's story is a carefully researched and brilliantly written study of crime, corruption, violence, and ignorance.[147]

In the case of both tenant farmers and peonage, the burden fell most heavily on black people, but discrimination extended into other areas too. Raymond Wolters verified the discrimination that agency after agency imposed upon the blacks. Harvard Sitkoff, while recognizing how the New Deal helped black people, found the decade a time of planting for civil rights—"the sprouts of hope prepared the ground for the struggles to follow." At the time, however, Roosevelt's unwillingness to take a clear stand on lynching was particularly difficult to justify, as Robert L. Zangrando pointed out.[148] Moreover, recently edited research that Ralph Bunche performed for Gunnar Myrdal's *The American Dilemma* confirmed the way in which local politicos repressed blacks in the Southeast.[149]

147. Theodore Saloutos, *The American Farmer and the New Deal* (Ames: Iowa State University Press, 1982), 270; J. Wayne Flynt, *Dixie's Forgotten People: The South's Poor Whites* (Bloomington: Indiana University Press, 1979), xvii; Pete Daniel, *The Shadow of Slavery: Peonage in the South, 1901–1969* (Urbana: University of Illinois Press, 1972). The problems of the Dust Bowl are only indirectly related to "southern politics," but note should be taken of Donald E. Worster, *Dust Bowl: The Southern Plains in the 1930s* (New York: Oxford University Press, 1979); and Paul Bonnifield, *The Dust Bowl: Men, Dirt, and Depression* (Albuquerque: University of New Mexico Press, 1979).

148. Raymond Wolters, *Negroes and the Great Depression: The Problem of Economic Recovery* (Westport, Conn.: Greenwood Publishing Corp., 1970); Harvard Sitkoff, *A New Deal for Blacks: The Emergence of Civil Rights as a National Issue*, Vol. I, *The Depression Decade* (New York: Oxford University Press, 1978); Robert L. Zangrando, *The NAACP Crusade Against Lynching, 1909–1950* (Philadelphia: Temple University Press, 1980). See also John A. Salmond, "The Civilian Conservation Corps and the Negro," *Journal of American History*, LII (June, 1965), 75–88. Less sympathetic to the New Deal than Sitkoff, Nancy J. Weiss focuses on the northern voter and shows how southern politicians affected the politics of the New Deal and how economic realities drew blacks to the New Deal (*Farewell to the Party of Lincoln: Black Politics in the Age of FDR* [Princeton: Princeton University Press, 1983]).

149. Ralph J. Bunche, *The Political Status of the Negro in the Age of FDR*, ed. Dewey W. Grantham (Chicago: University of Chicago Press, 1973). See also Larry W. Dunn, "Knoxville Negro Voting and the Roosevelt Revolution, 1928–1936," *East Tennessee Historical Society Publications*, XLIII (1971), 71–93.

Two other agencies that had a dramatic impact upon southern agriculture were the Tennessee Valley Authority (TVA) and the Rural Electrification Administration (REA). Although some of the glow has been taken off these agencies by recent research, they remain significant accomplishments. Preston J. Hubbard's clearly written narrative provided the background of how George W. Norris and others throughout the 1920s had developed the concept of multipurpose development of the nation's main river valleys. Then Wilmon Henry Droze showed the importance of navigation and flood control not only in the development of the region but in providing constitutional justification for the TVA, and Thomas K. McCraw, focusing on the power question, developed the clash of two "mutually hostile traditions," private power and public power. McCraw described the ambiguities of Roosevelt's positions, the maneuverings within the agency, and the breakdown of the ideal of a regional plan. He concluded, however, that "the unified development of the Tennessee River was a spectacular achievement, unmatched for any other stream in the world." Such an assessment, to be sure, does not include those whom Michael J. McDonald and John Muldowny have described as the "dispossessed."[150]

While the TVA was the most comprehensive regional development of the New Deal, the "Crusade to serve farms" carried out by the REA may have been equally significant in its effect throughout the United States. D. Clayton Brown found that though this crusade was a national effort stimulated by Jeffersonian ideals, the real drive was led by rural congressmen from the South and Southwest such as John E. Rankin of Mississippi and Rayburn of Texas. Philip Funigiello, in a larger study of the electric-utility industry, also stressed the importance of the REA and pointed, in addition, to Rayburn's role as chair-

150. Preston J. Hubbard, *Origins of the TVA: The Muscle Shoals Controversy, 1920–1932* (Nashville: Vanderbilt University Press, 1961); Wilmon Henry Droze, *High Dams and Slack Waters: TVA Rebuilds a River* (Baton Rouge: Louisiana State University Press, 1965); Thomas K. McCraw, *TVA and the Power Fight, 1933–1939* (Philadelphia: Lippincott, 1971), 160; Michael J. McDonald and John Muldowny, *TVA and the Dispossessed: The Resettlement of Population in the Norris Dam Area* (Knoxville: University of Tennessee Press, 1982). See also Arthur E. Morgan, *The Making of the TVA* (Buffalo: Prometheus Books, 1974); James D. Bennett, "Roosevelt, Wilkie, and the TVA," *Tennessee Historical Quarterly*, XXVIII (Winter, 1969), 388–96; North Callahan, *TVA: Bridge over Troubled Waters* (South Brunswick, N.J.: A. S. Barnes & Co., 1980); and Edward Felsenthal, "Kenneth Douglas McKellar: The Rich Uncle of the TVA," *West Tennessee Historical Society Papers*, XX (1966), 108–22.

man of the House Committee on Interstate and Foreign Commerce in fighting for the Public Utility Holding Company Act.[151]

An area in which southern congressmen were not in the forefront was labor relations, and, indeed, southern historians have only begun to scratch the surface of that topic during the New Deal. John Hevener's *Which Side Are You On?* recognizes the bind that southern coal operators were in with their struggle for existence with northern operators. In Harlan County, Kentucky, the struggle was not just for better labor conditions but against arbitrary power. Not until the Wagner Act, Hevener concluded, were the miners able to win their war.[152]

The story of the legislation of the New Deal from the perspective of the mid twentieth century raises the question as to why more was not done to right the wrongs that so obviously existed. Thomas A. Krueger, in a pathbreaking study, described the efforts of a galaxy of southern liberals such as Clark Foreman and Lucy Randolph Mason "to bring down the whole battered mansion of Southern reaction." Even more moving is Anthony Dunbar's study of Christian radicals who denounced the conditions of injustice and violence that they found in the South and who refused to accept compromise even when the regional culture was too strong for them. A section of Warren Ashby's thoughtful biography of Frank Porter Graham suggests the trials of one southern liberal during the New Deal; Charles W. Eagles described Jonathan Daniels as a cautious liberal; and John Salmond brilliantly showed how Aubrey Williams of Alabama, "probably the most important spokesman for its [the New Deal's] social democratic left wing," fought for liberal causes until 1965, the year of his death.[153]

151. D. Clayton Brown, *Electricity for Rural America: The Fight for the REA* (Westport, Conn.: Greenwood Press, 1980); Philip J. Funigiello, *Toward a National Power Policy: The New Deal and the Electric Utility Industry, 1933–1941* (Pittsburgh: University of Pittsburgh Press, 1973).

152. John W. Hevener, *Which Side Are You On? The Harlan County Miners, 1931–39* (Urbana: University of Illinois Press, 1978).

153. Thomas A. Krueger, *And Promises to Keep: The Southern Conference for Human Welfare, 1938–1948* (Nashville: Vanderbilt University Press, 1967), 37; Anthony P. Dunbar, *Against the Grain: Southern Radicals and Prophets, 1929–1959* (Charlottesville: University Press of Virginia, 1981); Warren Ashby, *Frank Porter Graham, a Southern Liberal* (Winston-Salem, N.C.: J. F. Blair, 1980); Charles W. Eagles, *Jonathan Daniels and Race Relations: The Evolution of a Southern Liberal* (Knoxville: University of Tennessee Press, 1982); John A. Salmond, *A Southern Rebel: The Life and Times of Aubrey Willis Williams, 1890–1965* (Chapel Hill: University of North Carolina Press, 1983), 289. Another element in the conflict over

These reformers found it difficult to work within the states where power frequently lay with what Jasper Shannon described as the "banker-merchant-farmer-lawyer-doctor-governing class." And James Patterson has added, "State reformers faced the same potent forces which eventually brought the New Deal to its knees: the durable appeal of materialistic pro-business ideology and the stubborn resistance to a strong central government."[154] As in the earlier period, however, the story is not told just in terms of the courthouse elites. It can also be told in terms of governors who were rash enough to stand for office during the depression. These governors varied from the populistic types that might be confused with demagogues to the more genteel business progressives. The most effective of these, Huey Long, who moved from governor to senator in the 1930s, has been the most popular with historians. Eugene Talmadge, three times governor of Georgia, is another whose name evokes an image of red galluses and the "wool hat boys." William Anderson concluded that Talmadge "haunted the political structure as few men have done in any state's history" and argued that he, though not doing much for the little man, provided a kind of conventional stability at a time of economic and political upheaval. Indeed, Anderson seemed to excuse Talmadge's abuse of power while writing an otherwise stimulating and balanced account.[155]

---

the New Deal is developed in Billy H. Wyche, "Southern Industrialists View Organized Labor in the New Deal Years, 1933–1941," *Southern Studies*, XIX (Summer, 1980), 157–71; James A. Hodges, "George Fort Milton and the New Deal," *Tennessee Historical Quarterly*, XXXVI (Fall, 1977), 383–409; Monroe Billington, "The Alabama Clergy and the New Deal," *Alabama Review*, XXXII (July, 1979), 214–25; Margaret E. Armbrester, "John Temple Graves II: A Southern Liberal Views the New Deal," *Alabama Review*, XXXII (July, 1979), 203–13. A study that clearly shows the problems of black leadership is Raymond Gavins, *The Perils and Prospects of Southern Black Leadership: Gordon Blaine Hancock, 1884–1970* (Durham: Duke University Press, 1977).

154. Jasper Berry Shannon, *Toward a New Politics in the South* (Knoxville: University of Tennessee Press, 1949), 44; James T. Patterson, "The New Deal and the States," *American Historical Review*, LXXIII (October, 1967), 70–84, and *The New Deal and the States: Federalism in Transition* (Princeton: Princeton University Press, 1969), 207. See also John Braeman, Robert H. Bremner, and David Brody (eds.), *The New Deal: The State and Local Levels* (Columbus: Ohio State University Press, 1975).

155. Hubert Humphreys, "In a Sense Experimental: The Civilian Conservation Corps in Louisiana, Part I: Origin and Nature of the Experiment . . . ," *Louisiana History*, V (Fall, 1964), 345–67, and "Part II: Conservation of Human Resources," *Louisiana History*, VI (Winter, 1965), 27–52; Donald Holley, "Old and New Worlds in the New Deal Resettlement Program: Two Louisiana Projects," *Louisiana History*, XI (Spring, 1970), 137–65; William Anderson, *The Wild Man from Sugar Creek: The*

An important supplement to the Talmadge biography is Michael Holmes's meticulous study, *The New Deal in Georgia* (1975). Holmes discussed internal politics only as it affected the operation of agencies of the New Deal. His goal was to study the functioning of each agency and thus to show how the state shaped the New Deal. The result is a thorough administrative study. With respect to black people in Georgia, Holmes found that where there was a central state office, as with the National Youth Administration (NYA), the record was far better than where local authority prevailed as with the "blatantly discriminatory" Civilian Conservation Corps (CCC).[156]

While Talmadge was adding a demagogic sparkle to Georgia politics, William H. ("Alfalfa Bill") Murray was performing even more colorfully in Oklahoma. Keith L. Bryant, Jr., in a fine biography, brought out the incredible antics of Murray as governor. With a public career longer than that of either Talmadge or Long, Murray was more like Long in avoiding racism in his campaigning but more like Talmadge in the absence of constructive accomplishments. Bryant concluded that Murray felt that he was engaged in a lifelong agrarian crusade and that his principal concern was the defense of the family farm against outsiders—particularly corporate outsiders.[157]

Southern governors during the 1930s were not all of the character

---

Political Career of Eugene Talmadge (Baton Rouge: Louisiana State University Press, 1975), xiv. See also James C. Cobb, "Not Gone, But Forgotten: Eugene Talmadge and the 1938 Purge Campaign," *Georgia Historical Quarterly*, LIX (Summer, 1975), 197–209.

156. Michael S. Holmes, *The New Deal in Georgia: An Administrative History* (Westport, Conn.: Greenwood Press, 1975), and "The New Deal and Georgia's Black Youth," *Journal of Southern History*, XXXVIII (August, 1972), 443–60. See also Charles H. Martin, "White Supremacy and Black Workers: Georgia's 'Black Shirts' Combat the Great Depression," *Labor History*, XVIII (Summer, 1977), 366–81.

157. Keith L. Bryant, Jr., *Alfalfa Bill Murray* (Norman: University of Oklahoma Press, 1968). See also Donald W. Whisenhunt (ed.), *The Depression in the Southwest* (Port Washington, N.Y.: Kennikat Press, 1980); Kenneth E. Hendrickson, Jr. (ed.), *Hard Times in Oklahoma: The Depression Years* (Oklahoma City: Oklahoma Historical Society, 1983); James Ware, "The Sooner NRA: New Deal Recovery in Oklahoma," *Chronicles of Oklahoma*, LIV (Fall, 1976), 339–51; Peter M. Wright, "John Collier and the Oklahoma Indian Welfare Act of 1936," *Chronicles of Oklahoma*, L (Autumn, 1972), 347–71. Relief was not handled effectively in Arkansas. See Gail S. Murray, "Forty Years Ago: The Great Depression Comes to Arkansas," *Arkansas Historical Quarterly*, XXIX (Winter, 1970), 291–312; and Nan E. Woodruff, "The Failure of Relief During the Arkansas Drought of 1930–1931," *Arkansas Historical Quarterly*, XXXIX (Winter, 1980), 301–13.

of Murray, Talmadge, and Long. A number were comparable to the "business progressive" type of earlier decades. In North Carolina, however, only O. Max Gardner has been treated to a full-scale biography, but Anthony J. Badger wrote a superb short history of the New Deal that clearly brings out the "ambiguity" of the constructive impact upon that state of the New Deal while leaving "untouched" "the basic economic, social, and political structure." [158] Mississippi had its "business progressive" in Governor Martin S. ("Mike") Conner, a graduate of Yale Law School, who, according to William Winter, made an unparalleled imprint on the state. Coming in 1932 when the state was in a desperate financial plight, he put through a sales tax and fought for improved schools, conservation of natural resources, and industrial development. [159] In Tennessee, where the career of Edward Hull ("Boss") Crump was coming to one of its periodic climaxes, David Lee argued that a victory for Crump's organization in the Democratic primary of 1932 had transformed him from a city into a state boss, a position that he would hold for the next sixteen years. Although the concept of Crump as a state boss was in accord with the impression given by V. O. Key, William Majors looked at Crump differently. Majors insisted that Crump made no attempt to build a statewide organization. Liking to be on the winning side, according to Majors, Crump "surveyed the field, determined the candidate most likely to win, and then announced for him." Majors found, in fact, that Senator Kenneth D. McKellar, whom Key considered a junior partner, really managed the state organizaton. Such an inter-

158. Anthony J. Badger, *North Carolina and the New Deal* (Raleigh: Department of Cultural Resources, 1981), 91. See also Ronald E. Marcello, "The Selection of North Carolina's WPA Chief, 1935: A Dispute over Political Patronage," *North Carolina Historical Review*, LII (Winter, 1975), 59–76; Thomas S. Morgan, Jr., "A 'Folly . . . manifest to everyone': The Movement to Enact Unemployment Insurance Legislation in North Carolina, 1935–1936," *North Carolina Historical Review*, LII (Summer, 1975), 283–302. A precedent for social security legislation can be found in Andrew Dobelstine, "The Effects of the Reform Movement on Relief Administration in North Carolina: The Contributions of Alexander Worth McAlister," *South Atlantic Quarterly*, LXXV (Spring, 1976), 245–57.

159. William Winter, "Governor Mike Conner and the Sales Tax, 1932," *Journal of Mississippi History*, XLI (August, 1979), 213–30; Larry Whatley, "The Works Progress Administration in Mississippi," *Journal of Mississippi History*, XXX (February, 1968), 35–50. Hugh White, likewise a business progressive, succeeded Conner as governor. Fielding L. Wright served under Bilbo, Conner, and White. See Elbert R. Hilliard, "The Legislative Career of Fielding Wright," *Journal of Mississippi History*, XLI (February, 1979), 5–23.

pretation may explain how, after a struggle for power with Crump in 1936, Gordon Browning emerged as the state's governor and, according to Majors, produced "one of the most productive sessions in the state's history." Furthermore, Majors, in a fine biography of Browning, clearly brings out how the struggle between Browning and Crump reflects "the continuing clash between rural and urban interests in Tennessee." Browning's success was, no doubt, aided by the generosity of the New Deal, which, according to John Dean Minton, "wrought a revolution in Tennessee." [160]

Meanwhile, New Dealers were elected governor in South Carolina, Florida, and Maryland. Burnet R. Maybank from Charleston was elected on a platform of economy and efficiency. In Florida, according to the pattern of V. O. Key, an outsider from Brooklyn, David Sholtz, won the governorship in 1932. And in 1934 in Maryland, a New Deal Republican, Harry W. Nice, overwhelmingly defeated the four-term, but anti–New Deal Democrat, Albert C. Ritchie. Dorothy Brown pointed out that though Nice's defeat of Ritchie seemed to vindicate Roosevelt's programs, "the confluence of local conditions and issues" makes questionable any broad generalization to explain the outcome.[161]

160. David D. Lee, "The Triumph of Boss Crump: The Tennessee Gubernatorial Election of 1932," *Tennessee Historical Quarterly*, XXXV (Winter, 1976), 393–413; William D. Miller, "The Browning-Crump Battle: The Crump Side," *East Tennessee Historical Society Publications*, XXXVII (1965), 77–88; Majors, "A Re-Examination of V. O. Key's *Southern Politics*," 117–35, "Gordon Browning and Tennessee Politics: 1937–1939," *Tennessee Historical Quarterly*, XXVIII (Spring, 1969), 57–69 (quotation on p. 67), and *The End of Arcadia: Gordon Browning and Tennessee Politics* (Memphis: Memphis State University Press, 1982), 7; John Dean Minton, *The New Deal in Tennessee, 1932–1938* (New York: Garland Press, 1979), 275; James A. Burran, "The WPA in Nashville, 1935–1943," *Tennessee Historical Quarterly*, XXXIX (Fall, 1975), 293–306. For a study of the administration of relief in Kentucky, see Robert J. Leupold, "The Kentucky WPA: Relief and Politics, May-November 1935," *Filson Club Historical Quarterly*, LXIX (April, 1975), 152–68; Donald W. Whisenhunt, "The Great Depression in Kentucky: The Early Years," *Register of the Kentucky Historical Society*, LXVII (January, 1969), 55–62.

161. Marvin L. Cann, "The End of a Political Myth: The South Carolina Gubernatorial Campaign of 1938," *South Carolina Historical Magazine*, LXXII (July, 1971), 139–49; Merlin G. Cox, "David Sholtz: New Deal Governor of Florida," *Florida Historical Quarterly*, XLIII (October, 1964), 142–52; Charles B. Lowry, "The PWA in Tampa: A Case Study," *Florida Historical Quarterly*, LII (April, 1974), 363–80; James Levin, "Governor Albert C. Ritchie and the Democratic Convention of 1932," *Maryland Historical Magazine*, LXVII (Fall, 1972), 278–93; Dorothy Brown, "The Election of 1934: The 'New Deal' in Maryland," *Maryland Historical Magazine*, LXVIII (Winter, 1973), 405–21 (quotation on p. 421); Charles M. Kimberly, "The

Any survey of historical writing about the South inevitably leads to the not-remarkable conclusion that southern history can be approached in various ways. The years of the celebration of the United States' bicentennial stimulated such series as the Kentucky Bicentennial Bookshelf (University Press of Kentucky) and the Tennessee Three Star Books (University of Tennessee Press in conjunction with the Tennesseee Historical Commission). Of particular significance is the States and the Nation series edited by James Morton Smith and Gerald George for the American Association for State and Local History. All books were published between 1975 and 1979 and were designed to be interpretative essays, rather than scholarly treatises. The authors were enjoined to be sprightly and to a remarkable degree they succeeded. For the general reader not looking for reference material, this library of fifty-one volumes could hardly be exceeded.[162] For those looking for early-twentieth-century political history, however, the search might be a long one, since most authors in the bicentennial series put much greater emphasis on the colonial period and the nineteenth century. Carl Bode's volume on Maryland, for example, is weak in reflecting the complexity of the political situation in that state. Fortunately James B. Crooks and Dorothy M. Brown have contributed excellent chapters on the early twentieth century in a fine cooperative history of Maryland that can be supplemented by Marc V. Levine's study of Maryland politics from 1872 to 1948. John Alexander Williams' volume on West Virginia in the bicentennial series does not discuss the Democratic factionalism that he himself explained in detail in his book on the "captains of industry"—a factionalism that included Redeemers, agrarians, the Charleston Gang, and the Davis-Camden-Elkins Ring.[163] The fourth volume in a series

Depression in Maryland: The Failure of Voluntaryism," *Maryland Historical Magazine*, LXX (Summer, 1975), 189–202.

162. David L. Lewis, *District of Columbia: A Bicentennial History* (New York: Norton; Nashville: American Association for State and Local History, 1976); John Alexander Williams, *West Virginia: A Bicentennial History* (1976); Carol E. Hoffecker, *Delaware* (1977); Carl Bode, *Maryland* (1978); Louis D. Rubin, Jr., *Virginia* (1977); Steven A. Channing, *Kentucky* (1977); Wilma Dykeman, *Tennessee* (1975); Paul C. Nagel, *Missouri* (1977); William S. Powell, *North Carolina* (1977); Louis B. Wright, *South Carolina* (1976); Harold H. Martin, *Georgia* (1977); Gloria Jahoda, *Florida* (1976); Virginia Van der Veer Hamilton, *Alabama* (1977); John Ray Skates, *Mississippi* (1979); Joe Gray Taylor, *Louisiana* (1976); Harry S. Ashmore, *Arkansas* (1978); H. Wayne Morgan and Anne Hodges Morgan, *Oklahoma* (1977); Joe B. Frantz, *Texas* (1976).

163. Richard Walsh and William Lloyd Fox (eds.), *Maryland: A History, 1632–*

sponsored by the Kentucky Historical Society (by 1986 not published) may fill the gap in the twentieth century left in Steven Channing's volume on Kentucky.[164]

Wilma Dykeman obviously had a delightful time writing her bicentennial volume on Tennessee, but, for that state, one of the better histories, that by Stanley J. Folmsbee, Robert E. Corlew, and Enoch L. Mitchell, several times revised, has been brought up to date by Robert E. Corlew. Corlew has clearly brought out how the minority Republicans have attempted to profit from Democratic factionalism. In addition to these general histories, Paul E. Isaac has written the history of prohibition in Tennessee and Lester C. Lamon, a comprehensive study of black people that shows, among other things, that some black Tennesseans were active in promoting progressive reforms.[165]

In the case of Virginia, Louis D. Rubin, Jr., used his literary talents to write the bicentennial history, but a more satisfactory treatment of the twentieth century is *Virginia: The New Dominion* (1971) by Virginius Dabney. Dabney put Virginia in national perspective in considering the Progressive Era, the First World War, the 1920s, and the New Deal.[166]

Like Virginia, Georgia and Florida are fortunate to have more detailed scholarly surveys to back up the bicentennial volumes. Six professors at the University of Georgia have contributed to a history of Georgia, with William F. Holmes writing excellent chapters on the

---

1974 (Baltimore: Maryland Historical Society, 1974); Marc V. Levine, "Standing Political Decisions and Critical Alignment: The Pattern of Maryland Politics, 1872–1948," *Journal of Politics*, XXXVIII (May, 1976), 292–325; John Alexander Williams, *West Virginia and the Captains of Industry* (Morgantown: West Virginia University Library, 1976).

164. The series was projected in 1973 by the society. The first volume was George M. Chinn, *Kentucky: Settlement to Statehood* (Frankfurt: Kentucky Historical Society, 1975). The second volume provides an excellent narrative of Kentucky history, though it is rather weak on the national scene. See Hambleton Tapp and James C. Klotter, *Kentucky: Decades of Discord, 1865–1900* (Frankfurt: Kentucky Historical Society, 1977).

165. Robert E. Corlew, *Tennessee: A Short History* (Knoxville: University of Tennessee Press, 1981); Isaac, *Prohibition and Politics;* Lester C. Lamon, *Black Tennesseans, 1900–1930* (Knoxville: University of Tennessee Press, 1977).

166. Dabney, *Virginia: The New Dominion,* 480. See also James W. Ely, Jr., *The Crisis of Conservative Virginia: The Byrd Organization and the Politics of Massive Resistance* (Knoxville: University of Tennessee Press, 1976); and Edward Younger *et al.* (eds.), *The Governors of Virginia, 1860–1978* (Charlottesville: University Press of Virginia, 1982), which includes excellent essays on the twentieth-century governors.

period from 1890 to 1940, and Numan V. Bartley has contributed a one-volume narrative, which, as Dwight Billings described it, departs from Woodward's model by interpreting "the New South as a triumph of the landlord class and their defense of a traditionalistic, paternalistic and static order." In Florida, Charlton W. Tebeau provided a balanced narrative covering the politics of the twentieth century. Yet more thought-provoking was the valiant attempt of two political scientists, David R. Colburn and Richard K. Scher, to place the state's twentieth-century governors in the complicated web of sectional, ethnic, and personal politics.[167]

Mississippi, Louisiana, and Oklahoma have three of the most useful bicentennial histories from the point of view of the twentieth century. The authors, John Skates, Joe Gray Taylor, and Wayne Morgan and Anne Morgan, used a chronological approach. Skates on Mississippi focused on Vardaman and Bilbo and concluded that "no more than white Mississippians of a later generation did the followers of Vardaman and Bilbo recognize the unbreakable link between black oppression and white poverty." For those who wish a more detailed chronological treatment, Richard Aubrey McLemore has edited a two-volume history, with chapters by Nannie Pitts McLemore, William D. McCain, and J. Oliver Emmerich on the period from the Progressive Era through the New Deal. Good on state politics, though perhaps unduly bland on race relations, the story moves from the age of Vardaman and Bilbo, the "progressive" governors, through the 1920s, and on to Bilbo, the disastrous leader in the 1930s.[168]

In *Louisiana: A Bicentennial History*, Joe Gray Taylor has provided a comprehensive narrative of twentieth-century state history. He pointed particularly to the changes brought about by Huey Long and described him as perhaps "the most remarkable American of the twentieth century." The balanced treatment that Taylor provided may encourage an unduly favorable reaction to Louisiana politics. It

---

167. Kenneth Coleman (ed.), *A History of Georgia* (Athens: University of Georgia Press, 1977); Numan V. Bartley, *The Creation of Modern Georgia* (Athens: University of Georgia Press, 1983); Billings, "New Ways of Telling the New South Story," 485; Charlton W. Tebeau, *A History of Florida* (Coral Gables: University of Miami Press, 1971); David R. Colburn and Richard K. Scher, *Florida's Gubernatorial Politics in the Twentieth Century* (Tallahassee: University Presses of Florida, 1980).

168. Skates, *Mississippi*, 127; Richard Aubrey McLemore (ed.), *A History of Mississippi* (2 vols.; Hattiesburg: University Press of Mississippi, 1973). See also Neil R. McMillen, "Perry W. Howard, Boss of Black-and-Tan Republicanism in Mississippi, 1924–1960," *Journal of Southern History*, XLVIII (May, 1982), 205–24.

would be difficult, however, to have such a reaction from a reading of Mark T. Carleton's pioneering study of the state's penal system. He showed how an insensitive public opinion, political patronage, budget-balancing mentality, and racism shaped the making of policy. In the cane fields, too, Thomas Becnel found the atmosphere far from harmonious. Within the framework of a "three-sided confrontation" among industry, union, and church were differences among growers, refiners, and manufacturers. The issue of class, he concluded, was most important, while the church was an inconsistent, though at times almost the only effective, source of encouragement to the workers.[169]

The Southwest (the states of Arkansas, Oklahoma and Texas) is variously served by bicentennial history. All are written by experts, but Harry Ashmore's beautifully written volume on Arkansas hardly touches the twentieth century. Wayne Morgan and Anne Morgan did much better on Oklahoma and summarized effectively the complex story of grass-roots socialism, as told elsewhere by James R. Green, as well as the five-decade battle between wets and drys, as told by Jimmie Lewis Franklin. The Morgans' brief narrative can be supplemented by a fine history based upon a dissertation by James R. Scales and revised by Scales and Danney Goble. Joe B. Frantz has contributed both style and interpretation to the bicentennial history of Texas, which has had no fewer than three other histories since 1965. In addition, Paul Casdorph has written a useful history of the Republican party in Texas, and Alwyn Barr, by writing *Black Texans,* has joined Andrew Buni and Lester Lamon in contributing state histories of black people. Barr's book is supplemented by Darlene Hine's study of the white primary. Hine showed how the Democratic primary, considered to be a progressive reform, became a principal tool in disfranchising blacks. Particularly significant is Hine's conclusion that

---

169. Taylor, *Louisiana,* 155; Mark T. Carleton, *Politics and Punishment: The History of the Louisiana State Penal System* (Baton Rouge: Louisiana State University Press, 1971); Thomas Becnel, *Labor, Church, and the Sugar Establishment: Louisiana, 1887–1976* (Baton Rouge: Louisiana State University Press, 1980), ix. Charles L. Dufour has written a "popular" history of Louisiana with approximately twenty pages on the twentieth century. See his *Ten Flags in the Wind: The Story of Louisiana* (New York: Harper & Row, 1967). See also James Bolner (ed.), *Louisiana Politics: Festival in a Labyrinth* (Baton Rouge: Louisiana State University Press, 1982); and Thomas Schoonover, "Quantification and Louisiana Historians: An Essay Review," *Louisiana History,* XVII (Spring, 1976), 210–14, who says that there should be more of it.

the justices who tried to deal with the early cases involving the white primary were really bewildered by the legal issues involved.[170]

In spite of the geometric increase in the writing of early-twentieth-century political history since 1965, gaps remain. General histories of the twentieth-century South or of the several states need continual updating. Much more could be done in linking labor history with politics, along the lines of Melton Alonza McLaurin in his study of southern cotton mill workers and Gary M Fink on the labor movement in Missouri. Only a beginning has been made on southern politics during World War I. Much has been done on business progressivism in the 1920s and on the New Deal in the 1930s, but even there, several states lack comprehensive studies. Numerous political leaders rate full-scale biographies. Carl Degler's suggestion of breaking the South into different regions is a fruitful one, as James Green's history of socialism in the Southwest has demonstrated. Stimulating possibilities exist in comparisons within the South or involving the South and other areas (as John Cell's comparative study of segregation in the South and South Africa). Jacquelyn Dowd Hall and Anne Firor Scott's essay on southern women in this volume legitimately points to a lack of attention to women in southern politics. Political historians of the early-twentieth-century South still have much to do. Approaches and insights that have developed within the past twenty years, while making the field more complicated, have also provided the means to enrich it.

170. Ashmore, *Arkansas;* Morgan and Morgan, *Oklahoma;* James R. Scales and Danney Goble, *Oklahoma Politics: A History* (Norman: University of Oklahoma Press, 1982); Frantz, *Texas;* Seymour V. Connor, *Texas: A History* (New York: Thomas Y. Crowell, 1971); Rupert N. Richardson *et al., Texas, The Lone Star State* (3rd ed.; Englewood Cliffs, N.J.: Prentice-Hall, 1970); T. R. Fehrenbach, *Lone Star: A History of Texas and the Texans* (New York: Macmillan, 1968); Paul D. Casdorph, *A History of the Republican Party in Texas, 1865–1965* (Austin: Pemberton Press, 1965); Alwyn Barr, *Black Texans: A History of Negroes in Texas, 1528–1971* (Austin: Jenkins Publishing Co., 1973); Darlene Clark Hine, *Black Victory: The Rise and Fall of the White Primary in Texas* (Millwood, N.Y.: KTO Press, 1979).

Southern Politics Since World War II

HUGH DAVIS GRAHAM

When *Writing Southern History* was published in 1965, Dewey W. Grantham, Jr., who was commissioned to write the final (seventeenth) chapter, was responsible for surveying the full range of literature on the twentieth-century South, which had already run two-thirds toward the twenty-first century. Yet Grantham complained that "historians are just beginning to produce scholarly books and articles on the early twentieth century, [and] they have scarcely ventured at all into the period after 1920." As Grantham was writing, Lyndon B. Johnson's Great Society was hammering home a timid legacy of the Kennedy administration, which amounted to a veritable Second Reconstruction of the South.[1] Desegregation, the civil rights movement, and southern white resistance produced a flood of new regional literature, and as V. O. Key, Jr., had observed in his classic *Southern Politics*, "Of books about the South there is no end." Yet Grantham's lament of 1965 is partially sustained even for the 1980s: "Most of the writing on recent southern politics has been the work of political scientists and popularizers."[2]

But some political scientists of the old school were historians at heart, and this would include the formidable Texan with the strangely unsouthern name, Vladimir Orlando Key, Jr. Key's magisterial analysis of southern politics was published in 1949, and two years later C. Vann Woodward published *Origins of the New South*,

---

1. Dewey W. Grantham, Jr., "The Twentieth-Century South," in Arthur S. Link and Rembert W. Patrick (eds.), *Writing Southern History: Essays in Historiography in Honor of Fletcher M. Green* (Baton Rouge: Louisiana State University Press, 1965), 410–44 (quotation on p. 424). See Carl M. Brauer, *John F. Kennedy and the Second Reconstruction* (New York: Columbia University Press, 1977); and Steven F. Lawson, "Civil Rights," in Robert A. Divine (ed.), *Exploring the Johnson Years* (Austin: University of Texas Press, 1981), 93–125. The extensive literature on postwar racial relations is assessed in this volume by Dan T. Carter.

2. V. O. Key, Jr., *Southern Politics in State and Nation* (New York: Knopf, 1949), ix; Grantham, "The Twentieth-Century South," in Link and Patrick (eds.), *Writing Southern History*, 424.

1877–1913, which was Volume IX of Wendell Holmes Stephenson and E. Merton Coulter (eds.), *A History of the South.* Both books advanced essentially Beardian analyses that emphasized economic conflict between the South's haves and have-nots, and both regarded race as essentially an artificial issue that irrationally divided the have-nots across color lines. Numan V. Bartley has adeptly summarized the main features of the "Woodward-Key synthesis" as follows:

> In Woodward's analysis, the Civil War and Emancipation broke planter domination of southern politics and transferred power to modernizing bourgeois elites composed of merchants, businessmen, and industrialists. The Populist movement was an assault by agrarian have-nots on the exploitive Redeemer policies at home and the short-sighted Redeemer Right Fork alliance with northeastern capitalism nationally. With the failure of the Populist revolt, town and business oriented middle class Progressives led the South back into national politics, albeit not before shackling the region with disfranchisement, the one-party system, and de jure segregation. Key's study focused on the debilitating results of these institutions [plus growing malapportionment]. For more than half a century they stunted southern political development and undermined the formation of a biracial New Deal coalition of have-nots.

The Woodward-Key synthesis contained within its assumptions (its authors hoped) the seeds of its own political self-destruction, for both of these southern white liberals assumed that the destruction of the South's unique political legacy of the turn of the century—*i.e.,* disfranchisement, malapportionment, the one-party system, and Jim Crow—should naturally usher in a belated southern New Deal, one sustained by a biracial coalition of the numerically dominant southern poor.[3] The guarded optimism that was inherent in Key's analysis was reflected in Jasper Shannon's contemporary *Toward a New Politics in the South,* with its classic portrait of the southern county-seat courthouse gang, and also in Alexander Heard's *A Two-Party South?* Woodward's own optimism, though always carefully hedged, was re-

3. C. Vann Woodward, *Origins of the New South, 1877–1913* (Baton Rouge: Louisiana State University Press, 1951); Numan V. Bartley, "In Search of the New South: Southern Politics After Reconstruction," in Stanley I. Kutler and Stanley N. Katz (eds.), *The Promise of American History: Progress and Prospects* (Baltimore: Johns Hopkins University Press, 1982), 150–63 (quotation on p. 150). On V. O. Key and *Southern Politics,* see William C. Havard, "V. O. Key, Jr.: A Brief Profile," *South Atlantic Urban Studies,* III (1979), 279–88. On C. Vann Woodward, see Sheldon Hackney, "*Origins of the New South* in Retrospect," *Journal of Southern History,* XXXVIII (May, 1972), 191–216.

flected in *The Strange Career of Jim Crow,* his controversial analysis of the evolution of *de jure* segregation in the South. Woodward's thesis that Jim Crow emerged not on the heels of slavery but rather in a burst of new laws around the turn of the century, and hence that William Graham Sumner's dictum that "stateways cannot change folkways" was disproved, invited the inference that racial segregation was not so deeply embedded in southern folkways as Jim Crow's defenders proclaimed.[4]

But what we got instead of racial cooperation in the 1950s was *Brown* v. *Board of Education* and massive resistance. Appeals to racial solidarity appeared to be not so "artificial" after all. Benjamin Muse chronicled Virginia's massive resistance as early as 1961, but by far the most comprehensive analysis of the turbulent interaction of southern race and politics in the 1950s was Numan Bartley's *The Rise of Massive Resistance.* Bartley's portrait of the 1950s is bleak. The major political casualty of the decade was rural liberalism, which had produced a promising crop of neopopulist governors (all Democrats, of course) in the James E. Folsom tradition. But white rural liberalism's vulnerability to race-baiting in the post-*Brown* era was fatal—witness the devolution from Folsom to George C. Wallace in Alabama, from Huey Long to Jimmie Davis in Louisiana, from James P. Coleman to Ross Barnett in Mississippi, from Eurith D. Rivers to Lester Maddox in Georgia. The title of Bartley's book, however, was slightly misleading, because the "rise" of massive resistance culminated ineluctably in its doom.[5] Even a conservative Republican ad-

4. Jasper Berry Shannon, *Toward a New Politics in the South* (Knoxville: University of Tennessee Press, 1949); Alexander Heard, *A Two-Party South?* (Chapel Hill: University of North Carolina Press, 1952). Heard and Donald S. Strong edited a spin-off data book from the Key project, *Southern Primaries and Elections, 1920–1949* (University: University of Alabama Press, 1950). C. Vann Woodward, *The Strange Career of Jim Crow* (3rd rev. ed.; New York: Oxford University Press, 1974). The first edition (1955) was based on a series of lectures delivered at the University of Virginia in the fall of 1954. See Woodward, "The Strange Career of a Historical Controversy," in Woodward, *American Counterpoint: Slavery and Racism in the North-South Dialogue* (Boston: Little, Brown, 1971), 234–60.

5. Benjamin Muse, *Virginia's Massive Resistance* (Bloomington: Indiana University Press, 1961); Numan V. Bartley, *The Rise of Massive Resistance: Race and Politics in the South During the 1950s* (Baton Rouge: Louisiana State University Press, 1969). See also Neil R. McMillen, *The Citizens' Council: Organized Resistance to the Second Reconstruction, 1954–64* (Urbana: University of Illinois Press, 1971). Francis M. Wilhoit has produced an exercise in political-science taxonomy in *The Politics of Massive Resistance* (New York: George Braziller, 1973), but its analytical power is not up to the standards of Bartley or McMillen.

ministration under Dwight D. Eisenhower could not tolerate the defiance of Arkansas or Virginia, nor could the federal courts accept such defiance under any administration. Grandstanding defiance paid handsome political dividends at home for an Orval Faubus or a George Wallace, but it was disastrous for the long-term economic health and social interests of the states involved. If the intransigent Byrd machine in Virginia could not understand this, "progressive" North Carolina could, and even historically fire-eating South Carolina largely and wisely followed that low-profile model. Token compliance proved to be a more effective means of resistance than the confrontational, massive variety, which only hastened the supervision by federal courts.

Bartley concludes that the southern retreat from massive resistance in 1958–1959 represented "a shift that was conservative rather than reformist, that sought social stability rather than social change." That judgment seems to suggest that the abandonment of massive resistance under a conservative banner was somehow more reprehensible than its abandonment under a reformist banner, and it also suggests that conservatives cannot be "reformers." Our modern understanding of the Progressive movement, for example, shouts of Progressives as conservative reformers.[6] But Bartley was writing in the Woodward-Key tradition of liberal reform, and his resentment at the sour turn of the 1950s is understandable within that familiar ideological context.

So we began with a striking first phase of postwar scholarship on southern politics, the Woodward-Key synthesis, that firmly established the dominant interpretative context. Then we had a rather abrupt second phase of massive-resistance scholarship that seemed to deny many of the fundamental assumptions that were implicit in the first—i.e., that a biracial coalition of the poor should create a southern New Deal based upon common economic interests and premised upon the destruction of such artificial impediments as disfranchisement, malapportionment, the one-party system, and Jim Crow. The 1960s brought a third phase, and an increasingly confused one. In

6. Bartley, *The Rise of Massive Resistance*, 320. See Otis L. Graham, Jr., *The Great Campaigns: Reform and War in America, 1900–1928* (Englewood Cliffs, N.J.: Prentice-Hall, 1971), esp. Pts. 1, 3 (pp. 1–51, 97–169). The considerable willingness of conservative southern businessmen to join reform efforts supporting desegregation against defiant politicians is explored in Elizabeth Jacoway and David R. Colburn (eds.), *Southern Businessmen and Desegregation* (Baton Rouge: Louisiana State University Press, 1982).

historical retrospect, it is clear that the 1960s represented the crucible of the Second Reconstruction, and hence the contemporary confusion was quite natural, since the early martyrdom of the civil rights movement in the South was transformed into sudden triumph in the mid-1960s, only to dissolve with stunning speed into a nationwide wave of race riots in which blacks were the aggressors and southern cities were largely immune. The moral and rhetorical transition from desegregation to integration to black power was breathtaking. The narrow electoral victory of John F. Kennedy led to a landslide for Johnson in which he lost the Deep South to Barry M. Goldwater, and four years later Wallace mounted a major third-party campaign and Richard M. Nixon won the election. Given such volatile and conflicting political signals, historians sensibly hunkered down, and social scientists studying southern politics collectively hedged their bets in symposia cautiously dedicated to an assessment of the precarious balance between continuity and change in southern politics. Indeed, historians were scarcely noticeable in the rash of mid-1960s symposia.

But a historian led off the decade with a blast. In 1964, James W. Silver published *Mississippi: The Closed Society*—the year after he was president of the Southern Historical Association. A native of New York, Silver was a transplanted southerner with deep roots; as a professor at Ole Miss, he had witnessed the chaos and racial hatred at Oxford in 1962, and his angry book ranged understandably but too quickly from serious historical inquiry to bitter polemic. More characteristic of the scholarship of the 1960s was the surge of social-scientific symposia. In 1963, Allan P. Sindler edited an anthology dominated by political scientists and sociologists and entitled *Change in the Contemporary South*. Change was indeed clearly in the air, but no one knew which way it was going. The following year Robert Highsaw edited a similar anthology, this one on the Deep South, but a close reading leaves one puzzled about precisely in what ways the Deep South was being transformed. Also in 1964, Avery Leiserson's collection, *The American South in the 1960's*, offered a varied menu of political perspectives, but it is chiefly notable today as a kind of benchmark, a reflection of the irritation of liberal academics with the political intransigence and conservatism of white southern political elites.[7] The best of the lot surfaced in 1965, when John C. McKinney

7. James W. Silver, *Mississippi: The Closed Society* (New York: Harcourt, Brace & World, 1964); Allan P. Sindler (ed.), *Change in the Contemporary South* (Durham: Duke University Press, 1963); Robert B. Highsaw (ed.), *The Deep South in Transformation: A Symposium* (University: University of Alabama Press, 1964). Avery Leiser-

and Edgar T. Thompson edited *The South in Continuity and Change.* In this collection, twenty-four scholars, most of them sociologists and economists, produced wide-ranging essays, most of which survived the potential strangulations of the Parsonian, "structural-functionalist" theoretical framework that was imposed upon them, and probed deeply into patterns of southern migration, urbanization, economic development, occupational structure, labor relations, agriculture, education, religion, race relations, and politics.[8] It is instructive to contemplate that in a retrospective assessment of this mid-1960s burst of social-science symposia, the historians were generally invisible, the political scientists and sociologists were most editorial and least helpful, and the few contributions of both contemporary insight and abiding value were made by economists and demographers—those scholars who were perhaps least blinded by the genuine pain of the racial confrontation.

The extreme racial polarization of the mid-1960s prompted two significant studies that were not symposia and that looked at the same phenomenon from opposite directions. In *Negroes and the New Southern Politics,* two political scientists from the University of North Carolina at Chapel Hill, Donald R. Matthews and James W. Prothro, were generously funded by the Rockefeller Foundation to spend six years with a host of research associates and assistants interviewing 618 voting-age Negroes and a control sample of 694 whites, collecting economic, demographic, and political data on more than a thousand southern counties, studying four (regrettably anonymous) communities intensively, and running all this through their Univac. The result was a sophisticated social-science analysis of black and white social and political attitudes and behavior in 1961. But for all of its behavioralist apparatus, it was a mere fleeting snapshot, taken at a moment of such accelerating transition that the study's generalizations, which had considerable clarifying effect at the time, nevertheless had little staying power. The authors immodestly compared their book to Gunnar Myrdal's *An American Dilemma* and Key's

---

son (ed.), *The American South in the 1960's* (New York: Praeger, 1964). The eleven essays had originally been published in a special issue of the *Journal of Politics,* XXVI (February, 1964), entitled "The American South: 1950–1970." Writing about 1970 in 1964 was not the proper work of historians, and none was represented in the Leiserson anthology.

8. John C. McKinney and Edgar T. Thompson (eds.), *The South in Continuity and Change* (Durham: Duke University Press, 1965). See also Thompson (ed.), *Perspectives on the South: Agenda for Research* (Durham: Duke University Press, 1967).

Southern Politics. But *Negroes and the New Southern Politics,* with its elaborate political sociology and its shallow historical roots, has faded rather quickly from memory, but Myrdal and Key remain giants.[9]

The second study was Bernard Cosman's *Five States for Goldwater.* Cosman's lean little book has much to recommend it. He began in 1920, with a substantial historical run at his target, which was the evolution of southern Republicans voting in presidential elections. His commitment to the 1960s' vogue of behavioralist methods is consistent, as Robert Highsaw explained and approved in the introduction. But Cosman did not overreach himself; he divided the South into only four basic political types of counties, described and accounted for only what had happened in presidential elections, and recognized that the Goldwater phenomenon was an oddity that might not be a trend setter (it was not).[10] His parsimonious yet convincing monograph remains a model to be emulated.

Three important books characterize the political historiography of the turbulent and uncertain 1960s, two of them produced by social scientists and one by a historian, and all three were published at the beginning of the 1970s. One is Perry Howard's admirable *Political Tendencies in Louisiana,* a model of political ecology (which political sociologist Howard attributed to the tutelage of Rudolf Heberle). First published in 1957 and revised in 1971, Howard's astute historical and political analysis of Louisiana, which begins in 1812, remains without peer as a study of state politics in the South. The second book is Numan Bartley's excellent study of Georgia politics from 1948 through 1968, *From Thurmond to Wallace.* Historian Bartley's use of candidate-to-candidate, product-moment correlations provided a more powerful analytical tool than did Howard's reliance on percentages. But Bartley's otherwise incisive analysis of modern Georgia suffered from the same inherent limitations that blurred the perspective of its companion literature in the 1960s—*i.e.,* contempo-

9. Donald R. Matthews and James W. Prothro, *Negroes and the New Southern Politics* (New York: Harcourt, Brace & World, 1966), is dedicated to Key and Heard. Gunnar Myrdal, *An American Dilemma: The Negro Problem and Modern Democracy* (2 vols.; New York: Harper & Brothers, 1944). See also Everett Carll Ladd, Jr., *Negro Political Leadership in the South* (Ithaca: Cornell University Press, 1966), which in many ways parallels Matthews and Prothro.

10. Bernard Cosman, *Five States for Goldwater: Continuity and Change in Southern Presidential Voting Patterns* (University: University of Alabama Press, 1966).

rary political trends were so contradictory and confused that the longer range of their evolution was obscured. Bartley was quite aware of this, and his concluding chapter "Trends and Prospects" was cautious. Georgia's old Talmadge/anti-Talmadge Democratic factionalism had been broken down by the demise of the county unit system, growing black enfranchisement, and the rise of two-party politics. But basic elements of a New Deal coalition were absent in Georgia: ethnic- and religious-minority blocs with a liberal Democratic voting tradition, strong labor unions, and urban political machines. Black Georgians were natural liberals, but the lower-class whites were their most virulent opponents in an era of racial tension. Given the divergent political inclinations of the three main voting coalitions, which Bartley estimated as 45 percent conservative, 30 percent progressive ("populist"), and 25 percent liberal, the three blocs seemed bound to whiplash an emerging two-party system, driving it potentially in several contradictory directions.[11] Indeed, the 1968 presidential election, which scrambled the two-party system in the South, nevertheless seemed ideally suited to its trifurcated electorate, with blacks voting for Hubert H. Humphrey, rural and blue-collar whites for Wallace, and suburban white-collar whites for Nixon.

The third book completed the contemporary political analysis of the turbulent 1960s in an appropriate fashion by saluting the legacy of V. O. Key without attempting to mimic his grand design. This was *The Changing Politics of the South*, edited by William C. Havard. In his preface, Havard explained his conviction that there could be no successor to Key's *Southern Politics*: "*Southern Politics* was a unique achievement by a unique student of politics, the book set a standard that other books on the subject stand little chance of reaching, and the conditions of time, research assistance, and institutional and personal cooperation available to the original project's director are unlikely to be matched even with the enlarged bases of research support for the social sciences that have been developed recently." So Havard wisely elected to edit an eclectic book, centering on state analysis by social scientists who were widely known for their state expertise and who respected historical analysis—*e.g.*, Perry Howard on Louisiana,

11. Perry H. Howard, *Political Tendencies in Louisiana* (Rev. ed.; Baton Rouge: Louisiana State University Press, 1971); Numan V. Bartley, *From Thurmond to Wallace: Political Tendencies in Georgia, 1948–1968* (Baltimore: Johns Hopkins University Press, 1970).

Donald Strong on Alabama, Joseph Bernd on Georgia, Manning Dauer on Florida. Havard grouped the states into those that appeared to be evolving away from the political stagnation that Key had described (Virginia, Florida, Tennessee, and Texas), those that were wavering (Arkansas, Georgia, and North Carolina), and those that were vigorously protesting the Second Reconstruction (Alabama, Mississippi, Louisiana, and South Carolina). Such a taxonomy is less convincing today than it was then, but given their inherently limited historical perspective, the state essays are generally of high quality. Wayne Shannon's chapter on the southern revolt in Congress seems a period piece today, but Havard's introductory essay still repays a careful reading.[12]

Like Key, Havard was a political scientist who possessed both a keen respect for historical analysis and a writing style that was at once graceful, clear, and powerful. Havard acknowledged the centrality in the southern character of a series of almost bizarre contradictions: "Radical individualism, amounting at times to broad tolerance of extreme personal eccentricity, is set off against a social conformity so stultifying that it has sometimes been equated with paranoia and has been described in terms ranging from 'garrison psychology' to totalitarianism. Personalism, with its preference for the concrete and for a traditional, direct way of handling human relations—as opposed to an abstract and legalized view of man and society—is in direct confrontation in the South with the vaguely universalized clichés of racial prejudice and an elaborate legal apparatus in support of segregation."[13] Havard also contrasted the South's free and easy egalitarianism with its subtle social stratification, its fierce sense of independence with its bizarre paternalism, its innate conservatism with its colorful populistic liberalism, its intense and defensive sectionalism with an aggressive and xenophobic nationalism. Finally, he cited the unifying, consensual base of the South's political life "as opposed to actual political diversity, conflict, opposition, and dissent." This confounding legacy had elicited from the troubled Wilbur

12. William C. Havard (ed.), *The Changing Politics of the South* (Baton Rouge: Louisiana State University Press, 1972), v–vi. Most of the state-by-state analyses by Havard's contributors were completed in time for a three-day symposium on southern politics held in New Orleans in the spring of 1969.

13. *Ibid.*, 5. In citing "garrison psychology," Havard acknowledged T. Harry Williams' essay, "Trends in Southern Politics," in Frank E. Vandiver (ed.), *The Idea of the South: Pursuit of a Central Theme* (Chicago: University of Chicago Press, 1964), 57–65.

J. Cash a scream of agony in his classic *The Mind of the South* in 1941, and as early as 1953, C. Vann Woodward—no fan of Cash's prognosis—had argued in his justly famous essay "The Irony of Southern History" that unlike the rest of America, the South had experienced defeat, occupation, Reconstruction, poverty, and collective guilt. Havard could only hope that the South's cultural conservatism could be fruitfully joined with political and economic liberalism "without sacrificing all moral and religious values on the altar of relativism, and that the South could preserve its individuality through such mediating institutions as the family, church, and local community even in the face of an increasingly collectivized and centralized society."[14]

The growing awareness of the remarkable persistence of the distinctive southern character, despite what Woodward called the "Bulldozer Revolution," a reawakening that was reflected in the writings of Bartley (1970) and Havard (1972), was reinforced in the early and middle 1970s by other scholars. In 1972, sociologist John Shelton Reed published *The Enduring South*, which documented persisting southern differences from national norms in such attitudes and patterns of behavior as cultural defensiveness, intense local loyalties, including close attachment to family and clan, tendencies toward violence, and Bible Belt religiosity.[15] In 1973, George B. Tindall's presidential address to the Southern Historical Association stressed many of the same themes in arguing that southerners were an ethnic minority. Similarly, in *Place Over Time*, Carl N. Degler observed that despite the extraordinary physical transformation of the South by 1975, contemporary studies still found southerners to be "more conservative, more nationalistic, more self-identified, more defensive, and more romantic than other Americans . . . [and also] less rich, less urban, less diverse demographically and religiously, and more likely to be black than the rest of Americans." And Charles P. Roland's balanced and comprehensive survey of the South since 1945, *The Im-*

14. Havard (ed.), *The Changing Politics of the South*, 35; W. J. Cash, *The Mind of the South* (New York: Knopf, 1941); C. Vann Woodward, "The Irony of Southern History," *Journal of Southern History*, XIX (February, 1953), 3–19.

15. John Shelton Reed, *The Enduring South: Subcultural Persistence in Mass Society* (Lexington, Mass.: Heath, 1972). Reed's chapter on violence was anticipated in 1969 by Sheldon Hackney, whose multiple regression analysis demonstrated that the South's greater incidence of personal violence could not be accounted for by socioeconomic variables in the absence of the South's distinctive history. See Hackney, "Southern Violence," *American Historical Review*, LXXIV (February, 1969), 906–25.

probable Era, concluded on a similar note and acknowledged the power of the South's persistent mythology.[16]

But how, in the 1970s, might this heightened scholarly awareness of the stubborn persistence of a distinctive southern character translate itself into political terms? At least the Woodward-Key synthesis had clearly prescribed a New Dealish (and presumably Democratic) biracial coalition of the poor, but we seemed to be getting largely the opposite, with the Republicans for the first time sweeping every southern state in 1972 and with Nixon receiving 71 percent of the vote in the southern states, as against a 61 percent national average and a 54 percent nonsouthern average. Black southerners generally remained true to George McGovern, but they represented only 17 percent of the southern electorate—and besides, they seem to have been excluded from "southernness" in the extended dissection of the unique regional character that had begun with Cash's *The Mind of the South.*[17]

What was needed to connect the inertia of historical character to powerfully disruptive contemporary political forces was a new theoretical model of the American electoral process that could accommodate in historical perspective the rapidly shifting partisan alignments that seemed to be occurring during the Second Reconstruction and that seemed to have occurred with some periodic regularity throughout U.S. history after prolonged periods of relative stability. And the political scientists, with help from several historians, had been busy providing it.

Most readers of this essay are doubtless generally familiar with the new party systems model that emerged from the 1960s and that in turn flowed initially from the discovery, through maturing survey research in the 1950s, of remarkably stable patterns of partisan loyalty.[18] This "normal" vote was customarily maintained, as with the

16. George B. Tindall, "Beyond the Mainstream: The Ethnic Southerners," *Journal of Southern History,* XL (February, 1974), 3–18. See also Tindall's *The Ethnic Southerners* (Baton Rouge: Louisiana State University Press, 1976). Carl N. Degler, *Place Over Time: The Continuity of Southern Distinctiveness* (Baton Rouge: Louisiana State University Press, 1977), 127; Charles P. Roland, *The Improbable Era: The South Since World War II* (Lexington: University Press of Kentucky, 1975). In 1981 the respected University of Georgia Press at Athens published an anthology revealingly entitled *Why the South Will Survive,* written by "Fifteen Southerners."

17. C. Vann Woodward is quick to make this point in his criticism of Cash in "The Elusive Mind of the South," in *American Counterpoint,* 261–83.

18. A convenient summary discussion of this development and its literature can be found in Chap. 1, "American Party Systems and the South," in Numan V. Bartley and

New Deal Democrats during the 1930s and 1940s, or it could be occasionally and temporarily deviated from, as with Eisenhower in the 1950s. But only rarely did it lead to fundamental partisan *realignment*, as with Roosevelt in 1932 and 1936. Scholars have identified five great American party systems, the fifth one being the New Deal system. But in southern political development a main problem with the New Deal realignment has been that, except for eventually detaching Negro loyalties from the party of Lincoln, it had essentially no transforming impact in a Democratic South that for so long had been locked into the pattern of one-party political stagnation that Key had so eloquently described.

In 1975, Numan Bartley and I published *Southern Politics and the Second Reconstruction*, which represented to date the most ambitious and comprehensive effort (at the regional, not the state level) to apply the party systems model historically to postwar southern political evolution by using quantitative as well as traditional techniques.[19] But in retrospect it also demonstrates the limitations of this approach, mainly that the causal connections between political trends in partisan competition, especially as they are reflected in candidate selection, in campaign rhetoric, and in winning and losing elections, are so weakly linked to policy outcomes—in short, to the *So what?* of political competition. The Bartley-Graham research design is described in the book's note on method and data sources, and the substance of the historical narrative is too complicated to summarize here. But in essence (and also in disappointment), we found great continuity beneath the obvious and often surface change—that is, we found more Wilbur Cash than Woodward and Key. To be sure, since 1948, *de jure* segregation had been belatedly but thoroughly smashed, and this was the single greatest vindication of the Woodward-Key synthesis. But this crowning achievement did not seem to have translated itself into the political liberation and transformation that had been expected. The South's disfranchisement of blacks was destroyed, pri-

Hugh D. Graham, *Southern Politics and the Second Reconstruction* (Baltimore: Johns Hopkins University Press, 1975), 1–23. Its leading developers were, in social science, V. O. Key, Jr., Angus Campbell, William Nesbit Chambers, Walter Dean Burnham, and Gerald Pomper; in history, Lee Benson, Charles G. Sellers, Jr., Richard P. McCormick, Michael F. Holt, Paul Kleppner, Ronald P. Formisano, and Richard Jensen.

19. The county and precinct data upon which *Southern Politics and the Second Reconstruction* was primarily based were subsequently published in Bartley and Graham, *Southern Elections: County and Precinct Data, 1950–1972* (Baton Rouge: Louisiana State University Press, 1978).

marily through the radical and effective Voting Rights Act of 1965. But as a result, far more southern whites than blacks were registered on the newly swollen voter rolls, and this goes far to explain the bizarre Wallace-Maddox era of the mid-1960s.[20] Malapportionment was doomed by *Baker* v. *Carr* and *Reynolds* v. *Sims,* but the initial euphoria of urban liberals was dampened by the essentially unchanged behavior of reapportioned legislatures.[21] The one-person/one-vote formula turned out to be in no way inconsistent with the most brutal partisan or racial gerrymandering.

As for the one-party system, by the middle 1970s it was dead, at least as the yellow-dog Democrats had so long known and cherished it. Clearly at the presidential level the Solid Democratic South had by 1972 become the Solid Republican South. In 1975, Louis Seagull made a careful, state-by-state case that a legitimate realignment had occurred in the southern presidential Republican vote and that it was rooted in the white-collar sector. But the past three presidential elections had all been flukes in their unique ways; it was perilous to generalize from them—and besides, it was sustained grass-roots strength that built a political party. Bartley and Graham cautioned that Kevin Phillips' logical argument (and fervent plea) that the South ought to be Republican ignored the powerful illogic of history.[22]

Finally, since the publication of the books by Bartley and Graham and by Seagull in 1975—and also of Earl Black's excellent analysis of southern governors and racial politics between 1950 and 1973—two large studies have emerged that assess the evolution of recent southern politics in different ways and with rather surprisingly different

20. By 1970, the percentage of the eligible southern blacks who were registered to vote was 66.3, but white registration had soared to 83.3 percent of the white voting-age population. In an urban test of biracial coalition politics, political sociologist Chandler Davidson analyzed selected precincts in twenty Houston elections between 1960 and 1966, and argued that black and lower-income white precincts voted consistently for liberal candidates while upper-income whites did not. But Davidson, a radical critic of liberal pluralist theory, did not claim that the biracial coalition voting was especially successful. See *Biracial Politics: Conflict and Coalition in the Metropolitan South* (Baton Rouge: Louisiana State University Press, 1972).

21. See Thomas R. Dye, *Politics, Economics, and the Public: Policy Outcomes in the American States* (Chicago: Rand McNally, 1966).

22. Louis M. Seagull, *Southern Republicanism* (Cambridge, Mass.: Schenkman, 1975); Kevin P. Phillips, *The Emerging Republican Majority* (New Rochelle, N.Y.: Arlington House, 1969). See also Kirkpatrick Sale, *Power Shift: The Rise of the Southern Rim and Its Challenge to the Eastern Establishment* (New York: Random House, 1975).

degrees of success. The first is *The Transformation of Southern Politics,* by journalist Jack Bass and political scientist Walter DeVries. The strengths of the book are several: it spans three decades back to 1945, includes chapters for each state, is written in a lively style that features frequent pungent quotations from the many interviews, is sensibly balanced in its judgments, and contains superior state maps in the appendix. Beyond that, the Bass and DeVries book is extremely disappointing. An unimaginative attempt to reproduce and update Key's *Southern Politics,* it relies too heavily on contemporary interviews and is otherwise methodologically primitive. Its scarce footnotes and mere two-and-one-half-page bibliography reflect a minimal grasp of the relevant and extensive literature. As a result, it tells us virtually nothing that was not already well known by students of southern politics and seems intended primarily for a large popular audience. Its mood is one of "cautious optimism," generally heralding the arrival of the South's "fresh new faces"—*e.g.,* Jimmy Carter, Dale Bumpers, Reubin Askew, Andrew Young, Barbara Jordan— "moderate" Democrats all.[23]

The second study, *The Two-Party South* (1984) by Alexander P. Lamis, begun as a doctoral dissertation in political science at Vanderbilt, is a comprehensive study of southern politics from 1964 through the congressional elections of 1982. Lamis was sufficiently distanced from the heady Republican gains through 1972 to wonder why such momentum was so easily blunted by the Democratic counterattack of the 1970s. His original hypothesis was that racial polarization split the Democrats in the 1960s, but that as the racial issue abated in the 1970s and economic recession grew, the southern Democrats capitalized on the trapped black vote and on the New Deal legacy of Democratic appeal to the lower economic orders. But when the class appeal of the 1970s proved to be weak, Lamis turned to a third variable, and an old one: traditional partisan loyalties, which kept the Republican appeal top-heavy at the presidential level, spotty in between, and thin at the grass roots.[24]

Lamis' research design and method combine arithmetic and re-

23. Earl Black, *Southern Governors and Civil Rights: Racial Segregation as a Campaign Issue in the Second Reconstruction* (Cambridge: Harvard University Press, 1976); Jack Bass and Walter DeVries, *The Transformation of Southern Politics: Social Change and Political Consequence Since 1945* (New York: Basic Books, 1976).

24. Alexander P. Lamis, "Southern Two-Party Politics: The Dynamics of Electoral Competition in the South Since Early 1960" (Ph.D. dissertation, Vanderbilt University, 1982), and *The Two-Party South* (New York: Oxford University Press, 1984).

gression analysis of both county and precinct voting returns in a sensible fashion that is neither quantitatively sophisticated nor elaborate but that balances the "hard" with such "soft" approaches as elite interviews and traditional published sources. He then asks why Democrats did better in some states than others and analyzes each state, ordering them neither alphabetically (which is to say, randomly) as do Bass and DeVries, nor in clusters as does Havard, but along a continuum of Democratic success, with the Deep South somewhat surprisingly leading off. The result is a deft, up-to-date, and convincingly solid analysis that should dominate the field—at least until the next such effort.

But this is part of the problem for contemporary historians: recent American political history has been so volatile that its interpretation has been dominated by political journalists and political scientists in a confusing pendular fashion. Following Lyndon Johnson's triumph in 1964, which conceded the Deep South to Goldwater, Richard Nixon in 1968 detached the Rim South from the Democrats, and George Wallace and his American Independent party further detached the Deep South, leaving only Texas for Hubert Humphrey. Kevin Phillips then proclaimed the emerging Republican majority. When George McGovern lost the entire South to Nixon in 1972, Kirkpatrick Sale chronicled the surge to dominance of the conservative Sun Belt. But when in 1976, James Earl Carter recaptured 118 of the South's 130 electoral votes, losing only Virginia's 12, Bass and DeVries announced the belated triumph of New South moderation. Indeed, Carter's victory and his administration's vigorous enforcement of civil rights policy seem to have freed the South from its post–Civil War consignment to vice-presidential Democratic ticket-balancing—much as John F. Kennedy had dispelled the myth of Catholic unsuitability for the presidency in 1960.[25] But when Ronald Reagan reversed the South's pattern of electoral response in 1980 (claiming 118 electoral votes to Carter's home-state 12), Wayne

25. Betty Glad, *Jimmy Carter: In Search of the Great White House* (New York: Norton, 1980), is a journalistic biography based primarily on approximately three hundred interviews, most of them attributed in the text and placed on file in the University of Illinois Library. Glad's book suffers from a present-tense discussion of President Carter and a psychobiographical flirtation with Karen Horney's theory of the narcissistic personality, but it is essentially fair-minded. Gary M Fink, *Prelude to the Presidency: The Political Career and Legislative Leadership Style of Governor Jimmy Carter* (Westport, Conn.: Greenwood Press, 1980), analyzes Carter's attempt to reorganize Georgia's state government and is based on Carter's gubernatorial papers in the Georgia Department of Archives and History.

Greenhaw celebrated the new wave of conservative southern Republicans in *Elephants in the Cottonfields*. Then yet again, when the off-year elections of 1982 reinforced the durability of the southern Democracy at the state and local level, Alexander Lamis produced a deeper and more sober perspective.[26]

Clearly, for contemporary historians, recent political history too easily degenerates into an open-ended race with the political scientists, and this is a race that historians cannot win, nor should they. The greatest strength of historians lies in the depth of both their hindsight and their evidence. Hence it is a reasonable prediction that in the coming years the large new insights into the tumultuous political events in the South since 1945 will be derived not so much from more voting studies and more sophisticated modes of quantitative analysis of election returns and socioeconomic and demographic variables, although these will and should continue, as from an accumulation of careful state monographs and penetrating political biographies that will suggest the broad outlines of a new synthesis.

Indeed, the popular analogy of a Second Reconstruction is itself both helpful and treacherous. This is partly because southern politics since 1945 remains frustratingly open-ended and hence hardly constitutes a definable epoch. Given our inescapable contemporary myopia, we have no equivalent to the Compromise of 1877, and we may never have such a convenient if melancholy benchmark. On the other hand, the parallel between Reconstructions may well be historiographically apt in that the full meaning of the first Reconstruction could not be fully grasped until historians had shed their racial and ideological blinders, with their implicit assumptions that Negroes and carpetbaggers and scalawags were incapable of worthy motive and contribution. Similarly, the young historiography of the Second Reconstruction is likely to remain immature until historians reach beyond the limiting functions of chronicler and cheerleader for federal civil rights laws. The post-1964 snarl of contradictions that has centered on affirmative action decrees and racial and ethnic quotas, set-asides, and entitlements should hasten this development while at the same time further muddling the parallel-Reconstruction analogy by broadening it into categories of rights-demands and national expansion that the first Reconstruction never dreamed of contemplating. As for the party systems model and partisan realignment theory,

26. Wayne Greenhaw, *Elephants in the Cottonfields: Ronald Reagan and the New Republican South* (New York: Macmillan, 1982), is a poorly organized series of portraits of conservative ideologues in Republican state and regional politics.

we clearly have been unable to identify a critical realignment leading to a stable sixth party system, and indeed we may never have one in the historical sense that political historians have come to know party systems.[27]

The Woodward-Key synthesis, then, has been sharply challenged in our time, but it has not yet been replaced by a convincing new synthesis. While students of southern politics since 1945 have concentrated on either vindicating or challenging Key's dominant-liberal interpretation, with strikingly mixed results, Woodward's Beardian interpretation of the post–Civil War era has recently been attacked from the Left by young scholars who have grounded their "Prussian road" revisionism in state monographs.[28] We clearly lack the necessary perspective on events and access to personal papers and archival evidence (in that order) to anticipate an early revisionist challenge of equivalent depth for the post-1945 era, although Bartley has made an ambitious beginning with his new revisionist history, *The Creation of Modern Georgia*. Similarly, major political biographies that broadly illuminate the underlying dynamics of the political system, its costs and its payoffs, have been understandably slow in coming, given the restrictions on access to the papers of such recent political actors. Tennessee has curiously taken the lead, with biographies of Edward Hull Crump, Estes Kefauver, Gordon Browning, and Frank Goad Clement. Able biographies or life-and-times political analyses also exist for Harry Flood Byrd, DeLesseps S. Morrison, and Leander

27. As early as 1969, political scientist Walter Dean Burnham was arguing that political parties and the partisan loyalties on which they were based were becoming so disaggregated that while critical realignment theory and the party systems model remained crucial to understanding the evolution of political domination by America's entrenched elites, they lacked predictive value for improbable future realignments. See Burnham, "The End of American Party Politics," *TransAction*, VII (December, 1969), 12–22, and *Critical Elections and the Mainsprings of American Politics* (New York: Norton, 1970). Whereas Key saw the South's one-party system as loaded against the region's have-nots, Burnham foresaw a fluid national no-party system that was loaded against the nation's have-nots.

28. This challenge to Woodward had come most notably from Jonathan M. Wiener, *Social Origins of the New South: Alabama, 1860–1885* (Baton Rouge: Louisiana State University Press, 1978); and Dwight B. Billings, Jr., *Planters and the Making of a "New South": Class, Politics, and Development in North Carolina, 1865–1900* (Chapel Hill: University of North Carolina Press, 1979). Both historians acknowledge their debt to the pathbreaking revisionism of Barrington Moore and Eugene Genovese. See Numan V. Bartley, "Another New South?" *Georgia Historical Quarterly*, LXV (Summer, 1981), 119–37; and the essay by Harold Woodman in this volume.

Perez.[29] Two biographies of James E. Folsom have recently been published, and two highly critical, first-volume studies have been published on Lyndon Baines Johnson: one by Ronnie Dugger, the former editor of the *Texas Observer*; the other by Robert A. Caro, the Pulitzer Prize–winning biographer of Robert Moses.[30] We continue to await the political biography of perhaps the likeliest candidate for revealing the contours and tensions that characterized this era of extraordinary transformation in the South: Richard B. Russell of Georgia.

In the meantime, while we are awaiting (and writing) those deeper and more distanced and reflective state monographs and political biographies, and awaiting also Numan Bartley's volume in the venerable *A History of the South* (and awaiting also his crucial decision about when to stop and why), we may comfort ourselves that Dewey Grantham's lament of 1965—that most of the writing on recent southern politics has been the work of political scientists and popularizers—still enjoys a familiar currency even in the mid-1980s. Godspeed to all those prolific political scientists, if not necessarily to the ephemeral popularizers. But history, not being a science, must look back long and hard before then looking forward. If the first Reconstruction is any historiographical guide at all, we are just beginning.

29. Numan V. Bartley, *The Creation of Modern Georgia* (Athens: University of Georgia Press, 1983); William D. Miller, *Mr. Crump of Memphis* (Baton Rouge: Louisiana State University Press, 1964); Joseph Bruce Gorman, *Kefauver: A Political Biography* (New York: Oxford University Press, 1971); Charles L. Fontenay, *Estes Kefauver: A Biography* (Knoxville: University of Tennessee Press, 1980); William R. Majors, *The End of Arcadia: Gordon Browning and Tennessee Politics* (Memphis: Memphis State University Press, 1982); Lee Seifert Greene, *Lead Me On: Frank Goad Clement and Tennessee Politics* (Knoxville: University of Tennessee Press, 1982); J. Harvie Wilkinson III, *Harry Byrd and the Changing Face of Virginia Politics, 1945–1966* (Charlottesville: University Press of Virginia, 1968); Edward F. Haas, *DeLesseps S. Morrison and the Image of Reform: New Orleans Politics, 1946–1961* (Baton Rouge: Louisiana State University Press, 1974); Glen Jeansonne, *Leander Perez: Boss of the Delta* (Baton Rouge: Louisiana State University Press, 1977).

30. Carl Grafton and Anne Permaloff, *Big Mules and Branchheads: James E. Folsom and Political Power in Alabama* (Athens: University of Georgia Press, 1985); George E. Sims, *The Little Man's Big Friend: James E. Folsom in Alabama Politics, 1946–1958* (University: University of Alabama Press, 1985). The standard study of Alabama politics during the Folsom years remains William D. Barnard, *Dixiecrats and Democrats: Alabama Politics, 1942–1950* (University: University of Alabama Press, 1974). Ronnie Dugger, *The Politician: The Life and Times of Lyndon Johnson: The Drive for Power, from the Frontier to Master of the Senate* (New York: Norton, 1982); Robert A. Caro, *The Years of Lyndon Johnson: The Path to Power* (New York: Knopf, 1982).

From Segregation to Integration

DAN T. CARTER

When George B. Tindall wrote "Southern Negroes Since Reconstruction" in 1965, he was able to point to a growing body of historiographical work dating back to the early twentieth century. While much of this historical literature was concentrated upon the events of the late nineteenth and early twentieth centuries, Tindall predicted that the 1960s and 1970s would see an "extensive historical invasion" of the more recent field of black history that had been dominated by polemicists, journalists, and social scientists.[1]

Tindall was right; one crude measure of the change the past decades have brought may be made by analyzing the increasing number of essays on twentieth-century black/southern history listed in the *Journal of Southern History*'s annual survey of scholarly articles published during the preceding year. Although most historians of the South continue to write on nineteenth-century themes, twentieth-century studies are no longer rejected as suitable only for the op-ed pages of the New York *Times,* and the book review section of the *Journal* reflects a similar shift. There remain important gaps in the historical literature of the age of segregation, but the problems of perspective and interpretation are far more troublesome.

Given the interest of earlier historians in establishing the origins of *de jure* segregation, it is surprising that so little has been written on the subject of legal segregation after 1900. That may be because the few studies that do exist suggest that segregation laws which carried racial separation to its logical extreme were of relatively low priority

---

1. George B. Tindall, "Southern Negroes Since Reconstruction: Dissolving the Static Image," in Arthur S. Link and Rembert W. Patrick (eds.), *Writing Southern History: Essays in Historiography in Honor of Fletcher M. Green* (Baton Rouge: Louisiana State University Press, 1965), 337–61 (quotation on p. 361). Among the historiographical essays dealing with the age of segregation that I found most helpful were George S. Burson, Jr., "The Second Reconstruction: A Historiographical Essay on Recent Works," *Journal of Negro History,* LIX (October, 1974), 322–36; and John B. Kirby, "An Uncertain Context: America and Black Americans in the Twentieth Century," *Journal of Southern History,* XLVI (November, 1980), 571–86.

after the system was in place. Clarence Poe's scheme for rural segregation during the Progressive Era gained little support. The more ambitious attempts legally to separate urban black and white communities were soon overruled by a United States Supreme Court uninterested in the problems of black Americans but anxious to preserve the property rights of buyers and sellers.[2]

In the two accounts that do exist for Virginia and Georgia during the first half of the twentieth century, it appears that southern lawmakers gave the issue little thought except on rare occasions. Public segregation laws were generally found in the city codes, but—even there—local officials were often surprisingly lax in establishing requirements for segregation in public facilities. The enactment and enforcement of Jim Crow laws after 1900 were hardly unimportant, and an examination of state laws and local city codes in other areas of the South might produce somewhat different results. Nevertheless, the findings of John Hammond Moore and Charles E. Wynes would suggest that explicitly segregationalist legislation was important after 1900 primarily as a reflection of the racial self-confidence of white southerners. As Derrick Bell pointed out in "The Racial Imperative in American Law," the courts and with them the rule of law were as much a mirror of white repression as an instrument for enforcing the overall social, political, and economic system that guaranteed the supremacy of whites over blacks.[3]

What is needed more than a summary of segregation laws is an analysis of the way in which various groups and elements in white southern society used the instruments of the law. A number of historians have explored that intersection between the legal/political system and the larger structure of white supremacy. One thinks immediately of Pete Daniels' account of peonage in the late-nineteenth- and early-twentieth-century South, or Carl V. Harris' exploration of the ways in which white interest groups in Birmingham, Alabama, jockeyed to "maximize their ability to utilize Negro labor efficiently or to

2. Jack Temple Kirby, *Darkness at the Dawning: Race and Reform in the Progressive South* (Philadelphia: Lippincott, 1972), 119–30; Roger L. Rice, "Residential Segregation by Law, 1910–1917," *Journal of Southern History*, XXXIV (May, 1968), 179–99.

3. John Hammond Moore, "Jim Crow in Georgia," *South Atlantic Quarterly*, LXVI (Autumn, 1967), 554–65; Charles E. Wynes, "The Evolution of Jim Crow Laws in Twentieth Century Virginia," *Phylon*, XXVIII (Winter, 1967), 416–25; Derrick A. Bell, Jr., "The Racial Imperative in American Law," in Robert Haws (ed.), *The Age of Segregation: Race Relations in the South, 1890–1954* (Jackson: University Press of Mississippi, 1978), 26–28.

minimize dangers and disadvantages which they believed they suffered because of the presence of large numbers of blacks." Harris' article "Reforms in Government Control of Negroes in Birmingham, Alabama, 1890–1920" is a thoughtful example of the way historians should evaluate the politics of "reactionaries" and "reformers" in the age of segregation.[4]

Underlying that system of legal oppression and coercion was the ultimate threat and use of force. John Shelton Reed's argument that southerners who avoided arguments and adultery were safer than their northern counterparts is probably true. But then so is his accompanying observation that southern murderers killed for "reasons both killer and killee understand."[5] One scarcely needs a Ph.D. in sociology—or in history—to understand the basic reason that lynch mobs put to death several thousand black southerners between 1890 and the 1940s.

During the last two decades, historians have provided us with accounts of some of the worst outbreaks of urban violence in the South during the age of segregation: Charles Crowe's account of the 1906 Atlanta race riot, John D. Weaver's re-creation of the "Brownsville Raid" (the alleged 1906 attack by black soldiers on the town of Brownsville, Texas), Robert V. Haynes's painstaking reconstruction of the Houston riot of 1917, Scott Ellsworth's recent description of the Tulsa, Oklahoma, race riot of 1921, and William Ivy Hair's study of the black marksman Robert Charles, who shot twenty-four white New Orleans residents (including four policemen) and touched off the first southern race riot of the twentieth century. Of these five accounts, Hair's is the most important for its evocative description of the racial tensions of the rural and urban South at the turn of the century.[6]

4. Pete Daniel, *The Shadow of Slavery: Peonage in the South, 1901–1969* (Urbana: University of Illinois Press, 1972); Carl V. Harris, "Reforms in Government Control of Negroes in Birmingham, Alabama, 1890–1920," *Journal of Southern History*, XXXVIII (November, 1972), 567–600 (quotation on p. 600). See also William Cohen, "Negro Involuntary Servitude in the South, 1865–1940: A Preliminary Analysis," *Journal of Southern History*, XLII (February, 1976), 31–60.

5. Merle Black and John Shelton Reed (eds.), *Perspectives on the American South: An Annual Review of Society, Politics and Culture*, I (New York: Gordon & Breach Science Publishers, 1981), 13.

6. Charles Crowe, "Racial Violence and Social Reform—Origins of the Atlanta Riot of 1906," *Journal of Negro History*, LIII (July, 1968), 234–56, and "Racial Massacre in Atlanta, September 22, 1906," *Journal of Negro History*, LIV (April, 1969),

Equally compelling is James R. McGovern's account of the 1934 lynching of Claude Neal. Although McGovern describes the brutal public murder of Neal with clinical detail, he has tried to relate this atrocity to the changing pattern of white-on-black violence in the South between 1900 and 1940. His thoughtful discussion of the Neal incident does much to explain the continuation of such barbarous spectacles into the twentieth century as well as some of the factors that led to a gradual decline in the number of public murders. After the 1930s, lynching ceased to be a public spectacle; like the civil rights turmoil of the 1960s, it was bad for the community "image." But often this simply meant that southern whites were satisfied with the more dignified setting of the state-operated electric chair. Not every black southerner executed by the state was innocent, just as some victims of mob law were probably guilty of capital crimes. And it was certainly preferable to have one's fate decided by the southern court system than by a mob of drunken, enraged whites. As I suggested in my study of the Scottsboro case, however, the distinction was not so clear-cut as southerners liked to believe.[7]

Neither McGovern nor other historians who have described the operation of white-on-black violence have been able to make more than a crude estimate of the impact of such violence in maintaining white supremacy. Perhaps, on the other hand, it is a meaningless

---

150–73; John D. Weaver, *The Brownsville Raid* (New York: Norton, 1970); Robert V. Haynes, *A Night of Violence: The Houston Riot of 1917* (Baton Rouge: Louisiana State University Press, 1976); Scott Ellsworth, *Death in a Promised Land: The Tulsa Race Riot of 1921* (Baton Rouge: Louisiana State University Press, 1982); William Ivy Hair, *Carnival of Fury: Robert Charles and the New Orleans Race Riot of 1900* (Baton Rouge: Louisiana State University Press, 1976). See also Arthur I. Waskow, *From Race Riot to Sit-In, 1919 and the 1960s: A Study in the Connections Between Conflict and Violence* (Garden City, N.Y.: Doubleday, 1966); and Ann J. Lane, *The Brownsville Affair: National Crisis and Black Reaction* (Port Washington, N.Y.: Kennikat Press, 1971). More than a decade after its publication, Sheldon Hackney's article on southern violence remains the best survey of explanations for the general propensity of southerners—black and white—to kill and maim each other with excessive statistical regularity. See Hackney, "Southern Violence," *American Historical Review,* LXXIV (February, 1969), 906–25. But see also Albert C. Smith, "'Southern Violence' Reconsidered: Arson as Protest in Black Belt Georgia, 1865–1910," *Journal of Southern History,* LI (November, 1985), 527–64.

7. James R. McGovern, *Anatomy of a Lynching: The Killing of Claude Neal* (Baton Rouge: Louisiana State University Press, 1982); Dan T. Carter, *Scottsboro: A Tragedy of the American South* (Rev. ed.; Baton Rouge: Louisiana State University Press, 1979).

question. As Herbert G. Gutman pointed out in his discussion of the number of whippings that took place under slavery, the quantity is far less important than the victims' knowledge that whites could whip blacks with impunity.[8]

There was resistance within the black community to these policies of legal and political repression. August Meier and Elliott Rudwick have rescued from undeserved obscurity the little-known story of the struggle of black southerners in the early twentieth century against segregated streetcars and racist white businesses. Raymond Wolters' account of black campus unrest in the 1920s gives us some insight into the dissatisfaction of post–World War I black students, and Pete Daniels' analysis of the dispute over the staffing of Tuskegee's Veterans' Hospital shows that the black community was not completely powerless in its fight for minimal rights.[9] Moreover, I suspect that in years to come, historians will follow in the footsteps of Lawrence W. Levine and Herbert Gutman, illuminating the rich subculture of black southern life that continued to exist despite segregation, just as it had developed in spite of slavery.[10]

But three state studies of black life at the height of the age of segregation tell a bleak story that reinforces the gloomy portrait of the public side of race relationships in the early-twentieth-century South. John Dittmer, writing on Georgia blacks, Lester C. Lamon on Ten-

8. Herbert G. Gutman, *Slavery and the Numbers Game: A Critique of "Time on the Cross"* (Urbana: University of Illinois Press, 1975).

9. August Meier and Elliott Rudwick, "The Boycott Movement Against Jim Crow Streetcars in the South, 1900–1906," *Journal of American History,* LV (March, 1969), 756–75; Raymond Wolters, *The New Negro on Campus: Black College Rebellions of the 1920s* (Princeton: Princeton University Press, 1975); Pete Daniel, "Black Power in the 1920s: The Case of Tuskegee Veterans Hospital," *Journal of Southern History,* XXXVI (August, 1970), 368–88. See, for example, the autobiography of the militant Ida B. Wells of Memphis, a black woman who tenaciously fought lynching in the region until her death in 1931 (Ida B. Wells, *Crusade for Justice: The Autobiography of Ida B. Wells,* ed. Alfreda M. Duster [Chicago: University of Chicago Press, 1970]).

10. Lawrence W. Levine, *Black Culture and Black Consciousness: Afro-American Folk Thought from Slavery to Freedom* (New York: Oxford University Press, 1977); Herbert G. Gutman, *The Black Family in Slavery and Freedom, 1750–1925* (New York: Pantheon, 1976). In this respect, one thinks almost immediately of the autobiography of "Nate Shaw" (actually Ned Cobb) compiled by Theodore Rosengarten. *All God's Dangers* is hardly the story of a typical Alabama black farmer in the first forty years of the twentieth century, but Cobb's reminiscences—in addition to their artistic merit—are a reflection of the rich texture of a black world hidden from the view of most whites. Rosengarten, *All God's Dangers: The Life of Nate Shaw* (New York: Knopf, 1974).

nessee, and I. A. Newby on South Carolina have different emphases in their books, but they share Newby's depressing conclusion. The story of black South Carolinians, insists Newby, was one of repression, powerlessness, and a resigned adaptation to these conditions.[11]

Even Raymond Gavins, who depicts a far more dynamic response by the black leadership of Richmond from 1900 to 1920, agrees that "segregation not only denied the black community an equal share of the city's prosperity; it deprived black leadership of the power to protect blacks' interests." As John Matthews concluded in his article "The Dilemma of Negro Leadership in the New South," in the "racial climate of the early twentieth century there was little a black man could do to make his life more secure and to win just treatment from society. He was without social, economic, or political power to resist the worst manifestations of Southern racism."[12] And if that was true in the urban areas of the South, it was an even greater and more oppressive reality in the rural South, where the great majority of black southerners lived until well into the twentieth century.

Given the repressive nature of southern society and the almost complete absence of support from any segment of white American society, the acts of resistance on the part of black southerners during this period reflect a courage we would do well to remember. Nevertheless, they were at best symbolic holding actions; at worst, futile cries of resistance against a system that seemed unyielding in its rigors.

And yet beneath that apparently immovable structure of the segregated society of the South there was change. In important ways it began after 1914 with the great migration of black southerners out of the region and into the cities of the North. While much of the most important work on this demographic shift dates from the 1930s and

11. John Dittmer, *Black Georgia in the Progressive Era, 1900–1920* (Urbana: University of Illinois Press, 1977); Lester C. Lamon, *Black Tennesseans, 1900–1930* (Knoxville: University of Tennessee Press, 1977); I. A. Newby, *Black Carolinians: A History of Blacks in South Carolina from 1895 to 1968* (Columbia: University of South Carolina Press, 1973).

12. Raymond Gavins, "Urbanization and Segregation: Black Leadership Patterns in Richmond, Virginia, 1900–1920," *South Atlantic Quarterly*, LXXIX (Summer, 1980), 257–73 (quotation on p. 272); John Matthews, "The Dilemma of Negro Leadership in the New South: The Case of the Negro Young People's Congress of 1902," *South Atlantic Quarterly*, LXXIII (Winter, 1974), 130–44 (quotation on p. 144). With some variations, this is also the theme of Nancy J. Weiss's "The Negro and the New Freedom: Fighting Wilsonian Segregation," *Political Science Quarterly*, LXXXIV (March, 1969), 61–79; and Theodore Hemmingway, "Prelude to Change: Black Carolinians in the War Years, 1914–1920," *Journal of Negro History*, LXV (Summer, 1980), 212–27.

1940s, there have been a number of additional studies during the past fifteen years. Although Florette Henri devotes three-fourths of her study *Black Migration* to the creation and development of black urban communities in the North, she does summarize the background to the migration and vividly describes the painful process of relocation. More useful in exploring the forces that sent black southerners northward is *Anyplace But Here*, Arna Bontemps and Jack Conroy's description of the movement that led more than four million black southerners to leave the region and move into the urban centers of the North.[13]

While the Great Depression temporarily slowed this massive outmigration, with wartime mobilization in the late 1930s it resumed at an even more accelerated rate. Between 1920 and 1960 the number of black Americans outside the eleven states of the former Confederacy (plus Maryland) had grown by ten million. The increase in the black population of the South was less than two million. By the passage of the Civil Rights Act of 1964 the population of black America would be divided almost equally between the South and the rest of the United States.[14]

Historians are understandably reluctant to use the term *watershed,* but it seems that the years between 1930 and 1954 constitute, if not a watershed, at the very least a turning point in the age of segregation. Certainly change came slowly and always in the face of bitter resistance from most white southerners. In such celebrated civil rights confrontations as the Angelo Herndon case in Georgia and the Scottsboro case in Alabama, state officials stubbornly and bitterly defended the most indefensible results of Jim Crow injustice. Nor is there any evidence that the administration of Franklin D. Roosevelt was willing to commit itself to undermining the structure of southern racial relationships. As Frank Freidel shows in his brief book about Roosevelt and the South, the well-meaning Roosevelt was always a captive of

13. Florette Henri, *Black Migration: Movement North, 1900–1920* (Garden City, N.Y.: Anchor Press, 1975); Arna Bontemps and Jack Conroy, *Anyplace But Here* (New York: Hill & Wang, 1966). Of particular value is Jack Temple Kirby, "The Southern Exodus, 1910–1960: A Primer for Historians," *Journal of Southern History,* XLIX (November, 1983), 585–600. There is some useful statistical information on the recent migrational patterns in the otherwise disappointing *Black Migration in America: A Social Demographic History,* by Daniel M. Johnson and Rex R. Campbell (Durham: Duke University Press, 1981). See also the journalistic account, Dwayne E. Walls, *The Chickenbone Special* (New York: Harcourt Brace Jovanovich, 1971).

14. T. Lynn Smith, "The Redistribution of the Negro Population of the United States, 1910–1960," *Journal of Negro History,* LI (July, 1966), 155–73.

his reliance upon the southern wing of the Democratic party. Time after time he skillfully evaded efforts to force him to take a position on such controversial issues as antilynching legislation. Under his administration, black rights were inadequately protected in the NRA programs while the policies of the first and second Agricultural Adjustment Administrations benefited landowners and often increased the problems of landless tenants. Even when he gave his tacit support to the racial liberals of the Southern Conference for Human Welfare in 1938 and attempted to purge conservatives from the southern Democratic party that same year, racial reform was never a major consideration for Roosevelt. Few historians are likely to disagree with Raymond Wolters' gloomy conclusion in his study *Negroes and the Great Depression*. Except in a political sense, argues Wolters, there was no New Deal policy as such toward the race question that extended beyond the idiosyncratic and personal views of individual New Deal administrators.[15]

Wolters' conclusion is well taken. On the other hand, any assessment of the New Deal will have to make its judgments within the context of the 1930s, not the 1960s, 1970s, or 1980s. In his study of race relations in the late-nineteenth-century urban South, Howard Rabinowitz has suggested that segregation was sometimes a halting step forward from absolute exclusion toward separate and unequal facilities. In much the same way, the sometimes discriminatory and contradictory policies of the New Deal often led to direct and indirect benefits for black southerners who suffered far greater and more systematic discrimination at the hands of state and local governments in the decades preceding the 1930s.[16]

15. Frank Freidel, *F.D.R. and the South* (Baton Rouge: Louisiana State University Press, 1965); Raymond Wolters, *Negroes and the Great Depression: The Problem of Economic Recovery* (Westport, Conn.: Greenwood Publishing Corp., 1970); Sidney Baldwin, *Poverty and Politics: The Rise and Decline of the Farm Security Administration* (Chapel Hill: University of North Carolina Press, 1968). For a discussion of Roosevelt's timidity on issues of race, see Robert L. Zangrando's *The NAACP Crusade Against Lynching, 1909–1950* (Philadelphia: Temple University Press, 1980); Carter, *Scottsboro;* and Charles H. Martin, *The Angelo Herndon Case and Southern Justice* (Baton Rouge: Louisiana State University Press, 1976).

16. Howard N. Rabinowitz, *Race Relations in the Urban South, 1865–1890* (New York: Oxford University Press, 1978). See, for example, Michael S. Holmes, "The New Deal and Georgia's Black Youth," *Journal of Southern History,* XXXVIII (August, 1972), 443–60; and Anthony J. Badger's comments on the unintentional effects of the New Deal's tobacco price support program on race relations in eastern North Carolina in *Prosperity Road: The New Deal, Tobacco, and North Carolina* (Chapel Hill: University of North Carolina Press, 1980). It is a point of view shared by most of the au-

In *Farewell to the Party of Lincoln,* Nancy J. Weiss concentrates upon the political dimensions of the New Deal and Roosevelt's policies toward black Americans. She does not dissent from the conclusion of Wolters and other recent scholars that the Roosevelt administration shied away from adopting any substantive civil rights policy; even Eleanor Roosevelt does not emerge unscathed from Weiss's critical assessment of the Roosevelt record on racial issues. But she points out that despite these deficiencies, black Americans overwhelmingly turned to the Democratic party between 1932 and 1940 and went on to become the most dependable link in the Roosevelt political coalition. Republican indifference and Roosevelt's skill at manipulating symbolic issues undoubtedly accelerated this process. As Weiss conclusively documents in her analysis of the campaigns of the 1930s, however, the overwhelming reason was economics. Upper-class black voters continued, for example, to support Republican candidates. But most black voters were poor and they benefited directly from New Deal work and relief programs.[17]

Moreover, there is growing evidence that—whatever the intention of New Deal administrators—the policies and political thrust of the Roosevelt regime directly and indirectly undermined the foundations of southern racial practices. In his study *Black Americans in the Roosevelt Era,* John B. Kirby is often critical of the way in which white New Deal reformers channeled and tamed the more radical instincts of black New Dealers and sympathizers in the 1930s. Such white liberals (and some black ones as well), concludes Kirby, were often naïve in their assumption that prejudice would fade as federal policies improved the economic well-being of all Americans. And New Dealers were oblivious to the danger (seen, ironically, by a number of black supporters of the administration) that the creation of a welfare state would thwart the development of black self-reliance and shift black Americans' dependency from "ole Massa to Uncle Sam." Nevertheless, after weighing the failures as well as the achievements of the Roosevelt years, Kirby concludes that the administration created a national context in which the discussion of social, economic, and racial issues led in directions that challenged the status quo. Harvard Sitkoff's *A New Deal for Blacks* is a much broader study of the

thors in the essays edited by James C. Cobb and Michael V. Namorato, *The New Deal in the South* (Jackson: University Press of Mississippi, 1984).

17. Nancy J. Weiss, *Farewell to the Party of Lincoln: Black Politics in the Age of FDR* (Princeton: Princeton University Press, 1983).

impact of the Roosevelt years, but it reaches essentially the same conclusions.[18]

While changes in the economic, political, and legal aspects of southern racial relationships were not always apparent, there was a gradual reemergence of the issue of civil rights on the national scene after 1930. For perhaps the first time since the racial "solution" of the 1890s, white southerners were forced to defend the system of white supremacy they had so carefully constructed. Even as the political efforts of Roosevelt and Harry S. Truman to "liberalize" the southern Democratic party faltered in the 1940s, the federal courts had begun to challenge the legal matrix of the Jim Crow system. It was a long way from the Court's decision in the Scottsboro cases during the 1930s to *Brown* v. *Board of Education* in 1954, but the direction seemed clear by the 1940s. Certainly the Court's decision in 1944 outlawing the Democratic white primary was more than a matter of symbolic importance. It may not have guaranteed the vote for blacks in the South, but it created an altogether different climate and mood, particularly in the emerging urban black communities of the region.[19]

While much of the local black and white civil rights leadership of this era remains unknown, we are coming to understand more of the interconnecting biographies of those black and white southerners who were drawn into the New Deal and then either returned to the

18. John B. Kirby, *Black Americans in the Roosevelt Era: Liberalism and Race* (Knoxville: University of Tennessee Press, 1980); Harvard Sitkoff, *A New Deal for Blacks: The Emergence of Civil Rights as a National Issue* (New York: Oxford University Press, 1978).

19. Darlene Clark Hine describes the long history of the white primary in *Black Victory: The Rise and Fall of the White Primary in Texas* (Millwood, N.Y.: KTO Press, 1979). But her study is most valuable for her discussion of the effect the struggle against the white primary had in mobilizing and ultimately uniting the black leadership of Houston. For a discussion of the early emergence of the civil rights issue in the 1940s and the response of the Truman administration, see Donald R. McCoy and Richard T. Ruetten, *Quest and Response: Minority Rights and the Truman Administration* (Lawrence: University Press of Kansas, 1973); William C. Berman, *The Politics of Civil Rights in the Truman Administration* (Columbus: Ohio State University Press, 1970); Donald R. McCoy and Richard T. Ruetten, "The Civil Rights Movement: 1940–1954," *Midwest Quarterly*, XI (October, 1969), 11–34; Peter J. Kellogg, "Civil Rights Consciousness in the 1940s," *Historian*, XLII (November, 1979), 18–41; Richard M. Dalfiume, "The 'Forgotten Years' of the Negro Revolution," *Journal of American History*, LV (June, 1968), 90–106; and Lee Finkle, "The Conservative Aims of Militant Rhetoric: Black Protest During World War II," *Journal of American History*, LX (December, 1973), 692–713.

South or continued their involvement in issues relating to the "southern question" while they remained in Washington. Given the search by white southern liberal academics for a usable past, it is not surprising that a number of studies have appeared on the white veterans of the liberal crusades of the 1930s and 1940s. Such studies collectively illuminate the awkward marriage of nineteenth-century paternalism and the cautious social gospel of the early twentieth century that produced twentieth-century liberalism. For most such "liberals," evasion had been a deeply ingrained response to any question dealing with race in the first decades of the age of segregation.[20]

For a handful of whites, the decade of the 1930s was the setting for a radical conversion on the issue of race. By 1942, segregation had become, to the southern writer Lillian Smith, far more than a legal system of discrimination or an economic method of exploiting black southerners. It was part of the stifling Victorian ethos that had gripped the South for much of its recent history. Jim Crow practices were only the most vivid examples of the way in which the white southerner had pushed not simply blacks but "everything dark, dangerous, evil . . . to the rim of one's life." Signs placed over doors or water fountains seemed natural enough to the children of the South, for "signs had already been put over forbidden areas of our body." The banning of books and ideas was simply another reflection of "the banning of our wishes which we learned early to send to the Darktown of our unconscious." The destruction of legal segregation would thus liberate white as well as black southerners.[21]

20. Morton Sosna's *In Search of the Silent South: Southern Liberals and the Race Issue* (New York: Columbia University Press, 1977) is the most successful effort thus far to evaluate and assess this group. Anthony P. Dunbar, Thomas A. Krueger, and Robert F. Martin deal with some of the more radical southerners during this period; Dunbar in *Against the Grain: Southern Radicals and Prophets, 1929–1959* (Charlottesville: University Press of Virginia, 1981); Krueger in *And Promises to Keep: The Southern Conference for Human Welfare, 1938–1948* (Nashville: Vanderbilt University Press, 1967); and Martin in "A Prophet's Pilgrimage: The Religious Radicalism of Howard Anderson Kester, 1921–1941," *Journal of Southern History,* XLVIII (November, 1982), 511–30. Irwin Klibaner carries that story into the 1970s in his "The Travail of Southern Radicals: The Southern Conference Educational Fund, 1946–1976," *Journal of Southern History,* XLIX (May, 1983), 179–202. For other biographies, see John A. Salmond, *A Southern Rebel: The Life and Times of Aubrey Willis Williams, 1890–1965* (Chapel Hill: University of North Carolina Press, 1983); Jacquelyn Dowd Hall, *Revolt Against Chivalry: Jessie Daniel Ames and the Women's Campaign Against Lynching* (New York: Columbia University Press, 1979); and Charles W. Eagles, *Jonathan Daniels and Race Relations: The Evolution of a Southern Liberal* (Knoxville: University of Tennessee Press, 1982).

21. Lillian Smith, *Killers of the Dream* (New York: Norton, 1949; Garden City,

Not many southern white liberals shared Lillian Smith's conviction that racism was simply the ultimate expression of sexual repression. Fewer still were willing to echo her uncompromising denunciation of segregation. Nevertheless, as Daniel Joseph Singal illustrates, in his important study of southern intellectual life between the wars, the opposition of southern liberals to Smith's outspokenness was as likely to be on tactical as philosophical grounds. The two most distinguished social scientists of the South of the 1930s, Guy B. Johnson and Howard W. Odum, publicly counseled caution on the subject and seemed reconciled to the prospect that segregation would end slowly and painfully. Privately, there was no ambivalence. By the mid-1930s, concludes Singal, Odum had become, "perhaps without even realizing it, an 'ultimate integrationist.'" [22]

Unfortunately we have far fewer studies of black southerners during these two decades preceding the public emergence of the civil rights movement. *The Narrative of Hosea Hudson,* about a black Communist organizer in Alabama in the 1930s and 1940s (ably edited by Nell Irvin Painter), casts new light on the attempts of the Communist party to recruit black members in the region. Among main-line black leaders in the South, however, there are only a few studies to equal the Hudson autobiography. Walter B. Weare's account of the North Carolina Mutual Life Insurance Company (and his biographical essay on the guiding figure, Charles Clinton Spalding) and Raymond Gavins' excellent account of the Virginia educator and community leader Gordon Blaine Hancock stand alone as scholarly portraits of black southern leaders in the years between Booker T. Washington and Martin Luther King, Jr.[23]

N.Y.: Anchor Books, 1963), 75 (first quotation), 76 (second and third quotations). Page references are to the 1963 edition.

22. Daniel Joseph Singal, *The War Within: From Victorian to Modernist Thought in the South, 1919–1945* (Chapel Hill: University of North Carolina Press, 1982), 146–47, 324–25 (quotation on p. 147).

23. Nell Irvin Painter (ed.), *The Narrative of Hosea Hudson: His Life as a Negro Communist in the South* (Cambridge: Harvard University Press, 1979); Walter B. Weare, *Black Business in the New South: A Social History of the North Carolina Mutual Life Insurance Company* (Urbana: University of Illinois Press, 1973), and "Charles Clinton Spaulding: Middle-class Leadership in the Age of Segregation," in John Hope Franklin and August Meier (eds.), *Black Leaders of the Twentieth Century* (Urbana: University of Illinois Press, 1982), 167–90; Raymond Gavins, *The Perils and Prospects of Southern Black Leadership: Gordon Blaine Hancock, 1884–1970* (Durham: Duke University Press, 1977). There are some exceptions to this blanket generalization. Benjamin E. Mays's *Born to Rebel: An Autobiography* (New York: Charles Scribner's Sons, 1971) is useful. Rackham Holt has written a study of Mary McLeod

Gavins' study, in particular, is a suggestive portrait of the emergence of an increasingly independent and (by early-twentieth-century standards) assertive black community leadership in the 1930s and 1940s. To some extent, Hancock followed the well-worn ideological path of self-help and racial solidarity laid down by Booker T. Washington. But his blistering condemnation of discrimination and public segregation reflected a new and more restive generation of black southerners. It was Hancock (and several friends) who sponsored the conference that led to the 1942 Durham Manifesto on race relations and, ultimately, the transformation of the Commission on Interracial Cooperation into the Southern Regional Council.[24]

Hancock, a professor at Virginia Union Seminary and the pastor of Richmond's Moore Street Baptist Church, was not a nationally prominent figure, but Gavins rightly sees him as an example of the leadership that had emerged in the South's growing urban black communities. At the beginning of the twentieth century, 85 percent of all black southerners lived in the countryside, the majority in the plantation belt from Virginia through east Texas. By 1940, however, more than three million black southerners—one-third of the Negro population of the region—lived in towns and cities. By 1960, the majority made the city their home. And yet we know far more about the 5 percent of the antebellum southern population of free blacks and slaves who lived in cities (or even the emerging black communities of Harlem, South Chicago, and Watts) than we know of these twentieth-century black urban southerners.[25]

Bethune, the most influential black southern advisor in the Roosevelt administration, *Mary McLeod Bethune: A Biography* (Garden City, N.Y.: Doubleday, 1964). And there is Linda O. McMurry's excellent *George Washington Carver: Scientist and Symbol* (New York: Oxford University Press, 1981). But Holt's study is disappointingly journalistic. (B. Joyce Ross's essay "Mary McLeod Bethune and the National Youth Administration: A Case Study of Power Relationships in the Black Cabinet of Franklin D. Roosevelt," in Franklin and Meier [eds.], *Black Leaders*, 191–219, is far more perceptive.) And, while McMurry demonstrates that Carver's career is important in understanding the history of black and white in the first forty years of the twentieth century, Carver hardly fits into the mainstream of developments.

24. There have been a number of theses and dissertations written on the Commission on Interracial Cooperation and the Southern Regional Council, but we still lack a full-scale published study of these two important organizations.

25. Smith, "The Redistribution of the Negro Population," 155–73. For a discussion of the scarcity of monographic studies on black southern urban life in the twentieth century, see Dan T. Carter, "Southern Political Style," in Haws (ed.), *The Age of Segregation*, 57–66.

It was in those urban communities that black political consciousness increased in the wake of the Supreme Court's decision against
the white primaries. Between 1944 and 1950, for example, the number of black voters quadrupled from 150,000 to 600,000. And almost all of this increase was in the urban South. In Atlanta, Durham,
Jacksonville, Richmond, and other southern cities, voter registration
drives became a dress rehearsal for the civil rights movement of the
1950s and 1960s. That voting rights movement was, from the outset,
a cautious and conservative force led by black ministers, educators,
and "traditional" community leaders. Nevertheless, the insistence on
the right of black southerners to exercise the franchise was a sharp
break from the accommodationism that had dominated black rhetoric in the South.[26]

It is not simply an accident that Daisy Bates of Little Rock became
involved in the civil rights movement after her participation in Henry
Wallace's 1948 Progressive party campaign, or that Rosa Parks of
Montgomery had attended a labor/civil rights workshop at the Highlander Labor School before she refused to give up her seat on the bus
in 1955. When the civil rights movement became front-page news in
the 1950s, many of its leaders were young and newly politicized, but
there was an older generation that had already begun the less glam-
orous task of voter registration in the new black urban communities
of the 1940s.[27]

To move from the 1940s and early 1950s into the post-1954 era of
southern race relations is to pass from famine to gluttony. During the
1950s (and particularly in the 1960s), publishers discovered that
black was green, and hundreds of personal accounts, journalistic descriptions, and pop-history/sociology texts soon cluttered the shelves
of America's bookstores. Ironically, as the public's interest and the
publishers' profit levels receded, we have finally begun to benefit from
that wave of scholarly works George Tindall predicted. In some areas
the quantity of materials is simply overwhelming. To cite just one ex-

26. Clarence A. Bacote describes the early stages of black urban political organization prior to the Brown decision in "The Negro in Atlanta Politics," *Phylon*, XVI
(Winter, 1955), 333–50. David M. Tucker has written a brief biography of the Memphis black politician George Washington Lee, *Lieutenant Lee of Beale Street* (Nashville: Vanderbilt University Press, 1971).

27. Patricia Ann Sullivan examines some of these forgotten figures in southern
interracial activism between World War II and the mid-1950s who moved into the
Progressive party ("Gideon's Southern Soldiers: New Deal Politics and Civil Rights
Reform, 1933–1948" [Ph.D. dissertation, Emory University, 1983]).

ample: since 1966, there have been at least a half dozen accounts of the desegregation of the various branches of the armed forces.[28]

With notable exceptions, much of the historical literature of the civil rights movement and the end of legal segregation has fallen into one of the following categories: accounts of the heroic struggle; descriptions of the disgraceful behavior of the defenders of a morally bankrupt institution; the brief celebration of victory in 1964, followed by disillusionment; and—finally—a growing number of works that reach behind the public accounts of the end of segregation to probe the inner history of the last decade of the legally segregated South.

The process of separating from the moral commitment of much of the early scholarship on the last years of legal segregation has not been an easy task. If the Second World War was the last unambiguously righteous military conflict for Americans, the civil rights movement may have been our last morally pure domestic crusade. That is hardly how it was described by segregationists in the 1950s and 1960s, but one would be hard pressed today to find a prominent figure—North or South—who would condemn the purposes and goals of the movement or who would question its ultimately positive effects upon southern society. During his last ill-fated reelection campaign in 1980, supporters of Georgia Senator Herman Talmadge removed from circulation dog-eared copies of *You and Segregation,* which he had written and proudly mailed to libraries in 1956. And even though there is no evidence that James J. Kilpatrick has tried to destroy copies of his 1962 book, *The Southern Case for School Segregation,* we may be reasonably confident he is not arranging a reprint edition.[29]

Many of the early accounts of the rise of the civil rights movement

28. Morris J. MacGregor, *Integration of the Armed Forces, 1940–1965* (Washington, D.C.: Center of Military History, 1981); Ulysses Lee, *The Employment of Negro Troops* (Washington, D.C.: Office of the Chief of Military History, United States Army, 1966); Alan M. Osur, *Blacks in the Army Air Forces During World War II: The Problem of Race Relations* (Washington, D.C.: Office of Air Force History, 1977); Richard M. Dalfiume, *Desegregation of the U.S. Armed Forces: Fighting on Two Fronts, 1939–1953* (Columbia: University of Missouri Press, 1969); Jack D. Foner, *Blacks and the Military in American History: A New Perspective* (New York: Praeger, 1974); Alan L. Gropman, *The Air Force Integrates: 1945–1964* (Washington, D.C.: Office of Air Force History, 1978).

29. Herman Talmadge, *You and Segregation* (Birmingham: Vulcan Press, 1956); James Jackson Kilpatrick, *The Southern Case for School Segregation* (New York: Crowell-Collier Press, 1962).

and the bitter defense of segregation by white southerners are marked by emotional commitment and righteous indignation. One need read only Leon Friedman's edited collection of essays caustically titled *Southern Justice* to gain a flavor of much of this earlier literature. While Friedman's collection represents the horrified response of (mostly) northern legal missionaries in the South, the tone was already established by the southern historian James W. Silver in his angry 1963 presidential address to the Southern Historical Association (and his book the following year) condemning Mississippi's closed society.[30]

There were always exceptions to this generalization. Neither Hugh Davis Graham nor Numan V. Bartley concealed his antipathy to Jim Crow in their studies of white southern resistance published in the late 1960s, but they tried to be impartial and evenhanded in their descriptions of the antics of white southerners. Neil R. McMillen was equally successful in avoiding moral indignation in his 1971 account of the white citizens' council movement, and even I. A. Newby generally managed to restrain his obvious contempt for the popular and scientific proponents of segregation in his two studies of Jim Crow's defenders in the twentieth century. But most of the initial accounts of the civil rights movement and the conflict in the South are read today primarily because of the insights they offer us into events as they were seen by committed participants rather than by impartial observers.[31]

More recent works have been characterized by a greater emphasis

30. Leon Friedman (ed.), *Southern Justice* (New York: Pantheon, 1965); James W. Silver, "Mississippi: The Closed Society," *Journal of Southern History*, XXX (February, 1964), 3–34, and *Mississippi: The Closed Society* (New York: Harcourt, Brace & World, 1964).

31. Hugh Davis Graham, *Crisis in Print: Desegregation and the Press in Tennessee* (Nashville: Vanderbilt University Press, 1967); Numan V. Bartley, *The Rise of Massive Resistance: Race and Politics in the South During the 1950s* (Baton Rouge: Louisiana State University Press, 1969); I. A. Newby, *Jim Crow's Defense: Anti-Negro Thought in America, 1900–1930* (Baton Rouge: Louisiana State University Press, 1965), and *Challenge to the Court: Social Scientists and the Defense of Segregation, 1954–1966* (Baton Rouge: Louisiana State University Press, 1967); Neil R. McMillen, *The Citizens' Council: Organized Resistance to the Second Reconstruction, 1954–64* (Urbana: University of Illinois Press, 1971). Among these early surveys still useful are Reed Sarratt's *The Ordeal of Desegregation: The First Decade* (New York: Harper & Row, 1966); Benjamin Muse, *Ten Years of Prelude: The Story of Integration Since the Supreme Court's 1954 Decision* (New York: Viking, 1964), and *The American Negro Revolution: From Nonviolence to Black Power, 1963–1967* (Bloomington: Indiana University Press, 1968); and Pat Watters, *The South and the Nation* (New York: Pantheon, 1969). Earl Black has made a significant addition to this literature with his

on understanding rather than condemning and upon probing behind
the headlines in order to explore the complex patterns of white reaction to the events of the 1950s and early 1960s. It is not that the historians of the 1970s and 1980s have suddenly rushed to embrace the
arguments of Leander Perez and Orval Faubus. A careful reading of
several of the essays recently edited by Elizabeth Jacoway and David
R. Colburn (*Southern Businessmen and Desegregation*) does little
to rescue the reputations of most white business leaders. But we do
gain a far better understanding of the forces that shaped the response of grudging accommodation in some cities and bitter resistance in others.[32]

William Chafe is still the morally committed liberal in his study
of the civil rights movement in Greensboro, but he skillfully uses traditional historical sources supplemented by oral interviews to describe with far greater subtlety than heretofore possible the range of
individuals and factions that made up the black community of that
city and the white leadership as well that lay behind the "mask of
civility" which had helped Greensboro avoid overt violence in the
early 1960s.[33]

Even as historians have moved to understand as much as to
condemn the southern white conservatives, they have gingerly approached the task of reducing the heroic exploits of the civil rights
movement to more human dimensions. In some respects, David L.
Lewis' 1970 biography of Martin Luther King, Jr., reflects the kind of
shift that has taken place in accounts of the civil rights movement

---

study, *Southern Governors and Civil Rights: Racial Segregation as a Campaign Issue
in the Second Reconstruction* (Cambridge: Harvard University Press, 1976), while
George Metcalf has attempted a survey of school desegregation from 1956 to 1980 in
From Little Rock to Boston: The History of School Desegregation (Westport, Conn.:
Greenwood Press, 1983).

32. Elizabeth Jacoway and David R. Colburn (eds.), *Southern Businessmen and
Desegregation* (Baton Rouge: Louisiana State University Press, 1982). For a biography
of Leander Perez, which some reviewers have criticized as *too* objective, see Glen Jeansonne, *Leander Perez: Boss of the Delta* (Baton Rouge: Louisiana State University
Press, 1977).

33. William H. Chafe, *Civilities and Civil Rights: Greensboro, North Carolina,
and the Black Struggle for Freedom* (New York: Oxford University Press, 1980). Although he concentrates on a relatively brief period, J. Mills Thornton's "Challenge and
Response in the Montgomery Bus Boycott of 1955–1956," *Alabama Review*, XXXIII
(July, 1980), 163–235, is indispensable. A less successful but still useful study of the
impact of the movement on a Deep South community (Panola County, Mississippi) has
been made by Frederick M. Wirt in his *Politics of Southern Equality: Law and Social
Change in a Mississippi County* (Chicago: Aldine, 1971).

itself. Despite his admiration and affection for King, Lewis argued that the head of the civil rights movement had made a number of serious political miscalculations in his leadership, and he questioned many of the assumptions underlying King's program of nonviolence and moral suasion. In part, Lewis simply reflected the disillusionment of black power advocates, and his assumptions about the future direction of race and politics in the South and the United States may well have been further from the mark than King's. But Lewis' willingness to suggest that the great moral leader of the movement had feet of clay indicated a new skeptical tone and outlook.[34]

This changed emphasis can be seen in Clayborne Carson's *In Struggle,* a history of the Student Non-Violent Coordinating Committee. Using a variety of available records supplemented by his extensive oral history interviews, Carson writes affectionately of the men and women who led the battle for civil rights in the South. Still he is more analytical than authors of earlier studies and much more willing to find the seeds of self-destruction within the movement's inability to impose self-discipline and subordinate personal liberation to the less exciting task of developing ongoing programs in the black communities of the South.[35]

While it is difficult to make predictions, we are likely to see a number of studies that approach the civil rights movement from a quite different perspective. With few exceptions, even the most recent accounts continue to be drawn toward "what might have been" and to

34. David L. Lewis, *King: A Critical Biography* (New York: Praeger, 1970), and *King: A Biography* (Rev. ed.; Urbana: University of Illinois Press, 1978). Stephen B. Oates's new biography of King, *Let the Trumpet Sound: The Life of Martin Luther King, Jr.* (New York: Harper & Row, 1982), is dramatically readable, but less insightful in some ways than Lewis' earlier study.

35. Clayborne Carson, *In Struggle: SNCC and the Black Awakening of the 1960s* (Cambridge: Harvard University Press, 1981). Carson's book would have been strengthened by use of the SNCC papers at the Martin Luther King Center Archives, but their processing was incomplete until after his study was in press. In a particularly prescient article first published in 1969, Allen J. Matusow anticipated many of Carson's observations. See Matusow, "From Civil Rights to Black Power: The Case of SNCC, 1960–1966," in Barton J. Bernstein and Allen J. Matusow (eds.), *Twentieth Century America: Recent Interpretations* (Rev. ed.; New York: Harcourt Brace Jovanovich, 1972), 494–521. See also Mary Aickin Rothschild's *A Case of Black and White: Northern Volunteers and the Southern Freedom Summers, 1964–1965* (Westport, Conn.: Greenwood Press, 1982). A number of scholars at the 1978 University of Mississippi symposium on recent black history and race relations point toward what are likely to be some of the new historical directions taken in viewing the 1950s and 1960s. See Michael V. Namorato (ed.), *Have We Overcome? Race Relations Since "Brown"* (Jackson: University Press of Mississippi, 1979).

assess the movement's short-term effectiveness and noneffectiveness, its tactical successes and failures from the standpoint of frustrated liberalism. The instinctive genius of the civil rights leadership was its collective understanding of the new role of the mass media and its ability to channel the courageous, independent spirit of a new generation of black southern youths. But the movement was successful (to the extent that it was) precisely *because* it was deeply religious, profoundly conservative, and committed by principle and by generations of pragmatic experience to accept compromise.

A critical approach may be developing in assessments of the role of the federal courts in ending legal segregation, but it is hardly from the Left. With the exception of a handful of early attacks by right-wing ideologues and segregationists, most historians have followed the lead of Richard Kluger's *Simple Justice* in praising the federal courts. Kluger's encyclopedic narrative covers far more than the decision of the Supreme Court to end legal segregation. In his adulatory treatment of Earl Warren, however, Kluger set the tone for much of the scholarship of the 1970s and early 1980s. In 1979, J. Harvie Wilkinson III was cautiously critical of the Court's attempt to guarantee school desegregation in his book *From Brown to Bakke,* but works such as Jack Bass's account of the New Orleans Fifth Circuit Court of Appeals and Tinsley E. Yarbrough's study of Alabama's Frank Johnson have affirmed the essential rightness—even the heroic stature—of those judicial activists who reshaped the segregated South. The theme of George Metcalf's study of school desegregation from the 1950s through the 1970s was the failure of executive leadership, not that of the courts.[36]

36. Richard Kluger, *Simple Justice: The History of Brown v. Board of Education and Black America's Struggle for Equality* (2 vols.; New York: Knopf, 1975); J. Harvie Wilkinson III, *From Brown to Bakke: The Supreme Court and School Integration, 1954–1978* (New York: Oxford University Press, 1979); Jack Bass, *Unlikely Heroes: The Dramatic Story of the Southern Judges of the Fifth Circuit Court Who Translated the Supreme Court's Brown Decision into a Revolution for Equality* (New York: Simon & Schuster, 1981); Tinsley E. Yarbrough, *Judge Frank Johnson and Human Rights in Alabama* (University: University of Alabama Press, 1983); Metcalf, *From Little Rock to Boston.* The secondary literature on the federal courts and desegregation is extensive. Among the most important works published in the past twenty years are Loren Miller, *The Petitioners: The Story of the Supreme Court of the United States and the Negro* (New York: Pantheon, 1966); Charles V. Hamilton, *The Bench and the Ballot: Southern Federal Judges and Black Voters* (New York: Oxford University Press, 1973); Catherine A. Barnes, *Journey from Jim Crow: The Desegregation of Southern Transit* (New York: Columbia University Press, 1983); and Frank T. Read and Lucy S. McGough, *Let Them Be Judged: The Judicial Integration of the Deep*

In the early 1980s, however, scholars began to raise critical questions about the role and wisdom of the federal courts' decisions, particularly those judgments that seemed to move beyond the prohibition of segregation and the active promotion of desegregation. As Ray Jenkins of the Baltimore *Evening Sun* remarked in a 1983 review of Bass's book, the moral purposes of the Supreme Court were so unassailable and their adversaries were men of such shabby motives that few historians had raised the question of whether racial inequality was a "unique social problem which so eluded conventional political accommodation that it required the application of a unique judicial response." In subsequent decisions, asked Jenkins, was it possible that the "judicial branch overexpanded its role in American government and overpoliticized the process of constitutional adjudication?"[37]

In *The Burden of Brown,* Raymond Wolters has no doubt that the answer to Jenkins' question was yes. Using the case study approach, Wolters describes the impact of court desegregation decisions on Washington, D.C.; Prince Edward County, Virginia; Clarendon County, South Carolina; New Castle County, Delaware; and Topeka, Kansas. Wolters accuses the federal courts of failures that range from "arrogance," "naivete," and judicial incompetence to destructive "social engineering" which, he suggests, have done much to weaken public school education in America. The courts, he seems to suggest at one point, have failed to recognize the reality of the vast social and "moral" distance between the white and black community where the rise in illegitimacy showed that a "new pattern of mating and breeding had emerged" among black women, a pattern "at odds with traditional standards."[38]

Wolters' attack on the federal courts is essentially from the Right.

South (Metuchen, N.J.: Scarecrow Press, 1978). Unfortunately we have far less available on the operation of the southern state and local courts and the southern bar beyond the case studies in Friedman (ed.), *Southern Justice.*

37. Ray Jenkins, Review of Bass's *Unlikely Heroes,* in *Journal of Southern History,* XLIX (February, 1983), 145. In his provocative essay "The Jurisprudence of *Brown* and the Dilemmas of Liberalism," Morton J. Horwitz has suggested that there was an inherent dilemma created in the attempts to use the courts to move beyond a simple end to segregation. While racial discrimination has clearly led to widespread economic inequality, the liberal tradition (and the legal one, for that matter) has rejected the notion that the courts should become involved with "problems of social and economic equality." Namorato (ed.), *Have We Overcome?,* 173–87 (quotation on p. 186).

38. Raymond Wolters, *The Burden of Brown: Thirty Years of School Desegregation* (Knoxville: University of Tennessee Press, 1984), 7, 206.

Most historians writing about the nation's political leadership have been critical, but hardly from Wolters' perspective. Carl Brauer's *John F. Kennedy and the Second Reconstruction* is cautiously favorable, but other recent historians, notably Steven F. Lawson and David J. Garrow, make the case that civil rights leaders and their followers were forced to invite martyrdom in order to end the inaction of leaders more interested in avoiding conflict than ending discrimination.[39]

Still, if we are now in a better position to understand more fully some of the complexities of race relations in the modern South, we continue to view race relations from the perspective of liberal disillusionment. There is the sense that, whatever its undeniable achievements, the civil rights movement failed to end the deeper patterns of de facto segregation or to solve the underlying problems of economic deprivation for black southerners. In some respects, the state of the literature is analogous to that of Reconstruction historiography at the end of the 1960s. We have stripped away many of the illusions of moral purity, but we are a long way from constructing an alternative framework for interpreting the transformation of southern race relations.

In discussing the historical writing on black Americans in the twentieth century, John B. Kirby has suggested that the absence of any controlling interpretive theme or themes is related to a larger failure of historical interpretation. "Disintegration, fragmentation, and segmentation are themes often employed to describe American life in this century," he observed in a recent essay in the *Journal of Southern History*. And these interpretations have been strengthened by "the popular sense of a declining core culture, distrust of public and private institutions, the impact of technology and science, and the upheavals wrought by constant wars, both hot and cold."[40]

---

39. Carl M. Brauer, *John F. Kennedy and the Second Reconstruction* (New York: Columbia University Press, 1977); David J. Garrow, *Protest at Selma: Martin Luther King, Jr., and the Voting Rights Act of 1965* (New Haven: Yale University Press, 1978); Neil R. McMillen, "Black Enfranchisement in Mississippi: Federal Enforcement and Black Protest in the 1960s," *Journal of Southern History*, XLIII (August, 1977), 351–72; Robert F. Burk, *The Eisenhower Administration and Black Civil Rights* (Knoxville: University of Tennessee Press, 1984). While Steven Lawson paints a relatively favorable portrait of Lyndon Johnson's administration in his study *In Pursuit of Power: Southern Blacks and Electoral Politics, 1965–1982* (New York: Columbia University Press, 1985), David Garrow's chilling account of J. Edgar Hoover's harassment of Martin Luther King, Jr., is detailed in *The FBI and Martin Luther King, Jr.: From 'Solo' to Memphis* (New York: Norton, 1981).

40. Kirby, "An Uncertain Context," 576–77.

While Kirby's observation still rings true, there have been a number of studies that do more than simply concentrate upon narrow topics and attempt to bring together the disparate threads of the twentieth-century story of southern race relations. One thinks of such ambitious works as S. P. Fullinwider's study *The Mind and Mood of Black America* and George Fredrickson's more successful comparative study of race relations in the United States and South Africa. While Fredrickson concentrates upon the pre-twentieth-century setting for both countries, he illuminates the economic, social, and ideological factors that helped to shape the evolution of the race question in both the United States and South Africa.[41]

Joel Williamson's *The Crucible of Race* is perhaps the most ambitious attempt to explain the emergence of segregation and its persistence well past the first half of the twentieth century. At the core of Williamson's study is a description of three traditions in white attitudes (particularly white *southern* attitudes) toward race: liberalism, conservatism, and a virulently antiblack form of radicalism. In the 1890s, it was the radicals who triumphed and shaped southern race relations for the next sixty years. Williamson attributes this critical development to a combination of factors, particularly the existence of deeply rooted sexual neuroses among southern white men, that in the midst of the depression of the 1890s led to the myth of the black "rapist" and a demand for the total repression of blacks. Race relations in the twentieth century, argues Williamson, are a legacy of this tragic heritage.[42]

Williamson's interpretation is likely to provoke dissent in many quarters (including historians who share his emphasis upon the psychology of racism), but some of the first attacks have come from neo-Marxists. In a scathing review in *Reviews in American History*, Jonathan M. Wiener dismissed the importance of studying "white racial attitudes." These attitudes were of "secondary significance" in explaining southern history, he argued, and the "psychological roots" of racism were even less important. The key to black-white

---

41. S. P. Fullinwider, *The Mind and Mood of Black America: 20th Century Thought* (Homewood, Ill.: Dorsey Press, 1969); George M. Fredrickson, *White Supremacy: A Comparative Study in American and South African History* (New York: Oxford University Press, 1981).

42. Joel Williamson, *The Crucible of Race: Black-White Relations in the American South Since Emancipation* (New York: Oxford University Press, 1984).

relations was to be found in "social and economic institutions and processes."[43]

Wiener's article reflects the views of a growing number of historians, many of whom have recently completed research projects on the nineteenth-century South. These historians have sought to de-emphasize race and emphasize the importance of class relationships in shaping the history of the South. Perhaps the most persuasive statement of this point of view can be found in Barbara J. Fields's recent essay, "Ideology and Race in American History." Fields has politely but firmly scolded most historians of race relations for their excessive use of the concept of racism as though it were a trans-historical explanation for the tragic course of events in American (and southern) history. The ideas or notions people have of each other—even when they are reflected in different physical and color characteristics—must always be viewed within the total social context, argues Fields. And in an assessment of that context, any attempt to understand the role these racial notions played in determining the course of historical developments must begin with the recognition that class and race are "concepts of a different order; they do not occupy the same analytical space, and thus cannot constitute explanatory alternatives to each other." Or, as she argues at another point, "class is a concept that we can locate both at the level of objective reality and at the level of social appearances." Race, on the other hand, is a concept that exists at the "level of appearances only."[44]

This is, of course, a variation on the arguments made by a growing number of Marxist historians of the southern (and American) experience, most notably Jonathan M. Wiener, in "Class Structure and Economic Development in the American South, 1865–1955," and Jay R. Mandle, in *The Roots of Black Poverty*. Both Wiener and Mandle are primarily interested in the course of economic development, but both suggest that class relationships played a more important role than "racism" in the development of southern history in the twentieth century. As Wiener argues at one point, black southerners did suffer the greatest exploitation and oppression, "but the system of labor restrictions centering on debt peonage . . . expanded to include whites

43. Jonathan M. Wiener, "The 'Black Beast Rapist': White Racial Attitudes in the Postwar South," *Reviews in American History*, XIII (June, 1985), 226.

44. Barbara J. Fields, "Ideology and Race in American History," in J. Morgan Kousser and James M. McPherson (eds.), *Region, Race, and Reconstruction: Essays in Honor of C. Vann Woodward* (New York: Oxford University Press, 1982), 150 (first quotation), 151 (second and third quotations).

as well." Thus the southern economic system of exploitation was not "exclusively racial in orientation . . . but a class system—white planters dominating tenants of both races, with blacks forming the most oppressed part of the working class."[45]

Arguing from a somewhat different perspective, Mandle finds the roots of black poverty and backwardness in the economic, political, and ideological hegemony of the planter class. Despite the upheavals of the Civil War and Reconstruction and the pamphleteering of New South boosters, insists Mandle, this group maintained its stranglehold on the southern economy by resisting typically bourgeois forms of agricultural development—particularly those pioneered in the Midwest—and by concentrating instead upon maintaining nonmarket mechanisms for mobilizing and forcing an exploited laboring class to perform agricultural work at unnaturally low wages. In this regard, such socially coercive practices as peonage, paternalism, and institutionalized violence were of critical importance, but they cannot be understood as primarily "racial" phenomena. Only after World War II, argues Mandle, did northern demand for labor finally overwhelm the system that had allowed planters to maintain a coerced plantation labor supply. At that point the planter class turned to modern, more capital-intensive forms of agricultural development—a movement symbolized by the widespread adoption of the cotton picker.[46]

While the relevance of some of this argument may be a bit unclear, I think it is fair to say that—if accepted by historians—it would make the civil rights movement and the events of the 1950s and 1960s an afterthought, an inevitable (though sometimes painful) development in the process of re-creating southern society along the patterns of national economic and social development.[47]

Wiener and Mandle are candid in acknowledging their point of

45. Jonathan M. Wiener, "Class Structure and Economic Development in the American South, 1865–1955," *American Historical Review*, LXXXIV (October, 1979), 970–92 (quotation on p. 978).

46. Jay R. Mandle, *The Roots of Black Poverty: The Southern Plantation Economy After the Civil War* (Durham: Duke University Press, 1978).

47. Wiener says as much. "Just as the Prussian Road [of the postwar South] united economic with political repression, so the newly won economic freedom of the classic capitalist path created the opportunity for blacks to organize and win democratic reforms" ("Class Structure and Economic Development in the American South," 992). For an extended argument that changes in American economic and institutional relationships are becoming more important than "racism" in shaping the conditions of the majority of black Americans, see William Julius Wilson's *The Declining Significance of Race: Blacks and Changing American Institutions* (Chicago: University of Chicago Press, 1978).

view. As Wiener said in an exchange with one of his most severe critics, Robert Higgs, "Neither of us is 'neutral'; each of us offers an interpretation that each tries to support with evidence."[48] Nevertheless, it seems to me that there is the tantalizing promise of freedom from the blind alleys of traditionally eclectic historical explanations. By understanding the material bases of the society we are studying, the way in which class relationships are established, and the mechanisms by which one or more classes exploit others, we can see the *real* underlying causes of the segregated society, the rise of the civil rights movement, the destruction of legal segregation, and the continuing patterns of economic and racial inequality in the modern South. In short, we can expose the very mainspring of the historical process itself.

Such a perspective does not imply moral neutrality. Quite the contrary, it helps to avoid the ambiguities of bourgeois historians by laying out a more explicit framework for making those moral judgments. The men and women who experience class exploitation and oppression, regardless of race, are those who deserve our sympathy and admiration. Those who engage in exploitation regardless of their personal qualities or their individual acts of decency are the villains.

One of the problems with this approach was captured by that amateur historian Jack Burden in *All the King's Men*. As Burden said of his friend Adam Stanton, Adam was a "scientist and everything is tidy for him, and one molecule of oxygen always behaves the same way when it gets around two molecules of hydrogen." Consequently he believed, in life, that the molecule of good "always behaves the same way. The molecule of bad always behaves the same way." The problem, as Burden had learned, was that human beings are very complicated contraptions. They were not simply "good" or "bad" but they were "good and bad and the good comes out of the bad and the bad out of the good, and the devil take the hindmost."[49]

I do not mean by this that we should abandon the search for broad interpretive frameworks, or that we should make a fetish of avoiding moral judgments. We badly need some intellectual mechanism that will help us to understand the changing social, economic, and political relationships that have existed in the South and have shaped the conflicts that revolve around issues of race. If we are to understand

48. Jonathan M. Wiener, "Class Structure and Economic Development, Reply," *American Historical Review*, LXXXIV (October, 1979), 1002.

49. Robert Penn Warren, *All the King's Men* (New York: Harcourt, Brace, 1946), 248.

the transformation of the South from a legally segregated society to that bundle of de facto contradictions that exist today, we will need to think and write boldly and imaginatively. Still, we should be prepared to be confounded by the way in which events so often fail to conform to our expectations and our theories.

When Arthur F. Raper published his powerful study *Sharecroppers All* in 1941, he reflected the views of many of his generation of American—and southern—intellectuals who believed that exposing the mechanisms of economic exploitation would help Americans understand that there were no "deep and dark mysteries" about such disparate social phenomena as "lynchings, homicide, kidnapping, and unemployment." They were "as American as the cotton plantation, . . . as the acquisition of wealth through exploitation of natural resources and people, as the chain store and the assembly line."[50]

Arthur Raper was not entirely wrong, but there remain—and there are likely to continue to remain—deep and dark mysteries. Even as we abandon "racism" as a central theme that will explain the complex web of ideas and actions that have bound black and white together in the twentieth-century South, we should learn from the alchemists' experience and remain skeptical that the "class struggle" will finally be the magic formula for understanding the region's troubled past.

50. Arthur F. Raper and Ira De A. Reid, *Sharecroppers All* (Chapel Hill: University of North Carolina Press, 1941), 215.

Sun Belt Prosperity and Urban Growth

CHARLES P. ROLAND

In 1965, Dewey W. Grantham, Jr., opened his splendid essay on the historiography of the twentieth-century South with the statement that historians had scarcely begun to deal with the subject. He offered the opinion that the swift disappearance of the old regional distinctions, "the very process of change and fragmentation" that stimulated the writings of social scientists and journalists, made more difficult the portrayal of the era by historians. Yet he expressed the belief that the region's drift toward national conformity challenged them to broaden their focus and write about their state "or region in a more meaningful context."[1]

Recent scholarly works on the topics of southern prosperity and urban development justify the conclusion that, at least in part, the challenge perceived by Grantham is being met. In no other activities has the twentieth-century southern drift toward what was once considered to be national conformity been stronger than in the growth of regional industry and prosperity and the movement of population from the country to the cities. In no other fields of scholarly endeavor have stronger efforts been made to describe the regional scene in a more meaningful context.

At the time of Grantham's writing, most works on southern economic and urban life dealt with the laggard South. By every index the region's economy was then significantly behind that of the rest of the country, and Grantham ended his discussion of the historiography of the subject with a reference to the work of William H. Nicholls, who argued that the South's lag in per capita income was the result of slow industrial-urban development, which he attributed in turn to the region's adherence to an outmoded set of cultural values.[2]

---

1. Dewey W. Grantham, Jr., "The Twentieth-Century South," in Arthur S. Link and Rembert W. Patrick (eds.), *Writing Southern History: Essays in Historiography in Honor of Fletcher M. Green* (Baton Rouge: Louisiana State University Press, 1965), 410–44 (quotations on pp. 410, 411).

2. *Ibid.*, 437; William H. Nicholls, *Southern Tradition and Regional Progress* (Chapel Hill: University of North Carolina Press, 1960).

Since the publication of Nicholls' book and Grantham's article profound changes have occurred in the economic and demographic life of the South. Changes perhaps even more profound have occurred in the prevailing image of southern life. During the last decade and a half, the regional rates of population growth, industrial-urban development, and per capita income have become markedly higher than the national averages while in much of the rest of the country, industries have fallen into the doldrums and there has been a significant movement away from the cities. Suddenly the South, a South expanded in the imagination all the way to the Pacific coast, has been hailed as a Sun Belt of dazzling prosperity and blossoming metropolises.

The two works most directly responsible for the creation of this image in the popular mind are Kevin P. Phillips' *The Emerging Republican Majority* (1969), in which the expression "Sun Belt" appeared for the first time, and Kirkpatrick Sale's *Power Shift: The Rise of the Southern Rim and Its Challenge to the Eastern Establishment* (1975). Both authors are journalists. Phillips described the phenomenon of recent southern growth and prosperity. "The persons most drawn to the new sun culture are the pleasure seekers, the bored, the ambitious, the space-age technicians and the retired—a super slice of the rootless, socially mobile group known as the American middle class." Sale was even less complimentary to the South. He pictured it invidiously as a parasitic region that was draining off an excessive amount of federal money and as a society fostering a reactionary "cowboy" culture that threatened the traditional liberalism of the Northeast.[3]

Shortly after the appearance of Sale's book, the New York *Times* carried a series of articles that inflated the Sun Belt image and tended to support Sale's economic generalizations. *Business Week* and the *National Journal* added their voices to the chorus with pieces bearing such titles as "The Second War Between the States" and "Federal Spending: The North's Loss is the Sunbelt's Gain."[4] So frightening was the Sun Belt chimera that various groups of nonsouthern con-

3. Kevin P. Phillips, *The Emerging Republican Majority* (New Rochelle, N.Y.: Arlington House, 1969), 437; Kirkpatrick Sale, *Power Shift: The Rise of the Southern Rim and Its Challenge to the Eastern Establishment* (New York: Random House, 1975), 55–88, 177–87, 207–71 (use of "cowboy" to describe the culture of the "Southern Rim" on p. 178).

4. New York *Times*, February 8–12, 1976; "The Second War Between the States: Special Report," *Business Week,* May 17, 1976, pp. 92–114; "Federal Spending: The North's Loss is the Sunbelt's Gain," *National Journal,* VIII (June 26, 1976), 878–91.

gressmen and governors hastened to form "Frost Belt" coalitions for the purpose of defending their region against the southern menace.

Professional economists and historians of southern economic development recorded the regional gains if they did not always agree with the journalists' perceptions. All general works dealing with the recent South discuss its economy.[5] The earliest comprehensive attempt to account for the southward drift of many northern factories in the years immediately before and after World War II was Victor R. Fuchs's *Changes in the Location of Manufacturing in the United States Since 1929* (1962). He attributed the movement to the relative abundance and inexpensiveness of nonunionized southern labor.[6]

The recent southern industrial and economic surge has coincided

5. Among these are Thomas D. Clark and Albert D. Kirwan, *The South Since Appomattox: A Century of Regional Change* (New York: Oxford University Press, 1967); Monroe Lee Billington, *The American South: A Brief History* (New York: Charles Scribner's Sons, 1971); I. A. Newby, *The South: A History* (New York: Holt, Rinehart & Winston, 1978); Charles P. Roland, *The Improbable Era: The South Since World War II* (Lexington: University Press of Kentucky, 1975); and Francis Butler Simkins and Charles Pierce Roland, *A History of the South* (New York: Knopf, 1972).

6. Victor R. Fuchs, *Changes in the Location of Manufacturing in the United States Since 1929* (New Haven: Yale University Press, 1962). The pros and cons of this proposition were discussed also in Victor R. Fuchs and Richard Perlman, "Recent Trends in Southern Wage Differentials," *Review of Economics and Statistics,* XLII (August, 1960), 292–300; T. E. McMillan, Jr., "Why Manufacturers Choose Plant Locations vs. Determinants of Plant Locations," *Land Economics,* XLI (August, 1965), 239–46; Joe Persky, "The South: A Colony at Home," *Southern Exposure,* I (Summer/Fall, 1973), 14–22; and Benson Soffer and Michael Korenich, "'Right to Work' Laws as a Location Factor: The Industrialization Experience of Agricultural States," *Journal of Regional Science,* III (Winter, 1961), 41–56. For a more extended discussion of the southern labor situation, see Robert Emil Botsch, *We Shall Not Overcome: Populism and Southern Blue-Collar Workers* (Chapel Hill: University of North Carolina Press, 1980); Philip Taft, *Organizing Dixie: Alabama Workers in the Industrial Era,* ed. Gary M Fink (Westport, Conn.: Greenwood Press, 1981); James G. Maddox *et al., The Advancing South: Manpower Prospects and Problems* (New York: Twentieth Century Fund, 1967); F. Ray Marshall, *Labor in the South* (Cambridge: Harvard University Press, 1967); Merl E. Reed, Leslie S. Hough, and Gary M Fink (eds.), *Southern Workers and Their Unions, 1880–1975: Selected Papers, The Second Southern Labor History Conference, 1978* (Westport, Conn.: Greenwood Press, 1981); Robert Cooney, "The Modern South: Organized Labor's New Frontier," *American Federationist,* LXVIII (May, 1961), 15–19; Emil Malizia, "The Earnings of North Carolina Workers," *University of North Carolina Newsletter,* LX (December, 1975), 1–4; F. Ray Marshall, "Impediments to Labor Union Organization in the South," *South Atlantic Quarterly,* LVII (Autumn, 1958), 409–18; Jim Overton *et al.,* "The Men at the Top: The Story of J. P. Stevens," *Southern Exposure,* VI (Spring, 1978), 52–63; and Cliff Sloan and Bob Hall, "It's Good to Be Home in Greenville. . . . But It's Better if You Hate Unions," *Southern Exposure,* VII (Spring, 1979), 82–93.

with the emergence of the computer, the field of econometrics, and the quantitative approach in the disciplines of history, political science, and sociology. The study of economic and demographic affairs lends itself to the new statistical techniques, which were employed in many of the recent books on these subjects. Leonard F. Wheat's *Regional Growth and Industrial Location* (1973) splendidly illustrates the trend. To the humanistic scholar, it is a bewildering exercise in econometrics, laden with such sentences as: "Looking again at absolute growth, we find that Y remains positive and significant when P is held constant—provided that E (or $E^{1.5}$) is also controlled so that Y does not become a proxy for E." His conclusions are, however, perfectly clear. He rejected the older theory that cheap labor is a region's strongest attraction for industrial location. "The findings leave no doubt that markets and climate are far ahead as the leading influences."[7]

Much of the research and writing on the postwar southern economy was done outside the academic community. For example, in 1971 the Public Affairs Research Council of Louisiana (PAR) brought out *Industry Rates Louisiana,* which presents the state's many industrial advantages (including an abundance of energy and water) but also recommends various reforms in industrial practices. The study emphasizes the need for improved technical education of the workers and for a solution to the problems of law enforcement in labor-management relations. It says that there was probable cause to believe that theft, extortion, bribery, and intimidation were prevalent in the state.[8]

In 1972 a group of southern liberal journalists, politicians, businessmen, scholars, and other professionals, naming themselves the L. Q. C. Lamar Society, produced an extraordinary volume with the extraordinary title *You Can't Eat Magnolias,* which shows the South as an area with many remaining problems but also as a potentially redemptive element in a tainted American society. Three chapters deal directly with the southern economy. F. Ray Marshall and Virgil L. Christian, Jr., pointed out both the strengths and the shortcomings of the human resources. Stewart Gammill III described the southern economy as colonial because it was still controlled by outside interests. Jack Bass emphasized the persistence of poverty and

7. Leonard F. Wheat, *Regional Growth and Industrial Location: An Empirical Viewpoint* (Lexington, Mass.: Heath, 1973), 184, 183.

8. *Industry Rates Louisiana* (Baton Rouge: Public Affairs Research Council of Louisiana, 1971), 77–78.

malnutrition in many segments of the population. Despite these critical views, the general tone of the book is optimistic. The writers evoked a vision of southern industrial growth without excessive pollution, southern urban expansion without pathological congestion, and southern racial accommodation without destructive violence. Terry Sanford, former governor of North Carolina, struck the high note with an essay that ended: "The South's time has come, after a century of being the whipping boy and the backward child. The time has come, finally come. The South can lead the nation, must lead the nation—and all the better, because the nation has never been in greater need of leadership."[9]

The L. Q. C. Lamar Society next joined with the Center for Southern Studies at Duke University to sponsor a work by economists Thomas H. Naylor and James Clotfelter, *Strategies for Change in the South* (1975), which applies the method of systems analysis to the economic, educational, political, and social institutions of the region. If the authors were aware of the emerging Sun Belt theme of southern affluence, they ignored it. They followed instead the traditional theme of the South as "the Nation's No. 1 economic problem": "Although in terms of overall economic development, the gap between the South and the rest of the nation has certainly been reduced in the past thirty years, the South is still the nation's poorest region." Their recommendations for getting the South "out of the quagmire and into the economic mainstream" (to borrow a line from the title of their chapter on the subject) called for increased action by the federal, state, and municipal governments to help achieve greater economic independence and vitality for the region.[10]

Two years after the appearance of *You Can't Eat Magnolias*, a Nashville journalist and author, John Egerton, published a fascinating but far more pessimistic work, *The Americanization of Dixie: The Southernization of America* (1974). He concluded that regional distinctiveness is fast disappearing, in part because the South is losing its traditional characteristics but in part also because the rest of the nation is becoming more like the South. He believed that each is adopting many of the worst traits from the other. His chapter on southern industry bears the sinister subtitle "The New Carpetbag-

9. H. Brandt Ayers and Thomas H. Naylor (eds.), *You Can't Eat Magnolias* (New York: McGraw-Hill, 1972), 231–58, 259–72, 273–83, 317–29 (quotation on p. 329).

10. Thomas H. Naylor and James Clotfelter, *Strategies for Change in the South* (Chapel Hill: University of North Carolina Press, 1975), 10, 64–76.

gers." "The South is the new industrial frontier," he said. "The cheap and abundant labor force is still there, and the unions are still weak, and the weather is still good." His discussion of southern agriculture ends with a lament over the demise of the family farm: "Agriculture as it has traditionally been practiced in this country is now out of phase with the times. Somehow, agriculture seems the poorer for it, and so do the times, and so do we all." [11]

One of the more noteworthy of the nonacademic sources of research into the regional economy is the Southern Growth Policies Board. This organization came into being through executive orders issued in December, 1971, by the governors of nine southeastern states. Beginning with a $225,000 challenge grant from the Ford Foundation, the Southern Growth Policies Board continues to function on matching grants from the various member states (now increased to fifteen) and from private contributors. With headquarters in the famed Research Triangle Park in North Carolina, the organization employs a full-time staff to administer its programs and carry out research.

One of the earliest products of this research was *The Future of the South* (1974). It is not a recipe for inducing southern industrial growth; it takes such growth for granted. As is said in the foreword, "It is clear that the long-term destiny of the South is growth." The study primarily concerns itself with the means of controlling this growth so as to avoid repeating the mistakes made by other regions in the course of their industrial expansion. It makes sweeping recommendations for the creation of agencies to study land use, energy resources, and transportation needs; it urges the southern states to assist their land-grant colleges in agricultural research and the application of means to improve production; and it suggests that the Southern Growth Policies Board itself be maintained to provide a forum for airing regional problems, to advise southern governors on regional development, and to survey recreational needs so that areas needing conservation and protection can be identified. [12]

In 1977 the Southern Growth Policies Board published a collaborative study designed to defend the southern position in the war of words (and the war for federal dollars) being waged with the Frost Belt. Edited by two economists, E. Blaine Liner and Lawrence K.

11. John Egerton, *The Americanization of Dixie: The Southernization of America* (New York: Harper's Magazine Press, 1974), 124, 47.

12. *The Future of the South* (Research Triangle Park, N.C.: Commission on the Future of the South, 1974), 7 (quotation), 100.

Lynch, and titled *The Economics of Southern Growth,* the study argues that the South's rapid rate of growth is primarily the result not of federal spending but rather of southern advantages in agriculture, energy, and the amenities of life. The final chapter, by C. L. Jusenius and L. C. Ledebur, "A Myth in the Making: The Southern Economic Challenge and Northern Economic Decline," emphasizes the continuing southern economic disparity and concludes: "The current debate which focuses on the rate of growth of the Sunbelt as a partial explanation of the economic difficulties of the Northern States is detrimental to the goal of achieving national policies that facilitate overall growth among all regions of the United States." [13]

Throughout the remainder of the 1970s the Southern Growth Policies Board vigorously continued its research. It published more than a score of books, booklets, and reports. Among these was Pat Watters (ed.), *Final Report of the 1980 Commission on the Future of the South* (1981). [14] Conceding the persistence of many of the region's old problems, the study is nevertheless optimistic. It acknowledges the remarkable recent growth of the southern economy and predicts that it will continue, though not at the swift "pell-mell" rate of the past decade. The book concludes with numerous recommendations for

13. E. Blaine Liner and Lawrence K. Lynch (eds.), *The Economics of Southern Growth* (Durham: Southern Growth Policies Board, 1977), 173.

14. Pat Watters (ed.), *Final Report of the 1980 Commission on the Future of the South* (Research Triangle Park, N.C.: Southern Growth Policies Board, 1981). These publications (all published at Research Triangle Park, N.C.) included Watters (ed.), *Executive Summary of the Final Report of the 1980 Commission on the Future of the South* (1981); Bernard L. Weinstein, *Report of the Task Force on the Southern Economy* (1981); Patricia J. Dusenbury, *Report of the Task Force on Southern Cities* (1981); Arthur J. Wacaster, *Report of the Task Force on Energy in the South* (1981); Paula M. Breen, *Report of the Task Force on Southern Children: Raising a New Generation in the South* (1981); *Data Book II: A Profile of the Southern States* (1981); *The Economics of Southern Growth* (1977); *Southern Urban Trends* (1978); *Municipal Fiscal Trends: Southern Cities in the 1970s* (1981); *Improving the Intergovernmental System* (1980); *Tax Reform and Southern Economic Development* (1979); *Suburbs in the City: Municipal Boundary Changes in the Southern States* (1981); *Data Tables* (1982); *Graphic Summary of Southern Economic Growth* (n.d.); and *A New Human Services Agenda for the South* (n.d.). The research reports (all published in 1980) included *Teenage Pregnancy in the South; Factors Associated With Infant Mortality; The Changing South; Current Issues on Immigration and Refugee Policy; Infant Mortality and Teenage Pregnancy; Southern Cities: Economies in Transition; The Fiscal Outlook for Southern Cities; An Urban Economic Development Strategy for Southern States; Regulatory Costs on State and Local Governments; Low Level Nuclear Waste and Hazardous Waste in Southern States;* and *Structural & Spatial Trends in Southern Manufacturing: Implications for the 1980s.*

enhancing and controlling this growth. These include banking reforms, increased financial support of education, and expansion of the port facilities.[15]

By the 1970s the South's industrial growth was causing many of its inhabitants to fear the threat to the region's environment. The Tennessee River was reported to be tainted with mercury; experts predicted that unless stream pollution was curbed, the Gulf of Mexico would one day become a dead sea. The ravages of strip-mining coal were exceptionally severe and highly visible, especially in Kentucky, where Harry M. Caudill, a lawyer-turned-environmental-crusader, wrote eloquent indictments in *Night Comes to the Cumberlands* (1963), *My Land is Dying* (1971), *A Darkness at Dawn* (1976), and *Theirs Be the Power* (1983). Frank E. Smith, director of the Tennessee Valley Authority—one of the biggest users of strip-mined coal—attempted to throw light on the problem in "Improving the Southern Environment" (1970). He admitted the dilemma facing the South and the rest of the nation. "We cannot achieve a satisfactory quality of life for all Americans, let alone the South, from our present inadequate economic base. To expand that base, we are going to have to continue to develop our natural resources. That, in turn, requires a completely candid appraisal of our environmental condition." How serious and far from solution the South's environmental problems are is made clear in William Reynolds' 1979 *Southern Exposure* article, "The South: Global Dumping Ground," describing the hazards of radioactive waste deposited in the region. His frightening title suggests his theme.[16]

15. Watters (ed.), *Final Report of the 1980 Commission on the Future of the South,* 11, 68.

16. Harry M. Caudill, *Night Comes to the Cumberlands: A Biography of a Depressed Area* (Boston: Atlantic Monthly Press, 1963), *My Land is Dying* (New York: Dutton, 1971), *A Darkness at Dawn: Appalachian Kentucky and the Future* (Lexington: University Press of Kentucky, 1976), and *Theirs Be the Power: The Moguls of Eastern Kentucky* (Urbana: University of Illinois Press, 1983); Frank E. Smith, "Improving the Southern Environment," *New South,* XXV (Fall, 1970), 63–69 (quotation on p. 65); William Reynolds, "The South: Global Dumping Ground," *Southern Exposure,* VII (Winter, 1979), 49–56. Other works on the problem of pollution include Leslie Allan, Eileen Kohn Kaufman, and Joanna Underwood, *Paper Profits: Pollution in the Pulp and Paper Industry* (Cambridge: M.I.T. Press, 1972); S. R. Jarrett, "How the States Stack Up in Pollution Control," *Industrial Development,* CXLI (September/October, 1972), 2–6; Linda L. Liston, "Fifty Legislative Climates Turn Stormy as States Fire Up Pollution Control Programs," *Industrial Development,* CXXXIX (November/December, 1970), 1–15, and "The Southeast: Economic Imperatives Bow to Environmental Integrity," *Industrial Development,* CXL (September/

In 1978, two economists, Bernard L. Weinstein and Robert E. Firestine, brought out *Regional Growth and Decline in the United States,* which featured elaborate statistical tables demonstrating the rapid recent growth of southern industry and the relative slowing down of industrial growth in the North. The authors argued that there is little evidence that the countless southern state promotional efforts such as tax incentives have had any significant effect on plant location. "Taken as a whole," they said, "these incentives represent a serious misallocation of resources. In the main, government is subsidizing firms for undertaking investments that would likely have been made in any case." The authors concluded also that most southern industrial growth has been in the form of newly established plants and is not the result of the migration of plants from other areas. They said: "An important implication of these findings . . . is that economic growth in the South and West does not necessarily imply a decline in the North." Finally, they echoed the warnings issued by various other students that the so-called Sun Belt states and cities ought to establish growth priorities that would help them avoid industrial mistakes made by other regions.[17]

The most recent historical accounts of southern economic growth since World War II were produced by James C. Cobb. They are *The Selling of the South* (1982) and *Industrialization and Southern Society, 1877–1984* (1984). The author joined other critics in questioning whether the region's strenuous promotional efforts have been decisive in its industrial advance. His conclusions also represented a careful balancing of hope and doubt as to the benefits of southern industrialization. In the first work he said: "The Sunbelt ballyhoo of the late 1970s suggested that the realization of Henry Grady's dreams might at last be close at hand. Like Grady's New South, however, the Sunbelt South retained its ties to a past characterized not only by bright hopes but by recurrent disappointments. Thus, it remained to be seen whether the region could actually reach the nation's economic mainstream in the 1980s and, in so doing, make prosperity a permanent feature of a new 'southern way of life.'" The later volume closed with: "The historical circumstances that shaped the destiny of the agrarian South also played a major role in forging the character

---

October, 1971), 6–21; and Suzanne Rhodes, "Barnwell: Achilles Heel of Nuclear Power," *Southern Exposure,* VII (Winter, 1979), 44–48.

17. Bernard L. Weinstein and Robert E. Firestine, *Regional Growth and Decline in the United States: The Rise of the Sunbelt and the Decline of the Northeast* (New York: Praeger, 1978), 139, 134, 151.

of an industrial South. Like the gloomy, defeated Dixie of 1877, the optimistic, skyscraper-studded Sunbelt South of the 1980s still reflected the influences of a complex heritage, a heritage whose best elements had recently become as difficult to preserve as its worst had been to overcome." [18]

An integral factor in the recent growth of southern industry and prosperity has been the growth of southern cities, the movement of

18. James C. Cobb, *The Selling of the South: The Southern Crusade for Industrial Development, 1936–1980* (Baton Rouge: Louisiana State University Press, 1982), 208, and *Industrialization and Southern Society, 1877–1984* (Lexington: University Press of Kentucky, 1984), 164. Other books that threw light on the recent southern industrial expansion included Daryl A. Hellman, Gregory H. Wassall, and Laurence H. Falk, *State Financial Incentives to Industry* (Lexington, Mass.: Lexington Books, 1976); Joan Hoffman, *Racial Discrimination and Economic Development* (Lexington, Mass.: Lexington Books, 1975); Pat Watters, *The South and the Nation* (New York: Pantheon, 1969), 71–134; and Robert J. Newman, *Growth in the American South: Changing Regional Employment and Wage Patterns in the 1960s and 1970s* (New York: New York University Press, 1984). Articles that discussed the rise of southern prosperity included Carl Abbott, "The American Sunbelt: Idea and Region," *Journal of the West*, XVIII (July, 1979), 5–18; Gurney Breckenfield, "Business Loves the Sunbelt (and Vice Versa)," *Fortune* (June, 1977), 132–46; Gene Burd, "The Selling of the Sunbelt: Civic Boosterism in the Media," in David C. Perry and Alfred J. Watkins, (eds.), *The Rise of the Sunbelt Cities* (Beverly Hills: Sage Publications, 1977), 129–49; Lynda Chastain, "A Dream Whose Time Had Come," *Impact: Technical Education in South Carolina*, XI (April-May, 1978), 1–20; James C. Cobb, "Colonel Effingham Crushes the Crackers: Political Reform in Postwar Augusta," *South Atlantic Quarterly*, LXXIX (Autumn, 1979), 507–19; "The South as the New America, Special Report," *Saturday Review*, September 4, 1976, pp. 8–41; "The New Rich South: Frontier For Growth," *Business Week*, September 2, 1972, pp. 30–37; "A Park That Reversed a Brain Drain," *Fortune* (June, 1977), 148–53; "Recruiting Industry Abroad," *South*, V (April 1, 1978), 31–32; Charles P. Roland, "The South, America's Will-o'-the-Wisp Eden," *Louisiana History*, XI (Spring, 1970), 101–19; "Surging to Prosperity," *Time*, September 27, 1976, pp. 72–73 (but see the entire special section, "The South Today," pp. 29–99); Roul Tunley, "In Spartanburg, the Accent Is on Business," *Reader's Digest* (January, 1974), 165–68; Lynn E. Browne, "Narrowing Regional Income Differentials," *Texas Business Review*, LV (July-August, 1981), 141–45; William J. Serow and Dudley L. Poston, "Demographic and Economic Change in the South," *Texas Business Review*, LVI (January-February, 1982), 30–33; Norval D. Glenn and Charles N. Weaver, "Regional Differences in Attitudes Toward Work," *Texas Business Review*, LVI (November-December, 1982), 263–66; Mancur Olson, "The South Will Fall Again: The South as a Leader and Laggard in Economic Growth," *Southern Economic Journal*, XLIX (April, 1983), 917–32; George Sternlieb and James W. Hughes, "Frost Over the Sunbelt," *American Demographics*, V (June, 1983), 17–19; James R. Adams, "The Sunbelt," in John B. Boles (ed.), *Dixie Dateline: A Journalistic Portrait of the Contemporary South* (Houston: Rice University Studies, 1983), 141–57; and William K. Stevens, "A New Culture Emerges in the Oil Patch," in Boles (ed.), *Dixie Dateline*, 129–39.

population from the country into the metropolises. Throughout the twentieth century, the rate of growth of these cities has been markedly higher than the national average. Yet so enduring has been the image of an immutably rural South that only in the last few years have scholars begun seriously to undertake a description and analysis of this vast demographic shift and its consequences. Grantham in his text saw fit to devote but a single sentence to a single book on the subject—Rupert B. Vance and Nicholas J. Demerath (eds.), *The Urban South* (1954). Grantham's footnote citation adds only two other titles on limited aspects of southern city development. Nor did he indicate urban affairs as a field beckoning to the region's scholars. Zane L. Miller's brief study, *The Urbanization of Modern America* (1973), contains only two passing references to southern cities and not a word about southern urban development since World War II.[19]

During the last two decades, the rate of southern urbanization has risen even higher above the national average than it was earlier in this century, and scholars are now awake to the significance of this development. One of the earliest works to consider the phenomenon of post–World War II southern urban growth is that by the sociologist Leonard Reissman, whose sweeping view of the region discerned five major metropolitan clusters—"conurbations," he called them. He defined them as almost continuous urban sprawls reaching out from one or more metropolitan centers. The five are the Gulf Coast (New Orleans–Houston), the Atlantic Coast (Charleston-Miami), the Eastern Inner Core (Atlanta and environs), the Western Inner Core (Dallas and surroundings), and the Carolinas (a complex of small cities). Reissman noted also two lesser constellations developing along the Nashville-Memphis axis and in the Shreveport area. He excluded the Newport News–Portsmouth-Norfolk chain as being a part of the Boston–New York–Washington megalopolis.[20]

In *You Can't Eat Magnolias*, public policy and urban affairs specialist Joel L. Fleishman addressed the issue of southern urbanization. In an essay with the provocative subtitle "Northern Mistakes in Southern Settings," he reminded his readers that southern cities have

19. Grantham, "The Twentieth-Century South," in Link and Patrick (eds.), *Writing Southern History*, 434; Zane L. Miller, *The Urbanization of Modern America: A Brief History* (New York: Harcourt Brace Jovanovich, 1973).

20. Leonard Reissman, "Urbanization in the South," in John C. McKinney and Edgar T. Thompson (eds.), *The South in Continuity and Change* (Durham: Duke University Press, 1965), 79–100, esp. 93. See also Dudley L. Poston, Jr., and Robert H. Weller (eds.), *The Population of the South: Structure and Change in Social Demographic Context* (Austin: University of Texas Press, 1981).

the advantages of being smaller, newer, less dense, and less industrialized than nonsouthern cities, and he urged the region to take steps to prevent its cities from becoming Pittsburghs. "We can still choose," he argued. "Most other parts of the country cannot."[21]

John Egerton's outlook in *The Americanization of Dixie* was less optimistic than Fleishman's. Egerton's chapter on the southern city uses Columbia, South Carolina, as a case study. It follows his general theme that the South was acquiring the worst of the national characteristics, and he warned southerners that they have precious little time left in which to choose whether their cities will become replicas of Pittsburgh. He gave this chapter the ominous subtitle "Recreating the Monster Metropolis."[22]

In 1974, Blaine A. Brownell led professional historians into the field of recent southern urban history with a brief, perceptive work, *The Urban South in the Twentieth Century*. Asserting that the major regional cities had "come of age" in the first three decades of the century, he showed that the Great Depression retarded their progress but the national economic resurgence after World War II stirred them into a new period of rapid growth. He argued that the principal factors were the products of national trends and not of local promotion efforts, and he said that the main differences between the cities of the South and those elsewhere were differences of scale.[23]

Brownell then qualified his statement, admitting that southern cities also possessed certain "peculiar features" that derived from regional customs and mores. These included a stronger emphasis on church and family and a record of greater violence growing out of what he explained as the "primitive bravado that often pervades both white and black lower classes." "If southern cities are different," he said, "these differences certainly lie primarily in those peculiar patterns of interpersonal relations that are deeply woven into the rich tapestry of southern cultural experience—patterns that continue in the southern metropolis." Yet, he concluded, southern cities have taken their essential characteristics "more from the fact that they are cities than from the fact that they are southern."[24]

A year after the publication of *The Urban South in the Twentieth*

21. Joel L. Fleishman, "The Southern City: Northern Mistakes in Southern Settings," in Ayers and Naylor (eds.), *You Can't Eat Magnolias*, 169–94 (quotation on p. 170).

22. Egerton, *The Americanization of Dixie*, 151.

23. Blaine A. Brownell, *The Urban South in the Twentieth Century* (St. Charles, Mo.: Forum Press, 1974), 8, 14, 23.

24. *Ibid.*, 24.

Century, Brownell brought out a much more nearly definitive work, *The Urban Ethos in the South, 1920–1930.* In this book he selected five major regional cities—Atlanta, Birmingham, Memphis, Nashville, and New Orleans—and studied their development in the frenetic period immediately after World War I. He found the beginnings of many of the processes of later southern urban growth. The regional "urban ethos," he concluded, was enunciated by the white commercial-civic elite, which drew its principal conceptions of the city's role from the New South ideals of such late-nineteenth-century figures as Henry W. Grady.[25]

A different aspect of southern urban development occupied the work of Wayt T. Watterson and Roberta S. Watterson. In *The Politics of New Communities* (1975), they traced the origin and early course of San Antonio Ranch, a federally assisted community located twenty miles northwest of San Antonio. The planned new community, which ultimately failed, was a product of the federal Urban Growth and New Community Development Act of 1970. This book is largely an account of the legal and political maneuvering that preceded the beginning of work on the town.[26]

Still another phase of the region's urban history claimed the attention of economist Leonard F. Wheat. In *Urban Growth in the Nonmetropolitan South* (1976), he employed a computerized analysis, replete with econometric formulas, independent variables, multiple correlations, and chi-square tables, to measure the causes for the growth of southern communities with populations from five thousand to fifty thousand. He concluded that the most significant factor was air service, though education, taxes, and access to highways were also important.[27]

By 1977, historians were sufficiently aware of the importance of southern urban history to bring out a collaborative volume on the subject. Brownell and David R. Goldfield edited *The City in Southern History,* which traces regional city development from the very be-

25. Blaine A. Brownell, *The Urban Ethos in the South, 1920–1930* (Baton Rouge: Louisiana State University Press, 1975), 216, 220. See also Brownell, "The Commercial-Civic Elite and City Planning in Atlanta, Memphis, and New Orleans in the 1920s," *Journal of Southern History,* XLI (August, 1975), 339–68; and Charles Paul Garofalo, "The Sons of Henry Grady: Atlanta Boosters in the 1920s," *Journal of Southern History,* XLII (May, 1976), 187–204.

26. Wayt T. Watterson and Roberta S. Watterson, *The Politics of New Communities: A Case Study of San Antonio Ranch* (New York: Praeger, 1975).

27. Leonard F. Wheat, *Urban Growth in the Nonmetropolitan South* (Lexington: Mass.: Heath, 1976).

ginning—the founding of Jamestown. The editors set the tone of the work by quoting approvingly a statement once made by Charles G. Sellers, Jr., who said: "'The traditional emphasis on the South's differences is wrong historically.'" Southerners "have been, and remain, simply 'other Americans.'" But having made this point, the editors jibbed rather sharply by saying that southern cities "reflect some of the languid, unhurried, personal atmosphere that is perhaps lacking in metropolises of the North and West"; that "although at first glance well-scrubbed Atlanta might be mistaken for Minneapolis, and Houston may be Space City, there is a substance and quality of life forever veiled to those whose understanding rests solely on census data." [28]

Two chapters in the Brownell-Goldfield volume are particularly germane. These are Brownell's essay "The Urban South Comes of Age, 1900–1940" and Edward F. Haas's essay "The Southern Metropolis, 1940–1976." Brownell set the stage for work on the post–World War II surge in regional urbanization by describing the earlier years as a "takeoff period" during which the southern population moved into the cities at more than three times the rate of movement into twenty-one selected northeastern and midwestern states. His findings anticipated those of students of the later years by showing that many of the urban problems of today—such as flight to the suburbs, erosion of the tax base, and increasing racial segregation—originated before World War II. He concluded: "It was in the urban South that the regional culture came into contact with the opportunities and demands of a modern era and where the largely static and homogeneous social life of the countryside broke into a welter of heterogeneity." [29]

Haas's article is a pioneer work by a professional historian on the nature of southern city life after World War II. Although he made a number of important generalizations about regional cities as a whole, his major emphasis was on New Orleans. Much of his information and many of his insights came from his earlier study of the career of the flamboyant New Orleans mayor DeLesseps S. Morrison. Haas's theme was the cities' search for ways to convert wartime industrial and financial gains into permanent peacetime growth. He discussed the importance of continued postwar military spending and of the

28. Blaine A. Brownell and David R. Goldfield (eds.), *The City in Southern History: The Growth of Urban Civilization in the South* (Port Washington, N.Y.: Kennikat Press, 1977), 6, 7. See also Watters, *The South and the Nation*, 137–320.

29. Blaine A. Brownell, "The Urban South Comes of Age, 1900–1940," in Brownell and Goldfield (eds.), *The City in Southern History*, 123–58 (quotation on p. 150).

transportation revolution brought about by the construction of the interstate highway system and the expansion of commercial aviation, especially the rise of Delta and Braniff. He showed the social and political effects of city growth, emphasized the emerging problems and the efforts of city governments to cope with them, and he ended by saying: "[They] only affirmed the South's entry into the national urban pattern. In 1976 southerners . . . realized that the present as well as the future of their region rested in its cities." [30]

The same year in which the Brownell-Goldfield work was published saw also the appearance of an extraordinary collaborative volume, *The Rise of the Sunbelt Cities*. It contains twelve essays by professors of government, history, economics, and metropolitan studies, a student of transnational corporations, and a journalist. It claims to be a departure from the usual bias of interpreting urban development through the experience of the Northeast. As the title suggests, it views the recent experience of the South's cities as a part of that of the region as a whole. Although in this respect the book claims more originality than it deserves, it does in fact place unusual emphasis on the importance of regional economics and culture. In explaining the rise of the region's cities, the essays represent a wide variety of viewpoints, including traditional, neoclassical, and Marxist economic theories. All agree, however, that the changes cannot be attributed simply to new developments in transportation, technology, or some other such variable. The changes result from the evolution of the capitalist system that enables certain regions to advance faster than others. [31]

The most intriguing pieces are by Walt W. Rostow and Murray Bookchin. Rostow attributed the rise of southern cities to what he called the "fifth Kondratieff upswing," which he explained as a cyclical economic theory propounded in the 1920s by the Russian economist whose name it bears. Rostow's gloss on Kondratieff says that the present changes in southern cities are the result of favorable shifts in the prices of food and raw materials in relation to the costs of manufacturing. [32]

Bookchin contended truculently that while New York has served

30. Edward F. Haas, *DeLesseps S. Morrison and the Image of Reform: New Orleans Politics, 1946–1961* (Baton Rouge: Louisiana State University Press, 1974), and "The Southern Metropolis, 1940–1976," in Brownell and Goldfield (eds.), *The City in Southern History*, 159–91 (quotation on p. 191).

31. Perry and Watkins (eds.), *The Rise of the Sunbelt Cities*, 15.

32. Walt W. Rostow, "Regional Change in the Fifth Kondratieff Upswing," *ibid.*, 83–103.

an authentic function as an entrepôt and melting pot for millions of immigrants, the cities of the South and Southwest represent a "quixotic form of failure . . . a curious form of urbanization without cities." In the regional cities, which, according to him, are not really cities, he said business became a cult, growth a deity, and money a talisman. They were "faceless structures" sprawling across the countryside without the "seasoning of history, of authentic cultural intercourse, of urban development and centering." [33]

In *Urban America: From Downtown to No Town* (1979), Goldfield and Brownell took a tack quite different from Bookchin's. They surveyed the entire urban history of the nation, but they reserved a special place for southern cities during the last quarter-century. They saw the extraordinary growth of these cities as the result of "a process of *regional succession*" that is altering the whole national urban system. The authors continued to exhibit the strong ambivalence that marked their earlier studies on southern urban affairs. They conceded that southern cities face serious problems, especially those growing out of racial segregation and the recent overbuilding of office space. But the authors described these cities as representing something of a fulfillment of Frank Lloyd Wright's vision of "Broadacre City," a community featuring spread-out residential areas and cultural facilities but with low-density commercial activities. Whereas the older cities in other areas give "'an atmosphere of sepulchral menace,'" they wrote, the feeling in the Sun Belt cities is quite different. "Take a walk through downtown Atlanta . . . and for sheer exuberance and chutzpah [a venerable southern expression] it is difficult to beat." [34]

Carl Abbott, in *The New Urban America* (1981), attempted to bring together all the different perspectives on the recent movement in the South. [35] His subtitle indicates an effort to present the southern cities as products of regional forces. He defined the Sun Belt region

33. Murray Bookchin, "Toward a Vision of the Urban Future," *ibid.*, 259–76 (quotations on p. 262).
34. David R. Goldfield and Blaine A. Brownell, *Urban America: From Downtown to No Town* (Boston: Houghton Mifflin, 1979), 335 (quotation), 399, 400 (quotation).
35. Carl Abbott, *The New Urban America: Growth and Politics in Sunbelt Cities* (Chapel Hill: University of North Carolina Press, 1981). See also *Growth and the Cities of the South: A Study in Diversity* (Washington, D.C.: White House Conference on Balanced Growth and Economic Development, 1977). Among the books on specific southern cities are Truman Hartshorn, *Metropolis in Georgia: Atlanta's Rise as a Transaction Center* (Cambridge, Mass.: Ballinger Publishing Co., 1976); Brett W. Hawkins, *Nashville Metro: The Politics of City-County Consolidation* (Nashville: Vanderbilt University Press, 1966); M. Kent Jennings, *Community Influentials: The Elites of Atlanta* (New York: Free Press, 1964); Warren Leslie, *Dallas Public and Pri-*

broadly enough to include the states of Delaware and Washington, though curiously he excluded an entire cluster of states along the lower Mississippi River because their metropolitan areas since World War II had failed to grow at what he established as the Sun Belt rate, that is, a rate above the national average. Indeed, his definition is so loose that the traditional South is indistinct. He conceded, however, that population growth since 1970 in the lower Mississippi Valley states might soon require their inclusion in his Sun Belt. Abbott concluded his study with a warning that the new prosperity of the Sun Belt cities is in jeopardy unless they can find ways to solve the problems of unemployment and inner-city decay: "The immediate crises of depopulation and bankruptcy that have made headlines in the sev-

vate (New York: Grossman Publishers, 1964); Harold H. Martin, *William Berry Hartsfield: Mayor of Atlanta* (Athens: University of Georgia Press, 1978); Carol Estes Thometz, *The Decision-Makers: The Power Structure of Dallas* (Dallas: Southern Methodist University Press, 1963); David M. Tucker, *Memphis Since Crump: Bossism, Blacks, and Civic Reformers, 1948–1968* (Knoxville: University of Tennessee Press, 1980); and David G. McComb, *Houston: A History* (Rev. ed.; Austin: University of Texas Press, 1981). The periodical literature on urban development in the recent South is voluminous. Among the articles on the subject are Margery Post Abbott and Carl Abbott, "Colonial Place, Norfolk: Residential Integration in a Southern Urban Neighborhood," *Urban Affairs Papers,* I (Fall, 1979), 1–17; Lynn Ashby, "The Supercities: Houston," *Saturday Review,* September 4, 1976, pp. 16–19; Carol T. F. Bennett and Charles P. Zlatkovitch, "San Antonio: A Military, Trade, and Service Center," *Texas Business Review,* LI (July, 1977), 144–48; Reese Cleghorn, "Atlanta," *City,* V (January-February, 1971), 35–37; Borden Dent, "The Challenge to Downtown Shopping," *Atlanta Economic Review,* XXVIII (January-February, 1976), 29–33; Linda Fates, "CZO: The Virginia Beach Land Use Hassle," *Metro Magazine* (August, 1973), 22–27; "Fulton-Atlanta Merger Debated," *National Civic Review,* LIX (February, 1970), 97–98; David R. Goldfield, "The Limits of Suburban Growth: The Washington, D.C. SMSA," *Urban Affairs Quarterly,* XII (September, 1976), 83–102; Truman Hartshorn, "Getting Around Atlanta: New Approaches," *Atlanta Economic Review,* XXVIII (January-February, 1978), 43–51; Virginia H. Hein, "The Image of a City 'Too Busy to Hate': Atlanta in the 1960's," *Phylon,* XXXIII (Fall, 1972), 205–21; "Houston Is Where They're Moving," *Fortune* (February, 1971), 91–97; John D. Hutchinson, Jr., and Elizabeth T. Beer, "In-Migration and Atlanta's Neighborhoods," *Atlanta Economic Review,* XXVIII (March-April, 1978), 7–14; Charles Little, "Atlanta Renewal Gives Power to the Communities," *Smithsonian,* VII (July, 1976), 100–108; Leonard Reissman, "Social Development and the American South," *Journal of Social Issues,* XXII (January, 1966), 101–16; Bill Schemmel, "Atlanta's 'Power Structure' Faces Life," *New South,* XXVII (Spring, 1972), 62–68; Daniel C. Thompson, "The New South," *Journal of Social Issues,* XXII (January, 1966), 7–19; Dana White and Timothy Crimmins, "How Atlanta Grew: Cool Heads, Hot Air, and Hard Work," *Atlanta Economic Review,* XXVIII (January-February, 1978), 7–15; Alexander S. Wright III, "The Office Market: Central City versus Suburbs," *Atlanta Economic Review,* XXVIII (January-February, 1978), 34–36; and Neal R. Peirce, "The Southern City Today," in Boles (ed.), *Dixie Dateline,* 97–111.

enties are still confined to the older cities of the industrial belt, but New Orleans, Jacksonville, Washington, Denver, Portland, Seattle, San Francisco, Oakland, and Los Angeles all show danger signs that promise increased financial vulnerability in the eighties."[36]

The most recent effort to present a comprehensive view of the southern city in historical perspective is David R. Goldfield's *Cotton Fields and Skyscrapers* (1982). His final chapter, "A Kind of Sunlight," covers the period from 1920 to 1980. In dealing with the post–World War II years, Goldfield focuses on the problems rather than the promises of growth, especially continuing racial segregation, worker resistance to unionization, and the shortage of public services. The chapter title notwithstanding, an atmosphere of doom seems to pervade the discussion; southern cities appear to have lost much of the "chutzpah" that Atlanta once held for Goldfield. He closed the chapter with a picture of an Atlanta citizen rocking on his front porch, gazing at the city's towering skyline and savoring the odor of magnolias and homemade biscuits.[37] To the author's apparent regret, the region's intractable rural ethos has triumphed after all.

Another indication of the kindling of regional scholarly interest in city development is the appearance of two southern publication series devoted to this subject. These are the *Journal of Urban History,* a quarterly periodical that began in 1974 under the sponsorship of Florida Atlantic University and later was transferred to the University of Alabama in Birmingham; and *South Atlantic Urban Studies,* which began in 1977 and is published annually by the University of South Carolina Press in collaboration with the Urban Studies Program of the College of Charleston. Both series contain articles that are not exclusively on southern cities; indeed, most of them address urban affairs beyond the region. But the publications do include a number of thoughtful pieces on the recent southern urban scene.[38] The February, 1976, issue of the *Journal of Urban History* was devoted to the topic "Urban Themes in the American South," because, as the editor Blaine A. Brownell explained, "cities in the American South have

36. Abbott, *The New Urban America,* 26, 254.

37. David R. Goldfield, *Cotton Fields and Skyscrapers: Southern City and Region, 1607–1980* (Baton Rouge: Louisiana State University Press, 1982), 196.

38. Among these were Joel Williamson, "The Oneness of Southern Life," *South Atlantic Urban Studies,* I (1977), 78–89; James C. Cobb, "Urbanization and the Changing South: A Review of Literature," *South Atlantic Urban Studies,* I (1977), 253–66; Carol E. Hill, "Ethnicity as a Factor in Urban Social Change," *South Atlantic Urban Studies,* III (1979), 107–21; Numan V. Bartley, "The Limits of Urban Reform in the New South," *Journal of Urban History,* II (February, 1976), 253–55; and Dana F.

been woefully neglected as subjects of study, and their importance has been slighted by urban and regional historians alike." [39] Perhaps these two series will help to remedy this neglect.

In sum, writers on the postwar South are generally agreed that the region and its metropolitan areas have experienced extraordinary growth in population, industrialization, and prosperity, and that this growth is likely to continue for the immediate future. The writers do not agree on the exact causes, whether cheap labor, an expanding market, pleasant climate, abundant natural resources, favorable amenities for living, regional promotional efforts, or the flow of federal funds. They discuss all of these possible causes, but there are sharp differences on the order of importance. The writers agree that the changes have been both good and bad for the region, though there is also a wide range of opinion as to how good or how bad. Certainly all agree that growth must be controlled if the ultimate result is to be beneficial.

Because the phenomenon of southern growth in industry, urbanization, and prosperity is relatively recent, it has not yet attracted a volume of scholarly work equal to that on such topics as southern politics or race relations. One may confidently predict, however, that students of the region will increasingly turn their attention to the new fields. If in doing so they heed Grantham's advice to broaden their focus and write more meaningfully, they will provide a valuable service to the study of southern history. Heeding this advice will not oblige them to ignore the continuing differences between the South and the rest of the nation. Indeed, an emphasis on these differences may well be salutary, because, as many of the studies already completed have shown, the differences themselves can be of vital importance to the region.

Unquestionably, the use of the computer and quantitative techniques of research and analysis will grow in the study of southern economic and demographic affairs. These techniques ought to add a significant dimension to the entire body of work. But historians will be challenged to use them in a manner that will appeal to the humanistic sensibilities and common understanding of their readers. Too often the present quantitative studies leave the reader with an impulse to repeat what John Randolph of Roanoke once said upon re-

---

White and Timothy J. Crimmins, "Urban Structure, Atlanta," *Journal of Urban History,* II (February, 1976), 231–52.

39. Blaine A. Brownell, "Introduction: Urban Themes in the American South," *Journal of Urban History,* II (February, 1976), 139–45 (quotation on p. 139).

ceiving one of the turgid essays by John Taylor of Caroline. To the publisher, Randolph praised the content and spirit of the piece, but he urged: "For heaven's sake, get somebody to render it into plain English."

The questions of the causes and effects of southern growth ought to continue to engage the interest of historians, as should the question of how to control that growth. Obviously, these issues have by no means been settled. A great deal of excellent work has been done, and much remains to be done.

Agriculture and farm life offer perhaps the most neglected fields in recent southern economic and social history. Not only are these areas worthy of study, but without the striking developments in agriculture—such as mechanization, the use of herbicides and insecticides, and the shift to grazing, dairy and beef production, poultry culture, the growing of soybeans, and tree farming—the remarkable developments in industry and urbanization could not have occurred. Or would not have occurred in the same manner in which they in fact occurred. Yet, though these agricultural changes have been briefly described in all the general works on the South, in a number of pioneering articles, and in three chapters of Gilbert C. Fite's *Cotton Fields No More* (1984), the comprehensive history of post–World War II southern agriculture and farm life has not been written.[40]

40. Gilbert C. Fite, *Cotton Fields No More: Southern Agriculture, 1865–1980* (Lexington: University Press of Kentucky, 1984), 163–231. Besides the general works, for brief discussions of southern agriculture since World War II, see Thomas D. Clark, *The Emerging South* (New York: Oxford University Press, 1961), 40–103; Roland, *The Improbable Era*, 20–26; Zenas Beers, "The New Face of Southern Agriculture: The Delta," *Farm Chemicals*, CXXX (October, 1967), 33–38; Wayne M. Cox, "The New Face of Southern Agriculture: The Southeast," *Farm Chemicals*, CXXX (March, 1967), 30–37; Pete Daniel, "The Transformation of the Rural South 1930 to the Present," *Agricultural History*, LV (July, 1981), 231–48; Gilbert C. Fite, "Mechanization of Cotton Production Since World War II," *Agricultural History*, LIV (January, 1980), 190–207; Harry D. Fornari, "The Big Change: Cotton to Soybeans," *Agricultural History*, LIII (January, 1979), 245–53; Gilbert C. Fite, "Southern Agriculture Since the Civil War: An Overview," *Agricultural History*, LIII (January, 1979), 3–21; Jack Temple Kirby, "The Transformation of Southern Plantations, c. 1920–1960," *Agricultural History*, LVII (July, 1983), 257–76, and "The Southern Exodus, 1910–1960: A Primer for Historians," *Journal of Southern History*, XLIX (November, 1983), 585–600; and Pete Daniel, "The Crossroads of Change: Cotton, Tobacco, and Rice Cultures in the Twentieth-Century South," *Journal of Southern History*, L (August, 1984), 429–56. See also Pete Daniel, *Breaking the Land: The Transformation of Cotton, Tobacco, and Rice Cultures Since 1880* (Urbana: University of Illinois Press, 1985); and Jack Temple Kirby's forthcoming study of southern agriculture since *ca.* 1920.

Women in the South

JACQUELYN DOWD HALL and ANNE FIROR SCOTT

Women appears three times in the index of Arthur S. Link and Rembert W. Patrick's *Writing Southern History* (1965). Hugh F. Rankin, in his essay on the historiography of the colonial South, noted: "And that ever-present female influence in society has been covered in Julia Cherry Spruill's *Women's Life and Work in the Southern Colonies.* She testifies that women were responsible for important and lasting contributions to southern culture." But what these contributions were Rankin forbore to mention. More than 200 pages later, Mary Elizabeth Massey, writing on the history of the Confederacy, suggested that most of the work relating to women was "romantic and eulogistic." She cited one scholarly monograph, Francis B. Simkins and James W. Patton, *The Women of the Confederacy,* and suggested that it was time for a new book on the subject. After another 150 pages, A. Elizabeth Taylor's work on the southern suffrage movement was cited in a footnote along with that of three other historians. Thus ended the historiography of southern women in 1965.[1]

In his essay in the same volume, George B. Tindall inadvertently explained this puzzling state of affairs: "With the best of intentions the historian cannot completely transcend the human limitations imposed by the temper of his times, his regional identification, his race, or causes that arouse his sympathies. His view of historical reality, the very selection of the facts with which he is concerned, inevitably will be shaped and distorted by the perspective in which he views them."[2]

---

1. Arthur S. Link and Rembert W. Patrick (eds.), *Writing Southern History: Essays in Historiography in Honor of Fletcher M. Green* (Baton Rouge: Louisiana State University Press, 1965), 22, 268, 422.

2. *Ibid.,* p. 337. Women who are historians will observe an irony within the irony in this quotation. The failure to recognize the existence of southern women is not confined to the past or to *Writing Southern History,* which could only report on existing scholarship. Most of the general histories of the South, including the magisterial multivolume *A History of the South,* are similarly blank on the subject. In the final two

In no way has the historical landscape changed more radically in the past two decades than in the emergence from the deep shadows of the other half of the population. Like the Island of Surtsey, which pushed its way to the surface in the North Atlantic in 1963, offering biologists a chance to discover how flora and fauna develop on a new addition to the earth's surface, the emergence of the history of women allows us to observe the process by which a new field takes shape and to see how new questions generate new answers, even when the sources are familiar.

The recent surge of writing in women's history also provides another example, if another were needed, of the close connection between the subjects historians choose to examine and the social context in which they live. Not context alone but the question of *who* writes history has an effect upon what research is carried out, what articles, monographs, and books come to be written, how the past is viewed.

In the case of women's history, the two have been closely related. After 1920, feminism, which had been a dynamic force in American culture and politics for three decades, went through a forty-year period of fragmentation and reshaping before it reemerged in the early 1960s. During that time, few women became historians, and fewer still became historians of women. From 1920 to 1960, only five major historical works dealt with the history of American women; three of these were devoted to colonial history, and only one had anything to say about the South.

This period of quiescent feminism and inattention to the history of women came to a sudden end in the early 1960s. As feminism once more grew into a powerful social movement, the demand for attention to women's past also grew. Old books were rediscovered, new books and articles began to multiply, the Berkshire Conference of Women Historians expanded from two dozen to two hundred members and mounted conferences that matched in size and surpassed in

---

volumes of that series, women are indexed five times. The Fleming Lectures at Louisiana State University have yet to be devoted to women's history. The first Lamar Lecture to approach the subject came in 1982 with Paul M. Gaston's "The Women of Fair Hope" (published as *Women of Fair Hope* [Athens: University of Georgia Press, 1984]). Also in 1982 the Chancellor's Symposium on Southern History at the University of Mississippi was devoted to women's roles. Papers presented at that symposium have been collected in Joanne V. Hawks and Sheila L. Skemp (eds.), *Sex, Race, and the Role of Women in the South* (Jackson: University Press of Mississippi, 1983). See especially Anne F. Scott's article in the collection, "Historians Construct the Southern Woman" (95–110).

enthusiasm those of established historical societies. The Association of Black Women Historians was organized in 1978. With the help of the National Endowment for the Humanities an excellent guide to sources was created, and four volumes of *Notable American Women* provided thousands of bibliographical leads along with more than seventeen hundred biographies of influential women who had lived between 1607 and 1975. New journals were created and old journals began, albeit cautiously, to publish articles dealing with women's history.[3]

This efflorescence of scholarship was largely the work of young scholars, mostly women, who had flocked into graduate programs in the 1960s. In the nature of things, they found few mentors in the traditional sense; most wrote their dissertations, perforce, with men trained in other fields.[4]

Along with the resurgence of feminism, developments in social history were stimulating a renewed study of women's past. As more and more scholars broadened their scope beyond formal, public, or political institutions and began to look closely at a wide variety of social developments and social structures (family, church, voluntary associations, for example) and began to learn from anthropologists, psychologists, and sociologists, it was less and less possible to believe that only male experience was worth examining.[5]

3. Andrea Hinding (ed.), *Women's History Sources* (2 vols.; New York: Bowker, 1979); Edward T. James, Janet Wilson James, and Paul S. Boyer (eds.), *Notable American Women, 1607–1950: A Biographical Dictionary* (3 vols.; Cambridge: Belknap Press of Harvard University Press, 1971); Barbara Sicherman and Carol Hurd Green (eds.), *Notable American Women: The Modern Period: A Biographical Dictionary* (Cambridge: Belknap Press of Harvard University Press, 1980).

4. For example, Nancy Cott wrote with John Demos, Jacquelyn Hall with Kenneth Jackson, Carol Berkin with Richard Morris, William H. Chafe with William Leuchtenberg, Ellen DuBois with Robert Wiebe, Mary Ryan with Lynn Marshall, Mary Beth Norton with Bernard Bailyn, Linda Kerber with Richard Hofstadter, Suzanne Lebsock with Joseph Kett, and so on and on. Of the seven scholars at work in the field before 1960—Julia Spruill, Eleanor Flexner, A. Elizabeth Taylor, Janet James, Gerda Lerner, Anne F. Scott, and Barbara Solomon—only Taylor, James, and Lerner had written dissertations in the field. Scott and Solomon had written on other subjects and turned to the history of women afterward. Eleanor Flexner had no academic connection; she worked on the model of the nineteenth-century "gentleman scholar." Julia Spruill, caught up in family responsibilities, had given up scholarship except as a warm encourager of her successors.

5. While social history is unquestionably an exciting part of the discipline, historians, of all people, should not succumb to the belief that their own generation invented all the important new ideas. In 1937, Michael Kraus was already writing: "Historians have increased enormously the scope of their narratives and have measur-

As is usually the case when a new way of looking at the past develops, it was only after a good deal of concrete work that historians of women began to examine their assumptions. When they came to do so, one of the most basic was the existence of a phenomenon that may be called "women's culture." Although women, like men, differ by class, ethnicity, age, and region, in any of these categories there are discernible differences between the life experiences, values, and world views of women and men. The significance of women's culture for the historian is not only that women's life experience, from birth to death, differs in many ways from that of men, but also that in the creation and maintenance of social institutions women often express different values, function differently, and exercise different kinds of social power. The social reality of the past includes both, and written history that does not recognize the existence of women is at best incomplete and at worst simply wrong.[6]

Women's history, then, is not so much a separate field of study comparable to the study of slavery or of the English constitution. It is, rather, an approach to the whole body of past experience that asks, What were women doing? What was their particular part in the phenomenon under consideration? Was there a discernible and separate women's role in the rise of religious movements, the development of public education, the growth of abolitionism, the creation of the textile industry, the development of the civil rights movement? At some point in the future, the concept of "women's history" may be obsolete. The time will come when no scholar of any subject will consider his or her task complete without careful examination of the differences in the ways men and women have participated in the phenomenon under study. However, since in every culture, roles differ on the basis

---

ably deepened their understanding of the past by levying upon the contributions of colleagues in archaeology, geography, anthropology, ethnography, economics, psychology, and, particularly, sociology. The line has been drawn rather thin between the historian and the sociologist; in fact, the dominant group writing history today may be spoken of as the 'sociological school of historians'" (*A History of American History* [New York: Farrar & Rinehart, 1937], 319). He cites in turn Carl Becker, "Some Aspects of the Influence of Social Problems and Ideas Upon the Study and Writing of History," *American Journal of Sociology*, XVIII (March, 1913), 641–75. See also Caroline F. Ware, *The Cultural Approach to History* (New York: Columbia University Press, 1940), 3–16.

6. In most social groups, there is a male culture from which women are generally excluded, a female culture from which men are generally excluded, and a larger common culture in which both participate. See Shirley Ardener (ed.), *Perceiving Women* (London: Malaby Press, 1975), 23.

of sex, historians will always need to recognize gender as a category for analysis.

In little more than a decade, the effort to determine what women were doing has led to important work in American history, inventive in conceptualization and careful in documentation. Historians of women have examined family life, education, work, legal status, and the "bonds of womanhood" in formal associations or in informal social and kin networks. A handful of labor historians has begun to construct the history of women workers, and legal historians are providing many new insights into the role and status of women. Efforts to explore the gap between the prescription or even the myth of women's role and their real life experience have produced some interesting questions if not, so far, many answers.[7]

A comparatively small segment of this growing body of work deals with southern women. At first glance this is surprising, since no other regional category of women has received so much attention in fiction, myth, and the popular imagination. Perhaps, however, this neglect is understandable, given the Northeast's predominance in the historical profession and the constraints on women's educational and professional opportunities in the South.

While southern women have shared many characteristics and experiences with women of other regions, they along with other southerners have been shaped by their relationship to chattel slavery and its aftermath. Moreover, the plantation system—along with the concept of patriarchy that provided its cultural rationale—had a large influence on women's life experience. Until World War II, the South's economy was primarily agricultural, and relatively few of its people were drawn into the urbanizing process. Until that time, it was the home of most black Americans, female as well as male. For these rea-

7. For general historiographical summaries of the work in women's history, see Barbara Sicherman, "American History," *Signs*, I (Winter, 1975), 461–85; Mary Beth Norton, "American History," *Signs*, V (Winter, 1979), 324–37; Albert Krichmar, *The Women's Rights Movement in the United States, 1848–1970: A Bibliography and Sourcebook* (Metuchen, N.J.: Scarecrow Press, 1972); Cynthia E. Harrison (ed.), *Women in American History: A Bibliography* (Santa Barbara: ABC Clio Press, 1979); Gerda Lerner, *Teaching Women's History* (Washington, D.C.: American Historical Association, 1981); Carl Degler in Michael Kammen (ed.), *The Past Before Us: Contemporary Historical Writing in the United States* (Ithaca: Cornell University Press, 1980), 308–26; Barbara Sicherman *et al.*, *Recent United States Scholarship on the History of Women: A Report Presented at the XV International Congress of Historical Sciences, Bucharest, Romania, 1980* (Washington, D.C.: American Historical Association, 1980).

sons, as well as the long historical habit of viewing themselves as a group apart, "southern women" constitute a definable group, though within the group they are further divided by race, class, and region. Both southern distinctiveness and scholarly neglect argue for putting southern women's history high on the research agenda for historians of the South and for historians of women. But what comes next will build on a substantial base.

The first historian of the South who recognized the existence of women was Captain John Smith. His discussion of Pocahontas might class him as a precursor of the late-twentieth-century historians who see that both women and native Americans helped form the new society that European colonization was creating in the New World. Like Smith, other seventeenth-century chroniclers occasionally noticed women, but not until the middle of the nineteenth century was there a self-conscious effort to record women's activities—generally in connection with the Civil War. The result was the creation of those "romantic and eulogistic" works of which Massey complained in 1965, important only because they saved from oblivion events and people that might be treated more analytically in our own day. The first modern scholarly study seems to have been an article by Virginia Gearhart Gray published in the *South Atlantic Quarterly* in 1928. Gray traced the "steady entrance of southern women into public affairs" in the years before the Civil War. Before it had become common to do so, she used census data and city directories to identify women workers and to delineate women's business activity. She made imaginative use of legislative records to document women's political involvement, discovered needlewomen forming early protective associations, and described women working in textile mills in Maryland, North Carolina, and Georgia before the Civil War. Gray opened a number of lines of inquiry that would not be followed again for nearly three decades.[8]

Six years later the same journal published "Southern Women of a 'Lost Generation'" by Marjorie Stratford Mendenhall, who traced the widening of women's sphere of activity in the thirty years after the Civil War. Mendenhall was interested in voluntary activity as well as paid work. Neither Gray nor Mendenhall found jobs in history departments. One became an indefatigable manuscript archivist and the other a part-time lecturer in a political science department. There

8. Virginia Gearhart Gray, "Activities of Southern Women: 1840–1860," *South Atlantic Quarterly*, XXVII (July, 1928), 264–79 (quotation on p. 267).

was no structure of support to urge them on to further work in the field in which they had pioneered.[9]

If anyone had been listening, the modern study of women's history might have been inaugurated with the publication in quick succession of Guion Griffis Johnson's *Ante-bellum North Carolina* (1937) and Julia Cherry Spruill's *Women's Life and Work in the Southern Colonies* (1938). The books complemented each other and, taken together, covered two and a half centuries. Neither of these excellent scholars, living in the presumed center of southern liberal thought, was seriously considered for appointment to the Department of History at the University of North Carolina. Support for their scholarship came from Howard W. Odum and the Institute for Research in Social Science, and from their husbands. Both worked new ground with patience and imagination. Spruill, for example, spent more than a decade examining every extant southern colonial newspaper, as well as wills, inventories of estates, deeds, marriage records, travelers' accounts, printed documents in state and local historical journals, county minutes, parish records, legislative records, and letters. Johnson was similarly diligent.[10]

The next sign of interest in southern women's past came in 1941 when Eleanor M. Boatwright summarized her Duke University dissertation in an article on the political and civil status of women in Georgia between the Revolution and the Civil War. Her findings showed that while married women were legally dead in the eyes of the common law and their condition in Georgia "before 1860 was always hazardous, frequently humiliating, and often tragic," the status of any individual could not be deduced simply from legal disability. It was, Boatwright concluded, "far more commonly determined by her character, that of the man she married, their personal relation to each other, the use they made of the laws, and even by public opinion, than by the statutes alone." As others before and since have found,

---

9. Marjorie Stratford Mendenhall, "Southern Women of a 'Lost Generation,'" *South Atlantic Quarterly*, XXXIII (October, 1934), 343–53.

10. Guion Griffis Johnson, *Ante-bellum North Carolina: A Social History* (Chapel Hill: University of North Carolina Press, 1937); Julia Cherry Spruill, *Women's Life and Work in the Southern Colonies* (Chapel Hill: University of North Carolina Press, 1938). Both books were enthusiastically received by reviewers. Since Johnson's book was of broad scope and could be used in courses in southern and North Carolina history, it was widely read, at least by scholars and students. Spruill's, in spite of the initial reception, disappeared into libraries. It was rediscovered and reprinted in 1972 and thereafter widely read.

women improved their situations through the use of equity courts, and the common sense of judges often significantly modified women's common-law disabilities.[11]

Shortly after Boatwright published her findings, A. Elizabeth Taylor inaugurated what would become her life work with a series of articles on the Tennessee and Georgia suffrage movements. By 1957 she had added a book and four additional articles on aspects of the suffrage movement in the South.[12] In 1962 the *South Atlantic Quarterly* again proved hospitable to the history of southern women when it published Anne F. Scott's "The 'New Woman' in the New South," and in 1965, Guion Johnson summed up her years of study in "The Changing Status of the Southern Woman." Gerda Lerner's *The Grimké Sisters from South Carolina* appeared in 1967, and in 1970 came Scott's *The Southern Lady*. Since that time the stream, while slow, has been steady.[13]

11. Eleanor M. Boatwright, "The Political and Civil Status of Women in Georgia: 1783–1860," *Georgia Historical Quarterly*, XXV (December, 1941), 301–24 (quotations on p. 324).

12. A. Elizabeth Taylor continued to write about the southern suffrage movement, building a state-by-state account. She plans eventually to write an interpretative volume covering the whole South. See, for example, "A Short History of the Woman Suffrage Movement in Tennessee," *Tennessee Historical Quarterly*, II (September, 1943), 195–215, "The Origin of the Woman Suffrage Movement in Georgia," *Georgia Historical Quarterly*, XXVIII (June, 1944), 63–79, "The Woman Suffrage Movement in Texas," *Journal of Southern History*, XVII (May, 1951), 195–215, "The Woman Suffrage Movement in Arkansas," *Arkansas Historical Quarterly*, XV (Spring, 1956), 17–52, *The Woman Suffrage Movement in Tennessee* (New York: Bookman, 1957), "Revival and Development of the Woman Suffrage Movement in Georgia," *Georgia Historical Quarterly*, XLIII (December, 1958), 339–54, "The Last Phase of the Woman Suffrage Movement in Georgia," *Georgia Historical Quarterly*, XLIII (March, 1959), 11–28, "The Woman Suffrage Movement in North Carolina, Part 1," *North Carolina Historical Review*, XXXVIII (January, 1961), 45–62, "The Woman Suffrage Movement in North Carolina (Concluded)," *North Carolina Historical Review*, XXXVIII (April, 1961), 173–89, and "The Woman Suffrage Movement in Mississippi, 1880–1920," *Journal of Mississippi History*, XXX (February, 1968), 1–34.

13. Anne Firor Scott, "The 'New Woman' in the New South," *South Atlantic Quarterly*, LXI (Autumn, 1962), 473–83; Guion Griffis Johnson, "The Changing Status of the Southern Woman," in John C. McKinney and Edgar T. Thompson (eds.), *The South in Continuity and Change* (Durham: Duke University Press, 1965), 418–36; Gerda Lerner, *The Grimké Sisters from South Carolina: Rebels Against Slavery* (Boston: Houghton Mifflin, 1967); see also Katharine Du Pre Lumpkin, *The Emancipation of Angelina Grimké* (Chapel Hill: University of North Carolina Press, 1974); Anne Firor Scott, *The Southern Lady: From Pedestal to Politics, 1830–1930* (Chicago: University of Chicago Press, 1970). See also William R. Taylor, *Cavalier and*

Research about women has changed and complicated our understanding of southern social history. Documenting the activities of a wide variety of southern women, from plantation mistresses to field slaves and indentured servants, from Charleston and New Orleans ladies to frontier women of the upland, from factory workers and schoolteachers to sharecroppers, from church and Woman's Christian Temperance Union (WCTU) leaders to radical labor organizers, is affecting the way we interpret economic development, sectional feeling, family structure, the importance of kinship, the institution of slavery, and the nature of southern urbanization. Most of the significant social developments historians seek to understand were partly shaped by women, who often, though not always, had a different angle of vision, different goals and motives, from southern men. In this essay we have tried to identify the work in women's history that has changed our understanding both of the history of the South and of the history of women and to indicate the very large areas still awaiting scholarly attention.[14]

A group of scholars studying the seventeenth-century Chesapeake have begun to reconstruct the experience of the first generation of women settlers in Maryland. Compiling data from shipping lists, wills, and county records of all sorts and using sophisticated statistical analysis, Lois Green Carr and Lorena S. Walsh have produced a picture of an immigrant society to which most women came initially as indentured servants with the prospect of working hard and dying young. Because the sex ratio was unbalanced, those who survived could expect to marry early and often. In these conditions family life was, to say the least, complex. Carr and Walsh tentatively conclude that while there were degrading aspects to indentured servitude, on balance these women experienced fewer restraints on their social conduct than did their counterparts in England and exercised more social power. Moreover, they suggest that some of these patterns developed in the first generation carried over as Maryland became a

---

Yankee: The Old South and American National Character (New York: George Braziller, 1961), which contains an interesting analysis of southern women's roles; and Winthrop D. Jordan, *White over Black: American Attitudes Toward the Negro, 1550–1812* (Chapel Hill: University of North Carolina Press, 1968), which examines the dynamics of interracial sex.

14. Space constraints have dictated selectivity. We have not discussed music, the domestic arts, and other aspects of women's creativity, nor have we been able to give adequate attention to literature, biography, and collections of primary documents, all of which are windows to women's consciousness and experience that deserve extended treatment in their own right.

growing and prosperous native-born society in the third and fourth generations.[15]

Eighteenth-century legal records allow historians to examine the relationship of married women to property. Marylynn Salmon has been interested in the degree to which women used the equity courts to overcome common-law disabilities. Her examination of an unusually complete run of South Carolina marriage settlements shows that the use of equity was common among women in wealthy families. She found widows more likely than women marrying for the first time to resort to marriage settlements—a situation that also prevailed in New Hanover County, North Carolina, in the same period. There, Alan Watson found that over 70 percent of marriage contracts were made by widows, an indication, he concluded, "of the desire of such women to preserve a measure of the independence gained via widowhood and to secure their property for the benefit of the children of the previous or forthcoming marriage." [16]

Joan R. Gundersen and Gwen Victor Gampel, making a comparative study of women's legal status in the colonies of Virginia and New York, found customary law initially to be more favorable to women than it had been in England. They concluded that the colonial *femme couverte* was far from passive and that married women were active participants in the legal system. Like John Murrin, they saw American society becoming more Anglicized as time passed: when trained lawyers appeared, married women's legal freedom was increasingly restricted. Linda L. Angle's thesis, "Women in the North Carolina Colonial Courts, 1670–1739," reinforces this conclusion.[17]

15. Lois Green Carr and Lorena S. Walsh, "The Planter's Wife: The Experience of White Women in Seventeenth-Century Maryland," *William and Mary Quarterly*, 3rd Ser., XXXIV (October, 1977), 542–71.

16. Marylynn Salmon, "'Life, Liberty and Dower': The Legal Status of Women After the American Revolution," in Carol R. Berkin and Clara M. Lovett (eds.), *Women, War and Revolution* (New York: Holmes & Meier, 1980), 85–106, and "Women and Property in South Carolina: The Evidence from Marriage Settlements, 1730 to 1830," *William and Mary Quarterly*, 3rd Ser., XXXIX (October, 1982), 655–85; Alan D. Watson, "Women in Colonial North Carolina: Overlooked and Underestimated," *North Carolina Historical Review*, LVIII (Winter, 1981), 1–22. See also Kathryn Allamong Jacob, "The Woman's Lot in Baltimore Town, 1729–97," *Maryland Historical Magazine*, LXXI (Fall, 1975), 287–95.

17. Joan R. Gundersen and Gwen Victor Gampel, "Married Women's Legal Status in Eighteenth Century New York and Virginia," *William and Mary Quarterly*, 3rd Ser., XXXIX (January, 1982), 114–34. See also Linda Speth, "More than Her 'Thirds': Wives and Widows in Colonial Virginia," in *Women and History*, No. 4 (New York: Institute for Research in History and the Haworth Press, 1982), 1–42; and James W.

While detailed studies of the kind Carr, Walsh, Salmon, and others have made add significantly to our understanding of white women's experience, Spruill's book remains the essential work for the broader picture. She ranged from the seventeenth century to the Revolution, reconstructing generations of colonial women with wit and insight. She was as aware of "the housewife of the back settlements," of artisans and "she-merchants," as she was of the aristocracy.[18] A child of her generation, however, Spruill saw African slaves solely as servants and workers, without inquiring into their own views of the world.

Even a historian very much concerned to understand slave life in the seventeenth and early eighteenth centuries must be imaginative in the search for data. Allan Kulikoff, in a number of studies, has tried to find out how slave families were organized in the early Chesapeake colonies and how family and household relationships changed over time. Using probate inventories, runaway advertisements, depositions in court cases, and records kept by white owners, he has begun to draw a picture in many ways parallel to the Carr-Walsh description of white indentured servants. In both cases, there were initially many more men than women, mortality was very high, and stable family life almost impossible to achieve. However, among African slaves as among English indentured servants, there was considerable change over the generations, and a native-born group came into existence and the sex ratio declined somewhat. Kulikoff sees a sharp change as native-born Afro-Americans began to form a majority of slaves, as plantations grew larger, and as intricate kin networks took shape. Through no fault of his but because of the nature of the surviving data, slave women are shadowy figures in his study. Kulikoff suggests that while in the seventeenth century few slave women had resident husbands, by the middle of the eighteenth century nearly half of the adult slaves lived in family groups, with both husband and wife present or living close enough to share child rearing. His work might usefully be replicated for other southern colonies and is one of the few studies that throw any light on the life experience of slave women before 1800.[19]

Deen, Jr., "Patterns of Testation: Four Tidewater Counties in Colonial Virginia," *American Journal of Legal History*, XVI (April, 1972), 154–76. John Murrin, "Anglicizing an American Colony: The Transformation of Provincial Massachusetts" (Ph.D. dissertation, Yale University, 1966), and "Review Essay," *History and Theory*, XI, no. 2 (1972), 226–75; Linda L. Angle, "Women in the North Carolina Colonial Courts, 1670–1739" (M.A. thesis, University of North Carolina, 1975).

18. Spruill, *Women's Life and Work*, 81, 276–92.

19. Allan Kulikoff, "The Beginnings of the Afro-American Family in Maryland," in

A few other books and articles dealing with colonial women should be noted. Some family history is useful—Edmund S. Morgan's *Virginians at Home* (1952), for example, and the more recent work of Daniel Blake Smith. Smith's study of family life in the eighteenth-century Chesapeake, organized around concepts borrowed from psychology and anthropology, contains much useful data. Many of its generalizations, however, rest upon a narrow base of evidence and its analysis of kinship overlooks women's kin networks almost entirely.[20]

Several recent articles or essays add to our knowledge of eighteenth-century women. One is Lee Ann Caldwell's study of mid-eighteenth-century land grants to Georgia women; another is Anne F. Scott's sketch of the life and work of Eliza Lucas Pinckney. In an essay composed as part of the bicentennial, Mary Beth Norton examined the effect of the War of Independence on southern women. She found women being changed by the war, but she argued that their experience contributed to the development of a more confining role in the early nineteenth century. Her larger study, *Liberty's Daughters* (1980), is one of the few works in women's history that ranges throughout the colonies and pays close attention both to black women and to white.[21]

Aubrey C. Land, Lois G. Carr, and Edward C. Papenfuse (eds.), *Law, Society, and Politics in Early Maryland* (Baltimore: Johns Hopkins University Press, 1977). Gary Mills's "Coincoin: An Eighteenth-Century 'Liberated' Woman," *Journal of Southern History*, XLII (May, 1976), 205–22, is a fascinating narrative documenting the legend of an eighteenth-century Louisiana slave woman of unusual energy and ability. See also Cheryll Ann Cody's excellent article, "Naming, Kinship, and Estate Dispersal: Notes on Slave Family Life on a South Carolina Plantation, 1786 to 1833," *William and Mary Quarterly*, 3rd Ser., XXXIX (January, 1982), 192–211; and Chester W. Gregory, "Black Women in Pre-Federal America," in Mabel E. Deutrich and Virginia C. Purdy (eds.), *Clio Was a Woman: Studies in the History of American Women* (Washington, D.C.: Howard University Press, 1980), 53–70.

20. Edmund S. Morgan, *Virginians at Home: Family Life in the Eighteenth Century* (Williamsburg: Colonial Williamsburg, 1952); Daniel Blake Smith, *Inside the Great House: Planter Family Life in Eighteenth-Century Chesapeake Society* (Ithaca: Cornell University Press, 1980). See also Jan Lewis, "Domestic Tranquility and the Management of Emotion among the Gentry of Pre-Revolutionary Virginia," *William and Mary Quarterly*, 3rd Ser., XXXIX (January, 1982), 134–49; Michael Zuckerman, "William Byrd's Family," *Perspectives in American History*, XII (1979), 255–311; Lorena S. Walsh, "'Till Death Do Us Part': Marriage and Family in Seventeenth-Century Maryland," in Thad W. Tate and David L. Ammerman (eds.), *The Chesapeake in the Seventeenth Century: Essays on Anglo-American Society* (Chapel Hill: University of North Carolina Press, 1979), 126–52; and Darrett B. Rutman and Anita Rutman, "'Now-Wives and Sons-In-Law': Parental Death in a Seventeenth-Century Virginia County," in Tate and Ammerman (eds.), *The Chesapeake in the Seventeenth Century*, 153–82.

21. Lee Ann Caldwell, "Landgrants to Georgia Women, 1755–1775," *Georgia*

Native American women living in the area that would come to be "the South" have been rediscovered along with other women. Mary Young and Theda Perdue, in particular, have written thought-provoking articles on Cherokee women who enjoyed more rights and privileges than did their European counterparts—at least until the Europeans arrived. The newcomers were curious about native American life and set down many observations, which were distorted by their tendency to analyze what they saw in terms of their own culture. Twentieth-century historians have the benefit of anthropological concepts that allow them to make better sense of these observations than did the observers themselves. Young and Perdue are perceptive about the effect of European culture on the Cherokees; no one has yet taken up the opposite question—what effect did the Cherokee culture have upon the invaders? [22]

Only recently have scholars begun to examine women's lives in the years from independence to the early days of southern nationalism. Catherine Clinton's study of mistresses of seaboard plantations with more than twenty slaves provides massive evidence about the nature of work, kinship, courtship, health, education, and sexuality. She deals with a narrow segment of the population and makes no effort to trace change over the fifty years when so much of the South was on the move. Nevertheless, her book argues forcefully for the importance of gender in comprehending antebellum social relations and provides compelling evidence of the hard work performed by mistresses on even the largest of plantations. Provocative quotations

---

Historical Quarterly, LXI (Spring, 1977), 23–34; Anne F. Scott, "Self-Portraits: Three Women," in Richard L. Bushman *et al.* (eds.), *Uprooted Americans: Essays to Honor Oscar Handlin* (Boston: Little, Brown, 1979), 43–79; Mary Beth Norton, "'What an Alarming Crisis is This': Southern Women and the American Revolution," in Jeffrey J. Crow and Larry E. Tise (eds.), *The Southern Experience in the American Revolution* (Chapel Hill: University of North Carolina Press, 1978), 203–34, and *Liberty's Daughters: The Revolutionary Experience of American Women, 1750–1800* (Boston: Little, Brown, 1980). See also Harriott Horry Ravenel, *Eliza Pinckney* (New York: Charles Scribner's Sons, 1896); David L. Coon, "Eliza Lucas Pinckney and the Reintroduction of Indigo Culture in South Carolina," *Journal of Southern History,* XLII (February, 1976), 61–76.

22. Mary E. Young, "Women, Civilization, and the Indian Question," in Deutrich and Purdy (eds.), *Clio Was a Woman,* 98–110; Theda Perdue, "The Traditional Status of Cherokee Women," *Furman Studies,* XXVI (December, 1980), 19–25. For guides to the study of native American women, see Rayna Green, "Native American Women," *Signs,* VI (Winter, 1980), 248–67, and *Native American Women: A Contextual Bibliography* (Bloomington: Indiana University Press, 1983).

from women's private writings bring the book and its subject matter vividly to life.[23]

An original and seminal addition to our knowledge of these years is Suzanne Lebsock's *The Free Women of Petersburg* (1984), a study based upon meticulous examination of legal records supplemented by newspapers, personal documents, and travelers' observations. As is always the case when one gets down to the fine grain, life is far more complicated than it had appeared when painted with a broad brush. Lebsock's study, which covers the years from 1784 to 1860, suggests a steady increase in women's economic autonomy revealed by the use of separate estates, assertiveness among widows, and the accumulation of property (under difficult conditions) on the part of free black women. She also traces the rapid growth in associational life after 1813 and the change in its nature over time. Her evidence for the existence of a women's culture is compelling, and the book is rich in leads for further study. For example, she discovered white and black women working in Petersburg factories as early as 1820—only a few years after women and children went into the mills in New England. She discovered and delineated a free black community of astonishing size and complexity and documented the existence of a considerable number of women workers who were completely overlooked by the census takers. This book is one of the rare ones that break new ground; it should inspire similar studies of other southern communities.[24]

Antebellum is a vague term that in practice has come to mean the forty years leading up to the Civil War, years that have preoccupied historians of the South. Historians of women, too, have long felt a need to understand those four decades. Guion Johnson's *Ante-bellum North Carolina* and Virginia Gray's pioneering article have already been cited, and part of Lebsock's study of Petersburg covered these years. The first half of Scott's *The Southern Lady* is a reconstruction of the inner world of white women, mostly of the landowning class, based largely on letters and diaries. The "lady" emerges from her pages as a hardworking, introspective, pious, versatile wife and mother who spent a good bit of energy trying to live up to the prescriptions set before her by men. Here, and in a later article, Scott

23. Catherine Clinton, *The Plantation Mistress: Woman's World in the Old South* (New York: Pantheon, 1982).

24. Suzanne Lebsock, *The Free Women of Petersburg: Status and Culture in a Southern Town, 1784–1860* (New York: Norton, 1984).

detailed the discontents these women shared: the institution of slavery, constant pregnancy and childbearing, the double standard, and their limited opportunity for education. She argued that the existence of so much discontent created a significant element of instability in a patriarchal society about which slave owners were becoming increasingly defensive under abolitionist attack.[25]

Young scholars are elaborating this picture in original ways. Jane Turner Censer, for example, used divorce records for the years 1800 to 1860 to examine the attitudes of southern judges toward women. She concluded that while the judges "believed in their social order, they did not mindlessly uphold the tenets of patriarchalism; and they significantly modified legal concepts and expanded women's abilities to gain divorces, alimony and property, and custody of their children."[26]

In a provocative study of the concept of southern honor, which he describes as the most important aspect of antebellum ethics, Bertram Wyatt-Brown offers a number of generalizations about women. Since his book is in many ways a study of antebellum masculinity, perhaps its significance in this context is that he uses gender as a tool of analysis.[27]

Other articles and dissertations push back the boundaries of our ignorance or offer thought-provoking theses: for example, Michael P. Johnson on Charleston planters, Irving H. Bartlett and C. Glenn Cambor on the psychodynamics of southern womanhood, Nancy A. White on female identity and male guilt, Dorothy Ann Gay on the relationship of romanticism and violence to both abolitionism and feminism, Steven M. Stowe on courtship, and Kathryn L. Seidel and John Carl Ruoff on feminine ideals. Nor should it be forgotten that U. B. Phillips, writing in the 1920s and 1930s, paid more attention to antebellum women than did his brethren who were preoccupied with politics.[28]

25. Scott, *The Southern Lady*, 45–79, and "Women's Perspective on the Patriarchy in the 1850s," *Journal of American History*, LXI (June, 1974), 52–64.

26. Jane Turner Censer, "'Smiling Through Her Tears': Ante-Bellum Southern Women and Divorce," *American Journal of Legal History*, XXV (January, 1981), 24–47 (quotation on p. 47). For a broader study of antebellum family life, see Censer's *North Carolina Planters and Their Children, 1800–1860* (Baton Rouge: Louisiana State University Press, 1984).

27. Bertram Wyatt-Brown, *Southern Honor: Ethics and Behavior in the Old South* (New York: Oxford University Press, 1982).

28. Michael P. Johnson, "Planters and Patriarchy: Charleston, 1800–1860," *Journal of Southern History*, XLVI (February, 1980), 45–72; Irving H. Bartlett and

One vital subject has attracted few modern scholars. Nothing in the long run has been more central to the changes in women's life experience than access to education. In the South as elsewhere in the United States, the first half of the nineteenth century brought a growing demand for such access, as well as the rapid growth of various kinds of schools for women. The beginnings of scholarship on this subject are few: Fletcher Green's perceptive essay on southern women's education; Christie Pope's University of Chicago dissertation on female seminaries in North Carolina; Catherine Clinton's chapter and an article on the subject; and a Harvard honors paper on the history of female academies across the South by Elizabeth Ellis are the sum of recent scholarship. An older work (1909) by I. M. E. Blandin provides data not found elsewhere, and Thomas Woody was an indefatigable gatherer of facts that could be used as a starting point for a new study. The whole subject lies waiting for an imaginative historian.[29]

C. Glenn Cambor, "The History and Psychodynamics of Southern Womanhood," *Women's Studies: An Interdisciplinary Journal*, II (1974), 9–24; Nancy A. White, "Idol, Equal and Slave: White Female Identity and White Male Guilt: A Study of Female Role Definition in the Antebellum Society" (Ph.D. dissertation, American University, 1980); Dorothy Ann Gay, "The Tangled Skein of Romanticism and Violence in the Old South: The Southern Response to Abolitionism and Feminism, 1831–1861" (Ph.D. dissertation, University of North Carolina, 1975); Steven M. Stowe, "'The Thing, Not Its Vision': A Woman's Courtship and Her Sphere in the Southern Planter Class," *Feminist Studies*, IX (Spring, 1983), 113–30; Kathryn L. Seidel, "The Southern Belle as an Antebellum Ideal," *Southern Quarterly*, XV (July, 1977), 387–401, and *The Southern Belle in the American Novel* (Tampa: University of South Florida Press, 1985); John Carl Ruoff, "Southern Womanhood, 1865–1920: An Intellectual and Cultural Study" (Ph.D. dissertation, University of Illinois, 1976); U. B. Phillips, *Life and Labor in the Old South* (Boston: Little, Brown, 1929), esp. 203, 205, 214–43, 244, 256, 259, 261–67, 270, 278, 285, 317.

29. Fletcher Melvin Green, "Higher Education of Women in the South Prior to 1860," in *Democracy in the Old South and Other Essays*, ed. J. Isaac Copeland (Nashville: Vanderbilt University Press, 1969), 199–219; Christie Farnham Pope, "Preparation for Pedestals: North Carolina Antebellum Female Seminaries" (Ph.D. dissertation, University of Chicago, 1977); Clinton, *The Plantation Mistress*, Chap. 7, and "Equally Their Due: The Education of the Planter Daughter in the Early Republic," *Journal of the Early Republic*, II (Spring, 1982), 39–60; Elizabeth Ellis, "Educating Daughters of the Patriarchy: Female Academies in the American South, 1830–1860" (Honors paper, Harvard College, 1982); I. M. E. Blandin, *History of Higher Education of Women in the South prior to 1860* (New York: Neal Publishing Co., 1909); Thomas Woody, *A History of Women's Education in the United States* (2 vols.; New York: Science Press, 1929). Henning Cohen (ed.), *A Barhamville Miscellany: Notes and Documents Concerning the South Carolina Female Collegiate Institute, 1826–1865* (Columbia: University of South Carolina Press, 1956), documents

The centrality of religion in the lives of antebellum southern women and the implications of that centrality for family and social development are just beginning to be reflected in the literature. In *Religion in the Old South,* Donald G. Mathews has traced the liberating implications of the spread of evangelicalism. He argues that the rise of family religion and the decline of clerical power invested women with new responsibilities, and the conversion experience gave them courage to defy man-made norms. He portrays an emerging ideal of an evangelical woman distinguished by her domesticity, piety, and commitment to benevolent action. Women, like slaves, he concludes, could use evangelicalism "to fend off oppression, secure their personal and group identity, and assert themselves in new and surprising ways." Building on Mathews' work, Jean E. Friedman has written the first full-length study of nineteenth-century southern women's religious experience.[30]

Antebellum women among what Frank Owsley labeled "the plain people"—those families who owned land but no or only a few slaves and who combined subsistence with small-scale market farming—have received much less attention than have plantation mistresses. Contemporary observers rarely noticed them, and modern historians have followed suit. In addition to Owsley's own work, two articles, both relying on prescriptive sources, represent the sum of such work so far. Victoria Bynum is presently breaking new ground in this area using North Carolina data, and when her dissertation is complete we may hope for a substantial addition to our meager present knowledge.[31]

---

the work of one of the most influential of the antebellum female seminaries. See also Florence P. Davis, "The Education of Southern Girls from 1750–1860" (Ph.D. dissertation, University of Chicago, 1951). Anne Firor Scott discussed preliminary thoughts on the subject in her unpublished lecture, "Two Forays in Women's History" (Lamar Lectures, Wesleyan College, Macon, Ga., 1975).

30. Donald G. Mathews, *Religion in the Old South* (Chicago: University of Chicago Press, 1977), 101–102; Jean E. Friedman, *The Enclosed Garden: Women and Community in the Evangelical South, 1830–1900* (Chapel Hill: University of North Carolina Press, 1985). See also James L. Leloudis II, "Subversion of the Feminine Ideal: The *Southern Lady's Companion* and White Male Morality in the Antebellum South, 1847–1854," in Rosemary Skinner Keller, Louise L. Queen, and Hilah F. Thomas (eds.), *Women in New Worlds: Historical Perspectives on the Wesleyan Tradition* (2 vols.; Nashville: Abingdon Press, 1982), II, 60–75; William L. Lumpkin, "The Role of Women in 18th Century Virginia Baptist Life," *Baptist History and Heritage,* VIII (July, 1973), 158–67; and Joan R. Gundersen, "The Non-Institutional Church: The Religious Role of Women in Eighteenth-Century Virginia," *Historical Magazine of the Protestant Episcopal Church,* LI (December, 1982), 347–57.

31. Frank Lawrence Owsley, *Plain Folk of the Old South* (Baton Rouge: Louisiana

In the 1970s, scholarship on nineteenth-century slavery shifted to the world the slaves made, stressing the achievements of Afro-Americans rather than the dehumanizing effects of bondage. Herbert Gutman in particular laid to rest the notion that the black family was a matriarchal tangle of pathology in which men were emasculated and children grew up without male role models. From this revisionist literature emerged a picture of a unique, resilient black culture, with the family as its central institution.[32]

Although books, and even scholarly articles, expressly devoted to slave women have been few, studies focused on the slave quarters inevitably illumined women's lives. We are shown an Afro-American community in which premarital sex was common and accepted, but in which women, by age seventeen or eighteen, had usually settled into lasting marriages. Giving birth every two and a half years, they raised their children in two-parent households embedded in a network of biological and fictive kin. Women shared the rigors of field work with men, but in the quarters a sexual division of labor prevailed, and skilled jobs on the plantation were reserved for men. Eugene Genovese concluded that all this added up to "a healthy sexual equality" but went on to surmise that women practiced "female deference" in order to "support their men."[33]

Deborah G. White, however, faults Gutman and Genovese for celebrating Afro-American success in creating patriarchal families and thus underestimating women's contributions and misunderstanding their roles. The new scholarship, like the old, tended to assume that any sign of female autonomy and assertiveness implied dominance over men; it defended slave culture by overemphasizing the degree to which sex roles in the black community mirrored white norms. In an original and clearheaded reading of familiar sources, she presents an

State University Press, 1949); D. Harland Hagler, "The Ideal Woman in the Antebellum South: Lady or Farmwife?" *Journal of Southern History*, XLVI (August, 1980), 405–18; Keith L. Bryant, Jr., "The Role and Status of the Female Yeomanry in the Antebellum South: The Literary View," *Southern Quarterly*, XVIII (Winter, 1980), 73–88. Victoria Bynum is writing her dissertation at the University of California at San Diego.

32. Herbert G. Gutman, *The Black Family in Slavery and Freedom, 1750–1925* (New York: Pantheon, 1976); Eugene D. Genovese, *Roll, Jordan, Roll: The World the Slaves Made* (New York: Pantheon, 1974). See also John W. Blassingame, *The Slave Community: Plantation Life in the Antebellum South* (New York: Oxford University Press, 1972); Leslie Howard Owens, *This Species of Property: Slave Life and Culture in the Old South* (New York: Oxford University Press, 1976); and John B. Boles, *Black Southerners, 1619–1869* (Lexington: University Press of Kentucky, 1983).

33. Genovese, *Roll, Jordan, Roll*, 500.

alternative view in which sex roles in the black community contrasted sharply with those in the white. Work roles were not consistently differentiated and where they were, men's work was not necessarily more highly valued than women's. The jobs of midwife, cook, and seamstress, for example, demanded as much skill and commanded as much respect as did those performed by male artisans. Black families were not "matriarchal" but were matrifocal: women in their role as mothers were the focus of family life. However strong the bonds between man and wife, black women relied for subsistence and protection more on their own resourcefulness than on their men and participated in a supportive women's culture in the slave quarters. The result was not a community in which women dominated or were the same as men, but one in which relative sexual equality prevailed and in which women's values and sense of self-worth were drawn primarily from their place in a black female world. White's approach is a needed corrective to studies that see slave women mainly as victims. She points, for example, to uniquely female forms of individual resistance. Childbearing might serve as a means of fending off the threat of sale and resisting work. Concubinage or sexual liaisons could be practical options, an active means by which women protected themselves and their families and exercised informal influence. Still needed is a full analysis of women's roles in slave revolts and other forms of collective action.[34]

Jacqueline Jones, in contrast, offers an interpretation that places even more stress than did earlier scholars on sexual asymmetry in the black community. Drawing a finely nuanced portrait of women's work at various life stages, she concludes that "within well-defined limits, the slaves created—or preserved—an explicit sexual division of labor based on their own preferences." Moreover, during the Reconstruc-

34. Deborah Gray White, *"Ar'n't I a Woman?" Female Slaves in the Plantation South* (New York: Norton, 1985), and "Female Slaves: Sex Roles and Status in the Antebellum Plantation South," *Journal of Family History,* VIII (Fall, 1983), 248–61. In "Free Black Women and the Question of Matriarchy: Petersburg, Virginia 1784–1820," *Feminist Studies,* VIII (Summer, 1982), 271–92, Suzanne D. Lebsock makes a similar point. She argues that employment, property holding, and female-headed households among free black women were symptoms of oppression; yet these conditions also encouraged women's autonomy and a relatively high degree of equality between the sexes. The best bibliography on black women's history published thus far is Janet Sims-Wood, *The Progress of Afro-American Women: A Bibliography* (Westport, Conn.: Greenwood Press, 1980). An exemplary curriculum guide is Nancy Faires Conklin, Brenda McCallum, and Marcia Wade, *The Culture of Southern Black Women: Approaches and Materials* (University: Archive of American Minority Cultures and Women's Studies Program, University of Alabama, 1983).

tion era, when black women sought to withdraw from field labor and men to assert male prerogatives in public and private life, both men and women paid "allegiance to a patriarchal family structure." Jones assumes that these postwar developments represented the culmination of the "African heritage as it applied to the American experience." Elsewhere, and more persuasively, she suggests that the sharecropping family was based on a peasant "ethos of mutuality" at odds with the dominant society's emphasis on possessive individualism and social mobility. Elaborating on an idea first expressed by Angela Davis in 1971, she sees these gender arrangements as strategies for resisting sexual and economic exploitation by whites but concludes that in the long run the black community "paid a high price" for the resulting denial of status and opportunity to women. Left unexplored is the possibility that men and women may have had conflicting views of gender roles or that, in the context of the post–Civil War South, the domestic submission of women may have represented a capitulation to white norms as well as a means of resisting white exploitation.[35]

Both White and Jones concentrate on the nineteenth century; neither has much to say about chronological change. Before we can resolve such differences of interpretation, we must attend to the formative eighteenth century, trace the transformation of West African customs of manhood and womanhood in the New World, and avoid reading postbellum developments back in time. Suzanne Lebsock's observations may serve as a guide to further work. It is time, she writes, to cease using the reduction of male authority as the "touchstone of scholarship on black family life" and come to terms both with the fact of black women's victimization and with the evidence of their strength and self-esteem.[36]

35. Jacqueline Jones, "'My Mother was Much of a Woman': Black Women, Work and the Family Under Slavery," *Feminist Studies,* VIII (Summer, 1982), 235–70 (quotations on pp. 258, 261), and, by the same title, Working Paper No. 45, Wellesley College Center for Research on Women, Wellesley, Mass., 1980. For the postbellum period, see Jones, "Freed Women? Black Women, Work, and the Family During the Civil War and Reconstruction," Working Paper No. 61, Wellesley College Center for Research on Women, 1980, and "A Bridge of 'Bent Backs and Laboring Muscles': Black Working Women in the Rural South, 1880–1915," Working Paper No. 67, Wellesley College Center for Research on Women, 1981. These working papers formed the basis for her *Labor of Love, Labor of Sorrow: Black Women, Work, and the Family from Slavery to the Present* (New York: Basic Books, 1985). Angela Davis, "Reflections on the Black Woman's Role in the Community of Slaves," *Black Scholar,* III (December, 1971), 2–15, and *Women, Race and Class* (New York: Random House, 1981).

36. Lebsock, "Free Black Women," 273. The slave narratives have been published in George P. Rawick (ed.), *The American Slave: A Composite Autobiography* (41 vols.;

Two additional monographs and one particularly original article deserve special note. Joseph Hugo Johnston's *Race Relations in Virginia and Miscegenation in the South, 1776–1860,* written in the 1930s, was not published until 1970. Based on detailed study of legislative records, Johnston's work throws a bright beam onto the often hidden subject of interracial sex during the era before emancipation. Joel Williamson provides a broader, more analytical treatment of the same subject. Tracing the history of miscegenation from the colonial period to 1965, he probes the changing role of the "new people" who were the product of sexual contact between the races. Michael P. Johnson's analysis of infant smothering deaths in the slave quarters provides unique insight into issues of health and nutrition that profoundly affected women's lives.[37]

For women, along with other southerners, the year 1861 inaugurated a period of trauma followed by the emergence of a new order different in many vital ways from earlier society, but in which much of the old was still embedded. Glorification of Confederate women and efforts to record their part in the war began before the war

---

Westport, Conn.: Greenwood Press, 1972–79). Gerda Lerner (ed.), *Black Women in White America: A Documentary History* (New York: Pantheon, 1972), is an invaluable source of both analysis and documentary information on all aspects of black women's history.

37. James Hugo Johnston, *Race Relations in Virginia and Miscegenation in the South, 1776–1860* (Amherst: University of Massachusetts Press, 1970); Joel Williamson, *New People: Miscegenation and Mulattoes in the United States* (New York: Free Press, 1980); Michael P. Johnson, "Smothered Slave Infants: Were Slave Mothers at Fault?" *Journal of Southern History,* XLVII (November, 1981), 493–520. See also Jessie W. Parkhurst, "The Role of the Black Mammy in the Plantation Household," *Journal of Negro History,* XXIII (July, 1938), 349–69; Sudie Duncan Sides, "Southern Women and Slavery," *History Today,* XX (January, 1970), 54–60, and (February, 1970), 124–30; Mary Ellen Obitko, "'Custodians of a House of Resistance': Black Women Respond to Slavery," in Dana V. Hiller and Robin Ann Sheets (eds.), *Women and Men: The Consequences of Power* (Cincinnati: Office of Women's Studies, University of Cincinnati, 1977), 256–69; Dorothy Burnham, "The Life of the Afro-American Woman in Slavery," *International Journal of Women's Studies,* I (July/August, 1978), 363–77; Richard S. Dunn, "A Tale of Two Plantations: Slave Life at Mesopotamia in Jamaica and Mount Airy in Virginia, 1799 to 1828," *William and Mary Quarterly,* 3rd Ser., XXXIV (January, 1977), 32–65; Michael P. Johnson, "Runaway Slaves and the Slave Communities in South Carolina, 1799 to 1830," *William and Mary Quarterly,* 3rd Ser., XXXVIII (July, 1981), 418–41; Darlene Clark and Kate Wittenstein, "Female Slave Resistance: The Economics of Sex," in Filomina Chioma Steady (ed.), *The Black Woman Cross-Culturally* (Cambridge, Mass.: Schenkman, 1981), 289–300; and Shepard Krech III, "Black Family Organization in the Nineteenth Century: An Ethnological Perspective," *Journal of Interdisciplinary History,* XII (Winter, 1982), 429–52.

ended, and by the 1890s a major organization—the United Daughters of the Confederacy—had pledged itself to preserve their records.[38] As early as 1936, Francis Simkins and James Patton published *The Women of the Confederacy,* a detailed study based on primary sources that is marred by the authors' unconscious condescension toward their subject. Their first serious challenger was Mary Elizabeth Massey, whose *Bonnet Brigades* had been commissioned as part of the Civil War centennial. She dealt with women on both sides of the conflict, and her southern material provided numerous bibliographical leads for those who wanted to examine the wartime experience of southern women. Four years after Massey's book appeared, Scott's chapter "The War" offered what has become a familiar thesis: that when the men went off to fight or to serve in the Confederate government, women began to function as administrators, workers, organizers, farmers, nurses, and artisans and to set up soldiers' aid societies to clothe the Confederate army. She argued that for the women who took on these new responsibilities, significant changes in personality and self-image were apt to take place, with long-run consequences for the future of the society. An excellent brief article has recently adumbrated this thesis with respect to five women of the North Carolina planter class; a longer work by Henry E. Sterkx documents the same phenomenon for the state of Alabama. The possibilities for more detailed studies, based on community records, abound.[39]

38. On the Daughters of the Confederacy, see Gaines Milligan Foster, "Ghosts of the Confederacy: Defeat, History, and the Culture of the New South, 1865–1913" (Ph.D. dissertation, University of North Carolina, 1982).

39. Francis Butler Simkins and James Welch Patton, *The Women of the Confederacy* (Richmond: Garrett & Massie, 1936); Mary Elizabeth Massey, *Bonnet Brigades* (New York: Knopf, 1966); Scott, *The Southern Lady,* Chap. 4; Terrell Armistead Crowe, "'As Thy Days, So Shall Thy Strength Be': North Carolina Planter Women in War and Peace," *Carolina Comments,* XXVIII (January, 1980), 24–31; Henry E. Sterkx, *Partners in Rebellion: Alabama Women in the Civil War* (Rutherford, N.J.: Fairleigh Dickinson University Press, 1970). See also Bell I. Wiley, *Confederate Women* (Westport, Conn.: Greenwood Press, 1975); Nancy T. Kondert, "The Romance and Reality of Defeat: Southern Women in 1865," *Journal of Mississippi History,* XXV (May, 1973), 141–52; Hugh C. Bailey and William Pratt Dale II, "'Missus Alone in de Big House,'" *Alabama Review,* VIII (January, 1955), 43–54. Splendid documentary collections are adding a great deal to our resources for understanding the experience of women during the war. For example: Robert Manson Myers (ed.), *The Children of Pride: A True Story of Georgia and the Civil War* (New Haven: Yale University Press, 1972); Carol Bleser (ed.), *The Hammonds of Redcliffe* (New York: Oxford University Press, 1981); C. Vann Woodward (ed.), *Mary Chesnut's Civil War* (New Haven: Yale University Press, 1981). See also Elisabeth Muhlenfeld's fine study, *Mary Boykin Chesnut: A Biography* (Baton Rouge: Louisiana State University Press, 1981); and Syl-

While there has been little argument about the immediate effect of the war on southern women, questions have been raised about Scott's conclusions that many women after the war found themselves heads of families and that, due to the high mortality of the war years, a generation of women without men, forced to find ways to support themselves, created the first large group of self-supporting white women. Jonathan Wiener, using the manuscript census for five Black Belt counties in Alabama, challenged the view that there was an increase in the number of female planters and that there was a "generation of women without men." However, Wiener's evidence is drawn from an extremely narrow segment of the population. Until there are studies of a wide variety of agricultural counties we shall not be able to speak with authority on the question of women heads of household, and until painstaking demographic reconstruction is done we will not be able to describe what happened to the generation of women who were married to, or might have married, the 260,000 Confederate dead.[40]

If the postbellum era presented white women of the planter class with both hardships and opportunities, it drew former slaves and, increasingly, white yeomen farmers into a long struggle for a hold on the land. The "new economic history" has revealed a great deal about the transition from slavery to sharecropping, but we have no studies of women's part in this great social change. This is unfortunate because some of the best recent work in women's history has posed questions about the impact of modernization on early-nineteenth-century New England farm women and about sex roles on the western frontier. Work on southern rural women would not

---

vie Hoffert, "Mary Boykin Chesnut: Private Feminist in the Civil War South," *Southern Studies,* XVI (Spring, 1977), 81–89.

40. Jonathan M. Wiener, "Female Planters and Planters' Wives in Civil War and Reconstruction: Alabama, 1850–1870," *Alabama Review,* XXX (April, 1977), 135–49; Lebsock, "Epilogue," *The Free Women of Petersburg.* For an interesting illustration of the way women's status changed with no feminist intent, see Suzanne D. Lebsock, "Radical Reconstruction and the Property Rights of Southern Women," *Journal of Southern History,* XLIII (May, 1977), 195–216. See also Kathryn Reinhart Schuler, "Women in Public Affairs in Louisiana During Reconstruction," *Louisiana Historical Quarterly,* XIX (July, 1936), 668–750; Kathleen Elizabeth Lazarou, "Concealed Under Petticoats: Married Women's Property and the Laws of Texas, 1840–1913" (Ph.D. dissertation, Rice University, 1980); and Kathleen Christine Berkeley, "'The Ladies Want to Bring About Reform in the Public Schools': Public Education and Women's Rights in the Post–Civil War South," *History of Education Quarterly,* XXIV (Spring, 1984), 45–58.

only bring to visibility another neglected group, it would also make possible generalizations about how different patterns of regional development affect rural women's lives.[41]

Harold Woodman has termed sharecropping the South's other "peculiar institution." It represented a compromise between freed men and women eager for autonomy and former masters determined to reassert their control. Central to the creation of the "sharecropping family" was the desire of black women to devote themselves to family enterprise instead of to gang labor in the fields. The resulting decline in staple-crop production and white consternation over what one contemporary called the "evil of female loaferism" are testimony to the political impact of family strategies. Jacqueline Jones has addressed the consequences of black family decisions in some detail in her *Labor of Love, Labor of Sorrow*.[42]

Still missing from the historical record are accounts of black women's roles in achieving landownership and community autonomy. Elizabeth Bethel's study of black landowners in Promiseland, South Carolina, shows women inheriting land on an equal basis with men. The anthropologist Kay Young Day finds market women in the South Carolina Sea Islands playing independent economic roles and relying on networks of female kin, even after their position was undermined by the commercialization of agriculture and men's entry into wage labor.[43] Both studies illustrate the value of oral sources and attention to local diversity and change over time.

Initially a substitute for slavery, sharecropping increasingly caught

41. John Mack Faragher provides a framework for such a comparative approach in "History From the Inside-Out: Writing the History of Women in Rural America," *American Quarterly*, XXXIII (Winter, 1981), 538–57.

42. Harold D. Woodman, "Sequel to Slavery: The New History Views the Postbellum South," *Journal of Southern History*, XLIII (November, 1977), 523–54; Roger L. Ransom and Richard Sutch, *One Kind of Freedom: The Economic Consequences of Emancipation* (Cambridge, England: Cambridge University Press, 1977); Gutman, *The Black Family*, 167–68 (quotation); Jones, *Labor of Love, Labor of Sorrow*, 58–68. See also Noralee Frankel, "Women in Mississippi, 1860–1870" (Ph.D. dissertation, George Washington University, 1982).

43. Elizabeth Rauh Bethel, *Promiseland: A Century of Life in a Negro Community* (Philadelphia: Temple University Press, 1981); Kay Young Day, "Kinship in a Changing Economy: A View From the Sea Islands," in Robert L. Hall and Carol B. Stack (eds.), *Holding On to the Land and the Lord: Kinship, Ritual, Land Tenure, and Social Policy in the Rural South* (Athens: University of Georgia Press, 1982), 11–24. See also Marsha Jean Darling, "The Growth and Decline of the Afro-American Family Farm in Warren County, North Carolina, 1910–1960" (Ph.D. dissertation, Duke University, 1982).

white farmers in its snare. The best study of white tenant women remains Margaret Jarman Hagood's *Mothers of the South,* originally published in 1939. One of the finest products of the confluence between documentary realism and regional sociology, Hagood's book added a qualitative dimension to her dissertation on southern fertility patterns. Life stories in which women are allowed to "speak for themselves" enable the reader both to perceive women's pride in their productive and reproductive roles and the practical egalitarianism of farm life and at the same time to understand how both class and sex circumscribed their lives.[44]

Perhaps our most pressing need is for research that takes as its focus rural women as a group, thus enabling us to chart the commonalities and differences in black and white women's lives. Despite their reluctance to participate in gang labor, black women throughout the nineteenth century were more likely than whites to work for wages in the fields or in other people's homes; they were more vulnerable to sexual violence and less likely to be able to read and write. Yet in many ways a farm woman's daily rounds were determined more by economics than by race. Region, for example, was more important than race in determining fertility rates: rural white women as well as blacks married young, gave birth frequently, and spent most of their adult lives rearing children. White farm women in the South joined men in the fields more often than did their counterparts in other regions. Like black women, they took pride in physical strength and farming expertise. Whether black or white, sharecroppers or small landowners, women served their communities as midwives and healers, sold butter, eggs, and produce at nearby markets, took in laundry, and kept boarders. Their domestic skills were crucial to the family economy.[45]

44. Margaret Jarman Hagood, *Mothers of the South: Portraiture of the White Tenant Farm Woman* (Chapel Hill, 1939; rpr., with introduction by Anne F. Scott, New York: Norton, 1977), and "Mothers of the South: A Population Study of Native White Women of Childbearing Age of the Southeast" (Ph.D. dissertation, University of North Carolina, 1937). See also Ruth Alice Allen, *The Labor of Women in the Production of Cotton* (Austin, 1931; rpr. New York: Arno Press, 1975); James Agee and Walker Evans, *Let Us Now Praise Famous Men: Three Tenant Families* (Boston: Houghton Mifflin, 1939); and Bradford L. Jenkins, "Emma's Story: Two Versions," *Southern Exposure,* VII (Spring, 1979), 8–26. Norton Juster, *So Sweet to Labor: The Voices of Rural Women* (New York: Viking, 1979), contains some material on the South.

45. For comparative studies, see Dolores Elizabeth Janiewski, "From Field to Factory: Race, Class, Sex, and the Woman Worker in Durham, 1880–1940" (Ph.D. dissertation, Duke University, 1979), Chap. 1; Jones, "Freed Women?," "A Bridge of 'Bent Backs,'" and "Frayed Bonds of Womanhood: Black and Poor White Women in the

Women not only contributed to agricultural production, they also joined in efforts at reform. Of the many histories of agrarian insurgency only Julie Roy Jeffrey's article on the North Carolina Farmers' Alliance looks specifically at women's part in that movement. She finds that women accounted for as many as one-quarter of the organization's members and traces an Alliance concept of a women's sphere that stressed education and self-sufficiency and mocked false gentility.[46] Picking up where Jeffrey leaves off, Lu Ann Jones has ar-

Rural South, 1865–1940" (Paper presented at the annual meeting of the Organization of American Historians, Philadelphia, April, 1982); and Barbara Finlay Agresti, "Household and Family in the Postbellum South: Walton County, Florida, 1870–1885" (Ph.D. dissertation, University of Florida, 1976). For fertility rates of black and white southern women, see Hagood, "Mothers of the South," *passim;* Bernice Milburn Moore, "Present Status and Future Trends in the Southern White Family," *Social Forces,* XVI (March, 1938), 406–10; Ronald R. Rindfuss, "Changing Patterns of Fertility in the South: A Social-Demographic Examination," *Social Forces,* LVII (December, 1978), 621–35; Herman Lantz and Lewellyn Hendrix, "Black Fertility and the Black Family in the Nineteenth Century: A Re-Examination of the Past," *Journal of Family History,* III (Fall, 1978), 251–61; and Stanley L. Engerman, "Black Fertility and Family Structure in the U.S., 1880–1940," *Journal of Family History,* II (June, 1977), 117–38. See also Lonnie E. Underhill and Daniel F. Littlefield, Jr., "Women Homeseekers in Oklahoma Territory, 1889–1901," *Pacific Historian,* XVII (Fall, 1973), 36–47; and Shirley Abbott, *Womenfolks: Growing Up Down South* (New Haven: Ticknor & Fields, 1983), which traces the experiences of several generations of women in the author's rural Arkansas family.

46. Julie Roy Jeffrey, "Women in the Southern Farmers' Alliance: A Reconsideration of the Role and Status of Women in the Late Nineteenth-Century South," *Feminist Studies,* III (Fall, 1975), 72–91. The ideal woman envisioned by the Farmers' Alliance had much in common with the "Lady Knight" described in Susan Levine's article "Labor's True Woman: Domesticity and Equal Rights in the Knights of Labor," *Journal of American History,* LXX (September, 1983), 323–39. Unlike Jeffrey, who attributes the Alliance's allegiance to notions of female moral superiority to the "upper class" origins of some Alliance leaders, Levine offers a needed corrective to the tendency of women's history to misconstrue class differences in the use of Victorian ideals. She argues that rather than adopting values that trickled down from the upper class, the Knights of Labor drew on the nineteenth century's customary notions of female rights and obligations to oppose the competitive capitalist values that were encroaching on their lives. The important point is that while neither the Alliance nor the Knights challenged the sexual division of labor or resolved the tension between domesticity and female activism, both embraced a vision of the family as an integral part of public life, a vision abandoned by the bread-and-butter unionism of the twentieth century—to the impoverishment both of the labor movement and of the larger political culture. Other studies of prescriptive images and ideals are Pamela Tyler, "The Ideal Rural Woman as Seen by *Progressive Farmer* in the 1930s," *Southern Studies,* XX (Fall, 1981), 278–96; and Betty Arlene Matthews, "Frontier Women as Portrayed in the Humor of the Old Southwest" (Ph.D. dissertation, University of Arkansas, 1979).

gued that after populism's defeat, women voiced less solidarity with men and more discontent with the female lot. As even middling farmers channeled labor into cash crops and capital into new equipment instead of the household appliances that were beginning to lighten urban housework, their wives began to complain of isolation and to resent men's control of family resources. New South Progressives, Jones concludes, capitalized on women's discontent by urging them to practice scientific housekeeping, sell their own products in a wider market, and purchase more consumer goods.[47] Studies that test these hypotheses in other southern states will allow us to draw conclusions about the extent to which women's economic partnership could be translated into family-based collective action and to understand the consequences for women of the change from family to business farming in the twentieth-century South.

Southern Appalachia illustrates the complexities of writing about women in the process of regional development. Here the literature on women in developing nations is especially helpful, for Appalachia must be viewed as a region in transition from a semisubsistence to a market-dominated economy *and* as a region whose resources were peculiarly exploited by outsiders. Through this double lens, Appalachian women can be seen as creating a "culture of resistance" analogous to that forged by women in neocolonial situations. Recent reinterpretations of Appalachian history, for example, have argued that as men were drawn off the farms into occasional wage labor for the timber and railroad companies in the 1880s, women, always partners in productive enterprise, stayed on the land, passing on to their children a heritage at odds with industrial values and maintaining family farms as an alternative to complete dependence on the emerging market economy.[48]

47. Lu Ann Jones, "'The Task That is Ours': White North Carolina Farm Women and Agrarian Reform" (M.A. thesis, University of North Carolina, 1983). See also Joan M. Jensen, *With These Hands: Women Working on the Land* (Old Westbury, N.Y.: Feminist Press, 1981), 142–87. Similarly, in "From Field to Factory," Janiewski has argued that the transition from subsistence farming to sharecropping devalued women's skills.

48. Helen Matthews Lewis, Sue Easterling Kobak, and Linda Johnson, "Family, Religion and Colonialism in Central Appalachia or Bury My Rifle at Big Stone Gap," in Helen Matthews Lewis, Linda Johnson, and Donald Askins (eds.), *Colonialism in Modern America: The Appalachian Case* (Boone, N.C.: Appalachian Consortium Press, 1978), 114–39; Ronald D. Eller, "Land and Family: An Historical View of Preindustrial Appalachia," *Appalachian Journal*, VI (Winter, 1979), 83–109; Jacquelyn Dowd Hall, "Gender, Class, and Conflict in the Industrializing South: An Appalachian Case Study," *Journal of American History* (forthcoming). See also Sidney Saylor Farr,

The reorganization of agriculture proceeded symbiotically with the rise of industry. Coal companies entered the mountains, turning southern Appalachian farm women into miners' daughters, sisters, and wives. Heralded as the savior of poor whites and the solution to all the region's ills, the cotton mill campaign took off in the 1880s, dotting the Piedmont with small, company-controlled mill villages whose principal residents were women. During the 1920s the South's urban population grew more rapidly than any other region's, and women, both black and white, migrated to the cities in larger proportions than did men.

The fact that in the region as a whole, agriculture and domestic service remained the largest employers of women masks profound changes. Although Appalachian women, excluded from the mines, found few opportunities for wage labor, they were no less affected than men by the rigors of coal-camp life. More women were employed in manufacturing in North Carolina, where the textile and tobacco industries centered, than in any other southern state, and the wage work of the female mill hand attracted attention in a way that women's customary labor on the land and in the home had not. In cities like Atlanta, as in the urban Northeast, commerce drew significant numbers of white women into clerical occupations. Urban black women served as domestic servants and laundresses and made up a majority of the tobacco work force. Escaping from rural poverty, they found themselves at the bottom of the urban economic structure, excluded both from white-collar and most industrial jobs and more likely than their rural sisters to head their own families.

C. Vann Woodward noted in 1951 that "to a large extent the expanding industrialization of the New South was based upon the labor of women and children," yet historians have told us little about either group.[49] Indeed, because labor historians have largely neglected

---

Appalachian Women: An Annotated Bibliography (Lexington: University Press of Kentucky, 1981); and Kathy Kahn, *Hillbilly Women* (Garden City, N.Y.: Doubleday, 1973). For the term *cultures of resistance,* see Mina Davis Caulfield, "Imperialism, the Family, and Cultures of Resistance," *Socialist Revolution,* IV (October, 1974), 67–85. For an assessment of the literature on women and development, see the special issue of *Signs,* VII (Winter, 1981), "Development and the Sexual Division of Labor." The best revisionist overview of Appalachian history is Ronald D. Eller, *Miners, Millhands, and Mountaineers: Industrialization of the Appalachian South, 1880–1930* (Knoxville: University of Tennessee Press, 1982). The most helpful older work is John C. Campbell, *The Southern Highlander and His Homeland* (New York: Russell Sage Foundation, 1921).

49. C. Vann Woodward, *Origins of the New South, 1877–1913* (Baton Rouge:

the modern South, scholars studying female wage earners do not inherit even the conceptual framework that facilitates research on rural women. Nevertheless, unpublished papers and recent dissertations are beginning to yield a research agenda that puts women at the center of the New South industrial world.

As cotton shaped their lives on the land, so textiles dominated women's industrial employment. Recent work on the numerous New England mills where the Slater—or family labor—system prevailed has highlighted regional similarities in textile workers' lives. But there were significant differences as well. For one thing, while waves of immigrants succeeded one another at New England looms, southern mills were reserved for whites only, intensifying segregation and consigning blacks to agricultural labor. For another, the South had no equivalent of the Lowell mill girls: while the Waltham system allowed young women to leave farm homes for a brief sojourn in the mills, southern millowners from the first commanded the labor of families in return for a "family wage."[50]

Dolores Janiewski, Dale Newman, and Cathy McHugh have begun tracing the origins and the fluctuations of this labor system. Janiewski argues that because female-headed families and families without sons were the most vulnerable to the hazards of a cash-crop economy, the first resort of a farm family in trouble was often to send its daughters

---

Louisiana State University Press, 1951), 226. General studies that contain some information on the South are Alice Kessler-Harris, *Out to Work: A History of Wage-Earning Women in the United States* (New York: Oxford University Press, 1982); and Barbara Mayer Wertheimer, *We Were There: The Story of Working Women in America* (New York: Pantheon, 1977). A full picture of southern working women must include both an overview of the impact of the region's culture and political economy on women's values and opportunities and a recognition of the subregional diversity obscured by aggregate figures. A general framework for understanding the factors that influence women's work in different localities is provided by Susan J. Kleinberg, "The Systematic Study of Urban Women," in Milton Cantor and Bruce Laurie (eds.), *Class, Sex and the Woman Worker* (Westport, Conn.: Greenwood Press, 1977), 20–42. A general study of industrial workers in the North and South Carolina Piedmont incorporating women's perspectives is Southern Oral History Program, *"Like a Family": An Oral History of the Textile South, 1880–1940* (Chapel Hill: University of North Carolina, forthcoming).

50. Scattered but unsuccessful attempts were made to use the Waltham system in the antebellum period (at William Gregg's mill in Graniteville, South Carolina, for example); as late as the 1920s the Dan River Mills in Virginia had a boardinghouse for women reminiscent of Lowell. For a study of New England that most closely resembled the southern type, see Jonathan Prude, *The Coming of Industrial Order: Town and Factory Life in Rural Massachusetts, 1810–1860* (Cambridge, England: Cambridge University Press, 1983).

to the mills. As a result, in contrast to Appalachia, Piedmont women and children led the flight from the land. As agricultural conditions worsened after 1900, pushing male-headed families into the mills, the proportion of women workers fell, and a family wage economy developed in which adult men, along with adolescents and children of both sexes, labored in the mills while married women took in boarders, cultivated gardens, and performed unpaid domestic tasks. After 1920, technological change and minimum-wage laws diminished child labor and married women reentered the work force, often becoming, like southern black women in the cities, lifelong workers contributing both wages and domestic labor to the family economy.[51]

Women were clearly among the most exploited members of the textile work force, but we know only the bare outlines of that exploitation and little about how women themselves viewed their working lives. Janiewski points out that men's and women's jobs were more similar in textiles than in vertically organized tobacco factories. Yet even textile jobs that provided greater status and autonomy, such as supervisor or machine fixer, were monopolized by men. And where tasks were identical, a pattern of wage discrimination prevailed.[52] Carrying the double burden of home and work, women were susceptible to special forms of stress. The imposition of the "stretch-out" after World War I, for example, may have been especially hard on married women who depended on the slower pace of the early water-powered mills for combining their private and public roles.

How did industrialization affect working-class marriages and family life? McHugh, Janiewski, and Newman all point out that the first generation of mill workers maintained traditionally high fertility rates, and succeeding generations sharply curtailed family size. Valerie Quinney's oral history of three generations of women in the mill evokes the human complexity behind such demographic change, but no one has undertaken a qualitative study of birth control. Drawing on autobiographies written by participants in a unique workers' edu-

51. Janiewski, "From Field to Factory"; Dale Newman, "Work and Community Life in a Southern Textile Town," *Labor History,* XIX (Spring, 1978), 204–25, and "Textile Workers in a Tobacco County: A Comparison Between Yarn and Weave Mill Villagers," in Edward Magdol and Jon L. Wakelyn (eds.), *The Southern Common People: Studies in Nineteenth-Century Social History* (Westport, Conn.: Greenwood Press, 1980), 345–68; Cathy Louise McHugh, "The Family Labor System in the Southern Cotton Textile Industry, 1880–1915" (Ph.D. dissertation, Stanford University, 1981). Newman, however, does not focus explicitly on women and McHugh is more concerned with child than with female labor.

52. Janiewski, "From Field to Factory"; McHugh, "The Family Labor System."

cation center, the Southern Summer School for Women Workers, Mary Frederickson argues that the egalitarianism Hagood found among sharecroppers persisted in industrial settings. While Frederickson sees sex roles made fluid by "working-class pragmatism," however, McHugh and Janiewski believe that patriarchal authority in the home reinforced the owners' power in the mill.[53]

This diversity of interpretation points toward the need for studies that raise questions of consciousness and historical agency. Historians have begun chipping away at the notion that mill towns and coal camps were "total institutions" in which paternalistic owners structured the lives of cultureless mill hands, stressing instead communal solidarity and cultural creativity. Viewed in this light, women, whether workers or wives, become not simply victims but creators as well—keepers of rural values, sources of family stability, and maintainers of networks of friends and kin.[54]

The question remains whether this rural/industrial workers' culture provided a basis for resistance as well as solace and support. The sociologist Robert Blauner has stated most baldly the case for women's conservatism, arguing that their predominance in southern textiles encouraged docility in the region's work force. Yet even from standard histories legendary female activists emerge: Ella May Wiggins, the balladeer of the 1929 Gastonia strike; the young mountain women who led the walkout at Elizabethton, Tennessee, that same year; Florence Reece, the coal miner's wife who composed the famous labor-turned-civil-rights song "Which Side Are You On?"[55]

Gradually, as historians have begun to examine women's collective

---

53. Valerie Quinney, "Textile Women: Three Generations in the Mill," *Southern Exposure*, III (Winter, 1976), 66–72; Mary Evans Frederickson, "A Place to Speak Our Minds," in Marc S. Miller (ed.), *Working Lives: The Southern Exposure History of Labor in the South* (New York: Pantheon, 1980), 155–65, and "A Place To Speak Our Minds: The Southern School for Women Workers" (Ph.D. dissertation, University of North Carolina, 1981).

54. Douglas DeNatale, "Traditional Culture and Community in a Piedmont Textile Mill Village" (M.A. thesis, University of North Carolina, 1980); and Southern Oral History Program, *"Like a Family."* Where these studies see cultural creativity, Newman finds white workers in rural yarn mills burdened by a sense of inferiority and thoroughly dominated by paternalism (in contrast to blacks who entered the work force in the 1960s bolstered by a heritage of racial solidarity and self-help and, to a lesser extent, in contrast to workers in a nearby, northern-owned weave mill).

55. Robert Blauner, *Alienation and Freedom* (Chicago: University of Chicago Press, 1964), 58–68; Stephen R. Wiley, "Songs of the Gastonia Textile Strike of 1929: Model of and for Southern Working-Class Women's Militancy," *North Carolina Folklore Journal*, XXX (Fall-Winter, 1982), 87–98.

action on its own terms, the female world that produced these legendary figures is coming into view. Interpreting the wave of strikes that swept the Piedmont in 1929 as a reaction to an assault on traditional work rhythms and social relations, this new labor history sees no contradiction between women's "traditionalism" and their willingness to join in collective action. Although David Corbin's excellent study (1981) of black and white miners does not focus on women's roles, it raises important questions about female militancy. Mimi Conway's *Rise Gonna Rise* (1979) traces the renewed organizing efforts that followed the entry of blacks into the textile industry after 1964 and the campaign for occupational health and safety initiated by the brown lung movement in the 1970s. A fine melding of oral history and journalism, her book sheds much light on the mill village past as well as on present struggles. Although not concerned solely with women, it shows their contributions and, in the brown lung movement especially, their assumption of leadership roles.[56]

Black women workers have been almost as thoroughly neglected as whites, with several important exceptions: debates over the relative influence of Afro-American culture on the high labor-force participation rate of married women (although these have focused for the most part on migrants to northern cities); careful examinations of household structure (revealing that while most urban blacks lived in two-parent households, a significant minority did not); and studies of domestic service. Whatever weight one assigns to the various factors involved—discrimination against men, the propensity of their offspring to set up independent households at a relatively young age, a segmented labor market that reserved certain menial occupations

56. David Alan Corbin is following his *Life, Work and Rebellion in the Coal Fields: The Southern West Virginia Miners, 1880–1922* (Urbana: University of Illinois Press, 1981) with a study of women in mining communities. Mimi Conway, author of *Rise Gonna Rise: Portraits of Southern Textile Workers* (Garden City, N.Y.: Doubleday, 1979), is a journalist who has written extensively on contemporary southern labor. In *Paternalism and Protest: Southern Cotton Mill Workers and Organized Labor, 1875–1905* (Westport, Conn.: Greenwood Publishing Corp., 1971), 23, Melton Alonza McLaurin notes that women joined the Knights of Labor in large numbers and participated in all the period's major strikes. He finds no evidence that southern management considered women more "tractable" than men. Because McLaurin does not use gender as a category of analysis, however, he does not explore the implications of his observations. Still in progress or in the form of unpublished papers and dissertations are the following studies of collective action in the 1920s and 1930s: Linda Frankel, "Women, Paternalism and Protest in a Southern Textile Community" (Ph.D. dissertation-in-progress, Harvard University); Hall, "Gender, Class, and Conflict"; and Frederickson, "A Place To Speak Our Minds."

for them—black women were a major component of the southern work force.[57]

David M. Katzman's *Seven Days a Week* provides a helpful framework for understanding the most prevalent of black women's occupations. Surveying the period from 1870 to 1920, he underlines the uniqueness of domestic service as a form of labor relations in which women, engaged in a highly personalized relationship, functioned both as employer and employee.[58] Additional research on the South should yield a fuller picture of the black domestic in her multiple identities—as nurturer, economic provider, and community builder among her own people as well as interracial mediator and participant in the intimate dynamics of white family life.

The best study thus far of black women in the tobacco industry is Dolores Janiewski's *Sisterhood Denied* (1985). Janiewski's work is especially important because it encompasses both black women and white, compares the Piedmont South's primary industries, textiles and tobacco, and examines women's role in union organization. She begins with an original account of the tobacco-growing region from which Durham's workers came, traces the emergence of class relations in the town, and examines women's work within both the factory and the home. Her chief themes are the profound divisions between black women and white and the domination of the American

---

57. Gutman, *The Black Family;* Claudia Goldin, "Female Labor Force Participation: The Origin of Black and White Differences, 1870 and 1880," *Journal of Economic History,* XXXVII (March, 1977), 87–108; Harold D. Woodman, "Comment," in *Journal of Economic History,* XXXVII (March, 1977), 109–12; Jacqueline Jones, "Between Plantation and Ghetto: Black Women, Work, and the Family in the Urban South, 1880–1915," Working Paper No. 79, Wellesley College Center for Research on Women, 1981, and "'To Get Out of This Land of Sufring': Black Migrant Women, Work and the Family in Northern Cities, 1900–1930," Working Paper No. 91, Wellesley College Center for Research on Women, 1982; William Harris, "Work and the Family in Black Atlanta, 1880," *Journal of Social History,* IX (Spring, 1976), 319–30.

58. David M. Katzman, *Seven Days a Week: Women and Domestic Service in Industrializing America* (New York: Oxford University Press, 1978). See also Trudier Harris, *From Mammies to Militants: Domestics in Black American Literature* (Philadelphia: Temple University Press, 1982). A number of Knights of Labor local assemblies in southern cities consisted of black domestics, and washerwomen sometimes banded together to improve their working conditions. For one notable washerwomen's strike, see Carter G. Woodson, "The Negro Washerwoman, a Vanishing Figure," *Journal of Negro History,* XV (July, 1930), 269–77; and Howard N. Rabinowitz, *Race Relations in the Urban South, 1865–1890* (New York: Oxford University Press, 1978), 73–76.

Federation of Labor (AFL) by white male leaders who could neither mobilize nor represent the interests of women and blacks.[59]

Robert Korstad's ongoing work on the successful 1943 organizing effort of the Tobacco, Agricultural and Allied Workers-CIO in Winston-Salem, North Carolina, provides a suggestive contrast to Janiewski's analysis of the AFL's limitations. Given the opportunity by an egalitarian union, black women in the tobacco stemmeries drew on a supportive work culture and a sense of self forged in a vital community life to become leaders of the South's largest and most politically active tobacco union local. Initiating voter registration drives and social welfare campaigns as well as securing better working conditions, Local 22 paved the way for the following decade's civil rights movement, which drew once again on black women's organizing skills.[60]

Julia Kirk Blackwelder's research adds a further dimension to our understanding of the impact of race on working-class women's lives. Her survey of the female work force in major southern cities during the depression reinforces Janiewski's emphasis on sex segmentation in the labor market. She finds Anglo, black, and Hispanic women channeled into jobs rigidly labeled by gender and ethnicity. Because southern history has tended to be seen in black and white, obscuring other ethnic groups, her book on San Antonio, where single Hispanic women dominated the industrial work force, is especially welcome. In *Women of the Depression*, she argues that among Hispanic women, culture overrode necessity, keeping married women out of wage labor even though Hispanics were at the very bottom of the economic scale. At the same time young Hispanic women played prominent roles in the strikes of the 1930s, and in contrast to blacks they benefited from the post–World War II increase in clerical occupations.[61]

59. Dolores E. Janiewski, *Sisterhood Denied: Race, Gender, and Class in a New South Community* (Philadelphia: Temple University Press, 1985).

60. Robert Korstad, "Those Who Were Not Afraid," in Miller (ed.), *Working Lives,* 184–99, and "The Workplace and the Union in Tobacco: Winston-Salem, North Carolina, 1943–1950" (Paper delivered at the annual meeting of the Social Science History Conference, Rochester, N.Y., November 7, 1980).

61. Julia Kirk Blackwelder, "Women in the Work Force: Atlanta, New Orleans, and San Antonio, 1930 to 1940," *Journal of Urban History,* IV (May, 1978), 331–58, "Quiet Suffering: Atlanta Women in the 1930s," *Georgia Historical Quarterly,* LXI (Summer, 1977), 112–24, and *Women of the Depression: Caste and Culture in San Antonio, 1929–1939* (College Station: Texas A&M University Press, 1984). See also George N. Green, "International Ladies' Garment Workers' Union in Texas, 1930–

The same process of regional development that transformed the lives of black and white working women had far-reaching consequences for the middle class. It seems clear that by the twentieth century women's employment and educational opportunities had widened, but only comparative studies will tell us how southern women fared in comparison to men of their own class and to women of other regions. Nor have scholars turned their attention to the impact of urbanization and industrialization on domestic life. Sexuality, child rearing, women's status within the family—on these issues and more, we must simply say that everything remains to be done. What we do have, however, is a wealth of insights into women's activities in the public realm, together with suggestive evidence of the relation between women's private experience and their angle of vision on social ills.

Anne Scott has argued that the wave of voluntarism that culminated in national women's organizations and put women in the vanguard of the Progressive movement had a significant impact on the South. The change first became apparent in the churches. Evangelical women in the antebellum period had organized prayer groups and aid societies; in the cities they launched charitable projects comparable to those springing up in the urban Northeast. After 1865 these efforts grew rapidly in numbers and autonomy. By the 1880s, local groups began to merge in regionwide women's organizations devoted both to foreign missions and to benevolent reform at home. Southern Methodists led the way in expanding women's public roles, and thus far their activities have received the most extensive documentation.[62]

1970," *Journal of Mexican-American History,* I (Spring, 1971), 144–69; Melissa Hield *et al.,* "Union Minded: Women in the Texas ILGWU, 1933–1950," *Frontiers,* IV (Summer, 1979), 59–70; and Richard Croxdale and Melissa Hield (eds.), *Women in the Texas Workforce: Yesterday and Today* (Austin: People's History in Texas, 1979).

62. Anne Firor Scott, "Women, Religion, and Social Change in the South, 1830–1930," in Samuel S. Hill, Jr. (ed.), *Religion and the Solid South* (Nashville: Abingdon Press, 1972), 92–121; Kenneth E. Rose, *Methodist Women: A Guide to the Literature* (Lake Junaluska, N.C.: General Commission on Archives and History, United Methodist Church, 1980). A useful older study is Noreen Dunn Tatum, *A Crown of Service: A Story of Woman's Work in the Methodist Episcopal Church, South, from 1878 to 1940* (Nashville: Parthenon Press, 1960). In 1980 the Women's History Project of the United Methodist Church held a major conference in Cincinnati that yielded a two-volume collection of essays on women in the Wesleyan tradition. These volumes contain a number of illuminating essays on the South. Hilah F. Thomas and Rosemary Skinner Keller edited the first volume of *Women in New Worlds;* Keller, Queen, and Thomas edited the second volume. For Baptist women's activities, see *Baptist History and Heritage,* XII (January, 1977), a special issue devoted to the role of

Virginia Shadron has shown how Methodist women revised the antebellum ideal of benevolent action to justify the professionalization of women's religious work and win the right to vote in church affairs. She draws a sensitive portrait of Methodist women's pioneering but highly ambiguous attempts at interracial cooperation and finds a significant overlap between leadership of the laity rights movement and participation in the secular suffrage campaign. Similarly, John McDowell documents Methodist women's leadership in promoting the social gospel, but his work is marred by lack of familiarity with the insights of women's and religious history. He observes, for example, that women's discontent with the effects of New South capitalism stopped short of criticism of capitalists themselves, but makes no attempt to show how women's activities may have been shaped by the very forces whose consequences they sometimes deplored. His analysis of women's motives, moreover, lacks the subtlety of Mathews' and Shadron's earlier observations, and he misses a chance to explore the relationship between the ideas of regional leaders and the actions of local missionary societies.[63]

Anne Scott has outlined a pattern of female organization that led directly from the churches to the WCTU, to YWCAs, women's clubs, suffragism, and finally, in the 1920s and 1930s, to race relations reform. Having created a vast associational network, southern women used it to promote prohibition, initiate the social welfare wing of southern progressivism, open higher education to women, establish kindergartens and settlement houses, and create a variety of welfare

---

women in Baptist history; and especially Patricia Summerlin Martin, "Hidden Work: Baptist Women in Texas, 1880–1920" (Ph.D. dissertation, Rice University, 1982). See also Fred Arthur Bailey, "The Status of Women in the Disciples of Christ Movement, 1865–1900" (Ph.D. dissertation, University of Tennessee, 1979).

63. Virginia Shadron, "Out of Our Homes: The Woman's Rights Movement in the Methodist Episcopal Church, South, 1890–1918" (M.A. thesis, Emory University, 1976), and "The Laity Rights Movement, 1906–1918: Woman's Suffrage in the Methodist Episcopal Church, South," in Thomas and Keller (eds.), *Women in New Worlds*, I, 261–75; John Patrick McDowell, *The Social Gospel in the South: The Woman's Home Mission Movement in the Methodist Episcopal Church, South, 1886–1939* (Baton Rouge: Louisiana State University Press, 1982). See also Mary Frederickson, "Shaping a New Society: Methodist Women and Industrial Reform in the South, 1880–1940," in Thomas and Keller (eds.), *Women in New Worlds*, I, 345–61. Anastatia Sims, for example, argues that few local missionary societies in North Carolina implemented the interracial program of the Woman's Missionary Society ("Sisterhoods of Service: Women's Clubs and Methodist Women's Missionary Societies in North Carolina, 1890–1930," in Keller, Queen, and Thomas [eds.], *Women in New Worlds*, II, 196–210).

institutions.[64] Scott's observations have been given theoretical force by recent studies describing a nineteenth-century reform tradition rooted in a female subculture and based on interlocking ideals of sisterhood, sexual separation, and women's vanguard mission in transforming the social order. This cluster of ideas, variously termed "Sentimental Womanhood" and "popular women's culture," inspired the WCTU's leap from single-issue to broad-gauged reform and shaped women's participation in both the Socialist and Progressive movements.[65] Undoubtedly, it underlay the whole spectrum of women's public activities in the South and provides an ideological link between groups as apparently different as local literary societies, farmers' home demonstration clubs, and a women's campaign against lynching.

On the other hand, such continuities—between the South and other regions and among various regional women's groups—may also obscure important differences. No one has done for the New South what Anne Scott, Catherine Clinton, and others have done for the plantation patriarchy, that is, a thoroughgoing study of how the ideology of women's roles meshed with other cultural themes. In *The War Within* (1982), for example, Daniel Singal argues that Victorianism came full-blown to the region only after the Civil War when the "New South Creed" transposed "the Cavalier mythology

64. Scott, "The 'New Woman' in the New South," and *The Southern Lady*, Pt. 2. Among other studies of women's organizational activities are Margaret Nell Price, "The Development of Leadership by Southern Women Through Clubs and Organizations" (M.A. thesis, University of North Carolina, 1945); Clara L. Pitts, "Julia Strudwick Tutwiler" (Ph.D. dissertation, George Washington University, 1942); Anne G. Pannell and Dorothea E. Wyatt, *Julia S. Tutwiler and Social Progress in Alabama* (University: University of Alabama Press, 1961); William J. Breen, "Southern Women in the War: The North Carolina Woman's Committee, 1917–1919," *North Carolina Historical Review*, LV (Summer, 1978), 251–83; Linda Peavy and Ursula Smith, *Women Who Changed Things: Nine Lives That Made a Difference* (New York: Charles Scribner's Sons, 1983), chapter on Oklahoma's Kate Barnard; and Keith L. Bryant, Jr., "Kate Barnard, Organized Labor, and Social Justice in Oklahoma During the Progressive Era," *Journal of Southern History*, XXXV (May, 1969), 145–64. Albert Coates, *By Her Own Bootstraps: A Saga of Women in North Carolina* (Chapel Hill: n.p., 1975), is particularly helpful on changes in women's legal status.

65. Among the most important of these are Nancy P. Cott, *The Bonds of Womanhood: "Woman's Sphere" in New England, 1780–1835* (New Haven: Yale University Press, 1977); Estelle Freedman, "Separatism as Strategy: Female Institution Building and American Feminism, 1870–1930," *Feminist Studies*, V (Fall, 1979), 512–29; Barbara L. Epstein, *The Politics of Domesticity* (Middletown: Wesleyan University Press, 1981); and Mari Jo Buhle, *Women and American Socialism, 1789–1920* (Urbana: University of Illinois Press, 1981), esp. 49–103.

onto the framework of Victorian belief in morality and industrial progress." But except for a chapter on Ellen Glasgow, he offers few hints about the role of gender ideology in this belief system or how women participated in the post–World War I "modernist" impulse he credits with dismantling that system.[66]

Besides analyses of regional variations on national themes we need studies that distinguish more carefully among different women's organizations within the region. Ellen DuBois, Barbara Epstein, and others have argued against an interpretation of women's associations that sees no tension between women's culture and feminist politics. This distinction, between a popular women's culture that justified an expansion of female roles without necessarily challenging male power and a feminist movement that sometimes, but not always, emerged from or converged with it, may be particularly useful in future research on the South.[67]

Two very different views of local women's organizations demonstrate the opportunities at hand. Noting that women's leadership in Progressive educational reform has been overlooked because of a focus on prominent male reformers and national organizations, James Leloudis has brought to light the extensive activities of the North Carolina–based Woman's Association for the Betterment of Public School Houses. He examines the motives and backgrounds of the association's members and places the group in the context of the New South campaign to restructure the economy through scientific agriculture and factory production. He sees the women acting both from humanitarian concern and from a desire for broader public roles but concludes that in the end they posed no fundamental challenge to "woman's place" or to the economic arrangements that perpetuated the regional poverty they hoped "better school houses" would alleviate.[68]

66. Daniel Joseph Singal, *The War Within: From Victorian to Modernist Thought in the South, 1919–1945* (Chapel Hill: University of North Carolina Press, 1982), 374. See also Paul M. Gaston, *The New South Creed: A Study in Southern Mythmaking* (New York: Knopf, 1970).

67. For a discussion of the tension between women's culture and feminism, see Ellen DuBois *et al.,* "Politics and Culture in Women's History: A Symposium," *Feminist Studies,* VI (Spring, 1980), 26–64; Epstein, *The Politics of Domesticity;* and Darlene Rebecca Roth, "Matronage: Patterns in Women's Organizations, Atlanta, Georgia, 1890–1940" (Ph.D. dissertation, George Washington University, 1978).

68. James L. Leloudis II, "School Reform in the New South: The Woman's Association for the Betterment of Public School Houses in North Carolina, 1902–1919," *Journal of American History,* LXIX (March, 1983), 886–909. Additional studies that

Darlene Roth's 1978 dissertation on women's clubs in Atlanta between 1890 and 1940 is the first comprehensive local study of its kind. Beginning with war relief efforts in 1866, multiplying geometrically in the 1890s, growing through the 1920s, and dropping off in the 1930s, women's organizations played an integral role in the emergence of the premier New South city. Roth documents a vast array of institution-building and public welfare activities but concludes that class condescension and racism often accompanied the most well-meaning reforms. Coining the intriguing concept of "matronage," she stresses the cultural functions of women's clubs: their role in conferring status and maintaining status distinctions, enabling adult women to extend the authority derived from an inflated notion of motherhood into a female public sphere, and perpetuating a value system that reinforced sexual segregation. Roth's conclusions derive in part from the fact that she concentrates on women's clubs and patriotic societies, rather than on the suffrage groups, YWCAs, Leagues of Women Voters, and interracial associations that addressed themselves to more controversial issues. Nevertheless, her work, reinforced by Anastatia Sims's study of North Carolina women's clubs, serves as an effective counter to overgeneralization and as a vivid illustration of the distinction between women's popular culture and feminism.[69]

---

provide valuable insights into how women's charitable and reform activities could promote capitalist agendas are LeeAnn Whites, "Southern Ladies and Millhands: The Domestic Economy and Class Politics; Augusta, Georgia, 1870–1890" (Ph.D. dissertation, University of California, Irvine, 1982), and "The Charitable and the Poor: The Emergence of Domestic Politics in Augusta, Georgia, 1860–1880," *Journal of Social History*, XVII (Summer, 1984), 601–15; and David E. Whisnant, *All That is Native and Fine: Politics of Culture in an American Region* (Chapel Hill: University of North Carolina Press, 1984).

69. Roth, "Matronage," and "Feminine Marks on the Landscape: An Atlanta Inventory," *Journal of American Culture*, III (Winter, 1980), 673–85. Anastatia Sims also emphasizes the sometimes conservative nature of women's clubs in "Sallie Southall Cotten and the North Carolina Federation of Women's Clubs" (M.A. thesis, University of North Carolina, 1976), and "Feminism and Femininity in the New South: Women's Organizations in North Carolina, 1883–1930" (Ph.D. dissertation-in-progress, University of North Carolina). See also William Stephenson, "How Sallie Southall Cotten Brought North Carolina to the Chicago World's Fair of 1893," *North Carolina Historical Review*, LVIII (Autumn, 1981), 364–83; and especially Megan Seaholm, "From Self-Culture to Civic Responsibility: Women's Clubs in Texas, 1880–1920" (Ph.D. dissertation-in-progress, Rice University). A less critical look at women's activities in an area where Quaker influence was particularly strong is Paula Stahls Jordan and Kathy Warden Manning, *Women of Guilford County, North Carolina: A Study of Women's Contributions, 1750–1979* (Greensboro, N.C.: Women of Guilford, 1979).

Among Roth's most important contributions are her comparisons between black and white associational life. Her call for an integrated southern women's history goes to the heart of the matter: "The histories of black and white southern women—because of slavery and segregation—have been separate histories, experienced separately and written down in separate traditions. Yet the similarities between their public records are too numerous and the differences too striking (and too socially significant) not to take advantage of direct comparisons. Furthermore, the consciousness of race so permeates the public lives of women, that any discussion of their modern-day, post-1865 lives must include consideration of both racial experiences." She finds black Atlanta women creating parallel and contemporaneous organizational networks, subscribing to quite similar notions of "distinctive womanhood," and using associational ties to cement social status. On the other hand, the social welfare activities of black women took on special meaning in an era when their communities were systematically excluded from public services. No white organization in the city, for example, ever approached the scope of the Neighborhood Union, a settlement house and community organizing project founded by Lugenia Burns Hope in 1906.[70]

Looked at as a whole, black and white associational movements have even more striking differences. Founded in the 1890s to forward what Ida B. Wells termed "a defense of black womanhood as part of the defense of the race from terror and abuse," the National Association of Colored Women's Clubs had from the start explicitly political goals. Also from the start southern black women played leading roles on a national level. Wells, the Memphis antilynching crusader, helped found Boston's New Era Club; Margaret Murray Washington was the first southern woman, white or black, to head a national organization of secular women's groups; and throughout the region women like Charlotte Hawkins Brown, Lucy Laney, and Mary McLeod Bethune combined club work with the creation of educational institutions and campaigns of racial protest and self-help.[71]

70. Roth, "Matronage," 49 (quotation).

71. Wells quoted in Jones, "Between Plantation and Ghetto," 65; Ida B. Wells, *Crusade for Justice: The Autobiography of Ida B. Wells*, ed. Alfreda M. Duster (Chicago: University of Chicago Press, 1970); Thomas C. Holt, "The Lonely Warrior: Ida B. Wells-Barnett and the Struggle for Black Leadership," in John Hope Franklin and August Meier (eds.), *Black Leaders of the Twentieth Century* (Urbana: University of Illinois Press, 1982), 39–61; Roth, "Matronage," 81; Tera Hunter, "Charlotte Hawkins Brown" (Honors paper, Duke University, 1982), and "The Correct Thing:

Recorded first by pioneering black historians, black women's institution-building activities are only now being revealed in their full extent and continuity. Eleanor Flexner paved the way by devoting several chapters of her 1959 study of the women's rights movement to black women. Then in 1972, Gerda Lerner called attention to the community work of black club women, and especially to Atlanta's Neighborhood Union.[72] Sharon Harley, Cynthia Neverdon-Morton, and Tullia B. Hamilton have expanded this story, while Elsa Brown's dissertation on Richmond, Virginia, from 1890 to 1930 provides an intriguing view of gender roles in the black community. Brown shows women adopting an ideology of independence and self-help and then implementing that ideology through a woman's bank, a department store, and mutual aid societies in which washerwomen worked in concert with their more privileged sisters. She also describes a spirited debate on "the woman question" within the black community.[73]

Charlotte Hawkins Brown and the Palmer Institute," *Southern Exposure*, XI (September/October, 1983), 37–43. More historical attention has been focused on Mary McLeod Bethune than on any of her contemporaries. For this literature, see Delores C. Leffall and Janet L. Sims, "Mary McLeod Bethune—The Educator; Also Including a Selected Annotated Bibliography," *Journal of Negro Education*, XLV (Summer, 1976), 342–59. For these and other black women leaders, see Hallie Q. Brown, *Homespun Heroines and Other Women of Distinction* (Xenia, Ohio: Aldine, 1926); Gerda Lerner (ed.), *Black Women;* Bert James Loewenberg and Ruth Bogin (eds.), *Black Women in Nineteenth Century American Life: Their Words, Their Thoughts, Their Feelings* (University Park: Pennsylvania State University Press, 1976); and Marianna W. Davis (ed.), *Contributions of Black Women to America* (2 vols.; Columbia, S.C.: Kenday Press, 1982).

72. Eleanor Flexner, *Century of Struggle: The Woman's Rights Movement in the United States* (New York: Atheneum, 1959). Lerner's article has been reprinted as "Community Work of Black Club Women," in Gerda Lerner, *The Majority Finds Its Past* (New York: Oxford University Press, 1979), 83–93. See also Jacqueline Anne Rouse, "Lugenia D. Burns Hope: A Black Female Reformer in the South, 1871–1947" (Ph.D. dissertation, Emory University, 1983). More general studies of the intersections of race, class, and gender include William H. Chafe, *Women and Equality: Changing Patterns in American Culture* (New York: Oxford University Press, 1977); Davis, *Women, Race and Class;* and Bettina Aptheker, *Women's Legacy: Essays on Race, Sex, and Class in American History* (Amherst: University of Massachusetts Press, 1982).

73. Sharon Harley, "Black Women in the District of Columbia, 1890–1920" (Ph.D. dissertation, Howard University, 1981), and "Black Women in a Southern City: Washington, D.C.," in Hawks and Skemp (eds.), *Sex, Race, and the Role of Women in the South*, 59–74; Cynthia Neverdon-Morton, "Self-Help Programs as Educative Activities of Black Women in the South, 1895–1925: Focus on Four Key Areas," *Journal of Negro Education*, LI (Summer, 1982), 207–21, and "The Black Woman's Struggle for Equality in the South, 1895–1925," in Sharon Harley and Rosalyn Terborg-Penn

Still urgently needed are investigations of women's contributions to the Afro-American church.[74]

Before 1920 the most important point of contact between black and white women was the struggle for education. But for the most part the white women involved were the northern teachers who came south to establish schools for the freed men and women. Women's education in the South, like voluntary associations, must be viewed as two "separate histories, experienced separately and written down in separate traditions." About neither do we have more than the sketchiest outline. Fortunately, an excellent bibliographical essay by Virginia Shadron and others has raised the central questions and made accessible the major sources for studying both traditions. The authors argue that whereas before the Civil War "white women's education in the South appears to have been roughly equivalent in type and intention to that in the North," afterwards it significantly diverged. They emphasize the region's fierce resistance to coeducation for white women and point out the fallacy of the assumption that black women were better educated than their male counterparts. "The conditions of male-defined and male-oriented educational objectives operating in racially and sexually segregated institutions," they conclude, "have constrained women's professional expectations and opportunities more severely in the South than anywhere else in the country."[75]

(eds.), *The Afro-American Woman: Struggles and Images* (Port Washington, N.Y.: Kennikat Press, 1978), 43–57; Tullia Kay Brown Hamilton, "The National Association of Colored Women, 1896–1920" (Ph.D. dissertation, Emory University, 1978); Elsa Barkley Brown, "Uncle Ned's Children: Richmond, Virginia's Black Community, 1890–1930" (Ph.D. dissertation-in-progress, Kent State University). See also William J. Breen, "Black Women and the Great War: Mobilization and Reform in the South," *Journal of Southern History*, XLIV (August, 1978), 421–40; and Patricia A. McDonald, "Baltimore Women, 1870–1900" (Ph.D. dissertation, University of Maryland, 1976).

74. In "Nineteenth-Century A.M.E. Preaching Women: Cutting Edge of Women's Inclusion in Church Polity," in Thomas and Keller (eds.), *Women in New Worlds*, I, 276–89, Jualynne Dodson offers an enlightening glimpse into black women's religious life, but she touches only peripherally on the South. Her dissertation-in-progress ("Women's Collective Power in the African Episcopal Church," University of California, Berkeley) promises to be an important contribution. For an early survey, see Sara Jane McAfee, *History of the Woman's Missionary Society in the Colored Methodist Episcopal Church* (Jackson, Tenn.: Publishing House C.M.E. Church, 1934).

75. Elizabeth Jacoway, *Yankee Missionaries in the South: The Penn School Experiment* (Baton Rouge: Louisiana State University Press, 1980); Jacqueline Jones, *Soldiers of Light and Love: Northern Teachers and Georgia Blacks, 1865–1873* (Chapel Hill: University of North Carolina Press, 1980); Virginia Shadron et al., "The Historical

However limited, the postwar increase in women's educational, vocational, and organizational activities undoubtedly helped create the preconditions for a regional suffrage movement.[76] Confronted with the handicap of disfranchisement, reformers could appeal to a broad constituency armed with organizational skills and convinced that women had special responsibilities. By the 1890s, suffrage organizations had appeared in every southern state; a movement was under way that served as a powerful politicizing experience for two generations of southern women and had a significant impact both on regional reform and on the national women's rights campaign.

Over the last forty years, A. Elizabeth Taylor has compiled a massive state-by-state survey of this movement. Her work has been supplemented by Paul Fuller's biography of Laura Clay, articles on important leaders, and a number of excellent brief biographies in *Notable American Women.*[77] But even with this impressive documentation we

Perspective: A Bibliographical Essay," in Patricia A. Stringer and Irene Thompson (eds.), *Stepping Off the Pedestal: Academic Women in the South* (New York: Modern Language Association of America, 1982), 145–68 (quotations on p. 168). A perceptive early survey is A. D. Mayo, *Southern Women in the Recent Educational Movement in the South* (1892: repr., with introduction by Dan T. Carter and Amy Friedlander, Baton Rouge: Louisiana State University Press, 1978). See also the chapter on Orie Latham Hatcher in Peavy and Smith, *Women Who Changed Things.*

76. Ellen Carol DuBois's comment that the effect of women's involvement in the movement may have been more important than enfranchisement itself is especially relevant to the South, where only three states eventually ratified the Nineteenth Amendment. See DuBois, *Feminism and Suffrage: The Emergence of an Independent Women's Movement in America, 1848–1869* (Ithaca: Cornell University Press, 1978). See Adele Simmons, "Education and Ideology in Nineteenth-Century America: The Response of Educational Institutions to the Changing Role of Women," in Berenice A. Carroll (ed.), *Liberating Women's History: Theoretical and Critical Essays* (Urbana: University of Illinois Press, 1976), 115–26, for the argument that in the Northeast, college-educated women were not in the forefront of the suffrage campaign.

77. Paul E. Fuller, *Laura Clay and the Woman's Rights Movement* (Lexington: University Press of Kentucky, 1975). For a critical review of Fuller's narrowly conceived study, see Sara M. Evans, *Signs*, III (Winter, 1977), 491–93. Lee N. Allen, "The Woman Suffrage Movement in Alabama, 1910–1920," *Alabama Review*, XI (April, 1958), 83–89; Marie Stokes Jemison, "Ladies Become Voters: Pattie Ruffner Jacobs and Women's Suffrage in Alabama," *Southern Exposure*, VII (Spring, 1979), 48–59; Marirose Arendale, "Tennessee and Women's Rights," *Tennessee Historical Quarterly*, XXXIX (Spring, 1980), 62–78; Kathleen Christine Berkeley, "Elizabeth Avery Meriwether, 'An Advocate for Her Sex': Feminism and Conservatism in the Post–Civil War South," *Tennessee Historical Quarterly*, XLIII (Winter, 1984), 390–407; Kenneth R. Johnson, "Florida Women Get the Vote," *Florida Historical Quarterly*, XLVIII (January, 1970), 299–312; Clement Eaton, "Breaking a Path for the Liberation of Women in the South," *Georgia Review*, XXVII (Summer, 1974), 187–99; Jacquelyn Dowd

have barely begun to comprehend the range and complexity of southern feminism. We lack biographies of leaders that probe psychological complexity and link private to public life. We need additional local and state studies that explain the campaign's role in the political dynamics of the time. Most of all, we need to take the next step: an interpretive overview calling on the insights of women's history and putting suffrage in the context of both feminist reform and regional politics.[78]

The suffrage campaign provides an ideal laboratory for unraveling some of the major themes of southern women's history. Suffragists proposed to expand the electorate by half at a time when southern elites were restricting rather than expanding voting rights—for class and racial ends—and their cause was taken up by the Knights of Labor, the Populists, and the Socialists who challenged the New South order from below. On the other hand, suffragists confronted opponents whose most effective argument was that enfranchisement would open the way to federal interference and flood the polls with black women, and they won the vote only after racial exclusion was an accomplished fact. There is no question that most southern suffragists— whether they allied with the Populists and Socialists, fought for a federal amendment with the National American Woman Suffrage Association, adopted the more militant tactics of the Woman's party, or defected to the states' rights position of the Southern States Woman

---

Hall, *Revolt Against Chivalry: Jessie Daniel Ames and the Women's Campaign Against Lynching* (New York: Columbia University Press, 1979), Chap. 2 on Texas suffragism; Sophonisba Preston Breckinridge, *Madeline McDowell Breckinridge: A Leader in the New South* (Chicago: University of Chicago Press, 1921); Melba Porter Hay, "Madeline McDowell Breckinridge: Kentucky Suffragist and Progressive Reformer" (Ph.D. dissertation, University of Kentucky, 1980); Lloyd C. Taylor, "Lila Meade Valentine: The FFV as Reformer," *Virginia Magazine of History and Biography*, LXX (October, 1962), 471–87; Trudy J. Hanmer, "A Divine Discontent: Mary Johnston and Woman Suffrage in Virginia" (M.A. thesis, University of Virginia, 1972); Charlotte Jean Sheldon, "Woman Suffrage and Virginia Politics, 1909–1920" (M.A. thesis, University of Virginia, 1969); Mary Louise Meredith, "The Mississippi Woman's Rights Movement, 1889–1923: The Leadership Role of Nellie Nugent Somerville and Greenville in Suffrage Reform" (M.A. thesis, Delta State University, 1974); Nancy Carol Tipton, "'It is My Duty': The Public Career of Belle Kearney" (M.A. thesis, University of Mississippi, 1975); Patricia L. Spiers, "The Woman Suffrage Movement in New Orleans" (M.A. thesis, Southeastern Louisiana College, 1965); Barbara B. Ulmer, "Virginia Durant Young: New South Suffragist" (M.A. thesis, University of South Carolina, 1979).

78. Marjorie Spruill Wheeler is completing a dissertation at the University of Virginia that promises to address many of these issues.

Suffrage Conference—shared the prevailing racism of the time.[79] It is certain too that they drew eclectically on ideals rooted in Victorian women's culture. But beneath these generalizations lie hundreds of individual stories of women confronting, internalizing, or challenging their era's assumptions about race, class, and sex and forging ideologies and strategies in the context of special regional constraints.

As historians begin to trace the patterns these stories suggest, one-dimensional images disappear. In place of a monolithic view of conservative southern suffragism we see local and individual complexity and an intriguing process of generational change. At the turn of the century Ida Hayman Callery joined her father on the Populist lecture circuit in Indian Territory and then went on to become a leading advocate of both socialism and feminism in the Southwest. At the same time aristocrats like Laura Clay of Kentucky and Kate M. Gordon of Louisiana staunchly advocated states' rights and, in Gordon's case at least, willingly exploited racial prejudice. After 1910 they were succeeded by younger women like Sue Shelton White of Tennessee, who joined the Woman's party and went to jail for burning President Wilson in effigy, and Minnie Fisher Cunningham, who became a stalwart of Texas liberalism. In Georgia in the 1880s, Rebecca Latimer Felton, inspired in part by her passion for women's rights, led the forces of radical racism by advocating lynching to turn back the alleged menace of the black rapist. Forty years later, in Atlanta, a younger suffragist named Jessie Daniel Ames channeled her brand of feminism into an antilynching campaign that turned Felton's argument on its head by rejecting the "false chivalry" of lynching rather than demanding protection from rape. Tempered in the suffrage movement and spanning the period from 1880 to 1940, these activist lives tell us much about the emergence of a New South social order. Fully understood, they can help us trace the contours of feminist con-

79. On racism in the southern movement, see Scott, *The Southern Lady;* Aileen S. Kraditor, *The Ideas of the Woman Suffrage Movement, 1890–1920* (Garden City, N.Y.: Anchor Books, 1971), and "Tactical Problems of the Woman-Suffrage Movement in the South," *Louisiana Studies,* V (Winter, 1966), 289–307; Rosalyn Terborg-Penn, "Discrimination vs. Afro-American Women in the Woman's Movement, 1830–1920," in Harley and Terborg-Penn (eds.), *The Afro-American Woman,* and "The Historical Treatment of the Afro-American in the Woman's Movement, 1900–1920: A Bibliographical Essay," *Current Bibliography on African Affairs,* VII (Summer, 1974), 245–59; Adele Logan Alexander, "Grandmother, Grandfather, W. E. B. Du Bois and Booker T. Washington," *Crisis* (February, 1983), 8–11, and "How I Discovered My Grandmother . . . and the Truth about Black Women and the Suffrage Movement," *Ms. Magazine* (November, 1983), 29–33.

sciousness and see women as agents in historical change, as well as illuminating that change.[80]

Until recently, conventional wisdom held that the women's movement fell apart in the 1920s. Suffragists had pinned their hopes too single-mindedly to the vote; younger women, rejecting feminism's high-minded concerns, pursued self-expression and sexual liberation; losing ground in the professions, women returned to the home, loyal to domesticity until the reemergence of feminism in the 1960s. While historians of women concentrated mainly on the colonial and Victorian eras, this picture, with its elements of truth, sufficed. As attention begins shifting to the modern period, however, a more complex story is coming into view, and nowhere is the revision proceeding more quickly than in the American South.

There is no doubt that a new model of womanhood emerged in the 1920s. In the growing cities of the South as in the rest of the country, young women bobbed their hair and shortened their dresses. "We were throwing our weight around in small ways," wrote Lillian Smith (who later became one of the most serious critics of the South's racial system), "we were flaming youth." Indeed, Zelda Fitzgerald, the legendary flapper, hailed from Montgomery and set the pace for Atlanta and Charleston no less than for New York. But as Nancy Milford's biography makes clear, beneath the surface glitter even of Zelda's life ran a powerful striving for meaningful work. Frank Stricker has

---

80. Neil K. Basen, "The 'Jennie Higginses' of the 'New South in the West': A Regional Survey of Socialist Activists, Agitators, and Organizers, 1901–1917," in Sally M. Miller (ed.), *Flawed Liberation: Socialism and Feminism* (Westport, Conn.: Greenwood Press, 1981), 87–111; Kenneth R. Johnson, "Kate Gordon and the Woman-Suffrage Movement in the South," *Journal of Southern History*, XXXVII (August, 1972), 365–92; James P. Louis, "Sue Shelton White and the Woman Suffrage Movement in Tennessee, 1913–20," *Tennessee Historical Quarterly*, XXII (June, 1963), 170–90; John E. Talmadge, *Rebecca Latimer Felton: Nine Stormy Decades* (Athens: University of Georgia Press, 1960); Josephine Bone Floyd, "Rebecca Latimer Felton, Champion of Women's Rights," *Georgia Historical Quarterly*, XXX (June, 1946), 81–104, and "Rebecca Latimer Felton, Political Independent," *Georgia Historical Quarterly*, XXX (March, 1946), 14–34; Hall, *Revolt Against Chivalry*. It is becoming clear that the influence of Woman's party militants in the South was not as negligible as A. Elizabeth Taylor implied. See, for example, Sidney R. Bland, "'Mad Women of the Cause': The National Woman's Party in the South," *Furman Studies*, XXVI (December, 1980), 82–91, and "Fighting the Odds: Militant Suffragists in South Carolina," *South Carolina Historical Magazine*, LXXXII (January, 1981), 32–43. Amelia Fry of the Regional Oral History Office at the University of California, Berkeley, is completing a biography of Alice Paul that draws attention to the Woman's party's southern campaign.

documented the persistence of career commitments among college-educated women in the nation at large through the 1930s. No comparable research has focused on the South, but it seems that where opportunities for education had so recently appeared and where urbanization was accelerating, women who came of age in the 1920s would have been more, not less, likely than earlier generations to aspire to professional careers.[81]

In an article published in 1964, Anne Scott called attention to the continuation and expansion of women's reform efforts "after suffrage." Since then a series of monographs have shown not only a continuation but a significant change and expansion of women's social concerns. With the decline of organized feminism, women ceased to devote their best energies to explicit issues of women's rights. But in other ways they built on the gains of their predecessors, challenging the "New South Creed" of industrial progress and racial exclusion and building alliances across both class and racial lines.[82]

The first of these studies deals with Jessie Daniel Ames, who in the 1920s became a leader in the interracial movement and in the 1930s directed a white women's antilynching movement. Jacquelyn Hall's *Revolt Against Chivalry* traces the roots of female interracialism to the struggle for women's rights within the Southern Methodist church and for black representation in the YWCA, then shows Jessie Ames channeling women's racial concerns into a single-issue campaign against mob violence. Hall argues that Jessie Ames articulated an implicitly feminist antiracism. Her personal struggle for autonomy resonated with her rebellion against a "rape complex" that confined

81. Lillian Smith, *The Winner Names the Age: A Collection of Writings by Lillian Smith,* ed. Michelle Cliff (New York: Norton, 1978), 206; Nancy Milford, *Zelda: A Biography* (New York: Harper & Row, 1970); Frank Stricker, "Cookbooks and Law Books: The Hidden History of Career Women in Twentieth-Century America," *Journal of Social History,* X (Fall, 1976), 1–19. For a persuasive comment on the 1920s, see also Alice Rossi (ed.), *The Feminist Papers: From Adams to de Beauvoir* (New York: Columbia University Press, 1973). For three contemporary analyses, see Guion Griffis Johnson, "Feminism and Economic Independence of Woman," *Journal of Social Forces,* III (May, 1925), 612–16; Chase Going Woodhouse, "Married College Women in Business and the Professions," *Annals of the American Academy of Political and Social Science,* CXLIII (May, 1929), 325–38; and Faye Elizabeth Hancock, "Occupational Opportunity for Southern Women: A Descriptive Picture of Women at Work in the South in 1940" (M.A. thesis, University of North Carolina, 1946).

82. Anne Firor Scott, "After Suffrage: Southern Women in the Twenties," *Journal of Southern History,* XXX (August, 1964), 298–318. See also Mollie C. (Davis) Abernathy, "Southern Women, Social Reconstruction, and the Church in the 1920s," *Louisiana Studies,* XIII (Winter, 1974), 289–312.

white women even as it terrorized black men. Ames drew eclectically on the ideals and tactics of the female reform tradition. Under her direction, association members sought to exercise moral suasion over would-be lynchers in their own homes, use their newly won voting power over public officials, and influence opinion makers who created an atmosphere in which violence could flourish. Although Ames led her constituency toward a view of lynching that linked violence to segregation, economic discrimination, and disfranchisement, she could not transcend certain limitations both of character and of strategy. She never viewed blacks as agents of their own liberation, and her refusal to support federal antilynching legislation—the main tactic of the larger NAACP-led movement—eventually alienated her from the mainstream of southern liberalism. Under her leadership, the antilynching association remained tied to the "female public sphere" of women's clubs and missionary societies while young women were rejecting the notion of social transformation radiating outward from the home, and the association was preoccupied with race at a time when the plight of white workers was becoming the chief concern of regional reform. Consequently, no younger generation rose to leadership; as Ames and her cohorts retired from public life, the antilynching association passed from the scene.[83]

Marion Roydhouse's research on women and labor reform in North Carolina shifts the focus from race relations to questions of

83. Hall, *Revolt Against Chivalry*, and "'A Truly Subversive Affair': Women Against Lynching in the Twentieth-Century South," in Carol Ruth Berkin and Mary Beth Norton (eds.), *Women of America: A History* (Boston: Houghton Mifflin, 1979), 360–88. A number of master's theses and articles document the antilynching association's activities. See Laura Hardy Crites, "A History of the Association of Southern Women for the Prevention of Lynching, 1930–1942" (M.A. thesis, American University, 1965); Henry E. Barber, "The Association of Southern Women for the Prevention of Lynching, 1930–1942," *Phylon*, XXXIV (December, 1973), 378–89; and Kathleen Atkinson Miller, "The Ladies and the Lynchers: A Look at the Association of Southern Women for the Prevention of Lynching," *Southern Studies*, XVII (Fall, 1978), 221–40. Crites, who was Jessie Daniel Ames's niece, provides especially interesting firsthand information. Julius Wayne Dudley, "A History of the Association of Southern Women for the Prevention of Lynching, 1930–1942" (Ph.D. dissertation, University of Cincinnati, 1979), is the most detailed organizational history written to date. It is particularly valuable for its treatment of the tension between Ames and black leaders of the antilynching movement. For parallels between antilynching reform and the contemporary struggle against rape, see Jacquelyn Dowd Hall, "'The Mind That Burns in Each Body': Women, Rape and Racial Violence," in Ann Snitow, Christine Stansell, and Sharon Thompson (eds.), *Powers of Desire: The Politics of Sexuality* (New York: Monthly Review Press, 1983), 328–49.

class. She expands on earlier observations that the YWCA pioneered in the effort to bring southern women together across class lines and provides the first detailed study of the activities of a state legislative council in which major women's groups combined for political influence. Roydhouse's most important insights concern conflict along gender lines and among different groups of women. As long as YWCA workers limited themselves to welfare work in the mill villages, their efforts were welcomed by millowners. But when YWCA Industrial Secretaries raised questions about working conditions or advocated unions, they drew strong opposition and economic reprisals. Similarly, when the legislative council called for a survey of women workers in the textile industry and lobbied for protective legislation, it stepped outside the southern Progressive mainstream and confronted vested economic power. Roydhouse documents case after case in which the legislative council pursued activities that not only ran counter to the general interests of their class but also came into direct conflict with those of members' own husbands and fathers. This is not to say that organized women presented a united front. On the contrary, Roydhouse reveals ongoing conflicts between the young YWCA Industrial Secretaries and wealthy members of the YWCA boards and among the leadership of the legislative council. By the mid-1930s, conservative women had gained control of the council and the more radical students and workers had grown disillusioned with the YWCA. In Roydhouse's work we see once more, in sharp relief, both the tensions within the female world and the degree to which the values nurtured in that world could inform a significant critique of the male-dominated social order.[84]

84. Marion Winifred Roydhouse, "The 'Universal Sisterhood of Women': Women and Labor Reform in North Carolina, 1900–1932" (Ph.D. dissertation, Duke University, 1980). See also Emma Louise Moyer Jackson, "Petticoat Politics: Political Activism among Texas Women in the 1920's" (Ph.D. dissertation, University of Texas, 1980); Betsy Brinson, "The Shorter Workday," *Southern Exposure*, IX (Winter, 1981), 9–11; and Frances Sanders Taylor, "'On the Edge of Tomorrow': Southern Women, the Student YWCA, and Race, 1920–1944" (Ph.D. dissertation, Stanford University, 1984). For women in party politics, see Vinton M. Prince, Jr., "Will Women Turn the Tide? Mississippi Women and the 1922 United States Senate Race," *Journal of Mississippi History*, XLII (August, 1980), 212–20, and "Women, Politics, and the Press: The Mississippi *Woman Voter*," *Southern Studies*, XIX (Winter, 1980), 365–72; Jane Whiteside Elliott, "Lucy Somerville Howorth: Legislative Career, 1932–1935" (M.A. thesis, Delta State University, 1975); Sandra Gioia Treadway, "Sarah Lee Fain: Norfolk's First Woman Legislator," *Virginia Cavalcade*, XXX (Winter, 1981), 124–33; Lorraine Nelson Spritzer, *The Belle of Ashby Street: Helen Douglas Mankin and Georgia Politics* (Athens: University of Georgia Press, 1982). Joanne V. Hawks, M. Carolyn

Conspicuously absent from Roydhouse's account are examples of sustained cooperation with working-class women. Fortunately, the one exception to that rule, the Southern Summer School for Women Workers, a workers' education project that convened in the North Carolina mountains each summer after 1927, is the subject of another outstanding dissertation, Mary Frederickson's "A Place To Speak Our Minds," which analyzes interwar feminism in its finest hour. The conclusions of the dissertation are suggested in an article by the same title. Founded by two YWCA women, Louise Leonard McLaren and Lois MacDonald, the school "sought to provide young workers from textile, garment, and tobacco factories with the analytic tools for understanding the social context of their lives, the opportunity to develop solidarity with one another, and the confidence for full participation in the emerging Southern labor movement."[85]

Like the Women's Trade Union League (WTUL), the school pursued the sometimes conflicting goals of securing support for workers among middle-class women and lobbying for women's interests within a male-oriented union movement. Helping to forward the shift from craft to industrial unionism in the late 1930s, the school became increasingly allied with the CIO. This alliance, while broadening its base of support, also undermined the group's identity as a women's institution. Unlike many other interwar reform groups, the school survived World War II and attempted to expand its program for white workers to include the racial issues that came to the fore in the

---

Ellis, and J. Byron Morris, "Women in the Mississippi Legislature (1924–1981)," *Journal of Mississippi History,* XLIII (November, 1981), 266–93, a study of the forty-four women who have served in the Mississippi legislature, is particularly instructive. The authors find that many of these elected officials had teaching experience and a background of participation in women's organizations, especially in the Methodist church. Although several of those who entered politics in the 1920s had been suffragists, and the most well-known among them, Ellen Woodward, went on to lobby for women's causes in the New Deal, most refused to be identified with women's issues. The authors also observe that neither the press nor their fellow lawmakers treated these women legislators seriously and conclude that "the women were hardworking, conscientious public servants; few were innovators or supporters of unpopular issues. Few made notable lasting achievements" (p. 293).

85. Frederickson, "A Place To Speak Our Minds," and "A Place to Speak Our Minds," in Miller (ed.), *Working Lives,* 155. For other reform-minded women of the 1920s and 1930s, see Frederickson, "Myra Page: A Biographical Portrait," *Southern Changes,* V (January/February, 1983), 10–15; Lucy Randolph Mason, *To Win These Rights: A Personal Story of the CIO in the South* (New York: Harper & Brothers, 1952); and Katharine Du Pre Lumpkin, *The Making of a Southerner* (New York: Knopf, 1947).

1950s. Isolated by postwar reaction and the retreat of the labor movement, however, it disbanded in 1951 before the civil rights movement began.

In her portraits of the school's teachers, Frederickson introduces a network of southern women who came to maturity in the 1920s, graduated from the region's small women's colleges, gained their introduction to industrial and racial problems through the YWCA student movement, and went on to careers in social research and socialist reform. She also traces the life histories of the workers who attended the school, arguing on the basis of their autobiographical writings that they were class-conscious, committed to wage earning, and eager for individual and collective change. In contrast to the WTUL, a similar attempt at cross-class feminist alliance building, Frederickson finds relatively little tension between these middle-class reformers and worker-students. Perhaps the difference lay in the fact that labor insurgency in the South was cut short before it could gain a strong institutional foothold. The school succeeded in providing a "social space" where women could realize their common interests free from the pressures of the outside world. But it did not have to face the test experienced by the WTUL, whose worker-members sometimes rose to union leadership positions that pulled against their loyalty to feminist allies.[86] It might also be argued that the hos-

86. Frederickson, " A Place To Speak Our Minds," 132, 222; Nancy Schrom Dye, *As Equals and as Sisters: Feminism, the Labor Movement, and the Women's Trade Union League of New York* (Columbia: University of Missouri Press, 1980). One of the most notable of women's accomplishments in the interwar period—and an excellent source for probing women's consciousness—can be found in southern literature. Although biographers and literary critics have explored the lives and works of individual writers, Anne Goodwyn Jones, *Tomorrow Is Another Day: The Woman Writer in the South, 1859–1936* (Baton Rouge: Louisiana State University Press, 1981), is the first attempt to trace the emergence of a specifically female literary tradition. Jones focuses on seven white women novelists who were precursors of the Southern Renaissance, and her lead should be followed for the renaissance itself. For illuminating perspectives on Margaret Mitchell's work, see Elizabeth Fox-Genovese, "Scarlett O'Hara: The Southern Lady as New Woman," *American Quarterly*, XXXIII (Fall, 1981), 391–411; and Darden Asbury Pyron (ed.), *Recasting: Gone With The Wind in American Culture* (Miami: University Presses of Florida, 1983). See also Virginia Spencer Carr, *The Lonely Hunter: A Biography of Carson McCullers* (Garden City, N.Y.: Doubleday, 1975); Marie Fletcher, "The Southern Heroine in the Fiction of Representative Southern Women Writers, 1850–1960" (Ph.D. dissertation, Louisiana State University, 1963); and Kathryn Lee Seidel, "The Southern Belle: Her Fall from the Pedestal in Fiction of the Southern Renaissance" (Ph.D. dissertation, University of Maryland, 1976), now published as *The Southern Belle in the American Novel* (Tampa: University of South Florida Press, 1985). Black women writers came into their own only in

tile climate of the anti-union South encouraged a special solidarity. Marion Roydhouse points out, for example, that the Southern School for Women Workers maintained a more radical and less elitist stance than did its northern counterpart, the Bryn Mawr Summer School, founded by Hilda Smith and M. Carey Thomas. In any case, Frederickson's study makes clear that some women reformers were on the cutting edge of labor insurgency in the interwar period and that the consciousness of women workers can be assessed only when southern labor history is viewed independently of the trade unions' organizational success.

It might be argued that this female reform tradition lost force in the late 1930s and was silenced in the post–World War II era. Certainly, activist women who came of age during the depression were more likely to pursue their goals in concert with men than to form specifically female institutions. We have no studies of the women who organized for the CIO and the Southern Tenant Farmers' Union or who helped found and sustain such expressions of southern radicalism as the Southern Conference for Human Welfare (SCHW) and Highlander Folk School. What were the self-perceptions and political orientations of women activists in a period when both female institutions and feminist ideology were in eclipse? What role did female networks and female friendships play in such women's private and public lives? Were there elements of continuity between them and the suffrage generation? What were the links between their pursuit of racial justice and economic democracy and the civil rights and women's liberation movements of the 1960s?

Scattered references in books devoted to other subjects, interviews, biographies, and autobiographies indicate that women of this era, both within mixed-sex organizations and in local communities, did indeed help lay the groundwork for the great social changes to come.[87]

---

the 1970s, but they built on a foundation laid by such outstanding southerners as Zora Neale Hurston and Margaret Walker. For this black women's literary tradition, see Barbara Christian, *Black Women Novelists: The Development of a Tradition, 1892–1976* (Westport, Conn.: Greenwood Press, 1980); Rosianne Bell, Bettye J. Parker, and Beverly Guy Sheftall, *Sturdy Black Bridges: Visions of Black Women in Literature* (Garden City, N.Y.: Anchor Press, 1979); Robert E. Hemenway, *Zora Neale Hurston: A Literary Biography* (Urbana: University of Illinois Press, 1977); and J. Lee Greene, *Time's Unfading Garden: Anne Spencer's Life and Poetry* (Baton Rouge: Louisiana State University Press, 1977).

87. William H. Chafe, *Civilities and Civil Rights: Greensboro, North Carolina, and the Black Struggle for Freedom* (New York: Oxford University Press, 1980), makes the importance of women's post–World War II activities clear. Barbara Woods Aba-

Virginia Durr of the SCHW and Anne Braden of the SCHW's successor, the Southern Conference Education Fund, once "discovered" by the young feminists of the 1960s, helped broaden their vision and sustain their struggle.[88] Glimpses of Ella Baker, the NAACP field worker who became a leader of the Southern Christian Leadership Conference and a founder of the Student Non-Violent Coordinating Committee (SNCC), have appeared in essays and a documentary film. Pauli Murray's own writings remain the best introduction to the life of one of the most remarkable of these women. Poet, lawyer, and priest, Murray was also a co-founder of the National Organization of Women (NOW) and among the first to point out the "double jeopardy" of racial and sexual oppression.[89]

Mecha, "Black Woman Activist in Twentieth Century South Carolina: Modjeska Monteith Simkins" (Ph.D. dissertation, Emory University, 1978), is the first full-length biography of a female civil rights leader in this transitional period. See also Daisy Bates, *The Long Shadow of Little Rock: A Memoir* (New York: David McKay, 1962); Septima Poinsette Clark, *Echo in My Soul* (New York: Dutton, 1962); Sharon Mitchell Mullis, "The Public Career of Grace Towns Hamilton: A Citizen Too Busy to Hate" (M.A. thesis, Emory University, 1976); Arnold M. Shankman, "Dorothy Tilly, Civil Rights and the Methodist Church," *Methodist History*, XVIII (January, 1980), 95–108, and "Civil Rights, 1920–1970: Three Southern Methodist Women," in Keller, Queen, and Thomas (eds.), *Women in New Worlds*, II, 211–33; Marcia Kunstel, "Breaking the Conspiracy of Silence," *Southern Exposure*, VII (Summer, 1979), 77–83; Florence Mars, *Witness in Philadelphia* (Baton Rouge: Louisiana State University Press, 1977); Lillian Smith, *Killers of the Dream* (New York: Norton, 1949); Redding S. Sugg, Jr., "Lillian Smith and the Condition of Woman," *South Atlantic Quarterly*, LXXI (Spring, 1972), 155–64; Morton Sosna, *In Search of the Silent South: Southern Liberals and the Race Issue* (New York: Columbia University Press, 1977), chapter on Lillian Smith (pp. 172–97); Jo Ann Robinson, "Lillian Smith: Reflections on Race and Sex," *Southern Exposure*, IV (Winter, 1977), 43–49; and Margaret Rose Gladney, "A Chain Reaction of Dreams: Lillian Smith and Laurel Falls Camp," *Journal of American Culture*, V (Fall, 1982), 50–55.

88. Virginia Foster Durr, "The Emancipation of Pure, White, Southern Womanhood," *New South*, XXVI (Winter, 1971), 46–54; Anne Braden, *The Wall Between* (New York: Monthly Review Press, 1958), and "A View From the Fringes," *Southern Exposure*, IX (Spring, 1981), 68–74. Both Durr and Braden (along with other associates of Highlander Folk School) will appear in a forthcoming book of oral histories to be edited by Sue Thrasher and Elliot Wigginton.

89. Ellen Cantarow, with Susan Gushee O'Malley and Sharon Hartman Strom, *Moving the Mountain: Women Working for Social Change* (Old Westbury, N.Y.: Feminist Press, 1982). The film *Fundi: The Story of Ella Baker* is distributed by New Day Films. Pauli Murray, *Proud Shoes: The Story of an American Family* (New York: Harper & Row, 1956), and "The Liberation of Black Women," in Mary Lou Thompson (ed.), *Voice of the New Feminism* (Boston: Beacon Press, 1970), 88–102. For the emergence of a black feminist movement, see Diane K. Lewis, "A Response to Inequal-

Sara Evans, in *Personal Politics,* is the first scholar to deal explicitly with women's roles in these postwar movements for racial and sexual equality. She portrays the courageous leadership of young women in SNCC and argues that older black women, such as Fannie Lou Hamer, a sharecropper in Sunflower County, Mississippi, carried much of the burden of local organizing campaigns. Inspired by such models, southern white women joined the movement, gaining a sense of self that conflicted sharply with notions of feminine deference and propriety. Eventually they followed a trajectory traced by Sara Grimké and Angelina Grimké over a century before. Just as the Grimké sisters were the first to move from abolitionism to the defense of women's rights, so their spiritual grandchildren in the southern civil rights movement issued the first manifesto of modern feminism.[90]

In contrast to most studies of the civil rights movement, which focus on students, ministers, and other middle-class leaders, Derek Williams' study of a food workers' strike at the University of North Carolina at Chapel Hill in 1969 documents a labor conflict in which black women workers allied with student activists to challenge the policies both of the university and of the state. In Williams' narrative, a group of southern workers whose social and economic situation was determined by class, race, and sex seize the possibilities offered by the civil rights struggle to assert their claims to decent pay and working conditions, and, beyond that, dignity and respect. The outcome illustrates both the movement's power and its limitations. While civil rights agitation created the context in which such women could assert themselves and their needs, it could not bring about fundamental economic change. The food workers won redress of some of their grievances: wage increases, upgrading of job classifications, a

---

ity: Black Women, Racism, and Sexism," *Signs,* III (Winter, 1977), 339–61; and Bell Hooks, *Ain't I a Woman?: Black Women and Feminism* (Boston: South End Press, 1981).

90. Sara Evans, *Personal Politics: The Roots of Women's Liberation in the Civil Rights Movement and the New Left* (New York: Knopf, 1979), "Women's Consciousness and the Southern Black Movement," *Southern Exposure,* IV (Winter, 1977), 10–18, and "Tomorrow's Yesterday: Feminist Consciousness and the Future of Women," in Berkin and Norton (eds.), *Women of America,* 389–426. Another study of sexual dynamics in the civil rights movement, focusing mainly on white northern volunteers, is Mary Aickin Rothschild, "White Women Volunteers in the Freedom Summers: Their Life and Work in a Movement for Social Change," *Feminist Studies,* V (Fall, 1979), 466–95. For a young black woman's perspective, see Anne Moody, *Coming of Age in Mississippi* (New York: Dial Press, 1969).

new manager. But neither they nor the movement of which they were a part sought to alter the structure of occupational segregation by race and sex that ultimately determined their options and opportunities.[91]

One final work illustrates the crosscurrents of southern women's political activism. Jane De Hart Mathews and Donald G. Mathews have focused on the antifeminist backlash of the 1980s. In a forthcoming book on the controversy over ratification of the Equal Rights Amendment (ERA) in North Carolina, they argue that the social profiles of ERA proponents and opponents are much the same; that the controversy is essentially a "symbolic conflict" between two value systems; and that the ERA has mobilized "women to such an extent that we may now speak not only of the feminist movement but of the 'other women's movement'—what students of collective behavior would term a counter movement."[92]

Still urgently needed are studies of the social changes that underlie these varieties of political action. We know virtually nothing about the post–World War II developments that have brought southern women's lives into closer conformity to the American mainstream, or about the regional and subregional differences that remain. Only when scholars begin to lavish attention on the recent configurations

91. J. Derek Williams, "'It Wasn't Slavery Time Anymore': Foodworkers' Strike at Chapel Hill, Spring 1969" (M.A. thesis, University of North Carolina, 1979).

92. Jane De Hart Mathews and Donald G. Mathews, *The Equal Rights Amendment and the Politics of Cultural Conflict: Feminists and Traditionalists in North Carolina* (New York: Oxford University Press, forthcoming). Preliminary findings have been published by Mathews and Mathews, with Roxie Nicholson-Guard, as "Women in the Contemporary South: The Symbolic Politics of ERA," in *Furman Studies*, XXVI (December, 1980), 6–8. Other studies of the ERA's fate in the South are Theodore S. Arrington and Patricia A. Kyle, "Equal Rights Amendment Activists in North Carolina," *Signs*, III (Spring, 1978), 666–80; and David W. Brady and Kent L. Tedin, "Ladies in Pink: Religion and Political Ideology in the Anti-ERA Movement," *Social Science Quarterly*, LVI (March, 1976), 564–75. See also Carl M. Brauer, "Women Activists, Southern Conservatives, and the Prohibition of Sex Discrimination in Title VII of the 1964 Civil Rights Act," *Journal of Southern History*, XLIX (February, 1983), 37–56. Research is needed on women and contemporary electoral politics. Among the surveys to appear thus far are Hawks, Ellis, and Morris, "Women in the Mississippi Legislature"; Joan S. Carver, "Women in Florida [1890–1978]," *Journal of Politics*, XLI (August, 1979), 941–55; and Sarah Weddington (coordinator), Elizabeth Fernea and Marilyn P. Duncan (eds.), *Texas Women in Politics* (Austin, Texas: Foundation for Women's Resources, 1977); Judie W. Gamage, "Quest for Equality: An Historical Overview of Women's Rights Activism in Texas, 1908–1975" (Ph.D. dissertation, North Texas State University, 1982); Elizabeth Hays Turner, "Benevolent Ladies, Club Women, and Suffragists: Galveston Women's Organizations, 1880–1920" (Ph.D. dissertation-in-progress, Rice University); and Martha H. Swain, "The Public Role of

of women's public and private lives equal to that which has been paid to the colonial and antebellum periods will the modern "southern woman" come clearly into view.[93]

Speaking of the peculiar tangle of sex and race that shaped women's place in the American South—and formed the backdrop for their many challenges to the region's status quo—Jessie Daniel Ames remarked, "Someday someone is going to be bold enough to write fully and completely about the Southern white women through slavery up to the present, but that day is far off." In a more personal context Lillian Smith reiterated this theme: "I am patient; I know my worth; I know my historical value to this country."[94] Taken together, and extended to women of color and of all classes, the words of Jessie Ames and Lillian Smith might be taken as a clarion call for an enterprise that is only now gathering momentum. The works discussed in this essay represent models and breakthroughs, but they must be seen as only a beginning. As scholars of women's history turn their attention to the South and southern historians increasingly attend to issues of gender, we will be able to comprehend both the image and reality of women's lives, with far-reaching consequences not only for our vision of the past but for our creation of the future.

Southern Women," in Hawks and Skemp (eds.), *Sex, Race, and the Role of Women,* 37–58.

93. For demographic variations, see John W. Florin, "Varieties of Southern Women," *Southern Exposure,* IV (Winter, 1977), 95–97.

94. Ames quoted in Hall, "'A Truly Subversive Affair,'" 377; Smith quoted in Robinson, "Lillian Smith," 47.

The Discovery of Southern Religious History

JOHN B. BOLES

The issuance since 1980 of at least a dozen important books on southern religious history demonstrates the current interest in a topic sadly neglected in scholarship until recently. Religion in the United States—meaning primarily in New England, the Middle Atlantic states, and the Midwest—has at least since the 1930s been the focus of impressive research and publication. In 1964, Henry F. May argued in an influential essay in the *American Historical Review* that "for the study and understanding of American culture, the recovery of American religious history may well be the most important achievement of the last thirty years." Yet in his survey of the significant books published in the preceding three decades, May listed no works on southern religion. Of course many regional denominational and associational histories had been published, along with admiring biographies and occasional collections of documents, but these mainly represented traditional, narrative, uncritical institutional history that neither related their subjects to larger movements nor were concerned with ideas, theology, the folk culture of the people, or the role of religious beliefs. There were exceptions—the books of Hunter D. Farish, Wesley M. Gewehr, Charles A. Johnson, and Walter B. Posey, for example, are still widely used, and there are very perceptive chapters in several books by Francis B. Simkins and Clement A. Eaton, but the poverty of the historical imagination with regard to southern religion was stultifying until the early 1960s. The paucity of citations to volumes on southern religion in the landmark book on the region's historiography, Arthur S. Link and Rembert W. Patrick's *Writing Southern History*, emphatically documents the point.[1]

1. Henry F. May, "The Recovery of American Religious History," *American Historical Review*, LXX (October, 1964), 79; Hunter D. Farish, *The Circuit Rider Dismounts: A Social History of Southern Methodism, 1865–1900* (Richmond: Dietz Press, 1938); Wesley M. Gewehr, *The Great Awakening in Virginia, 1740–1790* (Durham: Duke University Press, 1930); Charles A. Johnson, *The Frontier Camp Meeting: Religion's Harvest Time* (Dallas: Southern Methodist University Press,

There are several possible reasons for the lag in the discovery, not recovery, of southern religious history as an academic interest. First, the largest and most methodologically advanced graduate schools were located outside the region, and graduate students often chose topics dictated by the easy availability of source materials. Second, the early ascendancy of political and economic history nationwide was particularly hard to break for a region whose heritage seemed dominated by the politics of secession and the economics of slavery and then sharecropping. Third, many educated southerners, especially in the 1920s and 1930s when the region's graduate schools began to expand and improve, either accepted the voguish Mencken-like disparagement of southern evangelical religion or tended, in the aftermath of Perry Miller and the resurgence of Puritan scholarship, to belittle the worth of studying southern churches with their less sophisticated theological traditions.

Moreover, the relative scarcity of printed sermons and the like seemed to confirm the futility of the effort. Even W. J. Cash, in his evocative *The Mind of the South* (1941), implied in contradiction to his title that the South had no mind, only feeling.[2] Intellectual historians studied the ideas of elites in society, and the important, culture-shaping religion in the South hardly seemed the faith of an educated elite. The southern clergy desired evangelical results, not systematic theology. Consequently Henry May's thirty-year period of recovering American religious history was an inauspicious era for the study of southern religion.

By the early 1960s the major impediments to the development of southern religious history had largely disappeared. By that date a number of good graduate schools, with significant archival collections nearby, had evolved in the region. Historiographical trends

1955); Walter B. Posey, *The Development of Methodism in the Old Southwest, 1783–1824* (Tuscaloosa, Ala.: Weatherford Printing Co., 1933), *The Presbyterian Church in the Old Southwest, 1778–1838* (Richmond: John Knox Press, 1952), and *The Baptist Church in the Lower Mississippi Valley, 1776–1845* (Lexington: University of Kentucky Press, 1957); Francis B. Simkins, *A History of the South* (3rd ed.; New York: Knopf, 1963), Chaps. 10, 26; Clement A. Eaton, *The Freedom-of-Thought Struggle in the Old South* (New York: Harper & Row, 1964; shorter ed., 1940), Chap. 12, and *The Mind of the Old South* (Baton Rouge: Louisiana State University Press, 1964; rev. ed., 1967), Chap. 10; Arthur S. Link and Rembert W. Patrick (eds.), *Writing Southern History: Essays in Historiography in Honor of Fletcher M. Green* (Baton Rouge: Louisiana State University Press, 1965), 30–32, 215–16, 270, 386–92, 427–28, 434n.

2. W. J. Cash, *The Mind of the South* (New York: Knopf, 1941), 99.

against the old "history is past politics" school had overwhelmed traditional history everywhere, including the South, and the innovative, exciting fields of history were intellectual, cultural, and later social. The growing fascination with the South even outside the region meant that students elsewhere were joining their southern colleagues in turning to the intellectual, cultural, and social history of Dixie. With the new vogues of history (and perhaps in part because religion itself had become more respectable in the 1950s), scholars turned more sympathetically to a study of religious beliefs and institutions. Intellectual and especially cultural history had been considerably broadened to encompass popular values, what is now called *mentalité*. Historians also gravitated to the field because it was practically unworked, and virgin territory attracts scholars the way the West did pioneer farmers. For these reasons and no doubt others, the nature and quality of southern religious history changed markedly in the 1960s.

In 1964, the very year in which Henry May's historiographical essay appeared, Kenneth K. Bailey published *Southern White Protestantism in the Twentieth Century*. Having done solid research in primary materials, Bailey stepped back from the typical denominational perch and viewed his subject with refreshing candor and in a critical though fair-minded perspective. He dealt seriously with ideas, discussed the southern situation within a national framework, focused on the mainstream Protestant churches, and sensitively analyzed the conservative southern evangelical reaction to outside forces. In his move away from narrative institutional history, Bailey wrote what might be labeled the first modern book on southern religious history.[3] Other scholars followed his example, though they often had different research strategies and reached their conclusions by independent paths. None of this new breed of southern religious historians has been more influential than Samuel S. Hill, Jr.

In 1966, Hill published *Southern Churches in Crisis*, a moving study of the challenges facing southern Protestants in the 1960s with a perceptive account of how their historical and theological traditions both shaped their identity and limited their response. The individualistic, conversion-centered focus of the popular churches was

---

3. Kenneth K. Bailey, *Southern White Protestantism in the Twentieth Century* (New York: Harper & Row, 1964). Another book that addresses the impact of modernity on southern religion is Robert Watson Sledge, *Hands on the Ark: The Struggle for Change in the Methodist Episcopal Church, South, 1914–1939* (Lake Junaluska, N.C.: Commission on Archives and History, United Methodist Church, 1975).

shown to make them de facto defenders of the status quo, even though—and in part because—their theology was otherworldly. In addition to this important book, in his role as chairman of the department of religion first at the University of North Carolina and later at the University of Florida, Hill has been a major influence on the development of southern religious studies. The growth and increasing maturity of the field was indicated by a book he edited in 1972. The essays by several scholars, including a woman historian (Anne Firor Scott), an anthropologist (Charles Hudson), a religious demographer (Edwin S. Gaustad), a sociologist (Edgar T. Thompson), and Hill himself, suggested what groups other than white male Protestants should be studied and what methodologies other than history had to offer in the evolving attempt to understand the complex nature of southern religious culture. In a number of ways this book set the agenda for future scholarship in the field.[4]

Also in 1972, John B. Boles published a monograph on the Great Revival, that series of religious awakenings about 1800 that set the South on the road to evangelical dominance. He used printed and manuscript materials from both church institutions and individuals, tried to make explicit the ideas and "belief system" that made possible the growth of the popular denominations (Baptist, Methodist, and Presbyterian), and attempted to characterize the resultant evangelical culture and survey its influence on southern history. This book dealt exclusively with white Protestants in Virginia, North and South Carolina, Georgia, Kentucky, and Tennessee.[5] Four years later, Boles

---

4. Samuel S. Hill, Jr., *Southern Churches in Crisis* (New York: Holt, Rinehart & Winston, 1966), and Hill (ed.), *Religion and the Solid South* (Nashville: Abingdon Press, 1972).

5. John B. Boles, *The Great Revival, 1787–1805: The Origins of the Southern Evangelical Mind* (Lexington: University Press of Kentucky, 1972). Other recent articles on the Great Revival and its background, leaders, and significance include John Opie, Jr., "James McGready: Theologian of Frontier Revivalism," *Church History,* XXXIV (December, 1965), 445–56, and "The Melancholy Career of 'Father' David Rice," *Journal of Presbyterian History,* XLVII (December, 1969), 295–319; Ralph E. Morrow, "The Great Revival, the West, and the Crisis of the Church," in John Francis McDermott (ed.), *The Frontier Re-examined* (Urbana: University of Illinois Press, 1967), 65–78; Donald G. Mathews, "The Second Great Awakening as an Organizing Process, 1780–1830: An Hypothesis," *American Quarterly,* XXI (Spring, 1969), 23–43; John Scott Strickland, "The Great Revival and Insurrectionary Fears in North Carolina: An Examination of Antebellum Southern Society and Slave Revolt Panics," in Orville Vernon Burton and Robert C. McMath, Jr. (eds.), *Class, Conflict, and Consensus: Antebellum Southern Community Studies* (Westport, Conn.: Greenwood Press, 1982), 57–95; Terry David Bilhartz, "Urban Religion and the Second Great

513

published a book that was more restricted geographically but that included more religious groups. Part of the Kentucky Bicentennial Bookshelf, *Religion in Antebellum Kentucky* examined the state's religious history within the context of regional developments and contained chapters on Kentucky Catholicism and black Christians. Its final chapter again strove to analyze the religious cultures that emerged, how they were both a response to the historical situation and a force shaping the actions of Kentuckians (read southerners).[6]

As these books suggest, one of the distinctive features of the new writing on southern religion has been the extent to which authors were willing to criticize trends and movements within the southern churches. An important series of books have as their central theme the failings of past religious leaders to break loose from conventional mores and sustain a prophetic tradition. Works such as Donald G. Mathews' *Slavery and Methodism* (1965), John Lee Eighmy's *Churches in Cultural Captivity* (1972), and H. Shelton Smith's *In His Image, But . . .* (1972) indicated that southern religious scholars were now thoroughly in the modern, liberal academic mainstream. While often quite critical of the racism and rigid social and religious orthodoxy that had so long survived in southern Christendom, these historians were sensitive to nuance and aware of the societal restraints that weighed so heavily on their forerunners. Of these three studies, Mathews' was the most wide-ranging interpretation—though still quite traditional methodologically—and Smith's the most conventional in conclusions.[7]

Awakening: A Religious Study of Baltimore, Maryland, 1790–1830" (Ph.D. dissertation, George Washington University, 1979); and Charles G. Steffen, *The Mechanics of Baltimore: Workers and Politics in the Age of Revolution, 1763–1812* (Urbana: University of Illinois Press, 1984), Chap. 12, "Mechanics and Methodism" (pp. 253–75).

6. John B. Boles, *Religion in Antebellum Kentucky* (Lexington: University Press of Kentucky, 1976). Robert M. Calhoon's similar bicentennial state history, *Religion and the American Revolution in North Carolina* (Raleigh: Department of Cultural Resources, Division of Archives and History, 1976), is essentially a documentary collection, though it has valuable introductory comments. Herman A. Norton's very brief, illustrated survey, *Religion in Tennessee, 1777–1945* (Knoxville: University of Tennessee Press, 1981), is a good example of popular history.

7. Donald G. Mathews, *Slavery and Methodism: A Chapter in American Morality, 1780–1845* (Princeton: Princeton University Press, 1965); John Lee Eighmy, *Churches in Cultural Captivity: A History of the Social Attitudes of Southern Baptists* (Knoxville: University of Tennessee Press, 1972); H. Shelton Smith, *In His Image, But . . . : Racism in Southern Religion, 1780–1910* (Durham: Duke University Press, 1972). Eighmy's book nicely complemented an older study, Rufus B. Spain, *At Ease in Zion: Social History of Southern Baptists, 1865–1900* (Nashville: Vanderbilt University

The old style of religious history, the trials and triumphs of particular denominations, was also revived in the 1960s, but the new versions were more interpretative, more sophisticated, and far less tied to the filiopietistic school. In some ways the most impressive of these modern denominational histories was the three-volume *Presbyterians in the South* by Ernest Trice Thompson. Carefully researched, encyclopedic in coverage, and cautious in judgment, the massive work was disappointing, however, in that it departed only a small step from the old W. W. Sweet–style of narrative institutional history. A more incisive, interpretative denominational history was David Edwin Harrell, Jr.'s two volumes on the Disciples of Christ. The account of his denomination was solidly grounded in social history.[8] This is a good model for denominational history to follow.

[Handwritten margin notes: "Thompson's Presb. in the South"; "Harrell's Disciples of Christ"]

Press, 1961). During the 1960s and 1970s a number of works addressed the complex and tragic issue of race in southern religious history. Representative titles are: Victor B. Howard, "The Southern Aid Society and the Slavery Controversy," *Church History,* XLI (June, 1972), 208–24; Patricia Hickin, "Gentle Agitator: Samuel M. Janney and the Antislavery Movement in Virginia, 1842–1851," *Journal of Southern History,* XXXVII (May, 1971), 159–90, and "'Situation Ethics' and Antislavery Attitudes in the Virginia Churches," in John B. Boles (ed.), *America: The Middle Period. Essays in Honor of Bernard Mayo* (Charlottesville: University Press of Virginia, 1973), 188–215; James Brewer Stewart, "Evangelicalism and the Radical Strain in Southern Antislavery Thought During the 1820s," *Journal of Southern History,* XXXIX (August, 1973), 379–96; Lewis M. Purifoy, "The Southern Methodist Church and the Proslavery Argument," *Journal of Southern History,* XXXII (August, 1966), 325–41; Ralph E. Luker, "The Social Gospel and the Failure of Racial Reform, 1877–1898," *Church History,* XLVI (March, 1977), 80–99; and Henry Y. Warnock, "Andrew Sledd, Southern Methodists, and the Negro: A Case History," *Journal of Southern History,* XXXI (August, 1965), 251–71. Early antislavery has received extensive treatment; see Arthur Dicken Thomas, Jr., "The Second Great Awakening in Virginia and Slavery Reform, 1787–1837" (Th.D. dissertation, Union Theological Seminary in Virginia, 1981); and James D. Essig, *The Bonds of Wickedness: American Evangelicals Against Slavery, 1770–1808* (Philadelphia: Temple University Press, 1982). Two important articles spell out the development of a proslavery social ethic among some southern Christians: Drew Gilpin Faust, "Evangelicalism and the Meaning of the Proslavery Argument: The Reverend Thornton Stringfellow of Virginia," *Virginia Magazine of History and Biography,* LXXXV (January, 1977), 3–17; and Jack P. Maddex, Jr., "Proslavery Millennialism: Social Eschatology in Antebellum Southern Calvinism," *American Quarterly,* XXXI (Spring, 1979), 46–62. Maddex discusses the decline of that ethic after the Civil War in "From Theocracy to Spirituality: The Southern Presbyterian Reversal on Church and State," *Journal of Presbyterian History,* LIV (Winter, 1976), 438–57.

8. Ernest Trice Thompson, *Presbyterians in the South* (3 vols.; Richmond: John Knox Press, 1963–73); David Edwin Harrell, Jr., *Quest for a Christian America: The Disciples of Christ and American Society to 1866* (Nashville: Disciples of Christ Historical Society, 1966), and *The Social Sources of Division in the Disciples of Christ,*

While historians of southern religion were beginning to use tools from the behavioral sciences, scholars from other disciplines were turning to the subject of religion in the South. Three important examples are Dickson D. Bruce, Jr.'s *And They All Sang Hallelujah*

1865–1900 (Atlanta and Athens, Ga.: Publishing Systems, 1973). Important denominational histories include Hugh George Anderson, *Lutheranism in the Southeastern States, 1860–1886: A Social History* (The Hague: Mouton, 1969); Lester G. McAllister and William E. Tucker, *Journey in Faith: A History of the Christian Church (Disciples of Christ)* (St. Louis: Bethany Press, 1975); Robert A. Baker, *The Southern Baptist Convention and Its People, 1607–1972* (Nashville: Broadman Press, 1974); Ben M. Barrus, Milton L. Baughn, and Thomas H. Campbell, *A People Called Cumberland Presbyterians* (Memphis: Frontier Press, 1972); Emory Stevens Bucke (ed.), *The History of American Methodism* (3 vols.; New York: Abingdon Press, 1964); and Durwood T. Stokes and William T. Scott, *A History of the Christian Church in the South* (N.p.: N.p., 1973). Good local studies are George Fenwick Jones, *The Salzburger Saga: Religious Exiles and Other Germans Along the Savannah* (Athens: University of Georgia Press, 1984), and Jones (ed.), *Detailed Reports on the Salzburger Emigrants Who Settled in America . . . Edited by Samuel Urlsperger* (8 vols. to date; Athens: University of Georgia Press, 1968–); Frances Keller Swinford and Rebecca Smith Lee, *The Great Elm Tree: Heritage of the Episcopal Diocese of Lexington* (Lexington, Ky.: Faith House Press, 1969); Kirk Mariner, *Revival's Children: A Religious History of Virginia's Eastern Shore* (Salisbury, Md.: Peninsula Press, 1979); William H. Williams, *The Golden Age of Methodism: The Delmarva Peninsula, 1769–1820* (Wilmington: Scholarly Resources, 1984); Joseph D. Cushman, Jr., *The Sound of Bells: The Episcopal Church in South Florida, 1892–1969* (Gainesville: University Presses of Florida, 1976); Samuel Horst, *Mennonites in the Confederacy: A Study in Civil War Pacifism* (Scottsdale, Pa.: Herald Press, 1967); Ray Holder, *The Mississippi Methodists, 1799–1983: A Moral People "Born of Conviction"* (Jackson, Miss.: Maverick Prints, 1984); Carter E. Boren, *Religion on the Texas Frontier* (San Antonio: Naylor Co., 1968), primarily about the Disciples of Christ; R. Douglas Brackenridge, *Voice in the Wilderness: A History of the Cumberland Presbyterian Church in Texas* (San Antonio: Trinity University Press, 1968); O. Kelly Ingram (ed.), *Methodism Alive in North Carolina: A Volume Commemorating the Bicentennial of the Carolina Circuit* (Durham: Duke Divinity School, 1976); Frank Baker, *From Wesley to Asbury: Studies in Early American Methodism* (Durham: Duke University Press, 1976); Walter N. Vernon *et al.*, *The Methodist Excitement in Texas: A History* (Dallas: Texas United Methodist Historical Society, 1984); and Louis B. Weeks, *Kentucky Presbyterians* (Atlanta: John Knox Press, 1983). W. Harrison Daniel has written too many articles to list, most of them dealing with Baptists, on a variety of topics. Although his work has never been collected into a volume, his articles easily equal a book and their careful concern with details has rendered them useful to other scholars. A tiny group of communal sectarians, the Shakers (the United Believers in Christ's Second Coming), established two settlements in Kentucky, and historians have been intrigued by them. See Julia Neal, *By Their Fruits: The Story of Shakerism in South Union, Kentucky* (Chapel Hill: University of North Carolina Press, 1947), and *The Kentucky Shakers* (Lexington: University Press of Kentucky, 1977); and Francis Gerald Ham, "Shakerism in the Old West" (Ph.D. dissertation, University of Kentucky, 1962).

(1974), John R. Earle, Dean D. Knudsen, and Donald W. Shriver's *Spindles and Spires* (1976), and Thomas Virgil Peterson's *Ham and Japheth* (1978). Bruce, an anthropologist, brought his discipline's concern with structure and function to the study of the camp meeting. While much that he said was either quite conventional or ahistorical, he did rightly emphasize the otherworldliness, indeed the antiworldliness, of the pietistic yeomen converts and indicated how such sources as hymnbooks could be utilized to reveal popular religious beliefs. *Spindles and Spires* is a sophisticated sociological updating of the role of religion in Gastonia, North Carolina, and as such is a valuable supplement to Liston Pope's classic sociological analysis of the Gastonia textile strike of 1929, *Millhands and Preachers: A Study of Gastonia* (New Haven: Yale University Press, 1942). Peterson, trained in theology and religious studies, utilized in his *Ham and Japheth* the anthropological insights of Clifford Geertz and Claude Lévi-Strauss, especially their concepts that religion is a model of and for reality—that is, perception and action—and that myth is a way of mediating contradictions within a society. The result is a thought-provoking structuralist interpretation of the role of the Hametic myth (the supposed biblical authority for the subjugation of the black race) in southern history. Both Bruce and Peterson are long on analysis and short on historical evidence, and as a consequence their books have not had the impact they might otherwise have had. Yet they do suggest the growing interdisciplinary nature of the field and ensure that later work will not be one-dimensional.[9]

Donald G. Mathews in 1977 published the most comprehensive history of religion in the antebellum South that has yet appeared.[10] Although Catholics and other non-evangelicals were practically ignored, and the geographical focus is almost entirely on the Southeast, the book has a long section on slave Christianity and sweeps from the eighteenth-century Baptist awakenings, which Rhys Isaac

---

9. Dickson D. Bruce, Jr., *And They All Sang Hallelujah: Plain-Folk Camp-Meeting Religion, 1800–1845* (Knoxville: University of Tennessee Press, 1974); John R. Earle, Dean D. Knudsen, and Donald W. Shriver, *Spindles and Spires: A Re-Study of Religion and Social Change in Gastonia* (Atlanta: John Knox Press, 1976); Thomas Virgil Peterson, *Ham and Japheth: The Mythic World of Whites in the Antebellum South* (Metuchen, N.J.: Scarecrow Press and American Theological Library Association, 1978). An important article on methods of studying southern religion is Donald G. Mathews, "Religion in the Old South: Speculation on Methodology," *South Atlantic Quarterly*, LXXIII (Winter, 1974), 34–52.

10. Donald G. Mathews, *Religion in the Old South* (Chicago: University of Chicago Press, 1977).

has so fruitfully explored, to the Civil War.[11] Mathews also continues the long-overdue analysis of the role of women in the evangelical movement, a subject first developed by Anne F. Scott in the afore-mentioned book edited by Samuel S. Hill, Jr. The research is more broad-ranging than the citations suggest, including printed sermons, private manuscripts, church records, the relevant secondary litera-ture, and wide reading in the behavioral sciences. Mathews' inter-pretations often seem strained and overly abstract, and in his efforts to emphasize the community-building nature of the evangelical move-ment and the religious chasm between blacks and whites—"their re-ligious experience and ultimate hopes differed as radically as their so-cial positions"—he pushes his argument too far.[12] Nonetheless, he has written the most discussed, most influential single book on the subject. He is especially provocative in his analysis of the relation-ships between religious and social processes.

The chapters on Afro-American Christianity in both Boles's (1976) and Mathews' (1977) books represented another important develop-ment in southern studies, the growing emphasis on the cultural and social history of slaves from the black perspective. Eschewing pri-mary reliance on source materials generated by whites, scholars such as George P. Rawick and especially John W. Blassingame had in 1972 revealed hitherto unrecognized riches and complexities in slave cul-ture. Both wrote books containing valuable chapters on slave reli-gion, but it was ironically the Marxist historian Eugene D. Genovese who first made black Christianity central to his analysis of the slave experience. In a 124-page section of his magisterial *Roll, Jordan, Roll,* Genovese emphasized how religion gave meaning and purpose to slave life, how it proved an alternative value system for blacks, how it contributed to the psychological strength necessary to prevent de-

---

11. Four articles by Rhys Isaac have collectively been so influential they must be cited: "Religion and Authority: Problems of the Anglican Establishment in Virginia in the Era of the Great Awakening and the Parsons' Cause," *William and Mary Quar-terly,* 3rd Ser., XXX (January, 1973), 3–36, "Evangelical Revolt: The Nature of the Baptists' Challenge to the Traditional Order of Virginia, 1765 to 1775," *William and Mary Quarterly,* 3rd Ser., XXXI (July, 1974), 345–68, "Dramatizing the Ideology of Revolution: Popular Mobilization in Virginia, 1774 to 1776," *William and Mary Quarterly,* 3rd Ser., XXXIII (July, 1976), 357–85, and "Preachers and Patriots: Popu-lar Culture and the Revolution in Virginia," in Alfred F. Young (ed.), *The American Revolution: Explorations in the History of American Radicalism* (DeKalb: Northern Illinois University Press, 1976), 127–56. Isaac in 1982 published his long-awaited book, which incorporates and subtly revises many of his early essays.

12. Mathews, *Religion in the Old South,* 185.

humanization in the face of chattel bondage. Genovese made no use of church records, underestimated the extent to which blacks and whites worshiped together, and revealed a simplistic understanding of the white evangelical religion with which he compared slave religion. Yet never again after his book would slave Christianity be dismissed as unimportant or as merely an "opiate" for hapless black masses.[13]

Perhaps the most satisfying brief account of slave religion to date is Chapter 1, "The Sacred World of Black Slaves," of Lawrence W. Levine's *Black Culture and Black Consciousness*. Making eloquent and anthropologically informed use of a wide range of black folk materials, including spirituals and folktales, Levine has produced a valuable analysis of the slaves' "sacred" world view, seeking not simply description or even interpretation but an evocation of black religion.[14] Like Genovese, Levine often compares his sophisticated portrait of black religion with a stereotype of white religion, but his depiction of black culture is unrivaled.

Albert J. Raboteau in 1978 produced the first comprehensive history of slave religion well grounded in both historical and anthropological literature, with a broad comparative sweep that included Africa and the Caribbean.[15] Showing parallels between African and Christian religions, Raboteau traced the evolution of Afro-American Christianity in the South, with careful attention to social forces and theological traditions. He carefully portrayed the function of religion in the slave community and related it to both rebellion and docility. Raboteau emphasized black autonomy in religious life, though—to

13. George P. Rawick, *From Sundown to Sunup: The Making of the Black Community* (Westport, Conn.: Greenwood Publishing Corp., 1972); John W. Blassingame, *The Slave Community: Plantation Life in the Antebellum South* (New York: Oxford University Press, 1972; 2nd ed., 1979); Eugene D. Genovese, *Roll, Jordan, Roll: The World the Slaves Made* (New York: Pantheon, 1974).

14. Lawrence W. Levine, *Black Culture and Black Consciousness: Afro-American Folk Thought from Slavery to Freedom* (New York: Oxford University Press, 1977), 3–80. For a rigorous analysis of folkloric materials with fairly conventional conclusions, see Olli Alho, *The Religion of the Slaves: A Study of the Religious Tradition and Behaviour of the Plantation Slaves in the United States, 1830–1865* (Helsinki, Finland: Suomalainen Tiedeakatemia, Academia Scientiarum Fennica, 1976).

15. Albert J. Raboteau, *Slave Religion: The "Invisible Institution" in the Antebellum South* (New York: Oxford University Press, 1978). Other worthwhile studies of slavery and religion include Lewis M. Purifoy, "The Methodist Episcopal Church, South, and Slavery, 1844–1865" (Ph.D. dissertation, University of North Carolina, 1965); and William C. Suttles, Jr., "A Trace of Soul: The Religion of Negro Slaves on the Plantations of North America" (Ph.D. dissertation, University of Michigan, 1979).

this author, at least—his limited utilization of church records led him seriously to underestimate the extent to which there was a biracial religious community in the Old South.[16] Moreover, the real value of Raboteau's book lies less in providing new interpretations than in bringing together and synthesizing what had been written on the subject before about 1975. That work of synthesis, while it makes his book less exciting to specialists, enhances its value to the general historical community. More recently Raboteau's *Slave Religion* has been supplemented by Mechal Sobel's *Trabelin' On*. Her analysis is similar, though she did make extensive use of antebellum *black* church records. Related to this interest in slave religion has been a new concern with the white-sponsored mission to the slaves.[17]

One of the implicit assumptions of the modern scholarship has been that, with regard to religion as all else, southern history cannot be understood without taking into consideration how blacks have influenced whites and vice versa. In no area of southern life was this interchange more important than religion. More recent work, and re-

16. *Cf.* Kenneth K. Bailey, "Protestantism and Afro-Americans in the Old South: Another Look," *Journal of Southern History*, XLI (November, 1975), 451–72; Larry M. James, "Life Together: Blacks and Whites in Antebellum Mississippi and Louisiana Baptist Churches" (M.A. thesis, Tulane University, 1986); David T. Bailey, "Slavery and the Churches: The Old Southwest" (Ph.D. dissertation, University of California, Berkeley, 1979), 143–63; and the papers by David Bailey, Larry M. James, and Clarence L. Mohr at the 1981 annual meeting of the Southern Historical Association. (David Bailey's much-revised dissertation has been published as *Shadow on the Church: Southwestern Evangelical Religion and the Issue of Slavery, 1783–1860* [Ithaca: Cornell University Press, 1985], but it came out too late for extended discussion here.) See also Boles, *Religion in Antebellum Kentucky*, 84–85, and *Black Southerners, 1619–1869* (Lexington: University Press of Kentucky, 1983), 153–68; Timothy L. Smith, "Slavery and Theology: The Emergence of Black Christian Consciousness in Nineteenth-Century America," *Church History*, XLI (December, 1972), 497–512; and Winthrop S. Hudson, "The American Context as an Area for Research in Black Church Studies," *Church History*, LII (June, 1983), 157–71. Dickson D. Bruce, Jr., argues for a more distinctive black Christianity in "Religion, Society, and Culture in the Old South: A Comparative View," *American Quarterly*, XXVI (October, 1974), 399–416.

17. Mechal Sobel, *Trabelin' On: The Slave Journey to an Afro-Baptist Faith* (Westport, Conn.: Greenwood Press, 1979). See Milton C. Sernett, *Black Religion and American Evangelicalism: White Protestants, Plantation Missions, and the Flowering of Negro Christianity, 1787–1865* (Metuchen, N.J.: Scarecrow Press, 1975); Erskine Clarke, *Wrestlin' Jacob: A Portrait of Religion in the Old South* (Atlanta: John Knox Press, 1979); Donald G. Mathews, "Charles Colcock Jones and the Southern Evangelical Crusade to Form a Biracial Community," *Journal of Southern History*, XLI (August, 1975), 299–320; and D. Blake Touchstone, "Planters and Slave Religion in the Deep South" (Ph.D. dissertation, Tulane University, 1973).

search still under way, now suggest that the normative worship experience for blacks in the Old South was in a so-called white church, which was thus a biracial church. Blacks heard the same sermons, took communion with whites, were buried in the same cemeteries, and participated in the church disciplinary procedures. Such relative equality existed nowhere else in southern society. Slave testimony against whites was heard and accepted—this in a society where slaves were not allowed to testify against whites in courts of law. Slaves found meaning and purpose for their lives, and a sense of moral worth, in their participation in the South's biracial churches. In fact the membership of a "typical" Baptist church in antebellum Mississippi might have been more than 50 percent black.[18]

Most of the scholarship on southern religious history has concentrated on popular evangelicalism and the religions of the folk, whether poor whites (as in Dickson Bruce) or slaves (as in Raboteau). Students such as Hill, Boles, Bruce, and Mathews had emphasized how the white evangelical faith had helped shape the white southern historical experience, how it had helped create a sense of purpose, or self-identity. Each of these earlier students had recognized a degree of rationality in the theology preached, but all had chosen to focus on the popular faith.[19] After all, they were writing what Rush Welter has labeled external intellectual history—"the pursuit of ideas in their relationship to events"—rather than internal—"the study of ideas for their own sake."[20] While they rightly stressed the dominant religious tradition and sought to characterize the southern religious mind, they neglected a minority movement of learned clergy clustered in the South's handful of cities.

E. Brooks Holifield has corrected that lacuna in the scholarship with his detailed and analytical account of urban ministers and the rational orthodoxy that characterized their theology. Holifield con-

---

18. See note 16.

19. Other works that emphasized the religion of the folk include Bertram Wyatt-Brown, "The Antimission Movement in the Jacksonian South: A Study in Regional Folk Culture," *Journal of Southern History*, XXXVI (November, 1970), 501–29, and "Religion and the Formation of Folk Culture: Poor Whites of the Old South," in Lucius F. Ellsworth (ed.), *The Americanization of the Gulf Coast, 1803–1850* (Pensacola, Fla.: Historic Pensacola Preservation Board, 1972), 20–33; and Charles A. Scarboro, "A Sectarian Religious Organization in Heterogeneous Society: The Churches of Christ and the Plain-folk of the Transmontane Mid-South" (Ph.D. dissertation, Emory University, 1976).

20. Rush Welter, "The History of Ideas in America: An Essay in Redefinitions," *Journal of American History*, LI (March, 1965), 599.

centrated on the work of one hundred influential ministers, examined their theological writings, and interpreted not only their ideas but also the role they aspired to in southern urban society. The result is a study not of typical or representative southern ministers, but rather atypical ones whose writings reveal unexpected erudition and familiarity with European theological currents.[21] The influence of these one hundred is stated, but Holifield does not show how their ideas affected the world view or the lives of the huge majority of southerners, white and black. The primary value of the book is its acknowledgment of the complexity of southern religious life. We should recognize the strength of the revivalist tradition while not forgetting the lesser though still important rational theological tradition that was its contemporary. Because many of us have been so preoccupied with spelling out the origins and consequences of the popular folk belief, it is very good to have Holifield's book with its preoccupation with the other side of southern religion.

Still another indication of the extent to which southern religious history has come of age is the proliferation of studies on different aspects of religious culture. Buell E. Cobb, Jr.'s authoritative *The Sacred Harp*, a study of the shape-note songbook first published in 1844 and still in use in the rural South, is a case in point. His book represented the growing interest in folk culture. Another richly detailed and elaborately researched study in folk culture is Dena J. Epstein's *Sinful Tunes and Spirituals*. Less interpretative than it might have been, and rather casually drawing examples from the West Indies for the eighteenth century when sources for the mainland are limited, it nevertheless is a storehouse of information.[22] Another important tradition in southern religion now receiving scholarly attention is the holiness-pentecostal movement. David Edwin Harrell, Jr., has pioneered the academic study of these movements in *White Sects*

---

21. E. Brooks Holifield, *The Gentlemen Theologians: American Theology in Southern Culture, 1795–1860* (Durham: Duke University Press, 1978). Another important study of southern theology is Neal C. Gillespie, *The Collapse of Orthodoxy: The Intellectual Ordeal of George Frederick Holmes* (Charlottesville: University Press of Virginia, 1972). See also Theodore Dwight Bozeman, "Science, Nature and Society: A New Approach to James Henley Thornwell," *Journal of Presbyterian History,* L (Winter, 1972), 306–25. A good urban study is Michael Stephen Franch, "Congregation and Community in Baltimore, 1840–1860" (Ph.D. dissertation, University of Maryland, 1984).

22. Buell E. Cobb, Jr., *The Sacred Harp: A Tradition and Its Music* (Athens: University of Georgia Press, 1978); Dena J. Epstein, *Sinful Tunes and Spirituals: Black Folk Music to the Civil War* (Urbana: University of Illinois Press, 1977).

and Black Men in the Recent South and his impressively objective *All Things Are Possible*. The geographical focus of the latter goes beyond the South. Another pathbreaking book is the balanced and sympathetic study of the general movement by Vinson Synan, *The Holiness-Pentecostal Movement in the United States*. Southern historians generally need to be aware of how these sectarian churches were in their formative years (roughly from 1880 to 1920) much more open to participation (including leadership) by both blacks and women than the mainstream evangelical churches were.[23] Much work needs to be done in this area, but Harrell has indicated the direction such scholarship will likely take. The forthcoming major study of radio and television evangelists, and the so-called Moral Majority, by sociologist William C. Martin will add still further to our understanding of the old-time religion updated and wedded to brand-new technology.

State studies on important episodes in religious history are filling in the outline of regional church history. Such skillfully executed books as Frederick A. Bode's *Protestantism and the New South* and Thomas E. Buckley, S.J., *Church and State in Revolutionary Virginia*, augur well for the growing maturity of the field.[24] Recent biographies

23. David Edwin Harrell, Jr., *White Sects and Black Men in the Recent South* (Nashville: Vanderbilt University Press, 1971), and *All Things Are Possible: The Healing & Charismatic Revivals in Modern America* (Bloomington: Indiana University Press, 1975); Vinson Synan, *The Holiness-Pentecostal Movement in the United States* (Grand Rapids, Mich.: William B. Eerdmans Publishing Co., 1971). The sectarian movement is now the focus of a growing scholarly literature. Several of the more important are W. J. Hollenweger, *The Pentecostals: The Charismatic Movement in the Churches* (Minneapolis: Augsburg Publishing House, 1972); William W. Menzies, *Anointed to Serve: The Story of the Assemblies of God* (Springfield, Mo.: Gospel Publishing House, 1971); Timothy L. Smith, *Called Unto Holiness: The Story of the Nazarenes. The Formative Years* (Kansas City, Mo.: Nazarene Publishing House, 1962). On the issue of racial liberalism among Pentecostals (A. A. Allen in particular), see Howard Elinson, "The Implications of Pentecostal Religion for Intellectualism, Politics, and Race Relations," *American Journal of Sociology*, LXX (January, 1965), 403–15. A good local study is Charles Edwin Jones, "Disinherited or Rural? A Historical Case Study in Urban Holiness Religion," *Missouri Historical Review*, LXVI (April, 1972), 395–412. For the broader cultural implications, see Stephen R. Tucker, "Pentecostalism and Popular Culture in the South: A Study of Four Musicians [James Blackwood, Johnny Cash, Tammy Wynette, and Jerry Lee Lewis]," *Journal of Popular Culture*, XVI (Winter, 1982), 68–80.

24. Frederick A. Bode, *Protestantism and the New South: North Carolina Baptists and Methodists in Political Crisis, 1894–1903* (Charlottesville: University Press of Virginia, 1975); Thomas E. Buckley, S.J., *Church and State in Revolutionary Virginia, 1776–1787* (Charlottesville: University Press of Virginia, 1979). Thomas O'Brien Hanley's *The American Revolution and Religion: Maryland, 1770–1800* (Washing-

of denominational leaders indicate even that shopworn mode of religious history is undergoing a welcome change. Thomas W. Spalding's *Martin John Spalding* is a landmark in Catholic historiography, just now emerging from the filiopietistic tradition.[25] Mark K. Bauman's *Warren Akin Candler* brings from obscurity an important turn-of-the-century Methodist bishop. George William Pilcher's biography of Samuel Davies does not adequately explain Davies' appeal to eighteenth-century Virginians, but does present a credible portrait of the man himself.[26] There are also many useful biographies that remain unpublished in their dissertation form.[27] The old uncritical style

ton, D.C.: Catholic University of America Press, 1971) is another, more pedestrian, state study.

25. Thomas W. Spalding, *Martin John Spalding: American Churchman* (Washington, D.C.: Catholic University of America Press, 1974). Though Thomas O'Brien Hanley's 3-volume edition of *The John Carroll Papers* (Notre Dame: University of Notre Dame Press, 1976) is useful, the collection is not completely satisfactory. See John J. Tierney, "Another View of the John Carroll Papers," *Catholic Historical Review*, LXIV (October, 1978), 660–70. More satisfactory are Hanley's *Charles Carroll of Carrollton: The Making of a Revolutionary Gentleman* (Washington, D.C.: Catholic University Press, 1970) and *Revolutionary Statesman: Charles Carroll and the War* (Chicago: Loyola University Press, 1983). The most promising work on southern Catholicism is being done by Randall M. Miller. See his "The Failed Mission: The Catholic Church and Black Catholics in the Old South," in Edward Magdol and Jon L. Wakelyn (eds.), *The Southern Common People: Studies in Nineteenth-Century Social History* (Westport, Conn.: Greenwood Press, 1980), 37–54, and Miller and Wakelyn (eds.), *Catholics in the Old South: Essays on Church and Culture* (Macon, Ga.: Mercer University Press, 1983). The best state studies of Catholicism are James L. Pillar, *The Catholic Church in Mississippi, 1837–1865* (New Orleans: Hauser Press, 1964); and Michael J. McNally, *Catholicism in South Florida, 1868–1968* (Gainesville: University Presses of Florida, 1982). See also Pillar's "Catholicism in the Lower South," in Ellsworth (ed.), *The Americanization of the Gulf Coast*, 34–43.

26. Mark K. Bauman, *Warren Akin Candler: The Conservative as Idealist* (Metuchen, N.J.: Scarecrow Press, 1981). Two good biographies appeared too late for discussion here: James O. Farmer, Jr., *The Metaphysical Confederacy: James Henley Thornwell and the Synthesis of Southern Values* (Macon, Ga.: Mercer University Press, 1985); and William Allen Poe, *Green W. Hartsfield: A Biography, 1833–1896* (Natchitoches, La.: Northwestern State University Press, 1984). George William Pilcher, *Samuel Davies: Apostle of Dissent in Colonial Virginia* (Knoxville: University of Tennessee Press, 1971).

27. See, for example, Doralyn Joanne Hickey, "Benjamin Morgan Palmer: Churchman of the Old South" (Ph.D. dissertation, Duke University, 1962); Thomas Erskine Clarke, "Thomas Smyth: Moderate of the Old South" (Th.D. dissertation, Union Theological Seminary in Virginia, 1970); Edgar C. Mayse, "Robert Jefferson Breckinridge: American Presbyterian Controversialist" (Th.D. dissertation, Union Theological Seminary in Virginia, 1974); Raymond M. Bost, "The Reverend John Bachman and the Development of Southern Lutheranism" (Ph.D. dissertation, Yale University, 1963);

of denominational biography is not dead, however, as indicated by the recent publication of Ray Holder's life study of William Winans.[28]

That Holder's book stands out for its old-fashionedness is evidence of the advance in southern religious studies. The more than thirty books discussed here indicate that southern religious history had been at a crest of popularity in the decade of the 1970s. The increase in the number of books published was paralleled by a marked increase in the number of dissertations and articles on the subject. A quick survey, for example, of the listings printed in the *Journal of Southern History*'s annual bibliography, "Southern History in Periodicals," published in each May issue, illustrates the point. But the changes in the religious history of the South are not merely quantitative. The level of analysis and the sophistication of research design, the breadth of research, have also improved significantly. More and better history is being written, in part because of the body of work that has gone before. Four recently published books of unusual significance suggest that the momentum in southern religious studies has not yet ebbed.

Southern evangelicals in the eighteenth century especially were wont to quote approvingly the biblical adage that "the last shall be first." Following that dictum, we shall first examine the most recently published of the four new books here given extensive coverage, Rhys Isaac's *The Transformation of Virginia, 1740–1790*, which won the 1983 Pulitzer Prize for history. His is surely the most methodologically sophisticated book in the entire field of southern religion, and though Isaac, Reader in History at La Trobe University in Australia, was formally trained as a historian, this book borrows substantially from the cognate discipline of cultural anthropology. Keith Thomas has defined the work of cultural anthropologists in a way that aptly characterizes Isaac's aims:

> The interests of the new generation of anthropologists tend to be not so much sociological, as linguistic, even philosophical. Their primary concern is the way in which language and symbolism determine human understanding and behavior. Their object is to reconstruct the various methods by which men impose conceptual order on the external world. They wish to identify the "programs," the "grammars," the "para-

---

Raymond C. Rensi, "Sam Jones: Southern Evangelist" (Ph.D. dissertation, University of Georgia, 1972); and David L. Holmes, Jr., "William Meade and the Church of Virginia, 1789–1829" (Ph.D. dissertation, Princeton University, 1971).

28. Ray Holder, *William Winans: Methodist Leader in Antebellum Mississippi* (Jackson: University Press of Mississippi, 1977).

digms," the "cognitive structures," on which social behavior, as they see it, is founded. Above all, they seek to reconstruct individual cultural systems in their entirety, and to understand particular notions by identifying their place in the system to which they belong.[29]

Informed by such an outlook, Isaac examines the impact of the evangelical social revolution on eighteenth-century Virginia.

The Transformation of Virginia consists of three sections. Part I, "Traditional Ways of Life," provides the best description in print of the physical, social, and cultural landscape of Virginia *circa* 1740. Isaac illuminates every corner of Virginia life to which he turns his focus, and the total portrait that emerges is one of a stable, traditional order, where courthouse and church were visible symbols of the rule of law and spiritual authority. There was one uppercase *c* Community to which all whites belonged; the long arm of authority both temporal and ecclesiastical bound everyone to a recognition of their proper roles. Every social fact, from the architecture of plantation houses to the etiquette of horse racing, legitimated the authority of the ruling establishment. In several senses the Anglican church was *the* established church.

Part II of the book, "Movements and Events," details a series of developments that together shook the foundations of the established order. This section, the heart of the book, treats imaginatively such familiar topics as the Parsons' Cause and the episcopacy controversy, but the critical event for Isaac's thesis was the development of the Separate Baptist movement in Virginia after the early 1760s. The earlier Presbyterian revival and the slightly later Methodist awakening are related to the Baptist upsurge, yet the Baptists are the ones through whom Isaac sees a profound social revolution occurring. As a result of the Baptist challenge, the social and cultural landscape of revolutionary Virginia was transformed.

Part III, "Afterview," briefly examines the immediate and long-range result of this transformation, with implications for much of the subsequent history of Virginia and the South. Isaac's explication of the nature of the Baptist revolt, and its effect on Virginia, is an interpretive *tour de force* and represents a subtle though significant revision of the view he first presented in a series of important articles.

29. Rhys Isaac, *The Transformation of Virginia, 1740–1790* (Chapel Hill: University of North Carolina Press, 1982); Keith Thomas, "An Anthropology of Religion and Magic, II," *Journal of Interdisciplinary History,* VI (Summer, 1975), 91–109 (quotation on p. 92).

Isaac interrelates political and religious history—a signal accomplishment—but it is to certain aspects of his analysis of the Baptist movement and its implications that we now should turn.

For Isaac's interpretation, it is important to keep in mind that the Baptist movement in a sense was, in relation to the establishment, a counterculture. He writes, "The social world of the Baptists seems so striking a negative image of gentry-dominated milieus that it must be considered to have been shaped to a large extent in reaction to the dominant culture." [30] In his earlier articles, the Baptist stance seemed merely a reflexive reaction to the "dominant culture"; in the present book he does admit that the "evangelical counterculture" was not "exclusively the growth of Virginia soil," and he mentions the New England background of the Separate Baptists. This itself is an improvement on the original article, but he should still go farther and elaborate the world view the evangelicals brought to Virginia. Events in Virginia did not create the Baptist outlook; rather, the Baptist outlook had been shaped outside Virginia and, when brought to the state, it caused persons to see differently what they had previously accepted with little questioning.

In one sense the Baptist movement was "a revolt against the traditional system," and from that perspective "evangelicalism can be seen as a popular response to a mounting sense of social disorder." [31] But if by such terminology one means that an underlying social reality (of disorder, corruption, extravagance, etc.) created the Baptist view toward society, one underestimates the causative role of ideas, of Baptist "cognitive structures." One may agree here with Keith Thomas, who has written: "From the anthropologist's point of view, much of what historians call social change can be regarded as a process of mental reclassification, of re-drawing conceptual lines and boundaries." Baptist evangelists invaded regions of Virginia where the Anglican church was weakest and, with their emotional, persuasive preaching, gained thousands of adherents who found in the heartfelt Baptist meetings a sense of fellowship and purpose lacking in the nominal Anglican establishment. From their new perspective what they had formerly accepted as normal behavior now seemed immoral, disorderly, worldly. That changed perspective—not a marked increase of

30. Isaac, *The Transformation of Virginia*, 163–64.
31. *Ibid.*, 168. Some of the larger parameters of the evangelical movement are suggested by David S. Lovejoy, *Religious Enthusiasm in the New World: Heresy to Revolution* (Cambridge: Harvard University Press, 1985).

social disorder—is why Isaac is correct when he writes that "popular perceptions of disorder in society—and hence by individuals in themselves—came now to be articulated in the metaphor of 'sin.'" The emphasis needs to be shifted still more from too heavy a concentration on society to an enhanced portrait of the theological views of the Baptists. With their different perspective, Baptists implicitly challenged the all-inclusive hegemony of the ruling establishment by offering alternative measures of the good (and the bad) life. Focusing on that aspect of the Baptist challenge has been the most original and important contribution of Rhys Isaac to southern religious studies.[32]

In his earlier articles on the "evangelical revolt," Isaac also emphasized the community-building nature of the evangelicals. In contrast to the established church, they formed warmly supportive communities (local churches), and hence were seen not as having an atomizing, individualizing influence but rather the opposite. This argument that the essence of the evangelical revolt was that it welded together individuals into a closely knit community is of course a main contention in Donald Mathews' *Religion in the Old South*. Rhys Isaac in his book has significantly revised his own earlier interpretation, and rightly so. While he sees that the evangelicals created "*a* community within and apart from *the* community," he now stresses "the ambivalence between communitarianism and individualism." In fact, he now writes that "increasing 'individualism' in the social and cultural system of England and America may well constitute an underlying 'cause' [and one might add also a result] of the rise of evangelicalism." There was a turning away from the larger society—with the courthouse and idea of one official religious community, the established church, that theoretically included everyone under the umbrella of

---

32. Thomas, "An Anthropology of Religion and Magic," 98; Isaac, *The Transformation of Virginia,* 169. Perhaps this changing perception, not an increase in real disorder, is a way of reconciling Isaac's interpretation of Virginia social history with those by Edmund S. Morgan, *American Slavery—American Freedom: The Ordeal of Colonial Virginia* (New York: Norton, 1975); and T. H. Breen, "Horses and Gentlemen: The Cultural Significance of Gambling among the Gentry of Virginia," *William and Mary Quarterly,* 3rd Ser., XXXIV (April, 1977), 239–57, both of whom see an increase of *order* after mid-century. As Thomas pointed out, the evangelicals because of their "mental reclassification" could be labeling hitherto unexceptional behavior as disorder and sin, and the evangelical rise to prominence would cause the establishment to see the evangelicals' existence as evidence of disorder. Moreover, evangelical critiques of gentry behavior might have caused a sensitized gentry to worry about notable excesses among themselves. However it might be explained, Isaac and Morgan in two powerful books present opposing portraits of late colonial Virginia.

the state—and a new concern with individuals drawn together by conversion into local fellowships that were voluntary and in a way private. The small, local congregation was the focus of attention, not the larger community. This represents a real break from the earlier colonial conception of the corporateness of society. As Isaac writes in his concluding section, "The principle of individual autonomy, only just establishing an ascendancy destined to last until the present, was reorganizing late eighteenth-century Anglo-Virginians' perceptions of their world and the expectations they had of it."[33]

Not the least of the changes caused by the evangelical movement was the sundering of the unitary view of community—there now were two legitimate, even institutionalized, but incompatible world views, which Isaac characterizes as "the humbling, soul-searching culture of the New Lights and the proud, assertive culture of the gentry and their adherents." Hence Isaac sees Virginia entering the nineteenth century as a "polarized" society "with a complex of cultures that was fractured by a widening ethnic rift and an enduring legacy of conflicting value systems."[34]

Along these lines he expresses a reservation about Donald Mathews' view in *Religion in the Old South* concerning the almost complete domination of southern religion by evangelicalism. Here, though, Mathews—and one could add Samuel Hill, John Boles, and Anne Loveland—has the better argument. One of the results of the Great Revival, whatever its causes and its individualistic or communitarian nature, was that, building upon eighteenth-century origins, it set under way the process of church growth that won almost complete dominance in the Old South for evangelical views. James Oakes and Jan Lewis, for example, in their recent books document the prevalence of the evangelical outlook. Jan Lewis, in *The Pursuit of Happiness* (1983), indicates that by the first quarter of the nineteenth century even the world view of Virginia aristocrats was suffused with evangelical values. Oakes's *The Ruling Race* (1982) includes a perceptive chapter entitled "The Convenient Sin," in which he discusses the dominance among slaveholders of evangelical religion, including the evangelical critique of materialism and its implicit criticism of

---

33. Isaac, *The Transformation of Virginia*, 166 (first quotation), 171n (second and third quotations), 311 (fourth quotation). One of the subsections of the final chapter is entitled "Community Diminished." See also Edward L. Ayers, *Vengeance and Justice: Crime and Punishment in the 19th-Century South* (New York: Oxford University Press, 1984), 56–57, 122.

34. Isaac, *The Transformation of Virginia*, 322.

slaveholding itself.[35] Guilt was one of the results, and it was as a guilt-haunted society that the Old South found itself drawn to an evangelical religion that provided periodic, institutionalized, "highly visible[,] and ritualized escapes from guilt—revivalism" and the concept of rededicating one's life.[36]

But despite some reservations about the long-range implications of *The Transformation of Virginia,* it is a marvelous book and shows more than any other work how religious movements and attitudes help shape political and social history, and vice versa. Because of it we will never look at colonial Virginia the same way again, for our "cognitive structures" have been transformed.

Anne C. Loveland's meticulously researched *Southern Evangelicals and the Social Order, 1800–1860* (1980) is a detailed portrait of the views and characters of white evangelical ministers.[37] Basing her work exclusively on private papers, articles and editorials in denominational periodicals, and a long bibliography of published sermons, essays, and biographies (all complemented by the relevant secondary literature), Loveland has written the most comprehensive catalog of antebellum ministerial viewpoints and positions available, concentrating on Baptist, Methodist, and Presbyterian clergy in the South Atlantic states. The result is a valuable quarry of information,

35. Jan Lewis, *The Pursuit of Happiness: Family and Values in Jefferson's Virginia* (Cambridge, England: Cambridge University Press, 1983), Chap. 2; James Oakes, *The Ruling Race: A History of American Slaveholders* (New York: Knopf, 1982), 96–122. See also Arthur Dicken Thomas, Jr., "Reasonable Revivalism: Presbyterian Evangelization of Educated Virginians, 1787–1837," *Journal of Presbyterian History,* LXI (Fall, 1983), 316–34; and Ayers, *Vengeance and Justice,* 119–20. A provocative forthcoming study of southern religion is foreshadowed by Elizabeth Fox-Genovese and Eugene D. Genovese, "The Old South Considered as a Religious Society," *National Humanities Center Newsletter,* VI (Summer, 1985), 1–6.

36. Boles, *Religion in Antebellum Kentucky,* 143. There is a long historical controversy over guilt among antebellum white southerners. For one of the best arguments for its presence, see Charles G. Sellers, Jr., "The Travail of Slavery," in Sellers (ed.), *The Southerner as American* (Chapel Hill: University of North Carolina Press, 1960), 40–71. For a penetrating analysis of the failure of southern religious leaders "to discern the nature and meaning of the tragic dimension in human experience," see Ernest Kurtz, "The Tragedy of Southern Religion," *Georgia Historical Quarterly,* LXVI (Summer, 1982), 217–47 (quotation on p. 217). Bertram Wyatt-Brown, *Southern Honor: Ethics and Behavior in the Old South* (New York: Oxford University Press, 1982), presents the most elaborate argument against feelings of guilt in the Old South, though his book practically ignores southern religion.

37. Anne C. Loveland, *Southern Evangelicals and the Social Order, 1800–1860* (Baton Rouge: Louisiana State University Press, 1980).

quotations, and summaries of the clergy's attitudes that other scholars will mine for a long time to come. Beginning with their conversion experiences and the idea of a "call," Loveland examines the
innermost motives and expectations of her subjects. When she turns
to clerical attitudes toward their profession, Loveland reveals the
various and sometimes contradictory roles ministers knew they had
to perform, and she shows subtle changes and tensions within the
ministry that evolved over the years. Their primary role, of course,
remained the conversion of sinners, so her next chapter analyzes ministerial participation in and the changing reputation of revivals. The
early, occasionally rowdy camp meetings were calmed down and
regularized and, in urban areas, largely replaced by protracted meetings. But as both became routine human instruments for promoting
conversion, many ministers became critical of them. Here Loveland
begins to emphasize a point she had previously implied, the southern
evangelical preoccupation with the sovereignty of God and the futility,
even error, of dependence on human agency. Such an attitude predated the Great Revival.

The evangelical stance toward the world was quite complex. For
most clergy, the world represented values antithetical to the gospel
commands; consequently ministers warned their listeners to withdraw from secular concerns at least to the extent of not letting themselves be dominated by the world. This was a constant struggle, and
ministers fought a never-ending battle against worldliness in the
churches. "Fashion" and "wealth" were the twin evils; both seduc-
tively attracted Christians toward behavior unbecoming their faith.
Ministers in the last decade of the antebellum period were increasingly upset by the compromises many clergy and the churches themselves seemed to be making with the world. Even though ministers
typically believed that the South was less contaminated by the forces
of money and modernity than the North was, they came to expect
some sort of national chastisement by God for the nation's sins. As
Loveland concludes, "The crisis of 1860–1861 would come as no sur-
prise to them. They were conditioned to look for divine retribution."[38]

Yet the evangelicals were not indifferent to the world. They recognized the evils and temptations that were present and to a limited
degree acted to minimize their effect on individuals. The southern
evangelicals never constructed a real social ethic or social gospel, re-

38. *Ibid.*, 129.

strained as they were by the presence of slavery and relatively un-
affected by the liberalizing theological currents flowing from Europe
to the North. Instead they sought to reform individuals through conversion (either to Christ or away from an "evil" like drinking) and
aid victims of society such as widows, orphans, and the urban poor.
Relief and regeneration were their goals, but a religious critique of
society never emerged. Loveland provides a useful summary of the
variety of benevolent reforms that existed and relates the movements
to the southern individualistic ethic and the evangelical worry lest
human agency preempt divine providence.

Nowhere were the strengths and weaknesses of the evangelical benevolent movement in the South better revealed than in its response
to slavery. Essentially subservient to the slaveholding interests, evangelical clergy generally accepted the status quo even when they were
unwilling to defend slavery in the abstract. The decline of religious
emancipationism in the South after 1800 contributed to the hegemony of the slaveholding minority. But the ministers did not always accept abuses of the ideals of the system. They worked to regularize
marriage relations between slaves, used moral pressure to minimize
physical and sexual mistreatment, and exhorted masters to care for
the spiritual needs of the slaves long before the rise of modern abolitionism. At the same time the evangelical clergy criticized northern
abolitionists for harming the cause of slave religion by making slave
owners suspicious of ministers.

The clergy subsequently avoided what they termed the civil issue of
whether slavery should be abolished and they focused on the religious issue of converting the bondsmen. Ultimately ministers refined
their scriptural defenses of slavery and ended up being firm supporters of the southern way of life. Because they genuinely believed one's
otherworldly destination more important than one's status in this
world, they saw no contradiction between accepting slavery and
mounting an extensive missionary campaign to the slaves. In part because of their evangelical successes with the slaves and in part because they compared the North's liberal theology and newfangled
sects so unfavorably with southern orthodoxy, the evangelicals began
to apotheosize their society. When sectional tensions mounted in the
1850s, they discounted political efforts and resigned themselves to a
providential cleansing and deliverance. As Loveland concludes in the
book's final sentence, "The belief in the sovereignty and omnipotence
of God and the dependence of man informed the whole of their

thinking, and more than any other single element, contributed to the distinctiveness of southern evangelical thought in the nineteenth century."[39]

Very little of what Loveland has to say on an interpretative level will be new to specialists in the field. Rather, she has added details, emendations, and nuances to a familiar story. Yet historians probably put too much emphasis on newness per se. This is a substantial, workmanlike book that confirms and corroborates the scholarship that came before it. In a developing field, a degree of confirmation is helpful, and in a way the fact that little is surprising here is another indication that southern religious history may be reaching maturity. If Loveland's findings were all that new now, one would be suspicious of them. More troublesome than what the author says is what she does not address. This is quite openly a book from the viewpoint of white male clerics; the religious life of women, of blacks, of layersons is only hinted at. Moreover, the life of the church itself as an institutional body, as a fellowship of believers, as a religious community, is missing, probably because church and associational minutes were overlooked. The book is also more descriptive than analytical, but it does make clear the importance, indeed the centrality, of religion to the larger history of the South. It will be a standard source for the study of antebellum southern religion.

There is more a sense of freshness, of new ideas, about Charles Reagan Wilson's *Baptized in Blood* (1980), in part because the period has been less worked by religious historians, and in part because of the perspective and the methodological skills Wilson brings to the task. His central thesis is that the myth of the Lost Cause became the means by which many postbellum white southerners found self-identity. The notion of a separate political identity had collapsed at Appomattox, but cultural identity based on a mythical interpretation of the past took its place. That identity was infused with Protestant evangelical values. The result was a southern civil religion, explicitly Christian, explicitly southern, explicitly critical of the North—a way of finding meaning and ultimate vindication in the crucible of Confederate defeat. The Lost Cause became an authentic expression of religion, celebrated with and perpetuated by its own rituals, mythology, and theology, and complete with its own heroes, evangelists, and promotional institutions. The search for southern identity has long

39. *Ibid.*, 265.

been a major theme in southern historiography. Wilson has made an important contribution to that quest.[40]

Historians as diverse as Charles S. Sydnor and Anne Loveland have commented on how antebellum southerners came to believe by the 1850s that theirs was a more Christian, more virtuous region than was the nation as a whole.[41] Wilson has traced the metamorphosis of that idea through the ordeal of defeat. Northern material power, it was argued defensively, won the immediate war, but the more virtuous southern culture would eventually be victorious if southerners kept the faith. The whole apparatus of a religious establishment arose to maintain that promise, and the Lost Cause became for many southerners a holy cause. Defeat was interpreted as a trial, a hammering on the anvil of life, a "baptism in blood" that presaged moral triumph. Richmond became the Mecca of this Lost Cause religion; the Confederate cause its creation myth; Robert E. Lee, Stonewall Jackson, and Jefferson Davis its saints; Confederate Memorial Day (along with funerals of former Confederates) the time of ritualistically recalling the Cause; and the various Confederate veterans' groups (along with the United Daughters of the Confederacy) the cult institutions that kept the eternal fire burning. The churches served the same function, lending their offices to the Lost Cause at every opportunity.

Virtue, purity, duty were the watchwords, and the southern heroes (Lee, Jackson, Davis) in particular and southern womanhood in general were portrayed as exemplars of Christian values, holding steadfast to principle through temptation and defeat. Emulation of their behavior was constantly exhorted, for only if southerners were true to their heritage could the greater southern destiny be claimed, to lead the nation to holiness. Hence revivalism and calls for reformation resulted, and the South became even more self-conscious about its Protestantism. God, it was assumed, had a plan, and He obviously used the Civil War as a cleansing to prepare the South for its true mission. Clearly, a sense of worth, of pride, a reinvigorated sense of southern identity, emerged from the depression and loss of morale that followed defeat. Equally important, the surging sense of a re-

40. Charles Reagan Wilson, *Baptized in Blood: The Religion of the Lost Cause, 1865–1920* (Athens: University of Georgia Press, 1980). See also Wilson's important article, "The Religion of the Lost Cause: Ritual and Organization of the Southern Civil Religion, 1865–1920," *Journal of Southern History*, XLVI (May, 1980), 219–38.

41. Charles S. Sydnor, *The Development of Southern Sectionalism, 1819–1848* (Baton Rouge: Louisiana State University Press, 1948), Chap. 15, "The Affirmation of Southern Perfection" (pp. 331–39).

gional religious mission produced a detailed and sustained critique of the New South movement, which was portrayed as conducive to mammonism and worldliness by the older Lost Cause ministers who were adults during the Confederacy. Younger Lost Cause clergy were less suspicious and tended to see evangelical opportunity in growth and prosperity, provided materialism was held at bay. Likewise, slavery was never really attacked. Rather, it was remembered as God's way of controlling, educating, and Christianizing blacks. Now a paternalistic segregation was the accepted method of race relations, though race never became a central concern of the Lost Cause religionists.

The major celebrant, even evangelist, of the Lost Cause was a Baptist minister, author, Civil War chaplain, and promoter extraordinaire, J. William Jones. Leading the campaign to write the history from a southern viewpoint, Jones was an indefatigable itinerant for the Lost Cause. Confederate champions also supported secondary schools and colleges that taught the true faith, and institutions like Alexandria's Episcopal High School, the University of the South, and Washington and Lee University were citadels of conservative Confederate mythology. Through such institutions, and the rituals and ceremonies described earlier, southerners proudly maintained a culture separate from the rest of the nation. Ironically, their attitude of Christian mission led them to a reconciliation with the nation during the two decades following 1898. The Spanish-American War, ostensibly a crusade for Protestantism and virtue against Spanish autocracy, was a means of seeing national and southern aims as consistent. Even more so was World War I a holy crusade, especially since the nation was led by a devout southern Presbyterian, Woodrow Wilson. Slowly, almost imperceptibly, southern clergy had redefined the Lost Cause, subtly shifting the emphasis away from a former Confederate crusade for virtue to a southern crusade for liberty. In the context of fighting Germany, that was an idea more conducive to national identification. And so was the victory in World War I. The people of the Lost Cause, almost without realizing it, had become promoters of liberty, success, military victory, and the American mission. National reconciliation had been achieved, but with still another irony. Rather than being prophetic critics of American values, the Lost Cause spokesmen had become uncritical proponents of Americanism, 110 percent superpatriots.

Charles Reagan Wilson's book, informed by aptly utilized anthropological and sociological insights, is a richly interpretative, immensely provocative contribution to southern religious history. While

535

JOHN B. BOLES

at times his preoccupation with Lost Cause rhetoric may lead him away from the heart of southern evangelical culture and while he does not indicate the popular, congregational reaction to all that ministerial fulmination, his book significantly adds to the civil religion debate among historians of American religion and to the long historiographical search for southern identity. The place in this tradition for southern Catholics and especially black Christians is not made clear. But we stand in Wilson's debt for a timely, well-written account of the religion of the Lost Cause.

Samuel S. Hill, Jr.'s book, *The South and the North in American Religion* (1980), is very different in scope and approach from Isaac's, Loveland's, and Wilson's works.[42] Hill first presented these three brief, interpretative chapters as the Lamar Memorial Lectures at Mercer University in the fall of 1979. Each chapter focuses on a fifteen-year period important in the shaping of the North-South dialogue in religion, Epoch A (1795–1810), Epoch B (1835–1850), and Epoch C (1885–1900). For each of these eras, Hill characterizes the religious situation in both the North and the South, though most of his discussion concerns the South. His comparative perspective highlights the distinctiveness of the South, the region he treats more perceptively. Hence this essay will focus on Hill's portrait of religion in Dixie.

Hill begins with several important assumptions. First, he recognizes that while the South is a part of the nation and shares many national traits, its distinctiveness is emphatic in religion and in other matters as well. Christianity in the North, for example, has consistently evidenced a concern for the health of the society as a whole while in the South the churches have largely lacked a social ethic. Second, Hill assumes that religion is an "independent variable" with causative force, not simply a reaction to the "real" forces of politics and economics. Third, despite the absence of anything like a social gospel in the South, regional religion ended up supporting the status quo, even sanctifying it. Southern religion was not quite in cultural captivity; it helped shape the very culture in which it existed.

Epoch A was a period of flux in southern religion. Out of this formative stage came an evangelical movement that soon gained cultural hegemony. Individualistic in thrust, more pietistic than doctrinaire, oriented primarily toward evangelism, the revivalist ethos neverthe-

42. Samuel S. Hill, Jr., *The South and the North in American Religion* (Athens: University of Georgia Press, 1980).

536

less created a sense of community for groups of like-minded converts, and in these church communities, among the fellowship of the saints, the common people found meaning and status for their lives independent of old social distinctions. In that sense the individualistic faiths helped a southern folk society to evolve, and a folk culture resulted. This regional folk culture solidified during Epoch B, and as the South's religion became more rigid and uniform, northern religion was diversifying and becoming less normative. Race, the indelible presence of large numbers of blacks, was a crucial factor, and as the cotton curtain fell across the South, limiting regional criticism, the churches were constrained to adapt to the region's peculiar institution. Yet the emergence of a religious defense of slavery was not simply a falling away from an abolitionist tradition and a succumbing to political pressure. It was in part that, as Hill says, but the theological underpinning for social criticism was so weak, and the pietistic tendency toward ignoring worldly "political" issues so strong, that the sacralization of southern society was almost a logical result of evangelical success. The mission to the slaves was more a theological imperative than a reaction to abolitionist charges.

And, as Hill shows, borrowing from Charles Sydnor again and confirming Anne Loveland, southern Christians by the end of Epoch B were convinced that theirs was a more Christian, more virtuous section than was the North. By backing "away from religious interpretations which would have mandated social reform" and "by converting individuals, black as well as white, the churches [believed they] were accomplishing God's will for society." [43] As a result, they accepted their society, indeed embraced it. An evangelical movement that was theologically otherworldly and individualistic became a legitimizing agent of an entire society and consequently supported that region as a religious good in the eventual secession crisis. Perhaps more than any other single ingredient, popular religion contributed to the rise of southern sectionalism and served as the glue holding Confederate "cultural nationalism" together.

As different as the South and North in American religion had been in 1850, by Epoch C they were further estranged. Southern culture had been almost fossilized by the Civil War, and as a defense mechanism, southerners became even more insistent on their religious superiority. Southern evangelicals were aggressive and sure of their beliefs, and with the rapid rise of black denominations, the South was the

43. *Ibid.*, 74.

more intensively "churched" region, further proof to Lost Cause supporters that theirs was a special society. This of course was in increasing contrast to the North, where immigration (and Hill might have
added urbanization and industrialization) was producing a far different society, one no longer predominantly Protestant. Much that Hill
says confirms Charles R. Wilson's interpretation of the relationship of
Lost Cause mythology, southern religion, and southern identity. Hill
concludes with a brief section describing the remarkable rapproche-
ment between religion North and South that has occurred since
1900, noting all the same that southern distinctions still remain.

There is little to quarrel with in Hill's interpretative sketch. He essentially confirms much that had been known and skillfully puts in
just enough comparative material to highlight regional distinctions as
well as the subtle changes over time. Hill does not indicate sufficiently
how much variety existed not only in southern religion but also in
that of the North. His book does point up the need for a comprehensive history of southern religion, one commencing with the period
before the Great Revival solidified the evangelical hegemony, continuing through to the election of a born-again southern president,
and covering developments in Texas and Louisiana as well as Virginia
and North Carolina. Such a book would include Catholics, blacks,
the sects outside the main-line churches, women, the mind of gentlemen theologians as well as folk beliefs.

Perhaps such a comprehensive book is just over the horizon. As the
number of monographs on discrete topics in southern religious history proliferates, the gaps in the larger story are being filled in. While
we have long known a great deal about Virginia Anglicanism, and
Rhys Isaac's recent work has challenged our understanding of many
aspects, S. Charles Bolton in *Southern Anglicanism* provides a detailed institutional history of the established church for another
colony. The story is similar to that in Virginia, but it differs as well,
and Bolton argues that despite its obvious failures, "the Church
of England was the major cultural force in South Carolina."[44] Ran-

44. S. Charles Bolton, *Southern Anglicanism: The Church of England in Colonial
South Carolina* (Westport, Conn.: Greenwood Press, 1982), 162. See also John Wesley
Brinsfield, *Religion and Politics in Colonial South Carolina* (Easley, S.C.: Southern
Historical Press, 1983). Two dissertations on southern colonial revivalism should
be noted: Ronald W. Long, "Religious Revivalism in the Carolinas and Georgia,
1740–1805" (Ph.D. dissertation, University of Georgia, 1968); and David T. Morgan,
Jr., "The Great Awakening in the Carolinas and Georgia, 1740–1775" (Ph.D. disser-
tation, University of North Carolina, 1968).

dall M. Miller has similarly broadened our view of southern religion in the late colonial era with his collection of Loyalist essays by John Joachim Zubly, a Swiss Presbyterian minister in Georgia.[45] Miller's emphasis is on Zubly's political writings, but he lists eleven other religious pamphlets in a bibliographical appendix, and perhaps that dimension of Zubly's thought will be elaborated upon subsequently by Miller or another scholar.

The history of Afro-American Christianity during the antebellum period has been sufficiently studied for historiographical disputes to have arisen, but hitherto we have known little about the processes by which freedmen withdrew from the "white" churches immediately after the Civil War and established their own separate congregations and denominations. Kenneth K. Bailey, in an important article in 1977, pointed the way toward seeing the separation as a significant break from antebellum practices.[46] Although blacks initiated the process of separation and white denominational officers at first protested and then cautiously experimented with ways to cooperate with their sister black denominations, racial attitudes quickly hardened and by the 1870s racial separation became practically complete and applauded by white religious spokesmen.

Clarence E. Walker, in *A Rock in a Weary Land* (1982), has detailed the experience of the African Methodist Episcopal church's coming into the South, arguing that its mission was a species of civil religion combined with an ideology of racial uplift. Its success was ultimately limited by forces (poverty, racism) beyond its control and by an unrealistic opposition to emotionally demonstrative worship. Walker's book depends too heavily upon the denominational newspaper *Christian Recorder* and inadequately appreciates the extent of antebellum biracial religious worship, but it helpfully explains how and why the AME church entered the region and gained adherents.[47]

---

45. Randall M. Miller (ed.), *"A Warm & Zealous Spirit": John J. Zubly and the American Revolution. A Selection of His Writings* (Macon, Ga.: Mercer University Press, 1982).

46. Kenneth K. Bailey, "The Post–Civil War Racial Separations in Southern Protestantism: Another Look," *Church History*, XLVII (December, 1977), 453–73. See also Katharine L. Dvorak, "Exodus: The Segregation of the Southern Churches" (Ph.D. dissertation-in-progress, University of Chicago).

47. Clarence E. Walker, *A Rock in a Weary Land: The African Methodist Episcopal Church During the Civil War and Reconstruction* (Baton Rouge: Louisiana State University Press, 1982). See also Harry V. Richardson, *Dark Salvation: The Story of Methodism as It Developed Among Blacks in America* (Garden City, N.Y.: Anchor Press, 1976), Pt. 3, pp. 191–250; Edward Lorenzo Wheeler, "Uplifting the Race: The

As referred to earlier, there has been a mild disagreement among scholars of religion in the South over the extent to which what might be called "a social gospel" existed in the region. Samuel S. Hill and to a lesser extent John B. Boles have been associated with the idea that, as Hill expressed it, the "central theme" of southern religion has been the conversion of individual sinners. Yet it was not the intention of either Hill or Boles to deny that southern churches occasionally offered charity to society's victims or opposed, for example, the sale of alcoholic beverages. As Hill wrote in 1966, "Although the southern church has never devoted its energies to the redemption of the social structures, and certainly warrants no identification with the 'social gospel' tradition, it has not been blind to the relation between the Christian faith and a number of social currents and responsibilities."[48]

Two recent monographs address the issue of the social gospel in the South by focusing on two major denominations, and they come to conflicting conclusions. John Patrick McDowell, in *The Social Gospel in the South* (1982), examines the rhetoric of the urban-oriented leadership of the Woman's Home Mission Society in the Methodist church and shows their concern with orphans, widows, the urban poor (both blacks and immigrants). Undoubtedly, a minority of women in the Methodist church spoke out for broader social concerns, and that is important to know. Yet they still were a minority of women, the men often opposed their actions, and the involved women seldom if ever constructed a consistent critique of the societal institutions that produced poverty. That critique of what Hill called "social structures" is the essence of the social gospel, not merely good works. James J. Thompson, Jr., generally sides with the Hill thesis in his *Tried as by Fire* (1982). Thompson's book is concerned with many issues other than the social gospel, and he has perceptive chap-

---

Black Minister in the New South, 1865–1902" (Ph.D. dissertation, Emory University, 1982); James M. Washington, "The Origins and Emergence of Black Baptist Separatism, 1863–1897" (Ph.D. dissertation, Yale University, 1979); Maxine D. Jones, "'A Glorious Work': The American Missionary Association and Black North Carolinians, 1863–1880" (Ph.D. dissertation, Florida State University, 1982); and Joe M. Richardson, "The Failure of the American Missionary Association to Expand Congregationalism Among Southern Blacks," *Southern Studies,* XVIII (Spring, 1979), 51–73. There is an interesting analysis of pre–Civil War separation from the white churches by fugitive slaves in Canada; see Jason H. Silverman, *Unwelcome Guests: Canada West's Response to American Fugitive Slaves, 1800–1865* (Millwood, N.Y.: Associated Faculty Press, 1985), Chap. 4, "The New Exodus: The Development of the Black Church" (pp. 81–104).

48. Hill, *Southern Churches in Crisis,* 73, 171.

ters on Baptist attitudes toward premillennialism, fundamentalism, evolution, the proper way of approaching biblical study, the Catholic question in the 1928 election, and so on. Yet a major topic implicit throughout is the church's role in the world, and Thompson concludes that "hostile to the Social Gospel and committed to an individualistic religion, Southern Baptists advanced spiritual cures for temporal ills." [49]

Yet clearly, on the very fringes of southern Protestantism, there were clerical radicals who broke free from cultural captivity within the South to post far-reaching critiques of the society that produced the extremes of poverty and racism that marked the South before World War II. Several books on southern radicalism have contained valuable sections on movements like the Fellowship of Reconciliation and the Fellowship of Southern Churchmen and groups like "the radical revivalists of the Southwest." [50] Robert F. Martin has published a moving analysis of one such religious radical, Howard A. Kester, yet the atypicality of Kester is striking. Martin himself says that the movement Kester represented "never consisted of more than a few hundred persons . . . [though they] were deeply committed to the causes they championed." The careers of reformers like Kester point up the dominant conservatism and religious conformity of the

49. John Patrick McDowell, *The Social Gospel in the South: The Woman's Home Mission Movement in the Methodist Episcopal Church, South, 1886–1939* (Baton Rouge: Louisiana State University Press, 1982); James J. Thompson, Jr., *Tried as by Fire: Southern Baptists and the Religious Controversies of the 1920s* (Macon, Ga.: Mercer University Press, 1982), 208. On the important issue of fundamentalism and evolution, see two older, standard studies: Willard B. Gatewood, Jr., *Preachers, Pedagogues & Politicians: The Evolution Controversy in North Carolina, 1920–1927* (Chapel Hill: University of North Carolina Press, 1966), and Gatewood (comp.), *Controversy in the Twenties: Fundamentalism, Modernism, and Evolution* (Nashville: Vanderbilt University Press, 1969). For the historical origins of what is a modern-day corollary, the creationism controversy, see Ronald L. Numbers, "Creationism in 20th Century America," *Science*, CCXVIII (November 5, 1982), 538–44. Such significant national studies as George M. Marsden, *Fundamentalism and American Culture: The Shaping of Twentieth Century Evangelicalism, 1870–1925* (New York: Oxford University Press, 1980); and Timothy P. Weber, *Living in the Shadow of the Second Coming: American Premillennialism, 1875–1925* (New York: Oxford University Press, 1979), neglect southern developments.

50. James R. Green, *Grass-Roots Socialism: Radical Movements in the Southwest, 1895–1943* (Baton Rouge: Louisiana State University Press, 1978), 166. See also Thomas A. Krueger, *And Promises to Keep: The Southern Conference for Human Welfare, 1938–1948* (Nashville: Vanderbilt University Press, 1967); and Anthony P. Dunbar, *Against the Grain: Southern Radicals and Prophets, 1929–1959* (Charlottesville: University Press of Virginia, 1981).

region. And there were also conservative religious forces, at least in the early national period, that organized to produce what they considered a Christian state. Fred J. Hood has aggressively argued that those in the Reformed church tradition sought to impose "social control" on the majority. John W. Kuykendall has countered such interpretations in his 1982 study of national religious societies' reform activities in the South.[51]

Nevertheless, there surely has been too strong a tendency in all southern studies to homogenize the region and flatten out the cultural contours. Titles or subtitles like "The Mind of the South" or "The Southern Evangelical Mind" express inadequately the diversity that has existed and does exist in the land of Dixie. As with Holifield's *The Gentlemen Theologians,* which usefully reminds us of a more substantial theological tradition than emphasis on revivalists had conceded, works like those by McDowell and Martin force us to keep our mental apertures wide. No more convenient admonitory volume exists than the essays edited by David Edwin Harrell, Jr., *Varieties of Southern Evangelicalism.*[52]

Consisting of essays originally presented at the University of Alabama's Hugo Black Symposium in 1979, *Varieties of Southern Evangelicalism* provides a thoughtful critique of the popular image of a religiously "Solid South." Martin Marty places southern evangelicalism in a national context and shows its paradoxical appropriateness for some of the conflicts of modernity; Joseph R. Washington, Jr., evokes the spirit of black religion; William Martin shows that Billy Graham has been more aware of social evils—particularly segregation—than his facile critics have admitted; and Samuel S. Hill in a provocative final essay probes the regional distinctiveness of "popular southern piety." But for the topic suggested by the book's title, the

---

51. Robert F. Martin, "A Prophet's Pilgrimage: The Religious Radicalism of Howard Anderson Kester, 1921–1941," *Journal of Southern History,* XLVIII (November, 1982), 511–30 (quotation on p. 511); Fred J. Hood, *Reformed America: The Middle and Southern States, 1783–1837* (University: University of Alabama Press, 1980). Hood earlier developed his thesis in "Revolution and Religious Liberty: The Conservation of the Theocratic Concept in Virginia," *Church History,* XL (June, 1971), 170–81. John W. Kuykendall, *Southern Enterprise: The Work of National Evangelical Societies in the Antebellum South* (Westport, Conn.: Greenwood Press, 1982), provides a persuasive critique of the social-control thesis for antebellum religion in general, not just the South.

52. David Edwin Harrell, Jr. (ed.), *Varieties of Southern Evangelicalism* (Macon, Ga.: Mercer University Press, 1981).

variety present in southern religion, the essays by Wayne Flynt and Harrell, the book's editor, are most important.

Wayne Flynt accepts the standard interpretation of southern religion as individualistic and conversion oriented; in fact, he states that "one has to admit the basic thesis of . . . Sam Hill . . . and many others, that southern Evangelicals have been more faithful to southern culture than they have been to the radical ethics of Christ." [53] Then Flynt goes on to show that here and there southern evangelicals protested some forms of economic and racial oppression. That did happen occasionally. He proceeds then to argue that the social gospel existed in the South, with here and there a minister or a women's church group advocating temperance or prohibition and providing charity for the impoverished or classes for the children of the urban and immigrant poor. Clearly, one can find such examples, but they represent traditional church charity of a type many centuries older than the social gospel. And Flynt gives no figures to suggest the typicality, or relative strength, of those southern evangelicals who critiqued their surrounding culture. One may accept his particular examples and still maintain the larger generalization. Surely there *were* subtle differences in outlook, as there were in social station, among the millions of southern evangelicals.

David Harrell has been the foremost student of religious sectarianism in the South, and his essay "The South: Seedbed of Sectarianism" is a useful corrective to those of us who often speak of the region as though there were no others besides Baptists, Methodists, and Presbyterians. He shows quite convincingly that "the South was clearly the most fertile source of sectarianism in the United States in the first half of the twentieth century." He also shows that these conservative, almost apolitical groups were never rebellious; rather, they tended to accept grinding poverty as a "permanent fact" and preached

---

53. Wayne Flynt, "One in the Spirit, Many in the Flesh: Southern Evangelicals," in Harrell (ed.), *Varieties of Southern Evangelicalism*, 34. Flynt has been the most systematic and influential analyst of southern religion (especially Baptists) and social reform. See his "Dissent in Zion: Alabama Baptists and Social Issues, 1900–1914," *Journal of Southern History*, XXXV (November, 1969), 523–42, "Baptists and Reform," *Baptist History and Heritage*, VII (October, 1972), 211–22, and "Alabama White Protestantism and Labor, 1900–1914," *Alabama Review*, XXV (July, 1972), 192–217. Samuel Claude Shepherd, Jr., has shown how at least in one southern city the mainstream Protestant churches addressed secular needs in "Churches at Work: Richmond, Virginia, White Protestant Leaders and Social Change in a Southern City, 1900–1929" (Ph.D. dissertation, University of Wisconsin, 1980).

a gospel that in a way was a "glorification of suffering." [54] In doing so they injected meaning, purpose, even a sense of moral grandeur into otherwise drab lives. But this is, it seems to me, essentially documentation of Hill's central theme of southern religious history. And while we must make room in our descriptions of religion in the South for this significant minority of sectarians, we should at the same time remember that they are a decided minority, as a glimpse at the pie charts and other data in Edwin S. Gaustad's religious atlas shows.[55]

Even more of a minority in the South have been the Jews, who have never equaled 1 percent of the region's total population. Nevertheless, their influence has certainly been felt, with individuals like Judah P. Benjamin playing a leading political role. Most southerners have only recognized the Jewish presence through the region's great mercantile establishments like Richs in Atlanta and Neiman-Marcus in Dallas or great philanthropic institutions like Touro Hospital in New Orleans. Eli N. Evans has provided an engaging popular history of southern Jews, and there have been three valuable books of collected essays.[56] Several useful local histories have also been written, and most of the literature on southern Jews has examined how the Jews have been both a people set apart and a people well integrated into southern

54. David Edwin Harrell, Jr., "The South: Seedbed of Sectarianism," in Harrell (ed.), *Varieties of Southern Evangelicalism*, 48, 56. Another good source for the variety present in contemporary southern folk religion is the collection of articles, interviews, and illustrations gathered by Paul F. Gillespie (ed.), *Foxfire 7* (Garden City, N.Y.: Anchor Press, 1982). Mercer University Press has also issued a revised and expanded version of the *Southern Exposure* issue on southern religion: *On Jordan's Stormy Banks: Religion in the South* (Macon, Ga., 1983). The University of North Carolina Press at Chapel Hill published two long-playing documentary phonograph records that are appropriate to cite here: Jeff Todd Titon, *Powerhouse for God: Sacred Speech, Chant, and Song in an Appalachian Baptist Church*, 1982; and Brett Sutton and Pete Hartman, *Primitive Baptist Hymns of the Blue Ridge*, 1982.

55. Edwin S. Gaustad, *Historical Atlas of Religion in America* (Rev. ed.; New York: Harper & Row, 1976), 48–51, 122–28. See also the detailed chart of church membership in Houston in Louis Moore, "People Who Go to Church Now Minority in Harris County," Houston *Chronicle*, October 2, 1982, sec. 6, p. 7.

56. Eli N. Evans, *The Provincials: A Personal History of Jews in the South* (New York: Atheneum, 1973); Leonard Dinnerstein and Mary Dale Palsson (eds.), *Jews in the South* (Baton Rouge: Louisiana State University Press, 1973); Nathan M. Kaganoff and Melvin I. Urofsky (eds.), *"Turn to the South": Essays on Southern Jewry* (Charlottesville: University Press of Virginia for the American Jewish Historical Society, 1979); and Samuel Proctor and Louis Schmier with Malcolm Stern (eds.), *Jews of the South: Selected Essays from the Jewish Historical Society* (Macon, Ga.: Mercer University Press, 1984).

society.[57] In New Orleans' Mardi Gras, for example, Jews are excluded from the most acclaimed Carnival krewes yet participate in
Mardi Gras via their own prestigious krewe, Bacchus.

The southern population has always consisted of more than whites
and blacks; there existed an Indian population before Europeans
"discovered" the New World, and these Indians possessed a complex
religious belief system. Early on, Indians began to interact with
whites and blacks, becoming a missionary field for white evangelists.
Part of this interesting subfield of southern religious history has begun to be examined, but much work remains to be done, particularly
for the post–Civil War era.[58] In religion as in many other areas, the
southern culture that from a distance looked homogeneous proves,
upon closer inspection, to be remarkably complex.

There are of course still subjects in southern religious history that
cry out for investigation. We know far too little about religion in the
colonial South outside of Virginia and South Carolina; for example,
there is no adequate study of the Great Awakening's (limited) manifestations in the southern colonies as a whole. We need more state
studies, more state denominational studies, and far more work on the
South outside the seaboard states. We need to know more about the
role of religion in the secession crisis, though C. C. Goen's *Broken
Churches, Broken Nation* (1985) does much to explain the relationship. We need to know more about religion and revivals during the
Confederacy, scholarship that would complement James W. Silver's

---

57. Charles Reznikoff and Uriah Z. Engelman, *The Jews of Charleston: A History
of an American Jewish Community* (Philadelphia: Jewish Publication Society of Amer-
ica, 1950); B. H. Levy, "The Early History of Georgia Jews," in Harvey H. Jackson and
Phinizy Spalding (eds.), *Forty Years of Diversity: Essays on Colonial Georgia* (Athens:
University of Georgia Press, 1984), 163–78; Bertram Wallace Korn, *The Early Jews of
New Orleans* (Waltham, Mass.: American Jewish Historical Society, 1969); Isaac M.
Fein, *The Making of an American Jewish Community: The History of Baltimore Jewry
from 1773 to 1920* (Philadelphia: Jewish Publication Society of America, 1971);
Elaine H. Maas, "The Jews of Houston: An Ethnographic Study" (Ph.D. dissertation,
Rice University, 1973); Leo E. Turitz and Evelyn Turitz, *Jews in Early Mississippi*
(Jackson: University Press of Mississippi, 1983).

58. The best introductions to southeastern Indian religion before interaction with
whites are Charles M. Hudson, *The Southeastern Indians* (Knoxville: University of
Tennessee Press, 1976), Chap. 3; and James H. Howard, *The Southeastern Ceremonial
Complex and Its Interpretation* (Columbia: Missouri Archaeological Society, 1968).
William G. McLoughlin has written several important articles on this topic, as have
several other scholars, but McLoughlin's recent book, *Cherokees and Missionaries,
1789–1839* (New Haven: Yale University Press, 1984), is magisterial.

older study and provide an introduction to Charles R. Wilson's volume.[59] We know far too little about religion among the sharecroppers, moreover. There needs to be additional scholarship on the various sects that arose in the last decades of the nineteenth and early decades of the twentieth century. The relationship between civil rights and religion is yet another topic we know far too little about.

The role of women in southern religion, now being noticed, still requires further work, and dissertations like Patricia Martin's show how much can be learned on such topics. Of especial interest is Martin's portrayal of the diverse ways women via church work enlarged their sphere of activities within a society that severely circumscribed women's roles. Her work also suggests that the Baptist General Convention of Texas is almost another denomination—we simply have to be more attuned to subregional variation within the South.[60] If too much of American history has been New England writ large, we need to be cautious of the Virginiazation and Carolinazation of southern history.

Valuable snippets of other books—like Suzanne Lebsock's *The Free Women of Petersburg* (1984)—suggest how important their religion and their church were to southern women. Lebsock in several pages shows the at times dominant role of women in local churches and the significant role of religion in the women's lives. In their multitude of church organizations and activities, women found creative ways to build a sense of community—even perhaps nascent sis-

59. C. C. Goen, *Broken Churches, Broken Nation: Denominational Schisms and the Coming of the American Civil War* (Macon, Ga.: Mercer University Press, 1985). See also his "Broken Churches, Broken Nation: Regional Religion and North-South Alienation in Antebellum America," *Church History,* LII (March, 1983), 21–35; and James W. Silver, *Confederate Morale and Church Propaganda* (Tuscaloosa, Ala.: Confederate Publishing Co., 1957). Sidney J. Romero's *Religion in the Rebel Ranks* (Lanham, Md.: University Press of America, 1983) only partly meets this need. See Drew Gilpin Faust, "Christian Soldiers: The Meaning of Revivalism in the Confederate Army," *Journal of Southern History* (forthcoming).

60. Patricia Martin, "Hidden Work: Baptist Women in Texas, 1880–1920" (Ph.D. dissertation, Rice University, 1982). See also Fred Arthur Bailey, "The Status of Women in the Disciples of Christ Movement, 1865–1900" (Ph.D. dissertation, University of Tennessee, 1979); Noreen Dunn Tatum, *A Crown of Service: A Story of Woman's Work in the Methodist Episcopal Church South, from 1878 to 1940* (Nashville: Parthenon Press, 1960); Bobbie Sorrill, *Anne Armstrong: Dreamer in Action* (Nashville: Broadman Press, 1984); and Jean E. Friedman, *The Enclosed Garden: Women and Community in the Evangelical South, 1830–1900* (Chapel Hill: University of North Carolina Press, 1985). A more extensive discussion of women and religion is in the essay in this volume by Jacquelyn Dowd Hall and Anne Firor Scott.

terhood—and minimize the monotony and loneliness that might otherwise have overwhelmed them.[61] Those who emphasize the "victimization" of southern white women without appreciating the powerful role of religion in their lives distort an important part of women's history.

Large overarching interpretative works typically appear first and they shape and direct the nature of the monographic work. That has not really happened in this case, though Samuel S. Hill's *Southern Churches in Crisis* has played that role in a sense. But that kind of paradigm-shaping book is still to be written. And perhaps we don't have to wait very long. David Harrell is currently preparing an interpretative overview to be published as part of the University Press of Kentucky's New Perspectives on the South series. Samuel S. Hill has recently edited the multi-authored *Encyclopedia of Religion in the South,* a most welcome reference volume.[62] Hill also edited a book entitled *Religion in the Southern States,* with brief histories of religion in sixteen southern states.[63] And in the spring of 1981, Hill was the director of an important multidisciplinary symposium on southern religion held at Florida State University; he is editing the papers for publication in a book that will sum up much of the recent scholarship. The 1984 Chancellor's Symposium on Southern History at the University of Mississippi also focused on religion, with the collected essays published as *Religion in the South* (1985), edited by Charles Reagan Wilson. So despite the absence of a standard comprehensive text, an overall interpretative work, the studies already published and those under way bode well for the future of the discipline.

61. Suzanne Lebsock, *The Free Women of Petersburg: Status and Culture in a Southern Town, 1784–1860* (New York: Norton, 1984), 214–28, also 142–43.

62. Samuel S. Hill, Jr. (ed.), *Encyclopedia of Religion in the South* (Macon, Ga.: Mercer University Press, 1984). Hill's *ERS,* as it is known, should be supplemented with another immensely useful reference tool, David C. Roller and Robert W. Twyman (eds.), *The Encyclopedia of Southern History* (Baton Rouge: Louisiana State University Press, 1979), and three indispensable bibliographical aids: Kenneth E. Rowe (ed.), *Methodist Union Catalogue: Pre-1976 Imprints* (5 vols. to date; Metuchen, N.J.: Scarecrow Press, 1975–); John D. Batsel and Lyda K. Batsel (comps.), *Union List of United Methodist Serials, 1773–1973* (Evanston, Ill.: Garret Theological Seminary, 1974); and Edward Caryl Starr (ed.), *A Baptist Bibliography: Being a Register of Printed Material By and About Baptists, Including Works Written Against the Baptists* (25 vols.; Philadelphia: The Judson Press, 1947 [Vol. I]; Chester, Pa.: American Baptist Historical Society, 1952–54 [Vols. II-IV]; Rochester, N.Y.: American Baptist Historical Society, 1957–76 [Vols. V–XXV]).

63. Samuel S. Hill, Jr. (ed.), *Religion in the Southern States: A Historical Study* (Macon, Ga.: Mercer University Press, 1983).

The maturity of that scholarship, combined with the treatment now accorded the South in such general histories as Sydney E. Ahlstrom's *A Religious History of the American People* and William G. McLoughlin's *Revivals, Awakenings, and Reform* suggest southern religion has become, since Henry May's seminal essay in 1964, a tradition recovered.[64]

64. Charles Reagan Wilson (ed.), *Religion in the South* (Jackson: University Press of Mississippi, 1985); Sydney E. Ahlstrom, *A Religious History of the American People* (New Haven: Yale University Press, 1972); William G. McLoughlin, *Revivals, Awakenings, and Reform: An Essay on Religion and Social Change in America, 1607–1977* (Chicago: University of Chicago Press, 1978). Perhaps the first indication that southern religious historians had become self-conscious of the coming of age of their field was Rosemary M. Magee's brief, perceptive article, "Recent Trends in the Study of Southern Religion," *Religious Studies Reviews*, VI (January, 1980), 35–39. See also Robert Calhoon, "Southern Evangelicalism," *Evangelical Studies Bulletin*, II (March, 1985), 7–9.

Contributors

JOHN B. BOLES, professor of history at Rice University and managing editor of the *Journal of Southern History*, served on the *Journal's* Board of Editors from 1979 to 1982. He is the author of *The Great Revival, 1787–1805: The Origins of the Southern Evangelical Mind* (1972), *Religion in Antebellum Kentucky* (1976), and *Black Southerners, 1619–1869* (1983).

RANDOLPH B. CAMPBELL, professor of history at North Texas State University, served on the Board of Editors of the *Journal of Southern History* from 1981 to 1984. He has written a number of articles on slavery and slaveholding in Texas and is the co-author of *Wealth and Power in Antebellum Texas* (1977). His most recent book is *A Southern Community in Crisis: Harrison County, Texas, 1850–1880* (1983).

DAN T. CARTER, Andrew W. Mellon Professor of Southern History at Emory University, was on the Board of Editors of the *Journal of Southern History* from 1976 to 1979. His first book, *Scottsboro: A Tragedy of the American South* (1969), won the Bancroft Prize in History for 1969. His newest book is *When the War Was Over: The Failure of Self-Reconstruction in the South, 1865–1867* (1985).

LAWANDA COX is emeritus professor of history at Hunter College of the City University of New York. Her best-known writings include the co-authored *Politics, Principle, and Prejudice, 1865–66: Dilemma of Reconstruction America* (1963) and her *Lincoln and Black Freedom: A Study in Presidential Leadership* (1981). From 1972 to 1975 she served on the Board of Editors of the *Journal of Southern History*.

CHARLES B. DEW is Class of 1956 Professor of American Studies at Williams College, and he served on the Board of Editors of the

Journal of Southern History for the period from 1979 to 1982. He has written a number of articles on industrial slavery and is the author of *Ironmaker to the Confederacy: Joseph R. Anderson and the Tredegar Iron Works* (1966).

DREW GILPIN FAUST, professor of American civilization at the University of Pennsylvania, is the author of *A Sacred Circle: The Dilemma of the Intellectual in the Old South, 1840–1860* (1977) and *James Henry Hammond and the Old South: A Design for Mastery* (1982), and the editor of *The Ideology of Slavery: Proslavery Thought in the Antebellum South, 1830–1860* (1981). She served on the Board of Editors of the *Journal of Southern History* from 1982 to 1985.

HUGH DAVIS GRAHAM, professor of history at the University of Maryland, Baltimore County, served on the Board of Editors of the *Journal of Southern History* from 1978 to 1981. He is the author of *Crisis in Print: Desegregation and the Press in Tennessee* (1967) and *The Uncertain Triumph: Federal Education Policy in the Kennedy and Johnson Years* (1984), co-editor of *Violence in America: Historical and Comparative Perspectives* (1969), and co-author of *Southern Politics and the Second Reconstruction* (1975).

JACQUELYN DOWD HALL is professor of history at the University of North Carolina at Chapel Hill and director of the Southern Oral History Program there. Her *Revolt Against Chivalry: Jessie Daniel Ames and the Women's Campaign Against Lynching* (1979) won the Francis B. Simkins Award of the Southern Historical Association. She presently (1985–1988) serves on the Board of Editors of the *Journal of Southern History*.

EVELYN THOMAS NOLEN was associate editor of the *Journal of Southern History*. She was primarily responsible for copy editing the articles, including verifying quotations and citations, published in the *Journal* from 1968 to 1972 and from 1975 through 1985. Prior to joining the *Journal* staff, she was a documentary editor for the Winthrop Papers project at the Massachusetts Historical Society and for Plimoth Plantation.

GEORGE C. ROGERS, JR., is Caroline McKissick Dial Professor of American History at the University of South Carolina. A member of the Board of Editors of the *Journal of Southern History* for the term 1973–1976, he is the author of *Evolution of a Federalist: William Loughton Smith of Charleston (1758–1812)* (1962), *Charleston in the Age of the Pinckneys* (1969), *The History of Georgetown County, South Carolina* (1970), and co-editor of *The Papers of Henry Laurens* (10 vols. to date; 1968–).

CHARLES P. ROLAND, Alumni Professor of History at the University of Kentucky, served on the Board of Editors of the *Journal of Southern History* from 1978 to 1979 and was president of the Southern Historical Association in 1980–1981. His books include *Louisiana Sugar Plantations During the American Civil War* (1957), *The Confederacy* (1960), *Albert Sidney Johnston: Soldier of Three Republics* (1964), and *The Improbable Era: The South Since World War II* (1975).

ANNE FIROR SCOTT is W. K. Boyd Professor of History at Duke University and in 1983 was president of the Organization of American Historians. A member of the Board of Editors of the *Journal of Southern History* for the period from 1980 to 1983, she has published *The Southern Lady: From Pedestal to Politics, 1830–1930* (1970), *Women in American Life* (1970), and *Making the Invisible Woman Visible* (1984), and is co-author of *One Half the People: The Fight for Woman Suffrage* (1974).

JOE GRAY TAYLOR is professor of history and Dean of the College of Liberal Arts at McNeese State University. From 1977 to 1980 he served on the Board of Editors of the *Journal of Southern History*. Among his books are *Negro Slavery in Louisiana* (1963), *Louisiana Reconstructed, 1863–1877* (1974), *Louisiana: A Bicentennial History* (1976), and *Eating, Drinking, and Visiting in the South: An Informal History* (1982).

BENNETT H. WALL, who for years was professor of history at the University of Kentucky and then at Tulane University, is now a lecturer in history at the University of Georgia. From 1952 through 1985 he was secretary-treasurer of the Southern Historical Association, sponsor of the *Journal of Southern History*. Author of many articles, he is co-author of *Teagle of Jersey Standard* (1974) and editor of *Louisiana: A History* (1984).

RICHARD L. WATSON, JR., is professor of history at Duke University. He served on the Board of Editors of the *Journal of Southern History* from 1969 to 1972 and was president of the Southern Historical Association in 1976–1977. He is the author of *The Development of National Power: The United States, 1900– 1919* (1976); editor of *Bishop Cannon's Own Story: Life As I Have Seen It* (1955) and *The United States in the Contemporary World, 1945–1962* (1965); and co-editor of *Interpreting and Teaching American History* (1961) and *The Reinterpretation of American History and Culture* (1973).

HAROLD D. WOODMAN is professor of history at Purdue University. He served on the Board of Editors for the term 1973–1976. The author of many articles on the economic and agricultural history of the postbellum South, he has also written *King Cotton & His Retainers: Financing & Marketing the Cotton Crop of the South, 1800–1925* (1968) and edited *Slavery and the Southern Economy: Sources and Readings* (1966) and *The Legacy of the American Civil War* (1973).

Index